Advances in

ARCHAEOLOGICAL METHOD AND THEORY

Volume 5

Advisory Board

Advances in
ARCHAEOLOGICAL METHOD AND THEORY
Volume 5

Edited by

MICHAEL B. SCHIFFER

Department of Anthropology
University of Arizona
Tucson, Arizona

1982

ACADEMIC PRESS
A Subsidiary of Harcourt Brace Jovanovich, Publishers
New York   London
Paris   San Diego   San Francisco   São Paulo   Sydney   Tokyo   Toronto

ACADEMIC PRESS, INC.
111 Fifth Avenue, New York, New York 10003

United Kingdom Edition published by
ACADEMIC PRESS, INC. (LONDON) LTD.
24/28 Oval Road, London NW1 7DX

LIBRARY OF CONGRESS CATALOG CARD NUMBER:

ISBN 0-12-003105-1

PRINTED IN THE UNITED STATES OF AMERICA

82 83 84 85   9 8 7 6 5 4 3 2 1

Contents

1   Cultural Resources Management

DON D. FOWLER

2   The Study of Impacts on Archaeological Sites

LESLIE E. WILDESEN

3 Advances in Urban Archaeology

EDWARD STASKI

4 Avenues of Inquiry in Historical Archaeology

KATHLEEN DEAGAN

5 Archaeological Applications of Computer Graphics

J. BARTO ARNOLD III

6 Quantifying Archaeological Research

G. A. CLARK

7 Ceramic Compositional Analysis in Archaeological Perspective

RONALD L. BISHOP, ROBERT L. RANDS,
and GEORGE R. HOLLEY

8 Archaeofaunas and Subsistence Studies

R. LEE LYMAN

Contributors

Numbers in parentheses indicate the pages on which the authors' contributions begin.

George J. Armelagos (395), Department of Anthropology, University of Massachusetts, Amherst, Massachusetts 01003

J. Barto Arnold III (179), Texas Antiquities Committee, Austin, Texas 78711

Ronald L. Bishop (275), Museum of Fine Arts, Boston, Massachusetts 02115; and Department of Chemistry, Brookhaven National Laboratory, Upton, New York 11973

G. A. Clark (217), Department of Anthropology, Arizona State University, Tempe, Arizona 85287

Kathleen Deagan (151), Department of Anthropology, Florida State University, Tallahassee, Florida 32306

Don D. Fowler (1), Department of Anthropology, University of Nevada, Reno, Nevada 89557

Alan H. Goodman (395), Department of Anthropology, University of Massachusetts, Amherst, Massachusetts 01003

George R. Holley (275), Department of Anthropology, Southern Illinois University, Carbondale, Illinois 62901

Rebecca Huss-Ashmore (395), Department of Anthropology, University of Massachusetts, Amherst, Massachusetts 01003

R. Lee Lyman (331), Department of Anthropology, University of Washington, Seattle, Washington 98195

Robert L. Rands (275), Department of Anthropology, Southern Illinois University, Carbondale, Illinois 62901

Edward Staski (97), Department of Anthropology, University of Arizona, Tucson, Arizona 85721

Leslie E. Wildesen (51), Leslie E. Wildesen and Associates, Portland, Oregon 97218

Contents of Previous Volumes

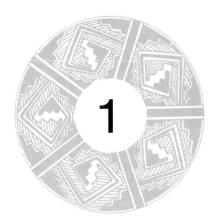

Cultural Resources Management

DON D. FOWLER

INTRODUCTION

Since 1974, cultural resource management (CRM) has become an increasingly important part of the discipline of archaeology in the United States. Cultural resource management has developed in response to federally mandated programs to inventory, to assess the significance of, and to manage cultural resources on public lands. Since 1960 a number of methodological and theoretical advances have been made within the field of archaeology that have various implications for the practice of CRM.

The term *cultural resources* began to be used within the National Park Service in 1971 or 1972 and soon thereafter by others. The term *management* was in use by 1974 (Lipe and Lindsay 1974). Whatever the origins of the phrase, a useful working definition of cultural resources is "physical features, both natural and manmade, associated with human activity. These would include sites, structures, and objects possessing significance, either individually or as groupings, in history, architecture, archeology, or human [cultural] development. . . . Cultural properties are unique and nonrenewable resources" (Fowler 1974:1467–1468).

Cultural resource management has been defined as "the application of management skills (planning, organizing, directing, controlling, and evaluating) to achieve goals set through the political process to preserve important aspects of our cultural heritage for the benefit of the American people" (Wildesen 1980:10). (See also Walka 1979:576–578.)

ADVANCES IN ARCHAEOLOGICAL METHOD AND THEORY, VOL. 5

These definitions encompass all resources relevant to the cultural heritage of the country. Ideally, CRM should encompass them all and become synonymous with, or subsume, historic preservation. In practice, CRM has focused principally on prehistoric and historic archaeological resources and the study and management thereof. Herein, that focus is maintained, with some discussion of the relationships between archaeology and other areas of historic preservation.

This chapter reviews the field of CRM, specifically the following areas: (*a*) the development of CRM as a field of endeavor, especially during the 1970s; (*b*) the legal context of CRM and the derivative implications for its practice; (*c*) the major management functions of CRM; and (*d*) some concerns for the future of the field held by professionals who are linked to it in various ways.

THE DEVELOPMENT OF CRM

As currently practiced, CRM is largely a product of a number of related concerns developed within the discipline of archaeology and the broader American society in which the discipline has functioned over the past 20 years (Moratto 1975). These concerns relate to the environment and the perceived detrimental changes being brought about by increasing urbanization, industrialization, and other land-altering activities. By the mid-1960s, threats to both natural and cultural resources were becoming increasingly severe, so much so that "crises" were declared in both the environmental and cultural realms (Clewlow *et al.* 1971; Davis 1972; Pastron *et al.* 1973; Rains *et al.* 1965; Whitaker 1976). One response to the problems was the passage of stringent, far-reaching legislation to attempt to cope with air and water pollution, endangered biological forms, general environmental degradation (U.S. Code 1977j) and dwindling cultural resources (U.S. Code 1977h,i).

These legislative acts are strongly conservation oriented, reflecting the ancient idea that each generation has stewardship of the earth and its resources (Glacken 1967; Graham 1971), which are to be used wisely and passed on to future generations. The conservation of nonrenewable resources—including cultural resources—is of particular concern. The central thrust of the legislation, especially the National Environmental Policy Act (U.S. Code 1977j), is to attempt to inject a strong element of systematic planning and evaluation into proposed land-altering or environmentally damaging projects. The act makes it federal government policy to ask if the project or development is really needed and to consider the alternatives. Furthermore, through the Environmental Impact Statement process, this act requires that these questions be posed in terms much broader than simply cost–benefit ratios.

The principal federal legislative response to the threat to cultural resources in general was the 1966 Historic Preservation Act (U.S. Code 1977i). As discussed in more detail in the following, this act provides a broad mechanism for the conservation of cultural resources through the process of placing "significant" resources on the National Register of Historic Places. Although listing on the register does not prevent the destruction of a site, building, or structure, it does serve to focus attention on the resource so that concerned individuals and groups can attempt to find ways to save it, if it is threatened by destruction.

Within the United States archaeological community, several specific concerns were developing during the 1970s. One was the already noted recognition that cultural resources, especially archaeological resources, were rapidly being depleted by federally supported activities, private land development, and vandalism (Davis 1972; Clewlow *et al.* 1971; Pastron *et al.* 1973). A second concern was the recognition that archaeological research, and attempts to protect and conserve archaeological resources, must largely be played out in the public arena. By 1970 almost all archaeological research in the United States was supported by public funds. The protection and conservation of archaeological resources require public laws—federal, state, and local. Archaeologists must interact with various segments of the public to carry on their work. McGimsey's (1972) *Public Archeology* highlighted all these factors. A third concern was the formulation of a conservation ethic within the archaeological profession, well expressed by Lipe (1974). The conservation ethic demands that all legal and other means should be used to protect and conserve extant archaeological resources for the future, rather than simply collecting or excavating any site threatened by a land-altering activity (see also the Management and Protection sections in this chapter).

The 1966 Historic Preservation Act and other legislation to be discussed later had caused federal land-managing agencies besides the National Park Service, to begin adding professional archaeologists to their staffs in the early 1970s. It became increasingly clear that the requirements of federal legislation and the realities of continued impacts on cultural resources by development activities and vandalism meant that the *management* of cultural resources had become a central concern of most members of the archaeological profession—both those in agencies and those in universities and museums.

In early 1974, a watershed conference was held at the Federal Center in Denver, Colorado (Lipe and Lindsay 1974). Major problems and issues were discussed and new approaches outlined. In response to the central concerns of the conference a new organization was formed, the American Society for Conservation Archeology. As of 1980, membership was 500. The society, through its *Newsletter* and annual symposia, has become a major forum for the discussion of CRM issues. Later in 1974, a series of seminars (the Airlie House seminars) were held in Virginia, sponsored by Interagency Archeological Services of the National Park Service. The seminars dealt with a variety of issues including the legal context of CRM, preparation and evaluation of reports, communication of research results, relations with Native Americans, professional certification, and the conduct of CRM per se (McGimsey and Davis 1977).

The burgeoning amount of field research required by federal legislation triggered a concern for the quality of research reports and highlighted the need for minimal fieldwork and reporting standards. This led to the formation in 1975 of the Society of Professional Archeologists (SOPA). The purposes of the society are to certify a minimal level of expertise in various areas of archaeological research and management and to promulgate a professional Code of Ethics. The latter defines responsibilities of a professional archaeologist regarding collection and interpretation of data, communication of research findings, and relationships with institutions and other professionals (Society of Professional Archeologists 1980).

As CRM continued to develop, sections devoted to the subject were added to major professional journals, including *American Antiquity* and the *Journal of Field Archaeology*. A section on CRM was established in the journal *Practicing Anthropology* beginning in 1978. In 1980 a new journal, *Contract Abstracts and CRM Archeology,* was established. The purpose of this journal is to disseminate abstracts of contract work and to provide an additional forum for the discussion of CRM problems. Other sources of current information on developments in CRM are the newsletters (*CRM Bulletin*) issued since 1977 by the National Park Service and *11593* issued (1978–1980) by the now-disbanded Heritage Conservation and Recreation Service.

In response to the increased need for trained personnel to carry out field, laboratory, and management tasks relating to contract research and CRM, several universities initiated graduate level training programs after 1974. In 1981, there were at least 35 universities in the United States providing graduate training in CRM, conservation archaeology, public archaeology, or salvage archaeology (American Anthropological Association 1980). A few of the programs award a master's degree; others are emphases within a master's program in anthropology.

In summary, the development of archaeological CRM in the United States has occurred principally since 1970. Prior to that time there were cultural resource managers, although they were not so called, in the National Park Service and other state or local agencies who were responsible for the management of public-owned areas containing cultural resources. But, CRM as currently practiced is structured by a set of federal laws passed before and after 1970. Attention is now turned to these laws.

LEGAL CONTEXT

It has been a declared federal policy since 1935 that the preservation of the nation's cultural resources is a public good to be sponsored and fostered by the federal government. However, the legal antecedents of that policy go back several decades earlier. Public concern in the United States for the preservation of cultural resources (Hosmer 1965) and conservation of natural resources (Graham 1971) developed in various (sometimes intertwined) ways throughout the nineteenth century. Until 1871, it was felt that such concerns were not the province of the federal government. But in that year the United States Fisheries Commission was established to aid in better management of fishery resources. In 1872, Yellowstone National Park was established to preserve the natural and historic resources of that area (U.S. Code 1977a:Section 21). In 1888 a law was passed extending the governmental power of eminent domain (U.S. Code 1977b) to acquire Civil War battlefields for historic parks. A United States Supreme Court (1896) decision upheld the use of eminent domain in this way and, in effect, established the preservation of cultural resources as an allowable federal activity. The Court also held that properties so acquired must have *national significance,* a ruling that had important implications in later federal legislation until 1966 (Fowler 1974:1471–1472). In 1889, the first federal step to preserve *archaeological* resources was taken when Congress set aside the Casa Grande site in Arizona (U.S. Code 1977c). Subsequent efforts to preserve and protect other archaeological resources in the Southwest and elsewhere, led finally to the passage of the 1906 Antiquities Act (U.S. Code 1977d). This act materially strengthened the federal involvement with cultural resources. The act has three major components:

1. It established a permit system for the excavation of archaeological remains on public lands (this is discussed further in relation to the 1979 Archeological Resources Protection Act in the following).

2. It gave the President the authority to set aside as national monuments cultural properties of national significance (reiterating the Supreme Court criteria of 1896) (Fowler 1974:1474; Lee 1970:87–109).

3. It delegated rule-making authority to the secretaries of Departments of the Interior, Agriculture, and War.

This placed CRM in the area of administrative law. The delegation of rule making to these three agencies highlighted the fact that federal responsibilities toward cultural resources were diffuse and uncoordinated.

In 1916 the National Park Service was created (U.S. Code 1977e:Section 1), and in 1933 a government reorganization gave the agency primary responsibility for the management of federally controlled cultural resources and natural resources.

In 1935 the United States Congress passed the Historic Sites Act, the cornerstone of all subsequent federal cultural resources legislation (U.S. Code 1977f). The legislation had been strongly supported by both President Franklin D. Roosevelt and Secretary of the Interior Harold L. Ickes (U.S. House of Representatives 1935:2–3) as part of a legislative package to reorganize the government. It was also strongly supported by a wide variety of historic preservation groups (Hosmer 1981:562–576). In several senses the act represented the culmination of efforts by various public and private groups over several decades to actively involve the federal government in cultural preservation (Hosmer 1965, 1981).

The Historic Sites Act gave the secretary of the interior, through the National Park Service, broad powers to survey and record cultural resources; to acquire, restore, and operate cultural properties or to enter into cooperative agreements with other entities for those purposes; to develop an educational program relating to cultural properties; and to cooperate with and seek assistance of federal, state, and municipal agencies, and educational and scientific institutions (U.S. Code 1977f:Sections 462–464).

The mandate to survey and record cultural resources legitimized the Historic American Buildings Survey (HABS), which had begun the previous year as one of the Depression-spawned New Deal make-work programs, and permitted the establishment of the Historic Sites Survey. (Under the same legislative authority, the Historic American Engineering Record was established in 1969. In 1978 the HABS and the Historic American Engineering Record were merged into the National Architectural and Engineering Record.)

In terms of subsequent developments, especially in archaeological CRM, two points should be made here. First, the emphasis on *national* significance of cultural resources put constraints on the kinds of cultural properties the government could acquire or protect. It also limited the assistance that the government could give to state, local, or regional groups concerned with the preservation of resources of less than national significance (Fowler 1974:1478). On the other hand, a broad construal of the authority to conduct surveys, and the authority to cooperate with and seek the assistance of educational and scientific institutions made it possible for the National Park Service after World War II to play an active (although at times uncertain) role in the "reservoir salvage" programs of the 1940s through the 1960s.

Following World War II and the advent of massive and accelerating urban redevelopment programs, large-scale highway construction, and a host of other land-altering activities, historic preservationists and archaeologists became increasingly alarmed at the rate of disappearance beneath the bulldozers of historic and prehistoric buildings, sites, and structures.

One response to the threat was the chartering in 1949 of the National Trust for Historic Preservation by the United States Congress (U.S. Code 1977g). Until very recently, the National Trust has been principally concerned with historic buildings and sites and with developing a large preservation constituency. Archaeology, especially prehistoric archaeology, has not been a major concern of the trust. Nonetheless, the existence of the trust has been of importance to CRM by creating a general awareness of cultural preservation and its importance within the country.

However, creation of the National Trust did not solve many preservation problems. There was a perceived need for a much stronger federal role, one that articulated federal, state, local, and private interests and concerns (Rains *et al.* 1965). The result was the Historic Preservation Act of 1966 (U.S. Code 1977i).

THE 1966 ACT

The 1966 Historic Preservation Act greatly enlarged the federal role in the preservation of cultural resources. It also marked a shift away from a strict concern with cultural properties of national significance. Sites, buildings, etc. of local, state, or regional historical or *cultural* significance also could be accorded protection. The act also gave the federal government a leading role in cultural resources protection activities and provided mechanisms to "encourage and assist" local and state governments, the National Trust, and private groups in preservation activities. The act (U.S. Code 1977i:Section 470f) authorized the expansion and maintenance of a "National Register of districts, sites, buildings, structures, and objects significant in American history, architecture, archaeology, and culture." It also established a grant program to states to prepare statewide historical surveys and plans, and a matching grant program to aid citizens in preserving eligible historic properties. These functions, and others discussed later, were to be administered on the state level by "liaison officers," later called state historic preservation officers. The act (U.S. Code 1977i:Sections 470i–m) also established the Advisory Council on Historic Preservation. The council membership included the secretaries of several cabinet-level agencies, the administrator of the General Services Administration, the chairman of the National Trust for Historic Preservation, and 10 citizen members. (The council membership was altered by the 1980 amendments to the 1966 act.)

For present purposes, the key provision of the 1966 act is Section 470f:

> The head of any federal agency having direct or indirect jurisdiction over a proposed federal or federally assisted undertaking in any state and the head of any federal department or independent agency having authority to licence any undertaking shall, prior to the approval of the expenditure of any federal funds on the undertaking or prior to the issuance of any licence, . . . take into account the effect of the undertaking on any district, site, building, structure or object that is included in *or eligible for inclusion in* the National Register. The head of any such federal agency shall afford the Advisory Council on Historic Preservation . . . a reasonable opportunity to comment with regard to such undertaking (U.S. Code 1977i; emphasis added).

This provision, together with the rules issued by the government to implement the act (U.S. Government 1980c–g), provides a significant portion of the basic legal structure and operating mechanisms for the conduct of CRM and historic preservation. But before turning to a review of how "the system" operates, it is necessary to outline other relevant pieces of federal legislation.

The mandate in Section 470f of the Historic Preservation Act to "take into account the effect of . . .[a federal] undertaking" on *cultural* resources was expanded in 1969 in the National Environmental Policy Act (NEPA) (U.S. Code 1977j). As previously noted, this act was designed to assess potential impacts of federal projects on the *total* environment, natural and cultural, and to assess alternative procedures by which the project could be undertaken. It (U.S. Code 1977j:Section 4332) established an "environmental review" process by requiring the development of Environmental Impact Statements. Such statements were to assess and evaluate all potential (social, economic, natural, and cultural) impacts of a proposed project, both adverse and positive, direct and indirect, and to discuss and evaluate feasible alternatives to the proposed project.

The assessment of adverse impacts on cultural resources and the provision for appropriate "mitigation measures" to avoid or lessen such impacts was required (U.S. Government 1980b).

The 1966 Department of Transportation Act [U.S. Code 1977m:Section 1653(f)] contains a provision relating to cultural resources similar to those in the NEPA. It requires that federally funded roadways shall not be built across land on which cultural resources of national, state, or local significance are located, unless (*a*) there are no "feasible and prudent" alternatives, in which case, (*b*) plans are formulated to minimize damage to such resources.

The 1966 Historic Preservation Act tacitly involved all federal agencies controlling land, buildings, or structures within the interests of cultural resources preservation. This involvement was given a positive direction by a presidential Executive Order, No. 11593, "Protection and Enhancement of the Cultural Environment" issued in May 1971 (U.S. Code 1977k). The order directs the federal government to provide leadership in preserving cultural resources, to take various steps to preserve cultural resources under federal control, and to "locate, inventory and nominate . . . all sites, buildings, districts and objects under their [federal agencies'] control that appear to qualify for listing on the National Register" (U.S. Code 1977k:Section 470).

The Executive Order created specific CRM responsibilities in federal agencies, especially land-managing agencies, such as the Bureau of Land Management (BLM) and the United States Forest Service. These responsibilities are discussed below.

In December 1980 the Congress passed extensive amendments (U.S. Code 1980c) to the 1966 Historic Preservation Act. Among other provisions, the amendments restructure the membership of the Advisory Council on Historic Preservation, codify Executive Order No. 11593, make various changes in the operation of State Historic Preservation Office programs, and reaffirm the federal leadership role in cultural resources preservation.

Other federal legislation pertaining to CRM includes the Reservoir Salvage Act of 1960 (amended 1974, 1978) (U.S. Code 1977h) and the Archeological Resources Protection Act of 1979 (U.S. Code 1980b); the latter is discussed in a subsequent section of this chapter. The Reservoir Salvage Act (U.S. Code 1977h) was designed to alleviate "salvage archeology" problems engendered by continuation of large-scale dam construction after World War II. Salvage archaeology within proposed reservoir areas actually began in the late 1920s behind Boulder (now Hoover) Dam, and continued in the 1930s in the Tennessee Valley Authority area in the Southeast and elsewhere. The history of "reservoir" salvage archaeology as an early form of CRM deserves much more extensive treatment than is possible here (Jennings 1963; Wedel 1981). The 1974 and 1978 amendments to the Reservoir Salvage Act established a firm funding base for mitigation of cultural resources impacted by large-scale federal projects—1% of project costs. The 1980 amendments to the Historic Preservation Act make it possible to exceed that limitation.

The Compliance Process

To implement the requirements of the 1966 Historic Preservation Act, the National Park Service in the late 1960s formed an Office of Archeology and Historic Preservation (OAHP). The major purpose of the office was to consolidate in one division all Park Service "external" cultural resources preservation functions (i.e., those not relating to national parks, monuments, etc.). The division includes the National Register of Historic Places, a grants administration section, Technical Preservation Services (primarily providing "how-to" information for preserving historic properties), the National Architectural and Engineering Record, the Historic Sites Survey, and Interagency Archeological Services.

As noted previously, the 1966 act also created the Advisory Council on Historic Preservation and gave it specific planning functions as well as some oversight on federal projects that may affect cultural resources. The oversight function, however, is limited to procedural reviewing and "commenting" on proposed federal actions. The council does not have legal authority to stop a federal project that may adversely impact cultural resources, a point returned to later.

Another set of entities created by the 1966 act is the State Historic Preservation Offices (SHPO). Under the federal regulations that implement the 1966 act (U.S. Government 1980d), the offices are established as a part of the state government of each state, the District of Columbia, and the various United States territories. The state governor is responsible for the appointment of the chief officer of the SHPO. The office staff is mandated to include qualified professionals in the fields of architectural history, architecture, history, and archaeology, although some state offices never have been fully staffed.

One of the major CRM functions of these three agencies—the SHPO, the Advisory Council, and the OAHP, especially the National Register division—is carrying out what is called the *compliance process*. That is, attempting to ensure that all parties involved in a proposed major federal project that might affect significant cultural resources are "in compliance" with the requirements of the pertinent historic preservation laws and regulations. The process is complex; a full discussion and examples are contained in King *et al.* (1977:65–93, 121–144). Here, only a simplified hypothetical example will be used to outline the working of the process.

A utility proposes to construct a pipeline from a fuel source to one of its power plants. The pipeline will cross public land, and a federal license is required for construction. Such a project clearly falls under Section 470f of the 1966 Historic Preservation Act. The project also will require an assessment of the potential environmental impacts of the pipeline as required by the 1969 National Environmental Policy Act. The utility planners propose several alternate routes for the pipeline. They consult with the appropriate SHPO to determine if any National Register eligible sites lie within or adjacent to the proposed rights-of-way. They also determine with the SHPO that surveys are needed to locate presently unknown cultural resources within the proposed rights-of-way. Depending on the planning process and the alternatives initially being considered, the level of survey (from some sample fraction to 100% coverage) will vary (U.S. Government 1980f).

The utility planners will also consult with the relevant federal cultural resource managers whose agencies control the lands being crossed as to the location of, and potential impact on, known cultural resources and the design and level of surveys to be undertaken at various stages in the planning process. The initial surveys are undertaken either by the agencies involved or under a contractual arrangement with a qualified organization. Based on data recovered from cultural resource and other environmental surveys, and on costs and other planning criteria, decisions are made on a specific right-of-way. (In reality, rights-of-way are often determined in advance, thus limiting options for avoidance of cultural resources.) Once the specific route is determined, an intensive survey is undertaken to locate the cultural resources within the route and to assess their significance (i.e., determine which of the resources are "eligible for inclusion" in the National Register). (The problem of significance determination, especially of archaeological resources, is very complex. It is discussed in the Management and Research section of this chapter.) Several cultural resource sites are found to be eligible for nomination. And, it is determined that those sites will be "adversely affected" by the pipeline construction.

Nomination forms for eligible sites are prepared by the federal agency involved and submitted to the SHPO. There they are reviewed for accuracy and adequacy by the SHPO staff and then submitted to a state-level advisory board for review and approval. On approval, the nominations are then forwarded to the National Register. If a site's eligibility is approved, the utility planners, the federal cultural resource managers, and the SHPO staff formulate a preservation plan, which is designed to avoid, or minimize, the adverse impact of the pipeline project on the cultural resources. The plan is forwarded to the Advisory Council on Historic Preservation for review and comment. Subsequently, a Memorandum of Agreement is signed by the Advisory Council, the utility, the SHPO, and the federal land-managing agency. The agreement specifies what will be done to protect the cultural resources (ideally by avoiding them entirely); if avoidance is not possible, various "mitigation measures" are agreed on. These may range from various forms of protection to partial or total excavation, depending on the exigencies of the situation and the location of specific resources. Following the execution of the agreement, the cultural resource managers assume a "watchdog" role to ensure that the agreement is upheld.

The foregoing is, admittedly, an over-simplified illustration. In practice, there are usually many hitches and complications to enliven the days of cultural resource managers, SHPO staff members, and the archaeologists who contract to carry out the research work associated with a project.

The compliance process takes on other dimensions in the case of projects being proposed by federal agencies whose personnel feel that compliance with cultural resources legislation impedes the "missions" of the agencies. Green (1980a) makes the following distinction:

> Management agencies are those [in] . . . possession . . . of actual cultural resources and [that] have both management and compliance responsibility toward them. . . . Project agencies are those that do not have possession . . . or [are] only temporarily in possession of cultural resources, and have compliance but no management responsibility toward them. . . . [The latter] tend to see cultural resources as entities which stand in the way of project completion and, therefore, [are] not worthy of management.

The purpose of the compliance process is to attempt to see that cultural resources threatened by a project are properly "managed" (i.e., recorded, evaluated, protected, or, if necessary, salvaged). The compliance mechanism is established by rules (U.S. Government 1980c) under which the Advisory Council can review and comment on proposed projects.

But the process is a fragile thing (King *et al.* 1977:65–94); it has depended in part on establishing informal working relationships by those concerned with CRM with staff personnel in project agencies. But, in the end, if all the review and commenting procedures outlined in U.S. Government (1980c) are exhausted, and the project agency refuses to comply, the project can still proceed as originally planned, and the cultural resources within the project area may well be destroyed or impaired.

Besides participation in the compliance process, the Advisory Council, the SHPOs, and the National Register have numerous other responsibilities (King *et al.* 1977:65–95). Some of these are touched on in subsequent sections.

MANAGING CULTURAL RESOURCES

The management of cultural resources is carried out by federal, state, and local agencies. But, since most of the CRM agencies are federal, the focus here is on them. The agencies have numerous CRM responsibilities under federal legislation and Executive Order No. 11593. How these responsibilities are implemented varies somewhat with the structure and "mission(s)" of the agency in question. The following is a brief description of the CRM functions of the major federal land managing agencies, followed by a discussion of how those functions are carried out.

Department of the Interior

National Park Service

The National Park Service, since its inception in 1916, has had a variety of mandated CRM functions. These include protecting, researching, and interpreting to the public the numerous and varied cultural resources found within the 287 national parks, monuments, historic sites, battlefields, recreation areas, parkways, preserves, scenic trails, lakeshores, and seashores (comprising over 11 million ha) under Park Service jurisdiction. These management functions take place at the various parks, monuments, etc. and are assisted by CRM specialists in the Washington, D.C. office, eight regional offices, two department-wide service centers at Harpers Ferry, West Virginia, and Denver, Colorado, and three archaeological centers, located at Tucson, Arizona, Lincoln, Nebraska, and Tallahassee, Florida. These several entities focus principally on internal Park Service CRM functions. Besides caring for the cultural resources, there is an active research program of cultural resources research within the parks, monuments, etc. The research activity in turn supports one of the Park Service's major functions—public education for the millions of persons who visit the various areas yearly.

A second division of the Park Service with CRM functions is the previously noted Office of Archeology and Historic Preservation. Its functions are external (i.e., not connected with national parks, etc.)—the National Register of Historic Places, the National Architectural and Engineering Record, Technical Preservation Services, administration of the State Historic Preservation Office program, and Interagency Archeological Services. The latter has specific archaeological functions relating to interagency coordination and contract archaeology.

Bureau of Land Management

The BLM is the nation's largest land manager, responsible for the administration of nearly 195 million ha plus the outer continental shelf. The BLM has a system of state offices with a CRM staff and district offices within each state, each district usually having at least one CRM person. The CRM functions are several. One is inventory, under Executive Order No. 11593. Given the land area that is administered, it is clear that the task is overwhelming. A variety of sample strategies have been applied in various districts and states to attempt to meet inventory requirements.

The BLM is a "multiple-use" agency; activities such as grazing, extraction of minerals and fossil fuels, and outdoor recreation are within its jurisdiction. Hence, bureau CRM personnel are engaged (usually simultaneously) in a wide variety of compliance, protection, planning, and research functions.

Fish and Wildlife Service

The Fish and Wildlife Service manages over 13 million ha of land and wetlands to provide refuge and protection for avifauna and various ungulates and to provide stock fish for lakes and reservoirs. Its principal CRM functions are inventory and protection of cultural resources on its lands.

Bureau of Reclamation

This agency (from 1978 to 1981 called the Water and Power Resources Service) is a major dam and irrigation project-building agency. By law it operates only in the 17 western-most states. The agency administers over 2.7 million ha. It is organized into a series of regional and project offices, each with at least one CRM staff person. The service has CRM inventory and protection functions, but also major mitigation functions—to survey, record, and, usually, salvage cultural resources to be inundated by a reservoir or impacted by related construction activities. A current example is the Dolores Project in southwestern Colorado (Breternitz *et al.* 1980; Madden and Weakly 1980).

Bureau of Indian Affairs

The Bureau of Indian Affairs (BIA) directly administers approximately 1.3 million ha of land. In addition, there are over 15 million ha of "tribally owned" lands (i.e., lands owned by tribal organizations, trust lands, and leased lands) in the contiguous 48 states. Cultural resource management on Native American lands is a highly complex matter, so much so that it requires separate treatment. It should be noted, however, that in recent years some tribal groups (e.g., the Zuni of New Mexico) have established their own CRM programs. Cultural resource management in relation to Native Americans is discussed in more detail in the following.

Department of Agriculture

The Department of Agriculture has recently formulated a strong policy toward the protection and management of cultural resources throughout all divisions of the agency (U.S. Government 1980a,k; Flamm and Friedman 1981). The largest of the department's land-managing agencies, the Forest Service, administers 76 million ha of forest and grasslands. The Forest Service has had an active and developing CRM program since 1970. The Forest Service is divided into 10 regions (each with a regional archaeologist) within which are the various national forests (each with at least one forest archaeologist). Like the BLM, the Forest Service is a "multiple-use" agency—activities such as timbering, grazing, mineral extraction, watershed management, and recreation come under its jurisdiction. Hence, it must undertake a variety of CRM functions—inventory, evaluation, protection, and compliance.

A second division of the Department of Agriculture that functions in a land-management capacity is the Soil Conservation Service. Its CRM role is complicated by the fact that most of its technical assistance operations are situated on private agricultural or grazing land. The Soil Conservation Service, however, does have CRM regulations governing the protection of cultural resources within its project areas (Flamm and Friedman 1981:189).

Department of Energy

The Department of Energy administers over .9 million ha of land, principally the Nevada Nuclear Test Site and the Los Alamos National Laboratory reservation in New Mexico. Cultural resource management functions are primarily inventory and mitigation in construction areas carried out under contract (Pippin, personal communication).

Department of Defense

The various components of the Department of Defense administer a total of 14 million ha of land. On lands administered by the Army, Air Force, and Navy, CRM functions have been primarily inventory and mitigation, usually under contract. The Corps of Engineers, which administers over 3.2 million ha of land, plays, and has played since World War II, a major CRM role. The corps is perhaps the largest construction agency in the country. It designs and builds dams, harbors, canals, flood control systems, irrigation systems, and a wide variety of defense installations. As such, it necessarily has a heavy impact on cultural resources in project areas. As a major dam builder, the corps has been involved in "reservoir salvage" programs since World War II. The corps is organized into districts, each with a variety of construction responsibilities. Its principal CRM functions are mitigation—usually salvage archaeology. A current example is the Tennessee–Tombigbee waterway project in Alabama and Mississippi (U.S. Army 1979a,b).

In the foregoing, various federal CRM functions are listed. Lipe and Lindsay (1974:vii–viii) define CRM as "the philosophy and methodology required to manage cultural resources as a cultural heritage of long-term worth" (see also McGimsey and Davis 1977:110). How the philosophy and methodology are implemented is the subject of the following discussion.

Land-management agency cultural resources personnel (e.g., those employed by the BLM, the Forest Service, or the Fish and Wildlife Service, etc., carry out a variety of management tasks. A major task is meeting the requirements of Executive Order No. 11593, inventorying cultural resources on lands under agency jurisdiction, evaluating the potential significance of those resources for nomination to the National Register of Historic Places, and protecting and otherwise managing the resources once identified.

A first major step in the identification and management of the cultural resources of a specified area is the formulation of a cultural resources *overview*. The purpose here is basically to determine what is known about the resources in an area and to make management and research recommendations for future implementation. A typical format for an overview includes sections on environment and ethnographic background, a presentation of the known culture history of the area, a history of previous research, an assessment of future research potential and an outline of relevant research problems, management recommendations, an extensive annotated bibliography, and assessments of, and guides to, pertinent archival resources and artifact collections. Properly done, overviews are highly useful baseline documents to guide future management and research efforts (e.g., Berman 1979; Cordell 1978; Glassow 1977; McClellan *et al.* 1980; McDonald 1976, 1979; Stewart 1980).

A second step in managing the cultural resources of an area is to undertake further inventory and assessment, leading to the formulation of an *archaeological* (or *cultural resources*) *assessment report*. To do this may include relocating and assessing previously recorded sites, as well as surveying for new sites. The level and intensity of the survey will be a function of area, time, funding, sample design, and management and research needs. In some instances, overviews and assessments are combined, particularly for relatively small land areas (e.g., Bousman 1974; Hartman and Wolf 1977; Schart 1977; Scurlock 1979).

Assessment reports are frequently formulated for areas in which a proposed land-altering project may impact cultural resources. These reports discuss known cultural resources within the project area and potential impacts on them, and they outline additional research required to evaluate adequately the significance of the resources and to suggest feasible mitigation alternatives. Such assessment reports usually feed into, or become part of, preliminary environmental impact reports. They are usually the bases on which *scopes of work* are formulated to acquire additional information to assess more fully potential impacts and alternatives or formulated mitigation plans (Vivian *et al.* 1977:74–75).

A third step is the formulation of a *management plan* for the cultural resources of an area. Such plans usually are incorporated into overall land management plans or environmental impact statements for specific areas or "planning units." These plans have a variety of functions, especially as proposed formulations for protecting, preserving, interpreting, and using cultural resources. Developing and implementing management plans for large areas is very difficult, especially "multiple-use" areas, such as those administered by the BLM or the Forest Service. A good example of the problems faced by cultural resource managers in such areas is the California Desert Conservation Area, which comprises nearly one quarter of the state of California (Bureau of Land Management 1980). The area contains large numbers of prehistoric and historic resources, but also has a multitude of other uses, which make the management (especially the protection) of those resources very difficult indeed.

Recently, Aten (1980) proposed an "integrative" management planning process to structure the inventory, evaluation, and protection "elements of preservation programs," on the state level. Basically, the process is an amplification of the overview, assessment, and management plan procedure just outlined and is designed to include *all* "important" cultural resources within a state.

Once produced, management plans should not be regarded as static, "cookbook" documents. This is particularly so for large areas in which many land-altering activities are ongoing or being proposed and in which many cultural resources are known (or suspected) to exist.

An example is an evolving management process for the San Juan Basin region in the Four Corners area of the Southwest. The region has a long culture history, from paleo-Indian times (ca. 10,000 B.C.) to the historic period. Historic tribes in the area include several Pueblo groups, and Navajo,

Apache, and Ute. The region has been the scene of extensive energy development, and much further development, especially uranium mining, is projected. Several CRM agencies have jurisdiction within the basin, including the National Park Service, the BLM, the Forest Service, the New Mexico and Colorado State Historic Preservation Offices, the Office of Strip Mining, the Department of the Interior, and the Navajo tribe. Starting from an assessment study by the National Park Service (1980), the several agencies are jointly developing a dynamic management system utilizing a computerized data base (Green 1981; Wait 1981) and extensive application of remote sensing (Drager and Lyons 1981) to monitor land-altering activities and as an aid in predicting probable site locations.

The San Juan Basin provides an example of a cooperative undertaking among several CRM entities. However, comprehensive management of cultural resources, particularly large land areas, requires considerable cooperation among *all* the land-managing entities within a particular state or region. For many and varied bureaucratic, legal, and (often) time reasons, such cooperation is difficult to achieve and even more difficult to maintain. The number of "players" involved, that is, representatives of agencies and groups that must be involved, often turns intended working task groups into conventions. Nonetheless, if properly structured, such task groups are an effective means of managing cultural resources within a state or a large region.

A model for this type of undertaking may be the Cultural Resources Subcommittee of the Alaska Land Managers Cooperative Task Force. This task force was established in 1978 to bring together all federal and state agencies and Native American groups with jurisdiction over, or interests in, land planning in Alaska. The task force functions as a consensus body for comprehensive land-use planning and management. One of its constituent committees, the Cultural Resources Subcommittee, deals with the full range of cultural resources within the state, from prehistoric archaeological sites to aircraft shot down during World War II. The subcommittee meets regularly with the full task force and hence is able to articulate CRM concerns with other land-management concerns statewide on a continuing basis.

In addition to the foregoing, CRM agencies have other management duties. These include protection of resources from vandalism (a complex and frustrating enterprise, which I discuss further later in this chapter) and the elements. Also, the *value* of cultural resources must be assessed. Green (1980a:2) makes a useful distinction between value and *significance*: "The value (not significance) of a cultural resource can be assessed in two ways: 1) whether its character is such that *in situ* preservation or adaptive reuse are merited, and 2) whether it has demonstrable scientific value." The latter is established within the text of a "valid" research design. In this view, *value* becomes a *function* of significance; the value of a resource is its potential likelihood of yielding data to confirm reputed significance versus *in situ* preservation. A third management element "refers to the mechanisms employed for deciding when and how a cultural resource will be preserved or used up" (Green 1980a:2), for example, deciding whether a "scientific need" is established to warrant the sampling or excavation of an archaeological resource, or deciding whether a structure or building warrants stabilization or other protection from the natural processes of decay.

Another side to decision making about "preserving" or "using" resources relates to threats to resources from land-altering projects. Here, the agency cultural resources manager becomes a pivotal figure in the compliance process (outlined previously), performing several tasks. These include,

1. formulating a scope of work to gather requisite inventory and significance assessment data;
2. overseeing the technical aspects of contract compliance;
3. participating in the formulation and evaluation of environmental impact statements;
4. establishing the value of resources relative to their preservation or "use";
5. negotiating with project agency personnel and, usually, staff personnel of the Advisory Council for Historic Preservation and the State Historic Preservation Office on memoranda of agreement and mitigation plans; and
6. keeping a sense of humor throughout the compliance process.

Another significant management task relates to the "utilization of cultural resources for the public good" (McGimsey and Davis 1977:110), that is, the *interpretation* of resources. As previously noted, CRM in the broad sense is a public collective good. Most of CRM, especially archaeological CRM, is preponderantly supported by public, or corporate, funds. In the American scheme of logic, it follows that the public should "get something" for its money—*understandable* information and enjoyment of that information. (It is not self-evident to an educated layperson what, if any, difference it makes if a flint artifact has an "edge angle" of 30° rather than 45°.)

The public may acquire cultural resources information by on-site visits to preserved resources or through "the media" (Green 1980a:2). For many years, the public has gotten a great deal of information from on-site visits to national, state, county, or municipal parks, monuments, historic sites, museums, battlefields, etc. The National Park Service, especially since its "Mission 66" upgrading program, has become a leader in on-site interpretation, as has also the National Trust for Historic Preservation. In recent years, both the BLM and the Forest Service have also established on-site cultural resources interpretive programs. Provision of information through publication, film, and broadcast is variable within CRM. In historic preservation, there is a wide variety of books, magazines, newspapers, and films available to the public. A significant percentage (possibly 30–40%) of the total funds utilized in historic preservation is for dissemination of public information. In archaeology, the percentage of funds for the same purpose is practically nil. Very little *public* information (as contrasted with technical reports) about archaeology is generated by anyone, least of all archaeologists. Many have recognized the "need to communicate" with those who pay the bills; few have done anything. It is more than symptomatic that the "Crisis in Communication" section (Woodbury and McGimsey 1977) of the Airlie House Report largely is devoted to lamenting the fact that archaeologists cannot communicate among themselves, let alone with the public. A major "management need" for archaeological CRM is to develop large-scale public information programs. To date, the only national efforts have been *Archaeology,* the magazine of the American Institute of Archaeology, and the recently established *Early Man* magazine, published by the Center for American Archaeology. Given the current levels of public support for archaeology, both magazines, commendable as they are, are not enough.

MANAGEMENT AND RESEARCH

Cultural resources may be thought of as "containers" of information, or potential information, about past human activities. In a very real sense, the principal thrust of the cultural resources preservation movement in the United States and elsewhere is to preserve the physical remains of the past for the information they yield or may yield. On this basis, a major function of CRM is determining the means through which information can (and ought to) be extracted from the resources—in other words, how research is to be conducted on managed resources.

There are at least four principal management considerations. One is the "conservation ethic" (Lipe 1974) of CRM, which holds that cultural resources are nonrenewable and, hence, a portion of the extant resources should be conserved for future research rather than being "used" now. The assumption is that in the future, new frames of reference, methods, and techniques will permit much more information to be extracted from resources than is presently possible. Therefore, one management consideration is deciding which resources should be conserved and which "used."

A second consideration relates to the reconciliation and coordination of management objectives and research objectives. In part, this centers around the question of whether data generated for planning and compliance purposes may also be used for research purposes and, if so, how?

A third consideration relates to the term "significance" as used in those federal laws and regulations that structure so much of CRM practice. For reasons outlined in the following the concept has proven to be difficult to handle when applied to archaeological resources.

A fourth consideration has to do with "quality control," that is, attempting to ensure that information generated is adequate for management and research purposes.

Conserving Cultural Resources

Previously, reference was made to the management function of deciding if a particular cultural resource should be "used" (Green 1980a:2), that is, establishing whether there is a "scientific need" to systematically collect a surface site or to excavate a site or a complex of sites. In an optimal situation, the site, or sites, is not threatened by immediate destruction. Rather, an archaeologist wishes to excavate a site to test one or more hypotheses. A key management function would be to assess the adequacy of the proposed research design (see the discussion on research designs) in relation to current knowledge and the number of known similar sites in the region. A decision can then be made to proceed or not. In a situation in which sites are threatened by land-altering projects, decisions as to how sites are to be "used" take on many additional dimensions. Project costs, feasible project design alternatives, mitigation costs, and secondary impacts on resources all should be weighed in deciding which cultural resources will be used, and how. No formula is possible given the wide variety of projects in which judgments and decisions must be made. However, the conservation ethic demands that sites should be conserved if possible. For most land-altering projects, this means that cultural resource managers must attempt to make the strongest possible case for a project design that avoids, or minimally damages, cultural resources within the project area (McMillan *et al.* 1977:40).

Secondary impacts are often a major problem in the protection and conservation of cultural resources. Even if a land-altering project is designed, and construction activities (*primary impacts*) controlled to avoid cultural resources, secondary impacts often serve to destroy them. Secondary impacts are spin-offs or indirect effects of a project. An example will illustrate the problem.

The proposed MX Missile Project in the Great Basin was to be constructed on the floors of some 23 valleys within the region, over some 32,260 km². A variety of cultural resources on the valley floors would have been affected by construction (primary impact). However, the majority of the resources lie in the foothills and uplands adjacent to the valleys. These resources increasingly would have been badly affected by surveying, seismic testing, and other activities and by recreational and leisure activities of the thousands of construction and military personnel scheduled to be in the region during construction of the project (D. Fowler *et al.* 1980). Here the secondary impacts would have been severe, possibly even more severe than the primary impacts on the valley floors. Whether workable CRM procedures would have been devised to protect and conserve the cultural resources was highly questionable. To date, many project agencies minimally consider secondary impacts, or see them as outside the mandates of CRM legislation.

Management versus Research

A central issue in CRM for several years centered on the apparent problem of reconciling management and research aims or goals. The problem really existed in the form of a dilemma: how to collect or develop scientifically useful data within the constraints of a contract specifying that only a highly delimited area be studied? For example, what contribution to general archaeological knowledge is made by an intensive survey of a 1.2-ha drill pad site, especially if any data generated cannot be linked to resources in the surrounding area? Or, what useful data are gained by intensively surveying tracts .2 × .8 km in size every 8 km along a 1930-km power line corridor? True, "compliance" requirements may be satisfied by such undertakings, but scientific, scholarly requirements are not. The matter remains an open question (e.g., Holden 1977; McGimsey 1980; Spiess 1978). Keel (1979) states the problem succinctly, pointing out that most "contract" archaeological research is necessarily circumscribed geographically and by data collection requirements, and that data so collected are basically for management or compliance purposes. If the collected data also contribute to the overall store of knowledge it is a serendipitous extra. From a strictly management perspective, this position is defensible; but it glosses over a much more basic question, one which underlies most of the management versus research quandary, that is, why are cultural resources being protected, conserved, and managed at all? As stated previously, cultural resources may be regarded as containers of information or potential information about past human activities. If public funds are expended to study a portion of the resources, should the results contribute only to management needs, or should some scientific results also be forthcoming? In short, can management and research needs be reconciled? The question has been widely discussed (Adams 1977; Fitting 1978; Gardner 1976; Grady and Lipe 1976; Holden 1977; King 1979, 1980a,b; Lindsay and Randall 1977; MacDonald 1976; Raab *et al.* 1980). The answer appears to be a qualified "yes." The key, however, is the formation of adequate regional research designs, within which data generated from small-scale, isolated projects—.4- or 16-ha surveys of drill pads or linear surveys of utility or transportation corridors—can be made to make some scholarly sense (Goodyear 1977; Schiffer and Gumerman 1977:363–444).

The other side of the coin is that *scopes of work*—statements issued by contracting agencies as to what research they wish to have undertaken—must be realistically written to permit the collection of useful and relevant data. Quite often, inappropriate sampling designs specified in scopes of work have led to the generation of spurious data (Dumond 1977).

Research Designs

As noted, a major key to reconciling management and research needs is the formulation of adequate research designs. Information derived from the study of cultural resources is not self-evident; its meanings are derived from the intellectual frame of reference within which the information is collected. Research designs are "frames of reference" in which conceptual assumptions, research goals, hypotheses, methodologies, and operations are explicitly laid out (Goodyear *et al.* 1978; Schiffer and House 1977).

The basic requirements for a good research design are (*a*) that the problems addressed are significant; (*b*) that proposed hypotheses or models are realistically testable, given the available resource base; and (*c*) that research procedures are rigorous, consistent, and justified (Grady 1977:44; Schiffer and Gumerman 1977:130–133).

Ideally, there should be several levels of research designs, each descending level dealing with an inclusive, smaller geographical area and increasingly finer-focused research questions. However, in many parts of the United States, overall state-level research designs are only beginning to be formulated (Aten 1980). (State-level research designs are artifacts of political boundaries and the existence of the State Historic Preservation Office system. In many instances, other boundary criteria are much more appropriate than state lines. Past cultural systems were rarely so bounded. Much more useful are regional research designs [Plog 1981]).

A "region" may be defined topographically, hydrographically, ecologically, or culturally. The Southwestern Anthropological Research Group (SARG) works primarily within a culturally defined regional framework. Given the diverse research interests of the group members, this is appropriate. Elsewhere, topographic or ecologic parameters may be used, for example, as in the Mojave Desert (Weide 1973), the Great Basin (Thomas 1969), or hydrographic basins, as in Illinois (Brown 1978).

However defined areally, a research design, whether regional or of smaller scale, minimally should contain the following elements:

1. A description of the resource base, that is, an outline of current knowledge about the distribution of resources, chronologies, and the culture history within the area of concern, should be included.

2. A statement outlining the "structure of inquiry," that is, the conceptual assumptions, or general theoretical approach of the investigators, is also necessary. In prehistoric archaeology, the approach may be that of cultural materialism (Thomas 1979:118–121; Willey and Sabloff 1980:185–191) or explicitly ecological (e.g., Hardesty 1980). Whatever the approach taken, it should be clearly delineated.

3. A third element is an outline of problem domains, that is, the general areas of research interest (Schiffer and Gumerman 1977:130–131). In research designs focusing on prehistoric cultural resources, problem domains might include, for example, chronologies, subsistence–settlement systems, paleodemography, technological systems, a variety of processual questions, settlement pattern networks. The range of domains is limited chiefly by the research interests of the investigators and whether certain questions are "feasible and relevant" (Grady 1977:44) given the extant data base. Each problem domain begins with a series of general questions followed by increasingly specific subquestions. The questions become the bases for the formulation of models or hypotheses to be tested.

Grady (1977:44) calls for an evaluation of "test implications" at this point. That is, a description of "the actual conditions that must hold in the archaeological record in order to evaluate the hypotheses" advanced. The concern is that oftentimes "hypotheses" are a reification of the obvious, or are tautological and hence lead to meaningless, or trivial, results; or that "hypotheses" are structured to meet agency goals rather than scientific goals.

4. A fourth element has to do with data quality and quantity control. Concern with data quality centers on the appropriateness and reliability of the data to be recovered. What kinds of data are needed to test specific hypotheses? Not all types of data potentially recoverable are relevant to the question at hand. In other words, what types of data are appropriate to the research questions and how is the quality of those data to be maintained? The quantity issue centers on how much data are required to address research questions properly, at what point are data redundant? (D. Fowler *et al.* 1980; James *et al.* 1980).

5. A fifth element, closely related to the fourth element, is the formulation of investigative strategies to meet the quality and quantity criteria. Here, reference is to sampling strategies in survey, collection, test, and excavation procedures. A central question is not the determination of which rote techniques are most easily applied, but which sampling strategies will be most productive given existing project constraints? Since 1970, the literature on the design and appropriateness of various sampling strategies and methods has

grown exponentially. Summaries and critiques may be found in King (1978), Lyons and Avery (1977), Mueller (1974, 1975), Plog *et al.* (1978), Schiffer *et al.* (1979), and Talmage *et al.* (1977). The choice of specific sampling strategies and methods often becomes a function of research design requirements balanced against agency goals, the area to be covered, and time and money constraints.

6. If a research design is meant to direct a specific project, operational procedures must be specified. That is, completing the field, archival, and laboratory research and ensuring data quality control in the process. Often, in archaeological CRM research, the fieldwork is conducted more or less adequately. But "carrying through," that is, carrying out all the tasks of analysis and report production within tight time and fiscal constraints has been a major problem (Keel 1979). Part of the problem is deciding at what point to quit "worrying" the data sets; that is, determining the point at which "enough" data have been extracted from an artifact, and the quantity of extractions that are necessary to answer adequately questions at some specified confidence level. No answer is proposed (or possible) herein—the point being that "operations management" or "research management" is a crucial exercise in CRM research, as well as in the implementation of specific research designs.

The foregoing "elements" are applicable to regional research designs and project-specific designs. There are other ways of organizing research designs. However they may be organized, their purpose is to lay out explicitly conceptual frameworks, research goals, hypotheses, methodologies, and operational procedures.

A major feature of research designs should be their dynamic nature. Research designs are not canonical documents. They are, at best, "state-of-the-art" assessments of current knowledge and speculation (hypotheses) and explicit guidelines for continued investigation. Research designs for large-scale CRM projects with multiple contractors selected on a low-bid basis (Weakly 1980) have additional requirements if the end results are to be scientifically useful. In such situations, as Canouts (1977:122) has pointed out,

(1) Each stage of a project's research program must be a refinement of the preceding stage;
(2) Research continuity must insure that a project is independent of a single researcher's commitment;
(3) Project research should be utilized as a cumulative base upon which subsequent contract projects can build.

Examples of research designs that attempt to meet these requirements include those for the Dolores Archeological Program in Colorado, the Tennessee–Tombigbee Project in Alabama and Mississippi, and the proposed MX Missile Project in Utah and Nevada (Breternitz *et al.* 1980; D. Fowler *et al.* 1980; James *et al.* 1980; Rodeffer and Chapman 1980; U.S. Army 1979a,b). Each of these designs must deal with the full range of cultural resources within the study area; each must cope with numerous problems of organizational coordination, data management, and data quality control. In doing these things, each must recognize the importance of the uniqueness of cultural data and the importance of context and relationship. Finally, each must attempt to maximize information recovery and project results within given fiscal and time constraints.

Significance

A central problem for several years in archaeological CRM has been how the "significance" of archaeological resources is to be established for compliance purposes, that is, determinations of eligibility for placement on the National Register of Historic Places, and hence, for protection and (if necessary) mitigation. The crux of the problem lies in the wording of the 1966 Historic Preservation Act (U.S. Code 1977i) and the rules implementing the act (U.S. Government 1980e:1202.6). Section 470a of the act authorizes the placement of "districts, sites, buildings, structures, and objects significant in American history, architecture, archaeology and culture . . ." on the National Register. The implementing rules set forth significance criteria that are basically humanistically derived. Only one criterion seems *directly applicable* to archaeological resources: properties "that have yielded, or may be likely to yield, information important in prehistory or history" [U.S. Government 1980e:1202.6(d)]. No specific *scientific* criteria are given. Attempts to remedy this oversight include an "Associated Memorandum," or addendum to the rules (U.S. Government 1980f) in which the term "research significance" is introduced. It is also suggested that such significance makes more sense if a "property" can be assessed within the context of a regional or state research design or overview "that will facilitate the development of arguments for and against the eligibility of specific properties and districts." According to an appendix to the "associated memorandum" (U.S. Government 1980f:Appendix A, Section VIIIB), "the following areas of significance are listed on National Register forms . . . *Archeology—Prehistoric:* The scientific study of life and culture of indigenous peoples before the advent of written records. *Archeology—Historic:* The scientific study of life and culture in the New World after the advent of written records." Thus were scientific considerations brought into National Register criteria.

However, the implementing rules appeared in 1976, 10 years after the passage of the Historic Preservation Act. And even when they did appear, they contained no explicit criteria as to what constitutes *scientific* significance. In the intervening decade, CRM archaeologists struggled mightily with "significance" and how it applied to archaeological resources. More importantly, they were often faced with providing a defensible definition to skeptical contracts officers and engineers in project agencies. Given the fairly clear-cut significance criteria applicable to historic houses ("George Washington slept here") or architectural set pieces ("designed by James Renwick"), the answer, "everything archaeological is significant—depending on the questions you ask," was less than satisfactory in the eyes of project managers eager to get on with construction. In some instances, credibility was further eroded when two reports on the same area disagreed as to the significance or potential significance of the sites recorded therein.

Numerous articles written between 1974 and 1979 resulted in no real agreement, but rather a recycling and reinterpretation of a small number of ideas (Thompson 1979:17). One way out of the dilemma is to recognize that archaeological resources have both humanistic and scientific significance (Dunnell and Dancey 1978:2–3). The former is a matter of cultural heritage and can be evaluated and explicated in terms of the usual National Register criteria of significance. The latter, scientific significance, relates to the totality of information in the archaeological record and is only explicated or realized within the framework of a properly formulated research design. The answer is still, "yes, it's significant, depending on the questions you ask." The difference must be that the questions (contained in research designs) must be asked ahead of time, before specific resources are assessed. Hence, the scientific significance of a specific cultural resource is its potential for providing answers to relevant research questions. Significance then becomes not an absolute concept, but a mechanism for structuring inquiry about cultural resources. A critical problem remains, that of translating the research significance of a resource into specific management recommendations (Schiffer and Gumerman 1977:243–244). This becomes one of the central tasks undertaken by cultural resources managers.

"Quality Control"

A fifth aspect of management and research in CRM relates to "quality control"—that is, the quality of fieldwork, of data generated and reports written, under CRM contracts. Hundreds of archaeological reconnaissances, surveys, and testing and excavation projects have been undertaken since 1966 to carry out the mandates of the various federal laws and rules. Many contracts specified inordinately tight time frames. In numerous instances, available field personnel were poorly, or only partially trained. The result has been many substandard project reports. The problem remains (Green 1980b; Kemrer 1980; Woodbury and McGimsey 1977). Aside from, but related to, the problem of poor writing is the problem of poor data collection and the analysis thereof. This is a matter of adequate training and supervision of field and laboratory personnel, which only academic archaeologists can resolve.

PROTECTION OF CULTURAL RESOURCES

A central problem facing CRM in the United States and other nations is the protection of cultural resources. Most federal legislation in the United States is designed to protect cultural resources from actions sanctioned by the federal government on public land. Equally urgent is the protection of cultural resources from theft or vandalism. The problem is worldwide, encompassing historic paintings, statuary, and other items, as well as "antiquities" (i.e., archaeological resources). The traffic in illegally obtained cultural objects runs to many millions of dollars a year. Equally objectionable from a scientific standpoint is the vandalism of archaeological sites to obtain salable antiquities.

The problem of vandalism, theft, and trafficking in antiquities is not new. Various Roman emperors issued edicts forbidding the defacement of monuments; in 1464, Pope Pius II forbade exporting works of art from the Papal States (Nieć 1976:1092); similar edicts or laws were issued by various European countries from the late sixteenth century on, usually for the preservation and conservation of monuments (Taylor 1948).

The problem of protecting cultural resources was exacerbated in the nineteenth century by the development of the great museums in Western Europe and the United States. To fill these great centers, the cultural resources of many nations were simply expropriated, one way or another. The Babylonian and Egyptian halls and the "shrine-room," containing the Elgin marbles (statuary fragments from the metopes and pediments of the Parthenon), in the British Museum symbolize this phase of antiquities "acquisition" and trafficking. Some museums in the United States and abroad are reputedly still acquiring "antiquities" illegally. Beginning in the late nineteenth century, many nations began enacting legislation (Nieć 1976) designed to halt the outflow of antiquities across their borders to the markets of Europe, the United States and elsewhere. In 1970, a general UNESCO conference adopted provisions of a Convention of the Means of Prohibiting and Preventing the Illicit Import, Export, and Transfer of Ownership of Cultural Property, since ratified by several nations, including the United States, which, however, has not passed any implementing legislation (Vitelli 1980) to make the convention enforceable. Other international developments include the resolution of the International Council of Museums, which recommends that member institutions not purchase art objects or antiquities of questionable provenience (Nafzinger 1972).

Official United States policy and legislation to control the import of foreign antiquities was, until recently, weak and inconsistent (Nieć 1976; Mark 1969). But in 1972, an act to control importation of illegal antiquities from Latin America (U.S. Code 1977l) was passed in part in response to the United States–Mexican Treaty of 1970 (U.S. Department of State 1970) and pressure from other Latin American countries to exclude or expel United States archaeological teams (Nieć 1976:1116) if the United States did not act. Until 1979 (U.S. Code 1980b), the United States did not prohibit the *export* of its own antiquities, making it relatively easy for collectors in Japan, Europe, and Arabia to relish Mimbres and other archaeological artifacts, and giving great financial impetus to vandalism of sites.

Within the United States, attempts have been made to control the vandalizing of archaeological resources since the 1880s when Congress first set aside Casa Grande and Chaco Canyon (Hosmer 1965:193). The 1906 Antiquities Act (U.S. Code 1977d) made unauthorized excavation a crime, although few, if any, cases were prosecuted before the late 1960s. In 1974 the Ninth Circuit Court declared the 1906 Antiquities Act unconstitutional (*U.S.* v. *Diaz,* 368 F. Supp. 856 [D. Arizona 1973] *rev'd.* 499 F. 2d 113 [9th Cir. 1974]). The decision highlighted the inadequacy of the legislation and the long overdue need for new legislation (Grayson 1976). The need was made increasingly urgent by the accelerating looting of archaeological sites for artifacts throughout the United States, but especially in the Southwest (Green and LeBlanc 1979; Rippeteau 1979; Williams 1978). In response to the problems, the Archeological Resources Protection Act (U.S. Code 1980b) was passed in late 1979. The act and implementing rules (U.S. Government 1981) provide federal cultural resource managers and prosecutors with stringent criminal and civil penalties that hopefully will impede the destruction of cultural resources on public lands.

Despite the new act, federal CRM is still faced with a monumental task in enforcing its provisions, especially in the West where there are hundreds of millions of hectares of public land. Land managing agencies have few enforcement officials (Peterson 1980) to cover vast areas. Local enforcement, at least in the West, may be unattainable for all practical purposes. The attitude toward enforcement was graphically brought home to the author during his work with the United States Congress on the 1979 Archeological Resources Protection Act, when an aide to a western senator informed him, ''the senator says to tell you he thinks that bill is an infringement on human rights.''

A particularly vexing problem is the protection of underwater cultural resources, principally shipwrecks, but also submerged maritime facilities (docks, etc.), middens, or occupational sites lying beneath coastal waters. The legal complexities surrounding jurisdiction over and protection of underwater cultural resources are staggering, complicated by admiralty law, international law, ambiguous state and federal laws, and recent adverse court decisions (Cockrell 1980). The formulation of workable legal mechanisms to protect submerged cultural resources, that is, laws that will stand up under challenge in court, is extraordinarily difficult. Meenan (1978) and Altes (1976) discuss the philosophical, procedural, and jurisdictional issues in detail. Meenan (1978:659–662), however, concludes that both state and federal jurisdiction over submerged resources can be legally established, and proposes a model underwater antiquities statute: States have jurisdiction within the "territorial sea," that is, the "three mile limit" (nine miles along the Gulf Coast of Florida and Texas) (Meenan 1978:642n.99); the federal government has jurisdiction beyond that to the limits of the outer continental shelf, as defined by international convention, "the seabed and subsoil of the submarine areas adjacent to coast but outside the territorial sea, to a depth of 200 meters" (U.S. Department of State 1958:Article 1[a]); and the outer continental shelf is under the jurisdiction of the BLM. The proposed statute is essentially the same as the current Florida state statute, which grants permits to salvors and splits the "take" between the salvors and the state (Cockrell 1980:334). Given the rapid despoliation of underwater resources, such a statute appears to be insufficient. However, getting "adequate" legislation through the Congress will be extremely difficult in the face of massive lobbying efforts by sports divers and others (Cockrell 1980:337).

Other Legal Protection Tools

In addition to federal antiquities legislation, there is a variety of other legal tools available that are potentially useful in protecting archaeological resources. These tools have been widely used in historic preservation to protect buildings and structures, but little used by archaeological CRM.

This "underutilization" may be because many archaeological resources are on public land, or lands within a "take area," an area that becomes public property in the course of a project.

The available legal "tools" include eminent domain, easements, zoning, transferable development rights, and tax incentives. Discussions of the applicability of these in historic preservation may be found in summaries by J. Fowler *et al.* (1980), Morrison (1974), Sackman (1979), Shull and Shull (1974), and Waters and Scott (1980). See also Kettler and Reams (1976) for additional bibliography. Recent works relating more specifically to archaeological CRM include Bauriedel (1980), Brothers (1975), Gyrisco (1980), Meenan (1978), Palacios and Johnson (1976), and Smith and Dryer (1976).

Eminent Domain

It was indicated in the preceding discussion that in 1896, the United States Supreme Court upheld the exercise of the power of eminent domain by the federal government for historic preservation purposes (Bosselman *et al.* 1973;

U.S. Supreme Court 1896). The exercise of eminent domain for the acquisition of archaeological properties has not been undertaken on the federal level, although the legal mechanism exists. Much more critical to CRM in general is the power of eminent domain on the state level, especially in mining law. Some portions of western states mining law is based on Nevada law, which grants the power of eminent domain to mining companies on the grounds that they are "paramount industries." The constitutionality of the law has been upheld three times by the Nevada Supreme Court and once, in 1922, by the United States Supreme Court (Rosha 1980). The current and projected upsurges in coal and oil-shale strip mining and precious and nonferrous open-pit mining in the West pose numerous threats to cultural resources on affected land areas (Vivian 1976). The existence of laws granting eminent domain to private corporations is a potential further threat. It should be noted that the eminent domain power is focused primarily on private lands. Whether it could be applied to state or federal public lands is moot at this time. As noted, the last test of the issue was in 1922, long before much federal or state legislation relating to public lands had been passed. (In May 1981, the Nevada legislature passed a law drastically curtailing the eminent domain powers of mining companies and recognizing CRM concerns.)

Zoning

Zoning is a police power delegated by states to county and municipal entities. Its primary function is to control types of land use and density of construction. In historic preservation, zoning has been used principally to create historic zones, districts, or overlays in urban areas (e.g., the Vieux Carré district in New Orleans, historic Savannah, Georgia). Few historic district or overlay ordinances include any consideration of archaeological resources, an exception being the recent ordinance passed in Oklahoma City (Gyrisco 1980).

Some local entities have antiquities ordinances not part of an overall historic district ordinance (e.g., Los Alamos county, New Mexico [LeBlanc 1979:363], Inyo and Marin counties, and the city of Larkspur, California [Gyrisco 1980:3]). Most such ordinances are designed to extend general protection to archaeological resources; others are limited to regulating the excavation of Indian burials.

Other types of zoning designed to preserve open space are potentially useful tools to preserve archaeological resources, for example, cluster zoning, which concentrates building density on a segment of a development parcel, leaving the remainder as open space. The review procedures adopted by San Diego and Orange counties in California, although they derive most directly from the California Environmental Quality Act, in effect utilize zoning powers as a means of protecting or mitigating cultural resources (Gyrisco 1980:7; May 1980).

Easements

Easements are interests or rights in property that are less than full, or fee simple, interests. They are most widely used to acquire access or use rights over private property for transportation, utilities, or communications purposes. In historic preservation, *facade easements* are widely used to preserve the historic or architectural character of an urban neighborhood or district. Owners of a historic building grant an easement of the exterior facades of their building to a public body, retaining the right to change the interiors as they wish. Such easements place restrictions on future alterations of the facades. Similarly, easements restricting development to preserve open space are widely used (e.g., in Maine and Maryland [Maryland Historical Trust 1975]). In California easements on archaeological sites have been donated to the state under provisions of the California Environmental Quality Act (Gyrisco 1980). Smith and Dryer (1976) propose an *archaeological easement* concept that may work in states lacking the land review powers inherent in the California situation. Briefly, the concept involves designation as a "state archaeological landmark" of any property containing "unique or significant sources of archeological data" identified during the review process or proposed land developments. The state then has the option of acquiring a 90-day "archaeological easement" to the property to permit time to evaluate the significance of the property, to work out a mitigation or preservation plan, or to see to its preservation and protection by selling the easement at fair market value for the land to a government body or appropriate nonprofit corporation or trust. An option is to give the power of eminent domain for acquisition of such properties to a state-appointed historic preservation committee; the committee may hold such a property for 2 years before disposing of it to an appropriate body (Smith and Dryer 1976:165).

Transferable Development Rights

The concept of transferable development rights (TDRs) was developed initially as a means of preserving historic landmark buildings in urban areas (Costonis 1974). The concept derives from the assumption that title to land is not a unitary right, but a collection of individual, severable rights, including development rights, that may be marketed apart from the land (Rose 1975:330). In urban areas, TDRs are defined, in effect, by zoning regulations that specify allowable density, bulk, and floor area of new buildings within a particular zone. The bulk or floor area of most existing landmark buildings is usually less than that allowed for the zone in which they are located. Since the economic return on a building is a function of total floor area, there is a strong economic incentive to tear down old buildings and erect new ones with floor areas that are as large as the zoning regulations allow. The TDR concept allows the owner of a landmark building to sell to another owner, for use elsewhere, the development rights to the differential between the actual floor space of the landmark building and the maximum allowed floor area for the zone. Once transferred, the "excess" and the right to develop the floor area is irrevocably withdrawn from the landmark lot; thus, in theory, preserving the extant landmark building. The sale income compensates the landmark owner for loss of income engendered by keeping the landmark. TDRs have been used in New York City and proposed in Chicago (Costonis 1974) to preserve landmark buildings.

The TDR concept has also been proposed (Rose 1974, 1975) as a means to preserve open space. Development rights to extant open land are transferred by sale to some other defined area within a local or county jurisdiction. The transfer extinguishes the right to further development and preserves the open spaces. Such an application could be used to protect archaeological resources on open, private land, perhaps as an additional tool to be used by such groups as the Archeological Conservancy (LeBlanc 1979), which is discussed in this chapter.

Tax Incentives

Under changes made in the United States Internal Revenue Code in 1976, 1978, and 1981 various federal tax incentives were created to encourage the preservation and restoration of privately held commercial buildings (Andrews 1980). Such incentives are inapplicable to archaeological resources. Applicable tax incentives are those federal and state laws governing donation of real property to charitable or educational institutions. Such donations would presumably be based on the value of the land per se rather than the value of the archaeological resources thereon. But, the result would be the protection of the resources. The donation of easements to archaeological resources, previously mentioned, in California is an example of the use of these forms of tax incentive.

Archeological Conservancy

The recently formed Archeological Conservancy (LeBlanc 1979; Michel 1981) holds some hope for cultural resources protection. Easements, donation, or outright purchases are used to protect sites (possibly also transferable development rights may be used). But clearly only a few "representative" archaeological sites can be obtained. And, the fact that a site is on private property rather than public land, especially in a remote area, is no guarantee it will remain inviolate. Nonetheless, the undertaking has great merit as one further means to protect cultural resources.

NATIVE AMERICANS AND CRM

In August, 1978 the United States Congress passed Joint Resolution No. 102 (U.S. Code 1980a), entitled the American Indian Religious Freedom Act, more properly perhaps the "Native American" Religious Freedom Act. The act states that it is

> the policy of the United States to protect and preserve for American Indians their inherent right of freedom to believe, express, and exercise the traditional religions of the American Indian, Eskimo, Aleut, and Native Hawaiian, including but not limited to access to sites, use, and possession of sacred objects and the freedom to worship through ceremonials and traditional rites.

The act also guarantees access to sacred sites, including cemeteries, visited for religious purposes, directs federal agencies to adjust their policies and procedures to meet the intent of the act, and requires a federal task force to report on means of implementing the act. Despite the apparent incongruity of guaranteeing Native Americans the right to practice Eskimo, Aleut, or Hawaiian religions (and presumably vice-versa), the intent of the act is clear, that is, to allow Native Americans full reign to practice traditional religions and to recognize the existence of sacred sites and areas (i.e., places or tracts of land that have significance and meaning within traditional belief systems) (Suagee 1980).

The Archeological Resources Protection Act of 1979 references the Native American Religious Freedom Act and contains specific provisions relating to exemptions for and issuance of permits to conduct cultural resources studies on Native American lands (U.S. Code 1980b:Section 4 [g]). The act (Section 4 [c]) *also* recognizes areas of tribal concern on nonreservation federal lands and specifies that if the issuance of an archaeological permit for work on public lands might result in harm to or destruction of a tribal religious or cultural site, the federal land manager must notify the tribe concerned prior to the granting of the permit (Suagee 1980:4). These rules are developed and extended in the Draft Rules and Regulations to implement the Archeological Resources Act of 1979 (U.S. Government 1981).

The revised regulations issued in 1979 by the Advisory Council on Historic Preservation, which implement the "streamlined" consultation procedures of Section 470f of the National Historic Preservation Act, contain a provision (U.S. Government 1980c:Section 800.10) requiring federal agencies with water resources responsibilities to formulate implementing procedures for

Section 470f review. As an alternative, agencies may formulate counterpart regulations. The BIA chose the latter course (U.S. Government 1980j). The BIA proposed regulations place Native American tribal governments clearly within the Section 470f consultation process, to the same extent as the State Historic Preservation officer. The regulations also encourage designation of a tribal official to act as a focal point in the consultation process and specify that the official should be able to "represent the views of or provide liaison with traditional religious leaders" (U.S. Government 1980j:Proposed Section 25 CFR 281.4; Suagee 1980:5). These several legislative acts and regulations will have far-reaching consequences for CRM, especially in the West and Southwest of the United States.

In part, the legislation attempts to address problems arising in archaeological CRM, especially the excavation of burials in Native American sites or cemeteries, a problem with a decade-long history (Johnson 1973; Johnson *et al.* 1977; King 1972; Sprague 1974) and with numerous legal (Cooper 1976; Rosen 1980; Wilson and Zingg 1974) and scientific (Bumsted 1980) implications. However, the problem is much broader than archaeological excavation of burials. In recent years, Native Americans have protested strongly against adverse impacts on sacred landscapes, areas, or sites in California, the Southwest, and elsewhere. The legislation also attempts to deal with those problems and, in so doing, has added a further dimension to the conservation versus development dichotomy, especially in the western United States. Clearly the impact of the legislation on CRM is considerable. It strengthens Native American influence on CRM and the historic preservation movement. And it also gives Native Americans considerable say in the conduct of CRM on public lands. Since a major portion of archaeological CRM is ostensibly devoted to an explication of Native American culture history and past lifeways, the legislation creates an interesting (and overdue) partnership.

The issues involved go well beyond Native American participation in CRM activities. What is involved are differing cultural values regarding human knowledge, how knowledge is generated and who should have access to it. Within the Euro-American intellectual tradition, scholarly research is regarded as an activity producing knowledge for the public good, and it is held that access to such knowledge is a universal human right (Johnson *et al.* 1977:91–92). In other societies with other cultural codes, this is not necessarily the commonly held view. Ritual or sacred knowledge is not universal; neither is there a view that ritual and sacred areas may be desecrated (i.e., studied, excavated, etc.) by "outsiders," even (or especially) if such activity adds to the outsiders' knowledge.

The "public good" stance toward knowledge is articulated clearly by McGimsey (1972:5):

> Knowledge of this [human] past, just as knowledge about our environment, is essential to our survival, and the right to that knowledge is and must be considered a human birthright. Archeology, the recovery and study of the past, thus is a proper concern of everyone. It follows that *no individual may act in a manner such that the public right to knowledge of the past is unduly endangered or destroyed*. This principle is crystal clear.

This statement presumably is meant to excoriate vandalism of cultural resources for private ends. However, within an anthropological frame of reference, which recognizes the validity of variant ethnic ideological systems, the statement takes on a very different meaning, certainly unintended by McGimsey. Rosen (1980:17) holds that the " 'principle' is neither precisely articulated nor automatically acceptable . . . for those to whom recognition of ancestral burials is an integral part of their continuing cultural identity, or for those who believe that curiosity and science are not self-satisfying ventures. . . ."

The implications for CRM of the American Indian Religious Freedom Act and associated legislation and regulations relating to cultural landscapes, sacred sites and areas, etc. remain to be seen. A central test will be whether CRM personnel really believe what they learned in anthropology classes about the validity of other value systems and epistemologies, and whether they take seriously statements of professional responsibility (e.g., American Anthropological Association [1973:1]) toward peoples of other cultural backgrounds.

THE PROFESSION OF CRM

The advent of CRM intensified and made more explicit two phenomena that have had profound impacts on archaeology as a profession, especially the emergence of "agency archaeologists" and "corporate archaeologists" (Butler and Niquette 1980; MacDonald 1976). Since 1960, archaeology in the United States has undergone a period of rapid theoretical and methodological change (Dunnell 1979; Gumerman and Phillips 1978). The magnitude of the change can best be described demographically. In 1960, perhaps 98% of all practicing archaeologists (those who earned a living "doing" archaeology) were in an "academic" setting (i.e., universities and museums). In 1980, there were 235 federal "agency archaeologists" listed in the American Anthropological Association *Guide* (not all federal agencies employing archaeologists are listed, especially those employed by the BLM) and there was an unknown, but possibly preponderant, number of archaeologists employed by profit and nonprofit corporations, research institutes, and consulting firms (Schiffer 1979). The biggest single direct employers of archaeologists are federal agencies and engineering firms.

These facts of demography and employment reflect the reality that archaeology is in rapid transition from a strictly academic profession to one in which consulting and implementing are major areas of endeavor. Archaeology's transition from an "ivory tower" profession to a "real world" profession closely parallels that of hydrology and geology. Colleagues in these fields report that both went through the same sort of transition some years ago. In both, the majority of the professionals are now in agencies and corporations; in both, the principal orientation of the academic side now is to train professionals for agency and corporate employment and to do "basic" research. Archaeology is, de facto, doing the same thing, but the difficult transition is still underway. There is a major difference, however, between hydrology and geology, and archaeology. The former are concerned with, and based in, extractive or productive industries or public services (e.g., mineral production, water supplies, sewage disposal) closely tied to the economy and infrastructure of the country. Archaeology is concerned solely with the production of knowledge—knowledge that is not immediately critical to the national economy nor to the operation of the national infrastructure, *and*, knowledge generated *only* because of the requirements of a suite of federal laws.

As the transition continues, it is probable that a pattern similar to that which occurred in geology and hydrology will emerge in archaeology as well, that is, a pattern of mutual feedback between academia and industry leading to improved curricula in academia and improved research goals in both areas, as Patterson (1980a:14) suggests. Patterson also makes a second major point: there are now many (at least several hundred) *full-time* archaeologists, that is, those who "do" archaeology full-time, rather than teach part-time, serve on university committees part time, and "do" archaeology part-time. The values, goals, and interests of the two "types" of professionals are not necessarily congruent. There has been a latent (i.e., verbalized, but not printed) antagonism toward agency and corporate archaeologists by some "elitist" academics, especially when the latter chafed at contract requirements that prevented their doing "real," "important" archaeology. But, as Keel (1979:168) rightly notes, agency and corporate archaeologists are trained by academic archaeologists.

The transition from academic to full time agency–corporate archaeology is marked by a trend toward a new kind of professionalization (Dincauze 1980). Fox (1980), citing Caplow (1954) and Elliott (1972), lists a series of similar steps by which professionalization proceeds in various occupation groups. Most of them echo developments within archaeology since 1970, for example,

the establishment of a professional association, with definite membership criteria designed to keep out the unqualified, . . . the development and promulgation of a code of ethics which asserts the social utility of the occupation, sets up a public welfare rationale, and develops rules which serve as further criteria to eliminate the unqualified and unscrupulous. The adoption of a code of ethics, despite certain hypocrisies, imposes a real and permanent limitation on internal competition (Caplow 1954:139–140).

(Regarding the establishment of a public welfare rationale, "there are lessons for all of us [in the archaeological record] if we can learn how to use them") (Dincauze 1980:71). Elliott (1972:143–144) sees in professionalization a series of contradictions including

> the contrast between individualism and the defense of common interests through guild-like organization . . . meeting narrow requirements of doing a professional job and following the wider implications of the profession's world view . . . [and] reconciling individualism and creativity at work with the routinisation following from professional norms and standards.

The formation of the American Society for Conservation Archeology and the Society of Professional Archeologists and the announced purposes and activities of these organizations clearly reflect the phenomena outlined by Caplow and Elliott. Other reflections are the increasing number of articles devoted to management and organizational considerations to cope with archaeology as a large-scale enterprise in need of management and operational guidance (Brown and Struever 1973; Cunningham 1974; Gardner 1976; Kemrer 1980; T.J. King 1980; Lindsay and Randall 1977; Patterson 1978a,b, 1980a,b; Portnoy 1978, 1980; Walka 1979).

SUMMARY AND CONCLUSIONS

As part of the information gathering process for this article, the author wrote to or talked with a number of colleagues who are concerned with CRM in various ways (some disavowed any concern with CRM). They were asked a number of questions about problems within CRM and future prospects. All responded, many at length and very forthrightly. What follows is a distillation of responses concerning a variety, but certainly not all, of the issues. No names are attached to specific issues; those who responded will, however, recognize their thoughts at various points.

1. A major concern is the continuing justification for CRM. The issue was posed in the same way by many: large sums of public funds are being expended on activities that appear to many decision makers and much of the public as elitist, dilettantish, and exclusivist. The public is getting very little usable information for its money. Others phrased the matter in terms of credibility or outreach: If CRM is supposedly a "public good," how can its practitioners maintain credibility with legislators and the public when they, by and large, seem to talk only among themselves (with little agreement!) at public expense?

2. A second concern is that of "scientism," that is, *playing at* or pretending to be scientific. This has two sides. One might be called the reinventing-the-wheel syndrome, that is, the requirement in every request for proposal or scope-of-work that vast amounts of redundant background data (geology, biota, previous research, etc.) be provided for areas already well described in published literature and innumerable previous project reports. The answer probably lies in felt needs of agency personnel that their information bases are fully covered in case of legal disputes arising out of environmental impact assessment requirements (Schindler 1976). This is, however, an excuse and not a solution. The other side of the "scientism" charge, and a charge made by many respondents, is the misuse and abuse of statistical methods in survey and sampling design formulation. As one respondent put it, "a sophisticated-looking apparatus of statistical probability often cloaks the merest tokenism, justified by 'cost-effectiveness.'" A related comment by several was that there is a need to "ground truth" many sampling and survey designs to determine whether *statistically defensible* information is being generated, or whether the designs are simply the results of scientism (see also Dumond 1977).

3. A third concern relates to the question of "salvage" versus "conservation" of cultural resources. As previously discussed, the conservation ethic (Lipe 1974) holds that cultural resources should be conserved for the future whenever possible. However, in many project situations, it is often more cost-effective, and time-effective, to "salvage" resource sites, rather than to avoid them. That is, from the mission agency project manager's viewpoint, it is much more cost-effective to "mitigate" cultural resources by excavating or otherwise "using" them, than to redesign a freeway or a major waterway around them. From a strictly economic viewpoint, it is difficult to argue that a freeway right-of-way should be moved, at the cost of several million dollars, to avoid an archaeological site that can be "mitigated" (i.e., satisfy the legal requirements) for $100,000 or less. The dilemma is, of course, that conservation of resources is desirable, but "salvage" excavation (or some other agreed on "mitigation" procedure) satisfies legal requirements. During the 1970s, a number of bitter battles were waged between CRM personnel and highway department or other construction agency personnel over this issue. Usually, the result was "mitigation" (i.e., salvaging the cultural resources to avoid their obliteration).

4. A fourth area of concern to many is the matter of "data." This has four facets: (*a*) "data deluge"—the fact that the amount of information (and artifacts and ecofacts) being generated is staggering, which leads to (*b*) "data retrieval" problems—how are these masses of verbiage, and objects to be digested, processed, and synthesized (if indeed this can be done) into "usable" formats for *either* research or planning purposes? This in turn raises

fact (*c*), data quality and quantity control—how to best generate *good* data, and how to determine when there are *enough* data? As many point out, the latter question is usually answered essentially by cost considerations.

5. A fifth area of concern centers on professional training. No one is happy with the quality of theoretical and technical training currently being dispensed by academic institutions. Interestingly, academic, agency, and corporate archaeologists all agree that students need to have business, management, and (some say) legal training in addition to (better) technical and theoretical training to become effective CRM personnel. On the other hand, no concrete curricula outlines were forthcoming.

6. A sixth area of concern relates to the increasing casuistry of project agencies: attempts ranging from random to concerted sidestepping, subverting, or avoiding the compliance process. Statements here were often coupled with expressions of hope that CRM will not get lost in "the energy shuffle", that is, the fear that as energy and other land-altering activities accelerate and costs escalate, all environmental legislation might be pushed aside as simply impediments and increasingly unaffordable luxuries. As noted previously, archaeology generates information, but the case has yet to be made as to how such information helps the gross national product or lowers the cost of energy.

The answer is, archaeological information does neither. Properly collected and interpreted, information about *any* cultural resource contributes to the "public good" in the same way as information from all other humanities and human sciences, that is, it seeks a better understanding of humanity, its history and behavior, and the environmental context within which human action takes place. This in theory, is what CRM and historic preservation is all about. The key will be to accomplish that purpose (to end with a bureaucratic phrase) in a timely, cost-effective and useful manner. Failing that, CRM will have been an interesting incident in the history of archaeology.

ACKNOWLEDGMENTS

A number of colleagues kindly provided unpublished documents, reprints and other materials as well as their thoughts on "whither CRM." They include Keith M. Anderson, Steven G. Baker, Calvin R. Cummings, Hester A. Davis, Robert C. Dunnell, Janet L. Friedman, Albert C. Goodyear, Dee F. Green, Roberta Greenwood, George J. Gumerman, Richard Hanes, Ronald Ice, Steven E. James, Jesse D. Jennings, Bennie C. Keel, Roger E. Kelly, Thomas F. King, Ruthann Knudson, Alexander J. Lindsay, Jr., William J. Mayer-Oakes, Lonnie C. Pippin, Stephanie H. Rodeffer, Michael B. Schiffer, Douglas H. Scovill, Susan M. Seck, Ernest W. Seckinger, Jr., Floyd W. Sharrock, T. Hal Turner, Walter Wait, and Rex L. Wilson.

I thank each individual and hasten to absolve them from any responsibility for errors of omission, commission, or any heretical ideas contained herein.

REFERENCES

Adams, E. C.
 1977 The changing nature of archaeological data, or, how to get along on a scarce resource. *ASCA Proceedings* 1977:36–42.
Altes, K.
 1976 Submarine antiquities: a legal labyrinth. *Syracuse Journal of International Law and Commerce* **4**:77–94.
American Anthropological Association
 1973 *Professional ethics.* American Anthropological Association, Washington, D.C.
 1980 *Guide to departments of anthropology, 1980–1981.* American Anthropological Association, Washington, D.C.
Andrews, G. E. (editor)
 1980 *Tax incentives for historic preservation.* Washington, D.C.: The Preservation Press.
Aten, L. E.
 1980 Resource protection planning process. *Heritage Conservation and Recreation Service Publication* No. 50.
Bauriedel, M. U.
 1980 Federal historic preservation law: uneven standards for our nation's heritage. *Santa Clara Law Review* **20**(1):189–217.
Berman, M. J.
 1979 *Cultural resources overview. Socorro area, New Mexico.* U.S. Department of Agriculture, Forest Service, Southwestern Region, Albuquerque, and Bureau of Land Management, New Mexico State Office, Santa Fe.
Bosselman, F., D. Cullies, and J. Banta
 1973 *The taking issue. An analysis of the constitutional limits of land use control.* Council on Environmental Quality, Washington, D.C.
Bousman, C. Britt
 1974 *Archeological assessment of Carlsbad Caverns National Park.* Southern Methodist University Archaeology Research Program for the National Park Service, Dallas.
Breternitz, David A., *et al.*
 1980 Research design and operations management, Dolores Project. *Contract Abstracts and CRM Archeology* **1**(2):17–21.
Brothers, L. L.
 1975 Preserving Indian archaeological sites through the California Environmental Quality Act. *Golden Gate University Law Review* **6**:1–21.
Brown, J. A., and S. Struever
 1973 The organization of archeological research: an Illinois example. In *Research and theory in current archeology,* edited by C. L. Redmond. New York: Wiley. Pp. 261–280.
Brown, M. K. (compiler)
 1978 Predictive models in archaeological resource management in Illinois. *Illinois Archaeological Survey, Circular* No. 3. University of Illinois, Urbana.
Bumsted, M. P.
 1980 CRM and the physical anthropologist. *ASCA Newsletter* **7**:2–9.
Bureau of Land Management
 1980 The California Desert Conservation Area. Plan alternatives and environmental impact statement. U.S. Department of the Interior, Riverside, California.

Butler, W. B., and C. N. Niquette
1980   In consideration of archeologists serving industry, cultural resources and the profession. Paper presented at the 45th Annual Meeting of the Society for American Archaeology, May, 1980, Philadelphia, Pennsylvania.
Canouts, V.
1977   Management strategies for effective research. In *Conservation archaeology,* edited by M. B. Schiffer and G. J. Gumerman. New York: Academic Press. Pp. 121-127.
Caplow, T.
1954   *The sociology of work.* Minneapolis: University of Minnesota Press.
Clewlow, C. W., Jr., P. S. Hallinan, and R. D. Ambró
1971   A crisis in archaeology. *American Antiquity* **36**(4):472-473.
Cockrell, W.
1980   The trouble with treasure—a preservationist view of the controversy. *American Antiquity* **45**(2):333-339.
Cooper, R. L.
1976   Constitutional law: preserving Native American cultural and archeological artifacts. *American Indian Law Review* **4**:99-103.
Cordell, Linda S.
1978   *Cultural resources overview, middle Rio Grande Valley, New Mexico.* U.S. Department of Agriculture, Forest Service, Southwest Region, Albuquerque, and Bureau of Land Management, New Mexico State Office, Santa Fé.
Costonis, J. J.
1974   *Space adrift: landmark preservation and the marketplace.* Urbana: University of Illinois Press.
Cunningham, R. D.
1974   Improve field research administration: how? *American Antiquity* **39**(3):462-465.
Davis, H.
1972   The crisis in American archaeology. *Science* **176**:267-272.
Dincauze, D. F.
1980   Planning, preservation and public policy—new demands on professional archaeologists. *Popular Archaeology* **9**(1-2):6-8.
Drager, D. L., and T. Lyons
1981   Remote sensing in cultural resource management: the San Juan Basin. In *The San Juan Tomorrow: Planning for the Conservation of Cultural Resources of the San Juan Basin,* edited by F. Plog. School of American Research, Santa Fe, in press.
Dumond, D. E.
1977   Science in archaeology: the saints go marching in. *American Antiquity* **42**(3):330-349.
Dunnell, R. C.
1979   Trends in current Americanist archaeology. *American Journal of Archaeology* **83**:437-449.
Dunnell, R. C., and W. S. Dancey
1978   Assessment of significance and cultural resource management plans. *ASCA Newsletter* **5**(6):2-7.
Elliott, P. R. C.
1972   *The sociology of professions.* New York: Herder and Herder.
Fitting, J. E.
1978   Client oriented archeology: a comment on Kinsey's dilemma. *Pennsylvania Archaeologist* **48**(1-2):12-15.

Flamm, B. R., and J. L. Friedman
  1981 United States Department of Agriculture: its role in protection of our heritage environment. *American Antiquity* **46**(1):188–191.
Fowler, D. D. *et al.*
  1980 *MX cultural resources studies, preliminary research design.* Woodward-Clyde Consultants, prepared for HDR Sciences, San Francisco.
Fowler, J. M.
  1974 Protection of the cultural environment in federal law. In *Environmental law,* edited by E. L. Dolgin and T. C. P. Guilbert. St. Paul: West Publishing Co. Pp. 1466–1517.
Fowler, J. M. *et al.*
  1980 Special symposium: preserving, conserving and reusing historic properties. *The Urban Lawyer, the National Quarterly on Local Government Law* **12**(1):1–147.
Fox, D. E.
  1980 A professionalization for archeology? Now wait just a minute! *Practicing Anthropology* **2**(4):26–27.
Gardner, M. C.
  1976 The role of business and the corporate archaeologist in conservation archaeology. *ASCA Proceedings* 1976:31–34.
Glacken, C. J.
  1967 *Traces on the Rhodian shore: nature and culture in Western thought from ancient times to the end of the eighteenth century.* Berkeley: University of California Press.
Glassow, M. A.
  1977 *An archaeological overview of the northern Channel Islands, California, including Santa Barbara Island.* National Park Service, Western Archaeological Center, Tucson.
Goodyear, A. C.
  1977 Research design in highway archaeology: an example from South Carolina: a guide for cultural resource management studies. In *Conservation archaeology,* edited by M. B. Schiffer and G. J. Gumerman. New York: Academic Press. Pp. 157–166.
Goodyear, A. C., L. M. Raab, and T. C. Klinger
  1978 The status of archaeological research design in cultural resource management. *American Antiquity* **43**(2):159–173.
Grady, M. A.
  1977 Research designs and cultural resource management: some practical considerations. *ASCA Proceedings* 1977:43–49.
Grady, M., and W. Lipe
  1976 The role of preservation in conservation archaeology. *ASCA Proceedings* 1976:1–11.
Graham, F., Jr.
  1971 *Man's dominion: the story of conservation in America.* New York: McGraw-Hill.
Grayson, D. K.
  1976 The Antiquities Act in the Ninth Circuit Court: a review of recent attempts to prosecute Antiquities Act violations in Oregon. *Tebiwa* **18**(2):59–64.
Green, D. F.
  1980a Brief analysis and advice on the Central Arizona Project to Water and Power Resources Service. Ms. on file, Central Arizona Project, Phoenix, Arizona.
  1980b Reporting standards for survey archeologists: what do you write and for whom? *New Mexico Archeological Council Newsletter* **3**(4):3–4.

1981   The SJBRUS data base: a look at its utility. In *The San Juan tomorrow: planning for the conservation of cultural resources of the San Juan Basin,* edited by F. Plog. School of American Research, Santa Fe, New Mexico, in press.

Green, D. F., and S. LeBlanc
1979   Vandalism of cultural resources: the growing threat to our nation's heritage. *USDA Forest Service, Southwest Region Cultural Resources Report* No. 28, Albuquerque.

Gumerman, G. J., and D. A. Phillips, Jr.
1978   Archaeology beyond anthropology. *American Antiquity* **42**(2):184–191.

Gyrisco, G. M.
1980   Legal tools to preserve archeological sites. *Information Related to Responsibilities of the Secretary of Interior, Section 3, Executive Order No. 11593,* Fall, 1980, Special Issue.

Hardesty, D. L.
1980   Historic sites archaeology on the western American frontier: theoretical perspectives and research problems. *North American Archaeologist* **2**(1):67–81.

Hartman, D., and A. H. Wolf
1977   *Archeological assessment of Wupatki National Monument.* Museum of Northern Arizona Archaeological Contract Section, for the National Park Service, Flagstaff.

Holden, C.
1977   Contract archeology: new source of support brings problems. *Science* **196:**1070–1072.

Hosmer, C. R., Jr.
1965   *Presence of the past.* New York: Putnam.

Hosmer, C. R., Jr.
1981   *Preservation comes of age. From Williamsburg to the National Trust, 1926–1949.* Charlottesville, Virginia: The University Press of Virginia.

James, S., A. Kane, R. Knudson, T. Kohler, and W. Lipe
1980   *The Dolores Project cultural resources mitigation design.* Water and Power Resources Services, Upper Colorado River Region, Salt Lake City.

Jennings, J. D.
1963   Administration of contract emergency archaeological programs. *American Antiquity* **28**(3):282–285.

Johnson, E.
1973   Professional responsibilities and the American Indian. *American Antiquity* **38**(2):129–130.

Johnson, E. *et al.*
1977   Archeology and Native Americans. In *The management of archeological resources: the Arlie House report,* edited by C. R. McGimsey III and H. A. Davis, pp. 90–96. Special Publication of the Society for American Archaeology, Washington, D.C.

Keel, B.
1979   A view from inside. *American Antiquity* **44**(1):164–170.

Kemrer, M. F.
1980   Quality in contract archeology: management, personnel and organizational consideration. *New Mexico Archeological Council Newsletter* **3**(4):2.

Kettler, E. L., and B. D. Reams, Jr.
1976   *Historic preservation law: an annotated bibliography.* Washington, D.C.: Preservation Press.

King, T. F.
1972   Archaeological law and the American Indian. *The Indian Historian* **5**:34–35.
1978   *The archeological survey: methods and uses.* U.S. Department of the Interior, Heritage Conservation and Recreation Service, Washington, D.C.
1979   The trouble with archeology. *Journal of Field Archaeology* **6**:351–360.
1980a   Responses to "the trouble with archeology": part one. *Journal of Field Archaeology* **7**:125–131.
1980b   Nobody knows the trouble I's seen. Responses to "The trouble with archeology." *Journal of Field Archaeology* **7**:233–241.
King, T. F., P. P. Hickman, and G. Berg
1977   *Anthropology in historic preservation: caring for culture's clutter.* New York: Academic Press.
King, T. J., Jr.
1980   The roles of the agency archeologist in managing large mitigation programs. *Contract Abstracts and CRM Archeology* **1**(1):12–15.
LeBlanc, S. A.
1979   A proposal for an archeological conservancy. *Journal of Field Archaeology* **6**:360–365.
Lee, R.
1970   *The Antiquities Act of 1906.* National Park Service, Washington, D.C.
Lindsay, A. J., Jr., and M. E. Randall
1977   Cultural resource management as a business, and its place in the business world. *ASCA Proceedings* 1977:28–35.
Lipe, W. D.
1974   A conservation model for American archeology. *The Kiva* **39**:213–245.
Lipe, W. A., and A. J. Lindsay, Jr. (editors)
1974   Proceedings of the 1974 Cultural Resource Management Conference, Federal Center, Denver, Colorado. *Museum of Northern Arizona, Technical Series* No. 14.
Lyons, T. R., and T. E. Avery
1977   *Remote sensing: a handbook for archeologists and cultural resource managers.* U.S. Department of the Interior, National Park Service, Washington, D.C.
MacDonald, W. K. (editor)
1976   Digging for gold: papers on archaeology for profit. *Museum of Anthropology, University of Michigan, Technical Reports* No. 5, and *Research Reports in Archaeology, Contribution* No. 2, Ann Arbor.
Madden, L., and W. Weakly
1980   The Dolores Project in historic perspective. *Contract Abstracts and CRM Archeology* **1**(2):14–16.
Mark, C.
1969   A study of cultural policy in the United States. *UNESCO Studies and Documents on Cultural Policies* No. 2.
Maryland Historical Trust
1975   *Preservation easements.* Maryland Historical Trust, Annapolis.
May, R. V.
1980   San Diego's cultural resource program: saving sites with land use law on private land at the local level. *ASCA Newsletter* **6**:26–29.
McClellan, C., D. A. Phillips, Jr., and M. Belshaw
1980   The archeology of Lake Mead National Recreation Area: an assessment. *Western Archeological Center, Publications in Anthropology* No. 9.

McDonald, J. A.
    1976   An archeological assessment of Canyon de Chelly National Monument. *Western Archeological Center Publications in Anthropology* No. 5.
    1979   *Cultural resources overview, Klamath National Forest, California.* U.S. Department of Agriculture, Forest Service, Klamath National Forest, Yreka, California.
McGimsey, C. R., III
    1972   *Public archeology.* New York: Seminar Press.
    1980   Letter to the editor. *Contract Abstracts and CRM Archeology* 1(1):31.
McGimsey, C. R., III, and H. A. Davis (editors)
    1977   The management of archeological resources. The Airlie House report. *Society for American Archaeology Special Publication,* Washington, D.C.
McMillan, B., M. Grady, and W. Lipe
    1977   Cultural resource management. In The management of archeological resources. The Airlie House report, edited by C. R. McGimsey III, and H. A. Davis, pp. 25–63. *Society for American Archeology Special Publication,* Washington, D.C.
Meenan, J. K.
    1978   Cultural resources preservation and underwater archaeology: some notes on the current legal framework and a model underwater antiquities statute. *San Diego Law Review* 15:623–662.
Michel, M.
    1981   The archeological conservancy. *Early Man* 3(1):27–28.
Moratto, M. J. (compiler)
    1975   Conservation archaeology: a bibliography. *San Francisco State University, Conservation Archeology Papers,* No. 1.
Morrison, J. H.
    1974   *Historic preservation law.* National Trust for Historic Preservation, Washington, D.C.
Mueller, J. W.
    1974   The use of sampling in archaeological survey. *Society for American Archaeology Memoir* No. 28.
    1975   *Sampling in archaeology.* Tucson: University of Arizona Press.
Nafzinger, A.
    1972   Regulation by the international council of museums: an example of the rule of non-governmental organization in the international legal process. *Denver Journal of International Law and Policy* 2:231–236.
National Park Service, Branch of Indian Cultural Resources
    1980   Cultural resources assessment for the San Juan Basin Regional Uranium Study. *San Juan Basin Regional Uranium Study, Working Paper* No. 50.
Nieć, H.
    1976   Legislative models of protection of cultural property. *Hastings Law Journal* 27:1089–1122.
Palacios, V., and R. L. Johnson
    1976   Overview of archaeology and the law: seventy years of unexploited protection for prehistoric resources. *Notre Dame Law* 51:706–721.
Pastron, A. G., P. S. Hallinan, and C. W. Clewlow, Jr. (editors)
    1973   The crisis in North American archaeology. *Kroeber Anthropological Society Special Publications* No. 3.
Patterson, L. W.
    1978a   Basic considerations in contract archeology. *Man in the Northeast,* Nos. 15–16: 132–138.

1978b   Contract archaeology: environmental and practical issues. *Archaeology* **31**(1):60–61.
1980a   Archeology in the real world. *Practicing Anthropology* **2**(4):14, 26.
1980b   Research deficiencies in contract archeology under environmental law. *ASCA Newsletter* **6**:9–25.

Peterson, R. M.
1980   Interagency meeting concerning protection and law enforcement. *ASCA Newsletter* **7**(1):35–37.

Plog, F.
1981   Regional archaeology and regional planning. In *The San Juan tomorrow: planning for the conservation of cultural resources of the San Juan Basin,* edited by F. Plog. School of American Research, Santa Fe, *in press.*

Plog, S., F. Plog, and W. Wait
1978   Decision making in modern surveys. In *Advances in archaeological method and theory* (Vol. 1), edited by M. B. Schiffer. New York: Academic Press.

Portnoy, A. W.
1980   The OP–BP framework. *Practicing Anthropology* **2**(2):9–10.

Portnoy, A. W. (editor)
1978   *Scholars as managers, or, how can the managers do it better?* U.S. Department of the Interior, Heritage Conservation and Recreation Service, Washington, D.C.

Raab, L. M., T. C. Klinger, M. B. Schiffer, and A. C. Goodyear
1980   Clients, contracts, and profits: conflicts in public archaeology. *American Anthropologist* **83**(3):539–551.

Rains, A., *et al.*
1965   *With heritage so rich.* New York: Random House.

Rippeteau, B. E.
1979   Antiquities enforcement in Colorado. *Journal of Field Archaeology* **6**:85–103.

Rodeffer, S. M., and L. N. Chapman
1980   Managing to manage: a case study of the Tennessee–Tombigbee Waterway. *Contract Abstracts and CRM Archeology* **1**(1):19–22.

Rose, J.
1974   A proposal for the separation and marketability of development rights as a technique to preserve open space. *Real Estate Law Journal* **2**:635–653.
1975   The transfer of development rights: a preview of an evolving concept. *Real Estate Law Journal* **3**:330–346.

Rosen, L.
1980   The excavation of American Indian burial sites: a problem in law and professional responsibility. *American Anthropologist* **82**(1):5–27.

Rosha, G.
1980   Eminent domain, mining law and historic preservation. Term project presented in Historic Preservation Laws and Policies course, University of Nevada, Reno, Spring 1980. Copy on file, Historic Preservation Program, University of Nevada, Reno.

Sackman, J. L.
1979   Landmark cases on landmark law. *1979 Proceedings of the Institute on Planning, Zoning & Eminent Domain, Southwestern Legal Foundation,* pp. 241–287.

Schart, W. L.
1977   *Archeological assessment, Aztec Ruins National Monument.* National Park Service, Southwest Cultural Resources Center, Santa Fe.

Schiffer, M. B.
  1979 Some impacts of cultural resource management in American archaeology. In *Archaeological resource management in Australia and Oceania,* edited by J. R. McKinlay and K. L. Jones, pp. 1–11. New Zealand Historic Places Trust, Wellington.

Schiffer, M. B., and G. Gumerman (editors)
  1977 *Conservation archaeology.* New York: Academic Press.

Schiffer, M. B., and J. H. House
  1977 Cultural resource management and archaeological research: the Cache Project. *Current Anthropology* **18**(1):43–68.

Schiffer, M. B., A. P. Sullivan, and T. C. Klinger
  1979 The design of archaeological surveys. *World Archaeology* **10**(1):1–28.

Schindler, D. W.
  1976 The impact statement boondoggle. *Science* **192**:4239.

Scurlock, D.
  1979 *Archeological Assessment, Hubbell Trading Post National Historic Site.* Center for Anthropological Studies for the National Park Service, Albuquerque.

Shull, J., and C. Shull
  1974 New inroads for historic preservation. *Administrative Law Review* **26**:357–373.

Smith, J. D., and R. L. Dryer
  1976 Preserving Utah's prehistoric past: a proposal for legislative reform. *Utah Law Review* **243**(1):143–171.

Society of Professional Archeologists
  1980 Code of ethics and standards of performance. *Directory of Professional Archeologists* (fifth ed.), pp. 3–6. Society of Professional Archeologists, Winston-Salem, North Carolina.

Spiess, A. E. (editor)
  1978 Conservation archaeology in the Northeast: toward a research orientation. *Peabody Museum Bulletin* 3. Peabody Museum of Archaeology and Ethnology, Harvard University, Cambridge.

Sprague, R.
  1974 American Indians and American archaeology. *American Antiquity* **39**:1–2.

Stewart, Y. G.
  1980 An archeological overview of Petrified Forest National Park. *Western Archeological Center, Publications in Anthropology* No. 10.

Suagee, D. B.
  1980 Indian tribal religious and cultural concerns and the implementation of federal archeology and heritage legislation. *CRM Bulletin* **3**(3):1, 4–5, 16.

Talmage, V., *et al.*
  1977 *The importance of small, surface, and disturbed sites as sources of significant archeological data.* Department of the Interior, National Park Service, Washington, D.C.

Taylor, F. H.
  1948 *The taste of angels: a history of art collecting from Ramses to Napoleon.* Boston: Little, Brown.

Thomas, D. H.
  1969 A pilot Great Basin research design. *University of California Archaeological Survey Annual Report,* 1968–1969, **11**:87–100.

Thomas, D. M.
  1979 *Archaeology.* New York: Holt.

Thompson, R. H.
    1979   Beyond significance. *ASCA Newsletter* **5**(6):15–20.
United States Army Engineer District, Mobile
    1979a   *Tennessee–Tombigbee Waterway, Alabama and Mississippi. Tombigbee River multi-resource district proposed mitigation plan. Vol. I, overall study plan.* Mobile District Corps of Engineers, Mobile.
    1979b   *General research design. Historic settlement in the Tombigbee River multi-resource district. Tennessee–Tombigbee Waterway, Alabama and Mississippi.* Mobile District Corps of Engineers, Mobile.
United States Code
    1977a   *An Act to Set Apart a Certain Tract of Land near the Headwaters of the Yellowstone River as a Public Park, 1872.* Title 16, Section 21 (17 Statute 32–33).
    1977b   *An Act to Authorize Condemnation of Lands for Sites of Public Buildings and for Other Purposes, 1888.* Title 40, Section 258 (25 Statute 357).
    1977c   *Repair of the Ruin of Casa Grande, Arizona, 1889.* Title 16, Section 431n (25 Statute 961).
    1977d   *An Act for the Preservation of American Antiquities, 1906.* Title 16, Sections 431, 433 (Public Law 59–209, 34 Statute 225).
    1977e   *Establishment of the National Park Service, 1916.* Title 16, Sections 1 *et seq.* (39 Statute 535 and amendments).
    1977f   *Historic Sites, Buildings, and Antiquities Act, 1935.* Title 16, Sections 461–467, (Public Law 74–292, 49 Statute 666).
    1977g   *National Trust for Historic Preservation Act, 1949.* Title 16, Section 468 (Public Law 81–408, 63 Statute 927).
    1977h   *Reservoir Salvage Act, 1960; Amendment 1974, 1978.* Title 16, Section 469 (Public Law 86–523, 94 Statute 220; Public Law 93–291, 88 Statute 174–175).
    1977i   *National Historic Preservation Act, 1966.* Title 16, Section 470 (Public Law 89–665, 80 Statute 915).
    1977j   *National Environmental Policy Act, 1969.* Title 42, Section 4321 *et seq.* (Public Law 91–190, 83 Statute 852).
    1977k   *Executive Order No. 11593. Protection and Enhancement of the Cultural Environment, 1971.* Title 16, Section 470 (36FR9821).
    1977l   *Importation of Pre-Columbian Monumental or Architectural Sculpture or Murals, 1972.* Title 19, Sections 2091–2095 (Public Law 92–587, Title II, Section 205; 86 Statute 1297).
    1977m   *Department of Transportation Act.* Title 49, Section 1653,(f) (Public Law 89–670, Section 4; 80 Statute 933).
    1980a   *American Indian Religious Freedom Act, 1978.* Title 42, Section 1996 (Public Law 95–341, 92 Statute 469).
    1980b   *Archaeological Resources Protection Act, 1979.* Title 16, Section 470aa–*11* (Public Law 96–95; 93 Statute 728).
    1980c   *National Historic Preservation Act Amendments of 1980.* Title 16, Section 470 (Public Law 96–515; 94 Statute 2987).
United States, Department of State
    1958   *Convention on the Territorial Sea and the Contiguous Zone,* Geneva, April 29, 1958. 15 U.S. Treaties 1606 (TIAS no. 5639).
    1970   *Treaty of Cooperation Between the United States of America and the United Mexican States Providing for the Recovery and Return of Stolen Archaeological, Historical and Cultural Properties.* 22 U.S. Treaties 494–497 (TIAS no. 7088).

United States Government, Code of Federal Regulations
  1980a *Department of Agriculture, Office of Environmental Quality; Enhancement, Protection, and Management of the Cultural Environment.* Title 7, CFR Part 3100.
  1980b *Environmental Protection Agency Implementation of Procedures on National Environmental Policy Act; Historical and Archeological Resources.* Title 44, CFR Part 216.
  1980c *Advisory Council on Historic Preservation: Protection of Historic and Cultural Properties; Final Amendments* 1979. Title 36, CFR Part 800.
  1980d *Criteria for Comprehensive Statewide Historic Surveys and Plans.* Title 36, CFR Part 1201 (formerly, Part 61).
  1980e *National Register of Historic Places.* Title 36, CFR Part 1202 (formerly, Part 60).
  1980f *Determinations of Eligibility for Inclusion in the National Register of Historic Places.* Title 36, CFR Part 1204 (formerly Part 63).
  1980g *National Historic Landmarks Program.* Title 36, CFR Part 1205.
  1980h *The Secretary of Interior's Standards for Historic Preservation Projects.* Title 36, CFR Part 1207.
  1980i *Tax Reform Act of 1976.* Title 36, CFR Part 1208 (formerly, Part 67).
  1980j *Bureau of Indian Affairs. Proposed Counterpart Cultural Resources Regulations.* 45 *Federal Register* 60923 (September 15, 1980).
  1980k *Department of Agriculture. National Forest Management Act Regulations.* Title 36, CFR 219.
  1981 *Department of Interior. Archaeological Resources Protection Act of 1979; Proposed Uniform Rulemaking and Notice of Public Hearings.* Title 36, CFR Part 1215. (*Federal Register* 46 (12), Part XX, January 19, 1981).
United States House of Representatives
  1935 Preservation of historic American sites, buildings, objects, and antiquities of national significance, and for other purposes. *76th Congress, 1st Session House of Representatives Report No. 1255.*
United States Supreme Court
  1896 *United States* v. *Gettysburg Electric Railway Company.* 16 U.S. 668ff. (1896).
Vitelli, R. D.
  1980 Implementing the UNESCO convention: a challenge for archeologists. *American Antiquity* **45**(3):558–561.
Vivian, R. G.
  1976 Archaeology, mining and the law. *Rocky Mountain Mineral Law Institute.* **22**:787–820.
Vivian, R. G., K. Anderson, H. Davis, R. Edwards, M. B. Schiffer, and S. South.
  1977 Guidelines for the preparation and evaluation of archaeological reports. In *The management of archeological resources: the Arlie House report,* edited by C. R. McGimsey III and M. A. Davis, pp. 64–77. Society for American Archaeology Special Publication, Washington, D.C.
Wait, Walter
  1981 The development and application of a computerized data base for the San Juan Basin, New Mexico. In *The San Juan tomorrow: planning for the conservation of cultural resources of the San Juan Basin,* edited by F. Plog. School of American Research, Santa Fe, New Mexico, in press.
Walka, J. J.
  1979 Management methods and opportunities in archaeology. *American Antiquity* **44**(3):575–582.

Waters, L. E., and R. W. Scott
 1980 The need for expanded initiatives: an overview of the ABA special symposium on "preserving, conserving, and re-using historic properties." *The Urban Lawyer, the National Quarterly on Local Government Law* **12**(3):413–428.

Weakly, W. F.
 1980 A contract sponsor's expectations of a researcher's administration. *Contract Abstracts and CRM Archeology* **1**(1):16–18.

Wedel, W. R.
 1981 Toward a history of plains archeology. *Great Plains Quarterly* **1**(1):16–39.

Weide, M. L.
 1973 An archaeological program design for the California desert. Ms. on file, Riverside District Office, Bureau of Land Management.

Whitaker, J. C.
 1976 *The swing of the pendulum: federal environment and natural resources development policy; the Nixon–Ford years, 1969–1976.* American Enterprise Institute for Public Policy Research, Washington, D.C.

Wildesen, L. E.
 1980 Cultural resource management: a personal view. *Practicing Anthropology* **2**(2):10, 22–23.

Willey, G. R., and J. A. Sabloff
 1980 *A history of American archaeology* (second ed.). San Francisco: W. H. Freeman.

Williams, L. R.
 1978 Vandalism to cultural resources of the Rocky Mountain West. *USDA Forest Service Southwestern Region, Cultural Resources Reports* No. 21.

Wilson, P. E., and E. O. Zingg
 1974 What is America's heritage? Historic preservation and American Indian culture. *University of Kansas Law Review* **22**:413–453.

Woodbury, N., and C. R. McGimsey, III (compilers)
 1977 The crisis in communication. In *The management of archeological resources: the Airlie House report,* edited by C. R. McGimsey III and H. A. Davis, pp. 78–89. Society for American Archaeology Special Publication, Washington, D.C.

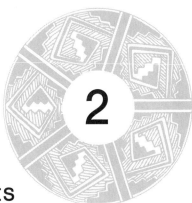

The Study of Impacts
on Archaeological Sites

LESLIE E. WILDESEN

INTRODUCTION

The United States contains about 895 million ha, of which an undetermined number exhibit evidence of historic or prehistoric human use in the form of anthropogenic landscapes and archaeological resources. Both types of evidence are subject to alteration over time by various natural and cultural processes. The workings of these processes define, at any given moment, the nature of knowable history of human land use and cultural development. Therefore, archaeologists need to know something of the nature of these processes, including the type, extent, duration, and intensity of change resulting from their operation.

This chapter explores aspects of natural and human-caused changes on that portion of the archaeological resource base consisting of archaeological sites. Although historic archaeological sites are included by implication, most of this discussion focuses on prehistoric sites because the bulk of existing research has been conducted on them. Current efforts in archaeological theory building, conservation and management of archaeological resources, and archaeological field research require better data and models than we now have of the operations of change-producing processes. Therefore, this chapter describes previous research, some applications of research results to theory building, management, and field studies, and a set of proposals for future research. First, it is necessary to describe a bit of recent history, and to introduce a vocabulary for the subsequent discussion.

ADVANCES IN ARCHAEOLOGICAL METHOD AND THEORY, VOL. 5

Archaeology at Mid-Century

Since the end of World War II, the emphasis in American archaeology has been shifting from classification and historical studies on limited geographical areas to a broader, "anthropological" mode of inquiry. Prompted by the seminal monographs of Taylor (1948), Wauchope (1956), Willey (1953), and Willey and Phillips (1958) and abetted by developments in dating technology, aerial photography, systems theory, and computer hardware, archaeologists began to examine their resource base for answers to new questions. These questions related more to what the archaeological data *meant* in terms of sociocultural phenomena than to the explicit nature of the artifacts, sediments, and faunal material found in archaeological sites.

At the same time, the postwar construction boom intensified the pressure on all land-based resources to provide housing, energy, recreation, and commodities for an expanding population. Factories, residential developments, highways, and dams were needed for "progress," and many archaeological sites were sacrificed to this cause. Limited "salvage" of archaeological resources was conducted as part of the Interagency Salvage program of the Smithsonian Institution and National Park Service (Committee for the Recovery of Archaeological Remains, 1958).

In the 1960s, archaeologists produced more theoretical and exhortatory monographs and articles (e.g., Binford 1962, 1964, 1968; Chang 1967; Clarke 1968; Struever 1968), while Congress enacted laws intended to alleviate some of the damage caused by the nation's mad dash into the future. The Reservoir Salvage Act (1960), the Wilderness Act (1964), the National Historic Preservation Act (1966), the Department of Transportation Act (1966), and the National Environmental Policy Act (1969) provided policy, procedures, and funding to carry out a vastly increased, federally mandated program of archaeological survey, planning, and research (Schumacher 1963).

During the 1970s, two major things happened; archaeologists began to ask questions of the "how do we know what we know" variety, and the federal government produced amendments and implementing regulations for legislation passed the previous decade. Monographs and edited works by Clarke (1973), Dunnell (1971), and Watson *et al.* (1971) were oriented toward epistemology and conceptual foundations of archaeology; methodological treatises dealt with faunal analysis (Chaplin 1971), chronometric dating (Michels 1973), sediments (Limbrey 1975), sampling strategies (Mueller 1975), and remote sensing applications (Lyons and Avery 1977); other archaeologists took to the field to study archaeological sites in the making, or to replicate earlier human technologies (Coles 1973; Gould 1978; Ingersoll *et al.* 1977; Kramer 1979); and still other archaeologists developed models of how sites form, and how the process of site formation and the developmental history of a site affect what is archaeologically knowable (e.g., Schiffer 1976; Wildesen 1973).

At the same time, as a result of legislative and regulatory mandates, archaeologists were asked to participate in land-use and project planning on an unprecedented scale. Such participation entailed locating previously unknown sites, evaluating them according to a set of prescribed criteria, and determining what "effect" a proposed government (or government assisted) project would have on them. If the "effect" was expected to be adverse, archaeologists were to provide recommendations to "mitigate" the "adverse effect" the project might cause. The Archaeological and Historic Preservation Act (1974) permitted government funds to be spent on such endeavors; regulations contained in Title 36 of the Code of Federal Regulations (Parts 800, 1201, 1202, 1204, and 1210) prescribe the procedures and criteria to be used. Federal agencies hired archaeologists, archaeologists formed consulting firms, colleges and universities launched graduate programs in "cultural resource management," new organizations were formed (the Society of Professional Archaeologists, the American Society for Conservation Archaeology), conferences were held (Fehon 1979; Lipe and Lindsay 1974; McGimsey and Davis 1977), and books were published (King *et al.* 1977; McGimsey 1972; Schiffer and Gumerman 1977). Not incidentally, a whole new vocabulary entered the archaeological lexicon: *conservation archaeology, mitigation, significance, compliance, data recovery, impact, adverse effect,* and acronyms by the score (ACHP, SHPO, BLM, HCRS, USFS, NPS, ad infinitum).

It is these two events—the resurging interest in archaeological "knowability," and the need to participate in government planning—that have led to an increased emphasis on the study of impacts to archaeological sites, particularly during the late-1970s. Unfortunately, much of the "literature" on impact studies exists as papers at meetings or in journals of limited circulation. Most of the accessible studies suffer from a vagueness of terminology and an irritating tendency to develop unique methods of "rating" impacts. Thus, an otherwise informative paper (such as Gallagher 1978) contains essentially nonreplicable results because its conclusions rest on incomplete definitions of impact intensity. I shall return to this point later, but want now to address the issue of terminology as it applies to the rest of this chapter.

Definitions

For the purposes of this chapter, I define the term *impact* as follows:

An *impact* is *a measurable change* in a characteristic or property of an archaeological site (as compared, say, with some prior condition of the characteristic or property).

Impacts are called *direct* if they are caused by an action and occur at the same time and place. They are called *indirect* if they are caused by an action, but occur later in time or farther removed in space (Council on Environmental Quality 1978). For example, removal of archaeological sediments by sheet erosion may be the direct result of an intense summer rainstorm, and an indirect result of removal of upslope vegetation due to road construction.

Impacts can be *discrete* or *continuous,* depending on whether the cause occurs only once, or recurs at intervals. Flash flooding usually causes discrete impacts, whereas seasonal colluviation causes continuous impacts.

Any impact can be classified as to *type*, of which there are a relatively small number; burial, removal, transferal, and alteration comprise the major categories (Wildesen 1973) under which specific impact types may be subsumed. For example, compaction, chemical changes in sediments, and churning of surface sediments are all instances of "alteration," as is the disappearance of soil silhouettes during immersion in a reservoir pool.

The causal *agent* of an impact can often be identified; most previous studies of impacts to archaeological sites focus on this aspect alone. For example, activities such as plowing, road construction, and timber harvest are known to be potential impact agents, which may cause various types of impacts (transferal of artifacts, removal of sediments by erosion, and alteration of sediments by compaction, respectively).

A complete description of an impact on an archaeological site will include not only the characteristics just listed, but also an indication of the *amount* of change, its *extent* in three-dimensional space, its *duration* (temporary, permanent, or as measured in hours or years), and something of its characteristic behavior (rapidity of onset, potential reversibility, and possible synergistic action with other impacts). In addition, for purposes of designing appropriate measures to mitigate impacts to sites, it is helpful to know whether the specific impacts are intentional (e.g., wanton vandalism) or unintentional (e.g., casual collecting by construction workers or recreationists).

It is important to distinguish physical properties of *impacts,* as defined here, on archaeological sites from *effects* on archaeological values embodied in those sites:

An *effect* is *a professional judgement about* a measurable change in a characteristic or property of an archaeological site, as it relates to the archaeological value(s) of the site.

Impacts on sites, therefore, are determined by physical observation, measurement, and description; effects on values are determined by reference to an outside philosophical, methodological, or regulatory standard. Impacts can be infinitely graded in a continuum (e.g., erosion may range from 0 to 10,000 kg/ha/year); effects are "either–or" phenomena (e.g., an effect either is, or is not, *adverse*). The concept of "effect," therefore, implies the existence of a *threshold*; measurable changes, in and of themselves, do not necessarily constitute an effect, but those of a certain type or in excess of a specified amount may cross the threshold and result in a judgment that an effect has occurred.

I return to these points in a later section of this chapter; a description of actual studies of impacts, as a basis for future discussion, follows.

STUDIES OF IMPACTS ON ARCHAEOLOGICAL SITES

This section focuses on the results of experimental or observational studies of impacts on various characteristics of archaeological sites. Although some research has been conducted on the disintegration of organic artifacts (see, e.g., Binford and Bertram 1977; Casteel 1971; Chaplin 1971; Chave 1964; Gifford 1978, 1981; Jewell and Dimbleby 1966; Lyon 1970; Ortner *et al.* 1972), and others have described various impacts on stone or ceramic artifacts (e.g., Ascher and Ascher 1965; Barnes 1939; David 1972; DeBoer 1974; Gero 1978; Goodyear 1971; Tringham 1974; Knudson 1973, 1974, 1979; Obear and Berg 1975; Roney 1977; Shepard 1956), detailed discussion of impacts on artifacts is not presented here for several reasons.

First, impact types most commonly observed are alteration, transfer, and removal. Although certain types of alterations to artifacts may impair their potential for providing data on original function or on manufacturing sequences, in general, the artifacts are still identifiable as such; their altered condition poses no insurmountable problem for analysis, that is, a sherd is still a sherd, and a flake is still a flake. Postdepositional edge damage to lithic artifacts or debitage may occasionally be misidentified as use–wear, but such difficulties diminish as archaeologists gain sophistication in lithic analysis (see, e.g., Hayden 1979; Keller 1966; Knudson 1973).

Second, transfer and removal of artifacts, without alteration, affects the integrity of the *site,* and the validity of the cultural inferences based on artifact location or descriptions. For example, correct identification and interpretation of artifact clusters as "activity areas" depends on their having remained more or less *in situ* since initial deposition. The ravages caused by rodents, tree roots, and relic collectors are well known, as are the actions of vertisols (self-mulching soils), and other geomorphic processes that transfer artifacts from place to place within a site, or remove them altogether (for an introduction to these processes, see Butzer 1971; Gladfelter 1977; Oakes and Thorp 1967; Soil Survey Staff 1975; Wood and Johnson 1978).

Finally, and despite David Clarke's assertions to the contrary (1968:13), description and study of artifacts per se are not the sole purposes of archaeology (see also, Rouse 1973). In the context of modern archaeological resource conservation and management, it is the integrity of the site, its potential for answering significant research questions, and its susceptibility to damage as the direct or indirect result of human activity that are crucial for decision making. Therefore, studies of transfer and removal of artifacts are more logically treated as impacts to sites, and are included in the discussion that follows.

Studies of Artifact Movement

After Redman and Watson (1970) explicitly tested the relationship of surface to subsurface materials by conducting excavations on prehistoric mounds in Turkey, archaeologists began to examine the actual movement of artifacts on surfaces and to attribute such movement to various causes (impact agents), particularly geomorphological processes and agricultural and other human activities. The issue of congruence between surface and subsurface assemblages also is beginning to receive the attention it deserves (see, e.g., Baker 1978; Hughes and Lampert 1977; Lewarch and O'Brien 1981). Clearly, whatever the "original" relationship between surface and subsurface expressions of site content, the present relationship depends on the amount, direction, and selectivity or distribution of impacts causing transfer of artifacts on the site surface.

Kirkby and Kirkby (1976) proposed a geomorphological model to account for the natural movement of ceramic sherds through time within and across the surface of prehistoric house mounds in semi-arid environments. On the basis of their model and data on sherd sizes, densities, and locations at archaeological sites in southern Mexico and southwestern Iran, they concluded that "over a 500-year period sherds less than 4 cm can be displaced by up to 5 m on slopes as low as 1 to 3 degrees" and that "larger sherds of 4–8 cm are displaced on similar slopes by less than 1 m" (1976:240–241). They propose that geomorphic processes such as wetting and drying or freeze–thaw cycles, although present, probably only impact artifact location in the top 50 cm of a site, and that "small, random disturbances tend to diffuse coarse material in all directions outwards from areas" of concentration, rather than directionally (1976:241). They conclude that "these geomorphic processes produce only very slow mixing of material which is probably always less significant than the rate at which the mound material is being eroded" (1976:241).

Rick (1976) also investigated natural downslope movement of artifacts, including stone, bone, and ceramics, by analyzing materials collected from the surface of a long variable slope below a rock shelter in Peru. He suggests that "if there is a finite upper weight limit in a given material, then there is a slope angle below which that material will not be moved" called the critical angle (1976:142). For example, his data show that "no significant number of projectile points" occurs in sample units with slopes less than 20° (1976:143). Artifact distribution and downslope movement are influenced by environmental factors such as paleoclimate, vegetation cover, and the thickness and stratigraphy of the archaeological site from which the materials are derived (Rick 1976:143).

After 4 years, the experimental earthwork at Overton Down showed evidence of erosion and downslope movement of surface materials; the crest had sunk 16.5 cm, with a concomitant compressing of the inner layers of the mound (Jewell and Dimbleby 1966:323). Although their text does not mention internal movement of artifacts placed in the earthwork during construction, it does indicate (1966:Figure 1) that some such movement took place between 2 and 4 years after mound construction.

The impacts caused by human actions such as plowing may be more or less severe than those caused by nature. For example, Talmage *et al.* (1977:24) quoted a study of a Maryland site by Robertson as showing that "plowing disturbs artifacts more than had previously been expected based on prior archaeological investigations of plowed sites." Yet Redman and Watson's mounds had been plowed for years, and they concluded

> though there is probably some lateral displacement, we do not believe it to be very great: calculations based on a random walk simulation . . . suggested that even with three thousand plowings, movement [of artifacts] would be five meters or less (1970:280).

In fact, Binford *et al.* (1970:7) used plowing as a method to help define site boundaries and to reveal "something of the internal structure of the site" at Hatchery West. Roper's (1976) study of the impacts of plowing at the Airport site in Illinois seems to bear out these latter studies. She estimated the mean lateral displacement of biface fragments on the surface of the Airport site to be 2.07–4.12 m; she believes that amount of movement is not enough to "distort spatial relationships" significantly (1976:373). Other papers, such as those by Fowler (1969) and Ford and Rolingson (1972), discuss, but do not quantify, the impacts of plowing on sites.

Several studies have been conducted to examine the impacts of specific kinds of ground-disturbing projects on archaeological materials, with particular attention to artifact movements on ground surfaces. Roney, in an unpublished study of grazing impacts, concluded that horizontal displacement of artifacts by cows "was less severe than had been anticipated," and would "probably leave intact spatial patterns relating to activity areas and isolation of individual campsites, but could obscure very fine patterning, as might be of interest in a study of motor habits" (1977:15). Roney suggests that moister soil might cause greater potential artifact displacement due to increased vertical mixing, and that artifacts might actually stick to the hooves of milling cattle, and be transported out of the area.

DeBloois, *et al.* (1975) studied the results of "pinyon-juniper chaining" at a site in eastern Utah. The chaining project consisted of dragging a 10-ton, 300-foot (9072 kg, 91 m) long section of anchor chain between two D8H caterpillar tractors, for the purpose of uprooting unwanted trees to encourage development of grasses and shrubs for grazing. A total of 367 brightly painted artifacts were placed in "test squares" and transects in the study area. Of these, "only 53 percent . . . were relocated, and only about one-third (124) were found undisturbed after chaining" (DeBloois *et al.* 1975:157). They measured the average displacement of 15 flakes recovered from the transects as 17.4 cm, in the direction of chain travel, but pointed out that the degree of impact was quite variable throughout the project area. Some parts of the study area were not disturbed at all. Density and distribution of trees apparently were important factors in determining extent of impact (DeBloois *et al.* 1975:158).

Gallagher (1978) used steel washers to simulate artifacts in a study of the impacts of "scarification" in southern Idaho. "To scarify" is defined as "to loosen the top soil in preparation for regenerating" a timber stand (Mifflin and Lysons 1979:17); it is usually done with a bulldozer, often with a toothed blade. Gallagher placed 396 steel washers in 99 postholes on a 6 × 6 foot (1.8 × 1.8 m) grid over the area; four washers were in each post hole, on the surface of the mineral soil, and at depths of 1, 3, and 6 inches (2.5, 7.6, and 15.2 cm). He reports that 14% of the surface washers had been horizontally displaced, 5% were vertically displaced, and 36% were lost altogether (not recovered even with the aid of a metal detector). The average horizontal displacement was 20.5 inches (52 cm), the average vertical displacement was −2.6 inches (6.6 cm) (1978:294). Smaller percentages of the more deeply buried washers were displaced, but 10% of those buried at the 6-inch (15.2 cm) depth were not recovered. As with the chaining project studied by DeBloois *et al.* (1975), the impacts from scarification were not uniform: "Some areas were heavily disturbed, while others were apparently untouched" (Gallagher 1978:293).

Wood (1979) reports on a study of the impacts caused by crushing brush (principally sagebrush and other unpalatable species) on grazing areas west of Prescott, Arizona. He cites studies by DeBloois *et al.* and Gallagher to propose that artifact damage per se "appears to be less of a factor in data loss than dislocation," at least "until the artifacts are so badly damaged as to be unrecognizable" (1979:29). Accordingly, Wood recorded displacement, as well as breakage, addition, and loss of surface materials, primarily ceramics, after one pass by a Marden brush crusher at four test squares in the project area. Of the original 52 specimens, 86.5% were impacted: "by far the most common impact was loss from the observable surface inventory. Out of 63 instances . . . 61.9% of the impact was loss . . . with breakage being the least frequent" (1979:94). Wood suggests that the amount of impact caused by the

Marden brush crusher depended on four factors: (*a*) contact with the blades; (*b*) soil texture; (*c*) depth of cultural materials; and (*d*) artifact size (1979:97). All of these factors determine the ease with which artifacts can be pushed by the blades down into the surface sediments and obscured from view. He points out (1979:94) that such "sudden" loss of surface materials, "with little replacement from the subsurface population" has implications for future recognition, description, and evaluation of sites based on surface signatures.

Phillips (1980), in an unpublished study of the impacts of tractor yarding of logs over a natural and cultural lag deposit of basalt, cryptocrystalline silica, and obsidian in eastern Oregon, noted that the factors causing the greatest disruption of spatial relationships include the number of trips made by the tractor, whether or not the tractor turned during its trip across the site, the percent of slope, the bulk density of the soil, the size and number of logs in a turn (load); and the size, shape, and material of the artifacts themselves (1980:5–6). He points out that rounded forms (such as nodules) suffer less mechanical damage, but are more likely to be displaced than more angular forms. Other specific characteristics of the impact agent created differential movement on different parts of the site, and in different soil types. For instance, flakes dropped out of the bulldozer blade sooner than did cores during piling of slash, and small flakes were swept away entirely by bundles of needles remaining on downed trees. Phillips concludes

vertical displacement was greatest in deeper soils with low bulk density and fine particle size. Horizontal displacement was greatest in the primary skid trails, deck and slash piling activities. Form modification [of cultural materials] was greatest in the rocky soils and least in low density ash/basalt soils (1980:8).

Studies of Internal Changes in Sites

Aside from studies of the movement of surface artifacts, few experiments have been conducted to determine the nature and severity of impacts on archaeological sites themselves, whether from natural or cultural causes. In North America, artificial sites have been constructed as teaching aids for classes in archaeological field methods, but little quantitative work has been reported (see Ascher 1970; Chilcott and Deetz 1964). I conducted a "hypothetical experiment in quantification" as part of an application of a site development process model, using data on organic decay rates to suggest how chemical constituents of archaeological sediments may be altered through time (Wildesen 1973), but no observational data were available to test the results. Roger Parsons and his coworkers have used archaeological sites in the Midwest and the West Coast as "soil genesis benchmarks" to provide limiting dates for the study of soil profile development (Parsons 1962; Parsons *et al.* 1962; Reckendorf and Parsons 1966), but no archaeologists have studied the impacts of pedogensis on the integrity of the archaeological record. Mattingly and Williams (1962) report on changes in chemical properties of soils buried since Roman times in England, again using the archaeological site to provide a limiting date for their study, but did not assess the impacts of prolonged burial on the archaeological sediments or their cultural contents.

The Overton Down experiment, mentioned previously, was designed to obtain quantitative data on natural processes because "monuments are continually being modified by nature and . . . evidence of weathering, denudation, and silting can be as informative as the artifacts sometimes found in them" (Ashbee and Cornwall 1961:129). The constructed earthwork was intended to be sampled at regular intervals for up to 128 years (Jewell and Dimbleby 1966; Proudfoot 1965) to enable quantification of geomorphic and decay processes acting on the mound, ditch, and included cultural materials.

Studies such as those reported by Hansen and Morris (1968) on the activities of pocket gophers, Hester (1975) on the natural introduction of mollusca into archaeological contexts, and Lane (1970) on differential compaction in natural and cultural deposits are suggestive, but are neither quantitative nor comparative. We need studies that are both.

"Imaginative" experiments (Ascher 1961) on chemical properties of archaeological sediments, inspired by the work of Heizer and Cook at Berkeley (see, e.g., Cook 1963; Cook and Heizer 1965; Eddy and Dregne 1964; Lotspeich 1961; Setzer 1947; Solecki 1951; Solokoff and Carter 1952; Solokoff and Lorenzo 1953; Storie and Harradine 1950; Van der Merwe 1972; Weide 1966) often lack sufficient comparative data, or average the results of an entire soil profile, and thus provide little observational insight on the specific changes associated with specific conditions (see Wildesen 1973). These studies remain significant today because they suggested a direction for future research, and introduced archaeologists to a new arsenal of analytic tools with which to approach the study of the past. But they did not provide specific data with which to quantify or predict impacts on sites from natural processes.

Qualitative and semiquantitative studies of site morphology can provide useful hypotheses for model building. Cook (1963:333) suggests that the "degree of surface weathering" might shed light on the age of artificially constructed mounds in western Mexico; Jewell and Dimbleby's work in England (1966) confirms that mound morphology does in fact change in measurable ways through time. Building upon these studies, Kirkby and Kirkby (1976) described a model to account for geomorphic processes acting on house mounds in arid environments. They suggested that a mound profile approximates a normal curve over time, and that "the absolute heights [at different times] of the mound can be seen to depend on both its original size and shape, but the spreading out of the mound . . . is independent of these factors"

(1976:233). They cautioned that the use of the slope profile as a relative dating tool depends on both the original size of the house mound and the local climate; in Iran, such a mound might retain surface expression for up to 2000 years, whereas in Oaxaca, it might survive for only 500 to 800 years (1976:236).

Human beings can alter their living space while they are occupying it, as Ascher (1968), Schiffer (1976, 1977), and others have pointed out. Schiffer's A–S and S–S processes treat those aspects of scavenging, reuse, and exchange as they operate within living communities (the "systemic context"). Matthews (1965) points out that a zone of disturbance travels upward in a stratified archaeological site; as humans occupy it, deposits accumulate and the "surface" rises. Both objects and sediments are subject to this upward migration through time. Although Matthews describes the type of impact, and something of its behavior, we are given no data on severity of mixing, its rate or extent, or on how its presence actually affects our ability to recover the systemic context of the cultural material so transferred.

As with studies of impacts on artifacts, most recent studies on sites describe percentages or numbers of sites impacted, or state the impact agent or type that results in damage or destruction. Papers by Clewlow *et al.* (1971), Davis (1972), Medford (1972), Moratto (1973), Newman (1971), Palacios and Johnson (1976), Schiffer and House (1975a,b), and Traylor *et al.* (1979) provide good examples of this approach. But all impact types can be classified as either burial, transfer, removal, or alteration regardless of the nature of the impact agent. All of these disturbances to the archaeological record, whether caused by natural or cultural processes, can and should be described. As Talmage *et al.* (1977) suggest, it is the *regularities* of these impacts that are important; few studies treat these regularities in any systematic or comprehensive way.

Garrison (1975) seeks to accomplish such systematic treatment by using data and theory from hydrology and engineering studies to describe the expected impacts on archaeological resources due to inundation in a reservoir. He suggests that the causes of impact are waves, currents, seiches, temperature (including variations), chemistry of the water, erosion, and sedimentation, and that these forces will behave differently in the active (upper), transitional, and static (lower) zones of any specific reservoir. The nature of each of these forces can be ascertained from relevant literature in hydrology and physics. For instance, waves are wind generated, and their height, length, and velocity depend on the expanse of the water body. The depth of expected disturbance is related to the depth of wave action, which varies with the height or length of the wave itself (1975:282–283). Some unquantified observational data from studies of previously inundated sites indicate that "the depth of surface water movements in the Active Zone is ... more extensive ... than originally conceived," and the existence of ''water currents and silting was more extensive in calm water areas such as embayments'' than expected (Garrison 1975:292). It remains to describe *how much* ''more extensive'' such impacts are, and what effect such changes have on the interpretation of the archaeological record.

Lenihan *et al.* (1977) built on Garrison's framework to develop a series of hypotheses for a National Reservoir Inundation Study. Unfortunately, most of the hypotheses they have developed are not quantitative, many of the sites they propose to study have little or no ''before'' impact data available, and the results of their work accomplished to date are not yet published.

Studies of Fire Impacts

Barnes (1939) provided a classic description of the morphological changes in stone artifacts when subjected to fire, and made ''pot-lid fracture'' a term in the vocabulary of every archaeologist who deals with lithics. Yet virtually nothing has been published on the impacts of fire on archaeological materials since his time. Unpublished proposals, single-issue contract reports or staff papers, and abstracts of papers presented at by-invitation-only meetings constitute the bulk of the ''literature'' at this time (e.g., Eisler *et al.* 1978; Fenn *et al.* n.d.; Kelly and Mayberry 1979; Manuel 1980; see also Switzer 1974). Traylor *et al.* 1979 discovered that fire altered the morphology of adobe bricks, but observed that the major impacts resulted from heavy machinery (mixing and transport of surface sediments and artifacts) and from vandalism by fire fighters (removal of artifacts).

Summary

Aside from removal of specimens or sediments altogether, extensive disturbance of strata or specimen location is the most detrimental impact the archaeological record can suffer. Studies of artifact movement already have been described; very few quantitative studies of actual surface disturbance due to human agents (the ''ground-disturbing project'' or the vandal) have been conducted. Many reports state that sites are, in fact, disturbed, but few archaeological studies provide any specifics. I shall turn, therefore, to studies conducted by other kinds of scientists to glean some suggestive data for our purposes.

STUDIES OF IMPACTS TO SOILS AND SEDIMENTS

A great deal of research has been conducted by environmental scientists in order to answer the question ''how much?'' with respect to erosion, compaction, disturbance, and sedimentation association with modern land-disturbing activities such as timber harvest, grazing, and recreation. In contrast to most archaeological studies, these studies go beyond identifying impact type, and approach assessments of impact degree, extent, and duration in quantitative terms.

Compaction Studies

Compaction of sediments can be measured in kilograms per square meter or by before-and-after measurements of soil bulk density and/or pore space. Compaction can be caused by any of several impact agents: heavy machinery, animals (including humans), and natural deposition. Compaction on an archaeological site may alter the nature of the sediments, and the inferences that can be drawn from them. It may also alter relationships among imbedded artifacts, and in some cases damage the artifacts themselves (especially bones and ceramics). Research on compaction has been conducted by recreation specialists, soil scientists, and logging engineers, with varying and sometimes contradictory results.

For example, visitor use at campgrounds and on trails results in increased compaction on heavily used areas (Brown *et al.* 1977; Liddle 1975; Merriam and Smith 1974). Liddle (1975:24) reports as much as 0.68 g/cm³ increase in bulk density on English walking paths over that of adjacent undisturbed sediments. Merriam and Smith (1974:629) report, however, that compaction amounts seem to level off after several years, and that further increases do not occur. Not surprisingly, the amount of use and the type and amount of initial vegetation cover appear to determine the amount of impact at any specific locality. Soil moisture, initial bulk density, and soil texture (especially the type and percentage of clay particles) affect the degree of compaction noted in these and other studies.

Grazing by large animals also may cause compaction to occur, but the amounts of measurable change vary widely, and other factors such as slope, soil texture, and initial bulk density play an important role in determining the degree of impact (see, e.g., Currie and Gary 1978; Read 1957; Rich and Reynolds 1963).

Several studies of compaction conducted by logging specialists have especially interesting implications for archaeological impact analysis. For instance, although some studies show little variation in soil bulk density after several passes with heavy equipment, Kuennen *et al.* (1979) found that compaction varied with depth, and that maximum compaction in their Montana study units occurred from 4 to 16 inches (10 to 41 cm) below the surface. They suggest (1979:5) that the nature of the parent material and genetic soil horizons are primary factors affecting the depth of compaction. Duration of compaction impacts is as little as 18 years in Virginia (Hatchell and Ralston

1971) but may last over 55 years in the Willamette Valley of Oregon (Power 1974). Froelich (1978) and King and Haines (1979) report that compaction increases with the number of passes by the equipment, and that soil moisture and soil texture affect the results of their tests.

The amount of compaction may vary in different parts of a site, and depends on at least four factors: (*a*) the nature of the impact agent, (*b*) the distribution of the compacting activity (i.e., whether it is confined to logging skid trails, or spread widely over the site area), (*c*) the number of separate "impact events" (e.g., passes by a tractor), and (*d*) the nature of the site sediments and included cultural materials. The question *how much* compaction constitutes an adverse effect cannot be answered without reference to these factors.

Erosion Studies

Numerous studies and syntheses exist that treat the erosional impacts of ground-disturbing projects, especially in the context of pollution abatement (see, e.g., Environmental Protection Agency 1976; McDonald *et al.* 1977). McDonald *et al.* (1977:7) distinguish between erosion hazard and erosion potential in a way that is useful to archaeologists: "Erosion hazard is an inherent property of the site while erosion potential relates to the effect of . . . activities upon that site." That is, erosion *hazard* relates to *n*-transforms, and erosion *potential* to *c*-transforms (Schiffer 1972, 1976). Based on this distinction, many versions of a *universal soil loss equation* (USLE) have been developed for estimating the erosion potential of certain activities, especially farming practices on cropland in the midwest (see, e.g., U.S. Department of Agriculture 1978); Curtis *et al.* (1977:2) point out that the USLE can be used to predict erosion from "skid trails, temporary roads, landings, burns, grazing, game and recreation areas, and planting sites on forested lands" as well. They include tables and graphs for computing the values of each factor in the equation for woodland situations.

Roads and road construction usually cause the greatest erosional impact of any ground-disturbing activity, as several studies have shown, and as some archaeologists seem to recognize. For instance, Lyneis *et al.* (1980:78) cite studies showing that 38% of the historic and prehistoric trail system in Death Valley National Monument has been destroyed by sheet and gully erosion since 1910, when the first roads were constructed near the trails (Hunt and Mabey 1966). Similarly, Megahan (1976:22) points out that in forested areas, it is "not simply the cutting of timber," but the entire "logging operation," including access road construction, that creates undesirable disturbance. Resulting changes may include disruption of soil structure, removal of protective vegetation, increased raindrop impact, and possibly reduced infiltration rates. He further noted that

> These . . . effects are particularly severe on roads. Roads have additional effects that tend to accelerate erosion: increased slope gradients on cut and fill slopes; interception of subsurface water flow zones; and concentration of overland flow of water on the road prism and in channels (1976:22).

Beschta (1978) also found that roads caused erosion in logging areas, but attributes high sediment yields to mass failures exacerbated by road construction, and states that "maximum sediment will usually follow immediately after treatment and will gradually decline over a period of years" (1978:1015). For an archaeological site downslope from such sources of sediment, the extent and duration of the impact are clearly of utmost importance. DeGraff (1979) points out that ground-disturbing activities are not necessary to produce mass movement if the hazard for gravity-induced movements (such as landslides) is already high. Thus, the amount of erosion is determined by both the erosion hazard and the erosion potential of an area, and the consequent impacts on archaeological resources will also be affected by these factors (Megahan 1977).

Surface Mixing Studies

Severe and widespread disturbance (mixing and transfer) of archaeological sediments can wreak havoc with interpretations of the internal structure of archaeological sites. Aside from the few studies of the impacts of various activities on surface movement of artifacts, no large-scale experiments on soil mixing have been conducted by archaeologists. The forestry literature, however, is replete with studies of surface disturbance of soils in a timber harvest unit caused by various logging practices. Only a few of these can be summarized here, but they illustrate the kinds of studies archaeologists need to conduct, if we are to control disturbance impacts on archaeological sites.

Most investigators report *extent*, as measured by the percentage of area subjected to disturbance, and also make an attempt to provide explicit, measurable criteria for *severity* of impact, although their definitions for each category of severity may differ. Each of the definitions in Table 2.1, however different from the others, provides operational criteria for assigning observable impacts to a specific category, either by defining a measurable threshold (greater than 5 cm, e.g.) or by providing an "either–or" criterion (e.g., mineral soil either is, or is not, exposed). By contrast, an otherwise useful study by Gallagher (1978), an archaeologist, includes no such criteria; "severe disturbance," for example, is defined as "mixing . . . over a wide area . . . [involving] considerable depths" with the result that "archaeological features

TABLE 2.1

Definitions of Surface Disturbance Categories

Category	Definition
Severe	Removal of litter, disturbance of soil >2.5 cm deep (Wooldridge 1960:371)
	Removal of the litter, A horizon, and a portion of the B horizon; burial of the soil surface by at least 0.25 m of soil material; or severe compaction of the mineral soil (Utzig and Herring 1975:61)
	Where A horizons are disrupted sufficiently to expose B horizons (Patric and Gorman 1978:33)
	Surface soil removed and subsoil exposed (Klock 1975:80; Dyrness 1967:2)
Moderate	Removal of litter, soil disturbed to <2.5 cm depth (Wooldridge 1960:371)
Slight	No removal of litter or soil (Wooldridge 1960:371)
	Litter disrupted sufficiently to expose, partly or wholly, mineral soil (Patric and Gorman 1978:33)
	Litter removed, soil exposed; litter and soil mixed 50–50; soil on top of litter or slash (Dyrness 1967:2)
	Undisturbed litter and topsoil still in place (Klock 1975:80)
	Litter; no compaction (Dyrness 1967:2)

would be extensively disturbed'' and ''interpretability would be reduced to a minimum'' (1978:297). The main questions have been begged: How wide is a ''wide area''? How deep is ''considerable depth''? Most important, what is meant by ''extensively disturbed''?

The results of 23 studies of degree and extent of surface disturbance associated with different log-yarding systems are presented in Table 2.2 (after Wildesen 1977). Haupt (1960) points out that factors such as the number of stems cut, whether an area is clear-cut or cut selectively, and the size of the tractor used for yarding affect the amount of surface bared during yarding. Because of the interaction of these factors, and the relationship of tractor size to the number of skid roads and haul roads needed, there is no simple formula to determine which method of cutting or yarding is *the least* disruptive to surface soils. As Klock's (1975:81) data suggest, ''adding the area of roads necessary for some cable skidding operations could raise the total area of severe soil surface disturbances to more than 50%,'' although Patric and Gorman (1978:34) assert that even with such additional area included, less than 3% of their study area in West Virginia would have exhibited ''severe'' disturbance (see also, Brown 1973; DeByle 1976; Hope 1979; Silen and Gratkowski 1953; Smith and Wass 1976).

Despite the variability in results, these and similar studies reaffirm the importance of treating impacts in terms of their *degree, extent,* and *duration* in addition to cause and type. It is crucial for archaeologists to be able to answer the ''how much'' questions for archaeological resources at least as well as soil scientists can for soil resources.

TABLE 2.2

Percent of Study Area in Each Disturbance Class

Yarding method	None	Slight to moderate	Severe	Compaction	Reference
Tractor or skidder on bare ground	7.2	5.9	15.9	—15.0—	Garrison and Rummell 1951
	35.6	6.3	8.9	26.8	Wooldridge 1960
	26.2	26.4	36.2	—	Dyrness 1965
	—	37.6	14.7–18.6	—	Klock 1975
					Utzig and Herring 1975
Tractor over snow	66.0	24.1	9.9	—	Klock 1975
Horse on bare ground		9.5		—2.3—	Garrison and Rummell 1951
High lead	57.2	15.8	9.7	9.1	Ruth 1967
		21.5		—1.9—	Dyrness 1967
		13.3			Garrison and Rummell 1951
			1.0	9.0	Fredrickson 1970
	58.1	21.0	9.6	9.6	Dyrness 1965
	50.7	24.5	13.6	7.1	Dyrness 1965
	62.7	18.9	5.8	10.7	Dyrness 1965
	23.5	44.5	32.0	—	Klock 1975
			7.2–9.4		Utzig and Herring 1975
Skyline	63.6	6.4	4.7	3.4	Ruth 1967
	5.7	24.4	3.2	—	Dyrness 1967
		2.2	5.0	3.0	Wooldridge 1960
			2.8	—	Fredrickson 1970
	74.8	22.4			Klock 1975
Balloon	78.1	15.8	2.6	1.7	Dyrness 1972
Helicopter	88.0	11.3	0.7	—	Klock 1975

Studies of Fire

Fire is a potent impact agent, not only for the damage it can cause directly, but also because it interacts with other impact agents to encourage or enhance their actions. Fire is known to cause destruction of organic matter in surface soils (Dyrness *et al.* 1957; Fenn *et al.* 1976; Packer and Williams 1976) and to alter other chemical properties of soils such as pH, cation exchange capacity, and percentage of nitrogen, potassium, and sulfur (DeBano *et al.* 1977).

Fire also creates enhanced erosion potential, especially in arid environments (Beaufait *et al.* 1975; DeBano 1977), and may increase a tendency toward compaction (Packer and Williams 1976). Wells and his coworkers (1979:16) sum up the current knowledge of fire impacts to soils as follows:

> Fire influences soil physical properties and erosion to a degree depending upon the intensity of the fire, the proportion of the overstory and understory vegetation destroyed, forest floor consumed, heating of the soil, proportion of the area burned, and frequency of fire occurrence. [In addition,] the changes wrought vary greatly with the conditions of the soil, forest floor, topography, and climate.

STUDIES OF VANDALISM ON ARCHAEOLOGICAL SITES

No discussion of impacts to the archaeological record can omit a description of the actions of vandals. Vandalism, including the results of thoughtless activities such as indiscriminate use of off-road vehicles (ORVs) takes an enormous toll of archaeological sites each year. This is especially true in the western United States, where estimates of numbers of sites severely damaged run upwards of one third of the total site inventory (Lyneis *et al.* 1980). Only recently have any studies of the actual magnitude of damage from vandalism been undertaken. As yet, comprehensive data on the actual type, extent, and degree of impacts do not exist.

Several studies have been conducted in the western United States to ascertain the amount of vandalism that occurs to archaeological resources on federal lands. Williams (1978:36) points out that different resource types are subject to differential vandalism, with rock art sites being the most vulnerable, followed by open camps or chipping stations, stone or adobe-walled dwellings, historic buildings, and rockshelters and caves, in that order. His study area included nine states in the "intermountain west"; his data show that the kind of sites most subject to vandalism vary by subregion within this broad area. Williams lists four "vulnerability factors" which seem to influence the amount and type of vandalism: resources that are well known, show signs of previous vandalism, receive high visitor use, or are obviously deteriorated are targets for further vandalistic acts (1978:49). He develops a "profile" of the typical vandal, based on characteristics reported by various federal land managers and archaeologists (1978:57, 60, 61, 63): Most vandals are over 30, vandalize in groups, are males from smaller towns (less than 25,000 people), are probably local residents or travel less than 100 miles to commit their acts of vandalism, and are repeaters (1978:71). Motives for archaeological and historical vandalism seem to be desire for personal acquisition of artifacts, followed by ignorance (of the law or of the destruction caused to the archaeological record), curiosity, recreation, profit, showing off, rebellion, and carelessness, in that order (1978:67). Increases in the rate of vandalism seem to be associated with an increased awareness of cultural resources, coupled with easy access and lax law enforcement; decreases in the trend seem to be associated with areas where the resources are scanty and law enforcement is vigilant. Williams suggests (1978:13) that "cultural resource vandalism . . . seems to be on the whole a characteristically different 'type' of depreciative activity" than other kinds, in part because collecting is a primary motive, rather than simple destruction per se. Therefore, archaeological vandals are likely to be "more methodical in their approach and older . . . than the youths damaging school buildings" (Williams 1978:13).

McAllister (1979) provides support for the idea that archaeological vandals are methodical; he lists some of the special tools such persons use to make their work more efficient and to help them escape detection by authorities. Among them are bottomless tents; aircraft spotters with radio communications to the vandals on the ground; special probes to locate burials without having to remove a lot of overburden; helicopter transportation in and out of the target area; and use of heavy equipment to move the greatest amount of dirt in the least amount of time (1979:35–36). Such tools are not inexpensive, and their use requires planning and attention to logistics beyond that expected of the casual recreationist. Of the known sites in McAllister's northern Arizona study area, 50% showed damage by vandals; in some subareas as many as 80% of the known sites were vandalized.

Lyneis *et al.* (1980) studied vandalism and natural impacts on archaeological resources in the California Desert Conservation Area, administered by the BLM in southeastern California. They found that accessibility of sites to population centers and roads was a major factor in the damage suffered from vandalism, and that different site types suffer different amounts and kinds of vandalism. For instance, only 36% of the aboriginal village sites are listed as in "good" condition, whereas 48% of the caves or rock-shelters are so listed (Lyneis *et al.* 1980:49). Overall, 38% of the rock features (alignments and ground figures) show damage by ORVs, and 25% of the rock art panels show damage by vandals (removal, use as shooting target, or enhanced exfoliation resulting from building campfires against the rock) (1980:49).

The BLM reported the results of before-and-after studies of the Barstowto-Las Vegas motorcycle race and its impacts on archaeological sites in the California desert. Of 50 known archaeological and historical sites within 3 miles (5 km) of the race course, 10 were in the "impact zone" of the race, and 3 were expected to sustain some impact as a result of the race (U.S. Department of the Interior, Bureau of Land Management 1975:83). Racers were directed by flagging and course marshals to steer clear of fragile sites, but of the 19 sites so protected, 11 received some impact from the race. The report describes a "disturbance scale," sorted into five classes apparently based on percentage of site area disturbed; no indication of depth of disturbance or degree of mixing is given (U.S. Department of the Interior, Bureau of Land Management 1975:90).

Although neither Lyneis *et al.* (1980) nor the BLM study provides quantitative data on actual impact type, degree, or extent caused by ORVs, Lyneis *et al.* (1980:2) point out that not only does the use of ORVs increase the accessibility of vulnerable sites and damage some sites simply from traveling over them, but there is a synergistic effect of ORV use on fragile desert pavement soils: Because the efficacy of wind as an erosive force depends on the degree of armoring on desert surfaces, destruction of vegetation and desert pavement by wheeled vehicles increases the danger of destruction by wind erosion (Lyneis *et al.* 1980:76). In addition, most sites damaged by human actions (vandalism or ORV use) are on slopes less than 6° (Lyneis *et al.* 1980:76). Coupled with the fact that 50% of the desert is within 1.6 km of a road, and 95% is within 4.8 km of a road, it seems unlikely that land managers will be able to limit access in order to reduce vandalism (Lyneis *et al.* 1980:78).

Sheridan (1979) summarizes much recent research on the impacts ORVs cause to natural resources. In addition to disruption of vegetation cover and the resulting increases in erosion, several studies report severe compaction on ORV trails, in some cases up to 1 m deep (Snyder *et al.* 1976; Webb *et al.* 1978). Thus, for compaction as an impact type, although the extent may be limited to trails, it certainly is severe, and it may not be reversible.

Behavioral studies of other kinds of vandalism do not provide much encouragement for those who would control archaeological vandalism, although Harrison's (1976:474) definition of vandalism is relevant to archaeological studies: Vandalism is "any willful act of physical damage that lowers the aesthetic or economic value of an object or area. In contrast to other categories of depreciative behavior, vandalism results in visible scars." Harrison lists exposure, access, and facility condition as three physical factors influencing the incidence of vandalism, and confirms that most acts of vandalism are performed by repeaters.

Clark *et al.* (1971:9) found that "more than 80 percent of the depreciative acts observed were committed when other people were present" and "in more than 90 percent of these cases, no perceptible reaction by adjacent campers could be observed.'' But part of the problem seems to be, as Clark (1976:65) points out, that

> many times an act of vandalism as defined by a manager may be very appropriate [behavior] from a user perspective. In some cases, recreationists who have little contact with the environment may really not know what is defined as vandalism by managers. In other cases they may know but disagree.

Harrison corroborates this point by suggesting that many acts of severe vandalism are "a result of thoughtlessness or ignorance on the part of visitors, and offenders seldom view their damage as vandalism" (1976:479).

Recent successful efforts to obtain new federal legislation applicable to "pot hunting" on public lands merely highlight the extent of this problem. In view of the fact that only archaeologists seem to consider surface collecting vandalism, the controversy over new antiquities legislation only points up what a poor job the profession has done in educating the public in the importance of *context* to interpretations from archaeological data (see Collins 1980; Collins and Green 1978; Grayson 1976; U.S. Congress 1979).

The study of motives of archaeological vandals, and the actual damage they cause is in its infancy. Without more detailed data, archaeologists cannot hope to develop effective measures to prevent or counteract vandalism. Inappropriately targeted educational programs will not work; fences and arrests are usually too late; and before-and-after studies of the archaeological resources themselves are nonexistent. As with other impact agents and types, it is clear that we need more specific, quantitative data on vandalism.

APPLICATIONS OF IMPACT STUDIES
TO ARCHAEOLOGICAL RESEARCH
AND RESOURCE MANAGEMENT

Despite the gaps and deficiencies in existing studies of impacts to archaeological sites (discussed in more detail later), there are several immediate applications for what little we know now. Results from the study of impacts can be applied to designing better strategies for locating sites; for developing intrasite sampling methods; and for predicting the accuracy and reliability of various analytical techniques.

Archaeological site survey is dependent on surface manifestations of sites; evaluation of research potential, and development of appropriate intrasite sampling methods is dependent on the nature of the relationship between surface expression and subsurface expression and content of a site. As Leeds (1975) points out, surface expressions of sites are subject to "pattern distortions" that may obscure the surface–subsurface relationship, or even prevent the site from being identified as such.

It is not within the focus of this chapter to engage in a comprehensive review of the recent literature on site survey strategy, or even to discuss the sudden resurgence of interest in surface–subsurface congruence. Those topics have been treated adequately elsewhere (see, e.g., Ammerman and Feldman 1978; Baker 1978; Bellis 1975; Binford 1975; Chartkoff 1978; Harrison 1972; Jeter and Reynolds 1975; King 1978; Lewarch and O'Brien 1981; Plog *et al.* 1978; Schiffer *et al.* 1978; Thomas 1975). It is appropriate, however, to describe the results of several interesting but not widely known studies that illustrate the points just made.

Leeds (1975) studied a large archaeological site in southeastern Missouri that had been subjected to plowing and land leveling during most of the twentieth century. His intent was to show that

a) the location and kind of soil movements distorting the [surface] sample can be specified, b) the degree of their effect on the sample can be evaluated and c) the specific location and original shape where possible, of mounds and other surface features can be mapped (1975:1).

By using color and color infrared aerial imagery, comparisons with early maps of the area, and interviews with local farmers, Leeds developed a "prehistoric landform estimate" (1975:3), so that he could determine "where excavations into the subsoil have taken place, where elevations have been removed and where depressions have been filled" (1975:4). He states that

In areas where the depth of filling exceeds the depth of plowing, the value of horizontal patterning of artifact classes will be . . . zero, except in cases where the original location of the material is precisely known. In areas filled to a depth less than the depth of plowing, patterns can be considered some fraction of the value of patterns in undisturbed areas, depending on the depth and artifact frequency of the fill. Similarly, areas from which higher elevations have been cut might be devoid of any sample. Just as often, the removal of soil will simply reveal artifacts previously not reached by the plow, and so, depending upon the equipment used, the artifact patterns will represent some fraction of those in undisturbed areas. Excavation will usually result in a total disturbance, but the location of excavations is generally obvious, both on the ground and in air photos, . . . and the horizontal extent will be small (Leeds 1975:6–7).

He concludes that, "although 25% of the sample area has been disturbed, only 9% of the area . . . should be considered *ipso facto* of zero value for horizontal patterning" (1975:7).

The point, of course, is that although the activities described certainly have created measurable impacts on the sites, the assessment of adverse effects depends on the research objective being considered, and on whether the nature of the prior impacts can be accurately determined. If no early maps, aerial imagery, or oral informants had been available, Leeds may well have found his research objectives impossible to fulfill, because there was no way to control for prior disturbance. But by identifying the regularities in the land-modification activities, Leeds was able to account for anomalous surface distributions of artifacts, and for seemingly "sterile" deposits where there should have been cultural materials. Therefore, less than 10% of the site area actually was made useless for the kind of study he wished to conduct. Clearly, in this case, assessment of research potential is one factor that *must* be included in defining the threshold of *effect*.

In another useful study, Kirkby and Kirkby (1976:229–230) tried to develop models to illustrate the impact of natural processes on house mounds in arid environments, to account for:

(1) the change in form of the house mound through time; (2) the alteration of the sherd scatter on the surface over time through the three interacting processes of accumulation, breakdown, and transportation; (3) the loss of sherds at the surface through natural alluviation and cultural accumulation over the original site; and (4) the combined effects of these and other factors on the probability of recovering early sites, or early periods, through surface survey, and thus the interpretations that may be made for apparent population change over time (emphasis in original omitted).

I described the results of some of their experiments on sherd trampling, sherd movement, and house-form changes earlier. Based on these experiments, and models of geomorphic processes, they conclude that:

within most archaeological areas . . . evidence of early periods will only be recovered at all with any certainty ($p > 0.95$) if there are more than 15 sites in the area dating from that time. Likewise, if an early period is represented by only a single site even if the area is later densely settled, the chances of recovering that period [are] only 20 percent even with a complete surface survey (emphasis in original omitted) (Kirkby and Kirkby 1976:251).

In addition, they suggest that if house mounds or other isolated prehistoric features are located more than 100 m apart, it is unlikely even with 20 test pits that they will be found (1976:248).

The logic and complexity of the Kirkbys' model merit close attention; I encourage the reader to peruse the entire paper, and the volume of which it is a part (Davidson and Shackley 1976). For our purposes here, it is important to realize that by developing a geomorphic model appropriate to the locality under consideration, and including explicit parameters for natural and cultural impacts on expected sites, one can design a survey strategy that takes into account the potential visibility of sites of different ages, or in different geomorphic situations in the local landscape. Without the estimates of impacts, selection of specific survey methods (including sampling intensity) must be based on guesswork, or on models from other localities that may or may not be appropriate.

The impacts of erosion and sedimentation on resource integrity and locatability often are crucial not only for interpreting the archaeological record but for developing intrasite sampling designs. Certainly, as Reid *et al.* (1975:221) point out, by attempting to model the processes of erosion and . . . deposition that operated on the cultural deposits to produce the surface of [a] site, 'target areas' can be defined where sub-surface deposits of secondary refuse might be expected to occur, [and] . . . the more known about how these processes formed the site under study, the more likely it is that one will be able to locate and sample the units containing data relevant to a systemic context question (1975:224).

These processes are important for all archaeological sites; they are especially relevant for studies of inundated sites. Despite the development of hydrologic models to estimate impacts on archaeological resources in reservoirs (e.g., Garrison 1975), the hypotheses proposed by the National Reservoir Inundation Study (Lenihan *et al.* 1977) do not include erosion or sedimentation except where they affect the "locatability" of sites. For example, Lenihan *et al.* (1977) imply that neither "standard survey procedures" nor aerial imagery will be very effective following inundation.

Few studies have been conducted specifically to determine the impacts of human-caused activities on analytical techniques (see Goodyear 1971). It is well known as Schiffer (1976) suggests, that characteristics of sediments affect the differential preservation of pollen grains (Faegri and Iverson 1964), and as we have seen, fire (including wildfire) can alter chemical properties of surface soils.

Lenihan *et al.* (1977) propose several hypotheses dealing with impacts of reservoirs on archaeologists' ability to analyze nonartifactual data from inundated archaeological sites. For example, they suggest that impacts on dating techniques will vary by technique: little change will be noted for radiocarbon, dendrochronology, archeomagnetism, or fission-track and alpha recoil dating techniques, but X-ray diffraction, amino-acid racemization, and fluorine dates will not be reliable, and obsidian hydration and thermo-luminescence techniques will have varying results depending on local factors, including length of immersion (Lenihan *et al.* 1977:84–106, passim).

Although these hypotheses are suggestive, they are not framed in such a way that testing them will provide sufficient data for specific descriptions of impact degree, extent, duration, rate of onset, or possible reversibility. *How much* will the dates vary after immersion? What is the *cumulative impact* of repeated drawdown on these analyses? We need solid experimental data to answer these questions.

PREDICTING AND MITIGATING ADVERSE EFFECTS ON ARCHAEOLOGICAL RESOURCES

In light of the foregoing descriptions of impacts on archaeological resources, consider the following statement about a 95,000-acre BLM "resource area" in Nevada:

The present range improvements include 100 miles [161 km] of fence, 11,000 acres [4472 ha] of crested wheatgrass seeding, 5 wells, 10,000 feet [3048 m] of pipeline for livestock watering, 500 acres [203 ha] of contour terracing and 5 check dams.

Future work will include: seeding, 5,000 acres [2032 ha]; chaining [junipers] 4,000 acres [1626 ha]; contour furrowing, 1,000 acres [407 ha]; spraying, 2,000 acres [813 ha]; water spreading, 1,000 acres [407 ha]; 60 gully plugs, 10 detention dams, 3 springs, 6 reservoirs, and 50 miles [80 km] of access road improvement (Eckert 1965:36).

What is the impact on the archaeological resource base of these activities? More important, what is the *effect* of these activities on the archaeological record of the area? What strategies can be proposed to mitigate any adverse effects? What data can be brought to bear on this problem?

As Lyneis *et al.* (1980:2) point out, "our society is accustomed to accept" the impacts of natural processes on archaeological materials, and it is very seldom indeed that we have taken measures to "slow or reverse these processes." But they continue, "our inclination to accept this damage is replaced by alarm . . . when we realize that the damages from each of these causes is accelerating *as the result of the interaction of natural processes and people's activities*" (emphasis added). For instance, we know, and tend to accept, that sites are subject to erosion, groundwater changes, and gradual decay of cultural materials contained within them. Some impacts of these processes may be preventable, but the processes themselves are inevitable. When erosion is aggravated by road construction, cattle grazing, or reservoir construction, however, the process itself is perceived as preventable: these activities do not *need* to occur on top of our resources, or if they must, there ought to be some way to minimize the damage, or reverse it once it has been done. To do so, of course, presupposes that we can accurately predict what the actual damage will be, and that the measures we choose to counteract it are appropriate.

We have seen that archaeological resources are subject to a wide variety of impact types, caused by a wide variety of impact agents. It is crucial now to have answers for the questions *how much? how bad? how long?* and *how rapid?* because we cannot develop *appropriate* counteractive measures simply by designating the impact agent and the resulting impact type. We also need to decide when it is worthwhile to spend our efforts in this way. That is, we need specific data on impact degree, extent, and duration, and a "threshold of concern."

Consider the situation just described. What types of impacts might 100 miles (161 km) of fence produce? The usual list probably would include surface disturbance, excavation (and perhaps removal), and disruption of subsurface materials from posthole digging; it might also include compaction or erosion from construction of a road for transporting materials or from trampling by horses. Depending on the proclivities of the fence builders, collection of artifacts may occur; and depending on the purposes for which the fence is being built, further trampling by cattle might take place. But *how much?*, and how seriously would the archaeological record be damaged if any or all of these impacts types actually occurred?

In this example, as in all such examples, the answer clearly is, *"it depends."* To establish the threshold of concern and to develop appropriate mitigation measures, one needs to know the nature and distribution of the local archaeological resource base; the specific location of sites with respect to the fence building activity; and the actual components of the fence building activity itself (handheld or mechanical posthole diggers? will access be by road or horses?) and the degree, extent, and duration of the impacts caused by each activity. The list of impacts above merely contains *labels* for impact agents and types; it therefore provides no data on which to base specific strategies for minimizing any specific impact with which to determine the overall effect of the project on any sites the fence must cross. Given such inadequate information, the "best" option for the manager in this instance seems to be to locate the fence building activity as far as possible from any archaeological resources. This is called "management by avoidance," and is becoming the standard recommendation of many archaeologists and managers faced with resolving resource conflicts.

But this option is simply pseudomitigation. It is neither good resource management, nor good decision making. It may prevent harm to a specific archaeological resource today, but what of tomorrow? What if the proposed activity was not the construction of a fence, which is, after all, a fairly geographically restricted, linear feature, but one of the other activities listed: seed drilling of 2024 ha, or juniper chaining of 1619 ha?

To answer these questions, it is crucial to have data on both the nature of the archaeological resource itself, and the purpose to which it is to be put. *These are the most important factors in defining a threshold of concern,* and thus in assessing the nature of "effect" in any specific case. Therefore, it is important to obtain sufficient data to characterize the physical properties of the archaeological site(s), either through test excavations, field mapping, collections analysis, or comparison with other known sites in the area. It is absolutely vital to have the specific, locally or regionally defined goals of archaeological resource management firmly in mind, as well. That is, one must know the range of purposes for which sites are to be managed: scholarly use (what are the relevant research questions?); public interpretation (what are the relevant visual and access characteristics it is important to preserve?); "banking" for future use (what will it be used for in the future?); and other purposes, which will have their own sets of questions in need of answers.

To some extent, it is not only the range of research questions, but the nature of the specific research strategies and methods that will influence the definition of the threshold of concern. The variety of opinions about the amount of harm caused to the archaeological record by agricultural activities, reviewed earlier, is a case in point. Of course "plowing" will have different degrees, extents, and durations of impact (assuming "surface disturbance–mixing" to be the impact type) depending on, for example, number of years the field has been plowed, depth of plowing, type of crop planted, manner of field clearing, type of equipment used, erosion potential of the land, slope of the surface, speed of the plow, moisture content and textural class of the soil, number of passes per episode of plowing, season, and so forth (Talmage *et al.* 1977:4). But *the nature of the effect also depends on what archaeologists expect out of the archaeological record.* Some archaeologists (e.g., Binford *et al.* 1970; Leeds 1975; Redman and Watson 1970) use plowing as a "visibility enhancement" tool (see Schiffer *et al.* 1978), contending either that the archaeological record is minimally disrupted, or that the regularities of the disruption can be defined and therefore can be accounted for in interpretation of archaeological data. If the focus of these studies had been on fine-grained behavioral patterns, such as knapping stations within a surface lithic scatter, such disruption might be excessive in degree, extent, and duration, and the value of the site *for that kind of study* might be permanently impaired. For as Aikens (1976:12) points out, "disturbance diminishes value in proportion to the extent and disruptiveness of that disturbance," with respect to one's *research objectives.*

The analysis of discrete characteristics of impacts in addition to impact type, the use of the concept of threshold, and an indication of the range of alternative mitigation measures that can be used in a specific situation can be illustrated with respect to a hypothetical example taken from Wildesen (1978) (see also U.S. Department of Agriculture, Forest Service 1978). Consider, for instance, the situation in which a surface scatter of obsidian artifacts has been identified in the middle of a proposed timber harvest area. Traditional "mitigation" measures dictate that either (*a*) the artifacts be collected, and thus removed from the area, or (*b*) the proposed timber harvest activity be moved elsewhere. Both of these alternatives eliminate the resource conflict, but the first does not meet the conservation archaeology objective to minimize the attrition of the archaeological resource base (Lipe 1974), and the second is temporary at best and may not meet the timber resource management objective for the area. What other options does the archaeologist have?

At this point, some archaeologists still would try to justify complete surface collection on the basis of "mitigating data loss"; others would reach for their lawbooks to try to halt the timber harvest activity altogether. But according to the principles I have outlined already, the next steps ought to be

1. to examine the components of the impacting activity to determine the potential type, degree, extent, and duration of specific potential impacts;

2. to determine the nature of the archaeological values in the site, and the management objectives for it;
3. to ascertain the "threshold of concern";
4. to discover what steps might be taken to reduce the impacts below the threshold, that is, to decide whether it is possible to change the impact type, or to decrease its degree, extent, or duration either before, during, or after project implementation; and
5. to choose from among the alternative strategies that seem to achieve both the archaeological and timber resource management objectives.

For instance, we have seen in Table 2.2 that certain yarding techniques create severe surface disturbance, including thorough mixing of mineral soil to a depth of several inches, whereas others do not create this type of impact. We also have seen that certain yarding techniques create severe disturbance over as much as 36% of the area. We note that displacement of artifacts on surfaces resulting from the action of heavy equipment ranges from a few centimeters to several meters, depending on factors such as slope, nature of ground cover, and type of equipment, and that all of these factors can be described for our study area. We know that, of the various kinds of equipment and techniques available for disposing of organic residue (slash), some of these are more likely to cause additional surface disturbance in the site than others, and, presumably, we can quantify their relative extent of mixing (see Harrison 1975; Ward and McLean 1976). We have several studies on edge damage to lithic materials that suggest that although damage may occur, it can be distinguished from "edge wear" caused by aboriginal human use of the tools; and we know that soil bulk density and textural class may influence the amount of edge damage that occurs. We know that the impacts of fire (if this is an alternative method for slash disposal) are likely to be concentrated on the top few centimeters of mineral soil, but that compaction impacts may go considerably deeper, depending on the initial characteristics of the sediments, the type of equipment used, the number of passes made over the site, and so forth.

We also must know what kind of research value the site now has: whether it can provide information on fine-grained behavior patterns; whether it can be expected to have retained integrity through the centuries since it was created, due to the actions and impacts of natural processes; or whether it is important primarily for the light it can shed on trade networks, lithic manufacturing, or edge-wear analysis. We need to know the depth and areal extent of the site and its location with respect to the expected actions of the potential impact agents. In other words, we need to know how *sensitive* the archaeological record is to the expected impact type(s), degree(s), extent(s), and duration(s) resulting directly or indirectly from the proposed activity.

Given these data and ideas, we can begin to define a threshold of concern, to select appropriate measures to reduce the impacts of *each* of the timber harvest activities, and thus to reduce the *cumulative impact* of these activities on the values of the archaeological resource we wish to conserve.

In our hypothetical example, we might define the threshold of concern at "20 percent severe disturbance," and seek a timber harvest practice that produces less than that extent. In another case, we might wish to limit the extent to 3% or permit up to 90% extent if certain portions of the site were not affected. *It is when the combined impacts exceed this threshold of concern that they may be said to have an adverse effect on the characteristics that make a site an important part of the archaeological resource base,* and it is at this point that we, as archaeologists and archaeological resource managers, need to develop measures to "mitigate" that effect.

Let us suppose, for the sake of argument, that we have selected 20% severe, permanent surface disturbance as our threshold of concern, and that the combined impacts of logging, yarding, slash disposal, and replanting as currently proposed, are on the order of 50%. If we remove the archaeological resource, we will have no site left to disturb, but we will also have no site left *in situ,* which might provide data 20 years from now. If we move the location of impacting project, we will have "saved" the site, only to be faced with the prospect of having to "save" it all over again 20 years from now, when the area is again selected for a timber project. I call these approaches *site exploitation* and *site conservation,* respectively (Wildesen 1978). On the other hand, if we can select some timber harvesting practices that reduce the cumulative impact extent or degree below our threshold of concern, we will have 80% of our site area relatively intact at the conclusion of the impacting activities, and can look forward to conducting research into the nature of the archaeological record there for years to come.

I call this approach *value conservation,* in contrast to the two more traditional approaches just described, because it seeks to define the nature of the archaeological *values* that are to be conserved rather than simply eliminating one or the other resource management opportunity from possibility. In other words, the value conservation approach attempts to find compatibility in what might at first glance appear to be incompatible land uses. Of course, in order to use this approach, one must know a great deal more about the expected impacts than, "there might be some," and a great deal more about the archaeological site than, "it exists."

One also needs to know those situations in which *no* level of a particular type of impact can be tolerated, regardless of how mild, how minute its extent, or how brief its duration. Most activities that might lower the water table near a wet site (Croes 1976) would probably fit this category, as would most activities that would literally level (that is, obliterate all evidence of) a Woodland mound. In these situations, site exploitation or site conservation could be justifiable approaches to conflict resolution, given today's state of the art in archaeological theory and method. But as Garrison (1975), Leeds (1975), Lenihan *et al.* (1977), and Talmage *et al.* (1977) have shown, activities that 20 years ago were assumed to cause irreparable harm to archaeological resources, today can be analyzed into their component parts. The impact type, degree, extent, and duration can be determined for each part, so that mitigation measures can be designed that are appropriate to each specific situation. More such pioneering work is needed, as are more hard data on the nature of impacts.

IMPLICATIONS FOR THE FUTURE

The study of impacts on archaeological resources has serious implications for archaeological theory building, archaeological resource management, and future research in both theoretical and applied archaeology (see Gunn 1978; Mayer-Oakes 1978; Wildesen 1979, 1980).

Archaeological Theory Building

Earlier in this chapter, I alluded to the nature of the site development process as it affects our ability to use the archaeological record to discover things about the past and discusssed how Schiffer's concepts (1972, 1976) of *n*-transforms and *c*-transforms apply to this endeavor (see also Schiffer and Rathje 1973). It should be clear that archaeologists have much to learn about how natural and cultural impacts affect this record. We know very little about the actual type of impact resulting from the action of a specific natural or cultural impact agent. We know even less about the characteristic features of each impact type, including degree, duration, extent, and distribution in time and space from the day the archaeological "site" was created until archaeologists find it again. And we know almost nothing about the degree of distortion introduced by those impacts into the archaeological record. It is essential to use an interdisciplinary approach to the study of impacts in which the results of separate studies by different specialists are integrated into the final interpretation of the archaeological record, rather than fragmented as individual reports with little or no feedback among researchers. It is not enough to know that pollen is differentially preserved; we need to know *how much* and in what way our data are likely to be distorted, and therefore in what directions our interpretations are likely to be in error.

We need to know more about how erosion removes or alters archaeological data and about how we can use that knowledge to help us locate house mounds, study soil profile development, or reconstruct past cultural behavior. We need to know how quickly organic cultural materials decay in a site, and whether any identifiable decay products might remain to help us determine the nature, quantity, and distribution of former organic cultural materials in the site matrix. We need to know the incidence of wildfire, tree windthrow, and slope wash to estimate the potential of a surface site for the study of specialized cultural activities such as flint knapping. Finally, we need to know *what really happens* to cultural materials, site features, and their sedimentary matrix under the plow, the bulldozer, the rising waters of a reservoir, or "pot-hunter pressure," so that we can factor that knowledge into our equation that defines the relationship between "archaeological" and "systemic" contexts.

Archaeological Resource Management

During the past two decades, we who would conserve archaeological resources for the future have been provided with some legal tools and planning models that require consideration of alternatives to archaeological resource destruction. Without hard data on the nature of impacts, we cannot use these tools efficiently. We need to be able to predict with some reliability and accuracy what effect a certain combination of impacts will have on the archaeological values we wish to conserve, so that we can develop effective strategies to mitigate adverse effects. We need studies of impacts so we can distinguish those situations in which there are *no* effective mitigation measures, and, therefore, in which site exploitation or site conservation are the appropriate conflict resolution strategies.

We need to know when the concept of "substitutability" may be applicable to our resource management decisions (Hendee and Burdge 1974; see also Green n.d.). As Hendee and Burdge (1974:161) emphasize, it is as important to know about those situations for which there are no substitutes, such as unique archaeological sites, because to foreclose policy and management options in these situations will be far more detrimental to the resource base than if substitutes are available. We cannot identify these situations without data both on the nature of the resource base itself, and on the expected impacts resulting from policy or project decisions.

"Mitigation measures" also need to be cost effective in this "real world" of increasing needs and limited finances. As I have pointed out in an earlier publication,

> conservation . . . often involves weighing the costs and benefits of using a given resource now, against the costs and benefits of using it in the future, or using a different resource now. . . . Put this way, the preservation of a site by not studying it now may in the long run cost us more than using it to increase our understanding of former ways of life (Wildesen 1975:11; emphasis in original omitted).

One of the most important implications that the study of impacts has for the future of archaeology is that only by knowing in some detail the nature of the threat to archaeological resources can we order our research priorities to correspond with the schedule of destructive impacts from outside impact agents. Those of use who "grew up," archaeologically speaking, in the era of "emergency salvage" know how far our profession has come in the past decade or so. We now have a real opportunity to participate in the land-use and project planning processes of federal agencies and other land and resource managing entities, but we need to develop some new paradigms if our participation is to be meaningful. In the face of our enormous ignorance of *what actually happens* to archaeological resources as a result of implementing a particular land-disturbing activity, our calls for "salvage" or "avoidance" increasingly will become scientifically and politically bankrupt.

Research Needs

It is clear that there are many important and fruitful areas for future archaeological research, and that we have reached a kind of turning point in our profession. I have touched on some of these areas in previous sections; I summarize them here as a "research agenda" of sorts for archaeologists in the coming decade.

1. We need both (*a*) more actual experimental research into the nature of specific impacts on archaeological resources, whether from natural or human causes, and (*b*) more application of data from other scientific fields such as soils, hydrology, and geomorphology to building models of the impacts caused by natural processes.

2. We need creative applications of these data to the prediction of impacts expected to result from specific kinds of land-disturbing projects, and much additional methodological research into the efficacy of various mitigation measures. That is, we need follow-through studies on our recommendations, to see how well they really work to minimize or reverse adverse effects on our resource.

3. We need additional behavioral research on vandals, and field studies on the effectiveness of various techniques intended to prevent vandalism, so that we can design appropriate strategies for protecting high-risk sites or areas from looting.

4. We need additional research into the nature of resource management decision making, so that we can participate effectively in the system that influences the future of all land-based resources, including archaeological resources.

5. We need additional large-scale substantive and methodological archae-

ological research. Answers to scientific questions about the past, about the relationship of the archaeological record to that past, and about the way we go about extracting archaeological data are crucial if we are to use the value conservation approach to resolving land-use conflicts, or to invoke the concepts of substitutability or of threshold of concern in our archaeological resource management decisions.

     6. We need to publish the existing studies in a form that will make them accessible to archaeologists and decision makers, so that the results of impacts research can be applied to conservation of our archaeological resource base.

The study of impacts on archaeological resources can provide a scientific, theoretical, and methodological underpinning for the future of our profession. As Talmage *et al.* (1977:5) stated it, "archaeologists must be willing to study the effects of disturbance on resources or must resign themselves to the cessation of archaeological fieldwork, since no intact pristine resources will remain."

Of course, we have *never* had any "intact pristine resources," strictly speaking, because all archaeological sites have been subject to natural and human-caused impacts since their creation. But the main point is well taken: we need to reexamine our assumptions about the nature of archaeological sites, and test those assumptions with real data, or we might as well hang up our trowels, our microscopes, and our lawbooks.

REFERENCES

Aikens, C. M.
    1976   Some archaeological concerns of the Bureau of Land Management in Oregon: observations and recommendations. Manuscript on file at Bureau of Land Management, Portland.
Ammerman, A. J., and M. W. Feldman
    1978   Replicated collection of site surfaces. *American Antiquity* **43**(4):734–740.
Ascher, R.
    1961   Experimental archaeology. *American Anthropologist* **63**(4):793–816.
    1968   Time's arrow and the archeology of a contemporary community. In *Settlement archaeology,* edited by K. C. Chang. Palo Alto, California: National Press Books. Pp. 43–52.
    1970   CUES I: design and construction of an experimental archaeological structure. *American Antiquity* **35**(2):215–216.
Ascher, R., and M. Ascher
    1965   Recognizing the emergence of man. *Science* **147**(3655):243–250.
Ashbee, P., and I. W. Cornwall
    1961   An experiment in field archaeology. *Antiquity* **35**:129–134.
Baker, C. M.
    1978   The size effect: an explanation of variability in surface artifact assemblage content. *American Antiquity* **43**(2):288–293.

Barnes, A. S.
    1939   The differences between natural and human flaking on prehistoric flint implements. *American Anthropologist* **41**(1):99–112.
Beaufait, W. R., C. E. Hardy, and W. C. Fischer
    1975   Broadcast burning in larch-fir clearcuts: the Miller Creek–Newman Ridge study. U.S. Department of Agriculture, Forest Service *Research Paper* INT-175.
Bellis, J. O.
    1975   The controlled surface pickup on the Mound House site in the lower Illinois River valley. Paper presented at the 40th Annual Meeting of the Society for American Archaeology, Dallas.
Beschta, R. L.
    1978   Long-term patterns of sediment production following road construction and logging in the Oregon coast range. *Water Resources Research* **14**(6):1011–1016.
Binford, L. R.
    1962   Archaeology as anthropology. *American Antiquity* **28**(2):217–225.
    1964   A consideration of archaeological research design. *American Antiquity* **29**(4):425–441.
    1968   Archeological perspectives. In *New perspectives in archeology,* edited by S. Binford and L. R. Binford. Chicago: Aldine. Pp. 5–32.
    1975   Sampling, judgment, and the archaeological record. In *Sampling in archaeology,* edited by James Mueller. Tucson: University of Arizona Press. Pp. 251–257.
Binford, L. R., and J. B. Bertram
    1977   Bone frequencies—and attritional process. In *For theory building in archaeology,* edited by L. R. Binford. New York: Academic Press. Pp. 77–153.
Binford, L. R., S. R. Binford, R. Whallon, and M. A. Hardin
    1970   Archaeology at Hatchery West. *Society for American Archaeology Memoir* No. 24.
Brown, G. W.
    1973   The impact of timber harvest on soil and water resources. *Extension Bulletin* 827. Corvallis: Oregon State University.
Brown, J. H., Jr., S. P. Kalisz, and W. R. Wright
    1977   Effects of recreational use on forested sites. *Environmental Geology* **1**(5):425–431.
Butzer, K. W.
    1971   *Environment and archaeology* (second ed.) Chicago: Aldine.
Casteel, R. W.
    1971   Differential bone destruction: some comments. *American Antiquity* **36**(4):466–469.
Chang, K.-C.
    1967   *Rethinking archaeology.* New York: Random.
Chaplin, R. E.
    1971   *The study of animal bones from archaeological sites.* London: Seminar Press.
Chartkoff, J. L.
    1978   Transect interval sampling in forests. *American Antiquity* **43**(1):46–53.
Chave, K. E.
    1964   Skeletal durability and preservation. In *Approaches to paleoecology,* edited by John Imbrie and Norman Newell. New York: Wiley. Pp. 377–387.
Chilcott, J. H., and J. Deetz
    1964   The construction and uses of a laboratory archaeological site. *American Antiquity* **29**(3):328–337.

Clark, R. N.
1976   Control of vandalism in recreation areas—fact, fiction, or folklore? In *Vandalism and outdoor recreation*. U.S. Department of Agriculture Forest Service General Technical Report PSW-17:62–72.

Clark, R. N., J. C. Hendee, and F. L. Campbell
1971   Depreciative behavior in forest campgrounds: an exploratory study. Pacific Northwest Forest and Range Experiment Station *Research Note* PNW-161.

Clarke, D. L.
1968   *Analytical archaeology*. London: Methuen.
1973   (Editor) *Models in archaeology*. London: Methuen.

Clewlow, C. W., Jr., P. S. Hallinan, and R. D. Ambro
1971   A crisis in archaeology. *American Antiquity* 36(4):472–473.

Coles, J.
1973   *Archaeology by experiment*. New York: Scribner.

Collins, R. B.
1980   The meaning behind ARPA: how the act is meant to work. U.S. Department of Agriculture, Forest Service *Cultural Resource Report* No. 32:1–9, Southwestern Region.

Collins, R. B., and D. F. Green
1978   A proposal to modernize the American Antiquities Act. *Science* 202:1055–1059.

Committee for the Recovery of Archaeological Remains
1958   *The inter-agency archaeological salvage program after twelve years*. Columbia, Missouri: University of Missouri.

Cook, S. F.
1963   Erosion morphology and occupation history in western Mexico. University of California *Anthropological Record* 17:281–334.

Cook, S. F., and R. F. Heizer
1965   Chemical analysis of archaeological sites. University of California *Publications in Anthropology* No. 2.

Council on Environmental Quality
1978   Regulations for implementing the procedural provisions of the National Environmental Policy Act, 40 CFR 1500-1508. *Federal Register* 43:55978–56007.

Croes, D. R. (editor)
1976   The excavation of water-saturated archaeological sites (wet sites) on the northwest coast of North America. National Museum of Man Mercury Series, *Archaeological Survey of Canada* Paper No. 50.

Currie, P. O., and H. L. Gary
1978   Grazing and logging effects on soil surface changes in central Colorado ponderosa pine type. *Journal of Soil and Water Conservation* 33(4):176–178.

Curtis, N. M., Jr., A. G. Darrach, and W. J. Sauerwein
1977   Estimating sheet-rill erosion and sediment yield on disturbed western forest and woodlands. U.S. Department of Agriculture, Soil Conservation Service *Technical Note* No. 10, Woodland.

David, N.
1972   On the life span of pottery, type frequencies, and archaeological inference. *American Antiquity* 37(1):141–142.

Davidson, D. A. and M. L. Shackley
1976   *Geoarchaeology*. Boulder, Colorado: Westview Press.

Davis, H.
1972   The crisis in American archaeology. *Science* 175:267–272.

DeBano, L. F.
1977 Influence of forest practices on water yield, channel stability, erosion, and sedimentation in the southwest. In *Proceedings of the Society of American Foresters National Convention,* Albuquerque. Washington, D.C.: Society of American Foresters. Pp. 74–78.

DeBano, L. F., P. H. Dunn, and C. E. Conrad
1977 Fire's effect on physical and chemical properties of chaparral soils. In Proceedings of the Symposium on the Environmental Consequences of Fire and Fuel Management in Mediterranean Ecosystems, Palo Alto. U.S. Department of Agriculture Forest Service, *General Technical Report* WO-3:65–74.

DeBloois, E. I., D. F. Green, and H. G. Wylie
1975 A test of the impact of pinyon–juniper chaining on archaeological sites. In *The Pinyon–Juniper ecosystem: a symposium, May 1975.* Logan, Utah: Utah State University, College of Natural Resources. Pp. 153–161.

DeBoer, W. R.
1974 Ceramic longevity and archaeological interpretation: an example from the Upper Ucayali, Peru. *American Antiquity* 39(2):335–342.

DeByle, N. V.
1976 Fire, logging and debris disposal effects on soil and water in northern coniferous forests. In *Proceedings of the XVI International Union of Forest Research Organizations World Congress,* Oslo. Pp. 201–212.

DeGraff, J. V.
1979 Initiation of shallow mass movement by vegetative-type conversion. *Geology* 7:426–429.

Dunnell, R. C.
1971 *Systematics in prehistory.* New York: The Free Press.

Dyrness, C. T.
1965 Soil surface condition following tractor and high-lead logging in the Oregon cascades. *Journal of Forestry* 63(4):272–275.
1967 Soil surface conditions following skyline logging. U.S. Department of Agriculture, Forest Service *Research Note* PNW-55.
1972 Soil surface conditions following balloon logging. U.S. Department of Agriculture Forest Service *Research Note* PNW-182.

Dyrness, C. T., C. T. Youngberg, and R. H. Ruth
1957 Some effects of logging and slash burning on physical soil properties in the Corvallis watershed. U.S. Department of Agriculture Forest Service *Research Paper* No. 19. Pacific Northwest Forest and Range Experiment Station.

Eckert, R. E., Jr.
1965 The Resource Conservation Area concept. *Journal of Range Management* 18(1):36.

Eddy, F. W., and H. E. Dregne
1964 Soil tests on alluvial and archaeological deposits, Navajo Reservoir district. *El Palacio* 71(4):5–21.

Eisler, D., D. Parrella, and L. Spencer
1978 Report on the investigation and analysis of cultural resources, Young's Butte fire, Paulina Ranger District, Ochoco National Forest. Manuscript on file at Ochoco National Forest, Prineville, Oregon.

Environmental Protection Agency
1976 *Forest harvest, residue treatment, reforestation, and protection of water quality.* EPA 910/0-76-020.

Faegri, K., and J. Iverson
  1964   Textbook of pollen analysis. New York: Hafner Publishing Co.
Fehon, J. R. (editor)
  1979   Proceedings of the compliance workshop, Chapel Hill, North Carolina, October
          1977. *North Carolina Archeological Council Publication* No. 9. Raleigh.
Fenn, D. B., G. J. Gogue, and R. E. Burge
  1976   Effects of campfires on soil properties. U.S. Department of Interior, *National
          Park Service Ecological Services Bulletin* No. 5.
Fenn, D. B., R. Kelly, and K. Davis
  n.d.   Evaluation of effects of controlled burning and wildfires on surficial archeological
          resources. Proposal on file, National Park Service, San Francisco.
Ford, J. L., and M. Rolingson
  1972   Site destruction due to agricultural practices in southeast Arkansas. Arkansas
          Archeological Survey, *Research Series* **3**:1–40.
Fowler, M. L.
  1969   Middle Mississippian agricultural fields. *American Antiquity* **34**(4):365–375.
Fredrickson, R. L.
  1970   Erosion and sedimentation following road construction and timber harvest on
          unstable soils in three small western Oregon watersheds. U.S. Department of
          Agriculture, Forest Service *Research Paper* PNW-104.
Froelich, H. A.
  1978   Soil compaction from low ground-pressure, torsion suspension logging vehicles on
          three forest soils. Oregon State University Forest Research Lab *Research Paper*
          36. Corvallis.
Gallagher, J. G.
  1978   Scarification and cultural resources: an experiment to evaluate serotinous
          lodgepole pine forest regeneration techniques. *Plains Anthropologist*
          23(82):289–299.
Garrison, E. G.
  1975   A qualitative model for inundation studies in archeological research and resource
          conservation: an example for Arkansas. *Plains Anthropologist* **20**:279–296.
Garrison, G. A., and R. S. Rummell
  1951   First-year effects of logging on ponderosa pine forest range lands of Oregon and
          Washington. *Journal of Forestry* **49**(10):708–713.
Gero, J. M.
  1978   Summary of experiments to duplicate post-excavational damage to tool edges.
          Lithic Technology **7**(2):34.
Gifford, D. P.
  1978   Ethnoarchaeological observations of natural processes affecting cultural
          materials. In *Explorations in ethnoarchaeology,* edited by R. A. Gould. Albuquer-
          que: University of New Mexico Press. Pp. 77–101.
  1979   Taphonomy and paleoecology: a critical review of archaeology's sister disciplines.
          In *Advances in archaeological method and theory* (Vol. 4) edited by M. B. Schif-
          fer. New York: Academic Press. Pp. 365–438.
Gladfelter, B. G.
  1977   Geoarchaeology: the geomorphologist and archaeology. *American Antiquity*
          42(4):519–538.
Goodyear, F. H.
  1971   *Archaeological site science.* New York: Elsevier.

Gould, R. A.
   1978 *Explorations in ethnoarchaeology.* Albuquerque: University of New Mexico Press.
Grayson, D.
   1976 A review of recent attempts to prosecute Antiquities Act violations in Oregon. *Tebiwa* **18**(2):59–64.
Green, E.
   n.d. Is this site worth saving? New arguments for the preservation of cultural resources. Manuscript on file, U.S. Department of Agriculture, Forest Service, Atlanta, Georgia.
Gunn, J. (editor)
   1978 *Papers in applied archaeology.* Center for Archaeological Research, University of Texas, San Antonio.
Hansen, R. M., and M. J. Morris
   1968 Movement of rocks by northern pocket gophers. *Journal of Mammalogy* **49**:391–399.
Harrison, A.
   1976 Problems: vandalism and depreciative behavior. In *Interpreting the environment,* edited by Grant W. Sharpe. New York: Wiley. Pp. 473–495.
Harrison, R. R.
   1972 The inventory survey in modern archaeology. Unpublished M.A. thesis, Department of Anthropology, Idaho State University, Pocatello.
Harrison, R. T.
   1975 Slash . . . equipment and methods for treatment and utilization. *Equipment Development and Test Report* 7120-7. U.S. Department of Agriculture, Forest Service Equipment Development Center, San Dimas.
Hatchell, G. E., and C. W. Ralston
   1971 Natural recovery of surface soils disturbed in logging. *Tree Planters Notes* **22**(2):5–9.
Haupt, H. F.
   1960 Variation in areal disturbance produced by harvesting methods in ponderosa pine. *Journal of Forestry* **58**(8):634–639.
Hayden, B. (editor)
   1979 *Lithic use–wear analysis.* New York: Academic Press.
Hendee, J. C., and R. J. Burdge
   1974 The substitutability concept: implications for recreation research and management. *Journal of Leisure Research* **6**(2):157–162.
Hester, T. R.
   1975 The natural introduction of mollusca in archaeological sites: an example from southern Texas. *Journal of Field Archaeology* **2**(3):273–275.
Hope, S. M.
   1979 *Surface disturbance in relation to highlead logging.* Unpublished M.A. thesis, Department of Forestry, University of Washington, Seattle.
Hughes, P. J., and R. J. Lampert
   1977 Occupational disturbance and types of archaeological deposit. *Journal of Archaeological Science* **4**(2):135–140.
Hunt, C. B., and D. R. Mabey
   1966 Stratigraphy and structure, Death Valley, California. U.S. Geological Survey *Professional Paper* 494-A.
Ingersoll, D., J. E. Yellen, and W. Macdonald (editors)
   1977 *Experimental archaeology.* New York: Columbia University Press.

Jeter, M. D., and W. E. Reynolds
   1975   *An evaluation of surface sampling intensities and designs.* Paper presented at the 40th Annual Meeting of the Society for American Archaeology, Dallas.
Jewell, P. A., and G. W. Dimbleby (editors)
   1966   The experimental earthwork on Overton Down, Wiltshire, England: the first four years. *Proceedings of the Prehistoric Society* **32**(11):313–342.
Keller, C. M.
   1966   The development of edge damage patterns on stone tools. *Man* **1**(4):501–511.
Kelly, R. E., and J. Mayberry
   1979   Trial by fire: effects of NPS burn programs upon archeological resources. Abstract, 2nd Conference on Scientific Research in the National Parks, San Francisco.
King, T. F.
   1978   *The archaeological survey: methods and uses.* U.S. Department of the Interior Heritage Conservation and Recreation Service, Washington, D.C.
King, T. F., P. P. Hickman, and G. Berg
   1977   *Anthropology in historic preservation.* New York: Academic Press.
King, T., and S. Haines
   1979   Soil compaction absent in plantation thinning. U.S. Department of Agriculture Southern Forest Experiment Station *Research Note* SO-251.
Kirkby, A., and M. J. Kirkby
   1976   Geomorphic processes and the surface survey of archaeological sites in semi-arid areas. In *Geoarchaeology,* edited by D. A. Davidson and M. L. Schackley. Boulder, Colorado: Westview Press. Pp. 229–253.
Klock, G. O.
   1975   Impact of five postfire salvage logging systems on soils and vegetation. *Journal of Soil and Water Conservation* **30**(2):78–81.
Knudson, R.
   1973   Organizational variability in late paleo-Indian assemblages. Unpublished Ph.D. dissertation, Washington State University, Pullman.
   1974   Inference and imposition in lithic analysis. Paper presented at the 39th Annual Meeting of the Society for American Archaeology, Washington, D.C.
   1979   Inference and imposition in lithic analysis. In *Lithic use–wear analysis,* edited by Brian Hayden. New York: Academic Press. Pp. 269–281.
Kramer, C. (editor)
   1979   *Ethnoarchaeology.* New York: Columbia University Press.
Kuennen, L., G. Edson, and T. V. Tolle
   1979   Soil compaction due to timber harvest activities. U.S. Department of Agriculture, Forest Service Northern Region, *Soil Air and Water Notes* 79–73.
Lane, R. B.
   1970   Soil compaction and cultural correlation. *Anthropological Journal of Canada* **8**(1):17–20.
Leeds, L. L.
   1975   Landform analysis at the Rich Woods site: controlling the effects of land levelling. Paper presented at the 40th Annual Meeting of the Society for American Archaeology, Dallas.
Lenihan, D. J., T. L. Carrell, T. S. Hopkins, A. Wayne Prokopetz, Sandra L. Rayl, and Cathryn S. Tarasovic
   1977   The preliminary report of the National Reservoir Inundation study. U.S. Department of the Interior National Park Service Southwest Cultural Resources Center, Santa Fe.

Lewarch, D. E., and M. J. O'Brien
1981   The expanding role of surface assemblages in archaeological research. In *Advances in archaeological method and theory* (Vol. 4), edited by M. B. Schiffer. New York: Academic Press. Pp. 297–342.

Liddle, M. J.
1975   A selective review of the ecological effects of human trampling on natural ecosystems. *Biological Conservation* 7:17–36.

Limbrey, S.
1975   *Soil science and archaeology*. London: Academic Press.

Lipe, W. D.
1974   A conservation model for American archaeology. *The Kiva* 39(3–4):213–245.

Lipe, W. D., and A. J. Lindsay, Jr.
1974   Proceedings of the 1974 cultural resource management conference. *Museum of Northern Arizona, Technical Series* No. 14. Flagstaff.

Lotspeich, F. B.
1961   Soil science in the service of archaeology. In Paleoecology of the Llano Estacado, assembled by Fred Wendorf, pp. 137–140. *Fort Burgwin Research Center Publication* No. 1.

Lyneis, M. M., D. L. Weide, and E. Warren
1980   *Impacts: damage to cultural resources in the California desert*. Department of Anthropology, University of Nevada, Las Vegas.

Lyon, P. J.
1970   Differential bone destruction: an ethnographic example. *American Antiquity* 35(2):213–215.

Lyons, T. R., and T. Eugene Avery
1977   *Remote sensing: a handbook for archaeologists and cultural resource managers*. Washington, D.C.: U.S. Government Printing Office.

Manuel, D.
1980   Prescribed burning and its effects on cultural resources within the Diablo and Sierra de Salinas mountain ranges of the interior central coast of central California. Manuscript on file, Bureau of Land Management, Folsom District Office, California.

Matthews, J. M.
1965   Stratigraphic disturbance: the human element. *Antiquity* 39:295–298.

Mattingly, G. E. G., and R. J. B. Williams
1962   A note on the chemical analysis of a soil buried since Roman times. *Journal of Soil Science* 13(2):254–258.

Mayer-Oakes, W. J.
1978   Applied and basic research in archaeology: implications for archaeology as part of the scientific community. In *Papers in applied archaeology,* edited by Joel Gunn. Center for Archaeological Research, University of Texas at San Antonio. Pp. 4–14.

McAllister, M. E.
1979   Pothunting on National Forest lands in Arizona: an overview of the current situation. In *Vandalism of cultural resources: the growing threat to our nation's Heritage,* edited by Dee F. Green and Steven LeBlanc, pp. 29–48. U.S. Department of Agriculture Forest Service Southwestern Region *Cultural Resource Report* No. 28.

McDonald, R., G. Alward, W. Arlen, R. Perkins, G. Parham, and L. Fansher
1977   Silvicultural activities and non-point pollution abatement: a cost-effectiveness

analysis procedure. Environmental Protection Agency, *Special Report* No. EPA 600/8-77-018. Washington, D.C.

McGimsey, C. R. III
1972 *Public archeology.* New York: Seminar Press.
McGimsey, C. R. III and H. Davis (editors)
1977 The management of archaeological resources: the Airlie House report. Society for American Archaeology, Special Publication.
Medford, L. D.
1972 Agricultural destruction of archeological sites in northeast Arkansas. Arkansas Archeological Survey, *Research Series* 3:41–82.
Megahan, W. F.
1976 Effects of forest cultural treatments upon streamflow. In *Proceedings of the 1975 Forest Acts Dilemma Symposium,* pp. 14–34. Montana Forest and Conservation Experiment Station, University of Montana.
1977 Reducing erosional impacts of roads. In *Guidelines for watershed management.* pp. 237–261. Food and Agriculture Organization of the United Nations, Forest Conservation and Wildlife Branch. Rome.
Merriam, L. C., and C. K. Smith
1974 Visitor impact on newly developed campsites in the Boundary Waters Canoe Area. *Journal of Forestry* **72**:627–630.
Michels, J. W.
1973 *Dating methods in archaeology.* New York: Seminar Press.
Mifflin, R. W., and H. H. Lysons
1979 *Glossary of forest engineering terms.* U.S. Department of Agriculture, Forest Service, Pacific Northwest Forest and Range Experiment Station, Portland, Oregon.
Moratto, M. J.
1973 Archeology in the far west. *The Missouri Archeologist* **35**(1–2):19–32.
Mueller, J. (editor)
1975 *Sampling in archaeology.* Tucson: University of Arizona Press.
Newman, T. M.
1971 The crisis in Oregon archeology. *Tebiwa* **14**(1):1–3.
Oakes, H., and J. Thorp
1967 Dark clay soils of warm regions variously called rendzina, black cotton soils, regur, and tirs. In *Selected papers in soil formation and classification,* edited by J. V. Drew. Madison: Soil Science Society of American Special Publication No. 1. Pp. 136–149.
Obear, M., and G. Berg
1975 Lithic edge damage: then and now. Paper presented at the Society for California Archaeology Annual Meeting.
Ortner, D. J., D. W. Von Endt, and M. S. Robinson
1972 The effect of temperature on protein decay in bone: its significance in nitrogen dating of archaeological specimens. *American Antiquity* **37**(4):514–520.
Packer, P. E., and B. D. Williams
1976 Logging and prescribed burning effects on the hydrologic and soil stability behavior of larch/Douglas-fir forests in the northern Rocky Mountains. In *Proceedings of the Montana Tall Timbers Fire Ecology Conference and Fire and Land Management Symposium* No. 14, 1974, pp. 465–479. Tall Timbers Research Station, Tallahassee, Florida.
Palacios, V., and R. L. Johnson
1976 An overview of archaeology and the law: seventy years of unexploited protection for prehistoric resources. *Notre Dame Lawyer* **51**:706–721.

Parsons, R. B.
    1962   Indian mounds of northeast Iowa as soil genesis benchmarks. *Journal of the Iowa Archeological Society* **12**(2):1–70.
Parsons, R. B., W. H. Scholtes, and F. F. Riecken
    1962   Soils of Indian mounds in northeastern Iowa as benchmarks for studies of soil genesis. *Soil Science Society of America Proceedings* **26**:491–496.
Patric, J. H., and J. L. Gorman
    1978   Soil disturbance caused by skyline cable logging on steep slopes in West Virginia. *Journal of Soil and Water Conservation* **33**(1):32–35.
Phillips, B.
    1980   An analysis of a timber harvesting operation's impact and effects on a basalt lithic scatter in N.E. Oregon: a synopsis. Manuscript on file at the Bureau of Land Management State Office, Portland.
Plog, S., F. Plog, and W. Wait
    1978   Decision making in modern surveys. In *Advances in archaeological method and theory* (Vol. 1), edited by Michael B. Schiffer. New York: Academic Press. Pp. 383–421.
Power, W. E.
    1974   Effects and observations of soil compaction in the Salem district. U.S. Department of the Interior, Bureau of Land Management *Technical Note* 256, Oregon.
Proudfoot, V. B.
    1965   The study of soil development from the construction and excavation of experimental earthworks. In *Experimental pedology,* edited by E. G. Hallsworth and D. V. Crawford. London: Butterworths. Pp. 282–294.
Read, R. A.
    1957   Effect of livestock concentration on surface-soil porosity within shelterbelts. *Journal of Forestry* **55**:529–530.
Reckendorf, F. F., and R. B. Parsons
    1966   Soil development over a hearth in Willamette Valley, Oregon. *Northwest Science* **40**(2):46–55.
Redman, C. L., and P. J. Watson
    1970   Systematic, intensive surface collection. *American Antiquity* **35**(3):279–291.
Reid, J. J., M. B. Schiffer, and J. M. Neff
    1975   Archaeological considerations of intrasite sampling. In *Sampling in archaeology,* edited by James Mueller. Tucson: University of Arizona Press.
Rich, L. R., and J. G. Reynolds
    1963   Grazing in relation to runoff and erosion on some chaparral watersheds of central Arizona. *Journal of Range Management* **16**:322–326.
Rick, J. W.
    1976   Downslope movement and archaeological intrasite spatial analysis. *American Antiquity* **41**(2):133–144.
Roney, J.
    1977   Livestock and lithics: the effects of trampling. Manuscript on file, Bureau of Land Management, Nevada State Office.
Roper, D. C.
    1976   Lateral displacement of artifacts due to plowing. *American Antiquity* **41**(3):372–375.
Rouse, I.
    1973   Analytic, synthetic, and comparative archeology. In *Research and theory in current archeology,* edited by Charles L. Redman. New York: Wiley. Pp. 21–31.

Ruth, R. H.
  1967   Silvicultural effects of skyline crane and high-lead yarding. *Journal of Forestry*
          65(4):251–255.
Schiffer, M. B.
  1972   Archaeological context and systemic context. *American Antiquity* **37**(2):156–165.
  1976   *Behavioral archeology*. New York: Academic Press.
  1977   Toward a unified science of the cultural past. In *Research strategies in historical
          archeology,* edited by Stanley South. New York: Academic Press. Pp. 13–40.
Schiffer, M. B., and G. Gumerman (editors)
  1977   *Conservation archaeology.* New York: Academic Press.
Schiffer, M. B., and J. H. House
  1975a   Direct impacts of the channelization project on the archeological resources. In *The
          Cache River archeological project,* assembled by Michael B. Schiffer and John H.
          House. Arkansas Archeological Survey, Research Series No. 8, 273–275.
  1975b   Indirect impacts of the channelization project on the archeological resources. In
          The Cache River archeological project, assembled by Michael B. Schiffer and
          John H. House. Arkansas Archeological Survey, Research Series No. 8, 277–282.
Schiffer, M. B., and W. L. Rathje
  1973   Efficient exploitation of the archeological record: penetrating problems. In
          Research and theory in current archeology, edited by Charles L. Redman. New
          York: Wiley. Pp. 169–179.
Schiffer, M. B., A. P. Sullivan, and T. Klinger
  1978   The design of archaeological surveys. *World Archaeology* **10**(1):1–28.
Schumacher, P. J. F.
  1963   The archeological salvage program in the United States. In Proceedings of the 1962
          Great Basin Anthropological Conference. Carson City: Nevada State Museum
          Anthropological Papers No. 9, 1–4.
Setzer, J.
  1947   Chemical analysis of Indian mounds. Unpublished M.A. thesis, Department of
          Soil Sciences, University of California, Berkeley.
Shepard, A. O.
  1956   *Ceramics for the archaeologist.* Washington, D.C.: Carnegie Institute of
          Washington, Publication 609.
Sheridan, D.
  1979   *Off-road vehicles on public land.* Washington, D.C.: Council on Environmental
          Quality.
Silen, R. R., and H. J. Gratkowski
  1953   An estimate of the amount of road in the staggered setting system of clearcutting.
          Pacific Northwest Forest and Range Experiment Station *Research Note* No. 92.
Smith, R. B., and E. F. Wass
  1976   Soil disturbance, vegetative cover and regeneration on clearcuts in the Nelson
          Forest District, British Columbia. Fisheries and Environment Canada, Canadian
          Forestry Service. Canada Pacific Forest Research Center, *Information Report*
          BC-X-151.
Snyder, C. T., D. G. Frickel, R. F. Hadley, and R. F. Miller
  1976   Effects of off-road vehicle use on the hydrology and landscape of arid en-
          vironments in central and southern California. U.S. Geological Survey *Water
          Resources Investigations* 76–99.
Soil Survey Staff
  1975   Soil taxonomy. U.S. Department of Agriculture, Soil Conservation Service,
          Agriculture Handbook No. 436. Washington, D.C.

Solecki, R. S.
  1951   Notes on soil analysis and archaeology. *American Antiquity* **16**(3):254–256.
Solokoff, V. P., and G. F. Carter
  1952   Time and trace metals in archaeological sites. *Science* **116**:1–5.
Solokoff, V. P., and J. L. Lorenzo
  1953   Modern and ancient soils at some archaeological sites in the Valley of Mexico. *American Antiquity* **19**(1):50–55.
Storie, R. E., and F. Harradine
  1950   An age estimate of the burials unearthed near Concord, California, based on pedologic observations. *University of California Archaeological Survey Report* 9:6–19. Berkeley.
Struever, S.
  1968   Problems, methods and organization: a disparity in the growth of archeology. In *Anthropological archeology in the Americas,* edited by B. J. Meggers. Washington, D.C.: Anthropological Society of Washington. Pp. 131–151.
Switzer, R. R.
  1974   The effects of forest fire on archaeological sites in Mesa Verde National Park, Colorado. *The Artifact* **12**:1–8.
Talmage, V., O. Chesler, and Interagency Archeological Services staff
  1977   *The importance of small, surface, and disturbed sites as sources of significant archeological data.* Cultural Resource Management Studies. National Park Service, Washington, D.C.
Taylor, W. W., Jr.
  1948   A study of archaeology. *American Anthropological Association Memoir* No. 69. Menasha.
Thomas, D. H.
  1975   Nonsite sampling in archeology: up the creek without a site? In *Sampling in archaeology,* edited by James Mueller. Tucson: University of Arizona Press. Pp. 61–81.
Traylor, D., L. Hubbell, N. Wood, and B. Fiedler
  1979   *The La Mesa fire study: investigation of fire and fire suppression impact on cultural resources in Bandelier National Monument.* Report submitted to National Park Service, Santa Fe.
Tringham, R., G. Cooper, G. Odell, B. Voytek, and A. Whitman
  1974   Experimentation in the formation of edge damage: a new approach in lithic analysis. *Journal of Field Archaeology* **1**(1–2):171–196.
United States Congress
  1979   *House report* No. 96–311.
United States Department of Agriculture
  1978   Predicting rainfall erosion losses. *Agricultural Handbook* No. 537. Washington, D.C.: U.S. Government Printing Office.
United States Department of Agriculture, Forest Service
  1978   *Yarding impacts on archaeological sites.* Request for proposals # R6-78-301. Portland, Oregon.
United States Department of Interior, Bureau of Land Management
  1975   *Evaluation report: 1974 Barstow-Las Vegas motorcycle race.* Sacramento: California State Office.
Utzig, G., and L. Herring
  1975   Forest harvesting impacts at high elevations: five case studies. British Columbia Forest Service *Research Note* No. 72.

Van der Merwe, N. J.
1972   Soil chemistry of postmolds and rodent burrows: identification without excavation. *American Antiquity* 37(2):245–254.

Ward, F. R., and H. R. McLean
1976   Burying forest residue—an alternative treatment. Pacific Northwest Forest and Range Experiment Station *Research Note* PNW-270.

Watson, P. J., S. A. LeBlanc, and C. L. Redman
1971   *Explanation in archeology: an explicitly scientific approach.* New York: Columbia University Press.

Wauchope, R. (editor)
1956   Seminars in archaeology: 1955. Society for American Archaeology Memoirs, No. 11. Salt Lake City.

Webb, R. H., H. C. Ragland, W. H. Godwin, and D. Jenkins
1978   Environmental effects of soil property changes with off-road vehicle use. *Environmental Management* 2(3):219–233.

Weide, D. L.
1966   Soil pH as a guide to archaeological investigation. University of California–Los Angeles Archaeological Survey *Annual Report* 8:155–163.

Wells, C. G., *et al.*
1979   *Effects of fire on soil: a state-of-knowledge review.* U.S. Department of Agriculture, Forest Service General *Technical Report* WO-7.

Wildesen, L. E.
1973   A quantitative model of archaeological site development. Unpublished Ph.D. dissertation, Department of Anthropology, Washington State University, Pullman.
1975   Conservation vs. preservation of archeological sites. *American Society for Conservation Archaeology Newsletter* 2(2):9–11.
1977   Analysis of project-related impacts on archaeological resources. Ms. on file Pacific Northwest Region, U.S. Department of Agriculture, Forest Service.
1978   Conserving archaeological values: an approach to impact assessment in archaeological resource management. Paper presented at the Oregon Academy of Sciences, Annual Meeting, McMinnville, Oregon.
1979   Coming of age in applied archaeology. *Reviews in Anthropology* 6(3):373–385.
1980   Cultural resource management: a personal view. *Practicing Anthropology* 2(2):10, 22–23.

Willey, G. R.
1953   Prehistoric settlement patterns in the Viru Valley, Peru. *Smithsonian Institution, Bureau of American Ethnology, Bulletin* 155. Washington, D.C.

Willey, G. R., and P. Phillips
1958   *Method and theory in American archaeology.* Chicago: University of Chicago Press.

Williams, L. R.
1978   Vandalism to cultural resources of the Rocky Mountain west. *Cultural Resources Report* No. 21. U.S. Department of Agriculture, Forest Service, Southwestern Region, Albuquerque, New Mexico.

Wood, J. S.
1979   Chaparral conversion and cultural resources on the Prescott National Forest: an experimental study of the impacts of surface mechanical treatment by Marden brush-crusher. *Cultural Resource Report* No. 27. U.S. Department of Agriculture, Forest Service, Southwestern Region, Albuquerque, New Mexico.

Wood, W. R., and D. L. Johnson
    1978   A survey of disturbance processes in archaeological site formation. In *Advances in archaeological method and theory* (Vol. 1), edited by M. B. Schiffer. New York: Academic Press. Pp. 315–381.
Woodridge, D. D.
    1960   Watershed disturbance from tractor and skyline crane logging. *Journal of Forestry* **58**(5):369–372.

3

Advances in
Urban Archaeology

EDWARD STASKI

INTRODUCTION

Although American urban archaeologists are a new breed, they are rapidly taking their place in the mainstream of archaeology. This is because of the volume of research they are carrying out—from such projects as excavating Archaic-period campsites about to face the impact of downtown redevelopment to studying such urban renovation as a subject in its own right.

This chapter reviews the current practice of urban archaeology in the United States. *Urban archaeology* is defined as the study of the relationships between material culture, human behavior, and cognition in an urban setting. An *urban setting* is defined as a permanent location in which the density of settlement and the amount of human energy expended per unit of land area are considerably greater than in the surrounding region. An *urban center*, or city, is a sociopolitical entity that exhibits the characteristics of an urban setting. The urban archaeologist studies societies from any time and located at any place where concentrations of people and energy are or were present.

Discussion is limited to the consideration of internal urban structure. Emphasis is given to the methods of doing archaeology *in* the city. Several historical archaeologists have debated the question of archaeology *in* the city versus archaeology *of* the city (Foley 1967; Ingersoll 1971; Salwen 1973). Archaeology *in* the city consists of addressing any research question in an urban setting. Archaeology *of* the city consists of using archaeological methods to contribute to an understanding of the specific processes of urban develop-

ADVANCES IN ARCHAEOLOGICAL METHOD AND THEORY, VOL. 5

ment (Staski 1980a). The former orientation involves viewing the city as an environment (such as a river valley or desert), which makes it necessary to apply a specific set of methods. The latter orientation, a subset of the former, involves viewing the city as both the environment and as the subject of research.

The primary purpose of this chapter is to describe accurately how urban archaeology is being conducted. First, the current status of urban archaeology in the United States is presented. The nature of the archaeological record in urban centers is next considered. Various urban land uses are discussed in order to present a general view of how the data lie in the ground. Emphasis is given to the degree of preservation and integrity of the material culture, and to the degree of accessibility afforded the archaeologist. This information sets the stage for a discussion of survey and sampling procedures appropriate in urban settings. Finally, consideration is given to the significance of cultural resources in terms of prevalent research interests current among urban archaeologists.

THE CURRENT STATUS OF URBAN ARCHAEOLOGY

The amount of archaeology being conducted in urban centers of the United States is increasing rapidly. The existence of urban archaeology has recently come to the attention of the general public (Lorber 1981). Yet, the results of most projects are not being well circulated within the discipline. There is no thorough review of the urban archaeological literature. As a first step toward such a review, I present a partial list and description of ongoing and completed projects (Table 3.1).

The scope of a project (the second column in Table 3.1) is the proposed investigative extent covered by the research design(s). A *major project* indicates the intent to integrate several sites so that an understanding of a larger area can be achieved. Where *various projects* have been investigated, several researchers have independently contributed to the archaeology of an urban center with no integration of effort. A *small project* indicates only one investigator contributing in a limited manner.

In a *contract* situation (the third column) archaeologists have worked under conditions imposed by a legal agreement with a government or private agency. A *noncontract* situation indicates that no such legal agreement exists, although the conditions of research are not necessarily less restricting.

Problem domains (the fourth column) are the research interests that tend to repeat in the research designs of urban archaeological projects. All projects listed have been based in part on an interest in *culture history,* that is, the recovery and description of data and an attempt at reconstructing behavior. This is a large and nebulous category and, when listed alone, indicates more than anything else that specific problem domains are not spelled out in the

TABLE 3.1

Partial List and Description of Urban Archaeological Projects in the United States

City	Scope of project	Contract or noncontract	Problem domains	References
Alexandria, Virginia	Major project	Both	Culture history Ethnicity Urban development	Beidleman 1979a, 1979b Cressey 1978, 1979a, 1979b, 1980 Cressey and Beidleman 1980 Henry 1980 Klein 1979a, 1979b Klein and Henry 1980 Klein *et al.* 1980
Atlanta, Georgia	Major project	Contract	Culture history Ethnicity Urban development	Carnes 1979 Dickens 1978 Dickens and Blakely 1978 Dickens and Bowen 1980
Baltimore, Maryland	Small project	Contract	Culture history	Basalik 1980
Boise, Idaho	Small project		Culture history	Jones 1981
Boston, Massachusetts	Various projects	Both	Culture history Ethnicity	Bower 1979 Bower and Rushing 1980 Johnson 1942
Dallas, Texas	Major project	Contract	Culture history Preservation	Skinner *et al.* 1978
Detroit, Michigan	Various projects	Contract	Culture history	Anonymous 1975
Dover, Delaware	Small project	Contract	Culture history Urban development	Wise 1976 Wise 1978
Kingston, New York	Small project	Noncontract	Culture history	Bridges 1974

(continued)

TABLE 3.1 (continued)

City	Scope of project	Contract or noncontract	Problem domains	References
Los Angeles, California	Major project	Contract	Culture history	Costello 1979 Los Angeles Department of Public Works ca. 1979
Lowell, Massachusetts	Major project	Noncontract	Culture history Urban Development	Schuyler 1974b, 1976
Milwaukee, Wisconsin	Major project	Contract	Culture history Ethnicity Urban development	Rathje and Thompson 1981
Newburyport, Massachusetts	Various projects	Noncontract	Culture history Preservation Urban development	Faulkner et al. 1978 Harris 1977
New Orleans, Louisiana	Various projects	Noncontract	Culture history	Prieto 1981 Shenkel and Hudson 1971
Newport, Rhode Island	Small project	Noncontract	Culture history Preservation	Mrozowski 1979
New York, New York	Various projects	Both	Culture history Ethnicity Preservation Urban development	Askins and Levin 1979 Bridges and Salwen 1980 Rockman 1980 Salwen and Bridges 1974a, 1974b Salwen et al. 1974 Salwen et al. 1981 Schuyler 1974a, 1977b, 1980a Solecki 1974 Staski 1976 Winter 1981 (and more)
Paterson, New Jersey	Major project	Contract	Culture history Urban development	Cotz 1975 Morrell 1975 Rutsch 1975

100

Philadelphia, Pennsylvania	Various projects	Both	Culture history Preservation	Basalik and McCarthy 1979 Cossans 1979 Cotter 1980 Cotter and Orr 1975 Hood 1973 Orr 1977
Phoenix, Arizona	Major project	Contract	Culture history Ethnicity Urban development	Stone 1981
Rensselaer, New York	Various projects	Contract	Culture history	Feister 1975 Feister et al. 1974 Huey et al. 1977
Rome, New York	Various projects	Noncontract	Culture history	Hanson 1974 Hanson and Hsu 1975
Roxbury, Massachusetts	Small project		Culture history Urban development	Bower 1980
Sacramento, California	Major project	Contract	Culture history Preservation	Landberg 1967 Praetzellis and Praetzellis 1980 Praetzellis et al. 1980
San Antonio, Texas	Small project	Contract	Culture history	Katz 1978
San Buenaventura, California	Various projects	Contract	Culture history Ethnicity	Greenwood 1975, 1976, 1980
San Diego, California	Major project	Contract	Culture history Preservation Urban development	Brandes 1978 Cleland 1980 Cleland et al. 1979 Cleland et al. 1980 Schaefer 1980 Schaefer and Cleland 1980

(continued)

TABLE 3.1 (continued)

City	Scope of project	Contract or noncontract	Problem domains	References
Santa Barbara, California	Various projects	Contract	Culture history	Costello 1976 Fagan 1976
Schenectady, New York	Small project	Contract	Culture history	Salwen and Lockhart 1975
St. Augustine, Florida	Major project	Noncontract	Culture history Ethnicity Urban development	Bostwick and Wise 1980 Deagan 1976, 1978 Deagan et al. 1976 Shephard 1975
St. Louis, Missouri	Major project	Contract	Culture history Preservation	Benchley 1975
Tucson, Arizona	Various projects	Both	Culture history Ethnicity Preservation	Ayres 1968, 1975 Betancourt 1978a,b Bradley 1980 Doelle 1976 Kinkade and Fritz 1975 Olsen 1978 Rathje 1974, 1979 Rathje and Hughes 1975 Rathje and McCarthy 1977 Wilk and Schiffer 1979 (and more)
Washington, D.C.	Various projects	Both	Culture history	Humphrey and Chambers 1977 Inashima 1980 Soil Systems, Inc. 1981
Waterford, Connecticut	Small project	Contract	Culture history	Hartgen and Fisher 1980
Wilmington, Delaware	Major project	Contract	Urban development	Wise et al. 1980

research design(s). *Urban development* indicates a specific intent to investigate the evolution of urban society. *Ethnicity* shows a special interest in studying the interaction and maintenance of ethnic groups in an urban setting. *Preservation* means that the nature of urban processes and their effects on the archaeological record is a major concern.

THE NATURE OF THE ARCHAEOLOGICAL RECORD IN CITIES

A number of the projects listed in Table 3.1 involve an attempt to understand the degree of preservation and integrity of the archaeological record. This is a particularly important research interest in urban archaeology because the city is a scene of major and numerous land alterations. Many archaeologists stress the adverse impacts such activities have on deposited material, though research results often point in an indirect way to the excellent preservation of much information.

In order to arrive at a substantive statement regarding preservation, it is necessary to consider the physical characteristics of the internal structure of cities. Physical characteristics are the actual uses to which the land is put and the material results of these uses. Nonphysical (social) characteristics include attitudes such as transiency, superficiality, and anonymity thought present among urban dwellers (Anderson 1959; Bourne 1971a,b,c; Chapin 1974; Hoover and Vernon 1959), and the demography of the city (Berry *et al.* 1963; Casetti 1967; Clark 1951, 1958; Newling 1969; Robson 1971). Attitudes and demographics might in part influence land-use patterns. Decisions concerning how to use any particular land parcel are based on site selection characteristics that reflect the behavioral norms of the developer (Bourne 1976). However, the nature and rate of debris accumulation in urban centers is directly dependent on land use (Gunnerson 1973).

The Classification System

Most land-use classifications, developed by urban planners, are designed to serve the needs of a single city or small number of cities. It is difficult to find a classification that has comparative applicability, though a few attempts have been made (Bartholomew 1955; Chapin and Kaiser 1979; Land Use Classification Committee ca. 1960; Northam 1979; U.S. Department of Transportation 1977). In this chapter, broad urban land-use categories are discussed, including single-family dwellings, multifamily dwellings, mobile dwellings, commercial land use, industrial land use, public land use, streets, and vacant land. Broad categories were chosen for several reasons. Data pertaining to very specific land-use categories are not easily available. The categories chosen are not restrictive and can be used no matter what the scope of project. Broad categories can be discussed in general terms.

The results of my survey of these land-use categories, and several subcategories, are found in Table 3.2. Degree of preservation (the sixth column) and accessibility to archaeologists (the seventh column) are the variables emphasized. Table 3.3, giving the average amount of urban land devoted to each land-use type, can be combined with the results of the survey so that a general statement concerning the degree of preservation and the possibility of investigation can be made. This statement is found in Table 3.4. These results are now discussed in more detail.

Single-Family Dwellings

The major structure present on this land is, of course, the house. Other, smaller structures are often present, such as garages and storage sheds. Yet, the overall impression one gets is of large amounts of open space. Information concerning the amount of open space relative to the area set aside for structures is not available, but could be obtained by studying aerial photographs, which many urban centers have. Such photographs are often found in county and city offices, libraries, universities, and the records of various planning agencies. If one were to gather such data, the most useful unit of research would be the socioeconomic neighborhood. Percent of open space most likely increases with greater household wealth.

The average percent of total urban land devoted to single-family dwellings is approximately one-third for cities of all sizes (Table 3.3). This land is not normally the scene of any significant disturbances to the archaeological record. Even with the presence of wells, cisterns, gardens, work sheds, and the like, the amount of earth undisturbed from *directly below the surface* is usually great. Recently developed neighborhoods are fertile grounds for the investigation of preurban prehistoric sites located both near the surface and buried deeply, assuming massive ground surface modification was not part of the construction process. Such modification is not as common as one might think. When it is planned, archaeologists can conduct small-scale surveys and tests such as those carried out by the Cultural Resource Management section of the Arizona State Museum (Susan Brew, Arizona State Museum, personal communication 1980).

Older neighborhoods of single-family dwellings add through time an archaeological record of their own. Historic urban material is deposited into archaeological context above whatever prehistoric remains are there initially. The record grows through time without significantly disturbing earlier material because disposal on such property is generally gradual and unplanned since the beginning of municipal sanitation services (Askins and

Levin 1979; Schuyler 1974a, 1980a). In all cases, preservation of the archaeological record can be considered excellent.

The prehistoric preurban material might consist of any kind of assemblage. Predictions of what kind of sites or artifacts will be found depend on a knowledge of preurban land-utilization patterns. The historic urban material, on the other hand, consists of that assemblage of artifacts used for domestic purposes. Recognizing domestic artifacts involves taking into consideration both the frequency and presence or absence of certain material objects, and their spatial context (Schaefer 1980; South 1977, 1979).

Models and theories concerning the locations of single-family dwellings within urban centers are complex. The general pattern indicates an increase in the percentage of land devoted to single-family dwellings as the distance from a city's spatial center increases (Staski 1980a). Most of this sort of land is privately owned by the residents. The ease of obtaining permission to investigate will vary depending on the attitudes of the owners.

Multifamily Dwellings

A multifamily dwelling is any structure designed to hold in separate quarters more than one family. Such dwellings range in size from small apartments that house two or three families up to massive apartment complexes that house hundreds. The discussion here focuses on the larger of such dwellings.

The average amount of land devoted to multifamily dwellings ranges from 3 to 5% of the total urban landscape (Table 3.3), a fortunately low percentage from the perspective of the urban archaeologist. Multifamily dwelling sites are places of intensive land use. Little open space remains for archaeological investigation. The larger the structure is, the deeper and more destructive the necessary foundation must be (Cressey 1980). Getting permission to investigate involves locating the often elusive property owner who many times has no interest in the history and significance of his land. Yet, the material record deposited in the alleyways, air shafts, courtyards, and early-period privies should not be ignored.

In all multifamily-dwelling locations, deposition is relatively rapid and unplanned. Assemblages from the historic urban period consist of domestic artifacts, the number of which is potentially great because of the high population density and the nature of construction (Staski 1980a). Although those few urban areas that have a high density of multifamily dwellings have a low overall investigative potential, they have a unique and long history that is of interest to certain urban archaeologists (Cressey 1980). Such neighborhoods through time have generally located near the spatial center of cities because of the proximity of transportation routes and employment locations (Johnston 1972; Quinn 1940).

TABLE 3.2

The Nature of the Archaeological Record in Cities

Present type of use	General location in the city[a]	Spatial configuration[b]	Type of material deposited[c]	Prevalent depositional pattern[d]	Degree of preservation[e]	Accessibility to archaeologists[f]
Single-family dwellings	Throughout, most in middle and periphery	Quadrat, extensive	PP: any HU: domestic	PP: various HU: gradual, unplanned	Excellent	Low-cost; permission varies
Multi-family dwellings	Throughout, most in center and middle	Irregular, limited	PP: any HU: domestic	PP: various HU: rapid, unplanned	Poor	High cost; permission difficult
Mobile dwellings	Unclear, most in middle and periphery	Quadrat, limited to extensive	PP: any HU: domestic	PP: various HU: gradual, unplanned	Excellent	Low-cost; permission varies
Commercial	Throughout, most in center	Various, most irregular, limited	PP: any HU: commercial	PP: various HU: rapid, unplanned	Mostly poor	High cost; permission difficult
Industrial	Throughout, along rivers	Linear, quadrat, extensive	PP: any HU: industrial	PP: various HU: rapid, planned	Various	Low cost; permission mostly easy
Recreation	Throughout	Quadrat, extensive	PP: any HU: park related	PP: various HU: gradual, unplanned	Excellent	Low cost; permission easy
Schools	Throughout	Quadrat, extensive	PP: any HU: school related	PP: various HU: gradual, unplanned	Fair to poor	Low cost; Permission easy
Cemeteries	Most in center and periphery	Various, most quadrat, extensive	PP: any HU: cemetery related	PP: various HU: gradual, planned	Good	Low cost; permission almost impossible
Churches	Throughout	Various	PP: any HU: church related	PP: various HU: gradual, unplanned	Good	Low cost; permission varies
Streets	Throughout	Linear, quadrat extensive	PP: any HU: any	PP: various HU: gradual, unplanned	Good to excellent	Cost varies; permission varies

Remnant parcels	Throughout, most in center	Irregular, limited	PP: any HU: any	PP: various HU: rapid, unplanned	Excellent	Low cost; permission varies
Unbuildable parcels	Throughout	Various	PP: any HU: little, if any	PP: various HU: gradual, unplanned	Excellent	Cost varies; permission varies
Corporate reserves	Throughout, most in center	Quadrat, extensive	PP: any HU: commercial	PP: various HU: rapid, unplanned	Excellent	Low cost; permission easy
Individual reserves	Throughout, most in periphery	Various	PP: any HU: little if any	PP: various HU: gradual, unplanned	Excellent	Low cost; permission varies
Institutional reserves	Throughout, most in periphery	Various	PP: any HU: little if any	PP: various HU: gradual, unplanned	Excellent	Low cost; permission varies

[a] General location in the city refers to where a land use is primarily found. Center, middle, and periphery: there are no sharp boundaries between these categories, which are not based on any theory or model of urban development. Throughout: significant amounts of a land use can be found in all areas of the city.

[b] Spatial configuration is the usual shape and extent of a land-use area that is available for archaeological study. Quadrat: available land approximates a rectangle in shape. Irregular: available land takes many shapes. Linear: available land approximates a transect in shape. Extensive: large open spaces are available. Limited: only small spaces are available. Various: the shape and/or extent of available land does not fall into one category.

[c] Type of material deposited refers to the predicted assemblage of artifacts one would find when investigating where a particular land use is present today. PP: the prehistoric preurban period. HU: the historic urban period. Any: there is no direct relationship between present land use and prevalent past behavior. The location of prehistoric preurban activities is directly related to environmental conditions, not to later urban development (Henry 1980). Domestic, commercial, industrial, park related, etc.; for historic urban period assemblages present land use can often suggest what will be found. "Urban inertia" (Johnston 1972; Quinn 1940) is common. Once a parcel of land is given over to a particular purpose, it is difficult to change use because of the great investment of energy and money that went into construction and the high cost of alteration. However, urban land uses do and can change occasionally. The rate and pattern of change is an empirical question that urban archaeologists can address (Salwen et al. 1981).

[d] Prevalent depositional patterns are very general indications of how material gets into the ground (Beidleman 1979a, 1979b; Cleland et al. 1979; Dickens and Bowen 1980). Various: prehistoric preurban depositional patterns are not directly related to current land use. Gradual, rapid: relative terms for the rate of debris accumulation. Planned: material was and is purposefully put into archaeological context at a particular location because of social norms. Unplanned: the site of debris accumulation was and is not designated by society as a place for deposition.

[e] Degree of preservation refers to a measure of the integrity of the archaeological record where a land use is present. Excellent, good, fair, poor: judgments are based on present land use, type of material deposited, prevalent depositional pattern, and other variables.

[f] Accessibility to archaeologists refers to a measure of the possibility for archaeological investigation where a land use is present. Low, high: relative measures for cost and/or ease of getting permission to investigate. Difficult, easy: relative measures for ease of getting permission to investigate. Varies: cost and/or ease of getting permission are determined for the most part by individual situations.

TABLE 3.3

Amount of Urban Land Put to Various Uses[a]

Land use	Urban population	Sample size	Average per capita total urban area (m²)	Average per capita urban area (m²)	Average percent total urban area (to the nearest 1%)
Single-family dwellings	100,000+	58	1439	516	36
	2,500–50,000	33	1872	627	33
Multi-family dwellings	100,000+	58	1439	77	5
	2,500–50,000	33	1872	51	3
Commercial	100,000+	58	1439	85	6
	2,500–50,000	33	1872	79	4
Industrial	100,000+	58	1439	163	11
	2,500–50,000	33	1872	220	12
Public	100,000+	58	1439	315	22
	2,500–50,000	33	1872	326	17
Streets	100,000+	58	1439	354	25
	2,500–50,000	33	1872	589	31
Totals[b]	100,000+	58	1439	1510	105
	2,500–50,000	33	1872	1891	100

[a] Data from Bureau of Municipal Research and Service (1961), Manvel (1968), and Northam (1979).
[b] Totals do not include vacant land or mobile dwellings.

TABLE 3.4
Investigative Potential of Urban Archaeology[a]

Average % (approximate)	Degree of preservation	Breakdown of accessibility	Investigative potential
40	Excellent	Cost low; permission easy and varies	High
30	Good	Cost low and varies; permission varies	Medium
3	Fair	Cost low; permission easy	Medium
10	Poor	Cost high; permission difficult	Low
10	Various	Cost low; permission easy	Medium

[a] Does not include data on vacant land and mobile dwellings.

Mobile Dwellings

A final kind of housing is that which includes potentially mobile dwellings that for the most part remain stationary in designated areas, such as mobile homes and trailers. There are no comparative data available on the average amount of urban land devoted to these dwellings, even though they are rapidly becoming a significant American housing type. This growth is especially rapid in western and southern states (Buel 1980).

This type of housing causes the least amount of disturbance to previously deposited archaeological material. These dwellings do not have foundations, and their impact on the archaeological record directly under them is minimal. What little there is derives from slight land modification to insure structural stability and the construction of roads. The entire area where mobile dwellings are located is thus potentially the scene of well-preserved prehistoric preurban remains. Little in the way of an historic-period archaeological record will be present, however, because of the recent development of most of these areas and their impermanent nature.

Areas of Commercial Use

Areas of commercial use are places on which are located establishments that dispense goods and services to the resident population and surrounding region. The average percent of total urban land area devoted to commercial use is relatively small (Table 3.3). This is a fortunate situation for the urban archaeologist, since commercial centers are scenes of intensive land use and processes disruptive to the archaeological record. Buildings and foundations are relatively large, leading to the presence of little open space and a subsurface level that is disturbed (Beidleman 1979a,b). Property owners, often difficult to find, many times consider the potential loss of profit an archaeological investigation might cause more significant than the history of their land.

Commercial establishments benefit by locating where there is access to pedestrian and vehicular traffic, and near wholesale suppliers, supporting industries, and complementary commercial businesses. Throughout American urban history, these benefits could be enjoyed to a maximum at the *point of minimum aggregate travel* (Porter, 1963) within the *central business district* (Burgess 1925, 1928, 1929). Located near the spatial center of the city, this area is the scene of the greatest temporal depth of any particular urban center. The earliest historic urban periods are most fruitfully investigated here. As with older neighborhoods of multifamily dwellings, the low overall investigative potential of this area is balanced by its potential to supply data that can help answer a select number of archaeological questions (Fowler 1979). Alleyways, hidden courtyards, and other locations *do* afford some protection to historic privies and living surfaces (Basalik 1980; Cleland *et al.* 1979). In addition, there are certain instances of good preservation of prehistoric resources (Stone 1981).

With changing transportation technology there has developed a hierarchy of urban commercial centers in recent times. The spatial arrangement and design of these centers reflects the model of central-place theory (Berry 1967; Christaller 1966). With the exception of specialized centers, such as ribbons, which cater to the needs of vehicular traffic (Berry 1959), the larger and more varied the commercial center, the more people it serves and the less frequently it appears (Figure 3.1).

Commercial centers outside the central business district are in general scenes of intensive land use and great disturbance to the archaeological record. Still, if resources are known to exist under them, chances are that some information could be recovered. Parking lots surrounding regional shopping centers, for instance, are extensive areas where there has been little disturbance and the archaeological record is protected by a veneer of asphalt.

Areas of Industrial Use

Areas of industrial use are places where raw materials are taken from the earth and/or processed into products. The average amount of urban land devoted to industry ranges from 11% to 12% of the total urban landscape (Table 3.3). Industrial land is the scene of the greatest range of land-use inten-

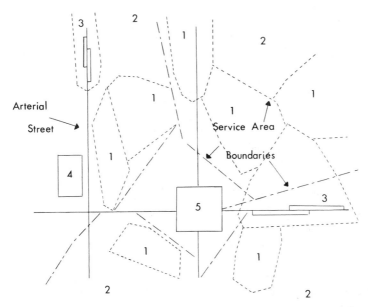

Figure 3.1. Schematic representation of the ideal spatial arrangement of commercial centers in the city. Neighborhood shopping center, 1; community shopping center, 2; ribbon development, 3; regional shopping center, 4; central business district, 5. (Adapted from Northam 1979.)

sity and degree of disturbance to the archaeological record (Betancourt 1978a,b), from no disturbance at all on industrial reserves to complete destruction in quarrying and mining areas. Determining this degree of disturbance involves consideration of the type of industry present, the degree of exploitation at any particular site, and the amount of time the industry has been practiced.

Environmental variables play a role in determining the location of any urban land use by setting constraints on how land parcels can be exploited (Bourne 1976). The environment is a major factor in the choice of an industrial site. Industrialists need to acquire property that affords access to transportation routes, raw materials, complimentary industrial establishments, and sources of energy. At the beginning of the American Industrial Revolution, both transportation and energy requirements were often met by locating near major rivers (Hamilton 1964; Parker 1940). In the early days of the railroad, in the nineteenth century, these rivers were recognized as inexpensive access routes across the country. The construction of railroad lines in river valleys increased contact between industries and encouraged more to settle nearby. By the time widespread use of steam power made the energy contribution of the rivers obsolete, the railroad had made the river valley an indispensable transportation corridor, and the concentration of industry made these locations profitable ones to settle in. By the mid-twentieth century, trucking took over the transportation role that the railroad had held. The same pattern was repeated, with highways following the established routes both for cost purposes and the good of industry (Heckscher 1977; Mumford 1963; Wheat 1969). The history of these functional relationships is spelled out in more detail elsewhere (Pred 1964). The resultant spatial intimacy of industry, railroad, and highway in urban centers is clear (Figure 3.2).

The same environmental variables that significantly help determine the location of urban industry were partly responsible for the location of past settlements. Any prehistoric preurban settlement or activity that required the nearby presence of a river will often leave evidence on land presently devoted to industrial uses. The *particular* archaeological materials found depend on the history of the area investigated.

Industrial archaeologists are interested in the history of industry in its own right. Their major approach to data stresses the need for preservation and the significance of America's industrial past (Cotz 1975; Morrell 1975; Rutsch 1975; Sande 1975). Obviously, much of their work will take them to the industrial areas of cities.

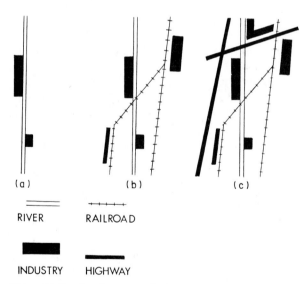

Figure 3.2. Stages in the development of urban manufacturing districts: (a) stage 1, waterfront district; (b) stage 2, railroad district; and (c) stage 3, highway district. (Adapted from Northam 1979.)

Areas of Public Use

Areas of public use include all land to which the general population has access. Also included are semipublic lands such as church grounds and the yards of private schools. Not included because of their unique spatial configuration, is the use of public lands for streets. Table 3.3 shows that a significant percent of urban land is public.

Northam (1979) defines four kinds of public land: recreational land, land for schools, land for cemeteries, and land for churches. His distinctions are based on the nature of the institution that owns the land, which leads to differences in how the land is used, the location of the land within the city, the degree of disturbance to the archaeological record, and the degree of accessibility given to archaeologists.

Recreation

Most recreational areas in cities fall under the rubric of "urban parks." These parks can be placed in a functional and spatial hierarchy in which the few larger parks serve a larger population, have a greater diversity of services, and are further apart from each other than smaller more numerous ones. As is the case with commercial centers, urban planners have reflected the concepts of central place theory in their attempt to most efficiently meet the urban population's recreational needs (Figure 3.3).

Many large urban parks found today in the center of cities were developed during the great "Park Movement" of the 1890s and early twentieth century or even earlier (Heckscher 1977). When first set aside, this land was at the outskirts of urban centers. Such parks experienced little encroachment through the years and remain, along with more recently developed parks, scenes of relatively undisturbed prehistoric, preurban material. Material remains from the historic urban period for the most part relate to behavior associated with park activities. One method of obtaining permission from municipal governments to investigate in parks involves the establishment of public displays of excavation procedures and results (Betancourt 1978b; Gregonis 1977; Gregonis and Reinhard 1979).

Schools

School properties have a spatial arrangement similar to that of urban parks (Northam 1979) and thus can be exploited by the urban archaeologist in a similar manner. However, school grounds are scenes of much more intensive construction and use activities. They should not be considered as valuable as parks in terms of investigative potential unless a particular location with known significant archaeological material is involved. Nevertheless, a factor

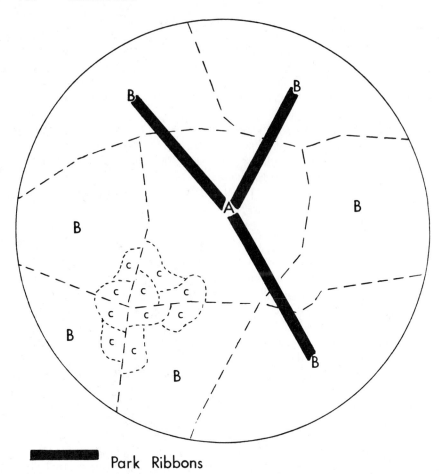

Park Ribbons

Figure 3.3. Ideal spatial hierarchy of urban parks, three orders: district park and service area. A (boundary, ——); community park and service area, B (boundary,---); and urban playground and service area, c (boundary,----). (Adapted from Northam 1979.)

to consider is the fine educational opportunities an on-school grounds excavation would provide.

Cemeteries

Older urban cemeteries that have developed in conjunction with a church or religious group and have grown with a city are usually found enduring in the center of the city. They are for the most part very small. Larger, more recently developed cemeteries are found generally on the outskirts of the city and on land that is unsuitable for other kinds of construction, such as a hillside (Northam 1979). Due to the small percentage (1.3%) of urban land taken up by cemeteries (Manvel 1968) and the obvious legal and moral problems of getting permission to excavate, this land should only be investigated when it is the surface material culture that is to be studied (Deetz and Dethlefson 1967) or when a cemetery is expanding into unused land parcels (Dickens and Blakely 1978).

Churches

Church grounds located near the spatial center of cities have been scenes of continuous protection of prehistoric, preurban material. Obtaining permission to investigate should not be difficult, though it will vary, as long as considerations of the church membership and administration are respected.

Streets

Streets are a unique type of public land, singular in their distribution and making up a significant portion of the urban landscape (Table 3.3). Streets appear everywhere in the city, many times preceding urban growth in an area. They are linear in form, though they occur in such high frequencies in some places to be considered areal in extent.

If major highways, which require massive alterations of the landscape for construction, are not included, streets are scenes of little disturbance to previously deposited archaeological material. Disturbance *will* occur where sewer pipes, electrical lines, and the like are located (Feister *et al.* 1974; Huey *et al.* 1977). There is no information available on the percentage of streets that have such facilities under them, though it is probably fairly low, particularly as distance from the spatial center of a city increases. In addition, paved streets offer more protection to the archaeological record than unpaved streets by preventing erosion and/or purposive digging. Repairs to paved streets for the most part involve the addition of more paving, and the gradual raising of street level above ground surface. The general conclusion is that streets are locations of well-preserved prehistoric preurban material culture.

The amount of historic urban material present under streets depends on the history of the location. It is believed that settlement has concentrated near streets in historic-period urban settings (Henry 1980). In general, however, the temporal relationships between streets and dwellings is unclear. One type of historic-urban-period behavior so far ignored by archaeologists involves the patterned littering that occurs along streets. The extent of littering varies according to the location of the street, the nature of surrounding land uses, and the amount of traffic.

The cost of investigating streets and what is under them depends on surface material. Ease of getting permission to excavate also varies. One needs permission from the municipal government, and getting it most often depends on the amount of traffic disturbance investigation would entail.

Vacant Land

It has been stated that close to 20% of the land area of cities with over 100,000 residents, and more than 33% of the land area of smaller cities, is put to no obvious use whatsoever and exists as vacant land (Northam 1971, 1979). However, Table 3.3 shows that the total average per capita input for individual land uses (Bureau of Municipal Research and Service 1961; Manvel 1968) already exceeds the approximate average total input (Northam 1979). This anomaly might be explained by the fact that I am summing average percents from a number of urban centers. Another and better explanation involves the fact that various data were only available from certain studies and had to be combined in this paper. Northam is the only scholar to discuss percentage of vacant land, and there is no way to check his figures by referring to other research results (see, however, Niedercorn and Hearle 1963).

Vacant areas in cities nevertheless do exist. Not included in this category is land with obvious features of past use and land for very extensive purposes such as open parks. Up to 70% of vacant land is suitable for development (Northam 1979).

Vacant urban land can be classified according to the reasons it remains vacant (Northam 1979), which affects the number, size, and location of the properties. *Type 1* consists of "remnant parcels" (Northam 1971) or "sinks" (Clay 1973). These are parcels that remain after platting and development have taken place. Most often they are not developed because they are small in size and irregular in shape. Though small, these areas of vacant land are the most numerous.

Type 2 includes parcels on land that, due to environmental characteristics, cannot be built upon. Lands that are left vacant because of social constraints are also included in this group. The latter type of vacant land is similar in size and number to type 1. Type 2 land that is the result of physical constraints tends to consist of larger and fewer areas.

Type 3 includes all urban land reserves. Corporate reserves develop when a business purchases a parcel of land with the intention of using it in the future for relocation or expansion and leaves it vacant for a time. There are relatively few of these areas, though size can be quite large. Individual reserves are kept by people in the private sector for speculation. These areas are relatively small in size. Institutional reserves are owned by such groups as churches, schools, and private clubs. The goal of the owners is somehow to use the land in the future for the purposes of the group. The range of sizes is considerable.

Each of the types of vacant urban land has a distributional pattern that is somewhat different from the others. Remnant parcels are found throughout the city, with slightly higher concentrations in the older central sections. Unbuildable parcels are located unevenly throughout the city, their location being determined by environmental conditions. Corporate reserves tend to concentrate near the center of an urban area where most commercial activities are located. Institutional and individual reserves are most often found at the periphery of a city, where land is less expensive and taxes are low. A common assumption once held by urban geographers was that the overall amount of buildable vacant land in a city increases as distance from the city's center increases (Burgess 1925; Hoyt 1939). Studies in Portland, Oregon (Northam 1979) and Tulsa, Oklahoma (Brown 1967) show this assumption to be false. The density of vacant land was shown to be dependent on ownership, shape, and size of parcels.

Although vacant urban land is the scene of various modern behaviors (Wilk and Schiffer 1979) it is also the scene of undisturbed archaeological remains. For the most part, the effect of current activity is restricted to the surface. Any prehistoric preurban material that is present is left intact. For historic-period data the situation is somewhat more variable and unclear (Schaefer and Cleland 1980). The different kinds of vacant land, being different sizes, occurring in different frequencies, and being located in different places, afford the urban archaeologist the opportunity to explore a wide range of questions and to use appropriately different survey and sampling methods.

Vacant urban land is largely in private hands. As city populations and demands on the land continue to grow there is no doubt that much of this land will eventually be put to use. Northam (1971, 1979) stresses the fact that vacant urban land is a *wasted* resource. The majority of urban geographers, city planners, politicians, and land owners undoubtedly agree with him (Sowell 1981). A leading planner views vacant land as:

> Useless slots of spaces between buildings, between parking lots and fences, so as inevitably to invite trash dumpers . . . useless back lots, inaccessible tracts, alley lots with no alleys, non-negotiable rights of way, the millions of geographic errors which lash together every urbanized landscape (Clay 1973:149).

The large amount of vacant land in cities is a promise to urban archaeologists but a bane to many with decision-making capabilities. Much urban vacant land will eventually be developed and archaeologists must play an active role in planning if archaeological data are to be saved.

Summary

Certain general conclusions about how the data lie in the ground and how accessible it is to archaeologists can be made. The urban archaeologist considers a number of characteristics of both present and past land uses when deciding where to investigate a particular research question. Such considerations lead him to discover that urban settings are the scenes of overall good preservation of the archaeological record (Table 3.4). This is an important and somewhat startling conclusion, considering the views of many urban scholars.

The fact that the archaeological record is not significantly disturbed in cities has been recognized by urban geographers for some time. However, because they do not have an archaeological perspective, investigative possibilities are seldom realized.

> Atlanta, originally a railroad town, has taken unique advantage of the almost ghostly residues of its central terminal. The tracks have long since been covered, first by bridges, which traversed them, and then by complete streets; a second city grew up at this new street level. Below, *like a city waiting to be unearthed by archaeologists,* lay the foundations of old railroad stations with their nearby hotels (Heckscher 1977:117; emphasis added).

It would probably never occur to Heckscher actually to investigate this rich supply of archaeological data. The material of Atlanta's past is viewed as *like* a city to be investigated by archaeologists, but not the real thing. The popular view limits such "archaeological cities" to those of the prehistoric and early historic periods of the world, most being located in Mesopotamia and Mesoamerica. The preservationist ethic that exists among urban geographers concentrates on maintenance of structures and not investigation of material–behavioral relationships (Ford 1979).

On the other hand, American archaeologists recognize the promise of doing research in cities, but because the integrity of the data is seldom recognized, they often fail to realize the possibility of such investigations. Roy Dickens, under contract with the Metropolitan Atlanta Rapid Transit Authority to evaluate the impact on cultural resources of constructing a subway system, discusses both promises and problems of urban archaeology (Dickens 1978; Dickens and Bowen 1980). The promises he emphasizes deal with theoretical contributions urban archaeologists can make. The problems he emphasizes deal with the supposed lack of preservation of the archaeological record. Skinner and his colleagues, though attempting to locate and evaluate prehistoric resources in the Dallas area so that future development can be directed in part by archaeologists, generalizes that "urbanization and other site disturbance factors" should be used to determine archaeological sensitivity zones within the region (Skinner *et al.* 1978:53). However, they do not discuss the various patterns and extent of such disturbance. Benchley, introducing her overview of the prehistoric resources of the metropolitan St. Louis area, makes the following generalization without empirical support:

> The priorities [of the overview] do not conform to the ideal of preserving a sample of all archaeological types in a region. Because of the *immediate threat posed by the expanding urban area,* the priorities focus on resources which are likely to contain well preserved data (Benchley 1975:2; emphasis added)

Contracts often take scholars to those urban areas that are the scenes of much disturbance, such as commercial centers. It is thus understandable why many archaeologists do not recognize the possibility of doing rewarding work in cities. There are nevertheless urban archaeologists who argue that the material record is many times intact, both American (Beidleman 1979a,b; King 1978; Salwen 1978, 1979; Salwen *et al.* 1981; Staski 1980a,b) and British (Addyman 1976, 1980; Biddle and Hudson 1973; Hall 1978; Heighway 1972). Until more summaries of the empirical evidence on preservation are available, resources will continue to be threatened more by the opinions of the archaeological community than by urban development itself.

SURVEY AND SAMPLING STRATEGIES FOR URBAN ARCHAEOLOGY

Intimately related to determining the nature of the archaeological record in urban centers are survey and sampling techniques appropriate for urban archaeology. The nature and extent of the material is measured by surveying and sampling. Knowledge of how the data lie in the ground in turn helps determine which survey and sampling techniques to use.

Survey and sampling have a role to play in all archaeological research, but they are particularly necessary when conducting urban archaeology because of the nature of cities and the requirements of modern archaeology. Cities are very large sites that exhibit high internal variability in terms of both material and behavioral components (Morris 1975). They are by definition concentrations of human activities and energy, and the quantity of artifacts and information potentially recoverable is tremendous. The material record is many times found in deep stratigraphic provenience sometimes buried beneath the manifestations of modern urbanization. The depositional configuration is often very complex (Askins and Levin 1979; Cressey 1980; Henry 1980).

These factors make investigation in the city a time-consuming and expensive undertaking. Still, a general knowledge of the nature and extent of the total urban material record is necessary if the results of particular projects are to contribute to an integrated understanding of any city, and if long-term mitigation plans for urban centers are to be developed (Cressey 1978). Trends indicate that contract archaeology will continue to be the dominant form of research, especially in urban settings where development is intense and impacts are constant. The urban archaeologist must have the ability to differentiate and evaluate the continuous distribution of cultural remains into workable units based on the patterns of impacts and the nature of the problem domains being investigated.

The necessity for multistage survey and sampling procedures in archaeology has been thoroughly discussed in the literature (Binford 1964; Doelle

1978; Redman 1973, 1974; and others). The guidelines discussed here are presented as a series of stages.

Stage 1

The first stage of all urban survey and sampling strategies involves finding out as much as possible about the history and dynamics of the city where investigation is going to occur. If such a presampling survey (King 1978) or overview (McGimsey and Davis 1977) has been attempted previously, the researcher uses it constructively and supplements it when appropriate. If it has not, the researcher must carry out such an overview to avoid having the project stand in isolation. Information for the overview will be found in the literature of disciplines other than archaeology.

Historical Documentation

All urban centers throughout time have had an administrative body that insures continuance of various functions. The administration of historic cities involves the keeping of a multitude of written records on many facets of urban life. The preservation of such records occurs almost exclusively in urban centers, where the proper facilities for storage and protection are available. Street plans, address directories, phone directories, almanacs, occupational standards, census data, all contribute to a detailed account of urban dynamics and growth. Careful use of these materials allows for a well-documented historical outline of the physical and social characteristics of a city (Askins and Levin 1979; Cleland *et al.* 1979; Harris 1977; Henry 1980; Schuyler 1974a,b, 1976, 1980a).

Also preserved are many contemporary accounts such as diaries, newspapers and letters, which tend to present more of the attitudinal qualities of urban life. An additional historical source is oral history, that is, knowledge of the past preserved in the minds of urban residents. The combined use of oral and documentary sources has been recognized as a valuable research technique by historical archaeologists (Brown 1973; Schuyler 1977a).

Historiography

The city has been a popular subject of study by historians. There is a multitude of literature on the history of particular cities and on urban development in general. Historiography has been considered by some of little use to the archaeologist because data collection and interpretations are generally unquantitative (e.g., Binford 1972). Yet, much recent historiographical methodology is scientific and quantitative. The disciplines of history and archaeology, though approaching the same subject matter from different perspectives, have much to contribute to and learn from each other (Cleland and Fitting 1968). In addition, archaeologists have found the amateur local historian not only knowledgeable about the history of a city, or part of a city, but also enthusiastic and very willing to help (Schuyler and Mills 1976).

Urban Geography

Almost all research in urban geography is quantitative in nature, and usually both data and interpretations are reported. Quantitative data can be interpreted in ways suitable to the problem domains of the urban archaeologist. In addition, many urban geographers have an interest in the material manifestations of the city, especially in terms of spatial arrangement. Particular contributions to urban archaeology are discussed later in this chapter and elsewhere (Staski 1980a).

Environmental Design

The emergence of the interdisciplinary field of environmental design has brought about communication between architects, urban planners, geographers, and sociologists. The object of such communication is the application of social-science theory to the pragmatic concerns of constructing an urban setting. Human behavior, needs, and desires are considered on an equal basis with engineering necessities so that the urban environment is not only functional, but also responsive to residents (Michelson 1970; Perin 1970; Zeisel 1975).

Although the field is broad and rather ill defined, five major areas of interest appear to have emerged (Gutman 1972):

1. the study of human physical characteristics, which generate building design requirements (Cooper and Hacket 1968; Vogdes 1974);
2. the impact of spatial organization on social interaction (Brolin 1972; Cook, 1973; Cooper 1975; Festinger *et al.* 1950; Rhodeside 1970; Saile 1971, 1972; Zeisel and Griffen 1974);
3. the impact of the man-made environment on mental and physical health (Cook, 1971; Griffen 1974; Kerpen and Marshall 1973);
4. the relationship between architectural design and cultural values (Boudon 1969; Cooper 1970; Saile 1972; Zeisel and Griffen 1974); and
5. the evaluation of the usefulness of using social-science theory when designing urban settings (Cooper 1975; Cooper and Hacket 1968; Ertel 1974; Zeisel 1972)

Certain studies consider more than one area of interest. Ideally, those environmental-design studies that are to have actual applications should include consideration of all five areas, since they are all interrelated. Most studies concentrate on the social implications of material–spatial arrangements, the area of interest most closely related to the perspective of archaeology.

Cartography

Maps, including aerial photographs, give the archaeologist information on the nature of the environment and the degree of development in areas where resources are believed to be located, and can even suggest the presence of material culture. As is the case with documentation, urban centers maintain a great number of maps because such records are necessary for administrative functions and cities have the facilities to preserve them. Those areas of a city that have been developed recently or are facing imminent development very often are recorded in map form to a degree of detail that far exceeds that which is available for any other location. Contour, geologic, and soil maps of great accuracy and precision must be available to developers so that construction requirements can be met. Rosebrock (1981) reviews the uses of maps in urban archaeology.

The preceding several disciplines and types of data are helpful to the urban archaeologist when developing an overview of the city in which an investigation will be carried out. These disciplines should continue to be relevant during later survey and sampling stages. However, such data are not a panacea for the various lacunae that must remain and the numerous problems that must be faced. The important point to remember is that it is an *archaeological* investigation that is taking place, and while other disciplines can contribute information, they cannot provide the archaeologist with all the background or research strategies that are necessary in an investigation. Most guidance will come from the discipline of archaeology itself, and the success of a project depends on the creativity of the investigator, along with an ability to select and combine various kinds of data while maintaining an archaeological perspective.

Stage 2

Stage 1 is completed when enough information has been gathered to stratify the city into areas differing in terms of the degree of investigative potential. This assessment requires equal consideration of the degree of accessibility afforded the archaeologist, the assumed degree of data preservation, and the likely presence of material necessary to answer research questions. These three measures will for the most part vary independently across the urban landscape.

Stage 2 requires a combined field and archival examination of areas with high investigative potential. The goal is to obtain enough information so that the possibility and nature of investigation can be estimated more accurately. Categories of information that are useful to most projects include:

1. land-use type at the level of the parcel;
2. surrounding land use;

3. approximate amount of accessible surface area;
4. configuration of accessible surface area;
5. structural descriptions, including estimates of age and present condition; and
6. opinions regarding the views of residents about the possibility of investigations taking place.

After the stage 2 assessments are completed, specific alternative areas of investigation are chosen. These areas are revisited so that information gathered previously can be confirmed and expanded. Owners of property are contacted at this time so that permission for study can be granted. Decisions are then made concerning which specific locations will be initially and actively investigated in the field. Of course, if the archaeologist has signed a legal contract to investigate a specific location, there is no such freedom of choice.

Stage 3

Stage 3 is the actual testing of the archaeological record. Subsurface material is now often being sampled in areas thought to have a uniformly high degree of investigative potential. In most cases, it is impossible to predict where specific resources are located. For the first time, it is therefore necessary to use a probabilistic sampling strategy to determine whether the chosen areas actually contain the required material and where.

Recently, archaeologists have begun to question how to measure the reliability of subsurface testing procedures that do not require large-scale excavation. Procedures include posthole digging and auguring at various intervals. Studies that consider the accuracy and proper use of the procedures involved include those interested in the location of sites within a region (Hole 1979; Scott *et al.* 1978), the artifact-type frequencies within a site (South and Widmer 1977), and the logistics of the techniques themselves (Casjens *at al.* 1978). No one, however, has considered quantitatively the consequences of having variable and independently patterned surface accessibility relative to the patterning of the archaeological record, a situation common in the urban setting. This is unfortunate, because urban archaeologists often have to investigate on small noncontiguous parcels of land (Bostwick and Wise 1980; Deagan *et al.* 1976; Henry 1980; Klein 1979a) in areas where ordinary excavation would be too costly and dangerous (Brown 1975). Because of the limitations of small-scale probes to answer site-wide questions, remote sensing techniques, such as resistivity (Clark 1969) and magnetometer surveys (Aitken 1969), are also used.

The archaeologist contracted to mitigate impacts of urban development will find the practice of construction monitoring very useful in determining the nature and extent of the resources. This technique has been used successfully during a number of projects (Cleland *et al.* 1979; Dickens and Bowen 1980).

Further Stages

After stage 3 testing is completed, the actual methods required for each project will be determined by specific field conditions and research questions. It is impossible to add any further general descriptions of survey and sampling techniques.

SIGNIFICANCE AND PROBLEM DOMAINS

Knowledge of the nature and extent of urban material culture and an understanding of how to survey and sample appropriately in urban settings are meaningless sets of information if divorced from a firm commitment to specific research goals. Such goals are stated in the form of problem domains to be investigated and are intimately related to the measurement of archaeological significance.

Several scholars have considered the meaning of significance (Glassow 1977; McGimsey and Davis 1977; Moratto 1975; Moratto and Kelley 1977, 1978; Schiffer and Gumerman 1977; Schiffer and House 1977; Scovill *et al.* 1977). Significance is a term used in most legislation pertaining to cultural resource management (CRM). All archaeologists, whether under contract or not, assess significance within the framework of evolving problem-oriented research (Lynott 1980; Raab and Klinger 1977). This is true for urban archaeology as well, though very few have explicitly done so (cf. Cleland 1980; Cleland *et al.* 1979; Schaefer and Cleland 1980).

There are no "cookbook" definitions that determine what significance is and there are no guidelines telling which resources are and are not significant for every project. There are frames of reference, nevertheless, against which significance can be measured. Problem domains current in urban archaeology are discussed according to these frames of reference.

Historical Significance

Historical significance involves property associated with a particular important person or historical event, or more broadly associated with important historical trends. A number of such trends are reflected and preserved in urban centers. In addition to being concentrations of people and energy, cities are also concentrations of human history. Many facets of the human past, especially that part of our history that occurred in complex societies, are restricted to urban settings. Many trends, such as immigration and assimilation (Schuyler 1980b), the evolution of transportation systems (Buchanan 1965; Mumford 1963), and the evolution of construction technology (Gottmann 1966), can be considered significant because they are directly related to our present lives. Perhaps the most promising of such historical studies in urban archaeology involves the evolution of urban centers. The greatest challenge for archaeologists trying to investigate urban development involves translating the social variables discussed by urban geographers and sociologists into material terms. Although certain scholars have attempted to do so (Cressey 1978, 1979a,b; Schuyler 1974b, 1976), no substantive suggestions have been made.

It is appropriate to discuss the explanations and models for urban development that have been proposed in the order of their inception, because each was formulated as a reaction to previous explanations and models (see Staski 1980a for a more detailed discussion). All are based on two assumptions: (*a*) socioeconomic variables are the most powerful determinants of the spatial organization of cities; and (*b*) an ecological–functional approach to understanding urban spatial organization is appropriate considering the interrelated nature of urban phenomena. These ecological and economic emphases began with Park (1916; see also, Haig 1926; Hurd 1924) and have continued to the present day (Cressey 1980; Wheatley 1972). Emphasis has also been placed on residential patterns, with the result that commercial, industrial, and public land-use types to a large extent have been ignored.

Park collaborated with Burgess. The latter's famous Concentric Zone Model (1925, 1927, 1928, 1929) assumes (*a*) constant urban population growth, with the addition of relatively poor migrant and minority groups near the spatial center of a city; and (*b*) the operation of a process called "filtering," by which is meant the tendency for many urban residents to acquire more wealth and social status through time and to move away from the urban center. These two assumed social trends are what Burgess saw as the main forces shaping urban spatial organization. Neighborhoods near the center of the city, he thought, become run down because only the poor occupy them. Concurrently, the wealthy continue to push the urban periphery out further and further, establishing new neighborhoods when necessary. People move as close to the wealthy "frontier" as they can, proximity being purely a function of economic ability. The result of this patterned movement of people was viewed by Burgess as a series of concentric rings of land containing residents of differing wealth and social status.

Burgess's explanation and model soon became the subject of both criticism (Davie 1938) and support (Quinn 1940). The first alternative to be widely accepted was Hoyt's Sector Model (1939). Hoyt suggested that a process exists by which high-status, wealthy residents proceed through time along established lines of travel outward from the spatial center of a city. The lines of travel were seen as being originally established by the nature of the physical landscape. High-status, wealthy individuals will naturally move away from the city, Hoyt thought, because more attractive property could be found at a city's periphery. At the same time, and for the same reason, less wealthy individuals move as close to the very rich as they can. A person's residential distance from neighborhoods of the very rich is determined by the amount he can afford for housing. The effect is a spatial organization made up of wedges, or sectors, of different socioeconomic wealth and status.

The third and final explanation and model of urban spatial organization and growth to gain widespread popularity was Harris and Ullman's Multinucleated Model (1945). They suggested that both Burgess and Hoyt were viewing urban development in simplistic ways. There is not, they claimed, any city with a single urban core around which land use is arranged. Different land uses attract and are attracted to various surrounding activities. At the same time, these land uses are detrimental to other activities, and tend to be located far from them. This mutual push and pull of land-use types was considered by Harris and Ullman as the force behind urban spatial organization. The result, as depicted by their model, is the emergence of separate urban nuclei around which particular urban growth patterns occur.

Such is the state of explanation for urban spatial organization and growth to the present day. Surprisingly, no major alternative explanations or models have been widely accepted since 1945! There have been many studies since then, but these for the most part have only served to gather more empirical and quantitative data. Little in the way of the development of theory has occurred. Those urban geographers who still believe that urban development can be studied scientifically continue to consider the earlier explanations and models but have not proposed new ones (Alonso 1964; Beeman 1969; Griffen and Preston 1966; Johnston 1972; Loewenstein 1965; Pickard 1962; Rodwin 1961; Steinlieb and Hughes 1980). Others have rejected the economic–ecological approach altogether and have decided that a scientific explanation of urban development is impossible (Anderson 1959; Bourne 1971b; Firey 1947; Gittus 1964; Hoover and Vernon 1959; Mumford 1938, 1961). Palm (1981) presents a review of recent work.

The present situation of uncritical acclaim versus outright rejection is especially astonishing considering the fact that all three explanations discussed are variations of a single theme. Constant growth and the desire for economic segregation are viewed in all three explanations as the force shaping urban spatial organization. Each contribution, from Burgess to Hoyt to Harris and Ullman, is merely the presentation of a more complex model that better fits actual urban conditions.

A major reason why there have been so few advances in the scientific study of urban development since Burgess involves the disciplinary perspectives that have predominated. The explanations and models that have been offered all assume historical processes as causes, yet these processes have universally been derived from the study of present-day urban conditions. The material record of the past, which reflects urban development, has not been studied by urban geographers, and thus the question of whether these processes occurred and were significant remains essentially unanswered. It is an archaeological perspective that is needed to determine if proposed explanations are acceptable or if new and innovative ones are necessary. Until archaeologists begin studying the development of urban centers, current explanations and models will remain the only alternatives to unscientific opinions (cf. Cressey 1980; Schaefer and Cleland 1980).

Scientific Significance

Scientific significance involves the potential of using cultural resources to establish facts and generalizations about the relationships between material culture, human behavior, and cognition. The degree of scientific significance of specific archaeological resources will thus vary according to the research interests of the investigator. All archaeologists, however, have a responsibility to avoid letting their evaluations of significance be affected by particular interests to an extreme degree. If this responsibility is ignored, certain information significant to the discipline will be overlooked and lost (Lipe 1974).

Obviously disturbed sites must not be ignored or assumed to be places of little or no scientific significance. This point is particularly salient for the urban archaeologist, who is working in an environment of current and sometimes intensive use. Disturbance of the archaeological record is often minimal in the city. Still, it is a factor with which the archaeologist must contend. In fact, no archaeological site, anywhere, is completely undisturbed. Assessment of the extent of disturbance is a research problem that requires archaeological testing. Studying the nature of urban disturbance, for instance, significantly contributes to an understanding of urban processes (Cleland *et al.* 1979) and to an appreciation of the potential of urban archaeology to recover information (Staski 1980a,b).

The contributions archaeology can make to other scientific disciplines are many. These potential contributions should also be considered when assessing scientific significance. The city is a specific and powerfully influencing material setting in which people live. Just as various fields can contribute to the development of an urban overview, urban archaeology can present a unique and important perspective and otherwise unobtainable information to disciplines with a focus on the city. The potential for such contributions will not be recognized until urban archaeologists begin to make substantive conclusions about urban phenomena, and communicate them.

Ethnic Significance

Ethnic significance involves the importance of certain cultural resources to the history and integrity of ethnic minorities. Many ethnic groups have been selectively ignored in the written record, and archaeological research is often the only avenue to the past of these groups. Research results are not only significant because they allow the history of a people to be known. They also play an important role when certain land-claims cases go to court by helping determine past land boundaries and by supporting contentions of the sanctity and value of certain areas. Archaeologists must directly involve ethnic group leaders and spokesmen when determining ethnic significance, because assessment depends on the attitudes and beliefs of the people. Ethnic groups in turn must realize that archaeological research can contribute accurate and valuable information about past conditions.

American cities are concentrations of many ethnic groups. It is in the urban environment that ethnic groups are most integrated, and that ethnicity as a boundary maintainer is most powerful, because of the intensive and constant contact between groups. Indications are that ethnic identity can continue for generations, despite the heterogeneous population (Glazer and Moynihan 1963; Lynch 1980; Shack 1973; Waldron 1980). As a result, both behavioral and material symbols of ethnicity, along with the material correlates of behavior, are most visible in the city. In addition, it has been suggested that the concept of ethnicity had little meaning to anyone until the emergence of complex societies with the power of political domination (Schuyler 1980b). Such complex societies were and are for the most part urban in nature.

Ethnic studies in American archaeology are proliferating. It has been stated that archaeologists should be interested in how they can best define ethnicity for their purposes and how ethnicity can be recognized in the archaeological record (Schuyler 1980b). These two methodological questions, however, are seldom if ever confronted in the sophisticated manner that the complexities of the ethnicity concept require. The two questions have been mentioned by several archaeologists (Baker 1980; Deagan 1973, 1976, 1978; Ferguson 1980; Kelly and Kelly 1980; McGuire 1979; Schuyler 1974a, 1980a; Shephard 1975; Staski 1976), but they have not yet been dealt with to the point that the dynamics of ethnic identification can be confidently confronted.

When trying to define ethnicity, archaeologists have consistently borrowed ideas and descriptions from other disciplines. However, there are as many ideas as to what ethnicity is as there are perspectives from which one can study social organization and differentiation (Greeley and McCready 1974). Two main approaches seem to have developed. One stresses the importance of behavioral distinctions that maintain boundaries between basic groups (Barth 1969; Spicer 1971, 1972). The other emphasizes identification through cognition, seeing "true" ethnicity based on specific thoughts and not necessarily on actions (Cronin, 1970, 1974; Schermerhorn 1969). The archaeologist will necessarily have to concentrate his efforts on behavioral aspects, since the material record more directly reflects what people do than what they think. An archaeological approach to the subject allows for an historical perspective (Spicer 1971) and this perspective allows for the observation of the emergence, continuance and eventual decline of ethnic identification within societies. It is more realistic than any static cross-cultural perspective could be, because ethnic identification is a continual process requiring effort through time if it is going to continue. Observation of ethnic groups at one point in time can result in a failure to recognize the dynamic qualities of group interaction and identification.

Material symbols of ethnicity are often scarce in the archaeological record, and material correlates of ethnically specific behaviors often must be studied instead (Clonts 1971). Distinguishing ethnic behavior from other social dimensions that are archaeologically reflected, such as economic status and religious affiliation, is often difficult. More work is necessary if we are to successfully identify ethnic identification. As with the study of urban development the problem lies in translating social phenomena into material terms.

One of the more practical ways for the urban archaeologist to study material symbols and behavioral correlates of ethnicity involves the investigation of architectural variation (Staski 1976). Cities are concentrations of architectural forms, and the amount of data available for study is great. Architectural features from both the past and the present are generally above ground, making investigation less expensive and time consuming than if excavation was required. The symbols or material correlates of behavior reflected in architecture are relatively permanent and preserved, more so, at least, than many other types of ethnic material symbols (Wobst 1977).

Public Significance

Public significance involves the benefits archaeology can have to society as a whole. These benefits include an increased understanding of America's cultural heritage. Contributions are not, however, exclusively in the direction from archaeology to the public. Once people appreciate the significance of archaeology they are willing to aid the discipline with financial and political support. The future of archaeology is indeed dependent on public awareness and appreciation (Lipe 1974). The more the public knows about the value of proper archaeological technique, the less the chance that looting and vandalism of cultural resources will occur.

Urban archaeologists are well aware of the public (e.g., Cressey 1980; Pendrey 1979). An urban excavation always draws a certain number of visitors. They are interested in the procedures and keep a watchful eye on the crew. Urban investigations expose archaeologists to a large part of the urban population. Unfortunately, this public contact is generally considered by archaeologists as a liability. It is often felt that since the area under investigation is still in use, getting permission for investigation will be difficult. In addition, vandalism and bottle hunting occur often, it is felt, because of the extreme visibility of the project within an area of dense population. In certain instances, these are very real problems. However, there is a positive side to the situation that is seldom realized. Archaeological investigations in an area where people live and work on a regular basis provide unprecedented opportunities for expanding public education. Greater visibility of an archaeological project, if handled correctly, can lead to greater public appreciation and support, especially for the archaeology of the recent past. In many urban centers where archaeological work is ongoing, guided tours of sites, talks and slide shows in libraries, and visits to schools by archaeologists serve to give the public a better understanding of what archaeologists are doing and why. Urban archaeologists obviously have the opportunity to show the discipline how important and beneficial a realization of public significance can be (Dickens and Bowen 1980; Schaefer 1980).

Legal Significance

Legal significance involves what is written into law concerning the protection and investigation of cultural resources. Various and important pieces of legislation are discussed elsewhere (McGimsey 1972; McGimsey and Davis 1977) and are not reviewed here. More recent legislation, not covered by these reviews, can only be found by scanning various legal documents and the Federal Register. In addition, many local and municipal laws exist throughout the country, with the result that legal significance varies from place to place.

Legal significance is a crucial frame of reference for all archaeologists, especially those working under contract. All other frames of reference were developed by archaeologists in order for the discipline to adequately deal with the vague definitions and directions of the law. The clearest legal statement of the significance of cultural resources is found in the criteria for evaluation for possible inclusion in the National Register of Historic Places. Significance is never defined in this Regulation, even though the term is used repeatedly. Criterion "d" theoretically allows every piece of material culture "that has yielded, or may be likely to yield, information important in prehistory or history" to be interpreted as significant (U.S. Code of Federal Regulations,

1976). This vagueness of the law was intentional and is both good and bad for archaeology. By not specifying what significance is, the law leaves the responsibility of definition to archaeologists, which is exactly where the responsibility should be. Members of the discipline, with their experience and expertise, are best suited to recognize significant cultural resources in terms of current and projected future problem domains and research needs (Klinger and Raab 1980; Raab and Klinger 1977, 1979; Schiffer and Gumerman 1977b; Sharrock and Grayson 1979). The criteria were not designed to *direct* archaeologists in their determination of significance, but only to *allow* them to reach such a determination (see also, Barnes *et al.* 1980; King 1977; King *et al.* 1977). Use of the criteria as a management tool has led to confusion, the necessity for archaeologists to work out irrelevant administrative details, and the neglect of the important role of research orientation when significance is to be determined. On the other hand, the ambiguity of legal significance makes it at times difficult to determine eligibility for inclusion in the National Register. The establishment of guidelines for the determination of significance by certain federal agencies, with archaeological research interests in mind, is helping to eliminate this ambiguity (Raab *et al.* 1980).

One aspect of the criteria for evaluation that is carefully noted by urban archaeologists is the obvious emphasis on standing and historic structures. Although archaeologists do not consider such factors exclusively when determining significance, they do keep in mind that a nomination to the National Register might be relatively easy in certain urban situations. If nomination is desired, the urban archaeologist might have an easier job merely because of the bias of the law.

It is impossible to consider the applicability of laws specifically related to urban research, because local and municipal legislation varies greatly from city to city and no compendium is available. Urban archaeologists become familiar with the legal structure of the city in which they are conducting research. The role that can be played by urban archaeologists in formulating and amending new legislation that would be useful to archaeologists on the local level must also be considered. There is, in general, a greater chance for the archaeologist to be able to influence local, municipal government than to tackle issues on the federal or state level, although the degree of possible involvement will vary greatly. Local legislation that might be introduced does not necessarily have to be solely or directly related to the protection of cultural resources to be of interest to archaeologists. For example, the recent enactment of certain urban zoning laws in Arizona has guaranteed that a percentage of land will be left vacant and/or open (Arizona Daily Star 1980). This legislation is meant to maintain a certain quality of life for urban residents, but it indirectly aids archaeology by curtailing certain land-use practices that are disruptive to the archaeological record.

Summary

Investigations of culture history, ethnicity, preservation, and urban development are prevalent in urban archaeology today. In the future, however, it is probable that other problem domains will be considered, and other data and information will be viewed as significant. Potential research interests include expanding sociopolitical frontiers, boomtowns, colonization, and the importation of Western urban society into non-Western rural regions of the world. When the number and type of research questions asked increases, urban archaeology will be more fully recognized as a legitimate and relevant field of inquiry.

CONCLUSIONS

Urban archaeology, a relatively new research area in America, is growing rapidly. Although communication of project results is fairly poor, the situation will necessarily have to change. More volumes of collected works and more general methodological statements of how to conduct archaeology in the city are needed.

Archaeologists are still surprised at the tremendous possibility and promise of conducting urban research, a surprise that is sensed usually long after projects are begun. The amount of available information is great because the processes of urbanization are not very destructive to the archaeological record. Appropriate survey and sampling procedures that allow the efficacious recovery of this information are available. When these potentials are realized, urban archaeology becomes the scientific study of significant resources and problem domains. In addition, archaeologists become more convincing and effective contributors to the planning stages of future urban development. When archaeologists view urban development as generally detrimental to the discipline, on the other hand, they artificially place themselves in an adversary relationship with urban planners, politicians, contractors, and the public, and put too much emphasis on recovering artifacts and not enough on addressing research questions.

Urban archaeologists need not merely salvage information. They study the relationships among material culture, human behavior, and cognition in a particular environment defined as urban. They are social scientists who many times attempt to understand a very relevant and immediate human condition known as the urban lifestyle. What can be contributed in the future to a general understanding of urban phenomena rests on the potential of archaeological investigations to add to human understanding. I believe this potential has not yet been realized fully.

ACKNOWLEDGMENTS

A number of urban archaeologists with whom I have corresponded have made valuable contributions to the development of my ideas. Conversations with additional members of the archaeological community, ranging from casual exchanges to heated imbroglios, have been very helpful. Special thanks go to Bill Askins, Paul Fish, Jed Levin, Randy McGuire, Bill Rathje, J. Jefferson Reid, Jerry Schaefer, Michael Schiffer, and Bob Schuyler. I of course take full responsibility for any faults, omissions, or other peccadillos in this paper.

REFERENCES

Addyman, P. V.
  1976   (Editor) *Excavations in York*. Council for British Archaeology, York Archaeological Trust.
  1980   Eburacum, Jorvik, York. *Scientific American* **242**(3):76–86.
Aitken, M.
  1969   Research laboratory for archaeology and the history of art. In *Science in archaeology,* edited by D. Brothwell and E. Higgs. London: Thames and Hudson. Pp. 681–694.
Alonso, W.
  1964   *Location and land use.*Cambridge, Massachusetts: Harvard University Press.
Anderson, N.
  1959   *The urban community: a world perspective*. New York: Holt.
Anonymous
  1975   Archaeology in Detroit. *Popular Archaeology* **4**(7):23–26.
Arizona Daily Star
  1980   Communities can use zoning law to save open space, justices rule. *Arizona Daily Star,* June 11, Tucson.
Askins, W., and J. Levin
  1979   Changes in function of a 19th century urban backyard. Paper presented at the 12th annual conference of the Society for Historical Archaeology, Nashville.
Ayres, J. E.
  1968   Urban renewal salvage: archaeology in Tucson, Arizona. Paper presented at the 33rd annual meeting of the Society for American Archaeology, Santa Fe.
  1975   Archaeological excavations in the art center block: a brief summary. Ms. on file, Arizona State Museum, Tucson.
Baker, V. G.
  1980   Archaeological visibility of Afro-American culture: an example from Black Lucy's garden, Andover, Massachusetts. In *Archaeological perspectives on ethnicity in America: Afro-American and Asian American culture history,* edited by R. L. Schuyler. Farmingdale, New York: Baywood. Pp. 29–37.
Barnes, M. R., A. K. Briggs, and J. J. Neilsen
  1980   A response to Raab and Klinger on archaeological site significance. *American Antiquity* **45**:551–553.
Barth, F. (editor)
  1969   *Ethnic groups and boundaries*. Boston: Little, Brown.

Bartholomew, H.
  1955   *Land uses in American cities.* Cambridge, Massachusetts: Harvard University
              Press.
Basalik, K. J.
  1980   Data collection and the bulldozer: salvage archaeology and the urban context.
              Paper presented at the annual meeting of the Council for Northeast Historical
              Archaeology, Albany.
Basalik, K. J., and J. P. McCarthy
  1979   Discerning patterns in an urban context: an example from Philadelphia. Paper
              presented at the 20th annual conference on Historic Site Archaeology, St.
              Augustine.
Beeman, W. J.
  1969   The property tax and the spatial pattern of growth within urban areas. *Urban
              Land Institute Reseach Monograph* 16.
Beidleman, D. K.
  1979a   Eight parking spaces at a time: pragmatism and research methods within the
              urban environment. Paper presented at the 12th annual conference of the
              Society for Historical Archaeology, Nashville.
  1979b   The 500 block King Street excavations: Alexandria archaeology's first "test
              square." Paper presented at the 9th annual meeting of the Middle Atlantic Ar-
              chaeology Conference, Rehaboth Beach, Delaware.
Benchley, E.
  1975   *An overview of the archaeological resources of the metropolitan St. Louis
              area.* National Park Service, Washington, D.C.
Berry, B. J. L.
  1959   Ribbon developments in the urban business pattern. *Annals of the Association
              of American Geographers* **49:**2.
  1967   Geography of market centers and retail distribution. *Foundations of economic
              geography series.* Englewood Cliffs, New Jersey. Prentice-Hall.
Berry, B. J. L., J. W. Simmons, and R. J. Tennant
  1963   Urban population densities: structure and change. *Geographical Review*
              53:389–405.
Betancourt, J. L.
  1978a   An archaeological synthesis of the Tucson Basin: focus on the Santa Cruz and
              its riverpark. *Arizona State Museum Archaeological Series* 116, Tucson.
  1978b   Cultural resources within the proposed Santa Cruz riverpark archaeological
              district. *Arizona State Museum Archaeological Series* 125, Tucson.
Biddle, M., and D. Hudson
  1973   *The future of London's past.* Rescue, a Trust for British Archaeology,
              Worcester.
Binford, L. R.
  1964   A consideration of archaeological research design. *American Antiquity*
              29:425–441.
  1972   Evolution and horizon as revealed in ceramic analysis in historical archaeol-
              ogy—a step toward the development of archaeological science. *The conference
              on historic site archaeology papers 1971* **6:**117–125.
Bostwick, J., and D. Wise
  1980   A sub-surface survey of the city of St. Augustine: historic precincts north of the
              plaza. *The Florida Journal of Anthropology* **5**(1).

Boudon, P.
1969 *Lived-in architecture: Le Corbusier's "Pessac" revisited.* Cambridge, Massachusetts: MIT Press.

Bourne, L. S.
1971a *Internal structure of the city: readings on space and environment,* edited by L. S. Bourne. London: Oxford University Press.
1971b Introduction. In *Internal structure of the city: readings on space and environment,* edited by L. S. Bourne. London: Oxford University Press. Pp. 3–10.
1971c Images: defining the urban realm. In *Internal structure of the city: readings on space and environment,* edited by L. S. Bourne, London: Oxford University Press. Pp. 11–16.
1976 Urban structure and land-use decisions. *Annals of the Association of American Geographers* **66**:4.

Bower, B. A.
1979 The historic development of Boston's 19th century Afro-American community. Paper presented at the 12th annual conference of the Society for Historical Archaeology, Nashville.
1980 Land use and urban development in Roxbury, Massachusetts 1700–1900. Paper presented at the annual meeting of the Council for Northeast Historical Archaeology, Albany.

Bower, B. A., and B. Rushing
1980 The African meeting house: the center for the 19th century Afro-American community in Boston. In *Archaeological perspectives on ethnicity in America: Afro-American and Asian American culture history,* edited by R. L. Schuyler. Farmingdale, New York: Baywood. Pp. 69–75.

Bradley, B. A.
1980 *Excavation at Arizona BB:13:74 Santa Cruz Industrial Park, Tucson, Arizona.* Oracle, Arizona: Complete Archaeological Service Associates Papers No. 1.

Brandes, R.
1978 The Quong building: historical and archaeological survey. Ms. on file, Department of Anthropology, University of San Diego, San Diego.

Bridges, S. T.
1974 The Clinton Avenue site, Kingston, New York. Unpublished M.A. thesis, Department of Anthropology, New York University, New York.

Bridges, S. T., and B. Salwen
1980 Weeksville: the archaeology of a Black urban community. In *Archaeological perspectives on ethnicity in America: Afro-American and Asian American culture history,* edited by R. L. Schuyler. Farmingdale, New York: Baywood. Pp. 38–47.

Brolin, B. C.
1972 Chandigarh was planned by experts but something has gone wrong. *Smithsonian* **3**(3):56–63.

Brown, J. A.
1975 Deep-site excavation strategy as a sampling problem. In *Sampling in archaeology,* edited by J. W. Mueller. Tucson: University of Arizona Press. Pp. 155–169.

Brown, M. III
1973 The use of oral and documentary sources in historical archaeology: ethnohistory at the Mott farm. *Ethnohistory* **20**:347–360.

Brown, R. C.
1967   Spatial variations of idle land in Tulsa, Oklahoma. Unpublished Ph.D. dissertation, Department of Geography, University of Oklahoma, Norman.

Buchanan, R. A.
1965   *Technology and social progress.* Oxford: Pergamon Press.

Buel, B. J.
1980   Mobile homes top growth in area housing market. *Arizona Daily Star,* August 5, Tucson.

Bureau of Municipal Research and Service.
1961   *Land use in 33 Oregon cities.* Bureau of Municipal Research and Service, University of Oregon.

Burgess, E. W.
1925   The growth of the city: an introduction to a research project. In *The city*, edited by R. E. Park, E. W. Burgess, and R. D. McKenzie. Chicago: University of Chicago Press. Pp. 47–62.
1927   The determination of gradients in the growth of a city. *Publications of the American Sociological Society* **21**:178–184.
1928   Residential segregation in American cities. *Annals of the American Academy of Political and Social Sciences* **140**:105–115.
1929   Urban areas. In *Chicago: an experiment in social science research,* edited by T. V. Smith and L. D. White. Chicago: University of Chicago Press. Pp. 114–123.

Carnes, L.
1979   Archaeological investigations of Atlanta's garbage dumps circa 1900: a preliminary statement. Paper presented at the 12th annual conference of the Society for Historical Archaeology, Nashville.

Casetti, E.
1967   Urban population density patterns: an alternative explanation. *Canadian Geography* **2**:96–100.

Casjens, L., G. Bawden, M. Roberts, and V. Talmage
1978   Field methods in New England cultural resource management. In *Conservation archaeology in the northeast: toward a research orientation,* edited by A. E. Spiess. Cambridge, Massachusetts: Harvard University, Peabody Museum of Archaeology and Ethnology Bulletin 3. Pp. 87–94.

Chapin, F. S., Jr.
1974   *Human activity patterns in the city: things people do in time and in space.* New York: Wiley.

Chapin, F. S., Jr., and E. J. Kaiser
1979   *Urban land use planning.* Urbana: University of Illinois Press.

Christaller, W.
1966   *Central places in southern Germany* (1933). Englewood Cliffs, New Jersey: Prentice-Hall.

Clark, A.
1969   Resistivity surveying. In *Science in archaeology,* edited by D. Brothwell and E. Higgs. London: Thames and Hudson. Pp. 695–704.

Clark, C.
1951   Urban population densities. *Journal of the Royal Statistical Society Series A* **114**:490–496.
1958   Urban population densities. *Bulletin Institute International de Statistique* **36**:60–68.

Clay, G.
  1973   *How to read the American city.* Chicago: University of Chicago Press.
Cleland, C. E., and J. E. Fitting
  1968   The crisis of identity: theory in historic sites archaeology. *The conference on historic site archaeology papers 1968* **2**:124–138.
Cleland, J. H.
  1980   Historical archaeology and cultural resource management: an example from downtown San Diego. Paper presented at the Southwest Anthropological Meeting, San Diego.
Cleland, J. H., D. Burkenroad, and J. C. Smith
  1979   *An archaeological and historical inventory of the Marina/Columbia residential development parcels, A, B and C.* San Diego: Wirth Associates.
Cleland, J. H., D. Burkenroad, C. L. Smith, and J. C. Smith
  1980   *Developing the bay, an archaeological overview of the Marina/Columbia redevelopment area.* San Diego: Wirth Associates.
Clonts, J. B.
  1971   Butchering analysis, a possible tool. Ms. on file, Arizona State Museum, Tucson.
Cook, B. E.
  1971   Survey evaluation for low-cost low rent public housing for the elderly, Pleasanton, California. Paper prepared for Hirshen and Partners, Architects, Berkeley, California.
  1973   Initial evaluation of Koffenger Place, Pleasanton, California. Paper prepared for Hirshen and Partners, Architects, Berkeley, California.
Cooper, C.
  1970   *Resident's attitudes toward the environment at St. Francis Square, San Francisco.* University of California, Institute of Urban and Regional Development, Working Paper 126, Berkeley.
  1975   *Easter Hill Village.* New York: The Free Press.
Cooper, C., and P. Hacket
  1968   Analysis of the design process at two moderate-income housing developments. University of California, Center for Urban Planning and Development Research, Working Paper 80, Berkeley.
Cossans, B. J.
  1979   An analysis of urban privy fills: Philadelphia, 1720–1850. Paper presented at the 12th annual conference of the Society for Historical Archaeology, Nashville.
Costello, J. G.
  1976   The royal presidio of Santa Barbara, phase 3: archaeology of the padre's quarters. Ms. on file, Santa Barbara Trust for Historic Preservation, Santa Barbara.
  1979   Archaeology in urban Los Angeles. Paper presented at the 12th annual conference of the Society for Historical Archaeology, Nashville.
Cotter, J. L.
  1980   Excavating Ben Franklin's house. *Early Man* **2**(2):17–20.
Cotter, J. L., and D. Orr
  1975   Historical archaeology of Philadelphia. *Historical Archaeology* **9**:1–10.
Cotz, J. A.
  1975   A study of ten houses in Paterson's Dublin area. *Northeast Historical Archaeology* **4**:44.

Cressey, P. J.
1978   The city as a site: the Alexandria model for urban archaeology. Paper presented at the 19th annual meeting of the Historic Sites Conference, Old Salem, North Carolina.
1979a   Studying the American city: the Alexandria urban archaeology project. Paper presented at a joint symposium at the 44th annual meeting of the Society for American Archaeology and the 12th annual meeting of the Canadian Archaeological Association, Vancouver, British Columbia.
1979b   The Alexandria urban archaeology project: an integrative model for systematic study, conservation and crisis. Paper presented at the 12th annual conference of the Society for Historical Archaeology, Nashville.
1980   Sharing the ivory tower. Paper presented at the 45th annual meeting of the Society for American Archaeology, Philadelphia.
Cressey, P. J., and D. K. Beidleman
1980   The development of a city's core: 500 King Street site, Alexandria, Virginia. Ms. on file, Alexandria Archaeological Research Center.
Cronin, C.
1970   *The sting of change: Sicilians in Sicily and Australia.* Chicago: University of Chicago Press.
1974   Social organization and social change: Sicilian peasants in Sicily and Australia. In *Frontiers of anthropology,* edited by M. J. Leaf. New York: Van Nostrand. Pp. 165–188.
Davie, M. R.
1938   The pattern of urban growth. In *Studies in the science of society,* edited by G. P. Murdock. New Haven: Yale University Press. Pp. 131–161.
Deagan, K. A.
1973   Mestizaje in colonial St. Augustine. *Ethnohistory* 20:55–65.
1976   Archaeology at the National Greek Orthodox Shrine, St. Augustine, Florida: microchange in eighteenth-century Spanish colonial material culture. *Notes in Anthropology* 15, Florida State University, St. Augustine.
1978   The material assemblage of 16th century Spanish Florida. *Historical Archaeology* 12:25–50.
Deagan, K. A., J. Bostwick, and D. Benton
1976   *A sub-surface survey of the St. Augustine city environs.* St. Augustine: Restoration Foundation, Florida State University.
Deetz, J. F., and E. S. Dethlefson
1967   Death's head, cherub, urn and willow. *Natural History* 76(3):29–37.
Dickens, R. S., Jr.
1978   Problems and promises in urban historical archaeology: the MARTA project. Paper presented at the 43rd annual meeting of the Society for American Archaeology, Tucson.
Dickens, R. S., Jr., and R. L. Blakely
1978   Preliminary report on archaeological investigations in Oakland cemetery, Atlanta, Georgia. *The conference on historic site archaeology papers 1978.* 13:286–314.
Dickens, R. S., Jr., and W. R. Bowen
1980   Problems and promises in urban historical archaeology: the MARTA project. *Historical Archaeology* 14:41–57.
Doelle, W.
1976   Management plan: Santa Cruz riverpark. *Arizona State Museum Archaeological Series* 91, Tucson.

1978 A multiple survey strategy for cultural resource management studies. In *Conservation archaeology: a guide for cultural resource management studies,* edited by M. B. Schiffer and G. J. Gumerman. New York: Academic Press. Pp. 201–209.

Ertel, M.
1974 Evaluation and programing of urban teenage hanging places. Ms. on file, Harvard Graduate School of Design, Architecture Research office, Cambridge, Massachusetts.

Fagan, B. M.
1976 The royal presidio of Santa Barbara: archaeology of the chapel site. Ms. on file, Santa Barbara Trust for Historic Preservation, Santa Barbara.

Faulkner, A., M. Peters, D. P. Sell, and E. S. Dethlefson
1978 *Port and market: archaeology of the central waterfront, Newburyport, Massachusetts.* Newburyport: Newburyport Press.

Feister, L. M.
1975 An archaeological test survey in the front yard of Fort Crailo State Historic site, city of Rensselaer, New York. Ms. on file, New York Historical Places.

Feister, L. M., J. E. McEroy, and P. R. Huey
1974 Sewer line salvage archaeology under Riverside Avenue near Rensselaer, New York. Ms. on file, New York Historical Places.

Ferguson, L.
1980 Looking for the "Afro" in colono-Indian pottery. In *Archaeological perspectives on ethnicity in America: Afro-American and Asian American culture history,* edited by R. L. Schuyler. Farmingdale, New York: Baywood. Pp. 14–28.

Festinger, L., S. Schachter, and K. Back
1950 *Social pressures in informal groups.* New York: Harper.

Firey, W.
1947 *Land use in central Boston.* Cambridge, Massachusetts: Harvard University Press.

Foley, V. P.
1967 Pre-1800 historic sites—urban. *Historical Archaeology* **1**:43–44.

Ford, L. R.
1979 Urban preservation and the geography of the city in the USA. *Progress in Human Geography* **3**:211–238.

Fowler, G.
1979 Archaeologists hard at work at site of first city hall. *The New York Times,* October 25.

Gittus, E.
1964 The structure of urban areas. *Town Planning Review* **35**:5–20.

Glassow, M. A.
1977 Issues in evaluating the significance of archaeological resources. *American Antiquity* **42**:413–420.

Glazer, N., and P. Moynihan
1963 *Beyond the melting pot.* Cambridge, Mass.: MIT Press.

Gottmann, J.
1966 Why the skyscraper? *Geographical Review* **56**:2.

Greeley, A. M., and W. C. McCready
1974 *Ethnicity in the United States: a preliminary reconnaissance.* New York: Wiley.

Greenwood, R. S. (editor)
1975   *3500 years on one city block: San Buenaventura mission plaza project archaeological report, 1974.* Report prepared for the Redevelopment Agency, San
Buenaventura.
1976   *The changing faces of Main Street.* Ventura mission plaza archaeological project, Redevelopment Agency, Ventura.

Greenwood, R. S.
1980   The Chinese on Main Street. In *Archaeological perspectives on ethnicity in
America: Afro-American and Asian American culture history,* edited by R. L.
Schuyler. Farmingdale, New York: Baywood. Pp. 113–123.

Gregonis, L. M.
1977   Summary of excavations at AZ BB: 9:14: Fort Lowell County Park, September
1976 to May 1977. Paper prepared for Pima County Parks and Recreation
Department and Pima County Parks and Recreation Commission, Tucson.

Gregonis, L. M., and K. J. Reinhard
1979   *Hohokam Indians of the Tucson Basin.* Tucson: University of Arizona Press.

Griffen, D. W., and R. E. Preston
1966   A restatement of the "transition zone" concept. *Annals of the Association of
American Geographers* **56**:2.

Griffen, M. E.
1974   Mount Hope Courts: a social-physical evaluation. In *Proceedings of northeastern undergraduate conference on environment and behavior,* edited by
J. W. Vogt. Amherst: University of Massachusetts.

Gunnerson, C. G.
1973   Debris accumulation in ancient and modern cities. *Journal of the Environmental Engineering Division, Proceedings of the American Society of Civil
Engineers* **99**:EE3:229–243.

Gutman, R. (editor)
1972   *People and buildings.* New York: Basic Books.

Haig, R.
1926   Toward an explanation of the metropolis. *Quarterly Journal of Economics* **40**:
421–423.

Hall, R. A.
1978   *Viking age York and the north.* Council for British Archaeology, York Archaeological Trust, York.

Hamilton, E. P.
1964   *The village mill in early New England.* Meriden, Connecticut: Old Sturbridge
Village Booklet Series.

Hanson, L.
1974   Outhouses in Rome, New York. *Northeast Historical Archaeology* **3**(1):30–43.

Hanson, L., and D. P. Hsu
1975   Casemates and cannonballs: archaeological investigations at Fort Stanwix,
Rome, New York. *National Park Service Publications in Archaeology* **14**,
Washington, D.C.

Harris, C. D., and E. L. Ullman
1945   The nature of cities. *Annals of the American Academy of Political and Social
Science* **242**:7–17.

Harris, E.
1977   *Documents, legends and archaeology: unravelling the mysteries of
Newburyport's past.* Newburyport: Historical Survey Associates.

Hartgen, K. S., and C. L. Fisher
1980   Archaeological investigations in the Waterford historical district. Paper presented at the annual meeting of the Council for Northeast Historical Archaeology, Albany.

Heckscher, A.
1977   *Open spaces: the life of American cities.* New York: Harper.

Heighway, C. (editor)
1972   *The erosion of history: archaeology and planning in towns: a study of historic towns affected by modern development in England, Wales and Scotland.* Council for British Archaeology, Urban Research Committee.

Henry, S.
1980   An integrative survey for research and preservation. Paper presented at the 45th annual meeting of the Society for American Archaeology, Philadelphia.

Hole, F.
1979   Addendum to cultural resources evaluation, Vermillion 43, OCS-G-3544. Ms. on file, Outer Continental Shelf Office, New Orleans.

Hood, Graham
1973   *Bonin and Morris of Philadelphia: the first American porcelain factory.* Institute of Early American History and Culture, Chapel Hill.

Hoover, E. M., and R. Vernon
1959   *The anatomy of a metropolis.* Cambridge, Massachusetts: Harvard University Press.

Hoyt, H.
1939   *The structure and growth of residential neighborhoods in American cities.* Federal Housing Administration, Washington, D.C.

Huey, P. R., L. M. Feister, and J. E. McEroy
1977   Archaeological investigations in the vicinity of Fort Crailo during sewer line construction under Riverside Avenue in Rensselaer, New York. *Bulletin of the New York State Archaeological Association* **69**:19–42.

Humphrey, R. L., and M. E. Chambers
1977   Ancient Washington: American Indian cultures of the Potomac Valley. *G. W. Washington Studies* **6**:30–31.

Hurd, R.
1924   *Principles of city land values.* The Record and Guide, New York.

Inashima, P. Y.
1980   *Analysis and description of the artifacts from block 225, Washington, D.C.* Potomac River Archaeology Survey, Department of Anthropology, The American University, Washington, D.C.

Ingersoll, D. W.
1971   Problems of urban historical archaeology. *Man in the Northeast* **2**:66–74.

Johnson, F.
1942   The Boylston street fishweir. *Papers of the Robert S. Peabody Foundation for Archaeology* 2, Andover, Massachusetts.

Johnston, R. J.
1972   *Urban residential patterns.* New York: Praeger.

Jones, T. W.
1981   Boise's old Chinatown: an urban laboratory for the study of culture change. Paper presented at the 14th annual conference of the Society for Historical Archaeology, New Orleans.

Katz, P. R.
1978   Archaeological and historical investigations in the Arciniega Street area, downtown San Antonio, Texas. Archaeological Survey Report 61. Center for Archaeological Research, the University of Texas at San Antonio.
Kelly, M. C. S., and R. E. Kelly
1980   Approaches to ethnic identification in historical archaeology. In *Archaeological perspectives on ethnicity in America: Afro-American and Asian American culture history,* edited by R. L. Schuyler. Farmingdale, New York: Baywood. Pp. 133–144.
Kerpen, S., and D. Marshall
1973   *Health and user needs in low income housing.* People's Housing, Topanga, California.
King, T. F.
1977   Resolving a conflict of values in American archaeology. In *Conservation archaeology: a guide for cultural resource management studies,* edited by M. B. Schiffer and G. J. Gumerman. New York: Academic Press. Pp. 87–96.
1978   *The archaeological survey: methods and uses.* Heritage Conservation and Recreation Service, U.S. Department of the Interior, Washington, D.C.
King, T. F., P. P. Hickman, and G. Berg
1977   *Anthropology in historic preservation: caring for culture's clutter.* New York: Academic Press.
Kinkade, G. M., and G. L. Fritz
1975   The Tucson sewage project: studies at two archaeological sites in the Tucson Basin. *Arizona State Museum Archaeological Series* **64**, Tucson.
Klein, T. H.
1979a   Research potential and problems of an urban archaeological survey: Alexandria, Virginia. Paper presented at the 12th annual conference of the Society for Historical Archaeology, Nashville.
1979b   Integrating research and preservation needs through an urban archaeological survey: Alexandria, Virginia. Paper presented at the 9th annual meeting of the Middle Atlantic Archaeology Conference, Rehoboth Beach, Delaware.
Klein, T. H., and S. L. Henry
1980   Results of an urban archaeological survey in Alexandria, Virginia. Paper presented at the 13th annual meeting of the Society for Historical Archaeology, Albuquerque.
Klein, T. H., P. J. Cressey, J. H. Stephens, S. Henry, and E. Coleman
1980   *Archaeological preservation plan of Alexandria, Virginia.* Virginia Research Center for Archaeology, Williamsburg.
Klinger, T. C., and M. L. Raab
1980   Archaeological significance and the National Register: a reponse to Barnes, Briggs and Neilsen. *American Antiquity* **45**:554–557.
Land Use Classification Committee
ca. 1960 *A proposal for a standardized land-use classification system.* Land Use Classification Committee, North Carolina Section, Southeast Chapter, American Institute of Planners.
Landberg, L. C. W.
1967   Problems of post-1800 urban sites archaeology at Old Sacramento, California. *Historical Archaeology* **1**:71–77.
Lipe, W. D.
1974   A conservation model for American archaeology. *The Kiva* **39**:213–245.

Loewenstein, L. K.
 1965 *The location of residences and work places in urban areas.* New York: The Scarecrow Press.
Lorber, C.
 1981 Digging up our urban past. *The New York Times Sunday Magazine,* April 12:54ff.
Los Angeles Department of Public Works
 ca. 1979 An archaeological assessment of cultural resources in urban L.A., Ms. on file, Los Angeles Department of Public Works.
Lynch, O. M.
 1980 Political mobilization and ethnicity among the Adi-Dravidas in a Bombay slum. In *Urban life,* edited by G. Gmelch and W. P. Zenner. New York: St. Martin's Press. Pp. 229–237.
Lynott, M. J.
 1980 The dynamics of significance: an example from central Texas. *American Antiquity* **45**:117–120.
McGimsey, C. R. III
 1972 *Public archaeology.* New York: Seminar Press.
McGimsey, C. R. III, and H. A. Davis (Editors)
 1977 *The management of archaeological resources: the Arlie House report.* Society for American Archaeology Special Publication, Washington, D.C.
McGuire, R. H.
 1979 Rancho Punta de Agua. *Arizona State Museum Contribution to Highway Salvage Archaeology in Arizona* 57, Tucson.
Manvel, A. D.
 1968 Land use in 106 large cities. *Three land research studies,* Research report 12. United States Government Printing Office, Washington, D.C.
Michelson, W.
 1970 *Man and his urban environment.* Reading, Massachusetts: Addison-Wesley.
Moratto, M. J.
 1975 On the concept of archaeological significance. Paper presented at the annual northern California meeting of the Society for California Archaeology, Fresno State University, Fresno.
Moratto, M. J., and R. E. Kelly
 1977 Significance in archaeology. *The Kiva* **42**:193–202.
 1978 Optimizing strategies for evaluating archaeological significance. In *Advances in archaeological method and theory* (Vol. 1), edited by M. B. Schiffer. New York: Academic Press. Pp. 1–31.
Morrell, B.
 1975 The evolution of the Rogers locomotive company, Paterson, New Jersey. *Northeast Historical Archaeology* **4**(1–2):17–23.
Morris, G.
 1975 Sampling in the excavation of urban sites: the case of Huanuco Pampa. In *Sampling in archaeology,* edited by J. W. Mueller. Tucson: University of Arizona Press. Pp. 192–208.
Mrozowski, S. Jr.
 1979 Privy pits and refuse disposal at Newport, Rhode Island. Paper presented at the 12th annual conference of the Society for Historical Archaeology, Nashville.

Mumford, L.
1938   *The culture of cities.* New York: Harcourt.
1961   *The city in history: its origins, its transformations and its prospects.* New York: Harcourt.
1963   *The highway and the city.* New York: Harcourt.
Newling, B. E.
1969   The spatial variation of urban population densities. *Geographical Review* **59**:242–252.
Niedercorn, J. H., and E. F. R. Hearle
1963   *Recent land use trends in forty-eight large American cities.* The Rand Corporation, Memorandum RM 3665, Santa Monica, California.
Northam, R. M.
1971   Vacant urban land in the American city. *Land Economics* **47**:4.
1979   *Urban geography.* New York: Wiley.
Olsen, J. W.
1978   A study of Chinese ceramics excavated in Tucson. *The Kiva* **44**:1–50.
Orr, D. G.
1977   Philadelphia as industrial archaeological artifact: a case study. *Historical Archaeology* **11**:3–14.
Palm, R.
1981   Urban geography: city structures. *Progress in Human Geography* **5**(1):79–86.
Park, R. E.
1916   The city: suggestions for the investigation of human behavior in the urban environment. *American Journal of Sociology* **20**:577–612.
Parker, M. T.
1940   *Lowell: a study of industrial development.* Port Washington, New York: Kennickat Press.
Pendrey, S.
1979   Strawberry Banke: community involvement in archaeological research. Paper presented at the 12th annual conference of the Society for Historical Archaeology, Nashville.
Perin, C.
1970   *With man in mind: an interdisciplinary prospectus for environmental design.* Cambridge, Mass.: MIT Press.
Pickard, J. P.
1962   Property taxation in the United States, 1957, per capita levels and regional variation. *Urban land institute research monograph* 6.
Porter, P. W.
1963   What is the point of minimum aggregate travel? *Annals of the Association of American Geographers* **53**:2.
Praetzellis, A., and M. Praetzellis
1980   The old west in a new light. *Early Man* **3**(2):13–16.
Praetzellis, M., A. Praetzellis, and M. R. Brown III (editors)
1980   *Historical archaeology at the Golden Eagle site.* Anthropological Studies Center, Sonoma State University, Rohnert Park, California.
Pred, E. A.
1964   The intrametropolitan location of American manufacturing. *Annals of the Association of American Geographers* **54**:2.
Prieto, A. C.
1981   Faubourg Treme and the Vieux Carré: a comparison of ceramic and faunal data from two 19th century New Orleans neighborhoods. Paper presented at

the 14th annual meeting of the Society for Historical Archaeology, New Orleans.

Quinn, J. A.
1940   The Burgess zonal hypothesis and its critics. *American Sociological Review* **5**: 210–218.

Raab, L. M., and T. C. Klinger
1977   A critical appraisal of "significance" in contract archaeology. *American Antiquity* **42**:629–634.
1979   A reply to Sharrock and Grayson on archaeological significance. *American Antiquity* **44**:328–329.

Raab, L. M., T. C. Klinger, M. B. Schiffer, and A. C. Goodyear
1980   Clients, contracts, and profits: conflict in public archaeology. *American Anthropologist* **82**:539–551.

Rathje, W. L.
1974   The garbage project: a new way to look at the problems of archaeology. *Archaeology* **27**(4):236–241.
1979   Modern material culture studies. In *Advances in archaeological method and theory* (Vol. 2), edited by M. G. Schiffer. New York: Academic Press. Pp. 1–37.

Rathje, W. L., and W. W. Hughes
1975   The garbage project as a non-reactive approach. In *Perspectives on attitude assessment: surveys and the alternatives, Technical Report 2,* edited by H. W. Sinaiko and L. A. Broedling. Washington, D.C.: Manpower Research and Advisory Services, Smithsonian Institution. Pp. 151–167.

Rathje, W. L., and M. McCarthy
1977   Regularity and variability in contemporary garbage. In *Research strategies in historical archaeology,* edited by S. South. New York: Academic Press. Pp. 261–286.

Rathje, W. L., and B. Thompson
1981   *The Milwaukee Garbage Project.* The Solid Waste Council of the Paper Industry, Tucson and Milwaukee.

Redman, C. L.
1973   Multi-stage fieldwork and analytical techniques. *American Antiquity* **38**:61–79.
1974   Archaeological sampling strategies. Reading, Massachusetts: Addison-Wesley.

Rhodeside, Deana
1970   *Play observations on six council estates.* Ministry of the Environment, London.

Robson, B. T.
1971   *Urban analysis: a study of city structure with special reference to Sunderland.* Cambridge: The University Press.

Rockman, D. D. Z.
1980   Excavations at the Stadt Huys block, New York City: an interim report. Paper presented at the annual meeting of the Council for Northeast Historical Archaeology, Albany.

Rodwin, L.
1961   *Housing and Economic Progress.* Cambridge, Massachusetts: Harvard University Press.

Rosebrock, E. F.
1981   The use of maps in urban archaeological research. Paper presented at the 10th

annual conference of the Society for Industrial Archaeology, Hartford, Connecticut.

Rutsch, E. S.
    1975   Salvage archaeology in Paterson, New Jersey, 1973–1975. *Northeast Historical Archaeology* **4**(1, 2).

Saile, D.
    1971   Activities and attitudes of public housing residents: Rockford, Illinois. University of Illinois, Department of Architecture, Urbana–Champaign.
    1972   Families in public housing: an evaluation of three residential environments in Rockford, Illinois. University of Illinois, Department of Architecture, Urbana–Champaign.

Salwen, B.
    1973   Archaeology in megalopolis. In *Research and theory in current archaeology,* edited by C. L. Redman. New York: Wiley. Pp. 151–168.
    1978   Archaeology in megalopolis: updated assessment. *Journal of Field Archaeology* **5**(4):453–459.
    1979   Some comments on 'urban' archaeology. In *The Society for Historical Archaeology Newsletter* **12**(1):14–16.

Salwen, B., and S. Bridges
    1974a   The ceramics from the Weeksville excavation, Brooklyn, New York. *Northeast Historical Archaeology* **3**:13.
    1974b   Note on 'The ceramics from the Weeksville excavations'. *Northeast Historical Archaeology* **3**:8.

Salwen, B., and B. Lockhart
    1975   Report on the second archaeological reconnaissance of the 15-inch Mohawk River interceptor sewer project, Schenectady, New York. Report submitted to the Schenectady County Planning Department, Schenectady, New York.

Salwen, B., S. Bridges, and J. Klein
    1974   An archaeological reconnaissance at the Pieter Classen Wyckoff House, Kings County, New York. *Bulletin of the New York Archaeological Association* **61**:26–38.

Salwen, B., S. T. Bridges, and N. A. Rothschild
    1981   The utility of small samples from historic sites: Onderdonk, Clinton Avenue and Van Campen. *Historical Archaeology* **5**(1):79–94.

Sande, T.
    1975   A new adventure. *Industrial Archaeology* **1**(1):v–vi.

Schaefer, J.
    1980   *Changing urban adaptations, a research design for historic archaeology in San Diego.* San Diego: Wirth Associates.

Schaefer, J., H. Cleland
    1980   *The archaeology of urbanization in San Diego.* San Diego: Wirth Associates.

Schermerhorn, R. A.
    1969   *Comparative ethnic relations: a framework for theory and research.* New York: Random.

Schiffer, M. B., and G. J. Gumerman (editors)
    1977   Assessing significance. In *Conservation archaeology: a guide for cultural resource management studies,* edited by M. B. Schiffer and G. J. Gumerman. New York: Academic Press. Pp. 239–247.

Schiffer, M. B., and J. H. House
    1977   An approach to assessing scientific significance. In *Conservation archaeology:*

a guide for cultural resource management studies, edited by M. B. Schiffer and G. J. Gumerman. New York: Academic Press. Pp. 249–257.

Schuyler, R. L.

1974a   Sandy Ground: archaeological sampling in a Black community in metropolitan New York. *The conference on historic site archaeology papers 1974.* 7(2):12–52.

1974b   Lowellian archaeology. *Newsletter* of the Society for Industrial Archaeology 7:3–4.

1976   Merrimack Valley project: 2nd year. *Newsletter* of the Society for Industrial Archaeology, supplementary issue **8**:7–8.

1977a   The spoken word, the written word, observed behavior and preserved behavior: the contexts available to the archaeologist. *The Conference on Historic Site Archaeology Papers 1977* **10**:99–120.

1977b   Archaeology of the New York metropolis. *Bulletin of the New York State Archaeological Association* **69**:1–19.

1980a   Sandy Ground: archaeology of a 19th century oystering village. In *Archaeological perspectives on ethnicity in America: Afro-American and Asian American culture history,* edited by R. L. Schuyler. Farmingdale, New York: Baywood. Pp. 48–59.

1980b   Preface. In *Archaeological perspectives on ethnicity in America: Afro-American and Asian American culture history,* edited by R. L. Schuyler. Farmingdale, New York: Baywood. Pp. vii–viii.

Schuyler, R. L., and C. Mills

1976   The supply mill on Content Brook in Massachusetts. *Journal of Field Archaeology* **3**(1):61–96.

Scott, T. T., M. McCarthy, and M. A. Grady

1978   Archaeological survey in Cherokee, Smith and Rusk Counties, Texas: a lesson in survey methods. *Archaeological Research Program, Research Report* 116. Southern Methodist University.

Scovill, D. H., G. J. Gordon, and K. M. Anderson

1977   Guidelines for the preparation of statements of environmental impact on archaeological resources. In *Conservation archaeology: a guide for cultural resource management studies,* edited by M. B. Schiffer and G. J. Gumerman. New York: Academic Press. Pp. 43–62.

Shack, W. A.

1973   Urban ethnicity and the cultural process of urbanization in Ethiopia. In *Urban anthropology: cross cultural studies of urbanization,* edited by A. Southall. London: Oxford University Press. Pp. 251–286.

Sharrock, F. W., and D. K. Grayson

1979   Significance in contract archaeology. *American Antiquity* **44**:327–328.

Shenkel, J. R., and J. Hudson

1971   Historic archaeology in New Orleans. *The conference on historic site archaeology papers 1971* **6**(1):40–44.

Shephard, S.

1975   The Geronimo Jose de Hita y Salazor site: a study of Criollo culture in colonial St. Augustine. Unpublished M.A. thesis, Department of Anthropology, Florida State University, St. Augustine.

Skinner, S. A., J. J. Richner, and M. R. Johnson

1978   *Dallas archaeological potential: procedures for locating and evaluating prehistoric resources.* Archaeology research program, Institute for the Study of Earth and Man, Southern Methodist University.

Soil Systems Inc.

1981   *Historical archaeological reconnaissance and assessment: Barry's Farm, Washington, D.C.* Wilmington, Delaware: Soil Systems, Inc.

Solecki, R. S.

1974   The 'Tijger' an early Dutch 17th century ship, and an abortive salvage attempt. *Journal of Field Archaeology* **1**(1–2):109–116.

South, S.

1977   *Method and theory in historical archaeology.* New York: Academic Press.

1979   Historic site content, structure and function. *American Antiquity* **44**:213–237.

South, S., and R. Widmer

1977   A subsurface sampling strategy for archaeological reconnaissance. In *Research Strategies in historical archaeology,* edited by S. South. New York: Academic Press. Pp. 119–150.

Sowell, C.

1981   Infill Dilemmas. *Arizona Daily Star,* March 19. Tucson.

Spicer, E. H.

1971   Persistent cultural systems. *Science* **174**:795–800.

1972   Plural society in the Southwest. In *Plural society in the Southwest,* edited by E. H. Spicer and R. H. Thompson. New York: Interbook. Pp. 21–64.

Staski, E.

1976   Italian immigration to New York City and its material representation. Ms. on file, Department of Anthropology, City College of New York, New York.

1980a   Guidelines for the urban archaeologist. Ms. on file, Arizona State Museum, Tucson.

1980b   The preservation of archaeological material in urban settings. Paper presented at the 13th annual meeting of the society for Historical Archaeology, Albuquerque.

Steinlieb, G., and J. W. Hughes

1980   The changing demography of the central city. *Scientific American* **243**(2):48–53.

Stone. L. M.

1981   *Archaeological test excavations, Blocks 1 and 2 of the original Phoenix townsite.* Archaeological research services, Tempe, Arizona.

United States Department of Transportation

1977   *Standard land use coding manual.* Washington, D.C.: U.S. Government Printing Office.

United States Government, Code of Federal Regulations

1976   National Register of Historic Places, 36 CFR 60.

Vogdes, E.

1974   A social–physical comparison of two dormitory complexes at Harvard–Radcliffe: Mather and Currier houses. In *Proceedings of the northeastern undergraduate conference on environment and behavior,* edited by J. W. Vogt. Amherst: University of Massachusetts Press.

Waldron, S. R.

1980   Within the wall and beyond: ethnic identity and ethnic persistence in Havar, Ethiopia. In *Urban life,* edited by G. Gmelch and W. P. Zenner, New York: St. Martin's Press. Pp. 249–256.

Wheat, L. F.

1969   The effect of modern highways on urban manufacturing growth. Paper presented at the 48th annual meeting of the Highway Research Board, Washington, D.C.

Wheatley, P.
1972   The concept of urbanism. In *Man, settlement and urbanism,* edited by P. J. Ucko, R. Tringham, and G. W. Dimbleby. London: Duckworth. Pp. 601–637.

Wilk, R., and M. B. Schiffer
1979   The archaeology of vacant lots in Tucson, Arizona. *American Antiquity* **44**:530–536.

Winter, F. A.
1981   Excavating New York: Brooklyn. *Archaeology* **34**(1):56–58.

Wise, C. L.
1976   Data and status in 18th century Delaware: an archaeologist's view. *Transactions of the Delaware Academy of Science,* 1974 and 1975, Newark.

Wise, C. L.
1978   Cultural patterning in 18th century Delaware: excavations at Delaware's State House. M.A. thesis on file, Catholic University of America, Washington, D.C.

1980   Wilmington Boulevard archaeological mitigation program: research questions, models and hypotheses. Ms. on file, Delaware Bureau of Archaeology and Historic Preservation.

Wise, C. L., J. Keller, and C. Johnson
1980   Wilmington Boulevard archaeological mitigation program: an interim report. Paper presented at the annual council for Northeast Historical Archaeology, Albany.

Wobst, M.
1977   Stylistic behavior and information exchange. In *Papers for the Director: research essays in honor of James B. Griffen,* edited by C. E. Cleland. Ann Arbor: Anthropological papers, Museum of Anthropology, University of Michigan 61. Pp. 317–342.

Zeisel, J.
1972   Social/physical research and design: applied pre-design programing and post construction evaluation in South Carolina. Paper presented at the 3rd annual Environmental Design Research Association Conference.

1975   *Sociology and architectural design.* Russell Sage Foundation, Social Science Frontiers, New York.

Zeisel, J., and M. Griffen (editors)
1974   *Charlesview housing: a diagnostic evaluation.* Harvard Graduate School of Design, Architecture Research Office, Cambridge, Massachusetts.

Avenues of Inquiry
in Historical Archaeology

KATHLEEN DEAGAN

INTRODUCTION

Historical archaeology is not a new subfield of archaeology, although its
emergence as a legitimate subfield in the consciousnesses of most American
archaeologists is relatively recent. Much of the earliest archaeology conducted in Europe was historical archaeology because it was concerned with
civilizations documented in some form by written records. The origins of archaeology in the fifteenth century resulted in a tradition emphasizing the clas-
sical sites of Greece, Rome, and the Bible lands (Braidwood 1960:6–8; Daniel
1967:15; Rowe 1965) using both documents and objects as research tools.
Other branches of archaeology have, of course, developed in Europe since
then, emphasizing the study of both prehistory and history from a
developmental, cultural–historical orientation.

In North America as well, some of the earliest archaeological research concerned historic-period sites, such as the excavation of an historic-period
Algonquian grave in 1622 by the settlers at Plymouth (Schuyler 1976:27;
Young 1841). Applied historical archaeological methods in a quite modern
sense were used in 1797 to settle a political dispute between Britain and the
newly established United States. The dispute concerned the course of the St.
Croix River as mapped by Champlain, which established the boundary
separating American from British territory after the Revolutionary War. To
help solve this problem, a survey and test excavation were undertaken to find

ADVANCES IN ARCHAEOLOGICAL METHOD AND THEORY, VOL. 5
Copyright © 1982 by Academic Press, Inc.
All rights of reproduction in any form reserved.
ISBN 0-12-003105-1

the French settlement of St. Croix, which was recorded by Champlain but later abandoned. The remains of structures and artifacts were located and helped to solve the dispute over the boundary (Schuyler 1976:27–28).

Despite these examples of early historical archaeology in North America, the field has not had a continuous and active role since that time. Not until the mid-1960s did historical archaeology gain formal status, and even then, there was considerable confusion as to what historical archaeology actually was, did, or even ought to do. This resulted in the "crisis of identity" discussed in the following, which has remained with us to some extent.

This crisis of identity was reflected in the lack of agreement among historical archaeologists upon the proper name and proper definition of the field. These discussions resulted in the assignment of labels, with varying degrees of restrictiveness, to the potential subject matter of the field (Schuyler 1970). *Historical archaeology* has emerged as the most generally used term today, largely on the premise that the closest, and somewhat more cumbersome competitor, *historic sites archaeology,* implies that the field concentrates on sites of historical significance, as opposed to cultural significance.

A number of definitions of the field can be found, which more or less emphasize the presence of a documentary record as the distinguishing feature of historical archaeology. Examples include "the study of material remains from any historic period" (Schuyler 1970:119) and "the archaeology of the spread of European cultures throughout the world since the fifteenth century, and its impact on the indigenous people" (Deetz 1977a:5). Noël Hume defines archaeology as "the study of material remains from both the remote and recent past in relationship to documentary history and the stratigraphy of the ground in which they are found" (1969:12); whereas according to Stanley South, "those studies using both archaeological and historical data have come to be called historical archaeology" (1977:1).

None of these definitions have been entirely satisfactory to all historical archaeologists for various reasons of emphasis and subject-matter restriction. Schuyler's definition, for example, is perhaps too elegant, implying to the unwary that material remains themselves are the focus of historical archaeology, rather than the cultural systems that produced them. Likewise, South's statement could also describe several contemporary historical studies that use both historical and archaeological data (Hall 1981; Manucy 1978). Since the time when Deetz's definition was offered, several emphases in historical archaeology have emerged that would be difficult to encompass within that definition, such as the study of Black-American culture, Asian-American culture, and the Victorian period. Noël Hume's suggestion, aside from its puzzling construction, implies a stronger emphasis on documentary history as the focus of organization than many contemporary historical archaeologists are comfortable with.

All of these definitions, however, include reference to the use of both archaeological and historical data in research, and are thus in agreement that the time period covered by this discipline begins after 1492 for North America. The subject matter suggested includes material remains and past behavior. Thus, most historical archaeologists would probably agree that the field includes the study of human behavior through material remains, for which written history in some way affects its interpretation.

In only two decades, historical archaeology has made a rapid theoretical progression from descriptive and chronological concerns, through cultural-historical studies, to problems of culture process, cognition, and archaeological principles. The process has been in a sense additive in that the earlier goals continue to be addressed by historical archaeologists even as they pursue more contemporary problems and issues. Historical archaeology is today a complex discipline that incorporates principles from, and makes contributions to, a number of other disciplines both within and outside anthropology.

Because of its unique command of all the contexts of human behavior (Schuyler's "spoken word, written word, preserved behavior, and observed behavior" [1977]) (see also Brown 1974), historical archaeology has been able to make contributions that would not be possible through any other avenue of inquiry. Documented information about past social, temporal, and economic variables allows investigation of the cultural processes that affect those variables, and which are in turn affected by them. Furthermore, the simultaneous access by historical archaeologists to both emic statements (documents) and etic statements (archaeological data) about conditions in the past allows the study of behavioral processes involved in human perception, and the manipulation and means of coping with the environment.

It is partly due to these same circumstances, however, that historical archaeology today is in a difficult position. Most contemporary historical archaeologists are trying to establish the field as a subdiscipline of anthropology, both because of its unique potentials for understanding human behavior and because most American archaeologists are trained in anthropology departments. At the same time, however, the field is closely associated with other, nonanthropological disciplines that frequently can recover information relevant to their concerns only through historical archaeology. This is particularly true of such fields as applied history and architecture. Because historical archaeology, unlike prehistoric archaeology, shares its subject matter with other disciplines that ask very different kinds of questions about the same subject matter, the process of self-definition has been somewhat more complex.

The complexities involved in the recognition and understanding of historical archaeology as a field of scholarship were underscored also by the relationships between prehistoric and historical archaeologists during the

early development of these fields. Although by the 1960s most historical archaeologists had been trained in the same departments as prehistoric archaeologists, there remained a certain ambivalence toward historic-period sites in
American archaeology. Part of this was the bias in anthropological archaeology toward non-Western cultures as the proper focus of research (cf. Fontana
1965). This bias was due, at least in part, to the relatively abrupt and intrusive
appearance of literate societies in the culture history of North America, providing a natural historical division of subject matter. The directions of
American anthropology tended to support this division in that from the
nineteenth-century origins of the field through the middle of the twentieth
century, the major emphases in American anthropology were Native
American studies and the development of cultural–historical syntheses
(Willey and Sabloff 1974:Chs. 3 and 4). The ambivalent attitude toward
Euro-American sites as a legitimate emphasis has, however, been reduced and
perhaps resolved since the earliest decades of twentieth-century historical archaeology. This has been largely due to the American Bicentennial effort,
which not only made colonial America a popular and timely subject, but provided funds for historical archaeology on a major scale.

The strict separation of *history* from *prehistory* is in contrast to the attitudes of many archaeologists trained in Europe (cf. Noël Hume 1969). Probably due in part to the more gradual and variable spread of literacy in the Old
World, many European archaeologists do not use a specific point in time, or
even the presence of documents, to differentiate between history and prehistory. Christopher Hawkes, for example, suggested in 1951 that "prehistory, from the neolithic colonization of Europe onward, is classified according to the degree (as we ascend the scale) in which our knowledge of it
stands indebted to historic materials" (Hawkes 1951:1). Grahame Clark,
commenting on Hawke's discussion, offered a classification of prehistory
and history, which included *autonomous prehistory* (data for which no written references exist), *secondary prehistory* (nonliterate cultures that need to
be studied in reference to contemporary civilization), and *history* (civilization) (Clark 1954:7–9).

Among archaeologists in the United States during the early decades of this
century, there was little doubt that autonomous prehistory was the domain of
prehistoric archaeologists, and that history was the domain of historical archaeologists. Secondary prehistory was somewhat less well defined, and was
studied by both prehistoric and historical archaeologists.

The following discussion assesses the development of historical archaeology and the effects of this development on the work historical archaeologists
are doing today. It also identifies and evaluates the several approaches to
historical archaeology that are currently being taken, and that are contributing to a range of scholarly concerns.

DEVELOPMENT AND EMERGENCE OF HISTORICAL ARCHAEOLOGY IN AMERICA

Isolated examples of historical archaeology can be found throughout the nineteenth century. Such work as that of James Hill in 1856 at Miles Standish's home (Deetz 1977a:29–30) is characteristic of that early period in that the site was the home of an important historical figure, and Hall himself was a civil engineer rather than an archaeologist.

Near the end of the nineteenth century, investigations were undertaken by the New York Historical Society to recover information about military camp life and objects from the Revolutionary War and the War of 1812. Excavations were carried out in what are now the Washington Heights and Kingsbridge districts of the Bronx by officers of the Society, who carefully recorded and reported their finds (Calver and Bolton 1950).

Emphasis on historically important sites and the involvement of nonarchaeologists in the excavation of these also characterized studies in the early twentieth century. The development of a national program of Historic Preservation in the early decades of the twentieth century resulted in the entrenchment of historical archaeology as a recognized field of endeavor in this country. During the 1930s, particularly, programs aimed at relieving the effects of the Great Depression resulted in the first serious and large-scale investigations of historic-period sites (Harrington 1952). These covered a wide range of subjects, including British colonies such as Fort Frederica (Fairbanks 1956), Spanish missions (Montgomery 1949; Smith 1948), nineteenth-century forts (Smith 1939), and trading posts (Kelley 1939; Lombard 1953). These projects were particularly notable because of the serious emphasis on Euro-American sites for the first time in American archaeology.

Nearly all of these studies, however, were oriented toward recovering specific details useful for architectural reconstruction and the interpretation of what happened at the site. "The aim of the excavating was much the same as the Jamestown project, namely to rescue data that would permit the best possible interpretation of the site to the visitor" (Harrington 1952:342). Occasionally, such studies also solved problems of documentary ambiguity or the absence of information needed for reconstruction, such as Fairbanks's location of the Frederica town lot plan by locating the common wall between a duplex structure, thus pinning down the physical location of a known lot line (Fairbanks 1956).

While these projects brought recognition to historical archaeology as a field of research, their primary orientation toward questions of historical reconstruction rather than anthropological questions laid the groundwork for later conflict in the field. During the early decades of historical archaeology's development, prehistoric archaeology in North America was emerging in solid alignment with anthropology (Willey and Sabloff 1974:Ch. 2). Most American archaeologists were trained in departments of anthropology; however, it was not until the decades of the 1930s and 1940s that such anthropologically trained archaeologists became involved on a serious scale in the archaeology of historic-period sites. They have not, however, always dominated the field, and even today there are nonanthropologically trained archaeologists doing historical archaeology in America (Nöel Hume 1969; Webster 1974).

The first formal recognition in this country of historical archaeology as a discipline came in 1960, with the establishment of the Conference on Historic Sites Archaeology and the publication of its proceedings. This was followed in 1965 by the formation of the Society for Historical Archaeology and the publication of its journal, *Historical Archaeology*. Both of these organizations and publications remain the primary foci of professional activity in historical archaeology.

One of the first issues to be addressed in the early stages of the formalized discipline was the apparent "crisis of identity" (Cleland and Fitting 1968). This crisis revolved around the definition of what historical archaeology actually was, what its parent discipline was, and what its proper orientation should be.

The opposing points of view in the identity crisis were grounded in the question of whether history or anthropology was the parent discipline of the field, and by extension, whether historical archaeology was historical and particularizing in scope or anthropological and generalizing in scope. Anthropologically trained historical archaeologists, such as Cleland and Fitting (1968) and Griffin (1958), pointed out that there was little difference between the methods of observation, recovery, control, and analysis used by prehistoric and historic archaeologists. Most importantly, they pointed out that both areas of archaeology could (and should) ultimately address questions of human cultural adaptation and evolution. In this sense, historical archaeology shared the same guiding processual questions as cultural anthropology and anthropological prehistoric archaeology.

Another point of view was offered by several archaeologists (not all of whom were trained in departments of anthropology) and historians involved in historical archaeology. Dollar (1968), Harrington (1952, 1955), Noël Hume (1964), and Walker (1967) have suggested that the nature and extent of documentary information on historic sites render the analytical methods used by prehistoric archaeology inappropriate for historical archaeology (see particularly Dollar 1968). It was also suggested that due to the short time periods frequently characteristic of historical sites, some of the basic tools of archaeology—stratigraphy and seriation—are not as useful on these sites as on prehistoric ones (Harrington 1952:342). The basic point of view of the historically oriented researchers in this debate was that the best questions and most reliable answers in historical archaeological research were those organized around the need to "fill in the gaps" in history. This need included providing details of architecture and material culture that were not available in documents, such as Harrington's work at Fort Necessity (1957), as well as bringing to light the details of nonelite life so essential to the interpretation of the past.

The debate over the proper orientation of historical archaeology has not altogether been resolved, although most historical archaeologists today appear to claim an anthropological orientation (Deagan 1979:369). The needs of historians, however, and the goals of historically oriented archaeologists cannot be ignored, particularly since historical archaeology is often the only way to satisfy such needs and goals. The issue today resulting from the "crisis-of-identity" debates that marked the formal emergence of historical archaeology is to learn how to integrate the needs of both anthropology and history, rather than determining which of the two will emerge as a winner.

There are several practical and developmental reasons why this should be so. Cleland and Fitting (1968), Schuyler (1979:201), South (1977:5-13), and others have discussed the basic divisions of scholarship and the relationship of historical archaeology to them. They have identified these divisions as scientific (generalizing), historical (particularizing), and humanistic (aesthetic). If historical archaeology is a scientific discipline, it should be concerned with developing general principles that can explain regularities and variability in human culture and behavior. If it is essentially an historical discipline, it should be concerned with studying and illuminating the attributes, events, and processes of a particular time, place, and society; however, this does not preclude the use of scientific methods in the approach to these concerns. Finally, if historical archaeology is a humanistic discipline, it should impart an aesthetic appreciation of and an empathy with the human conditions of the past.

During the first decades of historical archaeological research in this country, one could confidently place historical archaeology in the historical category. Since the 1960s however, the placement has become somewhat confused, both because of the work done by historical archaeologists, and because of the fact that the same kind of confusion existed in the field of archaeology in general.

Prehistoric archaeology underwent a "crisis of identity" of sorts at about the same time as historical archaeology did; the main issue being whether culture history (particularizing) or culture process (generalizing) was the proper focus of archaeology (cf. Binford 1962; Deetz 1970; Willey and Sabloff 1974:Chs. 5 and 6). Attempting to share the goals and orientations of prehistoric archaeologists trained in anthropology departments did not help the newly emergent field of historical archaeology to resolve its basic crisis of identity. Anthropologists and archaeologists alike were studying and describing particular cultures at particular times and places, and in that sense, what anthropology was doing in 1960 was often little different from social history. This tended to confuse futher the determination of whether historical archaeology was historical or anthropological in origin, because in practice, it was frequently difficult to precisely distinguish between the two.

One result of these circumstances and developments is that historical archaeology today encompasses several different orientations. Not only have the "handmaiden-to-history," "reconstruction-of-past-lifeways," and "culture-process" concerns been retained both in stated intent and in practice, but certain newer emphases, unique to historical archaeology, have been added in recent years. These include the investigation of the relationships between patterned human behavior and patterned archaeological remains (cf. Deetz 1977b; Schiffer 1976, 1977; South 1977) and the testing of traditional archaeological principles developed to account for those relationships (cf. South 1977).

Some historical archaeologists have turned to questions that depend on the unique access of the field to both written and material by-products of behavior (Brown 1974; Schuyler 1977). These questions concern human perceptual systems and the role of patterned cognition in shaping the material world (see Deetz 1974, 1977a; Glassie 1969, 1975). This marks an unusual departure from the traditionally materialist explanatory framework of archaeology.

These new avenues of inquiry, as well as the research being conducted from the earlier orientations, are considered in the following sections. The emphases and accomplishments of this research and the mutual compatability of these various approaches within the field as a whole are also discussed.

HISTORICAL SUPPLEMENTATION

Historical archaeology as a "handmaiden to history" (Noël Hume 1964), that is, as a provider of supplementation for the historical record of the past, is most visible today in those projects carried out in support of historic reconstruction and restoration.

The large-scale retention of the historical supplementation goals in the field has also been influenced by the rapid expansion of cultural resource management needs during the 1970s. Historical archaeology conducted in support of architectural and historical reconstruction shares many of the potential contract-related problems faced by prehistoric archaeologists in that artificial restrictions are often placed on the scope of research because of the terms of a contract. Many historical archaeologists working on contracts, however, are doing research in conjunction with historians and architects in order to provide information on which to base the reconstruction interpretation of a site, which is frequently not endangered by anything other than the reconstruction activities. Unlike prehistoric archaeological contract work, the data recovered by the historical archaeologists under contract very often is crucially important to the successful completion of the project that provoked the issuance of the contract in the first place. Instead of (and occasionally in addition to) the narrow geographic restrictions often placed on prehistoric archaeological contracts, historical archaeologists are restricted in the questions they can ask: When was the east wing added? What was the evolution of the floor plan? There are hundreds of single-instance projects throughout the country that contractually restrict the historical archaeologist to supplemental data gathering, and historical archaeology to a service industry (Swannack 1975). It is difficult to gauge the full extent of such work because it is usually not published or presented at professional meetings. One suspects that if it were all gathered in one place, the major contribution of these projects would not even be to history, but rather to historical architecture. The many problems resulting from these circumstances in historic archaeology as well as in prehistoric archaeology can only be resolved through the ethical orientation of the archaeologists, who, as Schiffer and Gumerman (1977:16) and South (1977:294) have pointed out, must be willing to insist on the integration in the project design of problem-related goals with reconstruction needs.

That such integration is indeed possible has been demonstrated at a number of sites in the 1970s. Such contributions as Deetz's La Purisima study discussed previously, Lewis's study of frontier patterning (1977), House's documentation of squatters in the Ozarks (1977), Fergusons's work on the interpretation of artifact distributions at Fort Watson (1977b), Otto's status-variability study on St. Simon's Island (1975), Honerkamp's study of frontier adaptations at Frederica, Georgia (1980), and the community-patterning and acculturation studies at St. Augustine (Deagan 1978) have all been carried out within a cultural resource management framework.

This integration is perhaps most evident at major centers for public interpretation, such as Plimouth Plantation, St. Augustine, St. Mary's City, and Ft. Michilimackinac. At these centers, archaeology is generally supported specifically to recover data necessary for the reconstruction and interpretation of the sites. Because these sites represent communities, however, and because they have both long-term research and development plans and long-term commitments by academic institutions, it has been possible to integrate historical and anthropological studies into the framework of resource management (see also Stephenson 1977).

That there have also been positive contributions through a primarily historical orientation in historical archaeology cannot be denied. Archaeology has probably reached more nonarchaeologists through programs of public interpretation than through any other means, combating the field's potential for an "Ivory Tower" image. There is also certain historical information which simply cannot be retrieved through any means other than archaeology. This information can often enhance or even change traditional interpretations of social history. Such changes can include physical plans or constructions at a site, such as Harrington's at Ft. Necessity and Ferguson's discovery through archaeological data of the tactics involved in the battle at Ft. Watson (1977b:69). In St. Augustine, archaeological remains have indicated the extent to which colonists, despite claims to the contrary, indulged in illegal trade with the British colonies (Deagan 1978), and the foodways of the Spanish colonists in Florida (Reitz 1979). South (1977) has determined archaeologically that British colonists in the South disposed of their trash in a predictably patterned manner, a fact that could be of importance in the reconstruction of British colonial sites. The growth and expansion of settlement patterns in historic communities are also frequently documented only through archaeology (Deetz 1968; Fairbanks 1956). Another example of the illumination of historical interpretation through archaeology is found on slave sites, where documentary indications that firearms were prohibited and that food was cooked communally have been refuted archaeologically (Fairbanks 1972). The approach to historical issues through archaeological research can result in a more objective standard of measurement, as opposed to the frequently subjective standard of written history. This cannot be denied as one facet of modern historical archaeology.

RECONSTRUCTION OF PAST LIFEWAYS

Another orientation from which research is currently being conducted in historical archaeology addresses the reconstruction of a past society and conditions of the past. Although this orientation is certainly in keeping with anthropological tradition and practice, it is essentially similar to social history and to ethnography in that the focus of research is most often, although not always exclusively, on a particular time, place, and society. This is in contrast to the "processual" orientation, which has a primary research focus on general principles of behavior of culture process.

The emphasis on reconstruction of past lifeways in historical archaeology was paralleled by the methodological shift toward "backyard archaeology" proposed by Fairbanks in 1971 (Fairbanks 1977). This method de-emphasized historic structures and foundations, and the "Barnum and Bailey" syndrome (Noël Hume 1969:10) of concentration on the "oldest" or "largest" or "most historically significant'' site. Instead, emphasis was to be placed on the by-products of all aspects of behavior in the past, which were found most frequently in those locations where the behavior took place, namely the backyard.

One of the most visible and significant results of this emphasis on specific societies in historical archaeology has been the documentation of historically disenfranchised groups in our own culture, providing alternative images of national identity from those provided by written history (Schuyler 1976). The study of the roots of Black American culture—the written history of which has most often been incomplete and distorted—is a particularly evident example of this. Work done by Fairbanks in 1968 at the Kingsley Plantation slave cabins in Florida (Fairbanks 1972) was one of the first archaeological studies of American slavery from a nondocumentary point of view, and has been followed by numerous studies concentrating on Black American culture both in freedom and slavery (Deetz 1977a; Handler and Lange 1978; Otto 1979; Schuyler 1980; Singleton 1980; among others). Other undocumented, disenfranchised groups have also been the focus of historical archaeology, including Asian-Americans (Schuyler 1980); Native Americans of the historic period (Goodyear 1977; Kirkpatrick *et al.* 1980); Hispanic-American Creoles (Shephard 1975); and groups disenfranchised by poverty or disreputability such as mountaineers (House 1977; Price and Price 1978), hobos (Klein 1977), and miners (Deetz 1981).

With a few exceptions, such as the Hispanic-American sites in the southern and western United States, and some slave sites, such as those at Kingsley Plantation, Florida, most of the research on these groups has not been applied in the intensive public interpretation programs that characterize Anglo-American sites. These studies of disenfranchied groups are, however, being gradually included in the popular media (for example, *Odyssey,* a television series that communicates the contributions of anthropology to the general public) and in the research of other disciplines (Hall 1980 for example).

Such studies are quite often closely interrelated with processual concerns. Cross-cultural comparisons, for example, can reveal striking parallels and differences in the ways by which various groups adapted to relocation in a new environment and the mechanisms by which different groups became integrated into or excluded from American society. Archaeology has demonstrated, for example, that Spaniards in North America physically integrated themselves with the indigenous inhabitants of the New World, while British colonists resisted such integration. This resulted in a very different kind of adaptive pattern between the two groups (Deagan 1980).

Such ethnographically oriented studies have also occasionally resulted in a new perspective on historical and social processes traditionally cherished in those fields. ''The melting pot'' concept of the formation of America's national identity, for example, has recently been cast into doubt as an explanatory model. Deetz (1977b) and Schuyler (1976) have both suggested that the formation of American society was instead a process of systematic exclusion of non-Anglo groups from the mainstream of Anglo-American life, much in the same way that such exclusion is evident today. Research at the non-Anglo site of St. Augustine, however, has somewhat ironically indicated that the melting pot concept did indeed describe the process of formation for Hispanic-American society in the New World (Deagan 1980).

PROCESSUAL STUDIES

A third orientation in contemporary historical archaeology can be seen in those studies with a primary focus on the investigation of a cultural process, rather than on the investigation of a specific social group or set of events. The development of this orientation parallels the same development in American archaeology in general (Willey and Sabloff 1974:Ch. 6).

Processual studies in historical archaeology have most often concentrated on cultural processes operating at specific times and places, and are thus, strictly speaking, particularizing in result. They provide, however, the building blocks on which more general processual questions about human culture may be investigated. Most often, the studies have been approached through a hypothetico-deductive method of investigation.

The great advantage of historical archaeology in this research effort is the presence of the documentary record. In many cases, such social variables as ethnic affiliation, income, religious affiliation, occupation, family composition, economic network, and political restrictions of the social unit are known. Thus, it is frequently possible to investigate the specific mechanics of specific processes in a given unit, rather than simply identifying the presence of a certain phenomenon that might help interpret an archaeological pattern.

The use of documents as controls in this manner is, of course, subject to a considerably cautious assessment of their veracity and validity. Problems related to the nature of documentary evidence, and methods to cope with them have been concerns of archaeologists and historians alike (Barzun and Graff 1970).

One processual area to which historical archaeology has made particularly significant contributions is that of understanding acculturation. Many studies have been oriented, at least in part, toward the elucidation of this process due to the obvious advantage of having European–Native American contact sites available. Studies have concentrated on acculturation through trading relations (Brown 1978; Deetz 1965; Fairbanks 1962; Irwin-Mason 1963), religious conversion, (Cheek 1974; Deetz 1963; Loucks 1979) and racial intermarriage (Deagan 1974).

These studies have suggested that the sex of the people who provide the links between the two cultures in contact is a critical factor in determining the end results of acculturation. Among the eighteenth-century Creek Indians, for example, the primary link with Europeans was through the deerskin trade. In this trade, European men came into contact with the Creek men, and archaeological evidence indicates that it was the male activities among the eighteenth-century Creeks that showed evidence of European acculturation and alteration (Fairbanks 1962; Irwin-Mason 1963). Female-related activities, such as food production, pottery, and basketry, were little altered, and it has been suggested that the lag between technological change in male and female areas of eighteenth-century Creek culture was a causal factor in the personal stress leading to the Prophet's revitalization movement among the Creeks (Fairbanks 1962:53).

At the Spanish La Purisima mission, Deetz also found that male activity areas were subject to more intensive and rapid alteration through European influence than were women's activities (1963). This was also the case at the Florida missions (Loucks 1979). At these missions, however, both men and women were in direct contact with the male European friars.

These studies imply that because the Europeans who came into contact with Native American cultures were nearly always males, little innovative technology relating directly to female activities would result from European contact. In the Native-American cultures, therefore, technological innovation took place in male activity areas through trade and occasionally through gift-giving. In the Euro-American cultures, little alteration occurred through contact with Native Americans in male activity areas, but in those activity areas traditionally associated with women, the Europeans frequently incorporated the technologies of Native American women. This was particularly evident in situations involving concubinage or intermarriage (Deagan 1974).

Historical archaeology is also in a strong position with regard to revealing the impact of European technological innovation upon Native-American social systems. Social change in Native-American groups resulting from European interaction has been shown to be more closely linked to alteration of economic patterns than to either religious conversion or intermarriage. The example of the Arikara, cited previously, revealed a shift in kinship structure in response to a change from a farming economy to an economy based on middleman trade (Deetz 1965). Among the Algonquians, the implementation of the fur trade resulted in both a shift from small lineage-based villages to larger clan-based settlements; and a more pronounced structure of social differentiation, based in large part on differential access to European goods (Mainfort 1979).

Several other historical archaeological studies have investigated processes related to colonization and the establishment of Euro-American society. Lewis's work with the process of expansion by an established society into a wilderness has indicated that the frontier model developed by social scientists over the years (Lewis 1977:153–156) is an appropriate framework through which to understand the mechanisms and results of colonization. The frontier model and other studies based on it (for example, Honerkamp's application of the model at Frederica, Georgia [1980]) have not only illuminated the mechanics of adaptation by early New World colonists but also provided a model for the interpretation of early American history.

Certain other processual issues have also been noted as particularly appropriate foci for historical archaeology; however, little work has been directly oriented toward these. One of these processes is that of imperialism (Schuyler 1976). The circumstances under which imperialist expansion does or does not succeed, and the ultimate results of such expansion are relevant issues throughout much of the world. Such results can be objectively studied and assessed through historical archaeology. Another little-studied area in historical archaeology is that of the Marxian-derived dialectical relationships by which contemporary society is economically and socially organized, that is, production, distribution, and exchange mechanisms (Leone 1977b). Through historical archaeology's potential control through documents over the economic variables of past societies, the specific mechanisms of this dialectic could be predicted and tested in the archaeological record. Leone points out that historical archaeology's particular potential for explicating this dynamic process in the past can directly explicate the same processes as they operate in our own society.

ARCHAEOLOGICAL SCIENCE

One of the most uniquely productive and important aspects of historical archaeology is its ability to test principles of archaeological interpretation under controlled conditions. Although this is not a recent application in the field (for example, Deetz 1965:1), it has only been in recent years that studies concentrating on testing and verifying relationships between patterning in the material and behavioral spheres have become explicit (Ferguson 1977a; South 1977).

Historical archaeology studies oriented toward this end have been able to demonstrate that the associations between archaeological data and past behavior are indeed patterned and predictable in specific ways. Such studies focus on the development, testing, and verification of interpretive principles necessary for the scientific investigation of specific processes and events. Historical archaeology has been applied to the testing of a number of methods and assumptions commonly used in archaeological analysis and interpretation. One of the most prominent of these applications has been in testing the well-known assumption of a normal frequency distribution for stylistic traits through time (Flannery 1973; Kroeber 1919), or the *battleship curve of popularity*. In combination with the principles of stratigraphy and seriation, this assumption is basic to the description and interpretation of events in culture history. At least two historical archaeological studies using well-dated materials—gravestones (Deetz and Dethlefson 1967) and historic ceramics (South 1972)—have demonstrated that the battleship curve of popularity is a true description of a real and predictable diachronic phenomenon in the material world. It is a phenomenon that exists regardless of spatial and temporal location, and thus may constitute one of the very few general laws derived solely through archaeology. The most explicit proponent of this approach in contemporary historical archaeology has been South (1977). South has demonstrated that specific cultural phenomena are recognizably patterned and can be predicted in the archaeological record. Intersite function and intrasite activities, for example, are revealed through a statistical analysis pattern in South's discussion of the Carolina and frontier patterns (1977).

In his discussion of the Brunswick pattern of refuse disposal—a horizontal distributional pattern of artifacts associated with British colonists—South lays the groundwork for, and comes tantalizingly close to, explicating a basic postulate for archaeological interpretation; that is, the way in which refuse is disposed of is distinctly and recognizably patterned for specific groups of different ethnic background or cultural heritage. Such a postulate, if demonstrated and verified, could have considerable value in the interpretation of ethnic differentiation in the archaeological record, including that of prehistoric sites. Additional archaeological evidence related to this issue, such as Carillo's (1977) investigation of the German-American pattern, provides increasing support that the link between cultural heritage and patterned refuse disposal is indeed a valid observation.

Many historical archaeological studies have attempted to demonstrate the ways in which certain sociocultural variables are manifested in the archaeological record, using documentation about the nature of these variables as controls. One of the most frequently studied phenomena is the way in which variability in social status is reflected archaeologically. Otto's work at a Georgia plantation site (1975, 1977) indicated that ceramic type and form provided a reliable reflection of the status differences known to have been present in that society among planters, overseers, and slaves. Because of different dietary patterns among the groups, different ceramic forms related to type were used by each group despite the fact that the same basic ceramic assemblage was shared by all of the groups.

Similar results were obtained by Poe (1979) in Spanish Florida, where it was found that economic variability, as measured by income and occupation, was predictably linked to specific proportions of Hispanic, aboriginal, and other

European wares within the ceramic assemblage of each household. In this case, the patterns were believed to have been a function of differential access to scarce Hispanic goods.

Several historical archaeological studies have also tested the strength with which dietary remains reflect certain social subsystems. Work such as Cumbaa's (1975), Mudar's (1978), and Reitz's (1979) have shown that there is a predictable relationship between the specific components and proportions in a given faunal assemblage, and the function of the site from which it came, the ethnic affiliation of the site's inhabitants, and the economic status of the inhabitants.

Historic-period burial populations have also been tested through comparison with documentation to reveal their facility in reflecting certain social phenomena. Analysis of seventeenth- and eighteenth-century St. Augustine burial data has revealed that specific and sharply distinct mortuary patterns are associated with British-Protestant and Spanish-Catholic burials (Koch 1980), and Algonquian burial populations have been shown to reflect social changes, particularly status differentiation, brought about through the introduction of the European fur trade (Mainfort 1979).

In the pursuit of scientific principles that can help explain the relationship between behavioral variability and the archaeological record, historical archaeologists have turned to the study of contemporary groups. Such ethnoarchaeological studies in historical archaeology can simultaneously make use of material remains, oral accounts, documentation, and ethnographic observation. This has emerged in historical archaeology through the increasing awareness that the spoken word and observed behavior constitute categories of data equivalent to that of documents in the implementation of the many goals of the field (Brown 1974; Deetz 1977a,b, Schuyler 1977).

One of the best-known studies of this type is the Tucson garbage project (Rathje 1977; Rathje and McCarthy 1977). Using a combination of interviews and analyses of household garbage in Tucson, Rathje was able to directly observe and record the processes of discard in specific households over time. These households were sampled to reflect ethnic and economic differences within the community. Results of the study provided an indication of the ways in which economic stress was reflected in consumption patterns. In the case of Tucson, economic stress was accompanied by increased waste due to unfamiliarity with new and cheaper resources, and also by increased alcohol consumption. The project also suggested that while social variability was indeed visible after the formation of the archaeological record, the specific relationships between sociocultural variables, such as income or family size, and material patterns are not immutable, and are interrelated in ways that are not always recognizable in contemporary archaeological studies (Rathje and McCarthy 1977:284).

The observation of contemporary social and archaeological processes has considerably expanded the scope and potential of historical archaeology during the past decade. Not only can this allow cross-checking and verifications of principles developed through observation of the archaeological and written records (and vice versa), but it is the basis for the unique potential of historical archaeology toward understanding the relationships between material patterning, human behavior, and human perception.

The inclusion of contemporary societies in the focus of historical archaeology is related to a relatively recent conceptual self-image in the field, that of historical archaeology as the "science of material culture" (Deetz 1977b). This term describes archaeology essentially as the study of relationships between human beings and material things. One rather early statement of this point was provided by James Deetz in 1968 when he suggested that "archaeology must concern itself with material culture, regardless of its provenience, be it archaeological in the excavated sense or ethnographic in terms of present use" (1968:129).

An expanded statement of this point of view is found in Deetz's paper as well as in many of the other papers included in Ferguson (1977a). In these papers, material culture was treated as that segment of our physical environment that we modify through culturally determined behavior. While this expansion of the subject matter of the field has not received universal acclaim in the discipline, it has greatly expanded its scope, and created the potential for discovering enduring principles of behavioral–material relationships in human culture. As the garbage project has demonstrated, and as Leone (1977b) and Schuyler (1976) have pointed out, historical archaeology contributions are not restricted to our understanding of the past, but can help us to understand ourselves today, and possibly even predict our future behavior with regard to material things. This is not an insignificant potential when one considers the problems facing us from misuse or overconsumption of material resources.

Another important avenue toward archaeological science is also a potential focus for historical archaeology. This is the delineation of archaeological formation processes, the behavioral archaeology most visibly associated with Schiffer (1976, 1977). Although this was not a direct development from historical archaeological concerns, historical archaeology offers an important avenue of inquiry and investigation in support of it. Clearly, an understanding of the transformations through which the living material world passes in becoming an archaeological site is essential both to recognizing patterns in the archaeological record, and in understanding what those processes reflect. The controls offered by historical archaeology through its involvement in direct and indirect observation are of considerable potential for the definition of archaeological formation processes.

This orientation within historical archaeology toward the development, testing, and refinement of interpretive principles for archaeology is one of the field's more recent developments and one of the most useful for nonhistorical archaeologists. It also, however, presents a potential danger if it becomes the predominant goal in the field in that historical archaeology could evolve from a "handmaiden to history" to a "handmaiden to archaeology." The simple demonstration that material–behavioral patterns exist in a predictable manner (many of which are in any case intuitively obvious) is not in itself a desirable end result of research. Rather, these demonstrations hopefully will serve as a foundation for explaining why patterns and pattern variations exist in terms of human cultural adaptive behavior.

COGNITIVE STUDIES

A more recently evolved orientation in historical archaeology, also based on the simultaneous observation of the spoken, written, observed, and preserved contexts of behavior, is the attempt to discover and define the mental structures and cognitive systems of people through material culture. This, as noted above, is an extension of the "science-of-material-culture" definition of archaeology. Although in a very initial stage of development, if this approach can reveal general principles governing the relationships between cognitive processes and the shaping of the material world, it could offer tremendous potentials for contributing to explanation in many fields of the social sciences.

Much of the emphasis on cognitive studies has been due to the work of Deetz (1974, 1977a) and Glassie (1969, 1975). Glassie used principles of generative grammar to explain architectural regularity. Particular cultures hold in their collective unconscious basic units and deep structures (in the Levi-Straussian sense). These units are combined according to a set of transformations (rules) to generate all culturally acceptable forms and patterns. Glassie used folk housing as an example of this (1975), and Deetz extended the approach to ceramics, gravestones, and meals (1977a). The task of the archaeologist working from this stance is to reveal through archaeological methods such as quantification and pattern recognition these deep structures and cognitive systems.

The application of these ideas in historical archaeology has been extended to the concept of *mind set* by Glassie, Deetz, and their students. Mind set refers to a set of basic units which comprise a cognitive orientation. Such an orientation is shared by members of a group, and determines the way in which the material world is organized and shaped. It is, as yet, unclear whether the mind set is a racially, societally, culturally, or geographically specific phenomenon. Leone, in his work with Mormon material patterning, has suggested that religious affiliation carries with it a set of cognitive principles that are reflected in both sacred and secular architecture (1973, 1977a).

Deetz (1977a), in one of the principle statements regarding this orientation in historical archaeology, suggests that prior to the mid-eighteenth century, British-American colonists in New England had an essentially *medieval* mind set. This was characterized by an organic, informal, and unstructured pattern of organizing the material world. Houses were asymmetrical and grew in response to need rather than plan. Existence was corporate and privacy was not highly valued. This was reflected, according to Deetz, in house floor plans and the material culture of foodways, which did not emphasize individual place settings or serving pieces.

This cognitive model was replaced in the mid-eighteenth century by a new one known as the *Georgian* mind set, and characterized by an emphasis on the individual, separation of components, and tripartite symmetry. Symmetrical, Georgian-style formal houses, matched individual place settings at the table, and tripartite meat–potato–vegetable meals are suggested as examples of the manifestation of the Georgian mind set.

Two immediately apparent questions about this model are, why do the mind sets change? and how do they come to exist in the first place? In these questions, however, lies a possibility for the reconciliation of the mentalist approach taken by the proponents of the cognitive orientation and the materialist approach shared by the majority of American archaeologists. An obvious suggestion is that these cognitive structures function as part of the adaptive strategy of a group dealing with a specific set of techno-environmental circumstances. As Deetz (1977a) pointed out, as we come closer in time to the present the fit between humans and their physical environment becomes less tight, and social and ideological factors assume more obvious roles in the adaptive strategies of historic populations. Deetz, for example, noted that a distinctly American colonial cultural pattern developed in the mid-seventeenth century in response to the isolation of communities, the separation in time and space from the Old World origins, and the use and overuse of certain resources such as wood (1977a:37–43, 107–108). With the advent of better communications systems and the more effective dissemination of ideas through books—ultimately a result of the technological innovation of the printing press—the pattern of isolation and organic growth in response to need changed to a pattern of shared ideas and planned, formal growth.

Such a change is not only historically documented, but can be seen archaeologically in the patterns of the material world. The causal relationships between that material world and the cognitive structures behind it, however, remain unclear.

Another provocative aspect of the cognitive orientation can be seen in Deetz's treatment of the Parting Ways site, a Black community in New England (1977a). Material patterns at Parting Ways did not reflect the mainstream American-Georgian mind set, but was instead a separate and distinct pattern. The implication here is that different racial and social groups have different basic cognitive units and mental structures. Such a principle could be applied in contemporary society with unpredictable results. It could be interpreted to justify the separation and differential treatment of certain ethnic groups, or it could perhaps result in a heightened awareness of cultural differences and promote a spirit of understanding and compromise.

Whatever the ultimate application of such suggestions might be, the cognitive orientation in historical archaeology—made possible by access to written statements reflecting perception in the past—could offer a potential for the explanation of pattern. Shared cognitive orientations in a group, for example, might account for the different patterned refuse disposal practices of British, Spanish, and German-American colonists. It could also be offered as an explanation of why the "melting pot" concept discussed previously is an inaccurate description of the formation of American society, and why the systematic exclusion of minorities might be a more appropriate description of that process. Furthermore, this avenue of inquiry offers one of the very few possibilities in archaeology for investigating the interrelationships among the techno-environmental and ideological sectors of culture in shaping human cultural adaptations. Patterns reflecting such adaptation can be revealed and recognized through the application of scientific archaeological methods, exemplified by South's explication of quantification and pattern recognition (1977).

The programs of the 1980 and 1981 Society for Historical Archaeology meetings reflect the increasing and continuing interest in cognitive studies, with several sessions devoted to such questions, although there is some question about the assumption that "the proper emphasis of historical archaeology is the intellectual climates in which the artifacts and patterns our excavations discover once existed" (Hudgins 1980).

CONCLUSIONS

Historical archaeology today is actively contributing to a variety of problems and disciplines. From its emergence as a recognized area of research in the 1930s, the field has advanced from being essentially a set of techniques providing supplemental data for other disciplines, through being an anthropological tool for the reconstruction of past lifeways and the study of cultural process, to being a means of discovering predictable relationships between human adaptive strategies, ideology, and patterned variability in the archaeological record.

Certain aspects of historical archaeology should be particularly noted as having the potential for making contributions not possible through any other discipline. These contributions result from historical archaeology's unique ability to simultaneously observe written statements about what people said they did, what observers said people did, and what the archaeological record said people did. Inconsistencies and inaccuracies in the records of the past provided by written sources may be detected and ultimately predicted. Insights into past perceptions of human conditions provided by such written sources may be compared to the more objective archaeological record of actual conditions in the past in order to provide insight into cognitive processes. The simultaneous access to varied sources of information about the past also allows the historical archaeologist to match the archaeological patterning of a given unit against the documented social, economic, and ideological attributes of the same unit in order to arrive at a better understanding of how the archaeological record reflects human behavior.

The unique potential of historical archaeology lies not only in its ability to answer questions of archaeological and anthropological interest, but also in its ability to provide historical data not available through documentation or any other source. The inadequate treatment of the disenfranchised groups in America's past, excluded from historical sources because of race, religion, isolation, or poverty, is an important function of contemporary historical archaeology and one that cannot be ignored.

It is this very quality of relevance to a wide variety of problems and disciplines that is both a unique strength and an inherent danger to historical archaeology. Simultaneous attention to historical, anthropological, archaeological, and ideological questions has caused the field to be somewhat unfocused and erratic. The increased influence of reconstruction-oriented cultural resource management programs in historical archaeology has additionally exacerbated this condition. Different historical archaeologists ask very different kinds of questions, with little exchange of ideas in many cases. In this lies the possibility that historical archaeology could become a set of techniques applicable to a wide variety of concerns, but with no primary focus of its own.

On the other hand, the best studies in the field, and many of those discussed in the preceding sections, have not been restricted to a single orientation, but rather have made significant contributions to the concerns of anthropology, history, the humanities, and cultural resource management programs, all through the combined use of documented and archaeological sources and careful research design. Historical archaeology is in a state of rapid and unpredictable change, characterized by a hybridization of goals and ideas. The resulting hybrid vigor in the field has provoked its three-decade advance from a handmaiden to history to a branch of scientific archaeology that can pursue questions beyond the scope of any other subfield of archaeology, or of history. Although Schuyler's question, "Is historical archaeology a technique or a discipline?" (1979:202) cannot be finally and conclusively answered today, contemporary advances suggest that a distinct discipline is indeed emerging.

REFERENCES

Barzun, J., and H. Graff
1970   *The modern researcher* (revised ed.). New York: Harcourt.
Binford, L.
1962   Archeology as anthropology. *American Antiquity* **28**:217–225.
Braidwood, R.
1960   *Archaeologists and what they do.* New York: Franklin Watts.
Brown, I.
1978   Early 18th century French–Indian culture contact in the Yazoo Bluffs region of the lower Mississippi Valley. Unpublished Ph.D. dissertation, Department of Anthropology, Brown University.
Brown, M.
1974   The use of oral and documentary sources in historical archaeology: ethnohistory at the Mott Farm. *Ethnohistory* **20**(4):347–360.
Calver, W., and R. Bolton
1950   *History written with pick and shovel.* New York Historical Society, New York.
Carillo, R.
1977   Archaeological variability—socio-cultural variability. In *Research strategies in historical archaeology,* edited by Stanley South. New York: Academic Press. Pp. 73–90.
Cheek, A.
1974   The evidence for acculturation in artifacts: Indians and non-Indians at San Xavier del Bac, Arizona. Unpublished Ph.D. dissertation, Department of Anthropology, University of Arizona.
Clark, G.
1954   *The study of prehistory.* New York: Cambridge University Press.
Cleland, C., and J. Fitting
1968   The crisis in identity: theory in historic sites archeology. *Conference on Historic Sites Archeology Papers* **2**(2):124–138.
Cotter, J. L. (editor)
1958   Symposium on the role of archeology in historical research (mimeograph). National Park Service, Washington, D.C.
Cumbaa, S.
1975   *Patterns of resource use and cross-cultural dietary change in the Spanish Colonial period.* Unpublished Ph.D. dissertation, Department of Anthropology, University of Florida.
Daniel, G.
1967   *The Origins and Growth of Archaeology.* Penguin, Baltimore.

Deagan, K.
  1974   Sex, status and role in the Mestizaje of Spanish Colonial Florida. Unpublished
          Ph.D. dissertation, Department of Anthropology, University of Florida.
  1978   The archaeological investigation of first Spanish period St. Augustine. *El
          Escribano* **14**:1–351.
  1979   Self-awareness and coming of age in historical archeology: review of Schuyler's
          *Historical Archaeology: A Guide to Substantive and Theoretical Contributions.
          Reviews in Anthropology* **6**(3):365–372.
  1980   Spanish St. Augustine: America's first "melting pot." *Archaeology* **33**(5):22–30.
Deetz, James
  1963   Archaeological investigations at La Purisima Mission. *Annual Report of the Ar-
          cheological Survey of the University of California, Los Angeles*, pp. 165–209.
  1965   The dynamics of stylistic change in Arikara ceramics. *Illinois Studies in Anthro-
          pology* No. 4. Urbana: University of Illinois Press.
  1968   Late man in North America: archaeology of European-Americans. In *Anthropo-
          logical Archaeology in the Americas*, edited by Betty Meggers. Washington, D.C.:
          Anthropological Society of Washington. Pp. 121–130.
  1970   Archaeology as a social science. In Current directions in anthropology. *American
          Anthropological Association, Bulletin* **3**(2):115–125.
  1974   A cognitive model for American culture: 1620–1835. In *Reconstructing Complex
          Societies*, edited by Charlotte Moore. Chicago: American Schools of Oriental
          Research. Pp. 21–29.
  1977a   *In small things forgotten.* Garden City: Anchor Books.
  1977b   Material culture and archaeology—what's the difference? In Historical archaeol-
          ogy and the importance of material things, edited by Leland Ferguson. *Society for
          Historical Archaeology Special Publication* No. 2.
  1981   *Resurrecting the mining community of Somerville: mapping as a research strategy.*
          Paper presented at the Society for Historical Archaeology Conference, New
          Orleans.
Deetz, J., and E. Dethlefson
  1967   Death's head, cherub, urn and willow. *Natural History* **76**(3):29–37.
Dollar, C.
  1968   Some thoughts on method and theory in historical archaeology. *Conference on
          Historic Sites Archaeology Papers* 2(Part 2):3–30.
Fairbanks, C.
  1962   Excavations at Horseshoe Bend, Alabama. *Florida Anthropologist* **15**(2):41–56.
  1956   The Excavation of the Hawkins-Davison Houses. *Georgia Historical Quarterly*
          40:213–229.
  1972   The Kingsley slave cabins in Duval County, Florida, 1968. *The Conference on
          Historic Sites Archaeology Papers* **7**:62–93.
  1977   Backyard archaeology as a research strategy. *The Conference on Historic Sites Ar-
          chaeology Papers* **11**:133–139.
Ferguson, L.
  1977a   (Editor) Historical archaeology and the importance of material things. *Society for
          Historical Archaeology Special Publication* No. 2.
  1977b   An archaeological-historical analysis of Fort Watson: December 1780–April
          1981. In *Research strategies in historical archeology*, edited by Stanley South. New
          York: Academic Press. Pp. 41–72.
Flannery, K.
  1973   Archeology with a capital S. In *research and theory in current archeology*, edited
          by C. Redman. New York: Wiley. Pp. 47–53.

Fontana, B.
  1965   On the meaning of historic sites archaeology. *American Antiquity* **31**(1):61–65. Reprinted in *Historical archaeology: a guide to substantive and theoretical contributions,* edited by Robert Schuyler. Farmingdale: Baywood (1979). Pp. 23–26.
Glassie, H.
  1969   Pattern in the material folk culture of the eastern United States. *Folklore and Folklife,* 1. Philadelphia: University of Pennsylvania Press.
  1975   *Folk housing in Middle Virginia: a structural analysis of historical artifacts.* Knoxville: University of Tennessee Press.
Goodyear, A. C.
  1977   The historical and ecological position of protohistoric sites in the Slate Mountains, south central Arizona. In *Research strategies in historical archaeology,* edited by Stanley South. New York: Academic Press. Pp. 203–240.
Griffin, J. W.
  1958   End products of historic sites archeology. In *Symposium on the Role of Archeology in Historical Research,* edited by John Cotter, pp. 1–6. Reprinted in *Historical Archaeology: A Guide to Substantive and Theoretical Contributions* (1979), edited by Robert Schuyler. Farmingdale: Baywood. Pp. 20–22.
Hall, R.
  1981   Varieties of Black religious experience in Florida, 1565–1906. Unpublished Ph.D. dissertation, Department of History, Florida State University.
Handler, J., and F. Lange
  1978   *Plantation slavery in Barbados: an archaeological and historical investigation.* Cambridge: Harvard University Press.
Harrington, J. C.
  1952   Historic sites archeology in the United States. In *Archeology of Eastern North America,* edited by J. B. Griffin. Chicago: University of Chicago Press. Pp. 295–315.
  1955   Archaeology as an auxillary science to American history. *American Anthropologist* **57**(6):1121–1130.
  1957   *New light on Washington's Fort necessity.* Richmond, Virginia, Eastern National Park and Monument Association. Reprinted in *Historical archaeology: a guide to substantive and theoretical contributions* (1979), edited by Robert Schuyler. Farmingdale: Baywood. Pp. 91–138.
Hawkes, C.
  1951   British prehistory half-way through the century. Proceedings of the Prehistoric Society. XVII: pp. 1–9, London.
Honerkamp, N.
  1980   Frontier process in eighteenth-century colonial Georgia: an archeological approach. Unpublished Ph.D. dissertation, Department of Anthropology, University of Florida. University Microfilms, Ann Arbor, Michigan.
House, J.
  1977   Survey data and regional models in historical archeology. In *Research strategies in historical archeology,* edited by S. South. New York: Academic Press. Pp. 214–260.
Hudgins, C.
  1980   Every man's house and home: archaeological perspectives on the mental life of earlier generations (abstract). Symposium presented at the Society for Historical Archaeology Meetings, Albuquerque.

Irwin-Mason, C.
  1963   Eighteenth century culture change among the lower creeks. *Florida Anthropologist* **16**(3):65–80.
Kelley, A. R.
  1939   The Macon trading post, an historical foundling. *American Antiquity* **4** (4): 328–333.
Kirkpatrick, D., *et al.*
  1980   Studies of Navajo culture from northwestern New Mexico. Symposium presented at the Society for Historical Archaeology Meetings, Albuquerque.
Klein, J.
  1977   20th century archeological sites: are they eligible for the National Register? Paper presented at the Society for Historical Archaeology Meetings, Ottawa.
Koch, J.
  1980   Mortuary behavior patterning in colonial St. Augustine. Unpublished M.A. thesis, Department of Anthropology, Florida State University.
Kroeber, A. L.
  1919   On the order of change in civilization as exemplified by changes in fashion. *American Anthropologist* **21**(3):235–263.
Leone, M.
  1973   Archeology as the science of technology: Mormon town plans and fences. In *Research and theory in current archeology,* edited by Charles Redman. New York: Wiley. Pp. 125–150.
  1977a   The new Mormon temple in Washington, D.C. In Historical Archaeology and the Importance of Material Things, edited by Leland Ferguson, pp. 43–61. *Society for Historical Archaeology Special Publication* No. 2.
  1977b   Foreward. In *Research Strategies in Historical Archaeology,* edited by Stanley South. New York: Academic Press. Pp. xvii–xxi.
Lewis, K.
  1977   Sampling the archaeological frontier: regional models and component analysis. In *Research Strategies in Historical Archaeology,* edited by Stanley South. New York: Academic Press. Pp. 151–202.
Lombard, P.
  1953   *The Aptucxet Trading Post.* Bourne, Massachusetts, Bourne Historical Society.
Loucks, L. J.
  1979   Political and economic interactions between Spaniards and Indians: archeological and ethnohistorical perspectives of the mission system in Florida. Unpublished Ph.D. dissertation, Department of Anthropology, University of Florida.
Maintfort, R. C.
  1979   *Indian Social Dynamics in the Period of European Contact.* Publications of the Museum, Michigan State University 1(4):269–418.
Manucy, A.
  1978   Toward recreation of 16th century St. Augustine. *El Escribano* **14**:1–5.
Montgomery, R., W. Smith, and J. Brew
  1949   Franciscan Awatovi. *Papers of the Peabody Museum, Harvard University* 36.
Mudar, K.
  1978   The effects of socio-cultural variables on food preferences in 19th century Detroit. *The Conference on Historic Sites Archaeology Papers* **12**:323–391.
Noël Hume, I.
  1964   Archaeology: handmaiden to history. *The North Carolina Historical Review* **41**(2):215–225.

1969   *Historical archaeology.* New York: Knopf.
Otto, J. S.
    1975   Status differences and the archeological record: a comparison of planter, overseer and slave sites from Cannon's Point Plantation (1794–1861), St. Simon's Island, Georgia. Unpublished Ph.D. dissertation, Department of Anthropology, University of Florida.
    1977   Artifacts and status differences—a comparison of ceramics from planter, overseer and slave sites on an antebellum plantation. In *Research strategies in historical archaeology,* edited by Stanley South. New York: Academic Press. Pp. 91–118.
    1979   A new look at slave life. *Natural History* **88**(1):8–30.
Poe, C.
    1979   The manifestation of status in 18th century Criollo culture in colonial St. Augustine. Paper presented at the Society for Historical Archaeology Meetings, Nashville, Tennessee.
Price, C., and J. Price
    1978   Investigation of settlement and subsistence systems in the Ozark border region of southeast Missouri during the first half of the nineteenth century. Paper presented at the Society for Historical Archaeology Meetings, San Antonio, Texas.
Rathje, W.
    1977   In praise of archaeology: le projet du garbage. In Historical archaeology and the importance of material things, edited by Leland Ferguson, pp. 36–42. *Society for Historical Archaeology Special Publications* No. 2.
Rathje, W., and M. McCarthy
    1977   Regularity and variability in contemporary garbage. In *Research Strategies in Historical Archaeology,* edited by Stanley South. New York: Academic Press. Pp. 261–286.
Reitz, E.
    1979   Spanish and British Subsistence Strategies at St. Augustine, Florida and Frederica, Georgia, between 1563 and 1783. Unpublished Ph.D. dissertation, Department of Anthropology, University of Florida.
Rowe, J. H.
    1965   The renaissance foundations of anthropology. *American Anthropologist* 67(1): 1–20. Reprinted in *Historical Archaeology* (1979), edited by Robert Schuyler. Farmingdale: Baywood. Pp. 35–44.
Schiffer, M.
    1976   *Behavioral archeology.* New York: Academic Press.
    1977   Toward a unified science of the cultural past. In *Research Strategies in Historical Archeology,* edited by Stanley South. Academic Press, New York. Pp. 13–40.
Schiffer, M., and G. Gumerman (editors)
    1977   *Conservation archaeology.* New York: Academic Press.
Schuyler, R.
    1970   Historical and historic sites archaeology as anthropology: basic definitions and relationships. *Historical Archaeology* 4:83–89.
    1976   Images of America: the contribution of historical archaeology to national identity. *Southwestern Lore* **42**(4):27–39.
    1977   The spoken word, the written word, observed behavior and preserved behavior: the contexts available to the archeologist. *Conference on Historic Sites Archeology Papers* **10**(2):99–120.
    1979   (Editor) *Historical Archaeology: A guide to substantive and theoretical contributions.* Farmingdale: Baywood.

1980   (Editor) *Archaeological perspectives on ethnicity in America.* Farmingdale: Baywood.

Shephard, S.
1975   The Geronimo de Hita y Salazar site: a study of Criollo culture in colonial St. Augustine. Unpublished M.A. thesis, Department of Anthropology, Florida State University.

Singleton, T.
1980   The archeology of Afro-American slavery in coastal Georgia: a regional perception of slave households and community patterns. Unpublished Ph.D. dissertation, Department of Anthropology, University of Florida.

Smith, G. H.
1939   Excavating the site of Old Fort Ridgely. *Minnesota History: A Quarterly Magazine* **20**(2):146–155.

Smith, H. G.
1948   Two historical archeological periods in Florida. *American Antiquity* **13**(4):313–319.

South, S.
1972   Evolution and horizon as revealed in ceramic analysis in historical archaeology. *The Conference on Historic Sites Archaeology Papers* **6**:71–116.
1977   *Method and theory in historical archaeology.* New York. Academic Press.

Stephenson, R.
1977   A strategy for getting the job done. In *Research Strategies in Historical Archeology* edited by Stanley South. New York: Academic Press. Pp. 307–321.

Swannack, J.
1975   Mission-oriented agencies: means and ends of historic sites archeology. *Historical Archaeology* **9**:80–81.

Walker, I.
1967   Historical archaeology—methods and principles. *Historical Archaeology* **1**:23–34.

Webster, D.
1974   On the digging of potteries. *Antiques* 430–433.

Willey, G., and J. Sabloff
1974   *A history of american archaeology.* San Francisco: Freeman.

Youngm, A.
1841   Chronicles of the pilgrim fathers. Boston.

Archaeological Applications of Computer Graphics

J. BARTO ARNOLD III

INTRODUCTION

Computer graphics is one of the most rapidly advancing and growing aspects of computer science. This may be in part because, by reducing numerical and other computer output to a graphics format, the man–machine relationship is humanized to a great extent. If a picture is worth a thousand words, then a computer-generated graphic is worth 10,000 statistical tables. As with other aspects of the computer industry, hardware for computer graphics is becoming more sophisticated, less expensive, and more readily available. Software (or computer programs) to take advantage of these increased capabilities is also multiplying and increasing in sophistication and usability for the noncomputer specialist researcher. Many archaeologists are already using prepared statistical software packages such as the Statistical Package for the Social Sciences (SPSS) (Nie *et al.* 1975) and the Biomeds (BMDP) (Dixon and Brown 1979). In fact, in addition to the specifically graphics-oriented packages, the newer versions of these old friends, SPSS and the BMDP, now contain more complex statistical routines that have graphics output in the form of dendrograms, for example. Histograms, scattergrams, and other graphs are, of course, computer graphics, but the possible uses for computer graphics in archaeology extend far beyond the statistical applications. Indeed, many of the most exciting applications and techniques lie outside statistics. In this chapter I shall briefly consider the state of the art of com-

ADVANCES IN ARCHAEOLOGICAL METHOD AND THEORY, VOL. 5

puter graphics on a general level and then move on to examine current applications in archaeology. This section is followed by a suggestion on how the novice can approach computer graphics from a practical standpoint. Speculation on the possible future directions of computer graphics in our field concludes the chapter. By beginning with a general discussion of computer graphics capabilities and sources, it is hoped that researchers wishing to make computer graphics one of their research tools will encounter approaches that can be adapted to their own uses. The general discussion is subdivided into sections on hardware and software.

The bulk of the chapter is devoted to discussing examples of the ways archaeologists have used and are using computer graphics techniques as an aid in their research. Pulling together a variety of such examples in one chapter should assist in making the range of computer graphics applications in our field more easily realized. The efficiency of communication by graphic over verbal or numerical methods illustrated by these examples should be an inspiration to us all.

The definition of computer graphics can be stated as "the use of a computer to define, store, manipulate, interrogate, and present pictorial output" (Rogers and Adams 1976:1–2). Computer graphics are executed in two ways, one essentially passive and one interactive. Under the passive mode, that most frequently used by archaeologists, the user has no direct control over the picture being presented. With the interactive mode, the user can influence the picture being presented or communicate in real time with the computer to create or alter the picture. Rogers and Adams (1976:3) use the word picture "in its broadest sense to mean any collection of lines, points, text, etc. . . ." A more precise definition of *graphic* specifies "a picture, map, or graph used for illustration or demonstration" (Webster 1971:990). The benefits and effects of these illustrations are exciting, or graphic—meaning "marked by clear and lively description or striking imaginative power" (Webster 1971:990).

In addition to visual impact, improved efficiency of communication, data management, and reduction of errors, there are other practical reasons why computer graphics are of great value to archaeologists. Some tasks would be impractical if they had to be manually performed. The rotation of three-dimensional illustrations of artifacts or surfaces on the screen of a cathole-ray tube (CRT) is a prime example.

COMPUTER GRAPHICS HARDWARE

Computer hardware is the "physical equipment, such as mechanical, magnetic, electrical, and electronic devices" (Auerbach 1972:204). In contrast, software is "the collection of programs and routines . . . which facilitate the programming and operation of the computer'' (Auerbach 1972:206). In one very basic sense, even program listings or the tables of numbers produced by statistical routines are computer graphics in that they are visual displays produced by a computer. These cases deal with the most common and least sophisticated device for graphic output, the line printer. The results of statistical calculations can rapidly become too complex to comprehend in numerical form but can often be summarized visually by charts and graphs. The line printer, a typewriter-like device, is adequate for what might be thought of in terms of sophistication as middle-level graphics— statistical graphs such as histograms and scattergrams. The capabilities of line printers are somewhat strained when we consider the more sophisticated levels of computer graphics, such as contour plotting. With line printers, different densities of shaded areas composed of different letters or symbols must be used to indicate the levels in a contour plot (Figure 5.1), which is not always a satisfactory arrangement. Resolution and replicability are also problems (Samuels 1977).

Higher-level computer graphics from the more complicated graphs to contour and perspective, or three-dimensional, plotting require the use of an X-Y plotter. The X-Y plotter is a mechanical drawing device (Figure 5.2). Some can draw in a variety of colors. In size, they range from small models, accommodating legal size paper suitable for field or office use, to models as large as a drafting table. There are two basic types of X-Y plotters commonly in use: the drum plotter and the flatbed plotter. A drum plotter is set up so that the pen moves back and forth in only one direction, that is, along only one axis. Drawing on the second axis is accomplished by moving the paper back and forth over a drum that rolls at a 90° angle to the pen's axis of movement. Flatbed plotters are arranged so that the pen itself moves on two axes and the paper remains stationary. The limitation of plot sizes imposed by plotting surface dimensions can in part be overcome by producing the plot in segments and later pasting the segments together. Drum and flatbed plotters run a gamut from high speed and medium precision to low speed and high precision. Greater accuracy can be gained by using a plotter that draws with light from a photohead on special film. Some plotters can even produce scribed copy, a process involving the etching of a groove in coated material. This is an important technique in computerized mapmaking because, like that of the photographic process already described, it can be used directly to produce press plates (Fulton 1975:103).

The electrostatic plotter or printer that combines some of the capabilities of the line printer and the X-Y plotter is becoming widely available. Functioning in a manner similar to a photocopying machine, the electrostatic printer can produce subtly shaded areas superior to that of the line printer and can also produce lines like an X-Y plotter. Electrostatic printers are often used as a

KNIFE RIVER, MAIN VILLAGE, FIRE PIT NO. 1

FIRE PIT I, HOUSE CC

ONE METER

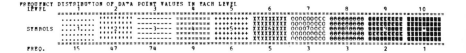

FREQUENCY DISTRIBUTION OF DATA POINT VALUES IN EACH LEVEL

LEVEL	1	2	3	4	5	6	7	8	9	10
SYMBOLS	...1.	|||2|||	---3---	====4===	◆◆◆5◆◆◆	XXXXXXXXX	000C000CC	●●●●●●●●	▓▓▓▓▓▓	████
FREQ.	15	47	74	9	6	5	3	3	2	1

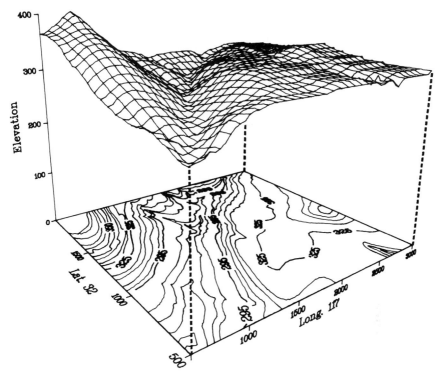

Figure 5.2. Example of a three-dimensional perspective plot of Sorrento Valley superimposed above the same topographic data rendered as a contour plot, a routine available in the DISSPLA® proprietary software of ISSCO, San Diego, California. (Reproduced by permission.)

convenient accessory for acquiring a paper copy of the display from a CRT terminal. In situations requiring large numbers of prints, the electrostatic printer is both cheaper and much faster than the $X–Y$ plotter.

Graphics terminals with CRT displays are particularly important for interactive computer graphics techniques. Interactive computer graphics involve the user creating a display in real time (i.e., with essentially instant reaction from the computer), perhaps with a light pen, cursor, or some other method, and then changing the display by adding, removing, or altering elements of the graphic or even rotating the display in three dimensions for

Figure 5.1. Example of a contour plot produced by line printer. The software used was SYMAP, and the plot is of magnetometer survey data from Sakakawea Village in North Dakota (Weymouth and Nickel 1977:115). (Reproduced by permission of the authors and *Plains Anthropologist*.)

views from different angles. There are many makes and models of graphics terminals. Lee (1975) summarizes the characteristics and capabilities of 64 graphics terminal models in a market survey and evaluation. He also covers expected future developments, many of which have already taken place since the publication of his book.

Preparing the geographical data for the computer is often done via a digitizer, an instrument much like a drafting board in appearance, the surface of which contains an electronic grid. A map is placed on the board and map data such as coastlines or river channels are traced with a cursor (sometimes called a mouse) that sends an electrical impulse to the grid below the map. The path of the cursor is automatically recorded in X and Y coordinates, enabling the computer to reproduce the map later. An added attraction is the ability of the computer to change the scale and orientation of the map or to reproduce only part of it and to overlay other data such as topography and vegetation.

Recently, there have been exciting advances in the field of color computer graphics hard copy. Hard copy refers to the production of graphics on paper instead of the temporary display on the screen of a CRT. Computer driven devices can now produce hard copy in several formats, including photographic prints, 35-mm slides, transparencies, and plain paper copies using techniques including xerography, dot matrix, ink jet, photography, and lasers (Klein and Nisen 1979a:1-2). Fine (1980) describes briefly and in understandable terms the use of a laser plotter for processing digitized images such as seismic data and remote sensing data such as Landsat digital data. The image is composed of resolution elements or pixels. Unlike the usual treatment of digital data in which each resolution element is an indivisible unit, in this laser process, each resolution element is composed of an array of 16 tiny dots. Each dot is burned into a special chemical substrate (in essence a sheet of plastic) by the laser. The number of dots in each resolution element made white or black provides the shades of gray in a gray scale of 17 values when viewed in mass. Similarly, overlays of three colors produce color images with literally thousands of shades possible. The unique advantage of this laser process is that, because it is computer controlled, the images are replicable with an exactness unknown with photographic processes.

Some computer graphics hardware is in the forefront of sophisticated and very expensive high technology. Other varieties are relatively inexpensive and portable, making it possible for archaeologists to take computer graphics capabilities with them to the field. Microcomputers such as the Apple II can present color graphics on a CRT. Small flatbed plotters are also available for such units. Popular publications on electronics even have "build-your-own" graphics hardware articles for the home computer buffs. A shoestring approach such as this may be of interest to many archaeologists on a limited budget.

Auerbach (1972) emphasizes the hardware aspects of computer graphics, covering plotters and digitizers in all varieties. Included are tables summarizing the characteristics of more than 50 plotters and 25 digitizers.

COMPUTER GRAPHICS SOFTWARE

More important than full understanding of the mechanics of computer graphics hardware for the nonspecialist user–researcher is a grasp of the capabilities of computer graphics in general terms and an acquaintance with the available software. Actually, writing programs (software) to produce sophisticated computer graphics is beyond the reach of most noncomputer scientists, but packaged graphics software programs are available, and it is within the capabilities of the nonspecialist and even the novice programmer to use these. They are only slightly more difficult to utilize than a statistical package like SPSS (Nie *et al.* 1975).

GENERAL COMPUTER GRAPHICS SOURCES

Inspiration can be had from viewing examples of the types of graphics available and contemplating their application to one's own research problems. Since archaeologists have not exploited the full potential of computer graphics, passing mention of sources outside the field is not inappropriate.

A general idea of the computer graphics capabilities currently available is easily obtainable from textbooks (Newman and Sproull 1979; Walker *et al.* 1975). The tremendous interest in computer graphics within the discipline of computer science itself is evidenced by the multiplicity of journals devoted to this topic exclusively. These include *Computers and Graphics, Computer Graphics and Image Processing,* and *Computer Graphics.* The Association for Computing Machinery (ACM), one of the largest computer science professional organizations, has a special interest group for computer graphics (SIGGRAPH–ACM) that produces a quarterly report similar to a journal that includes a listing of recent sources in computer graphics (Schrack 1980).

Locating generalized, state-of-the-art-type articles on computer graphics for the nonspecialist proved to be something of a problem with the exception of one article (Prueitt 1976). Possibly the best and most readily available general source on current trends in computer graphics is the *Harvard Newsletter on Computer Graphics.* In-depth analyses of the state of the art of computer graphics including both hardware and software are also available in the form of market and technology reports. A list of six examples of these sources, possibly the most valuable of all, appeared in the *Harvard Newsletter*

TABLE 5.1

Market Research Studies in Computer Graphics[a]

Title	Year published	Total pages	Price ($)	Publisher[b]
Computer Graphics Industry	1978	60	8.95	CS
Computer Graphics Software and Services Market	1979	243	8.25	F&S
Computer Graphics Equipment, Software and Services for the Manufacturing Industries	1978	187	7.75	F&S
Computer Graphics: A Study for Designers of Printed, Integrated, and Hybrid Circuits	1978	350	6.00	ITM
Computer Cartography: Worldwide Technology and Markets	1978	400	3.75	ITM
CRT Graphics Terminals & Systems Markets	1978	200	13.75	VDC

[a] From Klein and Nisen (1979b:4).

[b] CS: Creative Strategies, Inc., 4340 Stevens Creek Blvd., Suite 275, San Jose, CA 95129, (408) 249–7550. Contact: Tom D. Dexel.

F&S: Frost & Sullivan, Inc., 106 Fulton St., New York, NY 10038, (212) 233–1080. Contact: Robert Sanzo.

ITM: International Technology Marketing, 120 Cedar St., Wellesley, MA 02181, (617) 237–2089. Contact: Julius Dortman.

VDC: Venture Development Corp., 1 Washington St., Wellesley, MA 02181, (617) 237–5080. Contact Edward Ross.

on Computer Graphics (Klein and Nisen 1979b:4) and are reproduced in Table 5.1. One study contained an interesting statement on the benefits of applying computer graphics (International Technology Marketing 1974). Primarily these include cost reduction, time saving, improved accuracy, standardization of design and production elements, establishment of a data base, improved flexibility and speed of design changes, and improved design through availability of more strategies. One can easily see that these concerns are shared by archaeologists and, with the application of a little imagination, the same benefits will accrue.

COMPUTER GRAPHICS IN ARCHAEOLOGY

In considering the past and present applications of computer graphics in archaeology, three general reviews of computers in archaeology provide a perspective. Chenhall (1968), in an early article on this subject, had little to say about graphics, which were then in an embryonic stage of development by present standards. However, he made a general observation on our use of computers that remains true today. The only limitation on advances in applications of computer technology for archaeology is the lack of creative imagination (Chenhall 1968:23). Whallon's (1972) critical review of the use of computers in archaeology reflected the beginnings of an awareness of the possibilities of computer graphics for archaeology. He cited a few projects involving graphics under the heading of miscellaneous applications. During the past decade, the use of computer graphics in the representation of statistical results has multiplied apace, reaching a high level of sophistication as a result of increasing interest in ever more complex statistical methods. However, it is outside this limited application where the most exciting possibilities for archaeological application of computer graphics lie. The area of distributional studies holds great promise:

> Our visual pattern recognition capability can be exploited to help deal with spatial–temporal relationships. Graphics can be used to describe dynamic problems that are difficult to describe by conventional methods. We have an innate visual ability to scan and organize information as clusters and patterns, which can overcome some of the problems associated with the description of complex systems (Csuri 1977:53).

Individual archaeologists here and there have begun to exploit this potential. Perceptive reviewers are also beginning to take note, as witnessed by the following passage from the excellent article by Gaines and Gaines (1980:468):

> We have given some thought to the possible use of graphics terminals to display locational information, site coordinates, vegetation patterns, drainage patterns, etc. This would certainly be an aid to both fieldwork and analysis. It could quite possibly assist in establishing site locations and automatic plotting of sites on computer stored maps, to say

nothing of the potential for predictive research. This type of terminal is relatively expensive today and requires fairly sophisticated programming, but because of the tremendous potential as a research and analysis tool it deserves our attention.

Interest in computer graphics may have lagged among archaeologists as a whole, but considerable attention has been expressed for some time by those archaeologists sometimes referred to in an almost deprecatory tone as "computer jocks." This is apparent in reviewing the articles in the admirable but unfortunately defunct publication, *Newsletter of Computer Archaeology* (Arizona State University 1965–1979). In Great Britain, a similar publication entitled *Computer Applications in Archaeology* (University of Birmingham Computer Centre 1974–1977) presents the proceedings of annual conferences held from 1974 through at least 1977. A perusal of both of these series is highly recommended for any archaeologist interested in computer applications in our field in general and for computer graphics in particular. To keep up with current developments in this regard, the journal *Computers and the Humanities* provides a truly significant resource. Every year one of the issues of this journal has lists of articles that include examples of computer usage in the humanities. One section is specifically devoted to archaeology and typically contains citations of dozens of articles, including references from our European colleagues. Narrowing the frame of reference to computer graphics in archaeology, an important source is the collection of 11 papers from a symposium on that topic at the annual Society for American Archaeology (SAA) meeting in St. Louis in 1976 (Upham 1979). Several papers dealt with specific computer graphics applications and a discussion of these follows. At this point, it is appropriate to call attention to one of the papers that is a review of the application of two particular kinds of computer graphics in archaeology, the contour and three-dimensional perspective plots (Arnold 1979). A wide variety of plotting techniques and methods are covered and illustrated with examples in this review, and suggestions are made for future possibilities for further archaeological applications.

Instances of the use of computer graphics in archaeology are not new. Among the pioneers in the adoption of computer graphics techniques were Redman and Watson (1970), who used SYMAP to assist in the analysis of artifact distribution from two sites in Turkey. With good results they used and compared two variants of SYMAP plots produced by line printer, the contour plot and the proximal plot (Redman and Watson 1970:Figures 11 and 12). Interestingly, unfamiliarity with the graphic output led to a reversal of the captions by either the authors or the editors. Figure 12 (Redman and Watson 1970:289) is labeled as the proximity map, although it is actually the contour plot and vice versa for Figure 11. In their evaluation of the technique, the authors state: "Though these maps are very rewarding, the expense involved in getting sufficiently detailed maps limits the use of this program to the most important distributions'' (Redman and Watson 1970:289). However, the expenses involved in computer processing have decreased dramatically since this article was published. Another early use of computer graphics techniques in archaeology that continues today is associated with magnetometer surveys. Systematic magnetometer surveys can locate cultural features in an archaeological site and help to guide excavations. Scollar and Kruckeberg (1966) adapted computer graphics techniques to illustrate results of such surveys. Perhaps better known in this country is the early use of computer-drawn contour and three-dimensional plots by Breiner and Coe (1972) in presenting the results of their magnetometer survey at the Olmec site of San Lorenzo.

Having cited a few of the earliest examples of computer graphics in archaeology, we will proceed with consideration of the various applications of this technique in our field. The projects cited below are not intended to be all-inclusive, but merely serve as indicators of present activity in computer graphics applications. In turn, we will cover basic tabular and statistical graphics, artifact shapes, site distribution studies, map-base illustrations, artifact distribution studies, and contour and three-dimensional perspective plots. It is hoped that these citations will provide interested researchers with examples that they can personally view in light of the possible application of the techniques to their own projects.

Tabular and Statistical Graphics

On a very basic level, the tables of numbers printed out by a computer can be considered computer graphics. In 1979, a group of articles appeared on the computerized conversion of dates in the Maya calendar to their modern equivalents (Biese and Iannuccillo 1979; Doty 1979; Krowne et al. 1979). Each showed examples of the tables of date conversions. The first two showed reproductions of the actual computer printouts, the first by a thermal printer, which produces letters and numbers by burning the appropriate pattern of dots to make up each letter onto heat-sensitive paper, and the second by a traditional line printer. In the third example, the computer output was typeset. Perhaps the time saved by the editor to be realized in the direct reproduction of the computer output was offset by the poor or uneven quality of the output, which is often a problem with line printers. In each of these three examples, it was thought to be important to include the program listing (the actual step-by-step commands given to the computer). Gifford and Crader (1977) similarly presented their computer coding scheme for faunal remains. These listings themselves became basic computer graphics when reproduced directly. When quality allows, this is a more efficient method of presenting lengthy printouts than having them typeset. That camera-ready material can be produced by many of the other computer graphics plotters is one of the time- and cost-saving attractions of utilizing these techniques.

On a somewhat higher level of computer graphics, graphs of statistical output are being exploited by archaeologists on all levels from the most basic histogram or bar graph (Whallon 1971:126) (Figure 5.3) to some sophisticated techniques at the cutting edge of the state of the art of statistics and computer graphics. The results of nearest neighbor (Whallon 1971), cluster, and factor analysis (Tainter 1975) can often be visualized best by computer-produced graphs. Indeed, computer-produced cluster analysis results presented as dendrograms or treelike graphs of the hierarchical partitions of a set of similarity measures are quite common (Wood 1974; Hodson 1970). On an even more esoteric level, Olshan *et al.* (1977) presented a method of graphic display of high-dimensional (i.e., more than two-dimensional) variance revealed by multivariate statistical methods. They suggest and illustrate the mapping of each observation into a sine–cosine function (Figure 5.4). ''Thus, clusters and multivariate outliers may be visually assessed from a plot of the functions'' (Olshan *et al.* 1977:3). Another method of visualizing such relationships is through computer plotting of stero pairs. Graham *et al.* (1975) compared two packages of programs useful in data analysis through multidimensional scaling for archaeological seriation problems. The two packages are MDSCAL and LOCSCAL, and the output of both can be displayed as two- or three-dimensional graphics. The three-dimensional effect is achieved by plotting stereo pairs with lines drawn between plotted points.

Trace-element analysis of the material composing various types of artifacts has become an important technique for archaeology, and computer graphics have become an integral part of such studies. Nelson *et al.* (1977) presented a computer-drawn graph of the trace-element composition of obsidian artifacts obtained by X-ray fluorescence. Ekland (1977) showed the results of neutron-activation analysis on prehistoric ceramics that had been evaluated statistically by factor analysis. The factor scores were plotted by computer-drawn scattergram and demonstrated significant clusterings. Similarly, Kohl *et al.* (1979) offered the results of X-ray diffraction tests of Mideastern stone vessels analyzed by multiple discriminant analysis with the statistical results illustrated by a scattergram produced by line printer (Figure 5.5).

Artifact Shapes

Actual recording by computer of artifacts in visual form has been limited. IBM (1971) reported on a project utilizing their model 2250 graphics terminal and light pen to record vessel shape and decoration of about 2000 Egyptian

Figure 5.3. Example showing a portion of a line-printer-generated histogram or bar chart. The frequency of shipwrecks on the Texas coast is illustrated for the years around the time of the Mexican War (Arnold 1980:Figure 3a).

```
       I
 1838. ** (     1)
       I
       I
       I
 1839. ** (     1)
       I
       I
       I
 1842. ** (     1)
       I
       I
       I
 1846. ************** (    12)
       I
       I
       I
 1847. ************* (    11)
       I
       I
       I
 1848. ******** (    6 )
       I
       I
       I
 1849. ** (     1)
       I
       I
       I
 1851. *** (    2)
       I
       I
       I
 1852. ** (     1)
       I
       I
       I
 1853. ***** (     4)
       I
       I
       I
 1854. *** (     2)
       I
       I
       I
    0. *************************** (    29)
(MISSING) I  UNKNOWN
          I
          I.........I.........I.........I.........I.........I.........I
          0        10        20        30        40        50
          FREQUENCY
```

MEAN	1872.907	STD ERR	2.597	MEDIAN	1866.618
MODE	1867.000	STD DEV	37.985	VARIANCE	1442.864
KURTOSIS	1.139	SKEWNESS	1.023	RANGE	202.000
MINIMUM	1766.000	MAXIMUM	1968.000		

VALID CASES   214   MISSING CASES   29

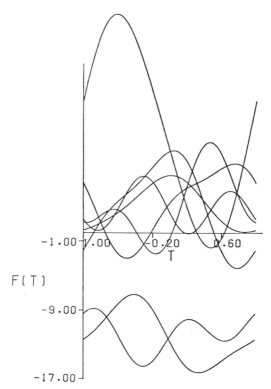

Figure 5.4. *X–Y* plotter-produced graph illustrating the plotting of sophisticated statistical results as an aid to understanding the output of such techniques. "The high-dimensional display represents five dimensions (canonical variates) that account for 99% of the cumulative variance available in the multivariate space. Careful examination of the plot will show the presence of three 'clusters' of canonical means. ... A two-dimensional plot of the canonical means failed to show this relationship" (Olshan *et al.* 1977:7, Figure 2). (Reproduced by permission of the authors and the *Newsletter of Computer Archaeology*.)

ceramic vessels in the Metropolitan Museum of Art in New York. Some of the advantages of a computerized approach to the study of large collections are explained in the following excerpt on that technique (IBM 1971:29–30).

Two attributes necessary to an adequate typology that are among the most difficult to deal with verbally, are classes according to vessel shape and decorative motifs. In this pilot project, the shape and decoration of some two thousand vessels were recorded. Some of the advantages of using the 2250 for this were: by using this device, drawings of vessels may be brought to the same scale; foreshortening from photographic input may be corrected; the size of the vessel on the screen may be enlarged or contracted; a detail, such as a spout, handle, or rim, may be displayed alone, enlarged or contracted; and several drawings and/or details may be retrieved on the screen simultaneously for comparison. One of the most fascinating achievements of the cathode ray tube is the so-called three-dimensional display. When plane views of an object have been entered on the screen, the computer joins the sides

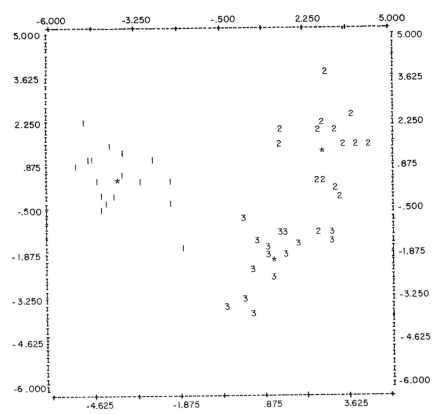

Figure 5.5. Line-printer-produced graph showing the results of multidiscriminant statistical analysis of three groups of artifacts. An SPSS routine was used to produce this graph of the results of X-ray diffraction tests (Kohl *et al.* 1979:Figure 6). (Reproduced by permission of the authors and *Archaeometry*.)

together, making the necessary corrections to produce perspective views of the drawing as it rotates on the screen to show the object in the round.

Along similar lines, Jones and Wilcock (1974) used the PLUTARCH package to automatically produce a typological sorting of projectile points and compare the assemblages from different sites. The study results include computer graphics diagrams of the group "planforms" (or outlines of the points) and also statistical graphics output in the form of dendrograms from cluster analysis and scalograms from multidimensional scaling.

Distribution Studies

Computer graphics techniques lend themselves very well to archaeological problems such as artifact distributions within a site. Croes *et al.* (1974) used an X–Y plotter to show distributions of woven artifacts within houses at the

Ozette site. Instead of abstract symbols to represent the different types of baskets, hats, and mats, the computer was programmed to draw shapes very similar to those of the actual artifacts. This greatly facilitated interpretation of the distributional plots. Using the SPSS scattergram routine (Nie *et al.* 1975), Copp (1977) produced maps of artifact distributions (Figure 5.6). He coded a number of variables for each artifact in addition to functional type and $x, y,$ and z coordinates such as raw material, modification technique, condition, and morphological characteristics. These could all be displayed as distribution plots.

Lees and Kimery-Lees (1979) used SYMAP distribution plots of European and non-European ceramics at Limerick Plantation to demonstrate that the majority of the non-European ceramics are from the historic period. Scheitlin and Clark (1978) analyzed a surface collection from Liencres, a prehistoric site in Spain (Figure 5.7). They used the SURGE 2 program, a three-dimensional plot program which allows surface rotation, enlargement, or reduction of plot scale, and scale changes in the z coordinate to "aid in the impressionistic evaluation of activities conducted on different parts of the site surface" (Scheitlin and Clark 1978:6). Analysis of spatial associations of artifact types through the graphic output of a nearest neighbor statistical program was used by Clark (1979) for the collection from Liencres. McNett (1979) examined artifact distributions through three-dimensional stereo pair computer graphics. In a very sophisticated application, Wobst (1979) developed a three-dimensional plotting routine with an orientationally adjustable cross-sectional, or profile, plot generation capability. This program is designed to aid the recognition of occupation levels with sloping surfaces within an archaeological deposit. Such sloping surfaces would be impossible to detect if only a single profile at the wrong angle to the slope was examined.

Map-Base Graphics

Cartographic, or map-based, studies carried out with the aid of computers are one of the most exciting applications of computer graphics in archaeology and will be one of the most significant for the future. The study of the distribution of sites across a given geographical area is one of the primary archaeological concerns, and several such studies have already made use of computer graphics techniques. SYMAP was used by Adovasio *et al.* (1975) in illustrating the distribution of cultural components within a river drainage in Cyprus. Green and Summer (1976), using computer graphics, conducted a study comparing the distribution of sites in an area with a randomly generated site distribution in order to test statistically the influences on the actual distribution of sites by such factors as distance from water. Effland (1978,

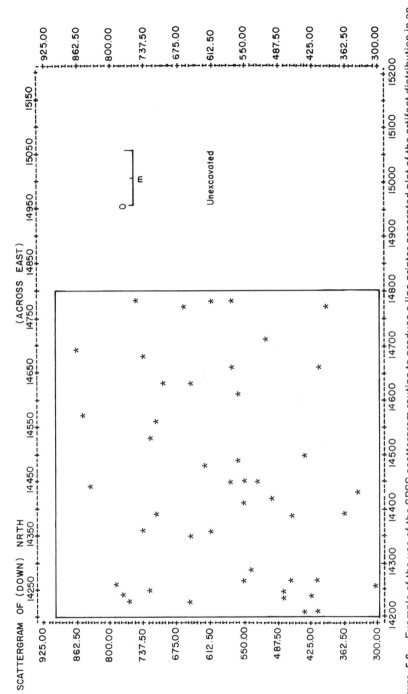

Figure 5.6. Example of the use of the SPSS scattergram routine to produce a line-printer-generated plot of the artifact distribution in an excavation unit (Copp 1977:Figure 3). (Reproduced by permission of the author and the *Newsletter of Computer Archaeology*.)

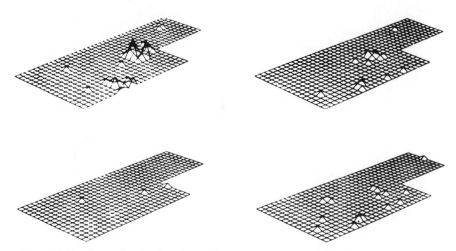

Figure 5.7. Example of using three-dimensional perspective plots to illustrate the distribution of four types of artifacts across an area sampled by controlled surface collections (Scheitlin and Clark 1978:Figure 3). (Reproduced by permission of the authors and the *Newsletter of Computer Archaeology*.)

1979) applied what he referred to as statistical distribution cartography in the statistical treatment of variable archaeological data across a defined site or region. The statistical methods used ranged from descriptive to correlative. Predictive modeling of site distribution is the aim of many computerized cartographic projects for both research and cultural resource management purposes (Arnold 1980). Computer graphics will play a vital role in these studies.

Samuels (1977) discussed in great detail the function and capabilities of digitizers in his article on the computerization of surface or land-contour data. He explained and advocated digitizing two-dimensional contour-map data to enable the computer to produce three-dimensional perspective drawings. The surface can then be viewed from any angle as an aid to archaeological analysis. Samuels has an enthusiastic but also realistic view of the applicability of his technique. He sites several, mainly hardware, limitations of the relatively simple system he used. Many of these limitations do not apply to more sophisticated digitizers.

Ehrenhard (1979) utilized a digitizer to aid a search for an historic fort. The eighteenth-century Fort William was located on Cumberland Island off the south Georgia coast. A series of maps dated at intervals from historic times to the present showed that the coastline of the island had substantially changed over time. The differing scales of the maps also made direct comparisons difficult, therefore the maps were digitized and a computer-produced map with overlays of the coastline of each map with scale corrections was prepared. This composite map demonstrated that the project's original unsuccessful search had been in the wrong area. The site was easily located with the help of the computer-generated map.

Some computer graphics software packages have map bases built in. Such a package was used to generate the computer graphics shown by Eighmy *et al.* (1980) (Figure 5.8) to illustrate the changing positions of the earth's geomagnetic pole. The software used, called SUPERMAP, presents specified portions of any of seven different global projections. Options allow plotting points or points with circles or ovals of confidence (Sternberg, personal communication). In an imaginative exploitation of computer X-Y plotter and statistical capabilities, Burton (1977) reported on a program for developing archaeological sampling strategies. Sampling methods available included simple random, systematic, stratified systematic unaligned, and random walk. Sampling unit size, shape, and orientation were variables specified by the user. "Numerous samples may be obtained easily either on actual survey data or on constructed situations created to test the efficiency of a sampling technique" (Burton 1977:1). The program can also be used to create a sampling design for a given project area.

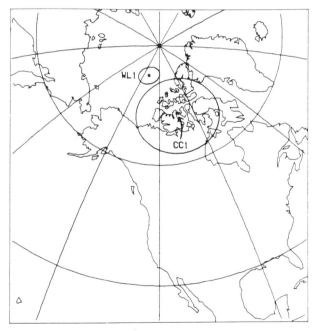

Figure 5.8.   Example of data plotted on a computer-produced map base, in this case past geomagnetic pole positions based on archaeomagnetic dating (Eighmy *et al.* 1980:Figure 2). (Reproduced by permission of the Society for American Archaeology from *American Antiquity* 45(3):511, 1980.)

In dealing with geographic data in computer graphics, bear in mind that it is much easier to deal with Universal Transverse Mercator (UTM) coordinates in meters or State Grid Plane coordinates in feet than with latitude and longitude. Also, the digitizing process can be time consuming.

Surface Representation by Contour, Three-Dimensional Perspective, and Other Plots

Plotting the quantity or intensity of various values, objects, or the results of electronic surveying techniques is a process of great interest to archaeologists, as it is to scientists of other disciplines. Considerable experimentation with different computer graphics techniques for representing intensity has been carried out by archaeologists. Among the software being used most successfully are packages such as SYMAP and SYMVU (Laboratory for Computer Graphics and Spatial Analysis 1971, 1975), packages by one of the major plotter manufacturers CALCOMP (1969a, 1969b), DISSPLA® (ISSCO 1978), and CPS-1 by Unitech (1973). All of these packages include capabilities to produce various kinds of contour and three-dimensional perspective plots. For a more in-depth evaluation see Arnold (1979).

One of the most imaginative and prolific writers on this subject is Scollar (1969, 1970, 1974). His specialty is archaeological magnetometer surveys and the automated analysis of the data from such surveys. After comparing related computer plotting techniques such as line printer (Scollar 1969) and X-Y-plotter contour plots (Scollar 1970), he selected and developed a method of dot-density plotting that represents the intensity of the magnetometer readings across a surface by a pseudo-half-tone technique (Figure 5.9). "Plots made using the dot technique appear to make very good use of the eye's ability to detect patterns in random arrays of points" (Scollar 1974:77). He also developed methods of enhancing the images through filtering out the background noise in the magnetic data (Scollar 1969) and eventually automated the entire survey process so that the data could be gathered in the field in machine-readable form, which tremendously accelerated the whole survey and graphics production process (Scollar 1974). Interestingly, his computer graphics output is produced by a microfilm plotter.

Archaeological magnetometer surveying was also the topic for Linington (1970), who used computer graphics to analyze the results of a survey and to extrapolate the expected magnetometer survey results for given buried structures under certain hypothetical situations (Figure 5.10). The excavation of several structures in a prehistoric pithouse village followed a successful magnetometer survey at a site in western Texas as reported by Arnold and Kegley (1977). Computer-drawn contour and perspective plots were used to illustrate the magnetometer survey results (Figures 5.11 and 5.12). In a review

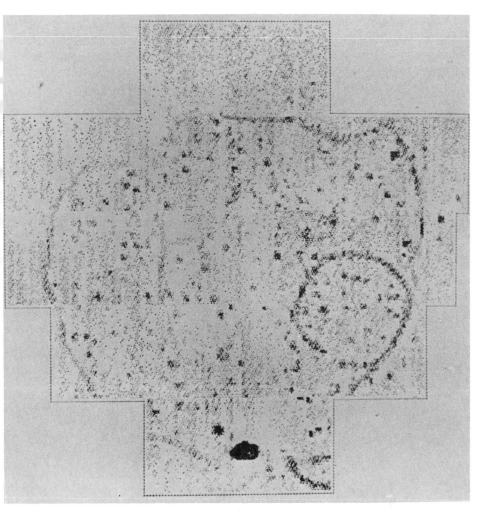

Figure 5.9. Example of a dot density plot used to illustrate the results of a magnetometer survey (Clark 1975:Figure 8). (Reproduced by permission of the author and the *Journal of Archaeological Science.*)

article on archaeological prospecting with electronic instruments, Clark (1975) presented a number of examples of different varieties of computer graphics that can be used to present similar data.

Dean and Robinson (1977) used computer-drawn contour plots to represent the changing spatial patterns of tree-ring growth and therefore variations in climate, such as rainfall and temperature, throughout the Southwest. The 128 maps each represent a 10-year period from 1970 back. The capabilities of

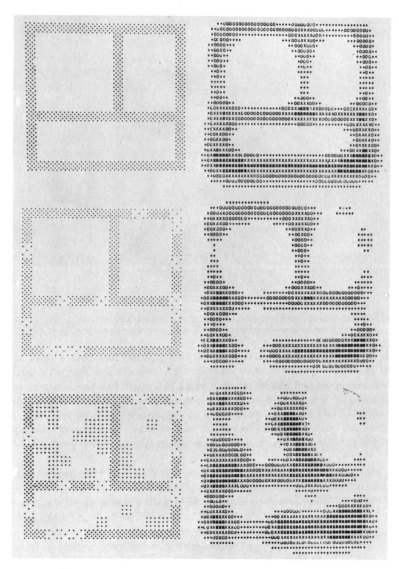

Figure 5.10. Example of the use of line-printer-generated plots to construct theoretical models of the magnetic anomalies to be expected from increasingly complex structural remains (Linington 1971:Figure 5). (Reproduced by permission of the author and the Royal Society of London.)

200

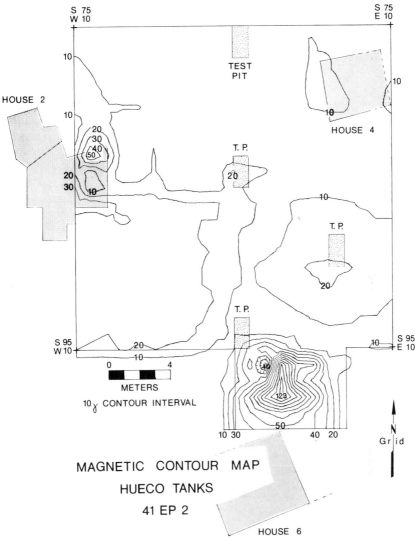

Figure 5.11. Contour plot of data from a magnetometer survey of a portion of a prehistoric pithouse village in West Texas. The structures subsequently excavated are shaded. (Reproduced by permission of the Texas Journal of Science.)

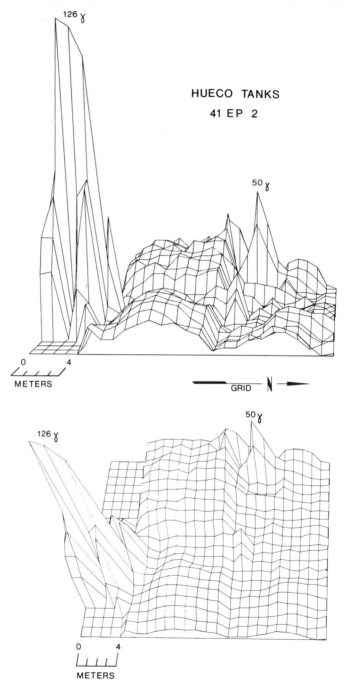

Figure 5.12. Two perspective views of the same magnetometer data shown in Figure 5.11. (Reproduced by permission of the Texas Journal of Science.)

the program used are discussed in an appendix (Dean and Robinson 1977:11–16). In a subsequent publication, Dean and Robinson (1979) present a more detailed discussion on the development of their project and compare their X–Y plotter contouring routine to SYMAP, examining the advantages and disadvantages of each.

That these particular computer graphics techniques can be used for less esoteric data is beginning to be realized by the archaeological community at large. Witness Frankel's (1980) discussion of using computer-drawn contour and perspective plots for topographic data from a shallow earthwork of aboriginal construction in Australia. The program is somewhat limited because of the necessity for taking the height readings on an evenly spaced grid across the site. Many of the more sophisticated software packages can accommodate data taken at irregular intervals and interpolate to the regular grid the computer needs before the computer can do the actual contouring. The only requirement is that there are sets of x, y (e.g., north and east grid coordinates), and z (in this case, the height measured by transit or alidade) coordinates. Frankel is absolutely correct in pointing out that, although one may need assistance from one's computer center staff the first time one uses such graphics software packages, thereafter, even the novice computer user should be able to proceed independently. Copp (1980) used computer-drawn contour and three-dimensional maps to illustrate the topography of the Beach Grove site (Figure 5.13). In an earlier study (Copp 1979), three-dimensional plots were used to show the contours of subsurface deposits or levels in an archaeological site compared to the adjoining undisturbed ground surface.

It should be mentioned that concern has often been expressed about the accuracy of the computer routines used to produce contour plots and other distributional graphics. The method of interpolation utilized is of critical concern as a source of possible distortion in computer plots. Hodder (1979) provides a rigorous critical review of several of these programs and methods. SYMAP is one of the most widely used program packages in archaeological applications of computer graphics. Jermann and Dunnell (1979) test the program through the range of its options on actual archaeological data. They evaluate the program package and make suggestions regarding the best of those options for archaeological purposes based on their test results, a particularly valuable contribution. In a discussion and appraisal article, Aldrich (1979) reviewed the articles and methods presented in the Upham (1979) volume, summarizing a number of the pitfalls in using SYMAP and contour plotting packages in general. Concerns include selecting the proper cartographic representation, selecting an appropriate interpolation routine to extrapolate continuous surfaces from discrete-point data distributions, and problems in achieving accurate area-density shadings with line-printer plots. Feder (1979) suggests that trend surface analysis, a statistical manipulation of

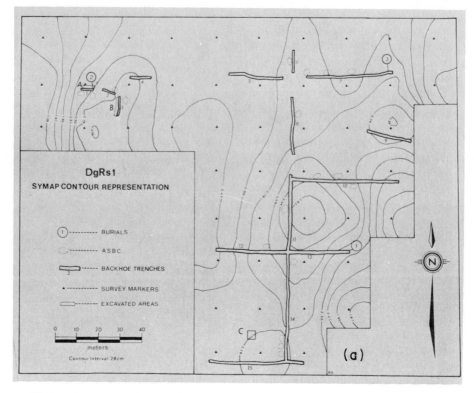

Figure 5.13. (a) Computer-drawn contour and (b) three-dimensional perspective plots of the topography of an archaeological site (Copp 1980:Figures 2 and 3). The vertical scale of the three-dimensional plot has been exaggerated to emphasize the topographical changes. (Reproduced by permission of the author and the *Datum: Heritage Conservation Branch Newsletter.*)

the data producing a best-fit model, is superior to the methods of interpolation commonly used in packages like SYMAP. Some packages give the user a choice of interpolation routines based on different formulas. CPS-1 (Unitech 1973) users, for instance, have a choice of six interpolation options or they can write their own. The consensus of reviewers, however, is an enthusiastic endorsement of computer contour plotting, given proper care by the user.

In underwater archaeology, computer graphics applications have gone hand in hand with the application and adaptation of marine geophysical survey techniques to the search for historic shipwreck sites. Arnold (1975, 1976) reports on a large-scale marine archaeological magnetometer survey with automated data acquisition and processing, heavily relying on computer drawn contour and three-dimensional plots to display the data. Pearson and

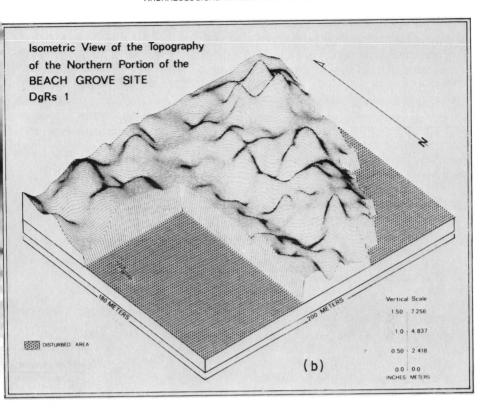

Rhodes (1980) used similar techniques in a more recent study conducted for the Corps of Engineers. In a very interesting project focusing on the Civil-War-period ironclad *CSS Georgia,* Garrison and Lowery (1980) used computer-drawn contour and perspective plots of water-depth data automatically recorded from a fathometer. Since the wreck protrudes above the bottom, the bathemetric maps are of as great an interest as the analogous topographic maps of an archaeological feature on land (e.g., Frankel's earthwork mentioned previously) would be. This is doubly true since underwater visibility is absolutely zero in the Savannah River where the wreck lies.

A substitution with many of the benefits of more formal computer graphics techniques is presented by the following three examples. Hand-held programmable calculators can be used to calculate coordinates that are then plotted by hand on graph paper, an ingenious and innovative adaptation for those archaeologists on a severely limited or nonexistent budget, as so many of us often are. Mazel and Riess (1979) used two transits, walkie–talkie radios, and a hand-held programmable calculator to plot the course of their survey vessel during a marine magnetometer survey in search of an historic shipwreck in

Maine. In a limited area close to shore, this obviated the need for leasing the extremely expensive electronic positioning equipment that would be needed for a larger-scale survey or one with a search area farther offshore. For underwater archaeologists, the accurate recording of a ship's structure is a key problem, particularly the interior profiles or cross sections of the hull. Such data are often initially obtained using a protractor and tape measure system. For easier, more accurate, and quicker production of plots of these data, Green (1980) developed a program for a hand-held programmable calculator to convert what were essentially polar coordinates into x and y coordinates. With the x–y coordinates, it was much simpler to produce a hand-drawn profile from the raw measurements. Henn (1976) used the same general idea to produce graph, or x–y, coordinates for hand-drawn star distribution charts showing change over time for the relative position of certain stars important in an astroarchaeological project.

APPROACHING COMPUTER GRAPHICS

Having decided computer graphics has a place in the archaeologist's repertoire, what is the next step? There is great variability among computer facilities in the level of sophistication and capabilities in computer graphics. It may seem self-evident, but the first step is to inquire at one's computer center about their graphics capabilities, both hardware and software. There will probably be an index of available software. It is unlikely that the archaeologist will be developing graphics software programs, but rather will be limited to using the packages available at the computer facility. The manual or manuals for the software package should be acquired and studied. These manuals will be very important references. One should be able to count on the advice and support of the local computer center in assisting one in getting started. I have always found such staff members enthusiastically cooperative and helpful. In budgeting, however, one should be aware that running graphics programs can consume more computer time than the typical statistical program. There are sometimes added charges for use of the plotters, and occasionally a royalty must be paid for the use of certain graphics packages. The product is worth the added cost when one considers the impact, not to mention the time and money saved, in comparison to that of manual drafting techniques.

Comparing the capabilities and the advantages and disadvantages of the major graphics software packages in detail is beyond the scope of this chapter. This question is addressed to some extent, however, in Arnold (1979). An examination of an industry-wide directory of software revealed almost 100 different graphics software packages (Datapro Research Corporation 1980). A detailed breakdown of the characteristics and capabilities of each package is provided. These programs are commercially available. They can be acquired at prices ranging from $35 for the Apple Data-Graph package, which produces color line graphs and scattergrams on an Apple II, to $25,000 for the CPS-1, which produces a variety of contour and three-dimensional plots using the largest computers and most sophisticated plotters.

FUTURE APPLICATIONS IN ARCHAEOLOGY

Some archaeologists have been so enthusiastic in adopting computer techniques that program packages specifically for archaeological uses have been assembled. Computer graphics are heavily emphasized in these efforts to make the use of computers more convenient for archaeologists. The British have put together the PLUTARCH (*P*rogram *L*ibrary *U*seful *to* *Arch*aeologists) package described by Wilcock (1974). This is an interactive graphics package utilizing light pen, key board, function keys, and disc storage. The package provides capabilities in information retrieval, statistical analysis, and graphics including three-dimensional plots, dendrograms, scalograms, histograms, pie charts, and distribution maps. Miscellaneous features include reduction of magnetometer data and pollen analysis. Aldrich and Effland (1974) reported an effort to integrate several programs into an archaeological package including SARG, MAPSARG, SYMAP, GIPSY3, SPSS, and a locally produced contouring program for archaeological data analysis and illustrative purposes. Although the latter case seems a bit unwieldy, increased numbers of "canned" program packages can be expected in the future. The major existing software packages can be expected to continue to evolve, as we have seen in the case of SPSS, becoming both more versatile and more convenient to use.

Perhaps a slightly more mundane application of computer graphics is the "form control terminal" discussed by Gaines and Gaines (1980:466). A special CRT is used on which frequently used computer coding forms are prepared once and then called to the face of the terminal at will. Flashing fields or cursors direct the user to each point where data must be entered. Aside from the convenience of avoiding the care and storage of countless paper forms, the data can be automatically checked by the computer for accuracy as it is entered. In the future, archaeologists will undoubtedly see the advantages of this method for coding large numbers of individual cases or items.

Data banks are becoming increasingly important in archaeology for research and cultural resource management. In Texas, the State Archaeologist's office is undertaking the centralization and coding for computer of the site files held by a number of institutions around the state. The tens of thousands of archaeological, historical, engineeering, and architectural sites recorded by many institutions, agencies, and programs will be available for research purposes such as predictive modeling and for cultural resource management purposes (Texas Heritage Conservation Plan 1981). The masses of data involved in these activities that will have to be faced eventually all across the country will necessitate ever increasing activities along these lines. Computer graphics will have a role to play. Imagine an archaeologist involved in a project review for cultural resource management purposes. First, instructions are typed in that call up on the CRT a previously digitized map base for the area in which a new pipeline or highway is proposed. The computerized site files are then accessed, and a sprinkling of site locations appears scattered across the map base. Different symbols or even different colors represent different types of sites. Then, looking at the plans for the proposed project route, the archaeologist types in the coordinates of the end points and any curves or bends. The coordinates can be latitude–longitude, state grid plane, UTM, or any of 8 or 10 other coordinate systems—the computer will automatically calculate any conversions necessary. The route will appear on the screen. If it appears that any conflicts in terms of damage to an archaeological site may occur, and a request for some action from the company or agency is needed, it may be desirable to have a paper copy of the map on file or to mail out with comments. If a somewhat informal version of the plot will do, a piece of special heat sensitive paper can be placed on the small printer or hard copy unit situated beside the CRT to make a copy on legal-size paper. Alternatively, the archaeologist can specify that the plot be prepared for later pickup in four colors and virtually any size on the large X-Y plotter at the computer center, the facilities of which can be used via a telephone linkup. The capabilities for this scenario exist today. It is up to us to take advantage of these and other possible computer applications.

Laser plotters are on the cutting edge of computer graphics technological development. Primary applications are still developing in such uses as the processing of data from satellite remote sensing systems and marine geophysical surveys. Archaeological applications will be spin-offs of these and other primary uses, but it is not too soon to start thinking about them. The color graphics processed from digitized marine seismic- or subbottom-profiler data are a truly mind-boggling improvement over the printouts of the same images available up till now. Previous printouts were produced with a gray scale of only three or four tones. The electronic instruments receiving the sound waves returning from the layers of the ocean bottom could distinguish a great many more shades or frequencies of sound than the machines on board were capable of plotting. The answer was to digitize that data and store it on tape for later more sensitive processing. The same technique is being considered for exploiting a similar latent potential of side-scan sonar imagery. The subbottom-profiling survey technique is already of great interest to archaeologists interested in prehistoric sites that have been inundated by lakes or rising sea levels. The side-scan sonar survey technique is of great interest to underwater archaeologists in searching for historic shipwreck sites because it produces what amounts to a photographic image of the ocean floor out to several hundred meters on either side of the survey vessel. Any advance that increases by a quantum leap the detail available from such survey instruments is also of archaeological significance. One wonders if perhaps the same image processing might be appropriate for a ground penetrating radar, a technique more familiar to archaeologists working on land.

The advances in remote sensing developed in the space program are beginning to have an impact on archaeology (Lyons and Avery 1977). Color infrared, multispectral scanner, and other types of images from aircraft are being used more and more by archaeologists in analyzing sites. Computer graphics techniques for handling and analyzing digital remote sensing data, particularly from multispectral scanner, have reached a very high level and are usually used for analyzing such matters of ecological or agricultural concern as crop conditions. A graphics package (Laboratory for the Application of Remote Sensing 1973a, 1973b) was specifically developed for such ecological analysis. The opportunity for archaeological exploitation of the mountains of unclassified, digitized satellite remote sensing imagery already existing is mainly in the area of studying regional environmental factors in relation to archaeological problems, since from space the scale is too small to distinguish individual archaeological features. However, dealing with this mass of digitized satellite data can be complicated.

Computer graphics can also be used to produce animation sequences, a capability that has potential for archaeological applications:

> No longer bound by the problem of the materialization of objects and the attendant problems of mass, gravity, friction, and the laws of mechanics and physics, man now explores and simulates alternative systems to deal with reality. With the technology of computer animation man creates powerful and compelling models to help explain his universe (Csuri 1977:4).

Animation by computer graphics is no longer an exclusive and esoteric area of research. It has become an economically practical application for more investigators due to advances in software and hardware. Archaeologists might use such animation sequences to illustrate the stages of development of a mound, a site, or a city. Computer graphics techniques developed by architects are not only used to illustrate structures, but can produce computer calculations on approximate cost of construction, heat loss and air circulation, daylight factors, etc. The nature of computer graphics makes it possible to extend this method to easy testing of alternative configurations (Walker *et al.* 1975). Archaeologists could well utilize these architectural computer graphics techniques in the analysis and reconstruction of historic and prehistoric structures.

Mapping activities and techniques are an integral part of the archaeologist's repertoire. Fulton (1975) presented an important review article exploring the importance and application of computers in mapping methodology, including a discussion of the integral role of computer graphics. Currently available techniques for digitizing topographic and shallow bathemetric data from stereo photographs seem to come to us directly from the realm of science fiction. Ellis (1978) goes into additional detail on these techniques of "semi-analytical aerotriangulation" through which are gathered digital x, y, and z axis measurements from stereo photos set up on a stereoplotter equipped with digital incoders. The advantages in time saved over the old alidade and plane-table methods for large sites is obvious, and the data is in machine-readable form, ready for the production of computer-drawn contour and perspective plots. The same x, y, and z coordinates, whether acquired by traditional surveying techniques or by the automated stereo photogrametric techniques just mentioned, could also be fed to a computer-controlled milling machine for production of a physical model of a site's topography. Imagine the applications for museum displays. Models of relatively complex objects can be produced by this technique (Newman and Sproull 1979:299), so it is conceivable that a model of even a complex site, such as a ruined pueblo or the in situ exposed hull remains of an historic ship, could be easily and rapidly produced.

The conclusion reached by the present author is that there is an incredible range and variety of computer graphics and concomitant techniques presently available. Even more are evolving all the time as high technology advances. It is up to us as individual archaeologists to make an effort to more fully exploit the resources available. The entire discipline will be the beneficiary of such efforts.

REFERENCES

Adovasio, J. M., G. F. Fry, J. D. Gunn, and R. F. Maslowski
    1975   Prehistoric and historic settlement patterns in western Cyprus (with a discussion of Cypriot Neolithic stone technology). *World Archaeology* 6(3):339–366.
Aldrich, F. T.
    1979   Comments on computer graphics applications in archaeology. In *Computer graphics in archaeology: statistical cartographic applications to spatial analysis in archaeological contexts,* edited by Steadman Upham. Anthropological Research Papers No. 15:145–148. Arizona State University, Tempe.

Aldrich, F., and R. Effland, Jr.
   1974   MAPSARG: a graphic display system. *Newsletter of Computer Archaeology*
           10(1):8-13.
Arizona State University
   1965-1979 *Newsletter of Computer Archaeology.* Arizona State University, Tempe.
Arnold, J. B. III
   1975   A marine archeological application of automated data acquisition and processing.
           Newsletter of Computer Archaeology **11**(1):5-11.
   1976   An underwater archeological magnetometer survey and site test excavation project
           off Padre Island, Texas. *Texas Antiquities Committee Publication* No. 3. Austin,
           Texas.
   1979   Archaeological applications of computer-drawn contour and three dimensional
           perspective plots. In *Computer graphics in archaeology: statistical cartographic
           applications to spatial analysis in archaeological contexts,* edited by Steadman
           Upham. Anthropological Research Papers No. 15:1-15. Arizona State University,
           Tempe.
   1980   Underwater cultural resource management: the computerized shipwreck reference
           file. Paper presented at the Eleventh Conference on Underwater Archaeology,
           Albuquerque, New Mexico.
Arnold, J. B. III, and G. B. Kegley III
   1977   Results of a magnetometer survey at Hueco Tanks, a prehistoric Mogollon village
           in western Texas. *The Texas Journal of Science* **28**:201-207.
Auerbach Publishers
   1972   *Auerbach on digital plotters and image digitizers.* New York: Auerbach
           Publishers.
Biese, L. P., and E. Iannuccillo
   1979   The reduction of Maya long count dates and calendar round position to their
           Gregorian equivalents. *American Antiquity* **44**:784-791.
Breiner, S., and M. D. Coe
   1972   Magnetic exploration of the Olmec civilization. *American Scientist* **60**:566-575.
Burton, R. J.
   1977   ARCHSAMP: a general purpose sampling simulation program. *Newsletter of
           Computer Archaeology* **13**(2):1-23.
CALCOMP
   1969a   General purpose contouring program. California Computer Products, Inc.,
           Anaheim, California.
   1969b   Three-D: a perspective drawing software system. California Computer Products,
           Inc., Anaheim, California.
Chenhall, R. G.
   1968   The impact of computers on archaeological theory: an appraisal and projection.
           Computers and the Humanities **3**:15-24.
Clark, A.
   1975   Archaeological prospecting: a progress report. *Journal of Archaeological Science*
           2:297-314.
Clark, G. A.
   1979   Spatial association at Liencres, an early Holocene open site on the Santander
           Coast, north-central Spain. In *Computer graphics in archaeology: statistical car-
           tographic applications to spatial analysis in archaeological contexts,* edited by
           Steadman Upham. Anthropological Research Papers No. 15:121-143. Arizona
           State University, Tempe.

Copp, S. A.
  1977   A quick plotting program for archaeological data. *Newsletter of Computer Archaeology* **13**(1):17–25.
  1979   Archaeological excavations at the McCall Site, South Okanagan Valley, British Columbia. Unpublished M.A. thesis, Department of Archaeology, Simon Fraser University, Burnaby.
  1980   Beach Grove: 3,000 years of prehistory. *Datum: Heritage and Conservation Branch Newsletter* **5**(3):4–9.
Croes, D., J. Davis, and H. T. Irwin
  1974   *The use of computer graphics in archaeology: a case study from the Ozette Site, Washington.* Laboratory of Anthropology Investigation No. 52. Washington State University, Pullman.
Csuri, C. A.
  1977   3-D computer animation. *Advances in Computers* **16**:1–55.
Datapro Research Corporation
  1980   *Datapro directory of software.* Datapro Research Corporation, Delrane, New Jersey.
Dean, J. S., and W. J. Robinson
  1977   *Dendroclimatic variability in the American Southwest A.D. 680 to 1970.* Laboratory of Tree-Ring Research, The University of Arizona, Tucson.
  1979   Computer cartography and the reconstruction of dendroclimatic variability in the American Southwest, A.D. 680 to 1970. In *Computer graphics in archaeology: statistical cartographic applications to spatial analysis in archaeological contexts,* edited by S. Upham. Anthropological Research Papers No. 15:79–94. Arizona State University, Tempe.
Dixon, W. J., and M. B. Brown (editors)
  1979   *BMDP-79: biomedical computer programs P-series.* Berkeley: University of California Press.
Doty, D. C.
  1979   A new Mayan long count Gregorian conversion computer program. *American Antiquity* **44**:780–783.
Effland, R. W.
  1978   Applications of computer graphic techniques to SARG data. In *Investigations of the Southwestern Anthropological Research Group,* edited by Euler and Gumerman. Museum of Northern Arizona, Flagstaff.
  1979   Statistical distribution cartography and computer graphics. In *Computer graphics in archaeology: statistical cartographic applications to spatial analysis in archaeological contexts,* edited by S. Upham. Anthropological Research Papers No. 15:17–29. Arizona State University, Tempe.
Ehrenhard, J. E.
  1979   Composite mapping for archeology. In *Proceedings of the First Conference on Scientific Research in the National Parks,* edited by Robert Linn. USDI-NPS Transactions and Proceedings Series No. 5:(2):955–958.
Eighmy, J. L., R. S. Sternberg, and R. F. Butler
  1980   Archaeomagnetic dating in the American Southwest. *American Antiquity* **45**(3): 507–517.
Ekland, C.
  1977   Neutron activation analysis of West Texas ceramics: a statistical evaluation. *Bulletin of the Texas Archaeological Society* **48**:119–131.
Ellis, M. Y. (editor)
  1978   *Coastal mapping handbook.* U.S. Department of Interior, Geological Survey;

U.S. Department of Commerce, National Ocean Survey, Office of Coastal Zone Management. Washington, D.C.: U.S. Government Printing Office.

Feder, K. L.
1979   Geographic patterning of tool types as elicited by trend surface analysis. In *Computer graphics in archaeology: statistical cartographic applications to spatial analysis in archaeological contexts,* edited by S. Upham. Anthropological Research Papers No. 15:95-102. Arizona State University, Tempe.

Fine, B. T.
1980   High resolution landsat for geophysical studies. Paper presented at the 14th International Symposium on Remote Sensing of the Environment, San Jose, Costa Rica.

Frankel, D.
1980   Contour-plans and surface plotting: aids for the field archaeologist. *Journal of Field Archaeology* 7(3):367-372.

Fulton, P.
1975   Mapping and computers. *Advances in Computers* 13:73-108.

Gaines, S. W., and W. M. Gaines
1980   Future trends in computer applications. *American Antiquity* 45:462-471.

Garrison, E. G., and L. Lowery, Jr.
1980   *The archaeological and engineering study of the C.S.S. Georgia, Part 1: abstract and executive management summary.* Cultural Resources Laboratory, Anthropology Program, and Structural Systems, Civil Engineering Department, Texas A & M University, College Station, Texas.

Gifford, D. P., and D. C. Crader
1977   A computer coding system for archaeological faunal remains. *American Antiquity* 42:225-238.

Graham, I., P. Galloway, and I. Scollar
1975   Model studies in seriation techniques. In *Computer applications in archaeology 1975: proceedings of the annual conference organized by the Computer Centre,* pp. 18-24. University of Birmingham, England.

Green, D. F., and E. L. Summer
1976   RADPLOT: a computer program for settlement analysis. *Newsletter of Computer Archaeology* 12(2):17-24.

Green, J.
1980   Maritime archaeology applications for a programmable calculator. *The International Journal of Nautical Archaeology and Underwater Exploration* 9(2):139-145.

Henn, J. M.
1976   Computer applications of astroarchaeological methodology. *Newsletter of Computer Archaeology* 12(1):1-31.

Hodder, I.
1979   Trends and surfaces in archaeology. In *Computer graphics in archaeology: statistical cartographic applications to spatial analysis in archaeological contexts,* edited by S. Upham. Anthropological Research Papers No. 15:149-153. Arizona State University, Tempe.

Hodson, F. R.
1970   Cluster analysis and archaeology: some new developments and applications. *World Archaeology* 1(3):299-320.

IBM
1971   *Computers in anthropology and archeology: IBM data processing application.* International Business Machines Corp., White Plains, New York.

International Technology Marketing
>   1974   *Final report: the computer graphics industry; a study for users and producers.* International Technology Marketing, Newton, Massachusetts.

ISSCO
>   1978   *DISSPLA: display integrated software system and plotting language users manual* (Current with Version 8.2.). Integrated Software Systems Corp., San Diego, California.

Jermann, J. V., and R. C. Dunnell
>   1979   Some limitations of isopleth mapping in archaeology. In *Computer graphics in archaeology: statistical cartographic applications to spatial analysis in archaeological contexts,* edited by S. Upham. Anthropological Research Papers No. 15:31–60. Arizona State University, Tempe.

Jones, P. A., and J. D. Wilcock
>   1974   Paleolithic "leafpoints"—an experiment in taxonomy. In *Computer applications in archaeology 1974: proceedings of the annual conference organized by the Computer Centre, University of Birmingham,* pp. 36–46, Birmingham, England.

Klein, S., and W. G. Nisen (editors)
>   1979a   Color hard copy: the barriers begin to fall. *The Harvard Newsletter on Computer Graphics* 1(1):1–2.
>   1979b   *The Harvard Newsletter on Computer Graphics* 1(2):4.

Kohl, P. L., G. Harbottle, and E. V. Sayre
>   1979   Physical and chemical analysis of soft stone vessels from southwest Asia. *Archaeometry* 21(2):131–159.

Krowne, C. M., R. V. Sidrys, and S. K. Cooperman
>   1979   A Lowland Maya calendar round-long count conversion computer program. *American Antiquity* 44:775–780.

Laboratory for Applications of Remote Sensing
>   1973a   *Guide to multispectral data analysis using LARSYS.* Laboratory for Applications of Remote Sensing, Purdue University, West Lafayette, Indiana.
>   1973b   *Remote sensing analysis: a basic preparation.* Laboratory for Applications of Remote Sensing, Purdue University, West Lafayette, Indiana.

Laboratory for Computer Graphics and Spatial Analysis
>   1971   *SYMVU manual—version 1.0.* Laboratory for Computer Graphics and Spatial Analysis, Harvard University, Cambridge, Massachusetts.
>   1975   *SYMAP user's reference manual, edition 5.0.* Laboratory for Computer Graphics and Spatial Analysis, Harvard University, Cambridge, Massachusetts.

Lee, K.
>   1975   *Evaluation of computer graphics terminals.* Environmental Design and Research Center, Boston.

Lees, W. B., and K. M. Kimery-Lees
>   1979   The function of Colano-Indian ceramics: insights from Limerick Plantation, South Carolina. *Historical Archaeology* 13:1–13.

Linington, R. E.
>   1970   Techniques used in archaeological field surveys. *Philosophical Transactions of the Royal Society of London* A(269):89–108.

Lyons, T. R., and T. E. Avery
>   1977   *Remote sensing: a handbook for archaeologists and cultural resource managers.* National Park Service, Washington, D.C.

Mazel, C., and W. Riess
>   1979   An inexpensive method for real-time, accurate navigational control of marine surveys. *The International Journal of Nautical Archaeology and Underwater Exploration* 8(4):333–338.

McNett, C. W., Jr.
   1979   Computer graphics in the analysis of an eastern Paleo-Indian site. In *Computer graphics in archaeology: statistical cartographic applications to spatial analysis in archaeological contexts,* edited by S. Upham. Anthropological Research Papers No. 15:69–77. Arizona State University, Tempe.
Nelson, F. W., K. K. Nielson, N. F. Mangelson, M. W. Hill, and R. T. Matheny
   1977   Preliminary studies of the trace element composition of obsidian artifacts from northern Campeche, Mexico. *American Antiquity* **42**(2):209–224.
Newman, W. M., and R. F. Sproull
   1979   *Principles of interactive computer graphics* (second ed.). New York: McGraw-Hill.
Nie, N. H., C. H. Hall, J. G. Jenkins, K. Steinbrenner, and D. H. Bent
   1975   *SPSS: statistical package for the social sciences* (second ed.). New York: McGraw-Hill.
Olshan, A. F., J. L. Hantman, and K. G. Lightfoot
   1977   The use of high-dimensional plotting in the analysis of multivariate archaeological data. *Newsletter of Computer Archaeology* **12**(4):1–13.
Pearson, C., and H. Rhodes
   1980   A magnetic survey of proposed channel improvement areas of the mouth of the Colorado River, Texas. Prepared for the Galveston District, U.S. Army Corps of Engineers (Contract DACW-64-79-1-0024). Coastal Environments, Inc., Baton Rouge, Louisiana.
Prueitt, M. L.
   1976   From data to dimension—computer-drawn graphics for science. *Functional Photography* **11**:18–25.
Redman, C. L., and P. J. Watson
   1970   Systematic, intensive surface collection. *American Antiquity* **35**:279–291.
Rogers, D. F., and J. A. Adams
   1976   *Mathematical elements for computer graphics.* New York: McGraw-Hill.
Samuels, S. R.
   1977   Investigations into computer graphics: archaeological applications. In *Occasional papers in method and theory in California archaeology.* Society for California Archaeology, No. 1:65–82.
Scheitlin, T. E., and G. A. Clark
   1978   Three dimensional surface representations of lithic categories at Liencres. *Newsletter of Computer Archaeology* **13**(3–4):1–13.
Schrack, G. F. (editor)
   1980   Current literature in computer graphics and interactive techniques: references. *Computer Graphics: A Quarterly Report of SIGGRAPH-ACM* **13**(4):381–394.
Scollar, I.
   1969   Some techniques for the evaluation of archaeological magnetometer surveys. *World Archaeology* **1**(1):77–89.
   1970   Magnetic methods of archaeological prospecting—advances in instrumentation and evaluation techniques. *Philosophical Transactions of the Royal Society of London* **A**(269):109–119.
   1974   Interactive processing of geophysical data from archaeological sites. In *Computer applications in archaeology 1974: proceedings of the annual conference organized by the Computer Centre, University of Birmingham,* pp. 75–80. Birmingham, England.
Scollar, I., and F. Kruckeberg
   1966   Computer treatment of magnetic measurements from archaeological sites. *Archaeometry* **9**:61–71.

Tainter, J. A.
   1975   Social inference and mortuary practice: an experiment in numerical classification. *World Archaeology* **7**(1):1–15.
Texas Heritage Conservation Plan
   1981   *Texas Heritage Conservation Plan Computerization Program Manual.* Texas Historical Commission, Austin, in press.
Upham, S. (editor)
   1979   *Computer graphics in archaeology: statistical cartographic applications to spatial analysis in archaeological contexts,* edited by S. Upham. Anthropological Research Papers No. 15. Arizona State University, Tempe.
Unitech, Inc.
   1973   *Contour plotting system (CPS-1)* (vols. 1 & 2). Unitech, Inc., Austin, Texas.
University of Birmingham Computer Centre
   1974–   *Computer applications in archaeology: proceedings of the annual conferences*
   1977   *organized by the Computer Centre, University of Birmingham.* Birmingham, England.
Walker, B. S., J. R. Gurd, and E. A. Drawneek
   1975   *Interactive computer graphics.* New York: Crane Russak.
Webster's Dictionary
   1971   *Webster's third new international dictionary of the English language, unabridged.* G. & C. Merriam, Springfield, Massachusetts.
Weymouth, J. W., and R. Nickel
   1977   A magnetometer survey of the Knife River Indian villages. *Plains Anthropologist* **22**(78-2):104–118.
Whallon, R., Jr.
   1971   Spatial analysis of Paleolithic occupation areas. In *The explanation of culture change: models in prehistory,* edited by Colin Renfrew. Pittsburgh: University of Pittsburgh Press. Pp. 115–130.
   1972   The computer in archaeology: a critical survey. *Computers and the Humanities* **1**(1):29–45.
Wilcock, J. D.
   1974   The PLUTARCH system. In *Computer applications in archaeology 1974: proceedings of the annual conference organized by the Computer Centre, University of Birmingham,* pp. 64–68. Birmingham, England.
Wobst, H. M.
   1979   Computers and coordinates: strategies for the analysis of Paleolithic stratigraphy. In *Computer graphics in archaeology: statistical cartographic applications to spatial analysis in archaeological contexts,* edited by S. Upham. Anthropological Research Papers No. 15:61–67. Arizona State University, Tempe.
Wood, J. V.
   1974   A computer program for hierarchical cluster analysis. *Newsletter of Computer Archaeology* **9**(4):1–11.

Quantifying Archaeological Research

G. A. CLARK

INTRODUCTION

This chapter concerns quantification in archaeological research; it consists of four parts. First, quantitative methods are examined from a historical perspective to outline the roles that statistics have played in past research and to shed some light on the nature of the relationship between theories, methods, and archaeological research designs. It seems to me that, for any given period of time, there are recurrent features that allow for a description of the research process in the discipline. These features often have a historical derivation and are influenced by developments in fields tangential to archaeology. They do not seem to be very different in archaeological research from procedures characteristic of research in other, more traditionally "scientific" fields.

Next, the major features of a proposed general design for confirmatory data analysis (CDA) in archaeological research are outlined. I think that such a research design should be founded on the principles of inferential statistics, and should specify

1. how propositions of broad anthropological interest are transformed into hypotheses that are meaningful in behavioral terms;
2. how behavioral hypotheses are converted into propositions that have empirical referents and that are amenable to statistical analysis using actual data sets;

ADVANCES IN ARCHAEOLOGICAL METHOD AND THEORY, VOL. 5

3. how those data sets are to be acquired and manipulated in a standard confirmatory mode;
4. what criteria are to be employed in making decisions about statistical hypotheses; and
5. how behavioral implications are to be extracted from decisions based on statistical conclusions.

The emphasis on hypothesis testing in the archaeology of the 1970s has overshadowed the development of alternative approaches to quantification in social science research, including that of exploratory data analysis (EDA) (Hartwig and Dearing 1979; Leinhardt and Wasserman 1979; McNeil 1977; Tukey 1977). The tenets of EDA are outlined in the section on alternatives to hypothesis testing. The utility of the approach is contrasted with the confirmatory model that underlies the classic Neyman–Pearson statistics discussed in the section on statistical hypotheses. The basis of the EDA perspective is formalized pattern searching using a variety of different techniques to assess the same body of data. Although testing is not a formal part of the approach, EDA techniques are not incompatible with a confirmatory mode of analysis. Instead, EDA techniques are regarded as useful procedures that are simple to do, that amplify understanding of data patterns, and that can be incorporated, under some conditions, in generalized procedures for the evaluation of research propositions.

In the final section, a concern with quantification in general and with the adoption of statistical modes of analysis is documented through the inspection of survey data (Schiffer 1977, 1978). Some suggestions are offered about how university curricula might be restructured at both the undergraduate and graduate levels in order to bring archaeological research designs more in line with those of other social sciences that have enjoyed a more long-standing commitment to quantified research.

QUANTIFICATION IN ANTHROPOLOGICAL RESEARCH

Some archaeologists have suggested recently that what separates contemporary archaeology from its predecessors is not the paradigm shift so often proclaimed in the literature, but rather an enormous proliferation of new methodology (Meltzer 1979; Zubrow 1972). If this is true, archaeologists might have more in common with respect to methodological concerns than with respect to any overarching archaeological theory of human behavior. In fact, there do appear to be broad commonalities about the proper conduct of archaeological research, and substantial agreement about methodological issues even in the absence of a clearly defined, unifying body of archaeological theory. This section examines the proposition that this methodological change has been primarily quantitative in nature. It outlines and discusses historical antecedents to quantified approaches in both anthropology and archaeology, and attempts to characterize the present status of quantification in archaeology.

The reader might wonder about the justification for quantification, for taking a statistical approach to the analysis of anthropological data, especially in view of the fact that some of the natural sciences have developed for centuries without employing statistical procedures to any significant degree. Blalock (1972:6) has noted that, in contrast with physics and chemistry, the social sciences are generally observational rather than experimental disciplines, and that the carefully controlled laboratory conditions characteristic of the natural sciences are usually absent in social science research. He regards "statistics [as] a poor man's substitute for contrived laboratory experiments in which all important relevant variables have been controlled" (Blalock 1972:6). But the need for generalization in *all* scientific research, whether observational or experimental is apparent, so that in fact a continuum is involved that has the laboratory sciences at one end and the social sciences at the other (see Figure 6.1). Social science statistical training requirements and reliance on statistical methods vary to a marked degree; this is also the case with anthropology. It is probably true that linguistic and cultural anthropology are closest to the observational end of the social

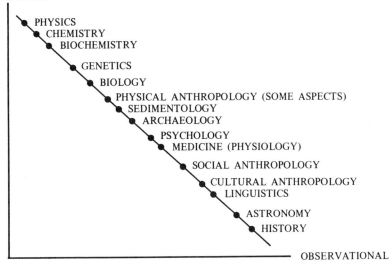

EXPERIMENTAL

PHYSICS
CHEMISTRY
BIOCHEMISTRY
GENETICS
BIOLOGY
PHYSICAL ANTHROPOLOGY (SOME ASPECTS)
SEDIMENTOLOGY
ARCHAEOLOGY
PSYCHOLOGY
MEDICINE (PHYSIOLOGY)
SOCIAL ANTHROPOLOGY
CULTURAL ANTHROPOLOGY
LINGUISTICS
ASTRONOMY
HISTORY

OBSERVATIONAL

Figure 6.1. A relative and somewhat arbitrary scale that orders some of the major social and natural sciences (and the subfields of anthropology) on a continuum from experimental to observational.

sciences part of the spectrum, but that physical anthropology (perhaps, in some aspects, the most experimental of the anthropological subfields) is closer to the other extreme. Archaeology falls somewhere in between (Figure 6.1). These observations are borne out to a considerable extent by the literature searches discussed in the following.

FUNCTIONS OF STATISTICS

Statistics has two general functions. The first is simple description—the summarizing or reduction of information in such a way that certain facts that data patterns suggest become readily apparent. Descriptive statistics may consist of nothing more complex than percentage graphs, frequency polygons, or histograms. More commonly, however, researchers desire to compress information further through the use of measures of central tendency (mean, median, mode), dispersion (standard deviation, variance) and association (correlation coefficients). Even the computation of these well-known summaries entails consideration of the problem of loss of information, and the scaling constraints that limit the appropriateness of all of them (Siegel 1956). Descriptive statistics are especially useful in situations where the effects of multiple variables are considered simultaneously, as is shown by the development of complex forms of multivariate analysis. It should be kept in mind that many multivariate procedures are little more than sophisticated pattern-search techniques most frequently used to *suggest* relationships among suites of variables. In a confirmatory mode of analysis, such relationships are typically subjected to the more rigorous kinds of evaluation implied by hypothesis testing.

The second function of statistics is induction—inferring properties of a population on the basis of known sample results or formulating general laws on the basis of repeated observations (Blalock 1972:4, 5). Inductive or inferential statistics is based on probability theory—the mathematical aspect of the discipline concerned with predicting outcomes of data generated from a given mathematical model. Inferential statistics is the branch of the discipline most crucial to those multifaceted aspects of archaeological research concerned with sampling strategies and designs, although some degree of generalization on the basis of limited sample information is required of most modern archaeological research, whatever form it might take. Practical reasons for making generalizations about populations from samples include time–cost factors (i.e., it may not be practical, given available resources, to describe some aspect(s) of a population), the inherent inaccessibility of a target population, or situations when the target population is theoretically infinite.

The extent to which statistical methods are employed in the social sciences is variable. Most psychology, sociology, and economics courses cannot be undertaken without at least some statistical preparation. This has not been the case with archaeology in the past, although it is becoming increasingly true today. Most people (including archaeologists) are somewhat leery of statistics, and resort to two rather extreme positions in attempting to cope with them. The first reaction is one of uncritical acceptance. To some, statistics possess a magical quality; data subjected to statistical analysis become "sacred," in Durkheim's sense of being beyond question. The other extreme is unilateral suspicion of statistical reasoning and statistical "facts." There are good reasons for this skeptical attitude, and there is little question that governments and other large corporate bodies have done much to foster it. Both extremes are unsatisfactory from the standpoint of the practicing professional, however, and there are really only two alternatives to them.

One is to rely exclusively on authority to resolve statistical questions (i.e., hire a consultant to develop the statistical aspects of the research design). However, qualified statisticians are not always available and are usually expensive, especially if hired on a short-term basis at an hourly rate. A far more serious drawback is that a properly executed statistical analysis can rarely if ever compensate for a piece of research that is poorly conceived initially. It is unrealistic to expect statisticians, however competent, to be more than the technicians they claim to be. The responsibility for the overall research design must rest with the social scientist. From this perspective, statistics is simply a tool but, as will be shown, an extremely useful one.

The second alternative, and one that is finding increased favor among archaeologists, is to try to learn enough about statistical reasoning and procedural frameworks to be able to use and to evaluate uses of statistics in one's area of interest. Most contemporary archaeological research projects are concerned with quantification because of the need for generalization and because of the rigorous descriptive capabilities of quantified analysis. Perhaps more than anything else, these departures from traditional methodological formats for data analysis constitute an advance over what has been done previously. Moreover, adoption of a statistical perspective carries with it a capacity to alter and expand our perceptions of the complexity of archaeological data. Thus, statistics becomes a much more flexible instrument for exploratory analysis than is commonly appreciated.

STATISTICS IN ANTHROPOLOGY AND ARCHAEOLOGY: A HISTORICAL PERSPECTIVE

Statistics has had a long-standing, although very partial, usage in anthropological research. Simple descriptive quantification goes back very nearly to the inception of the discipline and is evident in virtually all of its subfields.

However long overdue quantification might have been in archaeology, it is significant that, according to a recent survey, it has now become an important element of many, perhaps even most, archaeological research designs (Schiffer 1977, 1978). The general acceptance of a quantitative perspective is a phenomenon of the past 5 years, however, and one that remains to be integrated with any new paradigm for archaeological research that might emerge in the future. A brief historical consideration of statistical applications in anthropology is warranted here to provide a clearer idea of the kinds of quantification that have been used in the traditionally defined anthropological subfields (for a more extensive evaluation, see Clark 1981).

Anthropology

The most comprehensive survey of the general anthropological literature was accomplished by Thomas (1976:2-5), who examined the four major American anthropological journals for data relevant to the proportion of articles in the total run of each journal that was concerned with statistical inference. His survey covered the period from 1900 to 1970, and used *American Anthropologist* to monitor statistical inference in social and cultural anthropology, and in the field as a whole; *American Journal of Physical Anthropology* (AJPA) to assess inference in physical anthropology; *American Antiquity* for prehistoric archaeology; and *Language* for anthropological linguistics. His findings indicate a clear trend toward increasing quantification in all subfields except anthropological linguistics, with physical anthropologists clearly the vanguard users of inferential techniques (Thomas 1976:3). The post-World War II era is marked by a rather dramatic departure from the first half of the century in that the use of statistical inference begins in earnest in social–cultural anthropology and in prehistoric archaeology. This is part of a general proliferation of quantified research that can be directly attributed to the stimulus provided by World War II. In anthropology, it reflects the realization that anthropological questions and data are not intrinsically different from other behavioral science data. While it might seem unnecessary to make a point of the fundamental similarity of all observational (as opposed to purely experimental) science data, there are scholars (archaeologists among them) who seem reluctant to accept this basic congruity. Archaeological data differ from other social science data only insofar as conclusions that are meaningful in behavioral terms must be teased from the broken and discarded residual products of human activity rather than arrived at more directly through the observation and interrogation of living informants.

Thomas also assesses the relative importance of different degrees of anthropological quantification by examining a single volume (1972) in each of the four major subfield journals (1976:3, 4). For each, he determined the proportion of papers that were strictly qualitative, those that contained simple quantification (graphs, tables, etc.), those that relied on or used basic statistics (measures of central tendency, dispersion, basic probability theory, and the common probability distributions for discrete and continuous variables), and those which included advanced statistical methods (multivariate analysis). Again quantification was shown to be most advanced in physical anthropology; 86% of the papers published in AJPA were quantified at least to the extent that basic descriptive statistics were used. Archaeology in 1972 was still dominated by qualitative papers (58%), but a trend toward quantification was clearly evident from the results of Thomas' longitudinal study. What is perhaps somewhat surprising is the relatively low incidence (31%) of quantitative papers in the 1972 run of *American Anthropologist,* which Thomas regarded as a bellwether for the discipline as a whole. Given the increasing importance of demographic and simulation studies in social anthropology, one would have expected a larger proportion of quantitative papers—especially in view of the early and quite sophisticated pleas for quantification from Kroeber (1940, 1942) and more recent arguments for statistical approaches to the analysis of ethnographic data (White 1973). Anthropological linguistics continues to be an essentially qualitative discipline.

Archaeology

In order to monitor archaeological quantification, a survey was conducted by the author in which practically the entire run of *American Antiquity* was examined. The content of all "Articles," "Facts and Comments," and "Reports" was analyzed for the period 1935–1980. The objective was to try to assess with greater precision the kinds of quantification in which American archaeologists have engaged over the past 45 years. (*American Antiquity* was first published in 1935, the initial survey year.) To be included in the survey data, papers had to be characterized by at least simple quantification; purely qualitative essays, which account for about 81% of the total run, were excluded. To make the survey roughly comparable to Thomas' study, papers were scored according to whether they contained simple quantification, basic statistics, or advanced techniques (or any combination thereof), defined as in the preceding except for the last, which was expanded to include correlation coefficients (and techniques based on analysis of correlation coefficient matrices). Papers in which the only quantification consisted of lists of radiocarbon dates were scored as qualitative after 1955 (see the following). Memoirs dedicated to special topics were excluded.

Although *American Antiquity* is only a single data source, it is nevertheless a major one, and one that presumably would reflect "mainstream" developments in the field. I acknowledge that quantified approaches are also evident to various degrees *in certain aspects* of the archaeology of some European nations (e.g., France and Belgium). However, only in England and to some extent the Netherlands have quantified approaches become well-integrated features of *many* archaeological research designs. It is unfortunately the case that the work of continental scholars has had relatively little impact on American archaeology, and to provide a more exhaustive catalogue of quantitative applications would only make a lengthy paper even longer.

The results of the *American Antiquity* survey are presented in Figure 6.2. Several features of the exercise deserve special emphasis. First, it is apparent that simple quantification (counting and measuring things, arranging counts in lists or tables) goes back to the journal's inception, although enumeration of this sort was very differentially exercised by American archaeologists in the 1930s and early 1940s, and then only by a small minority of practicing (or publishing) professionals. Second and not apparent from an inspection of Figure 6.2 is the existence from 1940 to 1950 of a series of cumbersome, wholly qualitative papers outlining monothetic systems for describing artifacts using discrete (e.g., presence–absence) data categories. Third, many of the papers using basic statistics (means, standard deviations) in the 1950–1952 era do so in the context of discussions of radiocarbon dating. In fact, there was a special issue of *American Antiquity* dedicated exclusively to these then-novel methodological advances (Johnson 1951). Fourth, discussion generated by the well-known Ford–Spaulding debate on the nature of artifact types (Ford 1952, 1954a,b,c; Spaulding 1953a,b, 1954a,b) combined with the initial publications by Brainerd (1951) and Robinson (1951) (Lehmer 1951; Robinson and Brainerd 1952) describing the use of a similarity coefficient for chronological ordering, together account for most of the spate of papers dealing with comparatively advanced statistical topics in the 1950–1955 period. Interest in these methods appears to dwindle somewhat after 1955, at least as measured by pertinent *American Antiquity* citations. Fifth, the trend toward quantification shows a sharp upswing in American archaeology after 1970. Although the number of papers published in *American Antiquity* has increased gradually over the years, the figure has remained fairly stable for the past decade at an average of 17 per issue, or about 68 per year. However, the proportion of papers that are dedicated to quantitative topics or make use of at least elementary quantitative methods has risen from about 12% in 1965 to about 30% in 1975. For the past 5-year period (1975–1980), quantified papers account for about 54% of the total run. The survey disclosed the existence of a few comparatively sophisticated statistical papers, which appeared quite early (e.g., Kroeber 1940, 1942) but which seem to have had little discernible impact on the field. Noteworthy are essays by Merrill (1946:35–72) on Maya astronomy and Kroeber (1940:29–44) on statistical classification. The latter paper makes use of correlation coefficients, χ^2 and the probability distribu-

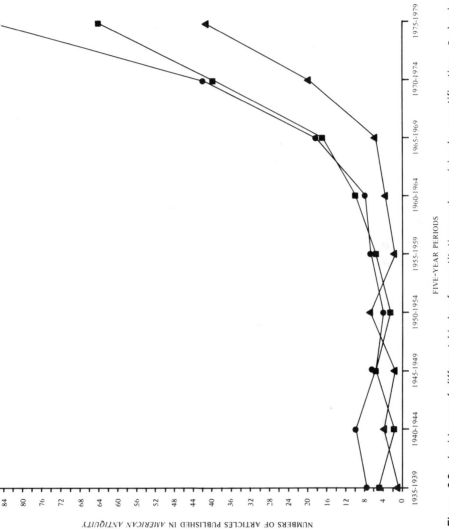

Figure 6.2. Incidence of different kinds of quantitative analyses (simple quantification, ●; basic statistics, ■; advanced statistics, ▲) in "Articles," "Facts and Comments," and "Reports" in *American Antiquity*, 1935–1979 (1980).

FIVE-YEAR PERIODS

NUMBERS OF ARTICLES PUBLISHED IN *AMERICAN ANTIQUITY*

tion of the standard normal variable to analyze a series of contingency tables cross-classifying artifactual trait data. Correlation is also discussed in subsequent papers by Fairbanks (1942:223–231) and Kroeber (1942:403–405).

1935–1950

In summary, most archaeological consumption of quantitative methods prior to 1950 consisted of simple enumeration of trait and artifact frequencies for the purposes of classification and/or description of assemblages. The objective of much of this research was chronological ordering and "cross-cultural" comparison, but although regional sequences were established in many areas, relationships among culture–historical units remained vague and ill defined. This lack of definition was due partly to fuzzy and conflicting notions of culture itself, and partly to a failure to recognize that culture could not be studied as a monolithic entity. Assumptions about culture, aspects of culture such as stability and change, the mechanisms of change, and, ultimately, the relationships that might exist between objects uncovered during excavations and concepts borrowed from anthropology were seldom scrutinized, yet were perpetuated in the literature as if they were commonly understood by everyone (Binford 1962). Implicit in the work of this period was the idea that all or most of the data could be collected to answer all or most of the questions regarded as "relevant" by the workers of the time. The earliest criticisms of a lack of independent conceptual development in archaeology were made during this period (e.g., Kluckhohn 1940; Steward and Setzler 1938).

Even by the end of this era, the massive quantification of science, which was an outgrowth of World War II, had not yet made much of an impact on archaeology. Although variety-minimizing, "normative" conceptions of culture were commonplace, they were most frequently expressed by nonquantified summations of shared material culture traits—modal suites of attributes that supposedly characterized a particular archaeological entity. A classic example is Anasazi, defined since the Pecos Conference (1927) by a specific geographical location and time range, an agriculture-based subsistence system, a distinctive burial configuration, certain ceramic and architectural types, etc. These criteria for delineating an "Anasazi Culture" are occasionally used today (e.g., Gumerman *et al.* 1972), although it has recently been suggested that they result in analytical units that limit, rather than expand, our capacity to understand prehistoric human behavior (Cordell and Plog 1979).

1950–1955

After 1950 and up until about 1955, there was increased interest in quantification, due to the development of radiocarbon dating techniques, and the publication of a number of controversial papers advocating the use of statistical procedures for type-discovery purposes and for seriating artifact frequencies for chronological ends. No significant increase in the use of basic statistical techniques was evident, but the first papers to make use of statistical inference were published during this period.

Willey and Sabloff (1974) characterize this period as one of increasing dissatisfaction with the limitations of the atheoretical "time–space systematics" of the preceding three decades, and point to an increased concern with context (the associational aspects of archaeological phenomena) and function (the ways in which artifacts were made and used). Archaeological remains came to be understood by an increasingly large segment of the discipline as the material remains of past human behavior, rather than as categories of objects to be studied in isolation. Settlement-pattern studies developed as a logical extension of a concern with function elevated to the level of sites (e.g., Willey 1953); primitive cultural ecological studies made their debut in the context of the first large-scale multidisciplinary research projects (e.g., Braidwood 1952, 1958; Braidwood and Howe 1960; Clark 1954).

1955–1965

The decade from 1955 to 1965 marked the first explicit recognition that complete data recovery is impossible and that particular kinds of data are required to resolve particular kinds of problems. A nascent concern with sampling was inevitable in this context, but explicit sampling designs are really a product of the 1970s. Archaeological usage of basic descriptive statistics increased at a slow and steady rate, although they were more often than not applied to traditional archaeological concerns, rather than to the processual objectives that were being articulated in the early 1960s (e.g., Binford 1962, 1965). The goal of all archaeological research was proposed to be the "discovery of regularities that are . . . spaceless and timeless" (Willey and Phillips 1958:2). This was a significant departure from previous research orientations because it lent to archaeology the notion of a quest for lawlike generalizations, motivated by a desire to bring archaeology back into the fold of general anthropology. In the absence of a strong concern with the relationship between methodology and objectives, however, there were problems regarding how one was to arrive at these "spaceless and timeless" regularities (Plog 1974:2). The much discussed "normative" orientation of the day had by now become a major liability. There was little appreciation of the existence of the enormous variability characteristic of the archaeological record, and still less understanding of how it might be monitored or controlled. Patterns were assumed to be intrinsic features of data, and it was widely held that data, suitably exposed, would somehow yield up their secrets to anyone prepared to observe them (Schwartz 1967). Thompson perhaps articulated the consensus view when, toward the beginning of this decade (1955–1965), he argued that the confidence placed in any particular archaeological reconstruction must ultimately rest on an assessment of the professional credentials of the archaeologist involved (1956:331).

Despite the quest for cross-culturally valid generalizations, and the edict that "archaeology is anthropology or it is nothing" (Willey and Phillips 1958:2), archaeology was in fact drifting away from the mainstream of anthropological thought. Research was based on analytical units which were by now so divorced from their anthropological counterparts that archaeological research no longer had any relevance for anthropologists. Willey and Phillips (1958) recognized that this was a problem, and sought to resolve it by proposing units of study that were supposedly comparable to those of the parent discipline. The result was a descriptive stage model (Lithic, Archaic, Formative, etc.), which expressed a chronological and developmental order, but which neither constituted an advance on the explanatory level nor was successful at reintegrating archaeological research into the broader context of anthropology. By the early 1960s, there was apparently some agreement about what constituted archaeological goals (i.e., the generation and testing of generalizations), but increasing discord about the conceptions of culture that framed archaeological goals, the appropriateness of different analytical units for the study of variability, and the methodology to be employed in research designs (Willey and Sabloff 1974).

1965–1970

This confused state of affairs was rectified somewhat in the 1965–1970 era by the recognition that goals and the procedures advocated for attaining them must be made compatible and explicit. The self-imposed constraints that had reduced archaeology to a sterile kind of time–space systematics were lifted by Binford's 1962 contention that the entire cultural system was preserved (at least in theory) in the archaeological record. It followed from this that any limitations to an understanding of the past were not inherent in the nature of archaeological data (as had often been claimed), but were instead to be attributed to flawed research designs and methodological naiveté (Binford 1968:23). The optimism generated by Binford's expansion of the realm of archaeological enquiry led to a number of explicit formulations of the ground rules that supposedly underlie "correct" research procedures (e.g., Watson *et al.* 1971). Pursuit of a "scientific" methodology led to the viewpoints whimsically characterized as the "law and order" (deductive–nomological) and "serutan" (systems theory) approaches (Flannery 1973). Although these and other models of scientific enquiry differed in many important respects, they all shared the notion that the past is empirically knowable, and that the formulation of lawlike generalizations is the goal of all science. Much had changed in the decade that had elapsed since Thompson's subjective appraisal of the quality of archaeological research. By 1967, Binford could argue that the formulation of hypotheses, the generation of test implications and their subsequent evaluation in probabilistic terms were the ways that archaeological research should proceed if the subjective element was to be minimized, and if independently replicable results were to be obtained (1967:10). Those replications would, presumably, constitute the basis for any generalizations that might ultimately achieve lawlike status.

Post-1970

As indicated in Figure 2, most of these changes in the archaeological metaphysic took place in the absence of a significant increase in quantitative methodology. After 1970, however, there is evidence of a proliferation of statistical methods in virtually all aspects of archaeological research. This is due (*a*) to the post-World War II quantification of research in general, which apparently only began to have an effect on archaeology after about 1965; and (*b*) the widespread availability of third-generation electronic computers in the late 1960s, which stimulated quantified approaches to data analysis in all areas and levels, and which made sophisticated multivariate procedures a viable option to many researchers for the first time.

In archaeology, consumption of inferential techniques received considerable impetus from the explicit concern with the development of regional sampling designs that dominated much of the literature in the early–middle 1970s (Chenhall 1975; Cowgill 1964, 1970, 1975; Judge *et al.* 1975; Matson and Lipe 1975; Mueller 1972, 1974, 1975; Plog 1980; Read 1975). The shift to a regional perspective has also been accompanied by the adaptation of geographical and economic models for describing and explaining distributions of sites and resources in space. These usually entail statistical comparison of observed patterns with idealizations constructed on the basis of minimization, maximization, or optimization principles applied to sets of economic variables monitored by quantified measures of interaction among human aggregates of various kinds (Bailey 1978; Blanton 1976; Cassels 1972; Clark and Lerner 1980; Clarke 1977; Crumley 1976, 1979; Euler and Gumerman 1978; Flannery 1976a, 1976b; Francis and Clark 1980; Hodder 1972a, 1972b, 1974, 1979; Hodder and Hassall 1971; Hodder and Orton 1976; Johnson 1972, 1973, 1975; Meiklejohn 1978; Mellars and Reinhardt 1978; Price 1978; Renfrew 1977; Roper 1979; Rossman 1976; Stark and Young 1981; Zarky 1976). Statistical approaches emphasizing nonparametric techniques are also being used to identify and compare artifact distributions at the intrasite level (Clark 1979; Clark *et al.* 1977; Dacey 1973; Hanson and Goodyear 1975; Hietala and Stevens 1977; Newell and Dekin 1978; Whallon 1973a,b; 1974, 1978). Use of these pattern search and comparison procedures has been facilitated by development of sophisticated software packages capable of manipulating large data matrices. The creation of computerized regional data banks (Chenhall 1971a,b, 1972; Cowgill 1967; Gaines 1978, 1981; Plog *et al.* 1978) should ultimately allow for increased application of these powerful methods to a wide range of problems. As Christenson (1979) and Thomas (1978) have observed, however, they also increase the incidence of inappropriately applied methods given the trendy nature of the discipline and a relatively low level of statistical expertise among archaeologists in general.

A parallel but unrelated trend is the focus on the quantification of artifact and attribute classification with the objective of refining and objectifying diverse sorts of classificatory schemes using the methods of numerical taxonomy (Sneath and Sokal 1973; Sokal and Rohlf 1969; Sokal and Sneath 1963). Renewed interest in the logic of classification was sparked by Dunnell (1971), who observed that all classifications are imposed constructs that function to order data so that the explanation of patterns of interest becomes possible. From this perspective, the justification for a particular classificatory scheme lies not in its ability to replicate some "native" or "natural" scheme (the existence of which is irrelevant), but rather in its capacity to address certain kinds of questions or to delineate certain sorts of problems of interest to the investigator. Statistical procedures brought to bear on classification problems range from comparatively straightforward contingency-table approaches analyzed with nonparametric techniques (e.g., Whallon 1974), to the use of different kinds of clustering algorithms (e.g., Hodson 1970, 1971; Hodson *et al.* 1966; Sibson 1971), factor and principal components analyses (e.g., Binford 1972; Binford and Binford 1966; Cowgill 1968), canonical variates (e.g., Graham 1970), regression (e.g., Binford 1962), and other powerful multivariate procedures. The rationale behind classification of different kinds of data has also been discussed at some length (e.g., Christenson and Read 1977; Clark 1976; Read 1974a,b).

As mentioned before, the incidence of misapplication of these methods (particularly multivariate analysis) is increasing proportionally to the overall use of them in the field. Archaeologists are not statisticians, nor is it reasonable to expect them to become statisticians. It does seem reasonable to expect them to be methodologically sophisticated enough to be able to understand and contribute to the corpus of ideas and substantive knowledge that make up the discipline. If there is at present an overuse of statistical procedures, it can only be hoped that a more reasonable perspective will be established in the future as the novelty of automated archaeological analysis wears off.

TOWARD A DESIGN FOR QUANTIFYING ARCHAEOLOGICAL RESEARCH

It would seem evident from the historical discussion just presented that what might be loosely termed "statistical reasoning"—thinking about problems in quantitative and/or statistical terms—has been part of at least some archaeological research designs for a long time, and that a quantified approach to data analysis is becoming increasingly common in the literature of the discipline. In this section, I delineate the main features of a research design which could be argued to characterize much (although certainly not all) quantified archaeological research regardless of the scale or nature of any particular research problem (obviously different aspects of the procedure will be emphasized depending upon the nature of a given piece of research). The design is based on classic Neyman–Pearson statistics and assumes that the generation of hypotheses and the evaluation of these in probabilistic terms is a legitimate perspective to assume in the conduct of scientific research. Clearly a confirmatory mode of analysis is *not* the only, nor even necessarily the most, productive design for quantifying the methodology of the "new" archaeology. However, this kind of analytical format *is* well represented in the work of contemporary professionals, it operates independently of any particular "theoretical orientation," and it contains all of the elements commonly understood to comprise proper research procedure. I think that "proper research procedure" itself is a relatively uniform phenomenon, shared implicitly by a large number of practitioners and here taken to underlie much contemporary archaeology.

In the context of these introductory remarks, I wish to make clear that no stand is taken here on general philosophy of science issues regarding what form such a research model should take, nor about the roles played by induction, abduction, deduction, and covering laws in such a model (e.g., Fritz and Plog 1970; Morgan 1973, 1974; Redman 1973a,b; Salmon 1975, 1976; Smith 1977; Tuggle *et al.* 1972; Watson *et al.* 1971, 1974). It is my opinion that rigid adherence to strictly defined models developed in philosophy of science contexts is neither necessary, realistic, nor even particularly productive in terms of the conduct of much archaeological research (see also Watson *et al.* 1974). Our capacity to contribute original insights to an elucidation of the general processes of human social behavior (which I take to be our singular, shared objective) is in no sense diminished by a failure to affiliate ourselves with a particular school of thought in the philosophy of science. This position comes from the realization that what had been widely represented to be relatively cut-and-dried philosophy of science issues (e.g., primacy of a deductive–nomological approach) are in fact increasingly revealed to be hotly contested within the boundaries of that very discipline (Morgan 1973, 1974; Tuggle *et al.* 1972; Watson *et al.* 1974).

To be viable, a confirmatory research design should be based on statistical inference and should specify how one goes from (*a*) a general proposition of anthropological interest, to (*b*) a series of hypotheses that are meaningful in behavioral terms, to (*c*) propositions that are amenable to statistical testing with empirical data, to (*d*) a procedure that defines how those data are to be acquired and manipulated, and in which decision-making criteria are made explicit, and finally back to (e) a reassessment of the behavioral implications of decisions based on statistical conclusions.

One form that such a model might take is represented by the flow chart in Figure 6.3. The diagram is based on various models for quantitative problem solving, and incorporates elements from papers by Fritz and Plog (1970:405–412), Redman (1973a:61–79), Siegel (1956:6–17), Thomas (1976:209–225), Wallis and Roberts (1967:309–340), Weaver (1977:3–6) and many others. I reiterate that nothing is said or implied about the (universal) generality of any conclusions that might be derived from the application of the model to actual data, nor are any conclusions derived that are not probabilistic in nature. Although the model is founded on the principles of inferential statistics, only parts of it necessarily involve statistical procedures; those aspects will be discussed later in greater detail. While inference can be argued to underlie all scientific generalization, statistical considerations enter in only (a) at the analysis stage of a project, after all data have been collected; (b) near the beginning of the research process, when initial plans for analysis are being formulated; and (c) whenever a sample is to be drawn and evaluated (Blalock 1972:5, 6).

Background Research and Mental Gestation

One usually initiates the research process already armed with a formidable *repertoire* of general anthropological knowledge, which is augmented and refined by undertaking "background research"—problem- and area-specific investigations of questions that are of interest to the investigator and are likely to be germane to more tightly focused research objectives.

At this stage, a good deal of mental gestation takes place, as the scientist evaluates plausible solutions in an informal way within the confines of habitual frames of reference (Figure 6.3:Boxes 1 and 2). There is a constant interplay of conscious reasoning on the one hand, and sudden flashes of insight on the other. Many false starts are made. Frustration may ensue when the problem involved resembles in some respects those confronted previously, but nevertheless contains some new elements of complexity that make its solution incompatible with the tenets of an established body of knowledge. Stress resultant from frustration might cause temporary abandonment of the problem as other events are allowed to intervene and, on the conscious plane at least, the issue is forgotten or shoved into the background. These intervals of distractedness (called "work avoidance behaviors" by a colleague) may be at times productive because subconscious rumination on the problem evidently

Figure 6.3. A flowchart identifying 11 stages in a generalized procedure for the evaluation of research propositions.

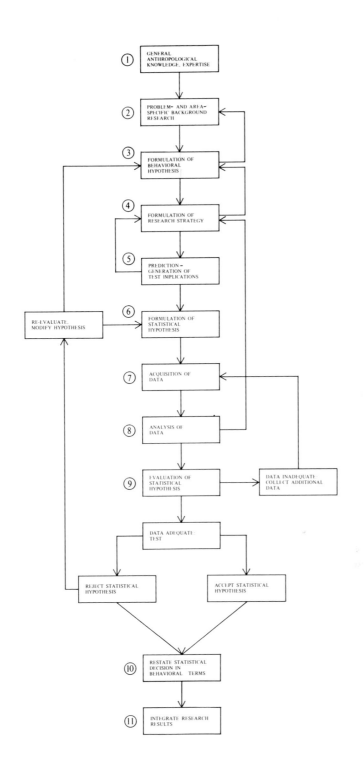

continues. During these episodes, allegiance to established paradigms may partially weaken, or in some dramatic cases, disappear altogether. A period of more or less random trial and error ensues, which at times can result in the discovery of hidden analogies between distinct conceptual categories. The discovery of these hidden analogies is what is commonly understood as creativity. Although the origins of meaningful insights are obscure, they appear to involve the capacity to shift habitual referential formats from one body (or "matrix") of knowledge to another in a creative way so that new and original relationships become apparent (Koestler 1964). It is in the variable capacity of people to shift formats of reference and to extricate themselves from habitual patterns of thought that differences in creativity lie, with the human tendency for automatized modes of thinking being perhaps the single most significant limiting factor.

The Behavioral Hypothesis

These complicated mental gymnastics sometimes culminate in the development of what I refer to as a behavioral hypothesis (Figure 6.3:Box 3). A behavioral hypothesis can be defined as a trial formulation derived from the complex factors just noted (i.e., background research, insight, intuition), which the investigator believes is likely to express a significant relationship between two or more variables. Such hypotheses might at this stage be vague and poorly defined, but should minimally contain as elements variables that refer to human behavior. The variables incorporated in a behavioral hypothesis must have phenomenological referents (i.e., they must be referable to or monitored by phenomena observable in the archaeological context). If they do not, there is no mechanism through which the plausibility of the hypothesis can ultimately be assessed. Behavioral hypotheses are generated from the theoretical conceptions that characterize a discipline. Some of these have observable implications; others do not (or at least it is not immediately apparent what those implications might be). While it is acknowledged that the observability of a given phenomenon is time dependent, in practical terms hypotheses that have no observable implications must be disallowed for the time being as untestable (although they might become testable in the future).

It is often remarked that much social science research appears to be founded on highly tentative theoretical propositions ("weak" theories) that are not directly amenable to evaluation. Consider, for example, the (anthropological) propositions that "patrilocal societies tend to practice female infanticide more than [do] matrilocal societies" (Thomas 1976:206); and "stylistic microtraditions in ceramic surface decoration tend to be inherited matrilineally, and thus should co-occur spatially with matrilocal post-marital resident units" (Longacre 1970). In neither case do these statements specify variables to be monitored in the event of a test (either in past or present contexts), nor do they identify sequences of analytical stages to be followed in any attempt to evaluate them. In short, they are imprecise statements that are understandable at a common sense level but that, in their present form, cannot be more rigorously assessed.

Formulation of the Research Strategy

With respect to creativity, the combination of reasoning and subconscious rumination are the most crucial aspects of the research process. Novelty lies in the restructuring of familiar elements, which, taken out of familiar contexts, can sometimes be transformed into a new synthesis. However, it is the *formal evaluation* of the tenability of an idea, and not its conceptualization, that is embodied in common conceptions of research design. The processes involved in getting from theoretical propositions of interest to statistical hypotheses, and from statistical hypotheses to the probability statements used in making inferences are by no means obvious or direct, and may in fact be exceedingly complex (Blalock 1972:11). This complexity is evident from the arrows connecting Boxes 3–5 in Figure 6.3. Whereas the fuzzy concepts and notions that are the currency of daily intercourse suffice in most ordinary situations, they must be considerably refined if they are to function in the context of a research methodology.

Theoretical and Operational Definitions

Following Bridgman (1938) and Northrop (1947), Blalock (1972:12–15) makes a distinction between theoretical definitions (Northrop's "concepts by postulation") and operational definitions (Northrop's "concepts by intuition"), which, he suggests, are both features of any scientific evaluation. In a theoretical definition, "a concept is defined in terms of other concepts, which supposedly are already understood" (Blalock 1972:12). In anthropology, for example, the concepts "culture" and "society" are often treated as theoretical definitions in the context of a given problem even though they are subject to debate in general terms. Theoretical definitions are arbitrary, although what constitutes the "given" terms in a problem (i.e., those concepts that are assumed to be understood) will vary (perhaps considerably) from one investigator to the next. In the first example cited (Thomas 1976:206), the concepts "patrilocal," "matrilocal," and "society" are theoretical definitions. Within the context of a single linguistic system (and across many linguistic systems), most ordinary definitions are theoretical rather than operational; yet despite their vagueness, they function with sufficient facility and precision to make possible everyday communication in a nearly infinite variety of experiential contexts.

Operational definitions, on the other hand, specify criteria for measurement. Since all measurement must entail classification of some kind, "an operational definition can be considered . . . a detailed set of instructions enabling one to classify . . . unambiguously" (Blalock 1972:12). An operational definition of "length" would specify exactly how the length of a particular class of objects is to be measured. An operational definition of the behavioral concept "microtradition" would indicate how a microtradition would be detected and monitored in the archaeological context. In a given classification, operational definitions should be sufficiently precise that any investigator acting independently would achieve essentially similar results by employing them (see also Thomas 1970:32–35).

Test Implications and Prediction

Ideally, for simplicity's sake, operational and theoretical definitions should be characterized by a close correspondence (Bridgman 1938:23–27). This is seldom realistic in *any* discipline, however, because of conceptual ambiguity and because there is typically an absence of full consensus about what constitutes an adequate operational definition of a given concept. It is a more common practice to generate a number of more or less acceptable operational definitions for a particular theoretical concept of interest; these are then argued to monitor, measure, or index—poorly or well—that theoretically defined concept or variable (Northrop 1947; Selltiz *et al.* 1959). The reader should recognize that operational definitions are the basis for the archaeologist's test implications, the imperfect reflections of theoretical variables that are themselves not directly measurable. The relationship between test implications and the theoretical variables they monitor cannot be reduced to an algorithm or formula. The adequacy of operational definitions must be grounded in air-tight "linking" or "bridging" arguments, which clearly establish that a particular operational definition does in fact provide a satisfactory measure of a particular theoretical concept.

Because multiple test implications can usually be generated for any theoretical concept, results can vary according to the particular test implications that are selected. It is important to keep in mind that actual tests are made by evaluating the concepts as operationally defined. While results should be reasonably consistent so long as the testing procedure is held constant and the test implications chosen are appropriate, discrepancies can indicate that the test implications are not measuring the same theoretical quantity or that the theoretical concept itself is ambiguous or even completely wrong (see, for example, Kepler's well-known attempts to compute a circular

Martian orbit). In this sense, the theoretical foundations of a discipline can be shaken or altered as a consequence of the testing procedure, subject, of course, to a consensus about what constitutes the theoretical foundation in the first place (Kuhn 1962, 1970a,b).

A research strategy, which has the function of operationalizing a test of the behavioral hypothesis, is formulated at this juncture (Figure 6.3:Box 4). Up to this point, relationships among anthropological variables may only have been conceptualized in rather vague terms, and test implications may or may not have been made explicit. Statistical procedures need not necessarily figure in the research process described thus far, although they may do so. Notice that in the flowchart (Figure 6.3), prediction (Box 5) is associated with the generation of test implications. I suggest that, in terms of the mental gymnastics that are characteristic of this phase of the research procedure, prediction is more of a process than an event. It can, for example, occur as part of the flash of insight that at times accompanies the crystallization of a behavioral hypothesis. If so, it might constitute no more than a vague expectation about what kinds of patterns would be observed in data yet to be gathered. Alternatively, prediction might be the outcome of conscious, deliberative cerebration. Regardless of their form, however, and the point at which they occur in the reasoning process, predictions are made concrete by the generation of test implications—expected patterns of variation in actual data sets—and hypotheses are considered confirmed to the extent that predictions derived from them are borne out by later events (Wallis and Roberts 1967:7).

The Statistical Hypothesis

With the formulation of the research strategy, statistical considerations become important in the generation and evaluation of the statistical hypothesis and in the development of the sampling design. *Adoption of a statistical perspective requires the investigator to define and measure variables in precise and explicit ways, and, in a confirmatory mode of analysis, to specify expected relationships among them.* As Read (1974a) has observed, attempts to employ statistical models in research can assist in the process of understanding and explaining phenomena because the investigator is compelled to scrutinize data in ways not demanded of nonquantitative approaches. Behavioral hypotheses cannot be evaluated directly, so it is necessary to transform them into statistical hypotheses. Put another way, "substantive research propositions must be translated into unequivocal statements of relationship between or among variables" (Thomas 1976:209).

Whereas the term hypothesis has, in social science research, a variety of different meanings, the notion of a statistical hypothesis can be circumscribed more rigorously. Blalock (1972:111) defines a hypothesis as "a statement about a future event, or an event the outcome of which is unknown at the time of prediction, set forth in such a way that it can be rejected." Ideally, hypotheses should be conditional statements of the form: if x, then y, given (conditions) z. However, it is immediately apparent that for very many research propositions, rigidly defined conditional statements implying deterministic relationships are so unrealistic as to be completely inappropriate. Rather than to hold that if x is true, then y must follow, it is more reasonable to restate the hypothesis in probabilistic terms: if x is true, then y will follow (with a probability of z). The implication of certainty is thus avoided, and we can admit to the possibility that, some of the time, y might be false even if x is true. The general form of a statistical hypothesis can be described as follows (Kruger 1976):

> Of all things that are M, m/n of these have property P.
> a is an M.
> Therefore, there is an m/n probability that a is also a P.

Here m/n is the a priori expectation based on "background research" (i.e., previous empirical work, theoretical suppositions, general knowledge of a problem domain) that a is (or has) P (Blair 1975).

A test of such a hypothesis would entail (a) prior agreement about the operational definitions of any theoretical variables or concepts that it might contain; (b) consideration of all possible outcomes of the test in advance of the test itself; and (c) agreement beforehand as to which outcomes would result in acceptance and which in rejection of the hypothesis (with rejection a possible result). The first criterion of a valid test is a particularly important one insofar as an absence of consensus about operational definitions would nullify *any* test because it could be argued that the operational definitions actually evaluated are not really effective or accurate monitors of some theoretical concept or variable of interest.

Because sampling of some kind is explicitly or implicitly involved in archaeological research, statistical hypotheses are generally statements about population parameters, which will be evaluated by comparing sample statistics with each other or with an estimate of some theoretical value. It is thus assumed that *some* degree of statistical generalization is characteristic of *all* research endeavors, and this is held to be true regardless of the nature of a particular problem and regardless of the discipline (or subdiscipline) involved. By statistical generalization, I mean the ability to arrive at conclusions about aspects of a population on the basis of facts known about a sample drawn from that population.

Whatever form the behavioral hypotheses might take, they should be amenable to transformation into pairs of statistical hypotheses, which should be mutually exclusive, maximally contrastive and exhaustive sets (i.e., the null and alternative hypotheses). Statistical hypotheses are either directional (if a relationship is postulated in which a parameter or statistic is greater than or less than some other parameter, statistic) or nondirectional (if a relationship of equivalence does or does not hold) (Siegel 1956). Multiple alternative hypotheses may represent the only realistic approximation of the complexity of a series of postulated relationships; and, if that is the case, tests for "goodness of fit" and criteria for choosing among competing "successful" hypotheses should be devised at this stage (Clark 1974, 1976).

The Statistical Model

It is at this juncture (Box 6) that consideration should be given to the selection of an appropriate statistical model. In a standard confirmatory mode of analysis, the statistical model comprises the set of assumptions about the data that are not likely to be the subject of much disagreement. The relationship between the common probability distributions and the level of scaling characteristic of measurement should be taken into account in the choice of a statistical model, because these factors will ultimately influence the choice of a test statistic. If, after due consideration, it is decided that a multivariate technique is required, the (often numerous) constraints and assumptions that are entailed in its proper application should be reviewed. Many multivariate methods are based on a multivariate normal distribution and make at least that assumption (i.e., that the data are intrinsically continuous and are multivariate normally distributed). Testing this assumption can be difficult, however, as variables may be marginally normal and yet are not necessarily multivariate normal in their joint distributions (Andrews *et al.* 1973). It has been claimed that when a method such as principal-components analysis is used only in a descriptive mode, such assumptions need not hold (Benfer 1979), although there would seem to be few instances when inferences from a sample to a population are not being made in archaeological research contexts. Similarly, assumptions, such as the equality of covariance matrices in discriminant analysis, generally have not been tested, and more appropriate potential alternatives, such as quadratic discriminant analysis, generally are not available.

Disregard for statistical assumptions is not restricted to multivariate methods. Misapplications of bivariate significance tests also occur with some regularity. Violations of assumptions are more problematic here than in multivariate applications because no appeal can be made to their use in a purely descriptive mode. Bivariate significance tests are clearly inferential in nature, and the validity of conclusions based on them are directly dependent on the appropriateness of the underlying model. Even these techniques produce conclusions that contain qualifiers of the form: "If the assumptions regarding the shape of the underlying population are valid, then we may conclude that...."

Given recent indictments of the tendency for archaeological misuse of complex multivariate procedures (Flannery 1973; Thomas 1978, 1980) and the fact that large numbers of inferential techniques exist that do not make as numerous or stringent assumptions about parameters (i.e., about the characteristics of the underlying populations from which the samples compared are being drawn), a strong case could be made for increased archaeological usage of nonparametric methods (Conover 1971; Hollander and Wolfe 1973; Siegel 1956). To overstate the case somewhat for comparative purposes, nonparametric tests produce conclusions of the form: "Almost regardless of the shape of the underlying population, we may conclude that. . . ." Although testing is emphasized here, it should be noted that nonparametric statistics are also useful and appropriate in point estimation, confidence interval, and multiple comparison contexts (Hollander and Wolfe 1973).

Nonparametric tests are often of the type referred to as "rank order" tests, referring to the level of scaling necessary for valid use of many of them. This highlights another important distinction between parametric and nonparametric tests—it is permissible to use the parametric techniques only on data that are truly numerical (i.e., where at least interval scaling is present). Nonparametric techniques do not have this constraint, and some may of course be used when only nominal or classificatory scaling is present. That many archaeological applications *do* utilize enumerated data (i.e., counts on categories of attributes, artifacts, sites, etc.) is a strong argument for the adoption of such methods. However, scaling is often not an intrinsic feature of measurement, but rather is imposed on it by the ways in which measurement is conceptualized. Many variables usually regarded as nominal or ordinal are capable of being intervally scaled. For example, it is a common practice to dichotomize Southwestern vegetation types into "pinyon–juniper" and "grasslands." Yet the variable "vegetation" can in fact be scaled along a continuum ranging from low grass density (i.e., pinyon–juniper) to high grass density (i.e., grasslands). Variables are typically conceived as nominal or ordinal for convenience, and a methodological trade-off is usually involved. To conceptualize measurement as nominal or ordinal allows for use of a wider range of statistical procedures, but sometimes at the expense of more powerful parametric alternatives. That expense might not be very great, however, since theoretical investigations indicate that many nonparametric procedures are only slightly less efficient than their normal theory counterparts given reasonably adequate data (Hollander and Wolfe 1973). Few readers would disagree that nonparametric statistics are typically underutilized in archaeology. They remain a vast, largely untapped methodological reservoir, which is likely to prove useful in many future research applications. The fact that they are comparatively straightforward and easily understood makes them preferable to complex multivariate parametric designs where substitution is legitimately possible. Quite useful sequences of nonparametric procedures can sometimes be constructed to evaluate hypotheses and, in a descriptive mode, to detect the existence and measure the strength of association among pairs of variables (e.g., Clark 1979; Clark *et al.* 1977; Francis and Clark 1980; Hanson and Goodyear 1975; Whallon 1974).

The foregoing has generally emphasized simplicity in data analysis, a plea made by a number of other authors (e.g., Christenson 1979; Thomas 1978). It should be stressed, however, that an extreme position should not be taken with respect to this issue, because there are relationships or data dependencies that cannot be detected in the univariate or bivariate case (Matson 1980). Insignificant results, for example, may be obtained in a series of t-tests on a given array of variables, yet significant results could be obtained on these same data using Hotelling's T^2, a multivariate equivalent. Jolicoeur (1975) provides an example in which multivariate and bivariate analyses failed to discriminate between three groups, whereas a projection of the same groups into two-dimensional discriminant space allowed the distinction to be made. Even when a multivariate statistic is used to reduce the dimensionality of a data matrix, significant relationships may exist at higher dimensions (e.g., Gnanadesikan 1977). Andrews' (1972) reevaluation of a discriminant analysis of fossil data using high-dimensional plotting techniques is a case in point.

Mechanical Aspects

Having selected an appropriate statistical model after due consideration of the nature of the data to be collected, the mechanical aspects of making a decision about the statistical hypothesis should be considered next. These are widely known, since they are common to all statistical tests, and are published in virtually every elementary statistics textbook (e.g., Henkel 1976; Ott 1977:70–83; Siegel 1956:6–34; Thomas 1976:205–226). They entail (*a*) selection of a level of (statistical) significance, which will define the critical region for acceptance–rejection of the null hypothesis (H_0) in the probability distribution of the test statistic involved (Figure 6.3:Box 6); (*b*) acquisition of the data (Box 7); (*c*) analysis of the data (computation of the test statistic—Box 8); and (*d*) evaluation of the statistical hypothesis (Box 9). It should be kept in mind that the decisions involved in step *a* should be made prior to the actual collection of any data. In essence, they provide the researcher with an unambiguous criterion for identifying those possible values of the test statistic that will allow for rejection and those that permit acceptance of H_0. In standard Neyman–Pearson statistics, research always proceeds by the successive elimination of false hypotheses (rather than by the confirmation of true ones), so that H_0 is in actuality established only to be subjected to the possibility of rejection. It is at this point that the importance of the "mutually exclusive and maximally contrastive" pairs of hypotheses mentioned earlier becomes evident, for rejection of H_0 should, ideally, entail acceptance of H_1 (the alternative or research hypothesis) as the only other reasonable possibility. However, what constitutes a "reasonable possibility" is in fact conditioned beforehand by the likelihood that the research hypothesis is true in the first place (Salmon 1973:112–115). It is worth remarking that hypotheses typically are not deduced in any formal sense from some proposition of interest, but rather are arrived at and evaluated inductively. The ability to rank (or, ideally, to assign probabilities to) research hypotheses is strictly a function of a priori expectations about the nature of structure in the data, which is in turn dependent on the statistical model chosen and the level of development of a particular discipline (see, for example, the following). In some highly developed experimental fields (e.g., in chemistry, physics), it is possible to derive deductively (i.e., assign probabilities to) a suite of research hypotheses. As far as archaeology is concerned, however, we are as yet rather far from that state of grace and can at best provide a crude ordering of research hypotheses in terms of their relative plausibility. Smith (1977:607) has observed that "such plausibility considerations in archaeological inference invariably take the form of argument by analogy (Binford 1967)," which is probably true as long as "analogy" is used in the generic sense and not in the narrower context of analogy with ethnographic situations. Wilcox and Sullivan (1979) make the point that such a restriction would unnecessarily preclude the eventual development of an independent body of archaeological theory.

The decision to "accept" or reject H_0 is usually based on an inference made from a sample, and because samples are always variable, there is some probability that an error will be made in the decision to accept or reject H_0. Because the characteristics of the population sampled are typically unknown, we are never really in a position to know with certainty whether a particular decision based on a sample statistic is the correct one or not. There are two possibilities for making an incorrect decision called, respectively, Type I and Type II errors. A Type I error occurs when H_0 is true but is mistakenly rejected; a Type II error occurs when H_0 is false but is erroneously accepted. The probability of Type I error is conventionally symbolized by alpha (α); the probability of Type II error is symbolized by beta (β). Given the unpalatable prospect of making an error of some kind a certain percentage of the time in the evaluation of *any* sample statistic, we have recourse to probability theory to allow for an assessment of the different error risks, which in turn allows these risks to be taken into account in establishing criteria for rejection of H_0.

Power Functions

In a relatively simple case, consideration of the power of a significance test will provide an objective means of assessing the relative importance of different sources of error in making the statistical decision (Cohen 1969; Siegel 1956). This aspect of the decision process has been increasingly recognized by archaeologists as an important part of any quantified research design (Cowgill 1977; Stafford and Stafford 1979). The power of a test is based on the fact that an inverse relationship exists between the probabilities of Type I and Type II error: a decrease in α will result in an increase in β for any given sample size. If we wish to reduce simultaneously the probabilities of both types of error, it can only be done by increasing the sample size. Ideally, one seeks to reduce the error probabilities to tolerable levels without increasing sample size to the extent that it becomes unwieldy. In normal practice though, the investigator commonly fixes α and disregards the fact that by doing so, β may be maximized—a procedure that might be quite justifiable in the context of a given problem.

The various statistical tests offer the possibility of different balances of error risks, which are measured in terms of the power function of the test. The power of a test is defined as the probability of rejecting H_0 when in fact it is false, which is a correct decision, and which is measured by $1 - \beta$. The power of a test increases as sample size increases for the fixed α level. Since the error probabilities are based ultimately on the probability distribution of the test statistic involved and are fixed only as long as sample size is fixed, about the only criterion that can be employed in balancing risk is an evaluation of the practical consequences of each type of error in the particular case involved. Error probabilities can be neatly summarized in simple statistical tests by use of an operating characteristic (OC) curve (Wallis and Roberts 1967:388–396). The probability of Type I error specifies the level of significance attached to the decision to reject H_0. It permits definition of the region of rejection of H_0 in the probability distribution of the text statistic involved, and it indicates how willing the investigator is to tolerate a risk of Type I error due solely to chance variation in a computed test statistic.

Sampling

If the foregoing has been undertaken in a careful and systematic way, it becomes a comparatively straightforward matter to acquire and analyze the data (Figure 6.3:Boxes 7 and 8). Considerations of sampling design are of course relevant here because inference is directly influenced by sampling methods. Are conclusions to be restricted to the sample evaluated, or are they to have wider implications (as is presumed to be the case here)? If the conclusions are to have implications beyond those restricted to the cases observed, one must determine how to choose the sample, bearing in mind that the pattern of sampling variability for any population is known if, but only if, the sampling technique results in a probability sample. A probability sample can be defined as a sample drawn in such a way that it is possible to assign a probability to every individual that might possibly be included in it. Probability samples are the very foundation of statistical inference, whereas nonprobability samples are of the very limited statistical interest. Probability sampling allows for estimates of the risk of error—the basis for all statistical inference; nonprobability sampling does not allow those estimates to be made; therefore, statistical inference is really not appropriate if based on nonprobability samples. Nonprobability sampling, however, can be employed to advantage in certain phases of an archaeological research design in which, for example, maximally representative (though biased) samples might be required, where preservational differences are marked, and to increase efficiency in the collection of rare but significant data (Asch 1975:170–191).

Sampling has recently occupied the attention of a number of archaeologists (e.g., Cowgill 1975; Judge *et al.* 1975; Mueller 1974, 1975, 1978; Plog *et al.* 1978; Plog 1976; Read 1975), so I will confine my remarks to a few general observations pertinent to statistical conceptions of sampling. These provide the basis for most archaeological discussions of the topic.

Probability sampling is commonly equated with simple random sampling, but there are actually four basic kinds of probability sampling, of which random sampling is only one (the others are systematic sampling, stratified sampling, and cluster sampling) (Blalock 1972:509–530). Systematic sampling is sometimes regarded by archaeologists as a form of nonprobability sampling, but if the selection process is initially random, then a probability sample can theoretically be attained (Blalock 1972:514, 515). The danger in systematic sampling lies in the introduction of bias in the sample selection process due to undetected trends or periodicity in the enumeration of elements in the population to be sampled. In practical terms, it usually does not matter very much as long as there is reason to believe that the ordering of elements is essentially random (this can often be checked by simple graphic means, etc.). If it is, a systematic sample will be the equivalent of a simple random sample. If it is not (i.e., if nonrandom patterns can be detected), then a systematic sample is best regarded as a form of stratified sample, and should be treated accordingly. In most research situations, stratified sampling is to be preferred over simple random sampling because it incorporates useful a priori knowledge about structure in data sets into the process of their evaluation. This in turn will improve both the sophistication (always) and the efficiency (often) of the sampling design. Blalock (1972:524) suggests that efficiency be measured by the relative size of the standard error of the estimate (the smaller the standard error, the higher the efficiency of the design). Cluster sampling, often unavoidable in archaeological contexts, can also improve efficiency over simple random samples as long as sample sizes are comparable and the clusters themselves are relatively homogeneous. Because cluster samples are often more easily obtained than other kinds of samples, cost factors might make cluster sampling preferable in some instances. Blalock (1972:526) observes that whenever costs that depend on the number of clusters selected are large in relation to costs that vary directly with the number of cases, cluster sampling will prove more economical than simple random sampling. In general, a balance between cost considerations and the efficiency of the design must be maintained. The design with the smallest standard error for a given cost should be selected.

Although it is possible to make use of statistical inference with each of these types of probability samples, it is also unfortunately true that the number of different kinds of tests that are appropriate for use with experimental designs utilizing nonrandom probability samples is somewhat restricted. While stratified and cluster sampling can often improve the sophistication and efficiency of a sampling design, and stratification in particular is conceptually simple and has obvious archaeological advantages, both can also be analytically complicated—especially with respect to computation of the probabilities to be assigned to individuals in strata or clusters. These probabilities are directly conditioned by decisions about how the strata and/or clusters are to be formed, what sampling fraction is regarded as "optimal" vis à vis the actual or theoretical population, whether stratified sampling is proportional or disproportional, and the like. Regardless of the nature of a probability sample, however, as long as it *is* a probability sample, accuracy, precision, bias, and representativeness should be taken into account (Cowgill 1975:263–266).

Restating the Statistical Decision

The statistical decision (to accept or reject H_0) follows from routine computational procedures, and all that remains is to restate the consequences of the statistical decision in behavioral terms (Figure 6.3:Box 10). Here, the major difficulty may lie in a failure to consider adequately the nature of the relationship between the samples actually evaluated, the population from which they were derived (sampled population), and the population about which conclusions are to be drawn (target population). It is particularly important that "archaeological context" variables be selected, and that test implications be generated from them, which monitor as accurately as possible variables of interest in the "systemic context" (the nonobservable behavioral system of which these remains were once a part and about which we are ultimately interested in drawing conclusions) (Schiffer 1972, 1973). Intervening "cultural and natural formation processes," which might influence the preservation and recovery and/or distort the relational aspects of archaeological remains should also be carefully controlled (Wilcox 1975). Failure to take depositional, postdepositional, and recovery factors into account would certainly diminish, and might vitiate altogether, the impact of any substantive results that might be forthcoming from a quantified research design, no matter how careful the design might have been as far as the statistical methodology is concerned.

ALTERNATIVES TO HYPOTHESIS TESTING

In the inferential model described in Figure 6.3 and the subsequent discussion of it, it has been assumed that the formal specification and evaluation of sets of paired hypotheses is or should be part of all quantified research designs. While many archaeologists appear to share this conception of the research process, it is important to note that it is not the only, nor even necessarily the most productive scenario for quantifying archaeology. Within statistics, hypothesis testing is recognized as an area of limited applicability, and some statisticians have argued that other statistical methodologies are both more powerful and more generally appropriate to a wider range of problems in data analysis than is the classic Neyman–Pearson inferential model for confirmation (e.g., Tukey 1977). Within archaeology, there is some diversity of opinion about the relative importance of significance testing, and the claim has been made that significance tests are unnecessarily limiting and prone to misinterpretation (Cowgill 1977). In this section, I give an assessment of significance testing and contrast it with the use of interval estimates. I then outline some of the major elements of a recently developed statistical perspective called exploratory data analysis, and offer some suggestions about where EDA methods and techniques might most appropriately be integrated with a design for evaluating research propositions.

Significance Tests and Interval Estimates: Some Pros and Cons

The litany of sins associated with significance testing is unfortunately a long one. Moreover, it is not confined to the interpretational difficulties cataloged by various authors (e.g., *ex post facto* manipulation of α, confounding with measures of association [see, e.g., Bettinger 1979; Cowgill 1977; Munday and Lincoln 1979; Stafford and Stafford 1979; Thomas 1976, 1978]). Despite these drawbacks, however, there are compelling reasons for the continued incorporation of significance testing in archaeological research designs. On the positive side, formulation of hypotheses amenable to statistical evaluation forces the investigator to devote attention to the selection of theoretically meaningful variables. At the same time, he is required to insure that those variables are monitored in some justifiable way by the archaeological variables examined through the generation of test implications. These concerns are not as apparent or even important in other branches of social science research where the hiatus between the "behaviorally meaningful" and the "directly observable" can be more readily narrowed.

The precision inherent in hypothesis-testing is often absent in the *ad hoc* pattern-search techniques commonly used in archaeology, and it could be argued that we have gone on long enough appealing to our lack of knowledge of archaeological phenomena to continue to justify the use of these methods in a purely inductive mode. As Read (1974b) has observed, a large number of dependency structures exist in any set of archaeological material. Whereas these are often implicit, a researcher benefits enormously from making them explicit by specifying a priori expectations about the nature of structure in the data. The results obtained from any statistical analysis reflect not only the structure that may exist *in* the data but the structure imposed *on* the data by the selection of a particular statistical model (for example, see Everitt [1974] regarding imposed structures in cluster analysis).

Interpretability of results is often the sole justification for accepting the results of the multivariate techniques often used in pattern searching (e.g., cluster analysis, factor and principal components analysis). Interpretability, however, is a necessary, but not a sufficient, condition for acceptance of a set of conclusions based on a statistical analysis. This is because the human mind is sufficiently flexible and inventive to make something of almost any set of results. The increased use of significance tests and confidence intervals in multivariate analysis is at least a partial solution to this dilemma (Christenson 1979), but when analysis takes place completely outside of a deductive framework, any procedure is likely to be problematic. As a first step in the analytical process, it is necessary to recognize the formal structures such procedures are designed to reveal in a data matrix (Degerman 1972).

Perhaps the most general argument in support of tests of significance, however, is one so obvious that it is seldom made explicit: correctly used, significance tests provide a mechanism for guarding against according substantive importance to results that can be explained easily by chance (Henkel 1976:87).

On the negative side, most problematic aspects of significance testing turn on its contribution, relative to other procedures, to the ultimate objective of scientific research in general: the development and validation of theories that allow for the explanation of empirical phenomena (Henkel 1976:83). It has been argued—by archaeologists (e.g., Cowgill 1977) as well as by statisticians and philosophers of science—that that contribution is likely to be rather meager. For one thing, because we cannot "prove" a hypothesis to be true, but can only falsify it, the substantive results of a test of significance can at best provide negative information insofar as they result in a decision to reject or to fail to reject some theoretical proposition.

Moreover, only exceptionally do tests of significance allow for generalizations to the hypothetical population of interest. This is because the property of generalizability is restricted to the sampled population, and cannot usually be extended to the target population (which is apt to be an abstract, theoretically infinite population). Only in the (unusual) situation in which sampled and target populations are identical would it be legitimate to make a direct statistical inference about the target population. If the target population is theoretically infinite, statistical inferences are not legitimately possible since, strictly speaking, there is no way to obtain a probability sample from it. (However, statisticians have few qualms about applying probability theory to finite but large populations. Certainly most archaeological populations are large but finite populations.)

Finally, null hypotheses typically evaluated in social science research are often limited, inefficient, and somewhat unrealistic insofar as parameters are usually posited as equal to zero or to some other specified value (i.e., two or a series of parameters or statistics, or a parameter and a statistic are compared, and then they are tested for differences between or among them). Since it is rather unlikely that the difference between the parameters of interest would be precisely zero (a point estimate), it has been observed that the ability to reject such null hypotheses does not really mean very much (Meehl 1967). In this context, Blalock (1972:209–212) advocates the use of confidence intervals (interval estimates). Placement of a confidence interval around an estimate indicates not only the degree of accuracy of that estimate but also and simultaneously constitutes an implicit and informal test of a whole range of hypotheses (Figure 6.4). Increased use of interval estimates has also recently been supported by Cowgill (1977), who argues that they are better suited to many kinds of archaeological problems than are testing approaches (see also Gross 1976).

It should be kept in mind that although hypothesis testing and interval estimates are closely related to one another, they are in fact conceptually distinct procedures. Although the same constraints and assumptions apply to the appropriate use of each (e.g., probability sampling), it is unnecessary in the latter case to hypothesize a specific value for a parameter to be estimated. In a single-sample problem in particular, placing confidence intervals about a parameter is often more reasonable than testing a hypothesis. However, confidence intervals are seldom used as alternatives to two- or k-sample tests in social science, mainly because in these situations, one is usually interested in simply establishing the existence of a relationship between two or among several variables; there is less concern with estimating the actual magnitude of that relationship. It has been suggested that this reflects the immaturity of the social sciences more than any other factor, and the prevalence of exploratory studies (Blalock 1972; Henkel 1976).

Exploratory Data Analysis

We have seen that the typical research project is characterized by a sequence of operations that progressively narrow the research focus. One defines the subject of study, generates hypotheses, collects appropriate data and analyzes them, and finally comes to some kind of substantive conclusion as a result of the analysis. In the standard confirmatory mode, data are *defined* in terms of hypotheses, and do not exist in any formal sense apart from them (i.e., what constitutes data is determined by the hypotheses evaluated; those hypotheses are formally defined). Some criticisms of the rigid analytical format of confir-

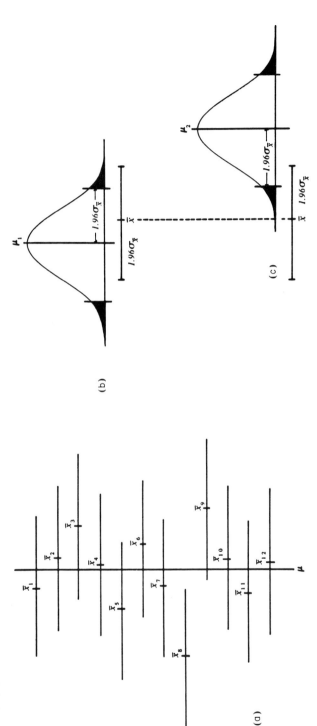

Figure 6.4. (a) Distribution of confidence intervals for 12 sample means about a parameter μ. Confidence intervals (defined as $1 - \alpha$) indicate the "confidence" that one will not commit a Type I error in the long run (i.e., over a repeated series of trials). If, for example, $\alpha = 0.05$, and we take a large number of samples, we know that we will get intervals for those sample means that would not include the parameter μ only 5% of the time. Conversely, the remaining 95% of the time, the procedure will give sample means close enough to the parameter that the confidence intervals obtained will include it (after Blalock 1972:207, 208). (b and c) Confidence intervals for a given sample mean $\bar{x}$. Confidence intervals are implicit tests of a whole range of hypotheses in that by establishing a confidence interval, we can determine what the results would have been had we actually tested any particular hypothesis. The figure is a comparison of the .95% confidence interval with tests of hypotheses at the 0.05 level of significance. The confidence interval in (b) implies nonrejection ("acceptance") of hypothesized μ_1, determined by the critical region of the normal curve, using the 0.05 level and a two-tailed test; μ_1 falls *within* the interval. The confidence interval in (c) implies rejection of hypothesized μ_2 determined as in (b); μ_2 falls *outside* the interval (after Blalock 1972:209–211).

matory data analysis have been voiced already. In statistics, these and other concerns have led to the development of an alternative mode of data analysis that emphasizes systematic pattern-search techniques. This perspective is called exploratory data analysis (Hartwig and Dearing 1979; Leinhardt and Wasserman 1979; Mosteller and Tukey 1977; Tukey 1977).

Exploratory data analysis is an empirical approach founded on the notion that as much as possible should be learned about structure in data *before* they are used to evaluate hypothesized relationships. Thus, EDA complements, rather than replaces, hypothesis testing. It employs visual methods and (visually represented) nonparametric measures of central tendency and dispersion. The techniques advocated are relatively simple and straightforward, and thus less likely to be abused than more complex procedures. Moreover, they can be used with qualitative (nominal, ordinal) as well as metric (interval, ratio) data. In an informal way, some EDA concepts and procedures have been used by data analysts for years in standard hypothesis testing contexts.

EDA developed because of dissatisfaction with the numerical summaries that are so marked a feature of the confirmatory mode of analysis (e.g., means, standard deviations, regression lines, etc.). The use of these measures is typically based on the assumption of a "normal" (Gaussian or quasi-Gaussian) distribution. Although it was recognized that such numerical summaries express certain important aspects of data patterning, it was also thought that they mask or conceal other (perhaps equally important) aspects (i.e., those that cannot be described by the standard statistical summaries) (Hartwig and Dearing 1979:9–12). An overemphasis on confirmatory analysis typically restricts explanation to only a few alternatives (i.e., those expressed in the null and alternative hypotheses). Explanation of other patterns that might exist is thus precluded (or at least discouraged).

The most fundamental conception of the exploratory approach is that all data are regarded as comprised of two components: the smooth and the rough.

$$\text{data} = \text{smooth} + \text{rough}$$

The *smooth* is the underlying simplified structure of a set of observations— the general shape of a distribution or relationship usually summarized by the standard measures of central tendency, regression lines, and the like. The rough constitutes the residuals—what is left behind after the smooth has been extracted (Hartwig and Dearing 1979:10, 11). Tukey (1977:205–235) has argued that traditional social science research typically ignores the rough, and that data that do not "fit" a preconceived model (e.g., a "normal" distribution) are as important in their own right as data that do. This is because the rough can suggest alternative explanations of patterns and reveal important structural characteristics of a data set that are likely to be minimized or ignored by an overemphasis on the smooth. From this point of view, all data analysis consists of the partitioning of data sets into smooth and rough components. What distinguishes EDA from CDA is a willingness to explore alternative models of relationship by the successive extraction of the smooth until nothing but unpatterned residuals remain.

The quest for structure is facilitated by "reexpression"—expressing the same information by some kind of transformation (e.g., logs, roots) (Tukey 1977:57–93). Measurement scales are regarded as arbitrary conceptions of the investigator imposed on data sets, and the use of a scale of measurement other than that in which a variable was originally recorded allows for the discovery of unanticipated patterns. Any transformation is considered acceptable as long as it can ultimately be related back to the original data. Tukey advocates as much reexpression as possible (although care should be taken that reexpression does not mislead the analyst later in the analysis). Usually, the more data are reexpressed (i.e., subjected to different transformations), the more smooth can be extracted.

Given the EDA emphasis on nonparametric methods, it is important that measures be "resistant" and "robust." A summary is considered resistant if changing a small portion of the data—no matter what part or how substantially—fails to change the value of the summary. Two qualities of robustness are (a) robustness of validity and (b) robustness of efficiency. Generally, robust measures lack susceptibility to the effects of nonnormality. The first type of robustness involves tolerance of nonnormal tails (e.g., confidence intervals for μ that have a 95% chance of including μ regardless of the population sampled). Robustness of efficiency involves high effectiveness in the event of nonnormal tails. An example would be confidence intervals for μ that tend to be almost as narrow for any roughly normal distribution as the best that could be achieved if the true distribution shape were known to a close approximation (Mosteller and Tukey 1977). The question of how well these "robust" and "resistant" measures perform is presently being addressed, often in a very sophisticated manner (cf. Gross 1976; Hampel 1978; Lax 1975). Studies of these kinds should ultimately lead to a more comprehensive understanding of these statistics and their roles in both EDA and CDA.

In a complete EDA scenario, analysis proceeds from the examination of single variables, to examination of relationships between two or more variables, to multivariate analysis. The rationale behind this incremental approach is to allow for as complete an understanding as possible of the structure of each variable as an entity, to understand pairs of variables as relationships, and ultimately, to understand groups of variables as models. Each stage in the process is characterized by a set of basic concepts and techniques. Most of these are familiar (or at least recognizable) to anyone with a basic statistical background; but they are modified to emphasize visual relationships, and they are described in terms of an unfamiliar vocabulary, which is likely to be a considerable obstacle to the novice reader (Tukey [1977] and Hartwig and Dearing [1979] provide glossaries).

The Univariate Case: Shape, Location, and Spread

As might be expected, analysis at the univariate level basically constitutes examination of the locational, spread, and shape characteristics of a distribution. Location refers to the point at which the distribution is anchored on a continuum from the lowest to the highest possible value of the range. Measures of location should identify the value most characteristic of a distribution, the single value that best describes the data set. In EDA, the location of a distribution refers to the dispersion of the observations, which is described in CDA by the standard deviation. Shape indicates the type of distribution (i.e., whether it is normal, symmetrical, unimodal, skewed to right or left, multimodal; whether it has outliers; etc.). Departures from normality are attributed to discreteness, gross shape differences, minor differences in "central shape," and patterning in a distribution's tails—the most difficult anomaly to detect (Mosteller and Tukey 1977:23). For each parametric concept, data displays are developed that are the visual equivalents of the standard statistical summaries. The objective is to simultaneously compress information and display more structure than is usually contained in a statistical summary.

Examples of such displays are Tukey's "stem-and-leaf" and "box-and-whisker" plots, shown in Figure 6.5. In EDA, a preliminary procedure for data analysis consists of "scratching down a batch" (organizing, condensing, and summarizing data prior to construction of a model). The stem-and-leaf display (Figure 6.5a) is the basic organizational device for doing this. A stem-and-leaf display is composed of a column of digits called starting parts (or stem values) that is separated by a vertical line from rows of digits. Each row is a stem; the individual digits on it are leaves. The batch displayed in the example is decomposed by tens. However, many other decompositions of a given batch are possible; other values can be used for starting parts (which themselves can be variously decomposed). A stem-and-leaf plot is superior to conventional data displays (e.g., histograms) because it focuses attention on shape—each leaf occupies a given amount of space, hence, the length of a line is proportional to the number of data entries for that particular stem. Besides general impressions regarding shape, spread, and location, the display clearly indicates where clustering occurs. It is also possible to use the stem-and-leaf display to make transformations of the data and to obtain the distribution of the transformed batch of numbers—by hand, and without a great deal of effort (Leinhardt and Wasserman 1979:317–319; McNeil 1977:3–6).

STEM: A ROW OF DIGITS

(a)

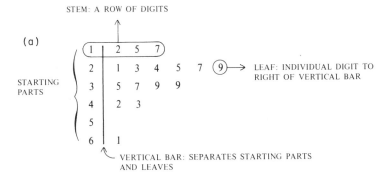

STARTING PARTS

LEAF: INDIVIDUAL DIGIT TO RIGHT OF VERTICAL BAR

VERTICAL BAR: SEPARATES STARTING PARTS AND LEAVES

(b)

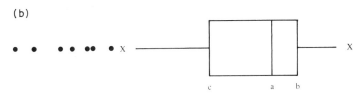

Figure 6.5. (a) "Scratching down a batch" (stem-and-leaf displays). The batch displayed here consists of the values 15, 17, 12, 43, 42, 61, 23, 39, 21, 39, 27, 24, 25, 37, 35, 29. The starting part 1 (here tens) consists of the (reordered) values 15, 17, 12. (b) A "box-and-whisker" plot. The median is a, b and c are the upper and lower "hinges," the Xs mark the observations farthest from but still within one midspread of the median. The darkened circles represent outliers (i.e., observations outside the midspread). (After Hartwig and Dearing 1979:34–36.)

In the "box-and-whisker" display (Figure 6.5b), the box represents the distribution of values that lie between the median, a, and the upper and lower "hinges" (the 25[b] and 75[c] centiles, respectively). Thus half the observations in the distribution lie within the box, with one-fourth distributed on either side of the median. The Xs mark the observations farthest from but still within one "midspread" of the hinges. The "midspread" of a distribution is the distance between the median and the lower and upper hinges. In each case it contains half the observations. The "whiskers" are the dashed lines connecting these observations to the box. Any observations that lie outside of one midspread are marked individually (the darkened circles in Figure 6.5b).

The "box-and-whisker" plot is only one of several basic schematic summaries developed by Tukey (who invites his readers to invent additional techniques). The major reason for displaying single variable distributions like this is that shape, rather than location or spread, might often be the most important characteristic of a data set. Shape is best perceived visually. The "stem-and-leaf" and "box-and-whisker" displays not only preserve the smooth—they also highlight the rough—detail at the ends of the distribution.

The Bivariate Case: Shape, Strength, and Direction

In the bivariate case, it is necessary to examine not only single distributions, but the relationship between two variables. From an EDA perspective, relationships between variables also have three important characteristics, one of which is shape (here the shape of the line formed by the smooth). The other two are strength and direction (Hartwig and Dearing 1979:31, 32). The strength of a relationship refers to the extent to which observed values on one variable can be predicted by observed values on the other. Strength assesses the relative importance of the smooth as compared to the rough. The closer the data points are to the smooth, the stronger the relationship (i.e., the smaller the residuals [the rough] after the smooth is extracted, the better values on one variable predict values on the other). Direction refers to whether or not a relationship is positive or negative (or both—a U-shaped distribution, for example, changes from a negative to a positive direction).

Bivariate relationships are displayed by scatter plots and summarized by modified forms of curve fitting. Scatter plots allow for the detection of patterns because they provide a complete picture of the relationship between the two variables (i.e., all three characteristics of relationships can be observed) (Tukey 1977:125–157). However useful scatter plots may be in an intuitive sense, though, only in exceptional cases do they allow for the partitioning of the data into its component parts (i.e., the rough and the smooth). More systematic techniques which are less sensitive to differences in individual perception are desirable if the subjective element in analysis is to be minimized. In CDA, those "more systematic techniques" typically involve fitting lines (usually straight ones) to the relationship and then making some kind of an assessment of how good the "fit" is (i.e., how well or poorly the line describes the relationship). Least-squares linear regression is probably the most common method for doing this (Blalock 1972:362–376). Least-squares regression lines are not satisfactory "smoothers" from an EDA standpoint, however, because they lack the property of "resistance" (i.e., they are sensitive to the effects of outliers). This is because means are used and residual values are squared and summed; the farther a case is from a regression line, the greater the effect it has on the location of that line. McNeil (1977) suggests that standard regression lines tend to "track" these outliers because they must come reasonably close to them to satisfy the least-squares criterion. Thus the position of the line in a scatter of points is influenced disproportionately by a few atypical cases. A nonparametric method that is a more resistant smoother would have obvious advantages.

An example of an EDA alternative to the least-squares regression line is the "Tukey line" (McNeil 1977). A Tukey line is contrasted with a least-squares regression line in Figure 6.6. In the point scatter shown, the locations of both lines are strongly influenced by the four cases in the upper left corner of the plot. Neither line describes the relationship for the majority of the cases very well (the swarm at the right side of the figure), but the Tukey line (T) does a better job than the least-squares line (R). In fact, the negative slope of the regression line is completely misleading (Hartwig and Dearing 1979:34–36).

A Tukey line is fitted to a data set displayed as a scatter plot by dividing the scatter along the horizontal axis into three nonoverlapping groups such that approximately one-third of the cases falls into each division. The medians of the x values in the first and third divisions are then obtained (MDx_1, MDx_3) as are those of the corresponding y values (MDy_1, MDy_3). The two cross-medians are located next. These are determined by the co-ordinates (MDx_1, MDy_1) and (MDx_3, MDy_3) which are connected using a transparent straightedge. The straightedge is then moved parallel to this line until one-half the cases are above and one-half are below the edge. A line is drawn—the

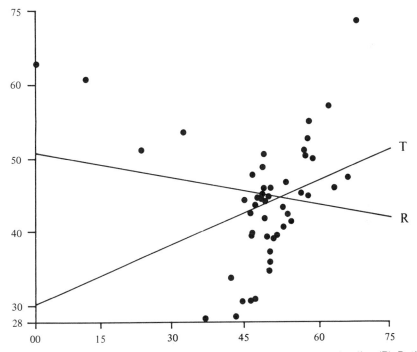

Figure 6.6. A Tukey line (T) compared with a least-squares regression line (R). Both are effected by outliers (especially the four points in the upper left part of the scatter). The Tukey line is more resistant to the effects of outliers (and is thus a better descriptor) than the regression line because it is based on medians (which are themselves more resistant) rather than means (after Hartwig and Dearing 1979:34–36).

Tukey line. The arithmetic equivalent is given by determining the slope b and the intercept a coefficients for the formula for a straight line:

$$\hat{y}_i = a + bx_i.$$

The slope is given by $(MDy_3 - MDy_1)/(MDx_3 - MDx_1)$. The intercept is the median of the values $D_i = y_i - bx_i$. The Tukey line can then be drawn in the scatter plot by a line between any two $x_i y_i$ points (McNeil 1977).

The property of resistance in a line used as a smoother is desirable because it is less likely than a nonresistant line to obscure the distinction between the smooth and the rough. The reason the Tukey line is more resistant than a regression line is that its location is based on medians. Medians are not as subject to the influence of outliers as are the means used in least-squares linear regression (Hartwig and Dearing 1979:35, 36).

In examining the relationships between pairs of variables, the Tukey line is used in conjunction with other smoothing sequences (e.g., running medians, "hanning," median and hinge traces, reexpressing nonlinear relationships) to develop a more thorough understanding of the network of relationships that are characteristic of a particular data set. In the bivariate case, outliers, asymmetries and nonlinear relationships of various kinds deserve special scrutiny because of the effect they can have on linear regression. As noted, exploratory data analysts are skeptical of least-squares linear regression without visual representation and reexpression because they believe that the method often results in misleading statistical summaries (cf. Figure 6.6). If asymmetrical distributions and nonlinear relationships are detected, the data should first be reexpressed in as many ways as possible to detect the possible presence of underlying linearity in the transformed variables. If successive smoothing still fails to produce linearity, outliers and other residuals should be isolated from the rest of the data (which can then usually be adequately summarized by the shape, strength, and direction of the relationship that characterizes them). Separate analysis of outliers is an entirely reasonable thing to do from an EDA standpoint since they are, by definition, not part of the same relationship as the other observations.

EDA advocates do not reject standard numerical summaries like regression, however, but instead use them in two ways: (a) to provide "first approximations" (initial smooths) of data, which are then subjected to further manipulation, and (b) to reanalyze reexpressed data. Reexpression facilitates further analysis by symmetrizing distributions of individual variables and by offering possible models for nonlinear relationships. In both cases, however, there are a number of possible reexpressions and no formal procedures for choosing among them. Tukey suggests that nonnormally distributed variables and nonlinear monotonic relationships (those in which the rate, but not the direction of the relationship changes) are most adequately transformed by reexpressions that adjust relative distances between variables while preserving their rank order (1977:309–329). The common nonlinear monotonic reexpressions include concave and convex transformations, and "hybrids" like the sine root function, odd-numbered roots and powers, and folded roots and logs (froots, flogs). Choice among these functions should be dictated by the particulars of the data set involved and by substantive considerations (i.e., some make more "sense" in given contexts than others). The transformed distribution should provide a better basis for further analysis (including analysis with standard statistical methods) than the untransformed data.

Multivariate Analysis

In the incremental approach advocated by Tukey, development of a multivariate model of the data is based on and derives directly from preceding univariate and bivariate analyses. The process is an iterative one, in which more and more structure (smooth) is extracted from successive sets of residuals by the creation through reexpression and analysis of new variables. When additional smooth can no longer be extracted from some final set of residuals (an "ultimate" rough), the multivariate model is considered to be complete. The rationale is that by pursuing the step-by-step interactive approach outlined above, a thorough understanding of the structure of variables is attained. Multivariate relationships are thus constructed from bivariate ones by adding additional explanatory variables that smooth (extract structure from) successive roughs (sets of residuals).

"Instant" multivariate methods like factor analysis and multiple linear regression are rejected in the early stages of analysis because they place too much emphasis on complex (and nonresistant) numerical summaries. These summaries might be based on erroneous assumptions of normal distributions, linear relationships, and the like, which—presumably—would be uncovered in the course of a complete EDA scenario. Tukey and his colleagues believe that an understanding of structure through interaction with the data at all levels is sometimes precluded in CDA by premature use of multivariate statistics (Tukey 1977). Multivariate methods can, however, be employed to advantage in the final stages of an EDA analysis to examine an ultimate rough for patterned residuals expected under a particular multivariate model (e.g., to compare residuals against the values predicted by the multiple linear regression equation (Hartwig and Dearing 1979:70–72). Although it is recognized that this conception of multivariate causality is somewhat at odds with that of standard CDA, EDA advocates suggest that relatively more is gained in terms of understanding by thorough structure searching than is lost from (premature and oversimplified) recourse to a "most comprehensive" multivariate statistical summary.

In summary, EDA is a way of looking at data with both an open mind and a healthy skepticism of traditional statistical summaries. It approaches the problem of understanding the network of relationships characteristic of a data set in a partitive fashion by decomposing that complex set of relationships into manageable pieces. At each level in the analysis, visual displays, resistant numerical summaries, and reexpression aid in the process of understanding. In one sense, EDA perspectives have always been a part of the research process (e.g., most introductory statistics texts encourage preliminary "data snooping"—data displays of various kinds—prior to analysis).

EDA and CDA: Some Observations

It is in regard to conceptions of data and the roles they play in hypothesis testing that an EDA perspective is perhaps most distinct from that of the confirmatory mode. In CDA, data are formally defined in terms of the requirements of the statistical hypothesis (Figure 6.3:Box 6), which in turn is ultimately determined by the statistical model chosen (Boxes 4 and 5). In EDA, data are more directly conceptualized in terms of the behavioral hypothesis (Figure 6.3:Box 3). Variables regarded as relevant are displayed, and a model of the smooth is *generated from the data set itself,* rather than imposed on the data set by the assumptions of a statistical model. No test in a formal sense is undertaken, although repeated smoothing may result in a series of data-generated models that are coherent and interpretable in terms of some theoretical model. This is confirmation in an EDA mode, and it is acknowledged that some readers might find it objectionable. The more similar the data-generated models are to some theoretical model, the more the data are considered to confirm the theory (Hartwig and Dearing 1979:12, 13).

Although EDA tends to suggest rather than confirm hypotheses, the procedures advocated are not incompatible with a confirmatory mode of analysis. All researchers engage in EDA to some degree. What EDA provides is a more formal way of structuring the exploratory phases of research. Clearly, the earlier such exploration occurs in the research process, the more likely it is to have a significant positive effect on subsequent stages in the research design. This is true whether or not confirmation is involved, but it is especially true if EDA techniques are integrated with a CDA design that has as its objective the formal evaluation of hypotheses.

One form such a "hybrid" research design might take is shown schematically in Figure 6.7. The diagram is a partial expansion and reordering of some of the elements in the CDA flowchart (Figure 6.3). It differs from Figure 6.3 in three respects.

First, compare the positions of the "data acquisition" boxes in the two diagrams. Data are defined in terms of a statistical hypothesis in a confir-

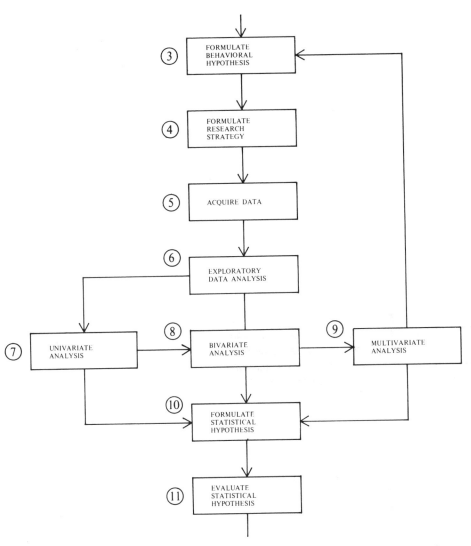

Figure 6.7. A flowchart incorporating an EDA pattern search in a CDA format for hypothesis testing.

matory mode of analysis. In EDA, they are acquired via a research design based more directly on a behavioral hypothesis. A behavioral hypothesis is a more fluid, less precise formulation than a statistical hypothesis. A correspondingly greater amount of latitude is thus allowable (and inevitable—maybe even to be encouraged!) in determining which data sets are relevant to its evaluation. As should be clear by now, EDA advocates stress openness to alternatives and a flexible "mix" of data display and pattern search techniques. They have not (to my knowledge) addressed the problem of data acquisition directly, but have instead concentrated on ways of searching for structure once "relevant" data have been acquired.

Second, although the complete EDA scenario calls for a progression from univariate to multivariate analysis (Figure 6.7:Boxes 7–9), it is clear that in many contexts only part of the procedure will be fully utilized.

Finally, notice that in Figure 6.7 an attempt is made to integrate EDA methods with a testing mode by using them to assist in the formulation of a statistical hypothesis (Box 10). There is some diversity of opinion as to precisely what role EDA should play in hypothesis testing. As noted, EDA methods can assist in the formulation of hypotheses. However, it has been suggested that the exploratory data analyst forfeits the right to evaluate the statistical significance of any models generated since they are not "formal, a priori hypotheses in a statistical sense" (i.e., the hypotheses are derived directly from the data sets evaluated; therefore, to test for significance would be meaningless) (Hartwig and Dearing 1979:78). This seems to be a legitimate constraint in those disciplines where formal, complete theories of relationships among variables are expressed in fully developed statistical models. However, in a field characterized by weak and partial theories of relationship, in which variables have many possible empirical referents, and many relationships among them are possible, it seems to me that a statistical hypothesis could be generated that was not incompatible with significance testing. Such an hypothesis would incorporate some characteristics of a relationship that were known from pursuing an exploratory mode of analysis, but would predict other characteristics of the data that were not known beforehand and that were not the direct result of an EDA pattern search. Weak theories, which do not specify completely *how* variables are related to one another, but only indicate that they *are* related in some way, are particularly susceptible to a "hybrid" analysis of this kind. Archaeology, it seems to me, is a discipline in which weak theories abound.

CONCLUSIONS

Statistical concepts and procedures have been discussed (*a*) from a historical perspective, in terms of the incidence of archaeological usage over the past 45 years; (*b*) in the narrower context of the role of inferential statistics in the formulation and testing of hypotheses (CDA); and (*c*) from the "display and pattern-search" point of view of EDA. Obviously, the treatment has been highly selective. Space limitations and the resolve of the author to limit the topics discussed have precluded a more general catalog of archaeological applications, which is a book-length subject in itself (cf. Doran and Hodson 1975). Some important research areas that have become heavily quantified in recent years have been ignored altogether (e.g., statistical artifact and attribute classification [Clark 1976; Read 1974a,b; Spaulding 1953b, 1960]). Discussion of complex multivariate analytical procedures and simulations has also been omitted and sampling designs slighted (cf. Cowgill 1968, 1970, 1975; Hodder 1979; Plog *et al.* 1978; Plog 1980; Redman 1973a; Thomas 1972). What has been said, however, makes it clear that quantification in the design of archaeological research is here to stay.

Preliminary results from a recent survey of current thinking in archaeological method and theory serve to underscore the widespread concern with quantification in general and with the adoption of statistical modes of analysis (Schiffer 1977).

1. Sampling and quantitative methods figure among the major areas of methodological expertise identified by many survey respondents (a sample taken from individuals listed in the AAA *Guide to Departments of Anthropology* who specified archaeological method and theory as an area of specialization).

2. The use and abuse of quantitative methods was identified as the second of a dozen major issues requiring urgent attention.

3. Quantitative applications, sampling designs, rigorous hypothesis testing, locational analysis, research designs in general, and multivariate statistics were among the top 16 topics suggested for inclusion in future *American Antiquity* issues devoted exclusively to method and theory.

Concerns with a lack of theoretical development within the discipline, and with the need to develop methods for obtaining a closer fit between models and data were also expressed in the context of a bewildering diversity of methodological and theoretical interests (179 different subjects were identified by the 94 respondents).

As Schiffer observes, the heavy emphasis on quantitative methods should lead to extensive restructuring of undergraduate anthropology curricula, so that initial exposure to quantitative modes of analysis becomes a part of the undergraduate preparation, just as it commonly has for the undergraduate sociology, psychology, or economics major. In anthropology, the present practice is to append, usually at the behest of a supervisory committee, some *ad hoc* knowledge of quantitative approaches to the methodological repertoire once admitted to graduate school. The result is that statistical procedures are grafted onto the dissertation proposal, and subsequent postgraduate research designs, more or less as an afterthought, rather than as a commitment to a quantitative approach right from the outset.

It is suggested that an exposure to basic quantification, descriptive and inferential techniques (i.e., univariate descriptive methods, basic probability theory, inductive statistics, the common probability distributions, and the common bivariate methods) would not be inappropraite by the end of the sophomore year and could be accommodated by the inclusion of a single introductory course in the undergraduate curriculum. With this basic foundation, at least three more courses would be helpful. One would consist of a survey of nonparametric approaches (e.g., Hollander and Wolfe 1973), which are of considerable utility to researchers because of wider applicability to archaeological data, fewer constraints (than multivariate techniques) on appropriate application, greater ease in comprehension, and a probable lower incidence of abuse.

The second course would consist of an intensive exposure to one or more advanced techniques (e.g., correlation, analysis of variance, simple linear regression), perhaps followed by an introduction to multiple linear regression and the more complicated ANOVA models (cf. Cooley and Lohnes 1971; Tatsuoka 1971). Such special topic courses can be found among the undergraduate "service" offerings of any average-sized mathematics or statistics department. Exposure to the more complex aspects of social statistics (e.g., factor and principal components analysis, multivariate ANOVA, etc.) should probably be deferred until graduate school, or be confined to optional courses available to the upper division undergraduate major.

The third course should provide an introduction to the EDA perspective. Although EDA is a recent development in statistics itself (the "definitive" texts [Mosteller and Tukey 1977; McNeil 1977; Tukey 1977] have appeared only in the past 4 years), universities with comprehensive, service-oriented mathematics and/or statistics departments have apparently been offering such courses since about 1979 (Young, personal communication 1981). At Arizona State University, which is perhaps typical of the large state-supported institutions in which most anthropology programs are found, EDA courses are offered by the Department of Mathematics and are assigned numbers that allow for both upper division undergraduate and graduate credit. Thus far, archaeologists have made only partial and eclectic use of EDA techniques, and they have not been formally incorporated into most archaeological research designs. This lack of penetration is due to the comparative "newness" of the approach, and to the bias in favor of CDA, which has been so evident in the literature of the past 15 years.

It is believed that curriculum restructuring of the kind suggested would bring anthropology more in line with other undergraduate social science curricula. At a minimum, the total student credit-hour investment would be on the order of three courses—not too great a price to pay for a more integrated conception of statistical reasoning and a better appreciation of the range of statistical methods, both of which are likely to pay dividends later on in graduate school and in subsequent professional life.

The regional orientation of many projects (e.g., SARG) and the related development of large, computerized archaeological data banks combine to create a situation in which broad sets of interrelated problems can be studied simultaneously and under the umbrella of a comprehensive research design. Because of the central role of sampling and the impact that descriptive and inferential statistics have had on the technical level of archaeological research in these regional contexts, the potential now exists for the acquisition of bodies of data useful for the evaluation of many different kinds of hypotheses. Statistical methods, appropriately applied, greatly expand the possibilities for manipulating these kinds of data in precise, sophisticated, and replicable ways, both to answer more limited questions of archaeological interest, and ultimately to produce conclusions that have some credibility within the broader field of anthropology as a whole.

ACKNOWLEDGMENTS

I want to thank N. Ackerly, F. Plog, C. R. Stafford, J. Hepworth, and D. Young (Arizona State University); D. H. Thomas (American Museum of Natural History); M. Schiffer (University of Arizona); and A. C. Spaulding (University of California at Santa Barbara) for taking the time to evaluate various drafts of this chapter. Thomas, Schiffer, and Ackerly were especially helpful and, quite apart from substantive matters, their encouragement and support did much to keep my morale up while struggling with the revision of the manuscript. The comments of these individuals, and those of five anonymous reviewers, have been incorporated wherever possible, and they have substantially improved the paper. P. Whitten (Eastern New Mexico University) helped me collect the *American Antiquity* data, for which I am most grateful. Barbara Bellamy typed the lengthy manuscript in short order, cheerfully, and with a minimum of errors. If, after all of this, any factual shortcomings or misconceptions remain, they are of course my responsibility.

REFERENCES

Andrews, D.
    1972   Plots of high-dimensional data. *Biometrics* **28**:125–136.
Andrews, D., R. Gnanadesikan, and J. Warner
    1973   Methods for assessing multivariate normality. In *Multivariate analysis* (Vol. III), edited by P. Krishnaiah. New York: Academic Press. Pp. 95–116.
Asch, D.
    1975   On sample size problems and the uses of nonprobabilistic sampling. In *Sampling in archaeology,* edited by J. Mueller. Tucson: University of Arizona Press. Pp. 170–191.

Bailey, G.
    1978   Shell middens as indicators of postglacial economies: a territorial perspective. In *The early postglacial settlement of Northern Europe,* edited by P. Mellars. London: Duckworth. Pp. 37–63.

Benfer, R.
    1979   Sample size in multivariate analysis: some corrections of Davis' review of *Sampling in Archaeology. Plains Anthropologist* **24:**71–73.

Bettinger, R.
    1979   Curation, statistics and settlement studies: a reply to Munday and Lincoln. *American Antiquity* **44:**352–359.

Binford, L.
    1962   Archaeology as anthropology. *American Antiquity* **28**(2):217–225.
    1965   Archaeological systematics and the study of culture process. *American Antiquity* **31**(2):203–210.
    1967   Smudge pits and hide smoking: the use of analogy in archaeological reasoning. *American Antiquity* **32**(1):1–12.
    1968   Archaeological perspectives. In *New perspectives in archaeology,* edited by S. Binford and L. Binford. Chicago: Aldine. Pp. 5–32.
    1972   Model building—paradigms, and the current state of paleolithic research. In *An archaeological perspective.* New York: Seminar Press. Pp. 244–294.

Binford, L., and S. Binford
    1966   A preliminary analysis of functional variability in the Mousterian of Levallois facies. *American Anthropologist* **68**(2):238–295.

Blair, D.
    1975   On purely probabilistic theories of scientific inference. *Philosophy of Science* **42**(3):242–249.

Blalock, H.
    1972   *Social statistics* (second ed.). New York: McGraw-Hill.

Blanton, R.
    1976   The role of symbiosis in adaptation and sociocultural change in the Valley of Mexico. In *The valley of Mexico: studies in prehispanic ecology and society,* edited by E. Wolf. Albuquerque: University of New Mexico Press. Pp. 181–201.

Braidwood, R.
    1952   *The Near East and the foundations of civilization.* Condon Lectures, Oregon State System for Higher Education, Eugene.
    1958   Near Eastern prehistory. *Science* **127**(3312):1419–1430.

Braidwood, R., and B. Howe
    1960   Prehistoric investigations in Iraqi Kurdistan. *Studies in Ancient Oriental Civilization* No. 31. Oriental Institute, University of Chicago.

Brainerd, G.
    1951   The place of chronological ordering in archaeological analysis. *American Antiquity* **16**(4):301–313.

Bridgman, P.
    1938   *The logic of modern physics.* New York: Macmillan.

Cassels, R.
    1972   Locational analysis of prehistoric settlement in New Zealand. *Mankind* **8:**212–222.

Chenhall, R.
    1971a   The archaeological data bank, a progress report. *Computers and the Humanities* **5**(3):159–169.

1971b   *Computers in anthropology and archaeology.* IBM Data Processing Application Manual GE 20-0384-0.

1972   Computerized data banks for archaeologists. *Archaologie,* 3, Berlin: B. Heslig.

1975   A rationale for archaeological sampling. In *Sampling in archaeology,* edited by J. Mueller. Tucson: University of Arizona Press. Pp. 3–25.

Christenson, A.

1979   On the virtues of simplicity: some comments on statistical analysis in anthropology. *Plains Anthropologist* **24**:35–38.

Christenson, A., and D. Read

1977   Numerical taxonomy, R-mode factor analysis and archaeological classification. *American Antiquity* **42**(2):163–179.

Clark, G.

1974   On the analysis of multidimensional contingency table data using log linear models. In *Computer applications in archaeology,* edited by J. Wilcock and S. Laflin. Birmingham: Computer Centre. Pp. 47–58. University of Birmingham.

1976   More on contingency table analysis, decision-making criteria and the use of log linear models. *American Antiquity* **41**(3):259–273.

1979   Spatial association at Liencres, an Early Holocene open site on the Santander coast, north-central Spain. In Computer graphics in archaeology, edited by S. Upham. *Anthropological Research Paper* No. 15. Tempe: Arizona State University. Pp. 121–144.

1981   Aspects of statistics in archaeological research designs. In *The design of archaeological research,* edited by L. Raab and T. Klinger. Chicago: Aldine.

Clark, G., R. Effland, J. Johnstone

1977   Quantitative spatial analysis. In *Computer applications in archaeology,* edited by S. Laflin. Birmingham: Computer Centre, University of Birmingham. Pp. 27–44.

Clark, G., and S. Lerner

1980   Prehistoric resource utilization in early Holocene Cantabrian Spain. In *Catchment analysis: essays in prehistoric resource space,* edited by F. Findlow and J. Ericson. Los Angeles: University of California. Pp. 53–96.

Clark, J. G. D.

1954   *Excavations at Star Carr.* Cambridge: Cambridge University Press.

Clarke, D.

1973   Archaeology: the loss of innocence. *Antiquity* **47**(1):6–18.

1977   Spatial information in archaeology. In *Spatial archaeology,* edited by D. Clarke. New York: Academic Press. Pp. 1–32.

Cohen, J.

1969   *Statistical power analysis for the behavioral sciences.* New York: Academic Press.

Conover, W.

1971   *Practical nonparametric statistics.* New York: Wiley.

Cooley, W. W., and T. R. Lohnes

1971   *Multivariate data analysis.* New York: Wiley.

Cordell, L., and F. Plog

1979   Escaping the confines of normative thought: a re-evaluation of Puebloan prehistory. *American Antiquity* **44**(3):405–429.

Cowgill, G.

1964   The selection of samples from large sherd collections. *American Antiquity* **29**(4):467–473.

1967   Computers and prehistoric archaeology. In *Computers in humanistic research,* edited by C. Bowles. Englewood Cliffs (N.J.): Prentice-Hall. Pp. 47–56.

1968   Archaeological applications of factor, cluster and proximity analysis. *American Antiquity* **33**(3):367–375.

1970   Some sampling and reliability problems in archaeology. In *Archeologie et calculateurs: problemes semiologiques et mathematiques*. Paris: Editions du Centre National de la Recherche Scientifique. Pp. 161–172.

1975   A selection of samplers: comments on archaeostatistics. In *Sampling in archaeology,* edited by J. Mueller. Tucson: University of Arizona Press. Pp. 258–276.

1977   The trouble with significance tests and what we can do about it. *American Antiquity* **42**:350–368.

Crumley, C.

1976   Toward a locational definition of state systems of settlement. *American Anthropologist* **78**(1):59–73.

1979   Three locational models: an epistemological assessment for anthropology and archaeology. In *Advances in archaeological method and theory* (Vol. 2), edited by M. B. Schiffer. New York: Academic Press. Pp. 143–174.

Dacey, M.

1973   Statistical tests of spatial association in the locations of tool types. *American Antiquity* **38**(3):320–328.

Degerman, R.

1972   The geometric representation of some structures. In *Multi-dimensional scaling: theory and applications in the behavioral sciences* (Vol. 1), edited by R. Shepard, K. Romney, and S. Nerlove, New York: Seminar Press.

Doran, J., and F. Hodson

1975   *Mathematics and computers in archaeology*. Cambridge, Massachusetts: Harvard University Press.

Dunnell, R.

1971   *Systematics in prehistory*. New York: Free Press.

Euler, R., and G. Gumerman (Editors)

1978   *Investigations of the southwestern anthropological research group*. Flagstaff: Museum of Northern Arizona.

Everitt, B.

1974   *Cluster analysis*. London: Heinemann Educational Books.

Fairbanks, C.

1942   The taxonomic position of Stalling's Island, Georgia. *American Antiquity* **7**(3):223–231.

Flannery, K.

1973   Archaeology with a capital "S." In *Research and theory in current archaeology,* edited by C. Redman. New York: Wiley Interscience. Pp. 47–53.

1976a   Empirical determinants of site catchments in Oaxaca and Tehuacán. In *The early mesoamerican village,* edited by K. Flannery. New York: Academic Press. Pp. 103–116.

1976b   Evolution of complex settlement systems. In *The early mesoamerican village,* edited by K. Flannery. New York: Academic Press. Pp. 162–172.

Ford, J.

1952   Measurements of some prehistoric design developments in the Southeastern states. *Anthropological Papers of the American Museum of Natural History* **44**(3).

1954a   Spaulding's review of Ford. *American Anthropologist*. **56**(1):109–111.

1954b   Comment on A. C. Spaulding's "Statistical techniques for the discovery of artifact types." *American Antiquity* **19**(4):390–391.

1954c   On the concept of types: the type concept revisited. *American Anthropologist* **56**(1):42–54.

Francis, J., and G. Clark
   1980   Bronze and Iron Age economies on the Meseta del Norte, north-central Spain. In
           Catchment analysis: essays in prehistoric resource space, edited by F. Findlow and
           J. Ericson. Los Angeles: University of California. Pp. 97–136.
Fritz, J., and F. Plog
   1970   The nature of archaeological explanation. *American Antiquity* 35(4):405–412.
Gaines, S.
   1978   Computer application of the SARG data: an evaluation. In *Investigations of the
           southwestern anthropological research group,* edited by R. Euler and G. Gumer-
           man. Flagstaff: Museum of Northern Arizona. Pp. 119–138.
   1981   *Data bank applications in archaeology,* edited by S. Gaines. Tucson: University of
           Arizona Press.
Gnanadesikan, R.
   1977   *Methods for statistical data analysis of multivariate observations.* New York:
           Wiley.
Graham, J.
   1970   Discrimination of British Lower and Middle Paleolithic handaxe groups using
           canonical variates. *World Archaeology* 1(3):321–327.
Gross, A.
   1976   Confidence interval robustness with long-tailed symmetrical distributions. *Jour-
           nal of the American Statistical Association* 71:409–416.
Gumerman, G., D. Westfall, and C. Weed
   1972   Archaeological investigations on Black Mesa: the 1969–1970 seasons. *Prescott
           College, Studies in Anthropology* No. 4.
Hampel, F.
   1978   Contributions to the theory of robust estimation. Unpublished Ph.D dissertation,
           Department of Statistics, University of California, Berkeley.
Hanson, G., and A. Goodyear
   1975   The shared tool method of spatial analysis: applications at the Brand Site. Un-
           published manuscript, Department of Anthropology, Arizona State University,
           Tempe.
Hartwig, F., and B. Dearing
   1979   *Exploratory data analysis.* Sage Quantitative Applications in the Social Sciences
           No. 16. Beverly Hills, California: Sage.
Henkel, R.
   1976   *Tests of significance.* Sage University Paper on Quantitative Applications in the
           Social Sciences, No. 4, edited by E. Uslaner. Beverly Hills, California: Sage.
Hietala, H., and D. Stevens
   1977   Spatial analysis: multiple procedures in pattern recognition studies. *American An-
           tiquity* 42(4):539–559.
Hodder, I.
   1972a   Interpretation of spatial patterns in archaeology: two examples. *Area* 4:223–229.
   1972b   Locational models and the study of Romano-British settlement. In *Models in ar-
           chaeology,* edited by D. Clarke. London: Methuen. Pp. 887–909.
   1974   A regression analysis of some trade and marketing patterns. *World Archaeology*
           6(2):172–189.
   1979   Trends and surfaces in archaeology. In *Computer graphics in archaeology,* edited
           by S. Upham. Anthropological Research Paper No. 15. Tempe: Arizona State
           University. Pp. 149–154.
Hodder, I., and M. Hassall
   1971   The non-random spacing of Romano-British walled towns. *Man* 6(2):391–407.

Hodder, I., and C. Orton
  1976   *Spatial analysis in archaeology.* London: Cambridge University Press.
Hodson, F.
  1970   Cluster analysis and archaeology: some new developments and applications. *World Archaeology* 1(3):299–320.
  1971   Numerical typology and prehistoric archaeology. In *Mathematics in the archaeological and historical sciences,* edited by F. Hodson, D. Kendall, and P. Tautu. Edinburgh: Edinburgh University Press. Pp. 30–45.
Hodson, F., P. Sneath, J. Doran
  1966   Some experiments in the numerical analysis of archaeological data. *Biometrika* 53(2):311–324.
Hollander, M., and D. Wolfe
  1973   *Nonparametric statistical methods.* New York: Wiley.
Huber, D.
  1975   Robust statistics: a review. *Annals of Mathematical Statistics* 43:1041–1067.
Johnson, F.
  1951   Radiocarbon dating. *American Antiquity* 17(1):1–65.
Johnson, G.
  1972   A test of the utility of central place theory in archaeology. In *Man, settlement and urbanism,* edited by J. Ucko, R. Tringham, and G. Dimbleby. London: Duckworth. Pp. 769–785.
  1973   Local exchange and early state development in southwestern Iran. *Anthropological papers, Museum of Anthropology, University of Michigan,* No. 51.
  1975   Locational analysis and the investigation of Uruk local exchange systems. In *Ancient civilization and trade,* edited by J. Sabloff and C. Lamberg-Karlovsky. Albuquerque: University of New Mexico Press. Pp. 285–339.
Jolicoeur, P.
  1975   Multivariate geographical variation in wolf *Canis lupus L.* In *Multivariate statistical methods: among groups covariation,* edited by W. Atchley and E. Dowder. Stroudsburg (PA): Hutchinson and Ross. Pp. 200–216.
Judge, J., J. Ebert, and R. Hitchcock
  1975   Sampling in regional archaeological survey. In *Sampling in archaeology,* edited by J. Mueller. Tucson: University of Arizona Press. Pp. 82–123.
Kluckhohn, C.
  1940   The conceptual structure in Middle American studies. In *The Maya and their neighbors,* edited by C. Hay *et al.* New York: Appleton. Pp. 41–51.
Koestler, A.
  1964   *The act of creation.* New York: Dell.
Kroeber, A.
  1940   Statistical classification. *American Antiquity* 6(1):29–44.
  1942   Tapajo pottery. *American Antiquity* 7(4):403–405.
Kruger, L.
  1976   Are statistical explanations possible? *Philosophy of Science* 43(1):129–146.
Kuhn, T.
  1962   *The structure of scientific revolutions.* Chicago: University of Chicago Press.
  1970a   Logic of discovery or psychology of research? In *Criticism and the growth of knowledge,* edited by I. Lakatos and A. Musgrave. Cambridge: Cambridge University Press. Pp. 1–23.
  1970b   Reflections on my critics. In *Criticism and the growth of knowledge,* edited by I. Lakatos and A. Musgrave. Cambridge: Cambridge University Press. Pp. 231–278.

Lax, D.
  1975   An interim report of a Monte Carlo study of robust estimators of width. *Technical Report* 93 (Series 2), Department of Statistics, Princeton University, Princeton.
Lehmer, D.
  1951   Robinson's coefficient of agreement—a critique. *American Antiquity* 17(2):151.
Leinhardt, S., and S. Wasserman
  1979   Exploratory data analysis: an introduction to selected methods. In *Sociological methodology 1979,* edited by K. Schuessler. San Francisco: Jossey-Bass. Pp. 311–372.
Longacre, W.
  1970   Archaeology as anthropology: a case study. *Anthropological papers of the University of Arizona,* No. 17. Tucson: University of Arizona Press.
Matson, R.
  1980   The proper place of multivariate techniques in archaeology. *American Antiquity* 45(2):340–344.
Matson, R., and W. Lipe
  1975   Regional sampling: a case study of Cedar Mesa, Utah. In *Sampling in archaeology,* edited by J. Mueller. Tucson: University of Arizona Press. Pp. 124–146.
McNeil, D.
  1977   *Interactive data analysis: a practical primer.* New York: Wiley.
Meehl, P.
  1967   Theory testing in psychology and physics: a methodological paradox. *Philosophy of Science* 34(2):103–115.
Meiklejohn, C.
  1978   Ecological aspects of population size and growth in late-glacial and early post-glacial northwestern Europe. In *The early postglacial settlement of Northern Europe,* edited by P. Mellars. London: Duckworth. Pp. 243–294.
Mellars, P., and S. Reinhardt
  1978   Patterns of Mesolithic land-use in southern England: a geological perspective. In *The early postglacial settlement of Northern Europe,* edited by P. Mellars. London: Duckworth. Pp. 243–294.
Meltzer, D.
  1979   Paradigms and the nature of change in American archaeology. *American Antiquity* 44(4):644–657.
Merrill, R.
  1946   A graphical approach to some problems in Maya astronomy. *American Antiquity* 12(1):35–72.
Morgan, C.
  1973   Archaeology and explanation. *World Archaeology* 4(3):259–276.
  1974   Explanation and scientific archaeology. *World Archaeology* 6(2):133–137.
Mosteller, F., and J. Tukey
  1977   *Data analysis and regression: a second course in statistics.* Reading, Massachusetts: Addison-Wesley.
Mueller, J.
  1972   The use of sampling in archaeological survey. Unpublished Ph.D. dissertation, Department of Anthropology, University of Arizona, Tucson.
  1974   The use of sampling in archaeological survey. *Memoirs, Society for American Archaeology,* No. 28.
  1975   *Sampling in archaeology,* edited by J. Mueller. Tucson: University of Arizona Press.
  1978   A reply to Plog and Thomas. *American Antiquity* 43(2):286, 287.

Munday, F., and T. Lincoln
  1979   A comment on Bettinger: problems in archaeological interpretation. *American Antiquity* **44**:345–351.
Newell, R., and A. Dekin
  1978   An integrative strategy for the definition of behaviourally meaningful archaeological units. *Palaeohistoria* **20**:7–38.
Northrop, F.
  1947   *The logic of the sciences and the humanities.* New York: Macmillan.
Ott, L.
  1977   *An introduction to statistical methods and data analysis.* North Scituate, Massachusetts: Duxbury Press.
Plog, F.
  1974   *The study of prehistoric change.* New York: Academic Press.
Plog, F., R. Effland, and D. Green
  1978   Inferences using the SARG data bank. In *Investigations of the southwestern anthropological research group,* edited by R. Euler and G. Gumerman. Flagstaff: Museum of Northern Arizona. Pp. 139–148.
Plog, S.
  1976   Relative efficiencies of sampling techniques for archaeological surveys. In *The early mesoamerican village,* edited by K. Flannery. New York: Academic Press. Pp. 136–158.
  1980   *Stylistic variation in prehistoric ceramics.* Cambridge: Cambridge University Press.
Plog, S., F. Plog, and W. Wait
  1978   Decision making in modern surveys. In *Advances in archaeological method and theory* (Vol. 1), edited by M. Schiffer. New York: Academic Press. Pp. 384–422.
Price, T. D.
  1978   Mesolithic settlement systems in the Nederlands. In *The early postglacial settlement of Northern Europe,* edited by P. Mellars. London: Duckworth. Pp. 81–114.
Read, D.
  1974a   Some comments on the use of mathematical models in anthropology. *American Antiquity* **39**(1):3–15.
  1974b   Some comments on typologies in archaeology and an outline of a methodology. *American Antiquity* **39**(2):216–242.
  1975   Regional sampling. In *Sampling in archaeology,* edited by J. Mueller. Tucson: University of Arizona Press. Pp. 45–60.
Redman, C.
  1973a   Multistage field work and analytical techniques. *American Antiquity* **38**(1):61–79.
  1973b   Research and theory in current archaeology: an introduction. In *Research and theory in current archaeology,* edited by C. Redman. New York: Wiley Interscience. Pp. 5–20.
Renfrew, C.
  1977   Models for exchange and spatial distribution. In *Exchange systems in prehistory,* edited by T. Earle and J. Ericson. New York: Academic Press. Pp. 71–90.
Robinson, W.
  1951   A method for chronologically ordering archaeological deposits. *American Antiquity* **16**(4):293–301.
Robinson, W., and G. Brainerd
  1952   Robinson's coefficient of agreement—a rejoinder. *American Antiquity* **18**(1):60, 61.

Roper, D.
1979   The method and theory of site catchment analysis: a review. In *Advances in archaeological method and theory* (Vol. 2), edited by M. B. Schiffer. New York: Academic Press. Pp. 120–142.

Rossman, D.
1976   A site catchment analysis of San Lorenzo, Veracruz. In *The early mesoamerican village,* edited by K. Flannery. New York: Academic Press. Pp. 95–102.

Salmon, Merrilee H.
1975   Confirmation and explanation in archaeology. *American Antiquity* **40**:459–470.
1976   "Deductive" versus "inductive" archaeology. *American Antiquity* **41**:376–380.

Salmon, Wesley C.
1973   *Logic* (second ed.). Englewood Cliffs, New Jersey: Prentice-Hall.

Schiffer, M.
1972   Archaeological context and systemic context. *American Antiquity* **37**(2):156–165.
1973   Cultural formation processes of the archaeological record: applications at the Joint Site. Unpublished Ph.D. dissertation, Department of Anthropology, University of Arizona, Tucson.
1977   Current directions in archaeological method and theory. *American Anthropologist* **79**(3):647–649.
1978   Taking the pulse of method and theory in American archaeology. *American Antiquity* **43**:153–158.

Schwartz, B.
1967   A logical sequence of archaeological objectives. *American Antiquity* **32**(4):487–497.

Selltiz, C., M. Jahoda, M. Deutsch, and S. Cook
1959   *Research methods in social relations.* New York: Holt.

Sibson, R.
1971   Computational methods in cluster analysis. In *Mathematics in the archaeological and historical sciences,* edited by F. Hodson, D. Kendall, and P. Tautu. Edinburgh: Edinburgh University Press. Pp. 59–61.

Siegel, S.
1956   *Nonparametric statistics for the behavioral sciences.* New York: McGraw-Hill.

Smith, B.
1977   Archaeological inference and inductive confirmation. *American Anthropologist* **79**(3):598–617.

Sneath, P., and R. Sokal
1973   *Numerical taxonomy.* San Francisco: Freeman.

Sokal, R., and F. Rohlf
1969   *Biometry.* San Francisco: Freeman.

Sokal, R., and P. Sneath
1963   *Principles of numerical taxonomy.* San Francisco: Freeman.

Spaulding, A.
1953a   Review: measurements of some prehistoric design developments in the southeastern states (Ford). *American Anthropologist* **55**(4):588–591.
1953b   Statistical techniques for the discovery of artifact types. *American Antiquity* **18**(3):305–313.
1954a   Reply to Ford. *American Antiquity* **19**(4):391–393.
1954b   Reply to Ford. *American Anthropologist* **56**(1):112–114.
1960   Statistical description and comparison of artifact assemblages. *Viking Fund Publications in Anthropology* **28**:60–83.

1971   Some elements of quantitative archaeology. In *Mathematics in the archaeological and historical sciences,* edited by F. Hodson, D. Kendall, and P. Tautu. Edinburgh: Edinburgh University Press. Pp. 3–16.

Stafford, C., and B. Stafford
1979   Some comments on the design of lithic experiments. *Lithic Technology* 8(2).

Stark, B., and D. Young
1981   Linear nearest neighbor analysis. *American Antiquity* 46(2):284–300.

Steward, J., and F. Setzler
1938   Function and configuration in archaeology. *American Antiquity* 4(1):4–10.

Sterud, E.
1978   Changing aims of Americanist archaeology: a citations analysis of *American Antiquity*—1946–1975. *American Antiquity* 43(2):294–302.

Tatsuoka, M.
1971   *Multivariate analysis.* New York: Wiley.

Thomas, D.
1970   Archaeology's operational imperative: Great Basin projectile points as a test case. In *Annual report, archaeological survey.* Los Angeles: University of California. Pp. 29–60.
1972   The use and abuse of numerical taxonomy in archaeology. *Archaeology and Physical Anthropology in Oceania* 7(1):31–49.
1976   *Figuring anthropology: first principles of probability and statistics.* New York: Holt, Rinehart and Winston.
1978   The awful truth about statistics in archaeology. *American Antiquity* 43(2).
1980   The gruesome truth about statistics in archaeology. *American Antiquity* 45(2):344, 345.

Thompson, R.
1956   The subjective element in archaeological inference. *Southwestern Journal of Anthropology* 12(2):327–332.

Tuggle, D., A. Townsend, and T. Riley
1972   Laws, systems and research designs: a discussion of explanation in archaeology. *American Antiquity* 37(1):3–12.

Tukey, J.
1977   *Exploratory data analysis.* Reading, Massachusetts: Addison-Wesley.

Wallis, W., and H. Roberts
1967   *Statistics: a new approach.* New York: Free Press.

Watson, P., S. LeBlanc, and C. Redman
1971   *Explanation in archaeology: an explicitly scientific approach.* New York: Columbia University Press.
1974   The covering law model in archaeology: practical uses and formal interpretations. *World Archaeology* 6(2):125–132.

Weaver, D.
1977   Prehistoric population dynamics and environmental exploitation in the Manuelito Canyon district, northwestern New Mexico. Unpublished Ph.D. dissertation, Department of Anthropology, Arizona State University.

Whallon, R.
1973a   Spatial analysis of occupation floors: the application of dimensional analysis of variance. In *The explanation of culture change: models in prehistory,* edited by C. Renfrew. London: Duckworth. Pp. 115–130.
1973b   Spatial analysis of occupation floors I: application of dimensional analysis variance. *American Antiquity* 38(3):266–278.

1974   Spatial analysis of occupation floors II: application of nearest neighbor analysis. *American Antiquity* **39**(1):16–34.

1978   The spatial analysis of Mesolithic occupation floors: a reappraisal. In *The early postglacial settlement of Northern Europe,* edited by P. Mellars. London: Duckworth. Pp. 27–36.

White, D.
1973   Mathematical anthropology. In *Handbook of social and cultural anthropology,* edited by J. Honigman. Chicago: Rand McNally. Pp. 369–446.

Wilcox, D.
1975   A strategy for perceiving social groups in puebloan sites. *Fieldiana: Anthropology* **65**:120–159.

Wilcox, D., and A. Sullivan
1979   Toward independent archaeological theory. Ms. available from authors, Department of Anthropology, Arizona State University, Tempe.

Willey, G.
1953   Prehistoric settlement patterns in the Viru Valley, Peru. *Bureau of American Ethnology Bulletin* No. 155. Washington, D.C.

Willey, G., and P. Phillips
1958   *Method and theory in American archaeology.* Chicago: Phoenix Books, University of Chicago Press.

Willey, G., and J. Sabloff
1974   *A history of American archaeology.* San Francisco: Freeman.

Zarky, A.
1976   Statistical analysis of site catchments at Ocós, Guatemala. In *The early mesoamerican village,* edited by K. Flannery. New York: Academic Press. Pp. 117–127.

Zubrow, E.
1972   Environment, subsistence and society: the changing archaeological perspective. In *Annual review of anthropology* (Vol. 1), Palo Alto, California: Annual Reviews. Pp. 179–206.

7

Ceramic Compositional Analysis in Archaeological Perspective

RONALD L. BISHOP, ROBERT L. RANDS,
and GEORGE R. HOLLEY

INTRODUCTION

The detailed study of ceramic composition requires a convergence of traditional archaeological interests with techniques of the natural and physical sciences. Unfamiliar methods of analysis utilize attributes of pottery that have been ignored generally or have lacked sophisticated treatment. Although potential benefits to archaeology are great, the procedures are not without costs in time and money. To capitalize on these potentials, the archaeologist must have some understanding of the techniques and methods of chemical and mineralogical analysis—their uses, strengths, and limitations. We consider these topics, calling attention to certain ways of achieving an articulation of compositional and cultural information.

Although detailed ceramic compositional analyses have generally been directed toward the investigation of trade, a requisite, logically prior level of inference concerns ceramic production. The selection and processing of raw materials are directly reflected in the compositional data, whereas inferences about exchange necessarily relate these data to other conditions. In keeping with current research undertakings, however, our primary focus is on compositional analysis as it helps to assess the possibility that nonlocal resources have been exploited and that some form of exchange, or perhaps enlargement of the zone from which raw materials were procured, has taken place.

The significance of compositional analysis is essentially spatial in nature

<hr />

ADVANCES IN ARCHAEOLOGICAL METHOD AND THEORY, VOL. 5

because, with varying degrees of precision, the analysis distinguishes among sources of raw materials used in pottery manufacture. This may be done directly, by establishing probable relationships of pottery to geographically localized raw materials, or indirectly, by demonstrating differences in ceramic pastes deemed to be sufficient to indicate the existence of geographically isolable resources. In either case, if compositional analysis is to be carried beyond the descriptive recording of similarities and differences, the resource procurement zone is a relevant concept, and it becomes operationally necessary in an attempt to infer places of ceramic production (Rands and Bishop 1980). Similar concepts in the literature are Arnold's "resource zone" (1978a) and Vita-Finzi and Higgs' "catchment areas" (1970), as discussed by Roper (1979).

A zonal concept is clearly necessary in the case of pottery because the raw materials—clay and temper—need not coincide in their place of procurement. Moreover, depending on geological and geochemical variables, these materials may exhibit considerable homogeneity over a fairly extended area. On the other hand, unless there is a strong, selective patterning in the exploitation of resources, great heterogeneity within a restricted region can result in fragmented procurement zones that are difficult to equate with the products of specific manufacturing centers. Under favorable circumstances, however, compositional analysis may be approaching a level of sophistication wherein microzones of limited geographical extent are assigned heuristically useful boundaries.

Time is not a principal focus in the compositional analysis of artifacts; it complicates studies of manufacturing sources in a way comparable to the effect of diffusion on temporal reconstruction. For example, differential exploitation or depletion of natural resources through time may result in changes in the paste composition of ceramics. Changing cultural choices in ceramic manufacture (e.g., selection and proportion of temper) may likewise affect ceramic paste. Trade routes may shift, and exchange networks may undergo modification, altering the compositional characteristics of a local assemblage. Aside from variations in paste composition introduced by time-related chemical or physical weathering, however, compositional studies focus on the spatial dimension, distinguishing among loci of raw material procurement and the inferentially associated centers of ceramic production. (Measured in geologic time, the effects of weathering on ceramic raw materials are enormous, resulting in a variability that distinguishes distinct resource procurement zones.)

Sources of variability, which are confounding factors in the analysis of exchange, are worthy of study in their own right. After mineralogical and chemical techniques of compositional analysis have been described and special characteristics of ceramic raw materials have been examined, attention is directed toward making inferences about exchange. Considered in less detail, vessel function and procurement pattern variability provide an enlarged focus for compositional analysis. Partially subsumed under the term "ceramic ecology" (Arnold 1975; Matson 1965; Rice 1978a), behavioral aspects encoded in paste composition are relevant to the transmission of technical information, as well as to the movement of pottery vessels from production source to place of deposition.

ANALYTICAL PROCEDURES

Regardless of the precise problem formulation, sophisticated techniques are necessary if compositional analysis is to be effectively employed. To varying degrees, the appropriate techniques are available only under specialized laboratory conditions. Because of this, compositional analysis of archaeological materials is generally an interdisciplinary undertaking. It should also be a collaborative one. Some specialized training in the physical and natural sciences is desirable, but, regardless of background, the archaeologist needs to learn as much as possible about the techniques in order to design a relevant research program, select appropriate specimens for analysis, and interpret analytical results. Likewise, the analytical specialist should gain a sense of archaeological problems, objectives, and relevance.

By no means does the investigation of all phenomena relating to paste composition require specialized techniques or settings beyond the capacity of the archaeological laboratory. The physical property of paste color, frequently employed in archaeological analysis, is a case in point. Color results from the combination of conditions during firing and constituents of the ceramic paste such as carbonaceous material, amount of temper, amount of iron, and other chemical characteristics of the clay. Use of the Munsell Soil Color Charts and an electric furnace for refiring can effectively exploit the attribute class of color (Matson 1971; Rye 1981; Shepard 1968) and this information may be articulated with compositional data derived from instrumental techniques of chemical analysis.

Our use of ceramic "composition" should be clarified. Although slips and pigments have physical substance and are of traditional importance in archaeology, their thinness is not well suited to the somewhat destructive analytical techniques generally employed in petrographic and chemical investigations. Rather, these techniques have tended to be used in analyzing ceramic paste or fabric. Unless otherwise qualified, therefore, references to composition are to the paste of the pottery, as this results from the cultural modification of natural resources. In research attempting to localize the place where a ceramic was manufactured, another reason exists for a focus on paste composition.

According to least-cost principles, the bulky materials used in fabricating pottery—the clay and temper—are less likely to have been obtained from a distant location in preindustrial societies than the clays or pigments used for finishing and decoration (Arnold 1976; Nicklin 1979:449). Centers of production, although not necessarily the ramifications of the resource procurement system, are more effectively determined by analyzing the ceramic paste.

Diverse procedures are used in ceramic compositional analysis to characterize pottery on the basis of its mineralogical or chemical constituents. Our discussion of techniques is by no means exhaustive, but does exemplify some of the currently most widely used means of ceramic paste analysis. The presentation here is in a sense hierarchical, moving from the general examination of an extensive number of specimens to the intensive analysis of selected pieces.

Sampling of Pottery

A sampling strategy is necessary for detailed compositional analysis, whether mineralogical, chemical, or a combination of techniques are employed. Clearly, sampling procedures will vary according to the specific problem formulation. In general, the attempt to reconstruct an exchange system requires the analysis of a large number of ceramic units. Sampling is more intensive than that which is necessary if the sole objective is to isolate broad patterns of "local" and "nonlocal" production. Yet, if the investigation focuses on the procurement of locally available resources, so that the site is defined in restricted terms—that is, excluding an outlying area having similar clay and temper deposits—covariation must be found in subtleties of cultural and compositional phenomena. This requires greatly expanded sampling.

In compositional analysis, chemical or mineralogical variability is assessed within one or more ceramic classes. Depending on the archaeological objectives, classes may, for example, be grouped into types based on selected attributes such as features of morphology or style, inferred functional classes, or "wares." Although ware is variously defined (e.g., Sabloff and Smith 1972; Rice 1976), the definition frequently involves a macroscopic level of paste characterization; conceptually related, but less commonly employed terms include "paste class" (Shepard 1963), "paste variant" (Ball 1980; Culbert 1973), and "fabric family" (Glock 1975).

The comprehensive characterization of a ware that is assumed to have been widely traded requires sampling of suspected imitations or temporal variants. This type of investigation is illustrated by Shepard's (1948) classic study of the Mesoamerican trade ware, Plumbate, with a stylistic and petrographic differentiation of the San Juan and Tohil groups. The investigation of a ware showing less pronounced stylistic variation may be facilitated by sampling that is geographically stratified. These are commonsense, archaeological decisions, determined by the nature of the individual investigation. Our suggested recommendations are fairly specific but cannot substitute for the perceptions appropriate to a particular research undertaking.

In the collaboration between archaeologist and analyst, the former should provide samples and information that will maximize the utility of the analytical data. If possible, small or weathered sherds should be avoided, even if they provide the minimal typological information required for a given archaeological investigation. Once the time and money have been invested in compositional analysis, the artifact has the potential to provide specialized information, in the current research or at some future time. Thus, the specimen is more than just another statistic; it holds promise for studies of design, morphology, function, or other properties that may lie outside the primary research orientation, and it should be accessible in the laboratory along with the basic analytical data. Also relevant to sampling, in addition to size and preservation, are archaeological contexts relating to chronology or function. At the same time, some attempt should be made to achieve proportionate representation within the designed ceramic units, or at least to be aware of problem-oriented departures from a random sample. Given that the number of specimens analyzed is usually relatively small, it may be difficult to meet these potentially conflicting standards.

Whatever compromise is reached in the sampling process, consideration must be given to the range of variation within the ceramic class or classes under immediate investigation. Sampling should be biased toward the most "typical" specimens, but it also should include less typical examples to provide the basis for compositional evaluation. Effective collaboration dictates that the analyst not be kept in the dark about archaeological problems, objectives, and provisional findings, and it is advisable for the archaeologist to share his evaluation of the "degree of typicality" of specific samples and to indicate the specific kind of comparisons that are of interest.

In the course of a single investigation, it may be useful to submit different samples at least twice, at first to obtain an overview and later to explore problem areas that have emerged following preliminary statistical analysis. It is sometimes useful for the analyst to select a subset of the initially submitted samples for preliminary analysis, permitting an early assessment of the relationships of compositional data to archaeological attributes. No magic number can be given for sample size. In chemical analysis, a rule of thumb is to initially submit 10–15 examples of each major class of interest from each site within a survey area and to prepare about half as many thin sections for initial petrographic analysis. Sampling will probably be biased toward a single site if it is the focal point of the investigation.

Most techniques of compositional analysis are slightly to moderately destructive, and if entire sherds or vessels are turned over to the analytical laboratory, technicians should assume the responsibility of preserving areas of design or special cultural information. These needs can be communicated by the archaeologist. In keeping with the view that the analyzed specimen constitutes a special resource, drawings or a photographic record should be maintained for reference throughout the analytical process and for publication with the analytical results.

Sampling of Clays

Supplemental information is obtained by sampling and analyzing clays from the region of archaeological interest. Under the most favorable conditions, a compositional "match" may be found between the raw material and the pottery under investigation; more likely, the clay analyses will provide a mineralogical and chemical perspective from which to view the variability found in the ceramic pastes. The sampled clays and pottery are frequently fired under standardized conditions to seek agreement in paste color. However, as emphasized by a multivariate compositional perspective, such matches apply only to a selected range of variability, and the clays will not necessarily coincide in other properties.

Clay sampling is sometimes guided by cultural precedent. Archaeological indications of intensive workshop activity such as kiln debris suggest that a clay known to occur in the same location may have been exploited by the prehistoric potters. Samples from clay deposits utilized by contemporary potters insure that the clay is workable, as well as directing attention to possible sources of prehistoric procurement. If tempering materials in current use are also collected, it is useful to sample the clay before and after temper has been added. In an investigation of ceramic continuity and change from prehistoric times, Rice (1978a) analyzed clays used for contemporary ceramic production in the Valley of Guatemala. Her study includes a detailed description of how the samples are processed in the laboratory, the ethnographic fieldwork being described by Arnold (1978b).

Existing information about regional geology should be utilized, but with or without this knowledge, an archaeologically oriented sampling of clay resources poses the problems of a pioneering undertaking. Perhaps an extensive clay bed, formed at approximately the same time from the same source lithology, is exposed discontinuously over a wide area. How homogeneous is this body, to what extent may a slightly different weathering history have affected each of the clay profiles? To assure coverage, one may be forced to obtain duplicate samples of the clay bed from multiple locations. Yet in the absence of detailed geologic information and thorough field investigation, a misleading impression of regional homogeneity can result from the replicate samples that have been taken. To achieve representative vertical sampling is a related problem.

Not all clays are equally useful for pottery manufacture. For example, because of their excessive swelling and shrinkage, montmorillonite and bentonite tend to be poor pottery clays, requiring mixing with other clays or temper for effective use (see, e.g., Shepard 1968:376). Familiarity with the working or plastic properties of clay is helpful in deciding which occurrences to sample. However, in an investigation designed not simply for the difficult-to-achieve location of specific sources but for an overview of regional variation, we prefer to sample all beds and outcrops that have been located. X-ray diffraction analysis and determination of plastic properties can then weight laboratory sampling for subsequent chemical investigation.

In general, existing geologic information is of greater use in locating the sources of regionally distinctive tempering materials than in locating the clay deposits exploited by prehistoric potters. Sampling procedures for both materials, as a basis for mineralogical or chemical analysis, are described by Rye (1981).

Mineralogical Analysis

Mineralogical Techniques of Paste Characterization

Beyond the utilization of a hand lens, an initial level of analysis can be accomplished with the use of a binocular microscope to yield information about the temper and textural relationships of the ceramic paste. Examination with a binocular microscope allows a large body of pottery to be assigned to general temper classes (e.g., volcanic, quartz sand, limestone, shell). It is possible to semiquantify these components, and special inclusions, whether part of the temper or occurring naturally in the clay, are frequently identified (e.g., ferruginous lumps, mica, igneous or metamorphic rock fragments). Additionally, a general assessment of the degree of vitrification or crystal formation is often feasible (Peacock 1977; Shepard 1968). Whereas all of these observations are also made with the more sensitive technique of thin-section analysis, the ease of binocular microscopic examination enables hundreds of sherds to be analyzed in a single day.

On a more detailed level of mineralogical analysis, thin sections are examined with the polarizing microscope (Figure 7.1). The mineralogical constituents of a ceramic are identified by using a combination of properties observed under polarizing light (Kerr 1959; Shepard 1968). Petrographic analysis is as much an art as a science, demanding considerable experience, especially if full quantification is required. Selective staining of the thin section may assist in mineral identifications such as differentiating calcite and

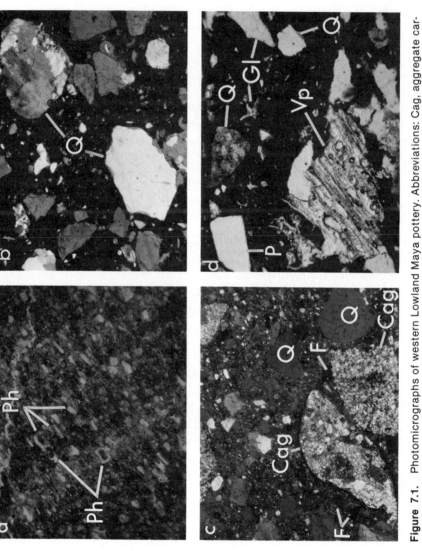

Figure 7.1. Photomicrographs of western Lowland Maya pottery. Abbreviations: Cag, aggregate carbonate grains; F, ferruginous lump; Gl, volcanic glass; P, phytolith; Q, quartz, Vp, pumice. (a) Fine paste; (b) quartz sand tempered; (c) carbonate tempered; (d) volcanics (glass and pumice). (a) Photomicrograph under plain light; (b–d) photomicrographs under polarized light. Original observations at approximately 100 magnification. (From Rands 1969.)

dolomite or distinguishing between potassium and sodium feldspars (Bailey and Stevens 1960; Dickson 1966). In staining a fine-grained paste, there is a tendency for colors to smear beyond the boundaries of the grains of interest, resulting in loss of detail.

Information pertaining to the geological history of the temper or clay is sometimes inferred from the kind of minerals present, their size, their association, and the extent of mechanical or chemical weathering the individual grains have undergone. The distribution of grain sizes in pottery is a possible diagnostic of some procurement location, reflecting natural factors such as source lithology and climate as well as depositional processes. In the case of quartz sand, surface characteristics, viewed under high magnification, may allow one to infer the type of environment from which the grains were derived, such as eolian, glacial, or shallow marine (Krinsley and Donahue 1968). Even so, assessments of this nature are generally too broad for routine archaeological purposes.

A more accurate quantification of petrographic data is achieved by point-count analysis (Chayes 1956; Griffiths 1967). With the use of an incrementing microscope stage and recording device, occurrences of grains and matrix under the optical cross hairs are identified and counted. From the counts, an estimate of the volume percentage of a constituent is calculated. The data, although more laborious to obtain than rank-order estimates, are continuous in nature. Thus, they are readily susceptible to rigorous statistical analysis, separately or in combination with other continuous data such as that provided by chemical analysis.

Generally described as a nonplastic, temper can refer to anything added to the clay in order to improve its workability and to impart properties desired in the final product. Given the frequent mixing within natural sediments, deliberate addition of temper is not always obvious. One approach to this problem determines the frequency distribution of grain sizes. In sediments, a general balance is obtained between erosion and transportation, resulting in good sorting of the grains (Inman 1949). As suggested by Rye (1981:52), a bimodal distribution of grain sizes, therefore, indicates the possible addition of temper, whereas a randomly sorted (normal tending) distribution could imply the use of a naturally occurring mixture. Caution is required in such an assessment because many natural and cultural factors influence the makeup of a ceramic paste.

Binocular microscope and thin-section examination can be used effectively in combination. In the hope of obtaining maximum ceramic variability, 20 sherds from the lower Chaco Basin were selected for thin-sectioning from geographically stratified sites (Loose 1977:568). Petrographic examination helped to establish temper categories that could then be sorted by using the binocular microscope. If detailed information about the range of mineral inclusions is known, paste classes can be established for identification with this instrument. But, which sherds should be used for initial thin-sectioning? In this case, comparative information resulting from previous investigations by Shepard (1939) and Warren (1967) was available. In the absence of prior information, possible groups to consider include multiple examples of dominant types, exotics, thin- and thick-walled vessels, and different form or stylistic classes. The more detailed the compositional data at hand, the more useful will be the broader, more general classification. It follows, therefore, that for a period of time, binocular microscopic and petrographic levels of examination should be closely linked, the specimens chosen being relevant to the basic research design.

Studied petrographically by means of thin sections, quartz-tempered pottery often reveals little more than the quartz embedded in a clay matrix, accessory grains being too few for characterization. In some instances, additional mineralogical information is obtained by heavy-mineral separation (Peacock 1967). Heavy minerals (e.g., zircon, tourmaline, rutile) are those exceeding a specific gravity of 2.9. Although occurring in relatively minor amounts in sand tempers, they may be removed from a sherd and concentrated. Their relative proportions, form, and nature sometimes characterize an assemblage relating to a fairly specific geologic source. Experimentation has shown that 150–200 individual grains are required for characterization, necessitating the destruction of 20–30 g of sherd material (Williams 1977). In addition to this loss, limitations of the technique include the small number of mineral species that are likely to serve as variables and the lack of detailed geologic information for many areas. Intraregional investigation would be virtually impossible in the absence of significant geologic variation.

Additional information about the major mineralogical constituents of pottery is derived from x-ray diffraction. This technique exposes a finely ground powder taken from a sherd to incident x-rays (Bloss 1971:454–527; Chen 1977). Depending on the interplanar spacing of the atomic planes of a crystal, the x-rays are scattered or diffracted selectively. The planes reflect x-rays only when a specific geometric relationship, formulated as Bragg's law, is satisfied. The reflections may be registered on a strip recorder moving in a set relationship to the x-ray detector. Relative intensities or peak height of the reflections essentially covary with the relative proportion of the minerals contained in the sample.

Only the major ($>2\%$) constituents are normally registered, severely restricting the utility of the technique for ceramic characterization. For example, Weymouth (1973) has attempted to use x-ray diffraction to differentiate 24 sherds representing four sites in Iowa and Missouri. Plots of the data points based on relative intensities of calcite–quartz and albite–quartz ratios indicated two sites to be indistinguishable; two separate groups characterized another site. Far more information is obtained by using the petrographic microscope (cf. Rice 1974).

X-ray diffraction is best considered an accessory technique rather than a direct approach to ceramic characterization. In the absence of thin section examination, for example, information is provided about the relative amounts of calcite to dolomite in carbonate-tempered pottery. In an innovative experiment, Isphording (1974) demonstrated that the clay minerals can be inferred by examining diffraction patterns of pottery refired above 1100° C. When a ceramic paste is held in that temperature region for a sufficient period of time, the clay minerals previously destroyed by the original firing form new, high temperature minerals. The primary application of x-ray diffraction is in identifying clay minerals, but the technique has also been useful in identifying pigments (Shepard and Gottlieb 1962; Shepard and Pollock 1971).

Supplementary Evidence in Mineralogical Analysis

Mineralogical analysis of pottery derives special importance from its direct applicability to field geology. Petrographic data may be related to geologic source areas, especially when the geology of the surrounding region is varied. The classic example of this approach is Shepard's (1942, 1965) investigation of Rio Grande glaze-paint pottery of New Mexico, in which andesitic dikes of localized occurrence were shown to be an important source of tempering material used in the widely traded ceramics. The identification of tempering materials has continued to be the major application of petrographic compositional investigation and has proved an effective means of discrimination when sources of the temper are of limited occurrence within the study area.

However, workers using temper as an indicator of manufacturing source face a fundamental problem. Was a nonlocal temper utilized in pottery production in the region of its natural occurrence, the finished vessels then being traded? or was the tempering material the subject of exchange, or of long-distance procurement expeditions? These questions cannot be answered satisfactorily simply with compositional evidence, but the major alternatives—movement of pots or movement of temper—are subject to systematic investigation. Correlations between paste color and tempering materials are potentially useful; if it can be shown that the suspected trade wares differ from the supposedly indigenous pottery in both respects, it appears extremely unlikely that the clay and temper were transported in raw form over appreciable distances. Thus, the evidence of paste color (sometimes requiring refiring of the pottery for adequate determination) may add substantially to the inferential power of temper as an indicator of artifactual exchange. This is especially true when clays are systematically collected and experimentally fired for comparison with ceramics (e.g., Loose 1977; Shepard 1942, 1965, 1971; Smith 1971; Toll et al. 1980; Windes 1977).

A tempering material having a common occurrence within a study area may, however, prove relatively difficult to characterize by petrography. This is often the case of quartz sands and sandstones (Shepard 1968). In the western Maya Lowlands, an investigation of regional ceramics by Rands and his associates has included the petrographic analysis of quartz-sand-tempered pottery, which dominated the Late Classic ceramics but within which mineralogical differences can be observed. Distinctions include angularity of quartz grains, amount and weathered state of feldspar, and micaceousness of the matrix among other variables relating extent of weathering in the raw materials to contrasting physiographic zones. One of the most sensitive indicators of different resource procurement areas is not a temper fragment, but rather minute siliceous inclusions recognizable within the clay by binocular microscope as well as thin-section analysis. The inclusions, opal phytoliths, accumulate in the clay profiles primarily as the result of the decay of grasses and sedges, providing an environmental indicator of the type of area in which the clays were procured (Figure 7.1a) (Rands 1967; Rands and Bishop 1980; cf. Rovner 1971). Such an investigation requires information about spontaneous vegetation zones (West 1966) as well as regional geology, and must consider the possibility that the former have undergone changes brought about by human occupation.

In general, a petrographic approach to identifying resource procurement zones and their associated manufacturing centers is most useful if distinctive geologic deposits were exploited. Yet great diversity within a highly localized area can be a complication; assuming that a production center utilized a number of different sources, the distinction between local and nonlocal pottery will be blurred. In any case, the availability of detailed geologic information will enhance the investigation. Of course, if nongeologic products such as crushed potsherds were used for temper in some of the pottery, petrographic examination will be useful in making the necessary identifications. But in such a case, the burden of proof falls squarely on the archaeologist to determine the place of manufacture by traditional archaeological methods.

Petrography and the Study of Exchange

In many respects, studies by Shepard of Rio Grande glaze-decorated ceramics present a model of what petrography can accomplish in an archaeologically well-known, geologically diverse area. A series of graphs and maps, covering 12 districts within a north–south area along the Rio Grande of approximately 300 km, relates temper percentages to geological occurrence of the tempering materials and to chronology (Shepard 1942:Figures 3–15; cf. Shepard 1965). Although the supporting data are not fully published, another study of glaze-decorated pottery is effectively mapped (Warren 1969:40; cf. Warren 1968). This shows a clinal distribution of glaze-paint pottery, as compared to other ceramics, extending across a north–south area of some 120 km. Such presentations suggest possible parameters of exchange from a single site (Tonque) or involving shifting loci of production and trade within the broader tradition of glaze painted pottery.

Shepard's studies of glaze-paint ceramics are of further significance because of her intent to clarify procedures combining archaeological and petrographic analysis and to evaluate steps in inferring ceramic trade. These detailed investigations illustrate and supplement her more widely read *Ceramics for the Archaeologist* (Shepard 1968). Also useful in this connection is her short study of contemporary pottery making in the Valley of Oaxaca, in which she explicitly addresses problems of interpretation faced by the archaeologist who fails to accord basic attention to paste classes (Shepard 1963).

In studying regional exchange, one may consider a total representative ceramic population rather than focusing on a single trade ware. This is exemplified by a research program of the Chaco Project, in which a model of a "complex cultural ecosystem" centering on Chaco Canyon is under investigation (Judge 1979; cf. Toll *et al.* 1980; Windes 1977). A number of years ago it was noted by Shepard (1939; Shepard in Judd 1954:236–238) that certain intrusive ceramics at Chaco are characterized by sanidine basalt and andesite tempers; these rocks do not occur at Chaco Canyon, where local formations are of sandstone. The closest known natural occurrences of sanidine basalt, or trachyte (Loose 1977:567–568), and of andesite–diorite occur at approximate distances of 70 km from Chaco Canyon. The frequent use of redfiring clays, known at a comparable distance from the canyon, supports the conclusion that "nonlocal" pottery at Chaco resulted from the importation of pots rather than temper. "Nonlocal" ceramics suggest sources toward the west if trachyte tempered and toward the north if tempered with andesite-diorite (Toll *et al.* 1980:Figure 1, Table 2). Although directionality can thereby be inferred, as is so often the case, it is easier to demonstrate that pottery is not of local production than to assign definite source areas. Identification of the pottery made in Chaco Canyon remains troublesome, although buff to yellowish red pastes with sandstone or sherd temper are candidates for local manufacture.

Shepard's petrographic investigations at Chaco showed that sanidine basalt (trachyte) temper occurred primarily in culinary pottery rather than in painted ceramics. Extensive trade in culinary ware appeared to be "archeological heresy" to Judd (1954:245), and Shepard responded that fine workmanship is required in the manufacture of corrugated cooking pots, which might have their own specialized centers of production (Shepard in Judd 1954:237). More recently, Windes (1977:294–296) has presented evidence indicating that an unusual combination of minerals in the red-firing, sanidine basalt-tempered culinary ware promoted vitrification at low temperatures, resulting in the production of exceptionally strong pottery. As exemplified by the Chaco research, the assumption that ceramic exchange tends to focus largely on luxury items or serving pottery may be misleading (cf., e.g., Nicklin 1971:17–18; Tourtellot and Sabloff 1972).

A different situation exists in the Pacific, where island groups are separated by vast distances and are characterized by fundamental distinctions in available tempering materials (Dickinson and Schutler 1968, 1971). Mineral differences reflect the tectonic provinces the various islands occupy; weathering results in four major classes of potential temper sands: oceanic basalt, andesite arc, volcano-plutonic, and tectonic-highland. Temper in pottery is identified according to tectonic province or island group or, under favorable conditions, for a specific island. Most of the petrographically examined pottery is believed to have been made on the island, or at least in the island group, where the minerals are indigenous. Characterized by quartzose sands, a few sherds from Tonga and the Marquesas are, however, identified as of probable Fijian source, perhaps as a result of trade or migration (Dickinson and Schutler 1974). Early dates are assigned the pottery, and it is suggested that migration would support the hypothesis of a Fijian homeland for the proto-Polynesians. Thus, under special circumstances, ceramic composition may have implications about colonization as well as about exchange. Whatever the historical realities in this case, the Oceanic investigations underscore two points: water transport is an efficient means of carrying pottery over long distances (see, e.g., Nicklin 1971), and the dissemination of ceramic vessels does not necessarily imply that the goods change hands, as indicated by the term "exchange." Beyond this, the situation is ideal for petrographic investigations on a macrolevel, as inhabited areas of relative internal homogeneity are set apart by sharp geologic boundaries.

Chemical Analysis

In the event of limited variation in the mineralogical inclusions within a ceramic paste, identification of pottery produced from different source areas may still be possible by means of chemical analysis. In any case, quantification of several elements, including those occurring in trace amounts, provides an extremely sensitive approach to problems of resource procurement, production, and exchange. In most respects, chemical analysis is a more powerful method than petrography, and it can distinguish more readily between clays. However, if carried out in isolation from mineralogical studies or without regard to geochemical principles, it is less likely than petrology to give the investigator readily recognizable information about the nature of the variation introduced by mineral grains. In the absence of such supplemental data, problems of basic interpretation may be compounded.

The increased sensitivity of chemical analysis comes at a further price. The need for more elaborate instrumentation and analytical training increases, together with initial expense. The elaborate technology also requires statistical analysis sufficiently powerful to reduce the analytical data to an interpretable level.

Ideally, cost should not be an overriding factor in the selection of an analytical technique, but it cannot be ignored. In general, the services of commercial laboratories for chemical analysis are beyond archaeological budgets. Assuming 10 elements are to be determined, prices range from $15 per sample for x-ray fluorescence to over $400 for neutron activation! Atomic absorption and emission spectroscopy average about $30 for an analysis. These restrictive costs may be largely removed, however, by a collaborative research program utilizing existing expertise and equipment such as are found in most university departments of chemistry and geology. We stress the word "collaborative," for few analysts are interested simply in providing service for archaeologists. Even for neutron activation analysis, collaboration, including partially offsetting expenses, may lower the cost for a 10-element determination to under $20. Assuming funding is available for the research, it is often the lack of personnel for the routine work of sample preparation and subsequent processing that constitutes the major hurdle to obtaining compositional data.

Chemical Techniques of Paste Characterization

The major techniques of chemical analysis have varying relationships to different parts of the atom. Most spectroscopic methods are based on the interaction of energy with matter, involving the electrons surrounding the nucleus, followed by the emission, absorption, transfer, or reflection of energy as light. The characteristics of that energy may be determined and the intensity used to calculate the concentration of a particular atom, hence element, present in a ceramic paste. Other techniques involve the excitation of the atomic nucleus. Although the choice of instrumentation is often guided by availability or cost, consideration must be given to the related aspects of sensitivity, precision, accuracy, and selectivity (see, e.g., Goffer 1980; Meschel 1978; Tite 1972).

Sensitivity in analytical chemistry relates to the ability to distinguish the difference of the response recorded as amounts grow smaller. If one is interested only in the major elemental concentrations, a technique sensitive to a few parts per billion is obviously unnecessary. *Precision* refers to the ability to reproduce the results of a measurement and represents the control the analyst has over the method being employed. *Accuracy* pertains to the sum of all absolute and relative errors and reflects such things as the choice of standards against which to calibrate the analytical determinations. Since standards, such as United States Geological Survey reference rocks, are frequently employed in ceramic investigations, accuracy depends on how well we know the actual elemental concentrations in those materials. Therefore, care should be given to the selection and reporting of the standards that are used, thus allowing other laboratories to compare analyses. Measurements must, however, be within acceptable limits of instrumental precision. Higher analytical precision becomes important for intraregional studies or when analyzing pottery from sites sharing a common geologic–geochemical history because fine differences in the pottery may otherwise be blurred (Prag *et al.* 1974). Finally, *selectivity* relates to the ability to discriminate the signal of interest from other possible interfering signals.

The need for a pure signal of high analytical precision and adequate sensitivity demands a series of compromises. These usually entail an experimental procedure that will yield, on the average, optimal conditions for the simultaneous determination of many elements. To assess patterns of chemical variation in the pottery of a region requires a large number of analyses, and selection of an appropriate technique must be guided by considerations of the time required to process and analyze a sample. A minimal amount of sample preparation is, therefore, advantageous.

One of the oldest techniques in pottery characterization is *emission spectroscopy*. A small amount of ceramic paste is vaporized by a flame or an electric arc. This results in the excitation of some of the atoms, which, as they return to a nonexcited state, emit radiation. The radiation characteristic of a particular element can be recorded on photographic plates; the amount of darkening of the spectral lines serves to indicate the relative concentrations of the elements. For this reason, results have frequently been reported as only relative intensities rather than absolute concentrations. More recently, instrumentation has increased the speed and objectivity of determinations by eliminating the step of photographic recording. In practice, emission spectroscopy is prone to large experimental errors and complex emission spectra, decreasing its sensitivity and precision. It has been utilized, however, in investigations of pottery for almost two decades, due primarily to the activity of the Oxford Research Laboratory (Catling *et al.* 1961; Catling and Millet 1965; Catling *et al.* 1963; Prag *et al.* 1974). The laboratory has since converted to atomic absorption spectroscopy (Hatcher *et al.* 1980).

The greater sensitivity and more direct quantification afforded by atomic absorption during the past 15 years slowed developments in emission spectroscopy. Recent developments in the use of plasma (ionized gases) are approaching a state that may lead to emission spectroscopy being more widely employed in archaeological investigations. In addition, advances in instrumentation enable 20–40 elements to be recorded simultaneously with few interferences. Although most samples are still introduced into the plasma as solutions, developments are aimed at the injection of solid samples (Van Loon 1980). When this stage of refinement is completed, plasma emission spectroscopy should provide a technique of elemental analysis at relatively low cost, low sample preparation time, and sensitivity over a range of simultaneously determined elements extending for some below the parts per million level. Unfortunately, these developments will probably require the attention of a full-time analyst rather than an archaeologist trained in the technique.

Atomic absorption also uses thermal energy, via a flame or carbon electrode, to decompose compounds (Slavin 1968). Nonexcited atoms absorb light of a particular wavelength, produced by a lamp containing the element of interest; the amount of light absorbed provides a measure of the elemental concentration in the sample. This technique has not been extensively utilized in archaeological ceramic studies, although it is capable of elemental determinations of high precision and accuracy down to a few parts per million. A major disadvantage lies in the need to place the sample into solution, thus risking lowered sensitivity by incomplete dissolution, loss of sample, or contamination. The procedure is also labor intensive, because only a single elemental determination is performed at one time. Examples of atomic absorption application in archaeology are found in Bower *et al.* (1975) and Tubb *et al.* (1980); specific procedures for ceramic analysis are discussed by Bomgardner (1981) and Gritton and Magalousis (1978).

In *x-ray fluorescence,* the exposure of a sample to X rays causes one of the innermost electrons of an atom to be ejected from its normal orbit about the nucleus. As that vacancy is filled by electrons from an outer orbit, a change in energy takes place, accompanied by the fluorescence of X rays characteristic of different atoms. Both energy dispersive and nondispersive systems are employed to record the X rays. In the former, a single measurement of a particular wavelength or radiation is made at one time. The latter utilizes a detector that simultaneously receives radiation of several wavelengths emitted by the sample, the signals being amplified and sorted according to their respective energies. The advantage of simultaneous measurement of several elements is somewhat offset by a decrease in the sensitivity. Limitations of the technique relate to the low penetration energy of the X rays; only the surface layer of a prepared specimen can be analyzed. Also, the technique is not useful for the determination of elements lighter than magnesium. However, it does offer potential as a multielement system at relatively low cost. X-ray fluorescence has been used in several investigations of ancient pottery, including those of Birgul *et al.* (1979), Egloff (1978), Picon *et al.* (1971), and Stern and Descoeudres (1977). The technique has been calibrated to results from atomic absorption analysis in the investigation of Chevelon pottery, Arizona (Waite, cited in Plog 1980).

X-ray fluorescence provides a technique for the determination of elements not susceptible to neutron activation analysis (e.g., magnesium, titanium). In addition, for elements such as potassium and calcium, the analytical precision of x-ray fluorescence is greater.

Of the currently available techniques of chemical analysis, only instrumental *neutron activation* combines low sample-preparation time, sensitivity below the parts per million range for some elements, and automated counting and recording. In contrast to the other techniques, neutron activation involves excitation of the atomic nucleus rather than the orbiting electrons (Kruger 1971). A small (40–100 mg) sample is bombarded by neutrons. Target nuclei capture a neutron resulting in a radioisotope for each element, each decaying with its own half-life and characteristic radiation. Of the various kinds of radiation, the gamma rays have special importance. The energy of an emitted gamma ray is specific to an isotope and may be measured, thereby determining the number of specific radionuclei. Although about 75 of the naturally occurring 92 elements may be detected by neutron activation, albeit with widely varying sensitivities, approximately 22 elements are usually determined. The actual number is a function of the neutron flux, length of irradiation, cooling interval, length of counting period, state of the instrumentation, and type and size of sample.

Although neutron activation and x-ray fluorescence are often characterized as nondestructive techniques, the compositional properties of a ceramic usually require destructive sampling and homogenization of the sample prior to analysis. The required amount is small, however; about 200–400 mg of powder provide an adequate sample. This is usually taken from the core of a sherd or from the base of a whole vessel after the exposed edge or surface has been removed by burring; it is important to obtain a sample that is as free as possible from contamination. Tungsten-carbide or diamond drills and burrs are frequently employed because these are resistant to abrasion during the sample preparation. In addition, pottery should not be selected if it has previously been subjected to treatments such as acid washing or to impregnation by epoxys.

The sample of ceramic material to be analyzed should be representative of the entire sherd. If only a small amount of the paste is to undergo chemical analysis, it is preferably drawn from a larger sample that has been homogenized. In general, the coarser the paste, the greater is the amount of pottery having to be sampled to guard against elemental variation due to inhomogeneity. If too small a sample is used, certain elements such as manganese, which tend to be heterogeneously distributed in nature, yield widely differing determinations in replicate analysis (Sayre *et al.* 1958; Abascal-M. 1974:37).

Microanalysis

Techniques of microanalysis are especially valuable if the highly localized concentration of elements, such as those in a single mineral grain, is sought. This is provided by the electron microprobe and, with greater sensitivity, by the laser and proton microprobes. The *electron microprobe* detects and counts emitted X rays in a manner similar to x-ray fluorescence, except that a beam of electrons, only 103 μ in diameter, is focused onto a sample. Due to high background, the electron microprobe is primarily used to determine the major elements with atomic numbers greater than 12. The *laser microprobe* employs an intense laser beam to vaporize part of the material. The vapor sets off a discharge between two electrodes; the emitted light is recorded, and the spectrum is analyzed as in optical emission spectroscopy. The sensitivity of the *proton microprobe* is much greater than that of the electron probe. The proton microprobe is employed with the use of a Van de Graaf accelerator, with beams of protons being tightly focused on a small target. This results in the emission of X rays characteristic of the elements in the affected area. Defocusing of the beam allows a larger area to be scanned, and the probe can in this way be used as a technique for paste characterization. Under ideal conditions, as many as 75 elements may be determined, using only a few milligrams of sample. Analytical sensitivity extends to a few parts per million for some elements (Kullerud *et al.* 1979).

Selecting a target area to avoid nonplastic inclusions, De Atley and Nelson (1981) have utilized the electron microprobe to investigate ceramic and clay variability in the southwestern United States. Expectably, the resulting characterization provides better agreement between source clays and pottery than is obtained by comparing raw clays to powdered samples composed of a mixture of clay and temper. Unfortunately, the separation of temper from other components of the ceramic body by sieving a crushed sherd or by employing heavy liquids is seldom sufficiently refined for the level of sensitivity desired in the chemical analysis. Although time consuming, the microprobe provides a promising approach for the comparison of raw and fired clays.

For the most part, these accessory techniques are used to address specific problems rather than for broad characterization. For example, we have employed the electron microprobe to determine that the abnormally high concentrations of titanium, found in a particular class of Maya pottery, was distributed throughout the clay matrix rather than occurring in the mineral grains. Because the conditions leading to high titanium adsorption onto the clay particles are rather specific (Beus 1971), the findings have given us an indication of a poorly drained, high oxidizing environment in which we might expect to find the requisite raw materials.

Clay Chemistry

A chemical approach to ceramic characterization takes cognizance of the fact that a chemical profile ("fingerprint") is a weighted average of all the mineralogical components of a ceramic specimen. Comprised primarily of clays, with varying amounts of nonplastic inclusion, the main chemical constituents are silicon, aluminum, iron, calcium, magnesium, potassium, and sodium. Although some of these major elements have been employed in various investigations, multiple sources of variation and overlapping concentration ranges between deposits (Poole and Finch 1972) decrease their utility for pottery characterization.

Clays represent an end point or geologic residue resulting from weathering or hydrothermal activity. The most important crystalline components of clays are the hydrous aluminosilicates, which have distinctive properties as a function of their structure, shape, and very small particle size (see, e.g., Blatt *et al.* 1972:Chapter 7; Grim 1968). The specific clay minerals and their mineralogical or chemical properties depend on the parent material from which they are derived. Frequently, these include multiple lithological sources, each with its own mineral and chemical composition. Additional factors include climate, geomorphological relief, biological agencies, and time (Jackson 1959).

During the various stages of weathering, elemental substitution takes place, with greater tendencies for some elements to be exchanged than others. Many of the trace elements (those occurring in amounts of less than 100 parts per million) tend to be fixed within a crystal structure. As minerals are broken down to finer particles, often continuing to clays, these trace elements become concentrated in the finer-sized fractions. Their proportions in a clay, therefore, reflect the more specific stages of weathering as well as a somewhat regional parent lithology (cf. Slatt 1974; Slatt and Sasseville 1976). For this reason, even in a region considered to be relatively homogeneous in its gross geologic characteristics, significant mineralogical and chemical differences may be discerned between clay deposits.

The chemical profile for pottery clay representative of a procurement deposit is usually modified to some extent during the stages of ceramic manufacture. If the clay is levigated, to separate fine materials in suspension from coarser particles, highly mobile adsorbed ions such as sodium or potassium are likely to be removed, thereby decreasing the amounts of these elements from what they had been in the clay deposit. Perhaps culturally induced levigation does not constitute a major problem in the analysis of most

Precolumbian New World pottery (Shepard 1968:52), although similar chemical effects are achieved by the transportation of sediments prior to deposition.

The effect of temper added to the clay is more serious. Because trace elements are generally concentrated in the clays, the addition of a relatively "pure" quartz sand to the clay will tend to bring about a proportionate lowering of the trace element abundances (cf. Olin and Sayre 1971). If, however, the quartz sand contains appreciable zircon, which is noted for its high rare earth element content, a complex interplay results between elemental dilution and enrichment; the proportional lowering of trace and minor elements caused by the silicon content of the quartz is partially offset by element enrichment due to the presence of zircon. This example, alone, illustrates the importance of petrographic information for the interpretation of ceramic compositional profiles. Additional examples of temper-related chemical variation are discussed by Bishop (1975, 1980) and Rice (1978b). In a very general sense, proportional similarity of trace elements tends to be less affected by the addition of quartz sand, calcite, crushed limestone, or vegetable fiber than it is by the addition of volcanic or crushed sherd material.

Choices in Chemical Analysis

Questions frequently concern the choice and number of elements that are most useful to determine. Theoretically, it is desirable to analyze a suite of elements of such a nature that some will have a very small range of concentration within a compositionally similar group of pottery from a production center but will have a much greater range when multiple centers are considered. Certainly, not all individual elements will have equal value in this regard. Basically, the problem is that the elemental patterns characteristic of a natural grouping of ceramics or the elements that best serve to separate groups cannot be determined until an investigation is completed. It seems advisable, therefore, to analyze as many elements as is operationally possible, the elements being determined by the chosen analytical procedures but representing a wide range in chemical properties (see, e.g., Winther-Nielsen *et al.* 1981; Widemann *et al.* 1975:46).

Under certain conditions, however, it does not seem advantageous to subject all of the available elements to statistical analysis. For example, minor alteration of the paste may have taken place due to postdepositional conditions such as pottery being saturated with ground water, which results in the deposition of calcium in the pores of the sherd. Similar deposition can occur regularly while a vessel for water storage is in use (Fontana *et al.* 1962:80). Under some environmental conditions, petrographic assessment of such possible contamination will be prudent.

Conversely, ground-water saturation of pottery can result in the leaching of particular elements such as sodium, potassium, magnesium, and calcium (Freeth 1967; Tubb *et al.* 1980). These major elements form oxides that are highly mobile in environments ranging from strongly oxidizing through reducing (Andrews-Jones 1968). To a great extent, the potential of these elements for substitution is influenced by factors such as ionic size and valence state (Bishop 1980:Figure 1). Under specific environmental conditions, elements of low mobility undergo minor substitution (Hedges and McLellan 1976), but on the whole, most of the *trace* elements routinely determined in ceramic analysis do not seem to reflect significant weathering or substitution effects.

The effect of firing has been studied in greater detail (Tubb *et al.* 1980; Rice 1978b:535). For pottery fired in the absence of a kiln, with temperatures below about 850° C, there does not appear to be a significant effect on many elements (Rice 1978b). If firing conditions were such that temperatures likely exceeded the point of an element's volatility, time spent refiring with replicate analyses might be repaid.

Perlman and Asaro (1969:31) have taken the general position that one seeks to measure independent variables, and Wilson (1978) and Rye (1981) consider it of dubious value to measure multiple elements that are strongly intercorrelated. The presence of several correlated elements may unduly weight the statistical calculations, by virtue of redundancy, in favor of particular chemical behavior. However, a somewhat different position turns these correlations to an advantage.

The underlying structure of a ceramic chemical data set reflects the pottery's mineralogical and textural characteristics. Within mineral assemblages such as clays and tempers, specific sets of elements tend to covary, following behavior relating to the substitution potential of the respective elements. This potential derives from the elemental valence and ionic radius, as well as from specific environmental conditions (Andrew-Jones 1968; Bishop 1980). Thus, pottery containing abundant potassium feldspar tends to be high not only in potassium, but also rubidium, cesium, and barium because these can substitute for the large potassium cation. Inspection of the trends of patterned elemental covariations can be more informative than noting the behavior of a single element. To some degree, the strengths of the relationships reflect the parent rock from which the materials were derived and weathering conditions, as well as the effects of manufacturing history, such as levigation or the addition of temper. Failure to determine multiple elements that covary in nature ignores the underlying mineralogical factors influencing the elemental profile of a ceramic.

Approaches and Problems in Chemical Analysis

Ceramic compositional analysis is not a static mode of investigation. Refinements in instrumentation, the use of more efficient methods of statistical analysis, and a firmer understanding of natural and cultural variables in pottery production contribute to an increasingly complex interdisciplinary endeavor. Accordingly, almost every chemical compositional investigation is, in part, a methodological exercise. Selected research is reviewed to illustrate alternative approaches to those previously outlined, problems that have been encountered in research design and data transformation, and questions that have been raised about prevailing assumptions.

Priorities in the Use of Analytical Techniques. Although we have described microanalysis as a special purpose technique, it has been employed in an effort to characterize the locally made pottery of Tepe Yaha, Iran (Kamilli and Lamberg-Karlovsky 1979). Thin-section analysis was also used in this investigation. Only 17 specimens were analyzed, but the study is extremely detailed in the mineralogical description of the ceramic pastes, the chemical data derived from microprobe analysis contributing to the mineral identifications. The level of detail should assist in placing Tepe Yahya in its geologic and cultural setting. However, the investigation changes the order that we have anticipated of first working toward a site or regional characterization based on extensive sampling, and in the course of this, identifying and exploring special problems.

Relating Instrumentation to Research Design. A general problem area alluded to previously concerns the selection and adequacy of various analytical techniques for specific research objectives. As long as the limitations of a particular technique or method are borne in mind in the interpretation of one's data, information that will make a positive contribution can be obtained from a variety of instrumental procedures. The results will be augmented if petrographic findings are successfully integrated with the chemical data. Investigations of Hellenistic ceramic relationships in southeastern Italy, carried out at the University of Oxford's Laboratory of Archaeology and Art and spanning approximately a decade are, nonetheless, instructive.

The initial program was thoughtfully conceived. Focused on black-glaze pottery that was apparently made in Athens and exported to Italy where it was locally imitated, the research had important implications about colonization, trade, and other economic relationships (Prag *et al.* 1974). Pottery from kiln sites was analyzed as a means of identifying local production centers, and the analytical and statistical techniques employed petrography (including heavy-mineral separation), optical mission spectroscopy, univariate statistics, and hierarchical cluster analysis.

The black-glaze pottery is finely textured, freeing the investigators from having to consider the effect of temper on the chemical data, but severely limiting the utility of the petrographic approach. Of nine sherds selected for heavy mineral analysis, three failed to yield a sufficient number of grains for a quantitative study. The weight of the investigation fell on the spectrographic data, which were primarily based on concentrations of the major elements.

Although the Greek control pottery separated from the other specimens in cluster analysis, certain anticipated levels of discrimination were not obtained, and it was concluded that this was due in part to the 5–20% analytical precision of the spectrographic technique (Prag *et al.* 1974:182). Several of the Hellenistic sherds were subsequently reanalyzed, using atomic absorption spectroscopy to determine concentrations for the same elements (Hatcher *et al.* 1980). When the reanalyzed sherd data were compared to the earlier optical emission results, large discrepancies were immediately apparent. Principal components plots revealed a much stronger separation of the Greek control pottery with the use of atomic absorption. In view of the lack of a single calibration factor to achieve comparability of the data derived from emission spectroscopy and atomic absorption, the study concludes with a call for reanalysis of the material from southern Italy before addressing specific archaeological questions (Hatcher *et al.* 1980).

From the advantages provided by a later perspective, we suggest the initial study suffered from more than instrumentation that was inadequate for the research objectives. Additionally, there was an overreliance on chemical patterning within the major elements and an overdependence on mineralogy in the investigation of finely textured pottery. It is worth remembering that the use of the more sensitive technique, atomic absorption spectroscopy, resulted in a stronger statistical separation of the pottery of Greek manufacture, in accordance with archaeological expectations. Although archaeological interpretations are prone to some degree of error, their convergence with chemically based findings should not be minimized in assessing the compositional data.

Heterogeneous Sampling and Data Manipulation.   Additional problems in compositional studies concern the comparability of the samples under analysis and the manipulation of the elemental data. Optimal separations tend to be on a broad level if great variation is present within a population, and some of this variability can frequently be detected in the absence of chemical analysis. Prior screening to remove logically separable compositional classes (e.g., temper) allows a clustering program to be directed toward finer levels of grouping according to similarity rather than toward the recovery of already identifiable divisions.

An attempt to differentiate locally produced from imported pottery, as well as to attribute some of the latter to specific sources, illustrates these problems (Hammond *et al.* 1976). The research was focused on the small Classic Maya ceremonial center of Lubaantún, Belize. Major, minor, and trace elemental abundances were derived by neutron activation and were submitted to hierarchical and iterative cluster analysis as well as multidimensional scaling. Sampling included 40 sherds representing the dominant ceramic types; also analyzed were 13 local clay samples, 22 examples of questionably local pottery, and 7 comparative ceramic specimens from two other sites. It was concluded that the dominant ceramic types were of local manufacture, with different raw materials being selected for the utilitarian and the elaborately decorated pottery.

Methodological weaknesses are inevitable in any developing field, and the Lubaantún study illustrates several. Summarized by a dendrogram, the hierarchical cluster analysis reveals several distinct groups separating essentially according to clay, grit-tempered pottery (with some subdivision apparently corresponding to the amount of temper) and pottery tempered with volcanic materials. The major divisions of the data are those easily achieved by examination with a binocular microscope. The indiscriminant use of samples with different kinds or amounts of temper, as well as clays, serves to obfuscate the statistical results. The iterative cluster program first employed a normalization that transformed the data to percentages, each elemental concentration being divided by the sum of all the concentrations determined for a particular sample. As was noted (Hammond *et al.* 1976:158), this procedure preserves only the proportions of the elements, not their absolute abundances. Unfortunately, the proportions of the major elements overpower the contributions of the trace elements in the clustering, and the relationships are therefore biased toward similarities among only a few of the elements. This situation carries over to the multidimensional scaling program. Although a primary objective of determining whether the major ceramic types are compositionally similar was partially achieved, specific relationships are difficult to assess.

Evaluation of Provenience and Data Transformation. Implicitly or explicitly, basic assumptions underlie provenience studies that attempt, by chemical analysis, to determine the place of manufacture of pottery objects. Such assumptions are examined in a series of related articles, in which it is correctly argued that analytical investigations of ceramic paste should consider behavioral variables (Arnold *et al.* 1978; Rice 1978a, 1978b). At issue in these studies is the utility of trace elemental data for linking manufacturing centers to the specific locations from which the raw materials were obtained. In combination, the compositional heterogeneity of a given clay bed, the practices of potters in preparing the clay, and postdepositional alteration of the ceramics are considered to mitigate severely the power of chemical analysis in establishing specific relationships between raw materials and finished products.

An intraregional perspective focuses on the Valley of Guatemala, and a number of hypotheses are tested relating to the degree of chemical correspondence between the sources of raw materials and the finished ceramics. The contemporary procurement of clays and temper from known locations, to be used in pottery making at identified villages, provides a control that is lacking in archaeological investigations. The frequent failure to find satisfactory chemical correspondences between raw materials and the pottery made from these materials leads to a rejection of various hypotheses and a dubious outlook about the value of neutron activation analysis for resolving problems of specific provenience.

From a mineralogical or chemical standpoint, Rice and her associates worked in a difficult region. The semiubiquitous nature of volcanic-derived sand and clay—and the complex alteration of the chemical profile of a ceramic as a result of the addition of volcanic temper—provides conditions under which the discriminatory power of an analytical approach may well be taxed in the attempt to distinguish patterns of variation. This still remains to be seen. In spite of the serious attempt that was made to provide a rigorous test, the potential of the studies for assessing compositional variability is limited because of sample size and fundamental weaknesses in transforming the elemental data.

One can always wish for a larger sample size. More serious was the decision to present the data in terms of a ratio of each determined element to a single element, scandium (Arnold *et al.* 1978:553; Rice 1978b:522–523). The multicomponent ceramic system makes such a choice intuitively unreasonable. While the transformation may preserve proportionality between that element and other elements concentrated in the same component of the ceramic system, i.e., clay, there is no a priori reason to assume the maintenance of that proportionality in another component. Further, one objective was to evaluate the chemical variation that could be introduced by temper; however, the effect of temper on the amount of scandium, the basis of the ratio transformations, is not determined or known. This fact alone would be sufficient to vitiate the statistical conclusions as to the extent of temper-induced variability. Finally, logarithms of the ratios were taken as the basis of the statistical analysis. Although trace elemental abundances may tend to be log-normally distributed in nature (Bieber *et al.* 1976a), indiscriminant extension of that observation to ratio data is unwarranted. Analytical or statistical weaknesses aside, these articles discuss important issues and make a positive effort to integrate compositional data within the cultural milieu.

A COMPOSITIONAL APPROACH TO THE STUDY OF EXCHANGE

Postulates

Fundamental problems of interpretation exist, including questions about the suitability of chemical analysis for specific source characterization. This level of precision can be critical for inferring directionality in exchange although, if relationships cannot be demonstrated between a finished pot and the zone from which the clay or temper was obtained, it may still be possible to distinguish pottery made from different sources of a raw material.

A relevant set of assumptions is formalized as the "Provenience Postulate" (Weigand *et al.* 1977:24). According to the postulate, identifiable chemical differences exist between sources of a raw material, and the analytical approach can recognize these differences. A corollary holds compositional variation within a source to be less than the variation between different sources. The Provenience Postulate was explicitly formulated in the study of turquoise, a material of greater within-source variation than most ceramic clays, but has since been extended to pottery (Bishop 1980).

Several problems exist in applying the Provenience Postulate to the investigation of ceramic exchange. As we have emphasized, the cultural modification and mixing of raw materials introduces ambiguity into the interpretation of analytical results. Moreover, the geographical extent of a source area, and its proximity to the place of pottery manufacture, are usually conjectural. Single or multiple production centers may have exploited the same source area; a single production center could have drawn on one or more sources; and the reciprocal transfer of goods, including pottery, might have taken place, undetected, within this zone. These problems are less severe in tracing long-distance trade than in reconstructing intraregional exchange (Arnold 1980; Hodder 1980; Rands and Bishop 1980; cf. Fry and Cox 1974).

An independent means of evaluating compositional variation is provided by the well-known "Criterion of Abundance." In its simplest form a ceramic unit strongly represented at a site is presumed to be of local manufacture, scarcely represented pieces being of nonlocal origin. A corollary holds that extended temporal continuity reflects the localized production of a given class of pottery. According to the basic assumption, a greater proportion of locally produced pottery is consumed locally than is disseminated to any other single site. Frequency of occurrence declines with distance, and, given certain provisos, this is formulated by Renfrew (1977:72–73) as the "Law of Monotonic Decrement." The general principle has obvious weaknesses, as discussed by Shepard (1942) among others, but relative abundance provides a reference point from which to assess the observed compositional patterning.

A related concept, based on elemental abundances rather than on the frequency of archaeologically defined pottery classes, identifies the chemical "center of gravity" (compositional or statistical centroid) of a site's ceramics. Statistical refinement of the data matrix may reveal a clustering that, in accordance with the assumptions of the Provenience Postulate and the Criterion of Abundance, represents locally manufactured pottery, the "nonlocal" examples diverging in multiple directions. A refined "center of gravity" does not automatically lead to precise interpretation. If the locally made pottery is of sufficient frequency, the centroid of the entire population is skewed in its direction, a pattern anticipated by the Criterion of Abundance. Additionally, the nonlocal pottery was, perhaps, produced within a region in which the chemical characteristics of the ceramic raw materials diverged gradually from those of the site under investigation. On the other hand, if the site has a distinctive environmental location relative to a homogeneous region from which the other ceramics were drawn, and if the latter pottery predominated in the sampling, one would not expect the locally produced materials to represent the center of gravity. This would probably be an exceptional case.

Ordination

Multivariate groups derived from elemental concentrations are increasingly employed in compositional analysis. Nevertheless, ordered relationships within the data set may be sought in the absence of discrete partitioning. Associations of chemical and nonchemical data provide an initial level of evaluation to guide the subsequent research, as well as constituting a major step in the compositional and archaeological synthesis.

The covariation of chemically patterned sherds and nonchemical variables can be shown effectively. One procedure generates a scattergram of ceramic specimens, plotted according to reference axes. Holding these positions in a constant relationship to coordinates on the x and y axes, petrographic or archaeological data may then be assigned the points occupied by the individual specimens. This can also be done in a triangular diagram, which has the advantage of showing the simultaneous contributions of three rather than two components. A series of these plots provides an overview of many complex relationships (cf. Bishop 1980:Figures 3–7). Additionally, if chemically established groups have already been formed and plotted, the diagrams facilitate a rapid assessment of the nonchemical patterning within and between groups (Figures 7.2 and 7.3) (Bishop and Rands 1982; Rands and Bishop 1980:Figures 3–5 and 11).

Reference Units

Especially when complexities are introduced by the use of temper, guidance for the interpretation of chemical data is necessary. As seen in the brief discussion of ordination, this is provided in part by petrography, a powerful sup-

---

Figure 7.2. Discrimination of chemical units of Maya pottery from the Palenque region, southeastern Mexico. Bivariate plot showing opal phytolith abundance, relative to chemically based discriminant functions. Clear discrimination on the first function allows vertical lines to be added to the computer printout, calling attention to almost perfect separation of three broadly defined CPCRUs (see Rands and Bishop 1980:Figure 3). Abbreviations for rank-order phytolith abundance: 0, absent; R, rare; C, common; A, abundant.

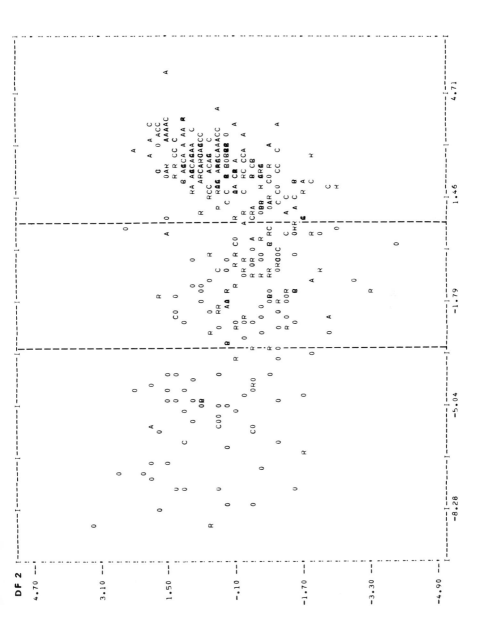

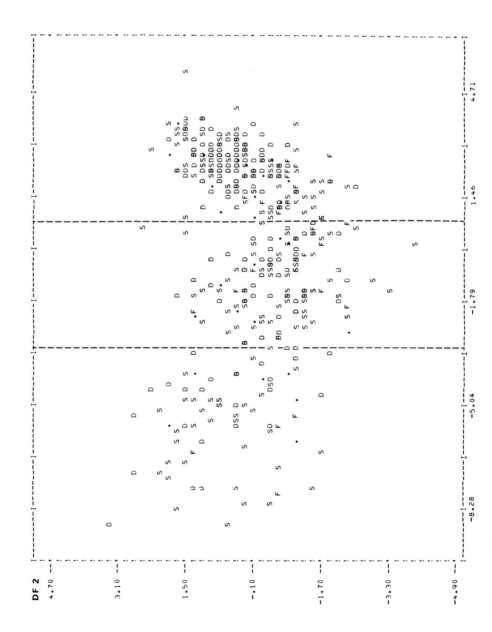

plementary and supportive tool. Additionally, interpretation of analytical data entails a consideration of cultural phenomena. It is inefficient and counterproductive to hold in abeyance the formal, temporal, and spatial dimensions of traditional archaeological concern until the compositional data have been fully analyzed. Using an expanded reference base to gain added perspective and feedback in the formation of compositional groups is preferable. Taking such a course, it is essential to make analytical steps explicit and to avoid the pitfalls of circular argument.

We suggest, therefore, the utility of a compositional approach that recognizes distinct levels of data integration. If chemical analysis has contributed substantially to the investigation of ceramic paste, this may be reflected in the formation of groups yielding statistically optimal divisions of the elemental data set. This level of grouping is effective if the archaeological problem requires simply a broad overview, but if a more detailed approach is required, as in the study of intraregional exchange, it will frequently be desirable to generate new groups from subsets of the original population. As in other archaeological practice, a "lumper's" or a "splitter's" approach is warranted, depending on objectives and research design. In either case, the primary level of analysis is based directly on the manipulation of elemental data, and we refer to the resulting groupings as *Chemical Paste Compositional Reference Units,* or CPCRUs (Bishop and Rands 1982). For convenience, one can differentiate between "global CPCRUs," representing optimal divisions of the entire data set, and "refined CPCRUs," which derive optimal separation after heterogeneity has been removed from the data set. Different levels of refinement, hence a hierarchy of "refined CPCRUs," may result.

The conceptual nature of the CPCRU is at the highest order of compositional sensitivity, the chemical data set. In formalizing the CPCRU as an operational category, it is explicitly recognized that the vicissitudes of nature and culture seldom permit maximum archaeological utility to be achieved by an interpretation of purely chemical data. By obtaining a better fit of a CPCRU with nonelemental data, a unit is derived that may prove more useful in archaeological analysis. We refer to such groups as *Paste Compositional Reference Units,* or PCRUs (Bishop and Rands 1982). A PCRU can result from merging two or more similar yet separable CPCRUs in order to achieve a new level of agreement with nonchemical data; in another approach, all specimens not belonging to a specific site provenience, form class, or other cultural or mineralogical category are removed. In some manner, we are mak-

Figure 7.3.   Bivariate plot of form-functional classes. Abbreviations: D, domestic or utilitarian pottery; S, serving vessels; F, figurines; dots, undesignated. Specimens occupy the same position in discriminant space as in Figure 2, permitting rapid assessment of chemical, mineralogical, and cultural data.

ing the original, chemically "homogeneous" class more homogeneous on some other level.

The paste compositional reference unit is problem specific, its membership being determined by the relationship of the "parent" CPCRU(s) to one or more variables selected by the investigator. The formation of the new unit is likely to be achieved at the expense of statistical rigor, although this need not be the case. For example, as those specimens removed from a CPCRU because of their poor agreement with petrographic data may also have had relatively low membership probabilities in this unit, the newly formed PCRU could prove to be more compact chemically as well as petrographically. Generally, this would neither be expected nor required in order to maintain the utility of the PCRU.

The PCRU and CPCRU have supplemental roles, at times being appropriate for different analytical procedures. Thus, redundancy would result from covariation between specific cultural or petrographic attributes and members of a PCRU that has been formulated with reference to those attributes. This is less a problem with the CPCRUs, the members of which are associable with any of the nonchemical variables. Notwithstanding this limitation, the PCRU is a flexible construct. It permits the direct association of a wide variety of archaeological attributes and chemical data, the latter having been deliberately weighted by external considerations.

Among other possible applications, the PCRU should prove useful in the analysis of ceramic populations in which chemical heterogeneity results largely from temper-induced factors. If these factors can be properly identified and evaluated, the remaining similarities may permit the merging of chemically isolable groups into a single PCRU, the new unit representing the products, both tempered and untempered, of a single manufacturing locality. The identification of temper-induced variability depends on an assessment of petrographic as well as chemical data, and other mineralogical information should support the essential uniformity of the ceramics. The possible input of cultural data in PCRU formation can be seen by supposing, in spite of the compositional similarities, that (a) contemporaneous stylistic differences are intensified when the CPCRUs are merged, and (b) the pottery of the tempered and untempered groups shows strongly contrasting geographical distributions. By introducing new levels of heterogeneity, such archaeological considerations would provide a telling argument against collapsing the CPCRUs into a single unit.

Group Formation and Refinement: A Statistical Overview

Chemically based ceramic compositional studies frequently lead to the formation of large data sets, each requiring a number of computer programs to analyze the information that has been generated. This analysis is usually directed toward the formation and refinement of groups such as the CPCRUs, although the groups have usually been conceptualized in somewhat different ways. A number of special purpose statistical programs have been developed for group formation or evaluation of archaeological materials (Bieber *et al.* 1976a; Perlman and Asaro 1971; Sayre n.d.). Additionally, several generalized systems of multivariate programs are available at most large computing facilities. These programs include SPSS (Nie *et al.* 1975), BMDP (Dixon and Brown 1977), Clustan (Wishart 1978), and NT-SYS (Rohlf *et al.* 1971). Textbooks such as that by Cooley and Lohnes (1971) also contain listings of various multivariate subroutines, including discriminant and classification options.

In selecting an appropriate series of statistical techniques, the investigator should recognize the structure imposed on a data set by the mathematical model. For example, if a technique utilizes a Euclidean definition of "closeness" to link samples, the end result will be the formation of spherical clusters (see, e.g., Everitt 1977:91). On the other hand, programs such as CLUS (Rubin and Friedman 1967) do not necessarily demand spherical clusters but do require partitions within the data set to be roughly of the same shape, spherical or ellipsoidal. Occasionally, specimens that are included under one procedure will be excluded under conditions imposed by the other. Many powerful techniques are likely to yield a residual body of ceramics lacking unequivocally assigned memberships, and it may prove difficult to interpret the relationships of these specimens unless the size and nature of the sample from which they have been drawn is modified.

Similarly, many statistical techniques are sensitive to initial data transformations, such as standardization, logging, or normalization by range. Although several clustering or refinement procedures are robust under transformation, fine levels of relationship are sometimes obscured. The need for a transformation and its resultant use must be as carefully considered as the selection of an appropriate multivariate technique.

It must not be forgotten that the chemical data are a reflection of the underlying mineralogy of the ceramic paste. Each component (the feldspars, micas, clays, etc.) contributes to the final chemical expression. A mixture of multiple constituents, each ceramic is variable in the proportions in which the ingredients have been combined. The components can, therefore, be conceived as ideal "end-members" present in the data set. Their position as end-members can be approximated by extracting a limited number of factors and ceasing once some level of cumulative variance is achieved.

Rather than representing relationships among chemical variables, techniques such as Q-mode factor analysis seek to portray relationships between the samples (Klovan 1975; Klovan and Imbrie 1971). When attempting to maximize information from mineralogical and chemical analysis, a Q-mode factor approach to the chemical data set appears to offer certain advantages.

The use of a proportional measure of similarity eliminates any problem of quartz temper acting as an "inert dilutant" (see, e.g., Olin and Sayre 1971) although complex, temper-related interaction of dilution/enrichment is still present (Bishop 1980). In effect, it appears that when the pottery under consideration is tempered, the theoretical end-members usually relate to the abundance of the various mineral inclusions, and when the pottery is finely textured the end-members often reflect those constellations of elements having similar substitution potentials. Testing of this approach and its implications for ceramic composition is continuing.

A special problem relates to small clusters of specimens too few in number to be evaluated by the more powerful statistical programs, such as those operating on a covariance matrix (Sayre n.d.). It is not always possible to obtain large groups of pottery from all sites or regions by the initial clustering procedures. Additionally, some small clusters are of special interest for the study of exchange, perhaps representing "exotic" ceramics that were traded infrequently over considerable distances. Many discriminant programs have options permitting calculations to be based on variance–covariance matrices pooled from all of the reference groups under consideration. Although less rigorous, the resulting probabilities of group containment are frequently useful in assessing problems likely to be encountered in compositional studies of exchange.

Single-Group Formation

The previous discussion of CPCRUs and PCRUs has assumed the existence of multiple reference groups. Only a single group is defined in some kinds of investigation, specimens that are not within the group's limits having an "outgroup" status. It is convenient, therefore, to consider the route to the formation of reference groups as dividing along two rather distinct paths, depending on whether one or more groups is sought.

The one-group approach has been discussed by Schneider *et al.* (1979) as a group established by reference to raw materials or artifacts of a known source. The authors rightly acknowledge the inherent difficulties of this approach. Clearly, the addition of temper to a clay or the mixing of one clay with another tends to produce a chemical profile differing from that of the original clay. Even if a complete characterization of raw materials could be achieved, there is, by virtue of ancient cultural practices, the possibility that no matches in profile could be obtained between the raw materials and the locally made pottery.

Another way of forming a single reference group is by the analysis of a large number of sherds known or inferred to be locally produced. These may consist of "wasters," pottery damaged during firing and discarded at an identifiable workshop site. This approach has been used by Poole and Finch

(1972) to infer postmedieval trade between continental Europe and Britain. In accordance with the Criterion of Abundance, the dominant pottery of a site, as exemplified by a ware or a sequential series of major ceramic types, may be sampled for chemical characterization. The "locality" of such a group is assumed rather than demonstrated.

The identification of a single reference group of "local" ceramics may also be based on a chemical "center of gravity." This is illustrated by an investigation of pottery from the Classic Maya site of Copán, Honduras (Bishop *et al.* n.d.). From each of the archaeologically sorted provisional types, 6–15 sherds were selected, carefully covering the ceramic sequence. Binocular microscopic examination was used to select only those with quartz-sand temper, eliminating volcanic or carbonate bearing pottery. The quartz-tempered specimens were analyzed by neutron activation and the resulting data submitted to statistical analysis. A restricted group was formed, serving as a reference unit against which to compare other pottery. This was done for Copador, a fine paste polychrome, to judge whether it was locally produced within the Copán Valley. The broad spectrum of classes from which the reference group was derived is considered more likely to include locally produced materials than the single class of Copador polychrome, the latter having a wider distribution on the southeastern Maya frontier. It was recognized that strict comparability had not been achieved between the quartz-tempered pottery of the reference unit and the finely textured Copador, but, with the elimination of the volcanic and carbonate-tempered sherds, appreciable heterogeneity was removed from the data set, leaving a more directly relevant body of reference material. Proportionality between the profiles for the Copán reference group and Copador suggests a common source. It should be noted here that to establish a single reference unit containing 60 specimens, it was necessary to utilize over 140 chemically analyzed samples.

If only a single reference group is established, it must be realized that excluded samples could have been derived from another production unit within the same site or locality. The sources for procurement may simply lie outside the allowed variation. Although this is a problem regardless of the number of reference units, lack of perspective characterizes the single-group approach. Whether based on raw materials or local pottery, this approach is not effectively oriented toward problems of exchange. It is strictly an "ingroup-outgroup" relationship; if not part of the reference group, the pottery is usually inferred to be imported.

Multiple-Group Formation

Alternative to the single-group approach is a strategy seeking to derive clusters of chemically similar pottery from within a given data matrix. The statistical methods used to form groups defined on the basis of chemical similarity have been considered frequently (e.g., Bieber *et al.* 1976a; Cabral and Gouveia 1979; Harbottle 1976; Sayre n.d.). As a general rule, if there are natural or discrete groups in the data set, most clustering procedures will recover them. Two major categories are commonly recognized, hierarchical methods, often taking the form of dendrograms, and iterative procedures.

The dendrogram is frequently employed (Bieber *et al.* 1976b). Closely similar examples are linked at a low level, the linkage continuing progressively until all specimens are merged into one large cluster. An enormous number of clustering variations exist. Each is based on some initial assumption about the underlying structure of the data set, but the appropriateness of the assumption is essentially unknown. Although the lower linkages of the dendrogram reflect the similarity of the joined specimens, the higher linkages are prone to considerable distortion (Rohlf 1970). Advantages of this method include the rapidity with which it can provide an overview of specimen relationships, but the interpretation of a dendrogram's structure is likely to be difficult.

Given a sample of sufficient size and internal heterogeneity, it could prove useful to resubmit major clusters of a dendrogram that are linked at a moderate hierarchical level. By reserving the power of the algorithm to seek linkages within a relatively homogeneous population, more subtle relationships may be seen. This is a possible step—although one complicated by additional assumptions—in the formation of "refined" CPCRUs.

In contrast, iterative partitioning procedures do not give a hierarchical relationship between the derived clusters. For example, in the CLUS program (Rubin and Friedman 1967), a search is made through a series of iterations for the number and membership of groups that contain the smallest amount of internal variation and that are most isolated externally. Groups satisfying these statistical requirements, which lead to a "global" solution, may be too generalized to meet the archaeological objective of identifying localized centers of ceramic production. Under these circumstances, it is desirable to resubmit each of the generalized groups to the program for further partitioning. From a global perspective, the more generalized groups are considered to represent the "optimal" classification, those units resulting from the subdivision having possible heuristic utility.

In the formation of the resulting "refined" CPCRUs, derived from a restricted data matrix, probabilities of membership for a given sherd usually change. Even if the probability of membership increases, some form of independent (nonchemical) evidence should be obtained to confirm archaeological usefulness. In the analysis of ceramics from the Palenque region, it was found that petrographic homogeneity tends to be considerably greater in a number of the units derived by subdivision than in the original, more generalized groups (Bishop *et al.* 1982). This stage of analysis is still at the level of CPCRU formation; specimens are not removed nor are groups merged to obtain greater homogeneity of a nonchemical nature, as in the case of the PCRUs. Yet, external information can be useful, helping the investigator to decide on a cutoff point for terminating further partitioning.

Group refinement by univariate or multivariate statistics is generally necessary to complete the formation of CPCRUs. Assuming an adequate number of samples, probability statistics can be calculated; these employ the specific group's correlation pattern of chemical elements and include the probability of group containment. Evaluation of multiple groups is possible by using discriminant functions (i.e., linear combinations of the original variates weighted maximally to separate the groups). Again, the probabilities of group containment may be obtained.

Decisions relating to the confidence interval selected during group membership refinement further illustrate the desirability of working outside a closed chemical system. The decision can be more adequately defended if, for example, there is an optimum agreement of petrographic and chemical data at approximately a 10% confidence interval than if this interval is arbitrarily selected (see, e.g., Bishop *et al.* 1982). In working toward the formation of CPCRUs, the investigator cannot judiciously close his mind to available outside evidence until a final day of reckoning. It is in the formation of the PCRU, however, that the convergence of chemical, petrographic, and archaeological data is maximized.

Local Use or Exchange

Whether the CPCRU or PCRU is of greater utility in addressing the alternatives of localized consumption or exchange depends on circumstances specific to a given research undertaking. It would seem that the more complex the data set, reflecting subtle differences brought about by clay processing or the existence of distinct but chemically similar source areas, the greater the dependence on the interpretive guidance provided by the PCRUs. In any case, covariation should be sought between the CPCRU, as the direct expression of chemical relationships, and archaeological data.

Whether the unit employed is a CPCRU or a PCRU, we call attention to the archaeological provenience of the pottery, referring to the proposition that more of a site's ceramic production is more likely to be consumed locally than to be distributed to any other site of equivalent size. Although this may not hold true in all circumstances, it is a useful rule of thumb, and to the extent that it is correct, there should be a positive relationship between a reference unit and the provenience of member specimens according to site or locality. *In effect, it is hypothesized that pottery is locally manufactured and used. The hypothesis is rejected in the case of specimens having membership in a given compositional reference unit but archaeological provenience in an area characterized by a distinct unit.*

The reference unit serves, then, as an operational device for refining test implications of the hypothesis that ceramic production and use were local. Independent evidence would need to be introduced to support the alternative hypothesis, that a negative correlation exists between a reference unit and the archaeological provenience of its member specimens. This would, of course, have profound implications about the nature and structuring of commercial activities.

A problem often exists in applying the test for covariation of a reference unit and its place of consumption: areas of human occupation and exploitation are frequently closely spaced and may be overlapping. In such cases, mutual utilization of ceramic raw materials may have taken place without seriously violating least-cost principles. In an unambiguous test of the utility of chemical analysis for the investigation of ceramic exchange, it is desirable that a number of reference groups are represented by the potential trade ware but that, in their totality, these units occur over a dispersed rather than compacted area.

An example is provided by the distribution of CPCRUs for the largely Terminal Classic to Early Postclassic Fine Orange and Fine Gray wares in the Usumacinta drainage of Guatemala and Mexico. As determined in this investigation (Bishop and Rands 1982; Rands *et al.* 1982), five CPCRUs are distributed linearly along an axis defined by the Pasion and Usumacinta rivers, including a lateral extension approximating one of the tributaries, the Chacamax. There is also a northern extension of one of the CPCRUs into the Yucatán Peninsula and another eastward to Belize. The geographical pattern of the CPCRUs is striking: Moving across the Petén and downstream, from east and south to north and west, Units 3, 4, 2, 5, and 1 occur sequentially, each concentrated in a geographically restricted area. Of over 50 specimens assigned to these reference groups, only 5 fail to have the distributions that would be predicted by an hypothesis that locally manufactured pottery remains within its zone of production or extends, with lower frequency, into an immediately adjoining zone. Although short-distance exchange may or may not have occurred regularly within each of the production zones, only the 5 specimens appear to have been widely traded. Previous hypotheses of a single Gulf Coast locus of manufacture are decisively rejected (see, e.g., Sabloff 1973; Sabloff and Willey 1967; Sayre *et al.* 1971).

In the Fine Orange investigation, CPCRUs served as effective reference units, without having to be transformed into PCRUs in order to achieve an unambiguous archaeological interpretation. Even so, selected aspects of interpretation were enhanced by the use of PCRUs. Two aspects should be borne in mind in considering the unusually clear-cut results that were obtained. First, the ceramics under investigation are fine paste, so the complicating effects of temper did not have to be confronted. Second, rather than being compacted into a small area, the zones as sampled are linear, following a few of the rivers in the Usumacinta drainage; variation on the spatial dimension could be readily controlled.

OTHER RESEARCH PROBLEMS

Although most of our discussion has been directed toward how mineralogical and chemical analyses may be used to investigate exchange, the general approach has additional promise. Vessel function and man–nature relationships in utilizing ceramic resources are considered briefly, occasionally amplifying earlier discussions.

Vessel Function

Pottery has varied functions, only some of which are probably reflected in paste composition. Two aspects are examined here, (a) the desirability of trade goods to be readily transported with minimal breakage and (b) the desirability of cooking vessels to withstand thermal shock. A least-cost strategy based on a considerable degree of trial and error is assumed.

To be efficient in bulk or long-distance exchange, especially in the absence of domesticated animals or water transportation, light weight and resistance to breakage are important considerations, and the traded pottery was perhaps desired as much for its strength as for other properties. A preference for technically superior pottery is suggested by Shepard (1968:355) to underlie the widespread distribution of the Mesoamerican Thin Orange, Fine Orange, and Plumbate wares (see, e.g., Nicklin 1971:19–20; Rathje et al. 1978). The importance of Tonque Pueblo as a major production center for the widely traded glaze-paint pottery is attributed by Warren (1969) to the local availability of high quality clay, suitable for the manufacture of thin-walled vessels, as well as to the proximity of lead ores for the glaze. The possibility that a mixture of basalt temper and iron-rich clay contributes fluxing impurities, lowering the point of vitrification and resulting in pottery of exceptional strength, is discussed by Windes (1977:294–295) for other Southwestern ceramics (see also Grimshaw 1971).

Regardless of exchange, the raw materials used in pottery manufacture impose constraints on functionally defined ceramic classes, these constraints being mediated by diverse technologies. The often-cited example of an earthenware water container that cools its contents by means of capillary action is a case in point; to achieve this effect a porous paste is needed. Clay can be transformed to the desired state by the addition of suitable temper. Similar constraints introduced by the intended use of the pottery can be considered in terms of the physical properties of a ceramic body and inferred from a number of ethnographic accounts.

Among these constraints, the susceptibility of fired pottery to thermal shock, resulting in cracking, splitting, and spalling, is perhaps best documented. As discussed by Shepard (1968:126), porous pottery has greater resistance to changes in temperature than finely textured ceramics because the grains have a greater freedom to expand, a state that can be achieved by the use of moderately large and uniform temper. Clays also differ in the porosity that results from firing within the upper ranges of temperature generally attained in nonkiln firing. It follows that raw materials promoting a high degree of porosity are efficient for cooking vessels and might be expected to be favored if potters had a choice of readily available materials (De Atley 1973:11; Ericson *et al.* 1972:86; Plog 1980:88).

Some of the physical properties required for efficiency in cooking pots, as contrasted to vessels for holding water, are summarized by Rye (1976:113). Thermal shock resistance, for example, is unnecessary in water pots, whereas it is essential in cooking pots. High porosity (permeability) and fine pores are desirable for cooling water in hot climates. In cooking pots, on the other hand, coarse pores provide protection against thermal shock, although permeability to fluids is undesirable. Rye (1976:114) further concludes that the optimum pore size for pottery used in a cooking fire of 300–500° C is between 7 and 9 mm; this is largely a function of the density of packing and the size of mineral grains, including temper and naturally occurring inclusions in the clay. Minerals with low thermal expansion, which are suitable in avoiding stresses within the fabric during repeated heating and cooling, include zircon, plagioclasse and other feldspars, augite, rutile, hornblende, and, under proper conditions, calcite (Rye 1976:116–117, 120–123).

Additionally, the mineral inclusions should have thermal expansions similar to that of the fired clay matrix, and this may be achieved by using temper that is prepared from crushed sherds made from the same clay as the pot that is being manufactured. That this optimal use of sherd temper was not always realized is indicated by the Yuma and Mohave of the American Southwest, who used sherd temper for most of their pottery but crushed rock (granite or sandstone) for cooking vessels (Rogers 1936:31, 37). In general, the acidic rocks, including granites, have greater thermal expansion than basic rocks (basalts, diorites, etc.; Winkler cited in Rye 1976:116). A number of instances in which the tempering materials used in cooking pots differ from those used in other functional vessel classes are cited in the ethnographic literature (see, e.g., Plog 1980:86–87).

Few archaeological investigations have been made of paste composition as it affects porosity. Within porosity ranges for a series of glaze-paint classes and other pottery at Pecos, New Mexico, Shepard (1968:128–130) was unable to find significant groupings by time, space, or composition until samples were refired experimentally at 1200° C. Of course, the differences observed on refiring did not affect vessel function, but they did indicate the use of distinct raw materials. Porosity tests of culinary ware at Chaco have revealed differences correlating with temper, although it is suspected that part of the variability reflects separate clays (Windes 1977:295–298). Plog (1980:88–93), in a study of Chevelon area ceramics, found that the tempering material covaried with vessel form; cooking pots were correlated with sand or crushed rock and noncooking vessels of various forms with fine sand or crushed sherd.

These considerations are not without relationship to compositional analyses directed toward ceramic exchange. In general, covariation of paste composition and attributes of vessel morphology and function would be seen as strengthening the distinctiveness of a ceramic class and, correspondingly, the probability that under appropriate conditions, it could be recognized as an item of exchange. The inference of trade, however, involves the proposition that the variables are independent rather than being linked by functional considerations. It is our experience, based on both chemical and petrographic analysis, that covariation often exists between aspects of paste composition and vessel shape. Serious consideration should be given to the possibility that the distribution of ceramic compositional groups within a localized region, although reflecting the spread of manufacturing concepts and techniques, is sometimes more informative about vessel function than about the movements of pottery vessels in short-distance exchange.

Although recognizing a possible functional relationship between paste composition and vessel use, the treatment in Rands (1979) of the strongly contrastive chemical patterning of serving and utilitarian vessels, the latter including many cooking pots, was too facile. Variables that are reasonably inferred to be truly independent are prized assets. In the Palenque region (Rands 1974:66–69; Rands and Bishop 1980), such a variable appears to be provided by opal phytoliths, a hydrous amorphous silica. Essentially, the phytoliths are not reflected in neutron activation analysis, are readily seen petrographically under magnification (Figure 7.1a), and represent a biogenic phenomenon not directly related to the normal geologic processes of rock weathering, diagenesis, and clay formation. Covariation of the phytoliths with cooking pots and other functional classes, or with CPCRUs and the minerals more traditionally used in petrographic analysis, therefore has a special, supportive role (see, e.g., Figures 7.2 and 7.3).

Raw Material Procurement Strategies

According to least-cost principles, a center of ceramic production should be situated in the general location of bulky materials used in pottery manufacture, such as clay, temper, and fuel for firing. These considerations may be augmented by an endeavor to obtain clay or temper having desirable, special purpose properties (e.g., superior materials for withstanding thermal shock). Utilization of clay and temper having properties that enhance strength might also promote selectivity in the choice of raw materials that were locally available or lead to an enlargement of the zone of resource procurement (cf. Nicklin 1979). These are complicating factors, suggesting that multiple compositional reference units may sometimes characterize a single production center. To be sure, this may be the case in the absence of production for exchange, but specialized selection in the procurement of raw materials is perhaps intensified under economic conditions of expansion or diversification in ceramic trade.

How far afield do preindustrial potters normally go to obtain their raw materials? Using an ethnographic sample of 61 cases, Arnold (1980) found that 64% of the communities obtain clay at a distance of 4 km or less and 91% at 7 km or less. Although marginal exploitation is recorded up to 31 km from a community, Arnold believes the preferred territory of exploitation has an upper limit of 1 km. Costs rise sharply beyond this distance. In a smaller sample of 28 communities, Arnold finds generally similar patterns for procuring temper. Fifty-seven percent obtain temper at a distance of 1 km or less, and 97% at 5 km or less; marginal exploitation extends up to 25 km from a community.

Arnold's findings are mixed. A general tendency exists for procurement zones and the place of ceramic manufacture to be in fairly close proximity. The possibility is underscored, however, that with the establishment of new settlements or other modification of the procurement system leading to "marginal" exploitation, pottery having ingredients from environmentally separated zones reflects procurement practices rather than exchange (Arnold 1980:148–149). Arnold further suggests that communities separated by less than 10–14 km are likely to have overlapping resource areas, each with a radius of 5–7 km. Considerable geologic variation may exist within such distances.

Differing patterns of exploitation take place within the suggested parameters of the resource zone. The quality of the ethnographic record varies greatly, and our suggested typology of five procurement strategies is by no means definitive.

We characterize the inferred strategies as nondiscriminating, discriminating, specializing, compounding, and importing. Environmental, social, and cultural constraints influence the form and choice of a particular strategy, or combination of strategies, that is employed. Thus, the availability of resources across the exploitable landscape is a major consideration, and not all of these clays are judged usable by the potter (Arnold 1971). Ownership and access, as well as competition from other land uses such as agriculture, impose social restrictions. The type or range of ceramics produced at a given locale may further influence the specific resources to be used, as has been discussed for cooking pots. Available technology also impedes clay selection. As Nicklin (1979:440) conjectures, potters who fail to levigate their clay would tend not to exploit impure deposits. This observation probably applies only to resource-rich or sophisticated potters, for there is ample archaeological evidence for the use of less than pure deposits.

Nondiscriminating Procurement Strategies. A wide number of available clay resources are exploited, with little preference being shown. There is not much ethnographic documentation for these strategies, perhaps as the result of disinterest or lack of perceptivity on the part of the observer. Kelly and Palerm (1952:216) note the abundance of clay at Tajin; it is collected from various sources by the local Totonac, different colored clays being regarded by some informants as equally usable. Arnold (1978b:331, 338) observes that many comal producers in the Valley of Guatemala do not have special places to obtain clay; they simply get it from their own yards.

Discriminating Procurement Strategies. Rather than collecting clay at any location, extraction efforts are concentrated at a valued clay resource. The clay may occur widely in the form of an eroding formation (Arnold 1978b; Rye and Evans 1976) or have a unique occurrence (Ogan 1970). Mining often accompanies this strategy (Freed and Freed 1963). In some cases, the ceramic workshop is placed at or near the source of the clay (Curtis 1962; Hanssen 1969). In their survey of Pakistan pottery making, however, Rye and Evans (1976:127) point out that the location of a kiln determines the clay source, not the reverse.

Specializing Procurement Strategies. A natural dichotomy exists in the distribution and compositional characteristics of clays, the flexibility afforded by the diverse resources being recognized and exploited by the potters (Arnold 1972a, 1972b, 1978b:336, 346–367; Handler 1963; Stone 1950). Clays resistant to thermal shock are employed when necessary; finely textured and coarse wares may be made with minimal preparation of appropriate clays; desired colors are achievable without the added use of slip.

Compounding Procurement Strategies. Distinct resources are available to the potter, but unlike specialized procurement, the clays are mixed to form a composite paste. Jar manufacturers on the island of Crete add a small portion of a highly refractory, poorly malleable clay to the common clay (Voyatzoglou 1974:19). An effective way of obtaining desirable properties, this pattern of clay procurement and preparation apparently has a peasant or modern focus (Foster 1957; Rye and Evans 1976; Taylor 1933). It may prove of greater general use in modifying the relatively uniform residual clays than in the preparation of sedimentary clays; the latter often have complex compositions, resulting from the mixing of materials derived from multiple lithological sources.

Importing Procurement Strategies.   Distant raw materials are purchased (Nicklin 1979:444–445; Rye and Evans 1976:73, 107; Wyndham 1971) or procurement parties are organized to acquire clays far from the site of ceramic production (Groves 1960; Nicklin 1979:445–446). These approaches are facilitated by the presence of modern or domesticate-based transportation, although canoe transport can effectively reduce problems arising from bulk and weight. If importing is a commonly employed strategy, implicit assumptions linking the resource procurement zone to an adjacent center of pottery production may give rise to false leads and surely will end in frustration.

In their own ways, the other strategies complicate the interpretation of compositional patterning; pottery considered to be of "local" manufacture will often be assumed to correspond to locally obtained clay samples. Other things being equal, discriminating procurement strategies should provide the most clear-cut ceramic characterization of a given site or locality, yet it may prove extremely difficult to locate the single clay source that was exploited. These factors contribute to our position that geologic survey is likely to be of more value for the perspective it provides than for the one-to-one matches it yields. However, if microanalytical techniques are developed to the point of rapidly and effectively distinguishing clay minerals and nonplastics in the ceramic paste, the potentials for obtaining meaningful agreements between paste and raw materials will be enhanced. Perhaps it will be possible to infer or even to detail the aboriginal strategy used for exploiting the resources of a particular procurement zone.

DISCUSSION

Chemical compositional studies are in flux and mistakes are being made, but instrumental analytical techniques are sensitive, statistical methods are powerful, and effective characterization of the pottery is more than a gleam in the eye of the analyst. In evaluating this approach, we especially note the potential of the workshop debris (kiln wasters) in establishing local reference groups (Fontes *et al.* 1979). Geographical patterning, in which multiple reference units tend to occupy axially adjacent, but mutually exclusive regions, constitutes another form of evidence that supports the integrity of the analytical procedure (Bishop and Rands 1982; Rands *et al.* 1982). As we have discussed, the exceptional ceramic specimens, having a site provenience within the territory characterized by another reference unit, constitute the compositional evidence for the exchange of pottery. With multiple sources characterized, geologically and by judicious application of the Criterion of Abundance, questions may be framed regarding the size, directionality, temporality, and centralization of a network of ceramic exchange (see Plog 1977).

Petrographic and chemical studies are strengthened by a knowledge of regional geology. The ability to match local and distant resources with the mineral grains of the pottery has, under favorable circumstances, produced outstanding examples of petrographic research. Even in the absence of a petrographic–geologic synthesis, the multicomponent nature of ceramics has implications for interpreting chemical data in terms of clays, their inclusions, and temper (Bishop 1980). Nevertheless, we are treading on poorly charted grounds, and such interpretations are far more successful with an understanding of ceramic petrography, regional geology, or, preferably, both. This information relates directly to the interpretation of the chemical data set, affecting judgments about the source of variability (e.g., the use of separate clay deposits, the addition of temper). The identification of resource procurement zones is partially dependent on such assessments.

Recognizing the power of chemical elemental data for multivariate analysis in compositional studies, together with dependence on an interpretive framework derived from petrology, geology, and geochemistry, we emphasize the need to develop methods promoting the integration of these data sets. The operational construct of the Chemical Paste Compositional Reference Unit (CPCRU) derives directly from chemical data, although, as has been discussed, archaeologically useful cutoff points in group formation are strengthened by an awareness of what is going on outside the closed chemical system. On another level, these "outside" considerations provide a means of weighting the chemical data, leading to the formation of the Paste Compositional Reference Unit (PCRU). In essence, analytical data are merged with accessory information. Cultural information may also be used in the derivation of PCRUs, but if it is, care must be taken to avoid circular reasoning and redundancy because the PCRU is associated with archaeological variables.

We have not attempted to address the full implications of this conceptual hierarchy. Different levels of refinement within the CPCRUs are recognized, an appropriate level being influenced by specific objectives of the research. However, we have not considered the possible variation in PCRUs (e.g., the number of these integrative units that may be used efficiently in a single investigation, whether a PCRU may be derived independently of chemical data). Rather than attempting to present a detailed system, we simply emphasize the need to move from maximum levels of analytical precision to units of analysis providing a wider, problem-oriented compositional perspective. The possibility that tempered and untempered ceramics were made from the same local clay illustrates the desirability of this dual approach.

As we have stressed—and has been pointed out by Rice, Arnold, and their associates (Arnold *et al.* 1978; Rice 1978b)—the processing of the raw materials during pottery production may induce complex chemical changes, resulting in a restructuring of the chemical profile such that the finished ceramic should be regarded as something more than simply the sum of its natural constituents. Variation on this level is not necessarily of major consequence in the investigation of long-distance exchange; regionally distinctive clays tend to provide distinctive chemical profiles. Frequently, the archaeologist will suspect the existence of trade wares, and a modest program of chemical analysis may put the problem in a greatly improved perspective.

The main challenge comes as we focus more sharply on intraregional exchange (Fry 1980). Here, supplementary geologic information of a detailed nature and a sophisticated geochemical perspective are of strategic importance, together with an awareness of subtle technical and stylistic patterning in the ceramics. We would add, however, that some of the more significant problems to be addressed in archaeology lie on the local level, and that obtaining hard data about exchange should prove among the most rewarding approaches to understanding a regional socioeconomic system. The challenge is great; for example, it has taken Rands a painfully long time to begin to reach initially sought-after levels of conclusions in his ongoing investigation of elite center–satellite exchange at the Maya site of Palenque (Rands 1967; Rands and Bishop 1980). It is reasonable to believe that future investigators, capitalizing on past mistakes and employing increasingly sophisticated analytical procedures, will move much more rapidly in the detailed investigation of localized exchange.

Indeed, at a time of budgetary austerity in which many laboratory facilities are increasingly treating archaeological analysis as an expendable luxury, it is of added importance that programs be thoughtfully designed, with input from both archaeologist and scientific analyst. Infrequently used techniques, such as those provided by microanalysis, should be exploited, exploring the special kinds of problems for which they are uniquely developed. Aside from reference-group formation, we have scarcely touched on archaeological relevance. As in much archaeological research, ceramic compositional analysis takes place at the interface of the natural environment with the social and cultural components of production. With modest improvement in our present body of methods and more judicious use of available techniques, we should soon be able to examine nuances of these relationships.

ACKNOWLEDGMENTS

We wish to thank the anonymous reviewers who commented on an earlier version of this paper.

REFERENCES

Abascal-M, R.
 1974   Análisis por activación de neutrones: una aportación para la arqueología moderna. Unpublished thesis, Ciencias Antropológicas, Universidad Nacional Autónoma de México, Mexico.
Andrews-Jones, D. A.
 1968   The application of geochemical techniques to mineral exploration. *Colorado School of Mines, Mineral Industries Bulletin* **11**:1–31.
Arnold, D. E.
 1971   Ethnomineralogy of Ticul, Yucatan potters: etics and emics. *American Antiquity* **36**:20–40.
 1972a Mineralogical analysis of ceramic materials from Quinua, Department of Ayacucho, Peru. *Archaeometry* **14**:93–102.
 1972b Native pottery making in Quinua, Peru. *Anthropos* **67**:858–872.
 1975   Ceramic ecology of the Ayacucho Basin, Peru: implications for prehistory. *Current Anthropology* **16**:183–205.
 1976   Ecological variables and ceramic production: towards a general model. In *Primitive art and technology,* edited by J. S. Raymond, B. Loveseth, C. Arnold, and G. Reardon. Alberta: Archaeological Association, Department of Archaeology, University of Calgary, Alberta. Pp. 92–108.
 1978a Ceramic variability, environment and culture history among the Pokom in the Valley of Guatemala. In *The spatial organisation of culture,* edited by I. Hodder. London: Duckworth. Pp. 39–60.
 1978b Ethnography of pottery making in the Valley of Guatemala. In *The ceramics of Kaminaljuyu, Guatemala,* edited by R. K. Wetherington. University Park: The Pennsylvania State University Press. Pp. 327–400.
 1980   Localized exchange: an ethnoarchaeological perspective. In *Models and methods in regional exchange,* edited by R. E. Fry. Society for American Archaeology, *SAA Papers* 1. Pp. 147–150.
Arnold, D. E., P. M. Rice, W. A. Jester, W. N. Deutsch, B. K. Lee, and R. I. Kirsch
 1978   Neutron activation analysis of contemporary pottery and pottery materials from the Valley of Guatemala. In *The ceramics of Kaminaljuyu, Guatemala,* edited by R. K. Wetherington. University Park: The Pennsylvania State University Press. Pp. 543–586.
Bailey, E. H., and R. E. Stevens
 1960   Selective staining of K-feldspar and plagioclase on rock slab and thin sections. *The American Mineralogist* **45**:1020–1025.
Ball, J. W.
 1980   The archaeological ceramics of Chinkultic, Chiapas, Mexico. *Papers of the New World Archaeological Foundation,* No. 43. Provo.

Beus, A. A.
1971   Titanium distribution in the lithosphere. *Chemical Geology* **8**:247–276.

Bieber, A. M., Jr., D. W. Brooks, G. Harbottle, and E. V. Sayre
1976a   Application of multivariate techniques to analytical data on Aegean ceramics. *Archaeometry* **18**:59–74.
1976b   Compositional groupings of some ancient Aegean and Eastern Mediterranean pottery. In *Applicazione dei metodi nucleari nel campo delle opere d'arte*. Rome: Accademia Nazionale dei Lincei. Pp. 111–143.

Birgul, O., M. Diksic, and L. Yaffe
1979   X-ray fluorescence analysis of Turkish clays and pottery. *Archaeometry* **21**:203–218.

Bishop, R. L.
1975   Western Lowland Maya ceramic trade: an application of nuclear chemical and geological data analysis. Unpublished Ph.D. dissertation, Department of Anthropology, Southern Illinois University, Carbondale.
1980   Aspects of ceramic compositional modeling. In *Models and methods in regional exchange,* edited by R. E. Fry. Society for American Archaeology, *SAA Papers* 1. Pp. 47–66.

Bishop, R. L., M. P. Beaudry, R. M. Leventhal, and R. J. Sharer
n.d.   Compositional analysis of Classic period painted ceramics in the Southeast Maya area. *Yax kin,* in press.

Bishop, R. L., and R. L. Rands
1982   Maya fine paste ceramics: a compositional perspective. In *Analyses of fine paste ceramics,* edited by J. A. Sabloff. *Memoirs of the Peabody Museum of Archaeology and Ethnology,* **15**, No. 2. Cambridge.

Bishop, R. L., R. L. Rands, and G. Harbottle
1982   A ceramic compositional interpretation of incense-burner trade in the Palenque area. In *Nuclear and chemical dating methods,* edited by L. A. Currie. Washington, D.C.: American Chemical Society. Pp. 411–419.

Blatt, H., G. Middleton, and R. Murry
1972   *Origin of sedimentary rocks.* Englewood Cliffs: Prentice-Hall.

Bloss, F. D.
1971   *Crystallography and crystal chemistry.* New York: Holt.

Bomgardner, D. L.
1981   Atomic absorption spectroscopy applications for ceramic analysis. In *Scientific studies in ancient ceramics,* edited by M. J. Hughes. *British Museum Occasional Paper* **19**:93–101.

Bower, N. W., R. H. Bromund, and R. H. Smith
1975   Atomic absorption for the archaeologist: an application to pottery from Pella of the Decapolis. *Journal of Field Archaeology* **2**:389–398.

Cabral, J. M. P., and M. A. Gouveia
1979   The application of neutron activation analysis and numerical taxonomic methods to the study of ancient fine grey pottery. *Portgal Physics* **10**:101–116.

Catling, H. W., A. E. Blin-Stoyle, and E. E. Richards
1961   Spectrographic analysis of Mycenaean and Minoan pottery. *Archaeometry* **4**:31–38.

Catling, H. W., and A. Millet
1965   A study in the composition patterns of Mycenaean pictorial pottery from Cyprus. *Annual of the British School of Archaeology at Athens* **60**:212–224.

Catling, H. W., E. E. Richards, and A. E. Blin-Stoyle
1963   Correlations between composition and provenience of Mycenaean and Minoan pottery. *Annual of the British School of Archaeology at Athens* **58**:94–115.

Chayes, F.
    1956   Petrographic modal analysis. New York: Wiley.

Chen, P.-y.
    1977   Table of key lines in X-ray powder diffraction patterns of minerals in clays and associated rocks. *Department of Natural Resources, Geological Survey Occasional Paper* 21. Indiana Geological Survey, Bloomington.

Cooley, W. W., and T. R. Lohnes
    1971   *Multivariate data analysis.* New York: Wiley.

Culbert, T. P.
    1973   The Maya downfall at Tikal. In *The Classic Maya collapse,* edited by T. P. Culbert. Albuquerque: University of New Mexico Press. Pp. 63–92.

Curtis, F.
    1962   The utility pottery industry of Bailén, southern Spain. *American Anthropologist* **64**:486–503.

De Atley, S. P.
    1973   A preliminary analysis of patterns of raw material use in plainware ceramics from Chevelon, Arizona. Unpublished M.A. thesis, Department of Anthropology, University of California, Los Angeles.

De Atley, S. P., and W. G. Nelson
    1981   Compositional variability of ceramic clays in the Moenkopi and Morrison Formations in the Southwest United States. Paper presented at *Archaeometry* 21, Brookhaven National Laboratory, Upton.

Dickinson, W. R., and R. Shutler, Jr.
    1968   Insular sands of prehistoric pottery from the southwest Pacific. In *Prehistoric culture in Oceania,* edited by I. Yawata and S. Sinoto. Honolulu: Bishop Museum Press. Pp. 29–37.
    1971   Temper sands in prehistoric pottery of the Pacific islands. *Archaeology & Physical Anthropology in Oceania* **6**:191–203.
    1974   Probable Fijian origin of quartzose temper sands in prehistoric pottery from Tonga and the Marquesas. *Science* **185**:454–457.

Dickson, J. A. D.
    1966   Carbonate identification and genesis as revealed by staining. *Journal of Sedimentary Petrology* **36**:491–505.

Dixon, W. J., and M. B. Brown (editors)
    1977   *BMD-77, Biomedical computer programs. P-series.* Los Angeles: University of California Press.

Egloff, B. J.
    1978   The Kula before Malinowski: a changing configuration. *Mankind* **11**:429–435.

Ericson, J. E., E. Reed, and C. Burke
    1972   Research design: the relationship between primary functions and physical properties of ceramic vessels and their implications for ceramic distribution on an archaeological site. *Anthropology UCLA* **3**:84–95.

Everitt, B.
    1977   *Cluster analysis.* London: Heinemann Education Books.

Fontana, B. L., W. J. Robinson, C. W. Cormack, and E. E. Leavitt, Jr.
    1962   *Papago Indian pottery.* Seattle: University of Washington Press.

Fontes, P., *et al.*
    1979   Analytical study of three Gallo-Roman white figurine workshops. In Proceedings of the 18th international symposium on archaeometry and archaeological prospection. *Archaeo-Physika* **10**:101–112. Rheinisches Landesmuseum, Bonn.

Foster, G. M.
    1957   Pottery making in Bengal. *Southwestern Journal of Anthropology* **12**:395–405.

Freed, R. S., and S. A. Freed
 1963 Utilitarian pottery manufacture in a north Indian village. *Anthropological Quarterly* **36**:34–42.
Freeth, S. J.
 1967 A chemical study of some Bronze Age pottery and sherds. *Archaeometry* **10**:104–119.
Fry, R. E. (editor)
 1980 Models and methods in regional exchange. Society for American Archaeology, *SAA Papers* 1.
Fry, R. E., and S. C. Cox
 1974 The structure of ceramic exchange at Tikal, Guatemala. *World Archaeology* **6**:209–225.
Glock, A. E.
 1975 Homo Faber: the pot and the potter at Taanach. *Bulletin of the American Schools of Oriental Research* **219**:9–28.
Goffer, Z.
 1980 *Archaeological chemistry, a sourcebook on the application of chemistry to archaeology.* New York: Wiley.
Griffiths, J. C.
 1967 *Scientific method in analysis of sediments.* New York: McGraw-Hill.
Grim, R. E.
 1968 *Clay mineralogy.* New York: McGraw-Hill.
Grimshaw, R. W.
 1971 *The chemistry and physics of clays and allied ceramic materials.* London: Ernest Benn.
Gritton, V., and N. M. Magalousis
 1978 Atomic absorption spectroscopy of archaeological ceramic materials. In *Archaeological chemistry II,* edited by G. F. Carter. Advances in Chemistry Series 171. Washington, D.C.: The American Chemical Society. Pp. 258–272.
Groves, M.
 1960 Motu pottery. *Journal of the Polynesian Society* **69**:3–22.
Hammond, N., G. Harbottle, and T. Gazard
 1976 Neutron activation and statistical analysis of Maya ceramics and clays from Lubaantun, Belize. *Archaeometry* **18**:147–168.
Handler, J.
 1963 Pottery making in rural Barbados. *Southwestern Journal of Anthropology* **19**:314–334.
Hanssen, G.
 1969 The pottery of Haut-Berry. *Pottery in Australia* **8**:7–13.
Harbottle, G.
 1976 Activation analysis in archaeology. In *Radiochemistry: a specialist periodical report,* edited by G. W. A. Newton. London: The Chemical Society, Burlington House. Pp. 33–72.
Hatcher, H., R. E. M. Hedges, A. M. Pollard, and P. M. Kenrick
 1980 Analysis of Hellenistic and Roman fine pottery from Benghazi. *Archaeometry* **22**:133–151.
Hedges, R. E. M., and M. McLellan
 1976 On the cation exchange capacity of fired clays and its effect on the chemical and radiometric analysis of pottery. *Archaeometry* **18**:203–206.
Hodder, I.
 1980 Trade and exchange: definitions, identification and function. In *Models and*

methods in regional exchange, edited by R. E. Fry, pp. 151–156. Society for American Archaeology, *SAA Papers 1.*

Inman, D. L.
1949   Sorting of sediments in the light of fluid mechanics. *Journal of Sedimentary Petrology* **19**:51–70.

Isphording, W. C.
1974   Combined thermal and X-ray diffraction technique for identification of ceramic-ware temper and paste minerals. *American Antiquity* **39**:477–483.

Jackson, M. L.
1959   Frequency distribution of clay minerals in major great soil groups as related to the factors of soil formation. *Clay Minerals, Proceedings of the National Conference on Clays and Clay Minerals* **6**:133–143.

Judd, N. M.
1954   The material culture of Pueblo Bonito. *Smithsonian Miscellaneous Collections* (Vol. 124). Washington, D.C.

Judge, W. J.
1979   The development of a complex cultural ecosystem in the Chaco Basin, New Mexico. In *Proceedings of the First Conference on Scientific Research in the National Parks* 2, edited by R. L. Linn, pp. 901–905. National Park Service Transactions and Proceedings Series 5.

Kamilli, D. C., and C. C. Lamberg-Karlovsky
1979   Petrographic and electron microprobe analysis of ceramics from Tepe Yahya, Iran. *Archaeometry* **21**:47–59.

Kelly, I., and A. Palerm
1952   The Tajín Totonac. *Smithsonian Institution, Institute of Social Anthropology, Publication 13.* Washington, D.C.

Kerr, P. F.
1959   *Optical mineralogy.* New York: McGraw-Hill.

Klovan, J. E.
1975   R- and Q-mode factor analysis. In *Concepts in geostatistics,* edited by R. B. McCammon. New York: Springer-Verlag. Pp. 21–69.

Klovan, J. E., and J. Imbrie
1971   An algorithm and FORTRAN-IV program for large scale Q-mode factor analyses and calculation of factor scores. *Mathematical Geology* **3**:61–67.

Krinsley, D., and J. Donahue
1968   Environmental interpretation of sand grain surface texture by electron microscopy. *Geological Society of America Bulletin* **79**:743–748.

Kruger, P.
1971   *Principles of activation analysis.* New York: Wiley.

Kullerud, G., R. M. Steffen, P. C. Simms, and F. A. Rickey
1979   Proton induced x-ray emission (PIXE)—a new tool in geochemistry. *Chemical Geology* **25**:245–256.

Loose, R. W.
1977   Petrographic notes on selected lithic and ceramic materials. In *Settlement and subsistence along the lower Chaco River: the CGP survey,* edited by C. A. Reher. Albuquerque: University of New Mexico Press. Pp. 567–572.

Matson, F. R.
1965   Ceramic ecology: an approach to the study of the early cultures of the Near East. In *Ceramics and man,* edited by F. R. Matson, Viking Fund Publications in Anthropology 41. Chicago: Aldine. Pp. 202–217.

1971 A study of temperatures used in firing ancient Mesopotamian pottery. In *Science and archaeology,* edited by R. H. Brill. Cambridge: MIT Press. Pp. 65–79.

Meschel, S. V.
1978 Chemistry and archaeology: a creative bond. In *Archaeological chemistry II,* edited by G. F. Carter. Advances in Chemistry Series 171. Washington, D.C.: The American Chemical Society. Pp. 1–24.

Nicklin, K.
1971 Stability and innovation in pottery manufacture. *World Archaeology* **3**:13–48, 94–104.
1979 The location of pottery manufacture. *Man* **14**:436–458.

Nie, N. H., C. H. Hull, J. G. Jenkins, K. Steinbrenner, and D. H. Bent
1975 *SPSS statistical package for the social sciences.* New York: McGraw-Hill.

Ogan, E.
1970 Nasioi pottery-making. *Journal of the Polynesian Society* **79**:86–90.

Olin, J., and E. V. Sayre
1971 Compositional categories of some English and American pottery of the American colonial period. In *Science and archaeology,* edited by R. H. Brill. Cambridge: MIT Press. Pp. 196–209.

Peacock, D. P. S.
1967 The heavy mineral analysis of pottery: a preliminary report. *Archaeometry* **10**:97–100.
1977 Ceramics in Roman and medieval archaeology. In *Pottery and early commerce,* edited by D. P. S. Peacock. New York: Academic Press. Pp. 21–33.

Perlman, I., and F. Asaro
1969 Pottery analysis by neutron activation. *Archaeometry* **11**:21–53.
1971 Pottery analysis by neutron activation. In *Science and archaeology,* edited by R. H. Brill. Cambridge: MIT Press. Pp. 55–64.

Picon, M., M. Vichy, and E. Meille
1971 Composition of the Lezoux, Lyons and Arezzo Samian ware. *Archaeometry* **13**:191–208.

Plog, F.
1977 Modeling economic exchange. In *Exchange systems in prehistory,* edited by T. K. Earle and J. E. Ericson. New York: Academic Press. Pp. 127–140.

Plog, S.
1980 *Stylistic variation in prehistoric ceramics: design analysis in the American Southwest.* Cambridge: Cambridge University Press.

Poole, A. B., and L. R. Finch
1972 The utilization of trace chemical composition to correlate British post-medieval pottery with European kiln site materials. *Archaeometry* **14**:79–91.

Prag, A. J. N. W., F. Schweizer, J. L. L. Williams, and P. A. Schubiger
1974 Hellenistic glazed wares from Athens and Southern Italy: analytical techniques and implications. *Archaeometry* **16**:154–187.

Rands, R. L.
1967 Ceramic technology and trade in the Palenque region, Mexico. In *American historical anthropology: essays in honor of Leslie Spier,* edited by C. L. Riley and W. W. Taylor. Carbondale: Southern Illinois University Press. Pp. 137–152.
1969 Mayan ecology and trade: 1967–1968. *Mesoamerican Studies, University Museum,* Southern Illinois University, Carbondale.
1974 The ceramic sequence at Palenque, Chiapas. In *Mesoamerican archaeology: new approaches,* edited by N. Hammond. London: Duckworth. Pp. 51–76.
1979 Comparative data from the Palenque zone on Maya civilization. *Actes du XLII Congrès International des Américanistes Vol. 8:*135–146.

Rands, R. L., and R. L. Bishop
    1980   Resource procurement zones and patterns of ceramic exchange in the Palenque region, Mexico. In *Models and methods in regional exchange,* edited by R. E. Fry. Society for American Archaeology. *SAA Papers* 1. Pp. 19–46.

Rands, R. L., R. L. Bishop, and J. A. Sabloff
    1982   Maya fine paste ceramics: an archaeological perspective. In *Analyses of fine paste ceramics,* edited by J. A. Sabloff. *Memoirs of the Peabody Museum of Archaeology and Ethnology,* Vol. 15, No. 2. Cambridge.

Rathje, W. L., D. A. Gregory, and F. M. Wiseman
    1978   Trade models and archaeological problems: Classic Maya examples. In *Mesoamerican communication routes and cultural contacts,* edited by T. A. Lee, Jr. and C. Navarrete, pp. 147–176. *Papers of the New World Archaeological Foundation* No. 40. Provo.

Renfrew, C.
    1977   Alternative models for exchange and spatial distribution. In *Exchange systems in prehistory,* edited by T. K. Earle and J. E. Ericson. New York: Academic Press. Pp. 71–90.

Rice, P. M.
    1974   Comment on Weymouth's X-ray diffraction analysis of prehistoric pottery. *American Antiquity* 39:619–620.
    1976   Rethinking the ware concept. *American Antiquity* 41:538–543.
    1978a   Ceramic continuity and change in the Valley of Guatemala: a technological analysis. In *The ceramics of Kaminaljuyu, Guatemala,* edited by R. K. Wetherington. University Park: The Pennsylvania State University Press. Pp. 401–510.
    1978b   Clear answers to vague questions: some assumptions of provenience studies of pottery. In *The ceramics of Kaminaljuyu, Guatemala,* edited by R. K. Wetherington. University Park: The Pennsylvania State University. Pp. 511–542.

Rogers, M. W.
    1936   Yuman pottery making. *San Diego Museum Papers* 2. San Diego.

Rohlf, F. J.
    1970   Adaptive hierarchical clustering schemes. *Systematic Zoology* 19:58–82.

Rohlf, F. J., J. Kishpaugh, and D. Kirk
    1971   *NT-SYS Numerical Taxonomy System of Multivariate Statistical Programs.* State University of New York at Stony Brook.

Roper, D. C.
    1979   The method and theory of site catchment analysis: a review. In *Advances in archaeological method and theory* (Vol. 2), edited by M. B. Schiffer. New York: Academic Press. Pp. 119–140.

Rovner, I.
    1971   Potential of opal phytoliths for use in paleoecological reconstruction. *Quaternary Research* 1:343–359.

Rubin, J., and H. P. Friedman
    1967   *A cluster analysis and taxonomy system for grouping and classifying data.* I.B.M., Scientific Center, New York.

Rye, O. S.
    1976   Keeping your temper under control: materials and manufacture of Papuan pottery. *Archaeology & Physical Anthropology in Oceania* 11:106–137.
    1981   *Pottery technology: principles and reconstruction.* Manuals on Archaeology 4. Taraxacum, Washington, D.C.

Rye, O. S., and C. Evans
    1976   Traditional pottery techniques of Pakistan. *Smithsonian Contributions to Anthropology No.* 21. Washington, D.C.

Sabloff, J. A.
  1973   Continuity and disruption during Terminal Late Classic times at Seibal: ceramic and other evidence. In *The Classic Maya collapse,* edited by T. P. Culbert. Albuquerque: University of New Mexico Press. Pp. 107–132.
Sabloff, J. A., and R. E. Smith
  1972   Ceramic wares in the Maya area: a clarification of an aspect of the type-variety system and presentation of a formal model for comparative use. *Estudios de Cultura Maya* **8**:97–115.
Sabloff, J. A., and G. R. Willey
  1967   The collapse of Maya civilization in the Southern Lowlands: a consideration of history and process. *Southwestern Journal of Anthropology* **23**:311–336.
Sayre, E. V.
  n.d.   Brookhaven procedures for statistical analysis of multivariate archaeometric data. In *Proceedings of the conference on the application of physical sciences to Medieval ceramics,* edited by J. D. Friedman and F. Asaro. Lawrence Berkeley Laboratory, Berkeley.
Sayre, E. V., L.-H. Chan, and J. A. Sabloff
  1971   High-resolution gamma ray spectroscopic analyses of Fine Orange pottery. In *Science and archaeology,* edited by R. H. Brill. Cambridge: MIT Press. Pp. 165–181.
Sayre, E. V., A. Murrenhoff, and C. F. Weick
  1958   The non-destructive analysis of ancient potsherds through neutron activation. *Brookhaven National Laboratory Report No. 508.* Upton.
Schneider, G., B. Hoffmann, and E. Wirz
  1979   Significance and dependability of reference groups for chemical determinations of provenience of ceramic artifacts. In Proceedings of the 18th international symposium on archaeometry and archaeological prospection. *Archaeo-Physika* **10**:269–285. Rheinisches Landesmuseum, Bonn.
Shepard, A. O.
  1939   Technology of La Plata pottery. In *Archaeological studies in the La Plata District,* by E. H. Morris, pp. 249–287. *Carnegie Institution of Washington, Publication* 519, Washington, D.C.
  1942   Rio Grande glaze paint ware, a study illustrating the place of ceramic technological analyses in archaeological research. *Carnegie Institution of Washington, Publication* 528, *Contribution* 39, Washington, D.C.
  1948   Plumbate, a Mesoamerican trade ware. *Carnegie Institution of Washington, Publication* 573, Washington, D.C.
  1963   Beginnings of ceramic industrialization: an example from the Oaxaca Valley. *Notes from a ceramic laboratory,* pp. 1–24. Carnegie Institution of Washington, Washington, D.C.
  1965   Rio Grande glaze-paint pottery: a test of petrographic analysis. In *Ceramics and man,* edited by F. R. Matson. Viking Fund Publications in Anthropology, No. 41. Chicago: Aldine. Pp. 62–87.
  1968   Ceramics for the archaeologist. *Carnegie Institution of Washington, Publication* 609, (fifth ed.). Washington, D.C.
  1971   Ceramic analysis: the interrelations of methods; the relations of analysts and archaeologist. In *Science and archaeology,* edited by R. H. Brill. Cambridge: MIT Press. Pp. 55–64.
Shepard, A. O., and H. B. Gottlieb
  1962   Maya blue: alternative hypotheses. *Notes from a ceramic laboratory,* pp. 43–64. Carnegie Institution of Washington, Washington, D.C.

Shepard, A. O., and H. E. D. Pollock
    1971   Maya blue: an updated record. *Notes from a ceramic laboratory,* pp. 65–100. Carnegie Institution of Washington, Washington, D.C.

Slatt, R. M.
    1974   Geochemistry of bottom sediments, Conception Bay, Southeastern Newfoundland. *Canadian Journal of Earth Science* 11:768–784.

Slatt, R. M., and D. R. Sasseville
    1976   Trace-element geochemistry of detrital sediments from Newfoundland inlets and the adjacent continental margin: application to provenance studies, mineral exploration, and Quaternary marine stratigraphy. *Canadian Mineralogist* 14:3–15.

Slavin, W.
    1968   *Atomic absorption spectroscopy.* New York: Wiley.

Smith, W.
    1971   Painted ceramics of the western mound at Awatovi. *Papers of the Peabody Museum of Archaeology and Ethnology* 38. Cambridge.

Stern, W. B., and J.-P. Descoeudres
    1977   X-ray fluorescence analysis of archaic Greek pottery. *Archaeometry* 19:73–85.

Stone, D.
    1950   Notes on present-day pottery making and its economy in the ancient Chorotegan area. *Tulane University Middle American Research Institute Publication* 15, *Middle American Research Records* Vol. 1, No. 16:269–280. New Orleans.

Taylor, P.
    1933   Making *cántaros* at San José Tateposco, Jalisco, Mexico. *American Anthropologist* 35:745–751.

Tite, M. S.
    1972   *Methods of physical examination in archaeology.* New York: Seminar Press.

Toll, H. W., T. C. Windes, and P. J. McKenna
    1980   Late ceramic patterns in Chaco Canyon: the pragmatics of modeling ceramic exchange. In *Models and methods in regional exchange,* edited by R. E. Fry, pp. 95–118. Society for American Archaeology, *SAA Papers* No. 1.

Tourtellot, G., and J. A. Sabloff
    1972   Exchange systems among the ancient Maya. *American Antiquity* 37:126–135.

Tubb, A., A. J. Parker, and G. Nickles
    1980   The analysis of Romano-British pottery by atomic absorption spectrophotometry. *Archaeometry* 22:153–171.

Van Loon, J. C.
    1980   Direct trace element analysis of solids by atomic (absorption, fluorescence, and emission) spectrometry. *Analytical Chemistry* 52:955A–963A.

Vita-Finzi, C., and E. S. Higgs
    1970   Prehistoric economy in the Mount Carmel area of Palestine: site catchment analysis. *Proceedings of the Prehistoric Society* 36:1–37.

Voyatzoglou, M.
    1974   The jar makers of Thrapsano in Crete. *Expedition* 16:18–24.

Warren, A. H.
    1967   Petrographic analysis of pottery and lithics. In An archaeological survey of the Chuska Valley and Chaco Plateau, New Mexico, by A. H. Harris, J. Schoenwetter, and A. H. Warren. *Museum of New Mexico Research Records* No. 4, Santa Fe.
    1968   Petrographic notes on glaze-paint pottery. In the Cochiti Dam archaeological salvage project. *Museum of New Mexico Research Records* No. 6, Santa Fe.

1969   Tonque: one pueblo's glaze pottery industry dominated Middle Rio Grande commerce. *El Palacio* **76**:36–42.

Weigand, P. C., G. Harbottle, and E. V. Sayre
1977   Turquoise sources and source analysis: Mesoamerica and the Southwestern U.S.A. In *Exchange systems in prehistory,* edited by T. K. Earle and J. E. Ericson. New York: Academic Press. Pp. 15–34.

West, R. C.
1966   The natural vegetation of the Tabasco lowlands, Mexico. *Revista Geográfica* **64**:107–122.

Weymouth, J. W.
1973   X-ray diffraction analysis of prehistoric pottery. *American Antiquity* **38**:339–344.

Widemann, F., M. Picon, F. Asaro, H. V. Michel, and I. Perlman
1975   A Lyons branch of the pottery-making firm of Ateius of Arezzo. *Archaeometry* **17**:45–59.

Williams, D. F.
1977   The Romano-British black-burnished industry: an essay on characterization by heavy mineral analysis. In *Pottery and early commerce,* edited by D. P. S. Peacock. New York: Academic Press. Pp. 163–220.

Wilson, A. L.
1978   Elemental analysis of pottery in the study of its provenance: a review. *Journal of Archaeological Science* **5**:219–236.

Windes, T. C.
1977   Typology and technology of Anasazi ceramics. In *Settlement and subsistence along the lower Chaco River,* edited by C. A. Reher. Albuquerque: University of New Mexico Press. Pp. 279–370.

Winther-Nielsen, M., K. Conradsen, K. Heydorn, and V. Mejdhal
1981   Investigation of the number of elements required for provenance studies of ceramic materials. In *Scientific studies in ancient ceramics,* edited by M. J. Hughes. *British Museum Occasional Paper* **19**:85–92.

Wishart, D.
1978   *Clustan user manual. Version 1C, Release 2.* Edinburgh University.

Wyndham, F.
1971   Potter's methods in Ceylon. *Pottery in Australia* **10**:39–41.

8

Archaeofaunas
and Subsistence Studies

R. LEE LYMAN

With the present focus in archaeology on adaptational and settlement–subsistence systems, the study of human subsistence as evidenced by biological remains is becoming a common endeavor (e.g., Cook 1975; Munson *et al.* 1971; Parmalee *et al.* 1972; Shawcross 1972; Smith 1974a, 1975a). Subsistence systems involve at a minimum the interaction of humans, technology, and floral and faunal resources. The study of these interactions through time and across space provides a description and an understanding of prehistoric ways of life.

This chapter explores the theoretical underpinnings of and analytic techniques used in studies of prehistoric subsistence practices. The discussion is restricted to faunal remains recovered from archaeological sites, but also applies in many cases to botanical remains. Evaluations of some basic theoretical and methodological issues underlying subsistence studies are made, and suggestions are offered that, if adopted, should lead to improvement in the validity of subsistence studies. These considerations have two basic functions: (*a*) to illustrate the "state of the art" to archaeologists who wish to discuss resource exploitation, subsistence, adaptational strategies, and the evolution of culture as an adaptive mechanism (e.g., Dunnell 1980; Kirch 1980), and (*b*) to synthesize much of the recent research on archaeofaunal analysis from a single, unifying perspective and thereby provide a starting point for detailed analyses of animal remains recovered from archaeological sites.

ADVANCES IN ARCHAEOLOGICAL METHOD AND THEORY, VOL. 5

I begin by defining some basic terms and concepts that are necessary to the discussion. The particular goals of faunal analysis are outlined, followed by a more detailed examination of subsistence analysis. Next, an in-depth evaluation of the theoretical perspective requisite to subsistence analysis is presented. This is followed by a consideration of six basic methodological issues. Finally, several subsistence analyses are briefly reviewed and the theoretical and methodological implications are summarized along with recommendations for improving subsistence analysis.

BACKGROUND

> The interpretation of archaeological faunal remains is usually directed towards
> . . . reconstruction of human activity patterns (Yesner 1978:338).

Terms and Concepts

Terms and concepts must be defined for discussion purposes. The definitions for particular terms are perhaps debatable, but much potential misunderstanding will be avoided if the semantics are clear from the outset.

A *fauna* is defined here as some predetermined set of animal taxa found in a geographic area of some predetermined size, kind, and location at some predetermined time. For example, there is a modern intertidal fauna of the Pacific Rim, a prehistoric terrestrial fauna of Europe, and a Pleistocene mammalian fauna of Colorado.

"Today we define *fossil* as the remains or trace of any organism that lived prior to recent time. The word *fossil* is derived from the Latin word *fossilis,* meaning 'dug up.' [But] by the late eighteenth century [*fossil* connoted] objects indicating the presence of prehistoric organisms" (Matthews 1962:1–2). Because the archaeological record includes not only Recent components, but Pleistocene (prerecent) components as well, fossil is defined for purposes of this chapter as any contemporary trace, remain, or part of an animal that died at some time in the past. The *fossil record* is that contemporary set of fossils *in situ* in some predetermined geographic and geologic space, such as the particular bones in a particular stratum found in the Southwest. A *fossil fauna* consists of those taxa represented by the fossil record at a given paleontological or archaeological site. A term that is nearly synonymous with fossil fauna is "local fauna" (Wilson 1974). I prefer the former because it serves to emphasize the distinction between a living fauna and a fauna represented by fossils.

The fossil record may be in a purely geologic context, or in a purely archaeological context. In the former case, there are no cultural materials associated with the fossils; these will be called *paleontological faunas*. In the latter case there are associated cultural materials; these fossils represent *archaeofaunas*. Paleontology is taken from the Greek words *palaios,* meaning ancient; *onta,* meaning existing things; and *logos,* meaning word or discourse. *Archaeo* is also derived from Greek and means ancient or primitive.

Although useful for discussion purposes, the distinction between paleontological faunas and archaeofaunas is not as clear-cut as it might first appear. To avoid ambiguity, the terms as they are used here are not meant to connote anything regarding the formation of the fossil records, but rather only the presence or absence of spatially associated artifacts with the fossils.

The analysis of fossils recovered from archaeological contexts has been called many things, the more common terms being archaeozoology, faunal analysis, osteoarchaeology, ethnozoology, paleoethnozoology, and zooarchaeology. Olsen and Olsen (1981) have made an attempt to define and evaluate these terms. On the basis of the Greek roots incorporated in the terms, they suggest that archaeozoology and paleozoology (and perhaps paleontology) are synonyms for "the study of ancient animals, without suggesting any association with humans or their culture" (Olsen and Olsen 1981:192). Osteoarchaeology is "the study of *bone* from archaeological collections" (Olsen and Olsen 1981:192). Ethnozoology "refers to the study of extant cultures and their relationships to the animals in their environment" (Olsen and Olsen 1981:193). Zooarchaeology is the term proposed "to describe the entire discipline of faunal studies in archaeology," admittedly "perhaps [because of Olsen and Olsen's] preference for emphasizing the importance for the cultural role of fauna" (Olsen and Olsen 1981:193). I shall use a slightly different nomenclature than Olsen and Olsen (1981), and note that my usage of faunal analysis nomenclature is for discussion purposes only.

Analysis of Archaeofaunas

> Often ten pages are devoted to the minutiae of pottery temper, paste, and so on, while one page or less describes subsistence and the relationship of the culture to the geographical environment (Steward and Seltzer 1938:7).

Analyses of archaeofaunas have been undertaken since the late nineteenth century in North America (Robison 1978). Although once scarcely more than a subsidiary endeavor, archaeological site reports now regularly contain a section on recovered fossils, often by a specialist, and many more independently published and in-depth studies of faunal remains are being prepared by specialists in zoology and archaeologists with zoological training (see Bogan and Robison 1978; Lyman 1979a). This reflects in part the holistic approach of archaeologists trying to understand and explain the human past (Schiffer 1978a, 1978b). Analysis of archaeofaunas is still in an infantile theoretical stage (Medlock 1975; Robison 1978). Most recent research efforts have focused on the development or testing of new analytic methods (Behrensmeyer 1978; Casteel 1976a; Hill 1979b; Yellen 1977) and on the evaluation of old methods (Binford 1978; Casteel 1977a, 1978; Grayson 1979b).

Within this subfield of archaeology, Smith (1976) contrasts two goals of fossil analysis: twitching, and ecology. *Twitching* involves the production of a list of taxa represented in an archaeofauna. Smith (1976:278, 283–284) contends that although these lists are of zoological interest, they are entirely descriptive and consequently prompt little interpretation or explanation and require very little in the way of "an explicitly scientific methodology." The actual construction of twitching lists requires following the taxonomic hierarchy of biology, the species concept, and the theory of evolution (Mayr 1970). Adherence to these principles generally results in a particular ordering in the list, commonly ascending complexity of anatomical structure (e.g., Gustafson 1972; Smith 1981), an arrangement that implicitly embodies the concepts of phylogeny and ontogeny (e.g., Hildebrand 1974).

The data represented by twitching lists can be interpreted using biogeographical theory, resulting in ecological or historical distributional interpretations (Ball 1975; Cox and Moore 1980; Grayson 1981a,d; Harris 1977; Langenwalter 1979; Platnick and Nelson 1978). These lists are sometimes interpreted as indications of which species were used as food (species in the list) and which were not (species not in the archaeological site but present in the habitat surrounding the site, such as those taxa found only in paleontological contexts) (e.g., Klein 1979). The lists may be ends in themselves, serving as gross descriptors of site contents to be compared to one another. There are several papers devoted to comparisons of twitching lists in the literature, mainly generated by paleontologists interested in comparing faunal community makeup or biogeography. Numerous analytic techniques have been developed for assuring that similarities and dissimilarities of two compared lists are statistically significant (see the review by Raup and Crick [1979]). That some of the uses of species lists involve analytic difficulties will become apparent in the following discussion.

The goal of ecology is to seek "to explain, in the form of predictive models, the interface that existed between prehistoric human populations and the faunal section of the biotic community" (Smith 1976:284; see also, 1974a). This goal of faunal analysis is anthropological in orientation because it addresses topics such as diet, procurement strategies, and predator–prey relationships. Because other analytic goals utilize ecological principles, I here refer to the ecological goal as the *subsistence* goal. This goal concerns the determination of human subsistence practices, and uses anthropological and ecological principles in analysis and interpretation.

A third goal (Lyman 1979b) is here termed *zooarchaeology* because goal attainment employs zoological data, methods, and theory to determine paleoenvironmental conditions (e.g., Casteel 1976a; Grayson 1976a, 1977b; Harris 1970). Zoological and ecological principles are paramount to answering questions of faunal turnover (Holbrook 1975, 1977), environment (Van Couvering 1980), and related issues.

The three goals do overlap in part. All three require taxonomic identification of the fossils, and analytic techniques such as quantification of the fossils may be similar. Interpretation generally requires use of ecological principles, such as predator–prey interactions and symbiosis, but the interpretive perspective is dictated by the research questions, which are in turn derived from the particular goal of analysis. The distinction between goals is useful to discuss, but is not mandatory in actual analysis because interpretation of a single archaeofauna may accomplish any two or all three goals (e.g., Gustafson 1972; King and Graham 1981; Scott 1977).

There is critical literature on twitching (Raup and Crick 1979; Smith 1976) and zooarchaeology (Findley 1964; Grayson 1981d; Redding 1978) but discussion of subsistence analysis to date has been limited largely to enumeration of analytic techniques (Chaplin 1971; Payne 1972; Smith 1976; Uerpmann 1973; Wing and Brown 1979). This deficiency will be remedied here.

Goals and Approaches of Subsistence Analysis

The study of subsistence practices seeks to ascertain how the people who originally deposited the fossils made a living in terms of animal-food subsistence. Questions often asked include: Which taxa were regularly eaten, which were rarely eaten, and which were never eaten? Which taxa contributed most to the diet? When were particular taxa hunted? How much food did different taxa provide? Were particular age groups or one sex of a taxon preferred over others? Did age, sex, or individual selection vary intertaxonomically? Where were food animals hunted and how were they hunted? Producing answers to these and similar questions constitutes attainment of analytic goals of subsistence studies.

The general approach to investigating subsistence patterns has been outlined by Gabel (1967) in a 20-page paper. Twelve years later, Wing and Brown (1979) produced a 200-page book on the subject. This tenfold increase in documentation is indicative of the increased interest in fossil analysis, and the increase in the number of approaches to subsistence questions. Some approaches are much more rigorous than others, but all entail certain traits. These include the need to distinguish culturally deposited bone from naturally deposited bone, to contend with sampling, to identify and quantify the fossils, and to interpret the data generated from the fossils. The analytic techniques used to deal with these traits and attain analytic goals will be discussed in later sections of this chapter. It should be pointed out here, however, that depending on the particular goals of a subsistence analysis, different analytic techniques may be employed to achieve similar results. For example, if an analyst is interested in determining the season that particular taxa were hunted, the fossils may be counted as individual specimens or individual animals (Lyman 1980c; Monks 1981). If determination of hunter selectivity is the analytic goal, the number of animals (Wilkinson 1976) or the represented biomass (Smith 1979) may be calculated. These different analytic techniques are seldom compared. The uninitiated and expert alike may have available a number of approaches to an analytic goal, but little basis for assessing which approach is best in a given situation, or even if there is a "best" technique for any situation. We as yet have no generally accepted compendium of approaches with which to compare techniques objectively. Perhaps the single exception is fossil quantification. Despite the large number of papers that evaluate quantification techniques (see references in Grayson [1979b] and Holtzman [1979]), many persist in using the old techniques with little regard for the problems that attend these methods. (e.g., Bayham 1979; Hastorf 1980).

As Medlock (1975) has pointed out, analytic techniques and approaches must be explicit if comparisons of two analyses are eventually to be possible. I would add that the analytic techniques must be comparable. Faunal analysis is *not* weak in the *number* of available analytic techniques but *is* weak in its ability to assess the reliability and validity of a particular analytic technique and the comparability of techniques. A later section of this chapter will examine in detail a number of analytic techniques, assess their respective validities and reliabilities, and suggest a way in which the incomparability of some analytic techniques may become a useful analytic and interpretive tool.

THEORETICAL ISSUES

> Although technological advancement is of the utmost importance, techniques alone neither state nor solve problems. Techniques are tools [and] may be perfected only with reference to their purpose (Steward and Seltzer 1938:5–6).

Subsistence studies, by the nature of their research questions, require knowledge of the formation of the archaeofaunal record (Lyman 1978a). Comparable knowledge is paramount to studies of paleontological faunas, but for different reasons (Behrensmeyer and Hill 1980b; Gifford 1981). Subsistence studies require that the fossils constituting the archaeofauna be sorted into at least two categories: fossils deposited as a result of human behaviors (subsistence), and naturally deposited fossils (Thomas 1971). The cultural fossils must be qualitatively and quantitatively representative of the fauna exploited, and quantification techniques must produce accurate relative abundances of economically important taxa. Because the goals of zooarchaeology, are different from those of subsistence studies, representative samples of *exploited* fauna are not required, but representative samples of the prehistorically *extant* fauna are. The exploited and extant faunas need not be comparable because humans probably selected only certain taxa and in different proportions than naturally available. Although these requirements are flexible in the sense that they have certain tolerance limits (e.g., a bison kill site probably does not include all the taxa exploited by a group of people, and a zooarchaeologist may focus only on the microfauna and ignore the large taxa in an archaeofauna), they do indicate the importance of controlling the formation of the fossil record. Sample representativeness may be controlled not only by recovery of the fossil record (Meadow 1981), but by formation of it as well (Collins 1975).

The study of the formation of the fossil record is called *taphonomy* (Efremov 1940). Gifford (1981) distinguishes two basic goals of taphonomic analysis: (*a*) "stripping away" the taphonomic overprint (or biases) from the fossil record to obtain accurate resolution of the prehistoric living fauna, and (*b*) determining the nature of the taphonomic overprint in order to be able to list the precise taphonomic mechanisms responsible for a given fossil assemblage and thus to be able to write taphonomic histories. The latter goal is similar to recent studies of the formation of the archaeological record (Schiffer 1976). The former goal is seen as a necessary step towards many paleontological and zooarchaeological goals because the target of analysis requires some knowledge of the prehistoric living fauna. But taphonomists are as yet unsure of the possibility of ever being able to completely strip away taphonomic overprinting, and are beginning to suggest that research might be better directed toward determining what kinds of questions can be asked directly of the fossil record and to be less concerned with faunas reconstituted from the fossil record (Behrensmeyer and Hill 1980a; Gifford 1981; Lawrence 1971).

The second goal of taphonomy, determination of the exact taphonomic mechanisms responsible for a fossil assemblage, is more frequently sought by archaeologists, particularly those interested in subsistence, than by paleontologists or zooarchaeologists due to the difference in the analytic goals of these disciplines. This becomes clear when the definition of taphonomy is considered. *Taphonomy* is a geobiological historical method of study of the transition, in all details, of animal organics from the biosphere into the lithosphere; it is the science of the laws of burial (Efremov 1940:93). The Greek roots are *taphos,* meaning entombment or burial, and *nomos,* meaning law. Descriptions such as Wheat's (1967, 1972) for the butchery process at the

Olsen–Chubbuck bison kill site are simply narrative models of taphonomic histories. Taphonomists seek an answer to the question "What are these bones doing here?" (Shipman 1979) whereas archaeologists want an answer to the question "What purposeful human behavior produced a given bone assemblage?" (Gilbert 1973:7). The questions are identical.

The two goals of taphonomic research are not mutually exclusive. To strip away the taphonomic overprint, it must be known. Once the taphonomic overprint is known, the prehistoric living fauna is readily determined by simply reversing the effects of the taphonomic mechanisms and tracing the taphonomic history back through time.

Taphonomy and Subsistence Analysis

Taphonomy is concerned with the differences and similarities between the fossil record and the prehistoric living fauna from which the fossil record derived. At a general level, differences are temporal and the presence–absence of animateness. Taphonomy concerns the differences and similarities between living faunas and fossil records in terms of relative taxonomic abundances, demographics of age, sex, and taxonomy, degree of representation of individual animals, anatomical integrity, taxonomic spatial relationships to habitats, etc. Because of the general differences, certain kinds of analysis are difficult. For example ecological and ethological studies of extinct taxa are impossible in the detail that living taxa are studied. Even those fossil taxa with living counterparts are not so easily dealt with because of difficulties in studying living taxa (Coe 1980).

Taphonomic differences and similarities also present analytic challenges. A fossil record generally represents a once living fauna that has been disarticulated, dispersed, and fragmented, and is only partially represented. Because paleoecological analysis employs principles used to study living faunas (Coe 1980; Van Couvering 1980; Western 1980), to answer many research questions the fossil record must be reconstituted into a fossil fauna at least, and perhaps into the untaphonomically affected prehistorically living fauna. This reconstitution involves first recording the fossil record as *primary data,* that is, the loci, context, associations, and anatomical and taxonomic identification of individual fossils. Then, these primary data are converted into *secondary data* that are meaningful to ecological analysis, such as the numbers of individuals of taxa, the abundances of browsers and grazers, or the taxonomic composition of faunas in different strata (Klein 1980b; Van Couvering 1980; Vrba 1980). The differences and similarities between the fossil record and the prehistorically living fauna are seen as the taphonomic overprint, which must somehow be controlled or eliminated to allow analysis and interpretation to proceed.

Subsistence studies face similar analytic challenges. Taphonomic differences and similarities occur between the fossil record and the prehistorically living fauna. However, because prehistoric humans did not sample the living fauna in the same manner that nature did, two levels of differences and similarities are detectable. First, it is likely that humans selectively killed members of an available fauna, whereas natural causes result in the eventual deaths of all individual constituents of a fauna. A consequence of this differential selection is differing potentials for accumulation of fossils in paleontological and archaeological contexts. Second, because the natural death of animals is not exclusive to paleontological contexts and may occur in archaeological contexts, both types of contexts have the potential for complete representation of the available fauna, both qualitatively (all available taxa) and quantitatively (fossil taxa proportions equaling that of faunal taxa proportions). Therefore, the analyst interested in human subsistence practices must determine which components of the archaeofauna represent natural deaths and which components represent culturally selected deaths. This is known as the "cultural versus natural bone" issue (Thomas 1971), and may be the most crucial issue in subsistence studies. This issue will be addressed in detail in the next section of this chapter.

The importance of taphonomy to zooarchaeology and subsistence studies is the concern for differences and similarities between the fossil record and the target of analysis—some sort of reconstituted fauna. How a fossil assemblage is accumulated is by definition taphonomic and may include catastrophic mortality, either artificial (e.g., Frison 1974) or natural (e.g., Voorhies 1969), which may preserve the demographic integrity of the living fauna much better than does attritional mortality. Taphonomy concerns burial processes, and anastrophic (catastrophic) burial (Kranz 1974) may preserve anatomical integrity, whereas slow burial such as that caused by butchery, transport, and storage (e.g., Binford 1978) may result in virtually no anatomical integrity (cf. Hill 1979a,b, 1980).

Following the definition of taphonomy and the considerations just mentioned, taphonomy can be conceived of as a necessary concept underlying the analysis of fossils. Every fossil record has a taphonomic history, that is, a formational history. These taphonomic histories are unique for each fossil record. Further, a particular fossil record may be biased in regards to a particular research question but not to others due to the taphonomic implications of the research questions and the taphonomic history of the particular fossil assemblage.

Many models of taphonomic histories have been published (see references in Gifford 1981), all of which entail certain elements. These include (*a*) mode of death (attritional versus catastrophic), (*b*) transport or dispersal (fluvial versus human versus ?), (*c*) accumulation (raptors versus carnivores versus humans), (*d*) disarticulation (butchery versus decomposition), (*e*) fragmenta-tion (marrow fracturing versus carnivores), (*f*) burial mode (anastrophic ver-sus slow), and (*g*) chemical alteration (fossilization, mineralization, petrifica-tion, erosion, weathering, etc.). It is apparent that humans are the major taphonomic agent involved in the formation of the archaeofaunal record, and this is called the "cultural filter" (Daly 1969). In most cases other (natural) agents are involved in forming the archaeofaunal record but perhaps to generally lesser degrees than the human agent (cf. Briuer 1977). Zooar-chaeological analyses must control for potential bias resulting from the cultural filter, whereas subsistence analyses must control for natural faunal deaths and determine what cultural filter is involved for a given archaeo-fauna.

Strategies and Logistics of Analysis

Although analysts have become more aware of the potential interpretive problems inherent in biased samples, the biases and consequently the inter-pretive problems may or may not be systematically dealt with by the analyst. Potential biases may be ignored (Klein 1980b; Van Couvering 1980), or ef-forts may be made to control or eliminate biases (Behrensmeyer 1975; Guil-day *et al.* 1978; Klein 1980a; Voorhies 1969). These two approaches to taphonomic considerations have been formalized by Medlock (1975), who outlined a simplified model of analysis and a model of analysis that incor-porates relevant taphonomic variables. In the first model, taphonomic biases are ignored. Interpretations may include inferences regarding the particular effects of the cultural filter, but other aspects of the fossil assemblage's taphonomic history are seldom dealt with in detail. For instance, the absence of particular skeletal elements are often attributed to butchery practices, such as having been left at the kill site (Perkins and Daly 1968) or having been broken beyond recognition during marrow fracturing (Noe-Nygaard 1977). Alternatively, absence of skeletal elements may be attributed to their use for tool manufacture and subsequent curation (Stein 1963). Binford (1978) has discussed in some detail the problems with such ad hoc arguments, pointing out that little systematic development or use of criteria for recognition of par-ticular human behaviors is apparent in the faunal analysis literature.

Medlock's (1975) second model of faunal analysis merely combines his simplified model with a model of taphonomic histories. Noting that the more complex the analytic model (i.e., the greater the number of included variables), the better the approximation of reality, Medlock (1975:226) sug-gests four methods to operationalize the relevant variable model: (*a*) im-proved techniques of analysis, (*b*) experimentation, (*c*) analogy, and (*d*) simulation research on the variables and their effects. The first method can only have a positive result if the relevant variables are understood, and this understanding derives from the other three methods. For example, determining which quantification technique (Grayson 1979b; Holtzman 1979) actually provides the most reliable and valid measure of taxonomic abundances requires knowledge of the taphonomic processes that control the integrity of the particular counting units.

Research to operationalize the relevant variable model has consequently focused largely on the last three methods, and has been termed an "actualistic" approach to taphonomy (Gifford 1981). Uniformitarianism denotes approaches that explain the past by reference to modern causes acting with the same intensity in the past as in the present, whereas actualism denotes "approaches in which past events are interpreted by analogy with processes observable in the modern world. . . . Actualistic approaches see causes of past geologic change as differing in energy but not [in] kind, or as differing neither in energy nor in kind, from those operating at present" (Grayson 1980:361). For taphonomists, actualism is a method of studying the past (cf. Hooykaas 1970). The actualistic method involves the observation of modern-day taphonomic histories as they occur and their resulting fossil records. Experimentation, ethnoarchaeology, and neotaphonomy (Hill 1978) are the common techniques of implementing the actualistic approach. Observations of empirical causes and effects are recorded and relationships of causes and effects are postulated.

Actualistic studies are now common in the literature (see references in Gifford 1981). Potential *signature criteria,* or archaeologically visible static phenomena indicative of particular prehistoric dynamics (Gould 1980) or particular taphonomic pathways and mechanisms are being developed and tested. Though quite rewarding in terms of providing cautionary tales (Gifford 1978), interpretive inspirations (Hill 1979a,b), and cost-efficient research techniques (Gifford 1980), these studies are as yet too new and too few in number to provide adequately tested signature criteria for most taphonomic mechanisms. Gifford (1981) argues, therefore, for an increased expenditure of research efforts and funds to exhaustively test potential signature criteria.

Although actualistic approaches are now quite fashionable, arguments have been published that question such approaches. Binford (1977) argues that the collection of actualistic data cannot result in scientific theories, but only in empirical generalizations. Willer and Willer (1973) argue that science uses laws and theories that are logically correct, whereas actualistic approaches are concerned with constructing empirical generalizations. Empirical generalizations are derived from commonly observed relationships between particular causes (taphonomic mechanisms) and particular effects (fossil signature criteria). Generalizations are "tested" by accumulating more and more cases of the observed relationship between a particular cause and a particular effect. When a contradictory case is encountered, that is, when a particular observed cause has an unusual observed effect, the generalization need not be discarded, but rather assigned a probability.

For example, it was originally believed that humans alone caused spiral fractures, because one could observe humans breaking bones (cause), and the bones humans broke were spirally fractured (effect) (Bonnichsen 1973; Dart 1957). But when it was realized that other agents such as carnivores could also cause spiral fractures (Haynes 1980; Myers *et al.* 1980), ad hoc arguments were appended to the empirical generalization resulting in an intuitively probabilistic generalization such as, "the larger the spirally fractured bone, the more likely humans broke the bone" (Morlan 1980).

Use of ad hoc arguments, particularly those phrased in probabilistic terms, results in retention of the empirical generalization as an explanatory hypothesis. It has been argued (Willer and Willer 1973) that because probabilities are generalizations, they cannot explain particular cases. However, if the population parameters of the variable are known, then the probability of a correct explanation can be calculated (Thomas 1976). We are as yet incapable of such explanations due to the paucity of data from which descriptive statistics, let alone population parameters, may be calculated.

Another reason for not using empirical generalizations is the argument that use of signature criteria that are not exhaustively tested may result in the fallacy of affirming the consequent (Hempel 1966). Finally, the use of nonexhaustively tested signature criteria does not allow for *equifinality,* "the property of allowing or having the same effect or result from different events" (Webster's Third International Unabridged Dictionary). Different taphonomic mechanisms may have identical signatures. This has only come to the attention of archaeologists since research interests turned to the formation of the archaeological record.

For example, Sullivan (1978:191) argues that the preeminent problem in archaeological methodology today is the determination of "how present-day properties of material remains are to be unambiguously partitioned according to the factors responsible for their production" and that "different formation processes can generate sites that have markedly similar properties." He suggests archaeology requires a theory of the formation of the archaeological record. Jochim (1979:99, 103) suggests that because "similar patterns of variable relationships can be produced by different underlying processes," and because "in most cases the archaeological materials available for measurement reflect only indirectly the variables sought," "archaeology might profit more at this stage from a systematic refutation of hypotheses than from the progressive accumulation of positive correlations" between archaeological data and interpretive models.

These points of view indicate that there is a dilemma in archaeology regarding how to deal with equifinality. Zoologists interested in the temporal and spatial distributions of taxa face a similar dilemma. Historical zoogeographers tend to favor one of two explanatory models, either (*a*) the vicariance model, in which taxon A is fragmented into at least two populations by the appearance of a barrier that precludes genetic exchange between the two populations and results in the evolution of population A1 into taxon B and population A2 into taxon C, or (*b*) the dispersal model, in which taxon A expands across a preexistant barrier and the two resultant populations subsequently evolve into taxa B and C (see Platnick and Nelson [1978] for a review of the two models). The observable results of the two historical processes are quite similar, and debate continues as to the viability of each model and as to which model is to be retained and which discarded (compare, e.g., Craw 1979 and McDowall 1978). Arguments against either model include equifinality, whereas arguments for either model include actualistic studies and polemic on how science works. Two solutions emerge however: (*a*) the question can be rephrased to a point where the historic mechanism or exact model responsible is a moot point, and/or (*b*) other, independent data sources can be used to corroborate the applicability of one or the other model in a particular case.

Gifford (1981) would solve the quandry of equifinality in archaeology by the completion of exhaustive testing of all potential signature criteria from which general principles and perhaps a theory of site formation or taphonomy could be derived. But how much is "exhaustive?" Is exhaustive testing in a literal sense possible (cf. Willer and Willer 1973), and is it necessary?

Regardless of one's theoretical and analytic perspective and research goals (compare, e.g., Gumerman and Phillips 1978 and Meltzer 1979, 1981 with Custer 1981 and Larson 1979), taphonomy must be addressed and Medlock's (1975) relevant variable model must be operationalized. The variables in the model are largely taphonomic and must be controlled and measured in a reliable and valid manner. *Reliability* "concerns the extent to which an experiment, test, or any measuring procedure yields the same results on repeated trials. [*Validity* concerns] the extent that [an indicator] measures what it purports to measure" (Carmines and Zeller 1979:11–12). For example, the length of a projectile point can be measured with dial calipers by one analyst and with a ruler by a second analyst. If the measurements are not significantly different, they are reliable. The measurement is valid if an index of projectile point size is desired. The type of stone from which the projectile point is made may not be a valid index of projectile point size even though some correlation between the size and mineralogy variables may exist.

Testing of signature criteria must focus on reliable and valid tests and measures of taphonomic mechanism effects. For example, many analysts can agree that a bone is spirally fractured (reliability), but the same analysts will argue about the agent of fracture (Bonnichsen 1979; Haynes 1980; Morlan 1980; Myers *et al.* 1980). The reliability–validity distinction must be considered in signature criteria testing. This plus mental, physical, and financial limitations as well as arguments of logic suggest that it will be many, many years before actualistic studies will provide the data necessary to taphonomic studies.

The ad hoc nature of most taphonomic studies, particularly those involving actualistic approaches, has resulted in very few general general principles and no theory of taphonomy (Olson 1980). Ad hoc results derive from equifinality and the "Black Box" approach of faunal analysts to taphonomy (Leach 1973). In the Black Box approach, we have some output fossil record Y, the creation mechanisms of which are signified by the Black Box (Figure 8.1). Paleoecologists are interested in the input fauna X, subsistence analysts are interested in X, the Black Box, the exploited portion of X, or some combination of these; and taphonomists are interested specifically in the Black Box. If X and Y are known, some correlation of the two may be observed, suggesting $Y = f(X)$. But as taphonomic data are accumulated, it becomes obvious that "in such circumstances we cannot infer with any confidence whatsoever what goes on inside the Black Box. There will ordinarily be an indefinitely large number of possible forms of mechanisms inside the Black Box that might produce the observed results" (Leach 1973:765). Statements on the structure and operation of the Black Box are inferences that are dependent on knowing both X and Y. Archaeologists only recover Y, and Y is all taphonomists have to work with, plus indirect data such as the geomorphic context of Y, etc. One could argue that certain taphonomic mechanisms might be eliminated from consideration when these indirect data suggest contrary mechanisms. For example, Dart's (1957) postulated osteodontokeratic culture has been questioned on the basis of natural weathering and carnivore attrition (Binford and Bertram 1977; Brain 1967, 1969; Shipman and Phillips-Conroy 1977). However, it is still unclear if the fossils in question are *totally* the result of hominid activity, carnivore activity, or natural weathering.

Because we may never know the exact taphonomic mechanism(s) responsible for a particular fossil record and thus be unable to strip away the complete

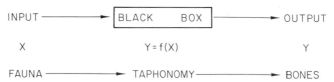

Figure 8.1.   The Black Box interpretive framework (after Leach 1973) compared to the taphonomy interpretive framework. (Reproduced with the permission of Gerald Duckworth & Co., Ltd., London.)

taphonomic overprint, some taphonomists are suggesting that research questions be rephrased to accommodate the limitations of the primary data of the fossil record (Behrensmeyer and Hill 1980a; Gifford 1981). Such an approach would not require exhaustive testing of all potential signature criteria and would circumvent arguments of equifinality and the fallacy of affirming the consequent. Not all archaeologists (Gifford 1981) agree completely with this approach, however.

It appears that three alternative approaches to the equifinality dilemma can be suggested

1. exhaustive actualistic studies leading to at least an operational relevant variable model,
2. alteration of research questions to accomodate the limitations of the fossil record, or
3. development of analytic techniques that control for what is known about taphonomic histories in general.

The first alternative is not yet available. Concerning the second alternative, actualistic studies will serve to define the limits of knowledge derivable from the fossil record and to suggest which questions can be most reasonably and realistically answered. Some general principles and approaches of the third alternative are outlined now and pursued in more detail in later sections of this chapter.

Controlling Taphonomic Histories in Subsistence Studies

It has been argued here that taphonomy defines the portions of the world with which subsistence studies must deal and the variables relevant to subsistence analysis. Realization that the fossil record has a taphonomic history that not only forms a vital part of subsistence analysis, but also may bias the fossil record leads to the conclusion that "efforts to fully understand prehistoric foodways are fraught with uncertainties. [But] insight into ways in which people have met their biological needs [seems possible]" (Wing and Brown 1979:10). Two basic yet interrelated issues must be dealt with. First, subsistence studies require examination of the fossil record. Second, the subsistence pursuits of people are entailed by their particular adaptation to an environment (Jochim 1979; Kirch 1980).

The first issue, examination of the fossil record, involves the concepts of taphonomy and formation of the archaeological record. Specifically, what are the appropriate archaeological units within which fossil data should be recorded? Subsistence analysts may certainly hope for a more specific conclusion than the "mean economic activities carried out during the whole period of accumulation of a deposit" (Uerpmann 1973:308). Such results may be unavoidable if the faunal analyst is not consulted prior to data recovery (Bonnichsen and Sanger 1977), and erroneous analytic assumptions such as "fossils are randomly distributed in a site" (Ziegler 1973) may be unavoidable as well.

Strata seem to be appropriate units for zooarchaeological endeavors because these natural units conform to some degree with the natural succession of faunas (Olson 1980). But they do produce "time-averaged" or asynchronic faunal units (Peterson 1977; Schindel 1980). Even if all other taphonomic factors are adjusted for, truly synchronic measures of species diversity and relative taxonomic abundances may be obscured, short-term fluctuations will be hidden (Peterson 1977), and the initiation and termination of change may be obscured. The resultant effect of asynchronic samples and units may be controlled in two ways. Fossil assemblages that are less asynchronic, such as single-instance catastrophic mortalities (Frison 1974; Kranz 1974; Voorhies 1969) may be sampled and compiled, but these are rare in time and space and will seldom allow production of local faunal histories (Schindel 1980). Alternatively, multiple sequences of asynchronous units over restricted geographic areas and long temporal spans may be compared for similar trends (Guilday *et al.* 1978). Although overall resolution may not be extremely detailed, general trends that may or may not have been identified in any single sequence may be apparent. If multiple sequences show similar trends, arguments of validity, as well as reliability, can be made because each sequence entails a different taphonomic history. Similar trends in parallel sequences would suggest that the particular taphonomic histories were not of sufficient effect to obscure all reflections of past faunal change, thus allowing arguments of validity (Grayson 1981c). Such control for taphonomy is permitted because the prehistorically extant fauna is the analytic unit that zooarchaeologists monitor.

Because subsistence analysts desire more detail than average economies, strata seem less appropriate than artificial units such as occupation surfaces or features such as rooms, house floors, or trash pits. Although also asynchronic to some degree, these artificial units may in many cases be much more synchronic than strata. Determination of the synchrony of occupation features falls within the realm of studies on the formation of the archaeological record.

Within this same realm, the subsistence analyst must consider which is the most appropriate horizontal unit. The finer the unit scale the more potential for greater resolution of such things as carcass utilization and other subsistence-related practices (Frison 1974; Lyman 1976, 1980b; Meadow 1978). But too fine a unit, such as a 2 × 2-m horizontal excavation unit, would split the fossil record into potentially meaningless sets of fossils. Taphonomy not only concerns what kinds and frequencies of fossils occur, but where they occur. Appropriate, fine-scale units, dictated by the questions being asked, are required for high resolution of taphonomic causes and effects. In some cases, such as synchronic mass-kill sites, the appropriate unit scale is site or stratum. In other cases, such as habitation or camp–village sites, the occupation feature may be more appropriate. Of course, some sites may require use of larger than desireable units due to poor visibility of site formation details.

Although comparison of faunal sequences and assemblages through time and across space will control for potential taphonomic biasing of faunal succession or paleoenvironmental data, such comparisons will not control for taphonomic biasing of subsistence data. This is because part of what subsistence analysts monitor is the cultural filter—the human accumulation of fossil materials. The cultural filter is not something to be controlled; rather, its nature is to be determined. This leads to the second issue, subsistence as part of an adaptational strategy. Control of taphonomic biasing need not derive from the fossils in this case; rather it may derive from the archaeological and paleontological records.

Because zooarchaeological and subsistence studies are so closely related through taphonomy, they must be dealt with simultaneously. For example, is a temporal change in the composition of the archaeofaunal fossil record due to cultural–subsistence-related factors, natural–zooarchaeology-related factors, or both? Klein (1980a) has suggested that temporal change in the fauna, either qualitative or quantitative, can be attributed to natural or environmental causes if

1. other environmental data such as pollen suggest environmental change,
2. there is no evidence of change in artifact assemblages,
3. intervals between faunal changes amount to thousands of years, and
4. changes are repetitive and cyclical.

The converse of these criteria would suggest faunal change was a result of cultural–adaptational change. But the third criterion is not an accurate assessment of all faunal turnover rates (Holbrook 1975, 1977; Van Couvering 1980), and the fourth criterion is not an accurate rendition of environmental change. Faunal change may occur seasonally, such as with migratory waterfowl (Grayson 1976a,b), anadromous fish (Schalk 1977), or migratory animals (Burch 1972). Changes may occur over a few years, such as cyclical population fluctuations in rabbits and their predators (May 1980). Faunal change may also occur over tens of thousands of years, such as from Pleistocene to Holocene times (Martin and Wright 1967). Temporal fluctuations and changes in climates and environments are extremely complex phenomena that are not so easily categorized as the third and fourth criteria imply. The response of fauna to environmental change is an equally complex process and only indirectly reflects environmental change (Casteel 1976a; Gauthreaux 1980; Redding 1978).

Klein's (1980a) first two criteria seem more reasonable, at least superficially. However the botanical and geologic records, which may be indicative of environmental change, must also be examined in light of formation processes (Bishop 1980; Delcourt and Delcourt 1980). Further, if culture is adaptational, then one potential adaptational response to environmental change is adaptational–cultural change (see references in Kirch 1980). Accessibility of resources may change due to environmental change (Shackleton and van Andel 1980) resulting in a change in the archaeofauna. Artifact types and their frequencies may change in response to the addition to or deletion from a fauna (Schroedl 1973). Finally, the archaeofauna may change as a result of changes in subsistence strategies resulting from changes in environment evidenced by the pollen record (Strauss *et al.* 1980). Sorting out particular causes for changes in the archaeofaunal record is *not* a simple matter.

Controls for taphonomic histories can be conceived for subsistence studies. Scott (1977) tested several analytic techniques by comparing models of subsistence and environment. One model was derived from the archaeological record and another was derived from historical records for the site (an historically occupied fort). Although no isomorphic correlations were found between the two models, correlations were found that suggested that very general characterizations of environment and subsistence were possible using the archaeological record. The majority of the archaeological record does not have historical documentation; consequently, other controls are necessary.

King and Graham's (1981:136) recommendation that "it is important to check environmental data derived from the archaeological site against an independent record such as a paleontological record of the same temporal and spatial context whenever possible" is easily adapted to subsistence studies. Such a technique of comparing natural and cultural deposits has also been recommended for paleoethnobotanical studies (Minnis 1981) focusing on subsistence. Several studies already exist that compare paleontological and archaeofaunas in similar settings.

Briuer (1977) compared plant and animal remain sequences and assemblages from natural and culturally occupied caves. He concluded that natural depositional processes are more important than traditionally thought, and that few obvious differences were apparent between cultural and natural samples. Relative abundances of several taxa were different between the cultural and natural samples, and Briuer (1977) believes these differences may be explained as the result of differences in accumulation mechanisms (people versus carnivores, raptors, and natural deaths). Although perhaps correct at some broad scale, Briuer's (1977) overly simplistic operational assumption (*all* differences are the result of *human* activity) does not allow for animal behavior toward caves occupied by humans *versus* animal behavior toward caves not occupied by humans; nor does it allow for the way in which the available faunal community is sampled by nature and people. A similar study was recently undertaken by McGuire (1980). Although some promising results were obtained by Briuer (1977) and McGuire (1980), much work remains to be done. Numerous, large, well-controlled archaeofaunal and paleontological faunal samples must be compared with the relevant variable model (Medlock 1975) in effect. Only with these multiple comparisons will the unraveling of taphonomic histories become possible.

The controls I have discussed thus far—the selection of appropriate units or aggregates of fossils, the use of multiple fossil records, both cultural and natural, and the use of all available paleoenvironmental and archaeological data—are neither truly new nor revolutionary. Their explicit use and expression in the literature is rare, largely due to the, as yet, paucity of multiple sequences in areas and to the only recently improving attempts at complete integration. The controls are logical considerations stemming in part from our overall perspective of the archaeological record. The controls are thus neglected quite regularly, but are gaining new expression, particularly in studies on the formation of the archaeofaunal record. In the following section, the more practical side of fossil analysis—analytic techniques—is considered and the theme of controlling for taphonomic biasing is continued by discussing the taphonomic underpinnings of some basic analytic techniques.

METHODOLOGICAL ISSUES

Faunal analysis is particularly weak in analytic techniques (Medlock 1975:223).

Six key methodological issues can be perceived that require detailed evaluation. There are, of course, other issues that may be recognized, but the chosen ones seem to be the main foundations of all analytic techniques used in subsistence studies. Each will be considered and evaluated in turn.

Natural versus Cultural Bone

The most critical analytic step is to determine which fossils were "deposited as the result of human activity" (Thomas 1971:366), and which were deposited by natural processes, or, cultural and natural bone, respectively. The distinction is necessary if accurate assessments of diet and predator–prey relationships are to be made. Further, a logical second step in the distinction process is the delineation of food and nonfood cultural bone. For example, a pet or beast of burden would be cultural bone in an archaeological context but may not have been eaten. This latter distinction is seldom acknowledged by analysts, the implicit operating assumption apparently being "if it is cultural bone then it is food bone" (Wing and Brown 1979). But a pet dog given a ritualistic burial on its owner's demise should not be delineated as food bone, although one can hardly argue that the pet's bones are natural. Such practices are common in the ethnographic and archaeological literature (Emslie 1978; Spinden 1908).

Criteria used to distinguish natural and cultural bone are many and varied, including: (*a*) burning and charring, (*b*) degree of weathering and mineralization, (*c*) butchering marks and mechanical alteration or fragmentation of bones, (*d*) ethnographic analogy, and (*e*) archaeological context. Bone may or may not be burned or charred when cooked depending on how the piece is cooked. Bone may be burned by a natural fire, and natural bone may be burned inadvertently by an artificial fire, such as when garbage is burned. Boiling would not result in charred bone, but as a method of extracting bone grease for, perhaps, pemmican, boiling may result in "comminuted bone" (Leechman 1951) or small bone fragments (Vehik 1977). The presence of extremely small bone fragments in large quantities might be interpreted as indicative of bone grease production and indicate that the taxa were exploited as a food resource. But two difficulties seem apparent: (*a*) very small fragments are seldom identifiable to genus or species, and (*b*) bone may have been broken or "crushed for other purposes" (Vehik 1977:169). Several lines of evidence that can be used to indicate bone grease production are (*a*) "the presence of many small pieces of unburned animal bone", (*b*) "negative evidence for the legs, feet, ribs, and vertebrae [which] would have been battered beyond recognition in preparation for boiling," (*c*) "hammerstones, anvil stones, fire pits, burned or unburned 'boiling-size' stones, [heat] fractured stone", and (*d*) "loss of collagen fibers from boiling [requiring] comparative analysis of unboiled bone from the same site" (Vehik 1977:172–173).

The presence of burning or charring is an important criterion in paleoethnobotanical studies. Minnis (1981) suggests only charred seeds should be considered as prehistoric, whereas uncharred seeds should be considered modern intrusives to site sediments unless data concerning the formation of the archaeological record suggest otherwise. Such an approach will certainly decrease any extraneous "'noise' in the archaeological seed assemblage due to the potentially large number of seeds found naturally in soils" (Minnis 1981:147). However, such a practice would so decimate the sample of most animal fossil assemblages that it is generally not followed by faunal analysts.

There are at least three possible sources of burned bone in archaeological sites: (*a*) brushfires, (*b*) cooking, and (*c*) human discard of meatless bones in fires (Balme 1980). Briuer (1977) found no burned bone in caves that were not occupied by people, whereas nearby caves that were occupied by people contained burned bones. Balme (1980) found burned bone in a cave that was not occupied by people, but in significantly less quantities than in a nearby cave that had been occupied by people. He goes on to imply that marked differences in the amount of burned bone per taxon may indicate which taxa were used as sources of human food; taxa with very little burned bone were probably not eaten. Due to the paucity of late Pleistocene and Holocene paleontological faunas, the kinds of comparisons made by Briuer (1977) and Balme (1980) can only be made in many cases when the research design incorporates the recovery of paleontological fossil records with temporal and spatial distributions that are comparable to the archaeofaunal records.

The degree of weathering, mineralization, and staining of bones occasionally varies between intrusive (natural) and *in situ* (cultural) bone. Pragmatics suggest that cultural bone will be more heavily weathered, stained, and/or mineralized than intrusive bone because the latter was deposited at a later time. But what of bones of a single taxon recovered from one stratum that display different degrees of weathering, staining, and mineralization? Simply because a bone is stained in a manner suggesting it is not intrusive does not mean it was deposited by cultural processes. A dog could introduce noncultural bone simultaneously with the deposition of cultural food bone.

The presence of butchering marks is a seemingly good criterion because the act of butchery presumably connotes food preparation. But not all cultural or food bone will display butchering marks because it is quite possible to butcher an animal of any size without leaving a mark on any bone (Guilday *et al.* 1962). Further, how are butchering marks to be distinguished from simple skinning marks and marks resulting from bone-tool manufacture when the desired end product from the carcass was only the hide or a bone tool, respectively? Two recent studies on tool marks, tool morphology, tool function, and tool efficiency (Walker 1978; Walker and Long 1977) do not address this problem although this is clearly a crucial question in this context. Walker and Long's (1977) data do suggest that marks made by tools used by humans will be more or less V-shaped in cross section, whereas data collected by Bonnichsen (1973, 1979), Haynes (1980), Miller (1969), and Morlan (1980) suggest marks created by carnivore and rodent teeth will be more or less U-shaped in cross section. These cross-sectional morphology data in conjunction with parallel striae in the V-shaped marks have been used to infer the activity of 2-million-year-old hominids (Bunn 1981; Potts and Shipman 1981). But because some of the marks interpreted as evidence of hominids were *not* located where the logic of butchery dictated they should be, are the V-shaped marks truly indicative of hominid activities other than butchery or meat exploitation, or were the marks perhaps not made by hominids? Much research is required before this question can be answered, and perhaps not only mark morphology, but mark orientation and distribution should be examined.

A set of bone modification criteria has been developed in the context of Early Man studies in North America that has applicability to the cultural versus natural bone distinction. Largely as a result of the discovery of undisputed bone artifacts that may date to 30,000 B.P. in the Old Crow Basin of Canada, much research has been devoted to developing criteria of bone alteration by humans (Bonnichsen 1973, 1978, 1979; Bonnichsen and Will 1980; Morlan 1978, 1980; Sadek-Kooros 1972, 1975) and other agents (Behrensmeyer 1978; Haynes 1980; Miller 1969, 1975; Tappen and Peske 1970). The literature is growing (see, e.g., Binford 1981), and the criteria developed thus far have still not met with general acceptance or approval by all archaeologists (Myers *et al.* 1980).

There are at least two reasons for the as yet debatable utility of the bone-alteration signature criteria. First, many of the criteria have not been exhaustively tested (Gifford 1981), and thus arguments are easily leveled against them. For example, spiral fractures were once thought to be exclusively the result of human intervention (Bonnichsen 1973; Dart 1957), but we now know this is in fact not the case and that spiral fractures may be created by carnivores and other agents (Haynes 1980). Second, because many of the criteria are not exhaustively tested and/or exceptions are known about the causes or agents, some of the criteria are applied in a limited manner, such as Morlan's (1980) suggestion that only spirally fractured elephant bones should be attributed to humans.

Alternatively, it is implied that the criteria are applicable on a probabilistic basis. Many of the criteria are qualified by modifiers such as "may be created by humans," "normally occur," "frequently occur," "generally occur," and "commonly occur." The criteria discussed by Bonnichsen and Will (1980) are discussed in these intuitively probabilistic terms. They suggest, that "like other historical disciplines, taphonomy is based on the principle of uniformitarianism" and present experimentally derived data "which can be used as interpretive analogs for resolving *which of several alternative processes might* account for bone modification" (emphasis added) (Bonnichsen and Will 1980:7). They initially qualify the data by pointing out that the data are "by no means comprehensive" and that "counter hypotheses that can explain the observed morphology must be discounted" (Bonnichsen and Will 1980:9). In the text describing the signature criteria we find the following qualifiers in the phrase "process A _____ cause result or signature B": may—16 times; usually and probably—twice each; and thought to, normally, apparently, and generally—once each. "Known to" is only used once (Bonnichsen and Will 1980:9–10). Although this use of intuitively probabilistic qualifiers may simply be attributed to writing style, admissions that the data are not comprehensive reflect the as yet uncertain tenor of this aspect of research in faunal analysis. For instance, Morlan (1980:57) ends his discussion of signature criteria with the statement "a rather large number of the Old Crow fossils have been placed in a category called 'natural or artificial' because I can find no means of deciding what produced the alterations in question." The research on this crucial topic is at an exciting stage, but until many more detailed attribute analyses are undertaken, the debates will continue.

To the best of my knowledge, no criteria for distinguishing butchering or food processing marks and technology or tool manufacturing marks have been posited and exhaustively tested. Even when such a set of criteria are developed, there remains the problem that not all bones, be they cultural food or nonfood, will display these marks. The distinction of artificial and natural marks on bones, when perfected, will permit an assessment of what animals and bones were utilized, but such criteria may not be applicable to the food versus nonfood cultural bone distinction.

Ethnographic analogy may be helpful in suggesting which taxa were eaten, but ethnozoological data may be ambiguous (Lyman 1979b). The use of ethnographically derived subsistence models has been criticized as restricting interpretations to ethnographic patterns (e.g., Walker 1978). When ethnographic subsistence models are compared to archaeological subsistence models, differences may be explained by ad hoc hypotheses or "arguments by anomaly" (Gould 1980). These differences force the archaeologist to realize that the past is at least at times different from the ethnographic present. "Perhaps in the end, it can be said that analogues are better at informing archaeologists about what they do not know about the past than about what they do know or can expect to know" (Gould 1980:36). This conclusion is surprisingly similar to the conclusion reached by some taphonomists (Behrensmeyer and Hill 1980a).

Thomas (1971) has proposed a quantitative procedure for distinguishing cultural and natural bone. The technique was derived from one outlined by Shotwell (1955), a paleontologist, who developed the technique to detect which taxa were locally derived and which lived far from the site. Shotwell (1958:272) believed that "the community of mammals with the greater relative [skeletal] completeness is the one nearest to the site of deposition." Thomas (1971:367) did not alter Shotwell's statistics appreciably, but rather shifted the focus to incomplete skeletons, assuming that "the dietary practices of man tend to destroy and disperse the bones of his prey-species"; therefore, the set of taxa with the lesser relative skeletal completeness is the one that can very likely be termed cultural bone. The Shotwell–Thomas method requires that the final decision be qualitative and subjective because the statistical manipulations merely result in a rank ordering of taxa by degree of skeletal completeness, but use of the technique is advocated by some (e.g., Wing and Brown 1979; Ziegler 1973).

The Shotwell–Thomas technique can be evaluated on two basic premises. First, the technique, as proposed, measures sample size, rather than any aspect of community membership (Grayson 1978b, 1979a, 1981b). This statistical problem can be circumvented, however, by treating the average skeletal completeness of an archaeological sample as a predicted, best-fit line. The residual values resulting from the fitting of a line are then analyzed to determine the degree of skeletal completeness (see Grayson 1978b, 1981b for a more detailed discussion). However, the second problem cannot be resolved as yet.

Numerous critics of the Shotwell–Thomas technique point out that it does not allow for differing taphonomic histories (Grayson 1978b; Voorhies 1969; Wolff 1973). For example, a dog that was buried would represent cultural bone, but would be represented by an essentially complete skeleton. Of course, in a scattergram such an outlier is easily discarded for statistical reasons (Kleinbaum and Kupper 1978), and thus this point would not be included in subsequent analysis of residuals. But what of more subtle differences? For example, Mellet (1974:349) notes that small mammal bones from carnivore scats "show little evidence (other than breakage) of what they have undergone" and scats may contain either complete or incomplete skeletons. Dodson and Wexlar (1979) show that owl pellets may contain complete or partial skeletons of small rodents, and it is clear that owl pellets do not accurately reflect owl diet (Lowe 1980). A measure of relative skeletal completeness can not distinguish these accumulation mechanisms, nor can it distinguish, for example, an incomplete rabbit skeleton deposited by natural processes from a complete rabbit skeleton deposited by cultural processes.

The final and perhaps most crucial criterion is archaeological context. That is, an archaeofauna, as defined, is in an archaeological context; it is spatially associated with indisputable cultural materials. Fossils may become spatially associated with artifacts via natural processes, such as the death of a burrowing rodent in a site. By definition, the dead rodent in a site is part of the archaeofauna, but the fossils representing the rodent are natural. The criteria discussed earlier are equivocal. When the criteria are used as a *set* and are applied to fossils constituting a paleontological fauna, such as that in the Old Crow Basin of Canada, many analysts quickly dismiss the criteria as being of questionable utility. But these same criteria may be used without question for fossils constituting an archaeofauna. It seems then, that a continuum of acceptability of these criteria exists. Few would agrue that spirally fractured, burned bone with striae at Olsen–Chubbuck (Wheat 1972) or the Casper site (Frison 1974) were not cultural. Similarly, few would argue that spirally fractured bone at North American paleontological sites over 1 million years old (Myers *et al.* 1980) was not natural. When the criteria are applied to fossils somewhere between these two extremes in terms of time and context or association with undisputable artifacts, debate follows (e.g., Bonnichsen 1979; Haynes 1980; McGuire 1980; Morlan 1980).

Though we can never be 100% sure that a fossil recovered from an archaeological site represents cultural or natural bone, we must strive for the closest approximation to the truth that is possible. Most criteria are independent of context. The use of the criteria in an archaeological context simply makes determinations more intuitively satisfying. To suggest that use of the criteria independent of archaeological context will increase the probability of a correct distinction of cultural and natural bone is to misconstrue probability theory. We do not know the range, mean, or distribution of any of the criteria and cannot assign ratio scale p values to the criteria. How do we assess the probability of an individual criterion? How are the probabilities for the various criteria converted to a cumulative probability? Are the probabilities additive or multiplicative, and are the criteria independent, dependent, or to some degree both? How are negative cases dealt with? A probability assessment of cultural bone is no simple matter, and for the present, it seems we must be satisfied with intuitively pleasing distinctions derived from use of the fossil and context criteria.

Archaeological context seems to be the paramount criterion in distinguishing cultural from natural bone. A rodent skeleton in a rodent burrow would seldom if ever be counted as a human food source even when in an archaeological site. But context is important in other regards as well. Zooarchaeologists examines the vertical distribution of fossils. Subsistence analysts must examine not only vertical, but horizontal distributions of fossils. Context becomes important in the delineation of food-processing areas, consumption areas, and waste-disposal loci, and involves study of the formation of the archaeological site (e.g., Bonnichsen and Sanger 1977; Lyman 1978b, 1980b; Wheat 1972). For example, Meadow (1978) examined the differential distribution of bovid and pig bones inside and outside buildings in conjunction with differential preservation, suggesting bones in buildings would be more protected from attritional agents. After calculation of various statistical tests to examine similarities and differences in bone assemblages, Meadow (1978:18) approached the "thorny problem of inference beyond the level of the [fossils] themselves" and postulated secondary disposal procedures and differential preservation to account for bone distributions.

The criteria reviewed were meant to be used for distinguishing cultural and natural bone. The distinction of food and nonfood cultural bone must also be made. One could argue that coprolites might be examined, but these are seldom recovered, and when they are recovered, they generally represent a very limited number of meals. Further, there is evidence to suggest that even if coprolites are available, the detectability of meat diet is still problematic because it involves the assumptions that the number of prey observed in coprolites is equal to the number consumed, and the relative abundances of different taxa are an accurate ratio-scale reflection of what was eaten. Studies with coyotes and wolves suggest these assumptions are probably unreasonable with these taxa (Floyd *et al.* 1978; Weaver and Hoffman 1979), and comparable studies with human feces suggest a similar conclusion (Poovaiah *et al.* 1977). Thus, even when large samples of coprolites are available for a single site or set of sites, ratio-scale percentage assessments of diet composition (e.g., Bryant and Williams-Dean 1975; Heizer and Napton 1969) may only be dim reflections of reality. Coprolites generally contain pollen and phytoliths, and may contain bone, shell, and hair (Bryant and Williams-Dean 1975). Sorting out which of the represented taxa were intentionally consumed and which were inadvertently consumed is a complex process (see Wilke and Hall 1975). Even chemical analysis is plagued with uncertainty, and several investigators were prompted to point out after a controlled experiment that "the fecal composition did not reflect even major differences in diet" (Poovaiah *et al.* 1977:51–52).

If the analyst wishes to determine how much of which taxon was eaten, we must distinguish food from nonfood cultural bone. This question has been indirectly addressed by distinguishing available meat (all parts of an animal minus bone and hide) from consumable meat (those portions of available meat that were probably eaten) through intensive analysis of butchery practices (Lyman 1979c). Much research has focused on the analysis of butchery practices (e.g., Binford 1978; Hill 1979a,b; Noe-Nygaard 1977; Yellen 1977), and results seem promising in regards to analysis of subsistence practices.

If we phrase our questions as testable hypotheses and use the criteria discussed as test implications, we may construct the following hypothesis: If a taxon underwent cultural modification, its bones should possibly display occasional charring and/or burning, display a consistent degree of weathering and mineralization indicative of deposition simultaneous with deposition of associated artifacts (i.e., should fit the archaeological context), and occasionally display artificial marks or modifications; local ethnographies may indicate that the taxon was utilized as a food source, and skeletons of this taxon should be relatively incomplete.

If none of the test implications are met or displayed by the sample under scrutiny, this does not mean all of the bone represents natural bone because the criteria used as test implications are not always universally distributed across all cultural bone (e.g., a butchered animal need not display butchering marks on any of its bones). If the test implications are met by a sample, "to argue that true implications confirm a hypothesis is to argue inductively, for it is logically possible for the implications to be true while the hypothesis is false" (Salmon 1976:377; see also Salmon 1966). For example, bones may display striae and charring, but these could have been caused by rodent gnawing and a brush fire, respectively, both of which are noncultural processes. Our results are thus only *plausible* explanations and our conclusions must be tempered accordingly. For example, the treatment of all bones of a taxon as cultural bone just because some of them display the test implications involves the implicit assumption that all the bones were in fact so exploited, a perhaps unreasonable assumption or inference on the basis of ethnographic data (e.g., Binford 1978; Bulmer 1976).

Sampling and Recovery

A major concern in all analyses involving samples of material is that the samples are representative of some target population. The target population is that group of things the analyst wishes to study, discuss, and make inferences about. The sample population is that fraction of the target population with which the analyst deals and from which the analyst extrapolates to discuss properties of the target population. For example, an archaeologist samples a site via excavation or surveys a sample of a region. The derived sample populations of site contents or discovered sites must be representative of the entire site or region, or conclusions will not accurately reflect the real world (Mueller 1975; Thomas 1976).

The appropriateness of a sample for answering particular questions must be assessed not only from the perspective that the sample may be taphonomically biased but from the perspective of recovery as well (Meadow 1981). Recovery can be controlled and modified by altering excavation strategies, which in turn must be dictated by the questions being asked by the archaeologist and the faunal analyst. Because the target population is determined by the research questions, if paleoecological issues are being addressed, the sample population must approximate the prehistorically extant fauna. If subsistence practices are the subject of study, the prehistorically extant fauna may or may not be the target population depending on the precise nature of the question, but the archaeofauna surely is a target population because we assume it reflects to some degree which taxa were exploited.

When the analyst studies subsistence practices, the archaeofauna may be both the sample and target populations. Regarding the relative dietary importance of different taxa, if the sample is representative of what was eaten and deposited in the site, then it is representative of the target population. Conversely, if the analyst wishes to determine if hunting was selective in regards to age, sex, and/or taxa, then he must somehow determine what was originally extant in order to compare it to the archaeological sample. The analyst may reconstruct the extant fauna from the archaeological data (Dasmann 1952; Selleck and Hart 1957), or may derive an estimate of the originally extant fauna from modern wildlife management data and project this estimate into the past (Smith 1979) for comparison with the archaeofauna. The originally extant fauna is a target population because the analyst acknowledges the cultural taphonomic accumulation factor of hunter selection resulting in the archaeofauna or sample population.

Gamble (1978) points out that the recovered fossils are a primary sample of the fossil record, whereas the identified and analyzed fossils are a secondary sample. The quality and quantity of the primary sample is directly controlled by recovery techniques. The secondary sample may be controlled by the expertise of the analyst for identifying fossils and by the scheme used to select a subsample of the recovered fossils for analysis. Furthermore, in generating primary samples, archaeologists sample geographic space, not bones. Given that the fossil record is not randomly distributed in space, and that distribution patterns and fossil finds are dependent on taphonomic histories, the sampled space may be representative of the target space, but the recovered fossils may *not* be representative of the fossil record in the target space.

Due to the assumption that the archaeofauna reflects subsistence practices, recovery of samples of archaeofaunas has been much discussed in the literature (e.g., Casteel 1972; Clason and Prummel 1977; Higham 1968; Payne 1972, 1975; Thomas 1969; Watson 1972). Thomas (1969), for example, suggests means of establishing correction indexes to account for large screen mesh size. However, because most analyses measure relative taxonomic abundances, these correction indexes would have to be calculated for every spatial analytic unit (e.g., stratum). And because taphonomic factors may result in nonrandom distribution of taxa and bones, the indexes would virtually have to be calculated repeatedly, that is, for each and every recovery unit. It would thus seem more pragmatic to use small screen mesh size throughout the excavation. Watson (1972) succinctly demonstrates that not only microfaunal remains, but remains of animals the size of sheep and cattle may also be missed by some collection procedures and recommends water sieving to aid in recognition and improve recovery of bone. It would thus seem best to direct excavations from a probabilistic perspective (e.g., Mueller 1975), to use small screen mesh size, and perhaps take random samples and process them via flotation (Struever 1968) as a test of sample adequacy only, *not* as a basis for developing conversion or correction factors. If the target population is the originally extant fauna, or if it is equivalent to the sample population, the representativeness of the sample must somehow be assessed. Wolff (1975) suggests that taxonomic diversity and size-trophic ratios documented for modern and fossil faunas may be compared to assess sample adequacy. This technique must be used with caution because we will never know if prehistoric size–trophic ratios were the same as present ratios, and because taxonomic diversity is a function of sample size in both living (Coe 1980) and fossil (Grayson 1981b; Wolff 1975) faunas.

It has been demonstrated many times that as sample size increases, the number of individual animals per taxon and the number of represented taxa increase (Grayson 1979b, 1981b; Thomas 1971; Wing and Brown 1979). Some research questions may be answerable regardless of the sample size (Grayson 1981c). If paleoenvironments are being assessed using fossils, then multiple-site or fossil records displaying similar trends in faunal succession would suggest that sample sizes were not obscuring major trends. When subsistence patterns are the subject of study, the analyst must be cognizant of potential interpretive problems given the particular questions of interest and the way in which nonrepresentative samples may affect analytic and interpretive results. In order to argue that fossil samples are representative of some target population, a rather crude test can be made. The analyst may begin with a fraction of the sample at hand and determine relative taxonomic abundances of frequently represented taxa, and other patterns of interest. The sample is then increased by 5% or 10%, and patterns are checked again. If patterns change with each successive increase in sample size, the sample is probably not representative. When several successive increases in sample size fail to significantly alter patterns, it can be argued that the sample is representative of the target population for the tested patterns.

Quantification

Several papers have examined the techniques commonly used to quantify faunal remains and their respective underlying assumptions (Casteel 1977a,b; Grayson 1973, 1978a, 1979b; Holtzman 1979; Medlock 1976; Watson 1979). One technique simply involves counting the number of identified specimens per taxon (NISP) (Casteel and Grayson 1977). A major problem with NISP in statistical manipulations is the unknown degree of interdependence of the counted elements (Grayson 1979b). For example, there is no known technique to determine if two deer bones or bone fragments are from one or two individual deer. Fragments could be fitted together much as ceramic vessels are reconstructed, but this would involve a great deal of time and would eliminate only a small fraction of the potential interdependence. The use of age and sex data (Chaplin 1971) also would eliminate only a small fraction of the interdependence.

A different, more frequently employed quantification technique is the determination of the minimum number of individual (MNI) animals necessary to account for the bones. This technique provides independent variables (Grayson 1979b) and can thus allegedly be used to determine the relative dietary importance of taxa. However, MNI values will vary depending on the calculation method used (e.g., Casteel 1977b; Perkins 1973; Watson 1979), the aggregation method used (Grayson 1973, 1979b), and most importantly, whether the MNI has been shown to be a function of sample size or the NISP value (Grayson 1978b). The actual number of individuals represented in a sample (ANI) may be any value between the NISP and the MNI inclusively! How the ANI may be derived from either the NISP or the MNI values is ultimately a taphonomic question, and how ANI relates to the prehistorically extant fauna and to the exploited fauna is also a taphonomic question. For instance, ethnohistoric research has shown that the frequencies of pelts traded by some human groups are not only poor reflections of natural taxonomic abundances, but poor reflections of abundances of taxa exploited for subsistence–consumption (see summary and references in May 1980).

The analyst could calculate and interpret the NISP and the MNI values independently and compare results and interpretations (e.g., Grayson 1977b; Lyman 1979b). Or, ordinal level relative abundances (Stevens 1946) may be the highest scale that can be hoped for, and even these must be demonstrably applicable in each case (Grayson 1979b). Different aggregation techniques (Grayson 1973) may alter even ordinal level measures. Grayson (1979b) recommends the comparison of MNI values derived from the site as a whole (maximum aggregation) to total NISP values (minimum aggregation). If ordinal scale relative abundances do *not* change, the analyst could then manipulate and interpret these relative ordinal scale abundances in zooarchaeological and human subsistence terms. Other techniques of quantification exist, but have been little used due to lack of acceptance or recency of introduction.

The quantification technique Binford (1978) has recently proposed, minimum numbers of anatomical parts, in part, builds on Shotwell's (1955, 1958) work, and results in more accurate reflections of the primary fossil data. Such an analytic result is possible using several different techniques (e.g., Lyman 1979c). The quantification results are intended to produce more realistic estimates of available meat. The basis for such techniques is the same as calculating the MNI, except that the scale of the quantification unit changes; that is, there are an infinite number of quantification unit sizes between a bone and an individual animal. One may define, for example, quantification units such as individuals, skeletal portions (Lyman 1976; Read 1971), butchering units (Lyman 1979c), anatomical portions (Binford 1978), and bones, from smallest scale (least resolution) to largest scale (most resolution). Other such units are possible both at smaller scales (e.g., fauna) and larger scales (e.g., bone fragments). All of these quantification units present similar analytic problems. How much of an anatomical portion, bone, or skeletal portion must be present for a tally of one to be recorded? If butchering units or bone fragments are being tallied, how is a complete, articulated skeleton or a complete bone, respectively, to be tallied? These problems plague all quantification techniques (see reviews in Chaplin [1971] and

Grayson [1979b]), and no generally accepted solution yet exists. The best solution to date is to outline explicitly the technique used and the reasons for deciding to use that particular technique. This will assure the comparability of samples quantified by the same technique.

Holtzman (1979) outlines the assumptions inherent in the NISP and the MNI measures regarding the taphonomic factors of fragmentation and differential preservation, and proposes a quantification technique called the *weighted abundance of elements* (WAE). The WAE measures are identical to Shotwell's (1955, 1958) *corrected number of specimens* (CSI), and even though allowances are provided for taphonomic factors, Holtzman (1979) does not explain how values are to be assigned to all the variables included in the equations. In computer simulation runs, WAE estimates are more accurate than MNI estimates, but whether or not WAE estimates are more accurate at interval scale levels than NISP or MNI estimates is unclear. The WAE approach does permit conversion of the WAE to the MNI, and the MNI to the WAE.

Watson (1979) suggests the definition of *diagnostic zones,* (i.e., particular bone fragment types). Diagnostic zones should be species specific, commonly preserved, suitable for all age classes of animals, and fragmented or partially represented as seldom as possible. "The vital rule is that it must not be possible to count the same bone twice within any one zone" (Watson 1979:129). At least half the zone must be present to be counted. "The advantage of the diagnostic zone approach is that it allows great flexibility in interpretation" (Watson 1979:135). Diagnostic zones are defined, listed, and tabulated for each sample of fossils. Such a list readily permits determination of the MNI, NISP, and WAE. The diagnostic zone technique is simply a sophisticated NISP technique, resulting in the definition of classes of specimens. It does not, consequently, resolve the problem of interdependence in NISP calculations, nor does it resolve the problems that attend MNI calculations.

Binford (1978), Watson (1979), and Holtzman (1979) have outlined new techniques to generate statistically meaningful quantitative data. These are not the first techniques to attempt to account for differential fragmentation (e.g., Lasota-Moskalewska and Sulgostowska 1977), an important taphonomic consideration to all quantification techniques; the underlying assumptions to the techniques are derived from Shotwell's work (1955, 1958). Each quantification technique entails slightly different assumptions regarding the taphonomic skewing of the fossil record (degree of fragmentation, identifiability, preservation, etc.), and consequently allows the analyst to cross-check results. Rather than using a single technique, it would be better for the analyst to use several techniques and derive an average quantitative value or a measure of relative abundances (e.g., ordinal-scale interpretations, even though data quantification techniques are interval or ratio-scale [Stevens

1946]). This may be the most reasonable approach at present due to the un-controlled nature of taphonomic histories.

Subsistence studies require some technique by which the relative dietary importance of different taxa may be assessed. Of course, such a technique must assume an accurate distinction of cultural and natural bone and of cultural food and nonfood bone. As pointed out earlier, this is a difficult distinction to make, particularly regarding individual bones. The common covert assumption is that if one bone of a taxon *seems* to represent food bone, then all bones of that taxon represent food bone. For the sake of discussion, let us assume that accurate assessments of natural and cultural bone and of cultural food and nonfood bone can be made. Relative NISP and MNI values calculated from the food bone are sometimes used for determining dietary importance, but a more logical technique has been developed and is regularly used. The realization that an NISP or MNI value of one deer represents more meat than a comparable value for a turkey or squirrel prompted the development of techniques for determination of amount of *available meat* (Lyman 1979c). These techniques (e.g., Casteel 1974; Smith 1975b; Stewart and Stahl 1977; White 1953) have been shown to be frought with difficulties that culminate in extremely gross estimates of meat amounts in most cases (Casteel 1978; Lyman 1979c). Further, these estimates are generally unrealistic from a cultural and nutritional perspective (Guilday 1970; Lyman 1979c). For example, Guilday (1970) has demonstrated that the amount of meat represented by archaeological bone from Fort Ligioner is a very poor estimate of what was actually present and required according to historical documentation. The determination of interval or ratio-scale estimates of meat amounts seems to be impossible, as does the determination of exact amounts of available meat. The approximation of ordinal abundances to the true values has yet to be tested.

Conversion of MNI values to meat weights is the most commonly used technique (Lyman 1979c; Smith 1975b; White 1953). This technique uses conversion factors that are averages, and consequently, no allowance for individual variation is made (Smith 1975b; Stewart and Stahl 1977). Therefore, the resultant meat-weight figures would have to be assigned a standard deviation to assure the probability of their accuracy, a practice that has not been developed (but see Higham 1968). Even if developed, such a practice would be tenuous at best because in order to assign a standard deviation value to a variable, the distribution of that variable must be known (Thomas 1976). Techniques to determine the distribution of the variable *meat weight* are not presently available, in part because of the difficulties in calculating meat-weight values. Finally, if relative ordinal-scale abundances are the desired result, standard deviation values may obscure rank-order abundances. A comparable analytic and interpretive challenge exists with radiocarbon dating, as in the case when the standard deviations of two dates overlap significantly. Are the two dates to be considered identical (contemporaneous) or different? This might be determined if the dates are from markedly different but contiguous strata, or if other dates are available that can be used to assure reliability and validity of the dates in question. But do comparable techniques exist for standard deviations of meat weight? They may if meat weights are calculated by using several different techniques and comparing rank-order abundances.

Another technique is to add a certain amount of meat to the sum for every particular skeletal element recovered (Pozorski 1979). Meat amounts are sometimes calculated by weighing bone and converting the bone weights to meat weights (Reed 1963; Uerpmann 1973). Statistical difficulties with the conversion factors have been detected (Casteel 1978), and differential weathering and mineralization of different bones for different taxa in different strata may skew bone weights. Both the meat-per-bone and bone-weight techniques may be affected by bone fragmentation, which, if varying intertaxonomically, may skew the proportions of identifiable fragments per taxon. Both these techniques require that standard deviations be assigned to derived values.

It may not be necessary to assign standard deviations in some cases. Comparison of meat amounts for different taxa using several of the techniques would suggest that ordinal abundances are valid if the rank orders between different techniques do not change (cf. Grayson 1979b).

Predator–Prey Relationships

Quantification is also required for assessing predator–prey relationships. In brief, this aspect of studying human subsistence requires a comparison of the archaeofauna (assuming it is representative of what was originally deposited) to the originally extant fauna. Derivation of the latter can take one of two basic forms or some combination thereof. The analyst can project modern figures into the past (Emerson 1980), or reconstruct the prehistoric fauna from the archaeofauna. To reconstruct a prehistoric fauna (target population) from an archaeofauna (sample population), it is necessary to ask how the target population was sampled by mechanisms that accumulated bones in the site. Phrased in this manner, it is clear that interpretations of predator–prey relationships involve taphonomic questions. Even though those concerned with wildlife-management have been discussing methods of calculating population figures from hunter-kill data for over 40 years (Kelker 1940, 1943), there is still some debate over the degree of accuracy that can be attained (Coe *et al.* 1980; Dasmann 1952; Selleck and Hart 1957). Even when these methods are perfected for application to contemporary populations, their applicability to archaeological data (e.g., Elder 1965) must be tempered by taphonomic considerations.

Prehistorians commonly hypothesize that hunters randomly killed their prey without regard for age and sex; or conversely, that prehistoric people selectively exploited their prey with respect to age and sex (I note that "taxon" may be substituted for "age and sex"). It is assumed that either case should "be reflected in the demographic structure of faunal samples from archaeological excavations" (Wilkinson 1976:322). Using "random-kill" data generated from commercial hunting of red deer in New Zealand, Wilkinson (1976) demonstrates the logical and practical problems of inferring selective or random hunting. First, one must know the exact, originally extant population size, density, and sex and age demography for each taxon as well as deriving the same data from the archaeological sample. This necessitates accounting for preservation (taphonomic) differences due to different ages of individuals (e.g., Binford and Bertram 1977; Brain 1967, 1969). More importantly, a technique for quantification of the archaeofaunal remains into values readily comparable to the extant fauna values is required because comparison of the two sets of values indicates the degree, if any, of selectivity in hunting. The two most commonly used quantification techniques (the NISP and the MNI) have already been discussed. There remains a third technique to consider.

Smith (1979:156) recommends using biomass (or the ratio of the standing crop to the weight of faunal organics per unit area) estimates to determine the degree to which a human population is selectively utilizing taxa. The procedure he advocates involves two steps: (*a*) "selection of a present-day biomass estimate for the different species being considered" and (*b*) comparison of this estimate with that suggested by the archaeological data. This approach then, provides one manner of projecting modern faunal figures into the past. Smith elaborates at some length on the problems inherent in step 1 of his procedure, such as the uncritical selection of biomass estimates by prehistorians (see also Bayham 1979), and the use of different approaches by different zoologists and ecologists to estimate contemporary biomass figures. Archaeologists should therefore "critically evaluate" how the biomass figures have been derived and use primary references (Smith 1979:158). The estimate employed should be from an undisturbed ecosystem, should have been derived from the geographic area of the archaeological site, and should be from an ecosystem similar to the prehistoric one. The problem here, of course, is one of "obtaining accurate and detailed descriptions of prehistoric ecosystems" (Smith 1979:158). A general description will suffice, but the seral stage of the ecosystem and the season of the year may affect biomass levels (I note that these same factors affect demographic data as well). The means recommended by Smith (1979) of circumventing these problems is to use a range estimate of biomass instead of a single-value estimate. Selective exploitation of taxa should be indicated by prehistoric values divergent from those estimated with contemporary data.

Several of the inherent difficulties in using biomass estimates have been alluded to in the discussion of calculating meat amounts from faunal remains. Other difficulties include selection of a contemporary biomass estimate to be projected into the past (Smith 1979). First, it is generally extremely difficult to determine if an ecosystem has been disturbed, even though the operating assumption *must* be that it has not been disturbed. The encroachment of Euro-Americans into the North American continent significantly disrupted most ecosystems and preceded in-depth studies of ecosystems. Although Native Americans also had effects on ecosystems, these were not of the same magnitude in most cases as the disruptive effects of Euro-Americans. Perhaps most importantly, how are we to test the accuracy of the contemporary estimate projected into the past? Does it accurately reflect what was present prehistorically? The relationship of the archaeofauna (and the paleontological fauna, for that matter) to the contemporary estimate is dependent on controlling the taphonomic history of the former. Are we to assume that the contemporary estimate is accurate and leave it at that? Kranz (1977) has outlined a model for estimating prehistoric biomass using the fossil record, but the model requires modern data in order to assign values to several key variables. He cautions that the model produces results not readily interpretable, and a low likelihood of error in results is not always produced. Kranz's (1977) model, within certain but as yet unspecified confidence limits, might be of some use in assessing the validity of contemporary biomass estimates to be projected into the past. But as King and Graham (1981:138–139) suggest, "plant and animal assemblages cannot be precisely reconstructed and projected into the past."

The underlying assumption in the zooarchaeology approach is that environmental parameters control the taxa present in a fauna and their respective abundances (e.g., Grayson 1977b), therefore controlling biomass as well (e.g., Guthrie 1968). The numerous studies using faunal remains to reconstruct past environments (e.g., Casteel 1976a; Grayson 1976a, 1977b; Gustafson 1972; Harris 1963, 1970; Holbrook 1977) could not logically acknowledge hunter selectivity. From the zooarchaeological perspective, faunal biomass differences are explained as being a result of change in environmental parameters; subsistence studies point to hunter selectivity as the explanation for faunal biomass differences (Smith 1979). One can never be sure, consequently, how much of the fossil collection reflects hunter selectivity and how much reflects environmental conditions, even allowing for an accurate distinction of cultural and natural bone (Grayson 1981d; Lyman 1980a; Medlock 1975). For example, Grayson (1981d) notes that bone accumulation mechanisms may change, while environmental conditions remain stable. (The converse—environmental and accumulation mechanisms both change, resulting in *no* change in the composition of the fossil assemblage—seems equally probable.) The resultant fossil assemblage may be interpreted as indicative of environmental change, or as a change in hunter selection, depending on which assumption one makes, and this in turn depends on the analytic goal.

When estimating prehistorically utilized biomass (Smith 1979), the common procedure is to convert MNI values into biomass. Techniques for determining meat weights are used to determine biomass. Another technique is to measure a bone, correlate the measurement with a live weight for control samples, and derive a regression equation from the correlations. Measurements from archaeological specimens are worked through the equation to derive a live weight (Casteel 1974; Emerson 1978; Parmalee and Klippel 1974). This technique allows for individual size variation, but many of the standard measurements (von den Driesch 1976) are between points subject to rapid weathering and distortion. "This approach does not allow the analyst to determine meat weights for all individuals in a faunal aggregate, since there is usually no way of knowing which specimens came from different animals" (Grayson 1979b:226). Finally, taphonomic factors such as bone fracturing may differentially affect taxa and/or skeletons, thus skewing the measureable sample. Biomass values would require standard deviations, and the comparison of prehistoric biomass values with standard deviations to range estimates of contemporary biomass is similar to the comparison of two radiocarbon dates outlined earlier. Comparing the means of a variable in two models (Emerson 1980) may suffice in some instances, but the important parameter here is the distribution of the variable. The distribution and standard deviation must be known, because these will dictate when the archaeological and modern models are significantly different and will allow the conclusion of hunter selectivity as the cause of faunal biomass differences.

Animal behavior patterns must be accounted for when planning a hunt (Binford 1978; Burch 1972; Frison 1978b). To determine exact hunting techniques requires more than simple documentation of animal behavior however (Flannery 1967). Archaeological data such as site location and weaponry systems are necessary, and in conjunction with knowledge of animal behavior, permit the analyst to make general suggestions regarding adaptive strategies and hunting techniques (Simmons and Ilany 1977). To suggest specific details about hunting techniques, such as "stalking," purely on the basis of faunal data seems tenuous at best.

Seasonality

A common aspect of analysis is the determination of the season of a site occupation (Bökönyi 1972; Monks 1981; Speth and Davis 1976). In instances where archaeofaunal samples represent synchronic events, such as in the case of kill sites (e.g., Frison 1978a; Wheat 1972), analysis is straightforward; but analytic procedures must be rigorous in the instance of fossil faunas representing diachronic accumulations (e.g., Smith 1978; Spiess 1979). Monks (1981) discusses the analytic techniques, data, and theory used to determine seasonality. To avoid problems of asynchrony or time averaging (Peterson 1977), the sample examined must be appropriately defined, such as the archaeofauna of a particular stratum or occupation feature. Because of intrataxonomic variation in seasonal indicators, large samples are necessary; and because of intertaxonomic variation in seasonal indicators, consideration of seasonal indicator accuracy is required. To quantify season-sensitive fossil data, Monks (1981) argues for use of the MNI because it controls for the possible interdependence of NISP values. Finally, all data should be used to increase the accuracy of seasonality determinations.

The study of season-sensitive phenomena in animals has gained much impetus in the past few years (compare references in Bökönyi 1972; Casteel 1976b; Monks 1981). For instance, studies of individual age phenomena, such as incremental growth evidenced in mammal teeth (Nellis *et al.* 1978; Rice 1980; Roberts 1978) and mollusk shells (Crabtree *et al.* 1980; Gordon and Carriker 1978; Hughes and Clausen 1980; Jones 1980, 1981), suggest that the precision of such phenomena for measuring individual age and season of death may not be as great as once thought. Another commonly used type of data in seasonality studies is the presence–absence of seasonally available taxa, such as migratory waterfowl and anadromous fish. There is some debate as to the stability of avian migration routes and timing (compare Bökönyi 1972; and Grayson 1976a, 1976b). The timing of anadromous fish migrations is highly dependent on water temperature (Schalk 1977). This brief review indicates that much work needs to be done to determine the reliability and validity of biological seasonal measures. Perhaps estimates of seasonality are much closer to relative assessments than absolute indicators.

Monks (1981) emphasizes two important theoretical issues in seasonality studies. First, the analyst must realize that the season of an activity—the animal's death—is being measured. This season of activity may or may not correlate with the season of site occupation due to differential transport and storage of meat foods (Binford 1978). Further, negative evidence for a particular season does not mean a site was not occupied during that season. Monks (1981) suggests that this two-sided problem can be dealt with by testing multiple working hypothetical models derived from ethnographic, ethnohistorical, environmental, and archaeological data on the temporal and spatial distributions and abundances of fauna.

Another approach would be to assume that not all animal taxa were exploited and consumed during the same or all seasons of the year. This assumption only needs to be made for occupation sites; single-instance game drives are approached differently (Frison 1978a; Monks 1981). The assumption allows for resource scheduling (Flannery 1968). More importantly, it allows for the differential accumulation (taphonomy) of potential fossil remains. It requires that each taxon, at whatever level in the taxonomic hierarchy, be measured separately; that is, the analyst may compare seasonal data from different classes, orders, families, genera, or species of animals. Seasonal data derived from fish, molluscs, birds, and mammals can be compared; or, seasonal data for deer, elk, bison, and pronghorn antelope can be compared. The utility of the assumption is that it can be argued that different taxa were quite probably differentially accumulated into the archaeofauna, both in terms of initial killing and introduction into a site. If all the taxa indicate the same season(s), it can be argued that the data are not only *reliable,* but *valid* because if the taxa were differentially accumulated, they are therefore independent measures of the same inferential result—seasonality of site occupation. Use of suites of taxa should theoretically control for taphonomic factors such as differential accumulation of the archaeofauna.

Ecology

Ecology has become a standard part of archaeological jargon in the past decade (see reviews in Hardesty 1980; Jochim 1979; King and Graham 1981), although the precise meaning and utility of the concept and all it entails (such as other concepts, principles, theories, etc.) for archaeology has not been agreed on. *Ecology* is defined here as "the study of the relation of organisms or groups of organisms to their environment, or the science of the interrelations between living organisms and their environment . . . the study of the structure and function of nature, it being understood that mankind is a part of nature" (Odum 1971:3). The concept of ecology is important to the attainment of subsistence and zooarchaeology analytic goals.

In regards to zooarchaeology, over 15 years ago, Findley (1964:23) outlined "five important problems which place obstacles in the way of meaningful use of data from vertebrate finds." First, difficulties exist in identification to a taxomonic level (species or subspecies) conducive to ecological interpretation. Statements such as "all bones, even the smallest fragments, may be identified with sufficient training in osteology" (Binford and Bertram 1977:125) display a remarkable naiveté. A skeleton may be composed of 100–200 complete bones, which, subsequent to taphonomic factors, may be variously fragmented, weathered, and deteriorated. Distinguishing one genus or species from another commonly requires the use of anywhere from one to a dozen criteria. Usually, several criteria are necessary; seldom is one enough. Adding the potential representation of virtually any number of taxa in an archaeofauna results in the requirement that the analyst be able to control a bewildering number of variables to derive generic and/or specific identifications.

The second problem Findley (1964) notes involves misconceptions about ecological ranges of taxa, those with the narrowest ranges (i.e., least tolerance) being of the most value to zooarchaeological analysis. However, some taxa have changed their range and preferred habitat since the introduction of Euro-Americans to North America (Murie 1957). Evolution may also result in taxa changing their ecological predilections through time (Mayr 1970), and extinct taxa may be incorrectly assigned to a particular ecology. Use of modern ecological data for particular taxa is common in attempts to circumvent these difficulties, but the ecology of modern taxa may be poorly known or understood (Coe 1980). Redding (1978) suggested that factors controlling the distribution of some taxa may not all be climatological and include dispersal, population fluctuations, water requirements, presence or absence of food resources, interspecific competition, and predation (see also Gauthreaux 1980). He suggests that the taxon that is used for monitoring paleoenvironmental conditions (*a*) must not have changed its habitat preferences, and (*b*) must not be domesticated or artificially managed; further, the remains must be (*a*) locally derived and (*b*) *in situ*. Obviously, the first factor is unknowable in a strict sense although we may be more confident in our interpretations if suites of taxa commonly found in association today are found in association archaeologically (Grayson 1979b; Holbrook 1977). Domestication, although difficult to assess from archaeological data (Ducos 1978; Olsen 1979), need only be considered when domestic animals may be present in the archaeofauna. The third and fourth conditions require a knowledge of the taphonomic histories of the fossils.

The concept of ecology is important to subsistence analysis as well. "Relationships between humans and their environments are most obvious in the realm of food procurement. This . . . has led to an overwhelming predominannce of subsistence studies in ecological archaeology" (Jochim 1979:84). One result of ecological archaeology and subsistence analysis is the development of the analytic technique known as "site catchment analysis" (Roper 1979; Vita-Finzi and Higgs 1970), the study of the relationship between technology and the natural resources occurring within the economic range of individual sites. Site-catchment analysis emphasizes the "availability, abundance, spacing, and seasonality of . . . resources as important in

determining site location," and assesses those resources "within a demar-
cated area surrounding a site" (Roper 1979:120). The underlying assumption
is simple and involves the concept of *optimization*—individuals exploiting a
resource will be efficient in their exploitation and will expend the least energy
for the greatest return of energy possible (Roper 1979; Vita-Finzi and Higgs
1970; see also Bayham 1979; Smith 1974a). In site-catchment analysis, this
translates as the farther resources of a given energy value are from the habitation site, the less likely they will be exploited, "other things being equal"
(Vita-Finzi and Higgs 1970:7).

To assess the prehistoric exploitation of faunal resources via site catchment
analysis, we must know where the faunal resources occurred in relation to the
site in order to determine the site catchment area for faunal resources. This requires reconstruction of the habitats that were available prehistorically, often
via interpretation of the faunal remains. The reconstructed habitats are
geographically located around the site based on analogy with modern habitat
distributions, and the catchment area is defined on the basis of taxa in the archaeofauna (e.g., Flannery 1976). The use of pollen or plant macrofossil data
for paleoenvironmental reconstruction would eliminate this tautological
reasoning, but such paleobotanical data may not be available (cf. Delcourt
and Delcourt 1980). Alternatively, the analyst could follow the suggestion
made by Vita-Finzi and Higgs (1970) that prehistoric resource distributions
are comparable to contemporary distributions. But as Roper (1979:127)
points out, because of "geomorphic change, climatic change, fluctuations in
sea level, and drastic changes in resource distribution with the introduction of
modern land-use practices, modern data may be highly unreliable." Resource
densities and locations may alter through time as well due to the process of
habitat succession (Daubenmire 1968). That alterations in faunal resources
correlate with climatic and successional change is well documented (e.g., Coe
1980; Western 1980).

The analyst draws concentric circles of certain diameters around the archaeological site, each circle demarcating the limits of a catchment area. The
potentially exploitable resources in each catchment are then measured. The
minimum diameter circle containing enough of the archaeologically
represented resources to support the site population optimally may then be
determined, or the maximum supportable human population is determined
from one circle size and compared to the suspected site population and a
measure of the intensity of resource use is derived (e.g., Rossman 1976). The
drawing of circles was originally suggested by Vita-Finzi and Higgs (1970),
who used ethnographic data as a baseline for suggesting a 10-km radius for
hunter–gatherers. This is curious because they acknowledge that existing
hunter–gatherer groups are "engaged in practicing the least productive of the
known techniques [of resource extraction] in the least advantageous areas,

whereas their prehistoric counterparts were exploiting the most rewarding of the known techniques in the most favourable regions" (Vita-Finzi and Higgs 1970:5). Vita-Finzi and Higgs (1970:7) suggest that use of a figure other than a circle to describe–define the catchment, such as a figure that tends to fit a particular area, would be misleading because it would imply that certain shapes are more desirable than others; *why* this should be so, however, is not clear. They later concede that the catchment model should eventually add a measure "to express how far the territory departs from the ideal of circularity" (Higgs and Vita-Finzi 1972:31–32) because the circular model assumes uniform resource distributions, a point they readily concede as incorrect. No such measure has yet been developed because each site would require a particular measure for its particular setting and associated resource distributions. And as clarified earlier, techniques to determine prehistoric distributions of mobile resources such as flora and fauna are still the subject of some debate.

It is conceivable that the prehistoric occupants of a site could exploit whatever resources they desired wherever they wanted to (Roper 1979). The circle drawn by the analyst is said to represent the occupants' catchment area because it allegedly contains all the archaeologically represented resources and follows the assumption of optimization. Thus, the concept of optimal use of resources requires further consideration, particularly in light of recent papers (Earle and Christenson 1980) presenting models that purport to explain subsistence. The major explanatory device in these models is the concept of optimal use of available resources. Bayham (1979), for instance, follows Smith (1974a:290), who defines optimization as an "exploitation strategy of maximization of return for energy expended." As presented, Bayham's (1979) model seems to be a reasonable construct, but it is hardly applicable to the study of human subsistence because it is assumed at the outset that occupants will exploit resources optimally; specifically, Bayham (1979) suggests people will exploit large taxa in preference to smaller taxa because of the maximum return of energy for energy cost. This assumption has been demonstrably false in several instances (e.g., Bulmer 1976) because it precludes certain kinds of selectivity such as taxonomic food preferences. Further, Lewontin (1978) has argued convincingly that optimization is unnecessary to a successful adaptation. Feeding behavior may be a compromise between the optimal strategy and some other consideration(s). Remember, for example, Vita-Finzi and Higgs (1970) suggest that "other things being equal" an optimal strategy will be followed. Seldom if ever are *all* other things equal.

Demonstration of optimization in prehistoric contexts requires that ratio-scale relative abundances of all prehistorically available taxa be determined and that the archaeofaunal taxa be expressed as biomass. As phrased by Bayham (1979), the concept of optimal use of faunal resources exclusively concerns the respective potential food value of different taxa. Hunters may select taxa for nonedible parts rather than or in addition to meat (e.g., Bulmer 1976), one kind of selectivity precluded by the requisite assumption of optimization for use as food and which in turn requires a distinction of cultural food and nonfood bone. To assume the most abundant taxa in an archaeofauna were preferred for their food value may be at best tenuous, and at worst incorrect.

Summary

Generally three stages are involved [in faunal analysis]: first classification, the manipulation of . . . results to determine either patterns or glaring irregularities, and finally that interpretive leap of faith, in which an attempt is made to explain observed results most often in cultural terms (Yellen 1977:276).

The techniques commonly used in the analysis of subsistence practices often lead to weak or questionable conclusions. This is largely a function of the fact that, potentially, numerous taphonomic histories can result in similar or comparable fossil assemblages (equifinality). This is of paramount importance because the subsistence questions we are asking of our data often involve reconstructing part or all of the taphonomic history of the fossils under scrutiny. At present, many of the most regularly used analytic techniques do not allow for the taphonomic history of particular fossil assemblages.

Our interpretations of hunting practices, season of resource exploitation and site occupation, butchery practices, and dietary preferences and practices are taphonomic explanations, because they concern formation of the fossil record. Wing and Brown (1979) distinguish primary and secondary data, and indicate that taphonomic factors directly affect primary data such as NISP values, ease of identification, and taxonomic level of identification and measurements. They conclude, "these data may be subject to inaccuracy in reflecting the animals that were used" (Wing and Brown 1979:123). Secondary data, such as MNI, biomass, and meat-weight values, are tantamount to speculation (Wing and Brown 1979). Because of the kinds of questions we are asking, analysis and interpretation must be preceded by conversion of the fossil record into meaningful, interpretable data, that is, primary and secondary data. As we have seen, this conversion process is not straightforward due to the theoretical underpinnings of taphonomy inherent in most analytic techniques. Methods of controlling for these taphonomic underpinnings have been outlined.

ARCHAEOLOGICAL FAUNAL ANALYSIS

The second type of failure of faunal analysis lies in the realm of theory, particularly the failure to develop sophisticated models (Medlock 1975:224).

Purpose and Goals

As noted at the beginning of this paper, three basic goals of archaeofaunal analysis can be delineated

1. "twitching," or species list construction—perhaps for biogeographical (e.g., Grayson 1977a, 1981a), subsistence (e.g., Klein 1979, 1979), or paleoenvironmental (e.g., Gustafson 1972) considerations;
2. zooarchaeology or paleoenvironmental reconstruction (e.g., Casteel 1976a; Grayson 1976a, 1977b); and
3. human subsistence pattern reconstruction (e.g., Smith 1975a; Spiess 1979; Wing and Brown 1979; Yesner 1978). The first two purposes–goals and their potential analytic results are now considered.

Biogeographers seek to explain taxonomic distribution by studying ecological requirements and distributional histories (Ball 1975; Platnick and Nelson 1978). Grayson's (1981d) treatise has succinctly dealt with the potential of archaeofaunas for testing predictive historical biogeographical models, and positive test cases are now available (Grayson 1977a, 1981a; Lyman 1981). If a taxon is discontinuously distributed in an area today, one may predict that archaeological (or paleontological) excavations between the two extant populations *may* produce remains of the taxon. I emphasize "may" because sampling and taphonomic factors may result in a failure to find any remains of the taxon. For this reason one could not predict the absence of a taxon at a particular place at a particular time. One must deal with and predict only the presence of taxa; their absence may be indicative of many things other than historic biogeography. Similarly, their presence may indicate trade or human transport, and this taphonomic implication must be controlled. Recovery of taxon remains predicted to have been in the recovery location in the past results in a positive test because the predicted results are observed. Multiple records of locally extinct taxa in both archaeological and paleontological contexts would increase the validity of biogeographical models.

Zooarchaeologists could produce predictive models of past climates that could subsequently be tested with empirical archaeological data. The problems of taphonomy, ecology, and quantification make measurement of environmental conditions with archaeofaunal data difficult, but again, multiple, well-controlled fossil records (i.e., good chronology, stratigraphy, and recovery) from both archaeological and paleontological sites would allow arguments of validity (e.g., Guilday *et al.* 1978). Pollen or plant macrofossil data could serve as independent checks, but taphonomic and quantification problems also plague analysis of botanical remains (Begler and Keatinge 1979; Dennell 1976, 1979; Ford 1979; Minnis 1981; Wing and Brown 1979). However, multiple sets of data indicating the same environmental trends would suggest that taphonomic factors were not adversely skewing all the data, because it is unlikely that any two data sets could have undergone identical taphonomic histories.

Subsistence Models

Perhaps one of the better known and most thoughtful analyses of human subsistence is Smith's (1974a,b, 1975a) work with faunal remains from Mississippian sites. He has presented a model that is extremely detailed and worthy of close scrutiny here because it involves many aspects of the discussion presented in the first part of this chapter, and because it allegedly involves predictive models.

In Smith's (1976) own terms, the primary research goal of subsistence analysis is the construction of predictive models that explain the interface between a fauna and the people who exploited the fauna. These models should be constructed prior to analysis. If the predicted values of the model match those observed archaeologically, then a positive performance judgment results. Predictions expressed in the model would include answers to the questions commonly asked by analysts interested in human subsistence and listed at the beginning of this essay.

The "predictive model" that Smith (1974a, 1975a) has published is derived from archaeological data, but the predictions Smith lists are not truly predictions. For example, "projected edible meat yields for 15 species/species groups" are compared to "projected annual productivity" values (Smith 1974a:286, 1975a:134) in order to *test an hypothesis* concerning human exploitative selectivity. The values do not match in some cases, resulting in the acceptance of the hypothesis that "Middle Mississippi populations selectively exploited animal populations" (Smith 1974a:287, 1975a:139) and the rejection of two alternative hypotheses. Consequently, the model Smith (1974a, 1975a) has presented can hardly be considered "predictive"; as originally phrased, it does not predict the observed values and only becomes predictive after several alternative hypotheses are considered. Even then, the model does not predict observed values; it merely states the kind of values that should be observed, not their magnitude. The resultant model sufficiently accounts for the data, but may well be incorrect.

For instance, in a related study, Smith (1974b) presents an age curve for white-tailed deer from one site, which he suggests indicates two things: intensive human exploitation of deer during winter months, and complementary, noncompetitive exploitation of deer by man and wolves (Smith 1974b). Specifically, the paucity of fawns in the archaeological sample is explained as a result of intensive wolf predation on this age class and human focus on older age classes. Ignoring for the moment the paucity of fawn bones, one would expect the intensive winter exploitation of deer by man to result in an age curve quite similar to a synchronic or catastrophic mortality curve such as that illustrated by Frison (1978b). Smith's (1974) age curve more closely resembles normal attritional mortality (Figure 8.2) as illustrated by Frison (1978b). The paucity of fawn bones in Smith's sample may as readily be explained using his own data: Since fawning season is in late Spring–early Summer, his proposed intense winter exploitation would result in few fawns being taken. Alternatively, one could also explain the paucity of fawn bones as being a result of other taphonomic factors that are highly correlated with bone density. The bones of younger individuals are less dense (Binford and Bertram 1977; Brain 1969) and, thus, much more readily affected by attritional agents.

In a study of an archaeofauna from Iran, Gilbert (1979) examines the correlation of bone recovery frequency, bone density, bone size, carnivore gnawing, butchering marks, and bone tools. Using path analysis, a form of multiple regression (see also, Duncan 1966), Gilbert examines bone-recovery fre-

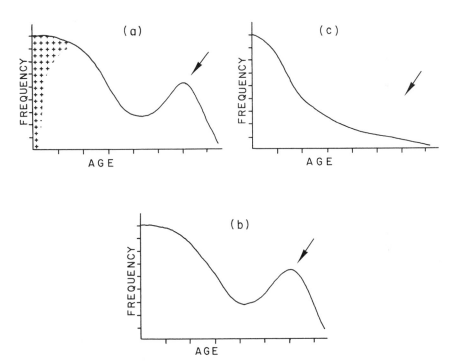

Figure 8.2. Comparison of (a) Smith's (1974b) archaeologically derived mortality curve with (b) natural attritional curve and (c) catastrophic mortality curve (after Frison 1978b). The shaded area under Smith's curve is attributed to wolf predation. Note in particular the curve portion indicated by the arrow. (Reproduced with modifications with the permission of Plenum Publishing Corp., New York.)

quencies—the dependent variable—in an attempt to determine which of the other—independent—variables account for most of the variance in bone frequencies. He found that not only do different particular independent variables account for different components of the archaeofauna, but that different independent variables account for different taxa within a given component. Gilbert (1979:428) suggests that "perhaps the most important application of taphonomic analysis and its quantitative member, path analysis, is the isolation of behavioral attributes of a faunal collection and their expression in standardized numerical form." Although significant strides have been made toward unraveling the taphonomic history of his fossil assemblage, Gilbert (1979:423) argues that "death assemblage level goals are too high and quite inappropriate." Specifically, (a) the analyst may not be able to strip away the taphonomic overprint, and (b) if the goal of subsistence analysis is to determine at some fine scale of resolution what was exploited and used (in terms of the death assemblage), the goal may not be attainable!

Finally, Spiess (1979) acknowledges the problems of taphonomy when comparing models of resource use to archaeological phenomena, and then describes three separate resource-use strategies in a two faunal species environment. He concludes that "one must *guess*" (Spiess 1979:243; emphasis added) which strategy was being followed by the hunter–gatherer group in question, regardless of whether or not the values predicted from the model match the archaeologically derived values.

The use of archaeofaunal remains for subsistence analysis has reached a new and exciting stage. Attempts to determine subsistence practices have been innovative and thought provoking (Cook 1975; Flannery 1967; Freeman 1973; Lyman 1976, 1977, 1980b; Munson *et al.* 1971; Parmalee 1979; Parmalee *et al.* 1972; Shawcross 1972; Straus 1977). However, research on animal behavior and physiology, and ethnoarchaeological research (Binford 1978; Bulmer 1976; Gould 1967; Haynes 1980; Morlan 1980; Yellen 1977) has begun to define the limits of what may be wrested from the fossil record and to suggest that earlier conclusions may not be as accurate as originally thought. Consequently, the "bottom line" of this chapter is that although there is a great deal of *talk* about the necessity for analysis to be scientific and rigorous, little seems to be happening in practice. Acknowledgement of analytic and taphonomic problems is quite common in the literature on analysis of archaeofaunas, but it is still rare that any attempt is made to deal with these problems in any scientific or rigorous fashion. Yet, this is precisely where the excitement lies, because the potential for developing new and innovative analytic techniques that can control these problems is largely unexplored. As the quality and quantity of data from actualistic studies (Gifford 1981) increases, new analytic techniques, hypotheses, and models will have to be constructed in order to deal with the fossil record in reliable and valid terms.

CONCLUSIONS

> I must differ with the methodology and conclusions [of osteoarchaeological pioneers], and with those who use uncritically some of [their] methods of analysis (Spiess 1979:67).

I have attempted in this chapter to present an evaluation of the way in which conclusions regarding prehistoric human subsistence are derived and their attendant validity. The literature displays an increasing awareness of many of the difficulties discussed above, but analysts tend merely to continue with analysis as if acknowledgement of the problems will serve to circumvent them. This is extremely frustrating not only to the expert, but to the novice as well.

In preparing this chapter, I read much of the literature, both old and new, on archaeofaunal analysis. The result was a clearer understanding of what those folks (including myself) who look at bones do and think. Much of what we do and think is implicit. No true text-book of faunal analysis exists. Chaplin (1971) and Casteel (1976a) may be exceptions to this—the former being concerned, in large part, with subsistence and the latter zooarchaeology; but although both focus on analytic techniques, they lack much in the way of any unifying principles or theories. Faunal analysis is undertaken by an increasing number of people, but the lack of unifying principles and guiding concepts has resulted in a literature that is extremely scattered in location (witness the references cited in this paper) and thought. Though not damning, this phenomenon is certainly a hinderance to research. Binford (1981), Behrensmeyer and Hill (1980b), Spiess (1979), and Wing and Brown (1979), among others, have made admirable attempts to consolidate much of the thinking on how to deal with the fossil record.

Throughout this chapter, I have outlined what seem to be reasonable steps toward dealing with the taphonomic history of the fossil record, while concurrently describing in some detail the importance of the formation of the fossil record for subsistence questions. The solutions offered may be summarized as follows: Taphonomy is the concept of the formation of the fossil record. Most analytic techniques currently in use involve assumptions (largely implicit) regarding taphonomic histories. Because these analytic techniques seldom control for different taphonomic histories, they must either be modified or used in a manner that controls for taphonomy. Some modifications are suggested; it is also suggested that the use of several techniques followed by a comparison of the results and the use of multiple sets of data followed by a comparison of the results will produce control of taphonomy and, if analytic results are comparable, will permit valid arguments. There are two related reasons for this: (a) no two fossil samples will have precisely the same taphonomic history, and (b) no two analytic techniques entail precisely the same taphonomic assumptions.

ACKNOWLEDGMENTS

Many people helped with the preparation of this paper. D. K. Grayson, D. J. Meltzer, S. Livingston, and M. B. Schiffer made helpful comments on various drafts. The *Advances* review process produced a very useful set of comments and ideas; I thank those referees. G. Holley, S. Livingston, D. J. Meltzer, and R. Whitlam were always willing to listen and quick to point out any errors in logic or references of which I was unaware. My wife, Barbara, was helpful and patient throughout. Responsibility for any errors of omission or commission are solely the author's. This chapter is dedicated to John David Lyman.

REFERENCES

Ball, I. R.
  1975   Nature and formulation of biogeographic hypotheses. *Systematic Zoology* **24**:407–430.
Balme, J.
  1980   An analysis of charred bone from Devil's Lair, western Australia. *Archaeology and Physical Anthropology in Oceania* **15**:81–85.
Bayham, F. E.
  1979   Factors influencing the archaic pattern of animal exploitation. *The Kiva* **44**:219–235.
Begler, E. B., and R. W. Keatinge
  1979   Theoretical goals and methodological realities: problems in the reconstruction of prehistoric subsistence economies. *World Archaeology* **11**:208–226.
Behrensmeyer, A. K.
  1975   The taphonomy and paleoecology of Plio-Pleistocene vertebrate assemblages east of Lake Rudolf, Kenya. *Bulletin of the Museum of Comparative Zoology* **146**:473–578.
  1978   Taphonomic and ecologic information from bone weathering. *Paleobiology* **4**:150–163.
Behrensmeyer, A. K., and A. P. Hill
  1980a   Conclusion. In *Fossils in the making,* edited by A. K. Behrensmeyer and A. P. Hill. Chicago: University of Chicago Press. Pp. 299–305.
  1980b   (editors) *Fossils in the making.* University of Chicago Press.
Binford, L. R.
  1977   General introduction. In *For theory building in archaeology,* edited by L. R. Binford. New York: Academic Press. Pp. 1–10.
  1978   *Nunamiut ethnoarchaeology.* New York: Academic Press.
  1981   *Bones: ancient man and modern myths.* New York: Academic Press.
Binford, L. R., and J. B. Bertram
  1977   Bone frequencies—and attritional processes. In *For theory building in archaeology,* edited by L. R. Binford. New York: Academic Press. Pp. 77–113.
Bishop, W. W.
  1980   Paleogeomorphology and continental taphonomy. In *Fossils in the making,* edited by A. K. Behrensmeyer and A. P. Hill. Chicago: University of Chicago Press. Pp. 20–37.
Bogan, A. E., and N. D. Robison (editors)
  1978   A history and selected bibliography of zooarchaeology in eastern North America. *Tennessee Anthropological Association Miscellaneous Paper* 2.

Bökönyi, S.
1972 Zoological evidence for seasonal or permanent occupation of prehistoric settlements. In *Man, settlement, and urbanism,* edited by P. J. Ucko, R. Tringham, and G. W. Dimbleby. London: Duckworth. Pp. 121–126.

Bonnichsen, R.
1973 Some operational aspects of human and animal bone alteration. In *Mammalian osteo-archaeology: North America,* by B. M. Gilbert, pp. 9–24. Missouri Archaeological Society, Columbia.

1978 Critical arguments for Pleistocene artifacts from the Old Crow Basin, Yukon: a preliminary statement. In Early man in America from a circum-Pacific perspective, edited by A. L. Bryan. *Occasional Papers of the Department of Anthropology, University of Alberta,* No. 1:102–118.

1979 Pleistocene bone technology in the Beringian Refugium. *National Museum of Man Mercury Series, Archaeological Survey of Canada Paper* No. 89.

Bonnichsen, R., and D. Sanger
1977 Integrating faunal analysis. *Canadian Journal of Archaeology* 1:109–133.

Bonnichsen, R., and R. T. Will
1980 Cultural modification of bone: the experimental approach in faunal analysis. In *Mammalian osteology,* by B. M. Gilbert. Laramie: privately published. Pp. 7–30.

Brain, C. K.
1967 Hottentot food remains and their bearing on the interpretation of fossil bone assemblages. *Scientific Papers of the Namib Desert Research Station* 32.

1969 The contribution of Namib Desert Hottentots to an understanding of Australopithecine bone accumulations. *Scientific Papers of the Namib Desert Research Station* 39:13–22.

Briuer, F. L.
1977 Plant and animal remains from caves and rock shelters of Chevelon Canyon Arizona: methods for isolating cultural depositional processes. Ph.D. dissertation, Department of Anthropology, University of California, Los Angeles. University Microfilms, Ann Arbor.

Bryant, V. M., Jr., and G. Williams-Dean
1975 The coprolites of man. *Scientific American* 232(1):100–109.

Bulmer, R.
1976 Selectivity in hunting and disposal of animal bone by the Kalam of the New Guinea highlands. In *Problems in economic and social archaeology,* edited by G. deG. Sieveking, I. H. Longworth, and K. E. Wilson. London: Duckworth. Pp. 169–186.

Bunn, H. T.
1981 Archaeological evidence for meat-eating by Plio-Pleistocene hominids from Koobi Fora and Olduvai Gorge. *Nature* 291:574–577.

Burch, E.
1972 The caribou/wild reindeer as a human resource. *American Antiquity* 37:339–368.

Carmines, E. G., and R. A. Zeller
1979 Reliability and validity assessment. *Sage University Paper, Quantitative Applications in the Social Sciences Series* 07-017. Beverly Hills: Sage Publications.

Casteel, R. W.
1972 Some biases in the recovery of archaeological faunal remains. *Proceedings of the Prehistoric Society* 38:382–388.

1974 A method for estimation of live weight of fish from the size of skeletal elements. *American Antiquity* **39**:94-98.

1976a *Fish remains in archaeology and paleo-environmental studies.* London: Academic Press.

1976b Incremental growth zones in mammals and their archaeological value. *Kroeber Anthropological Society Paper* **47**:1-27.

1977a A consideration of the behavior of the minimum number of individuals index: a problem in faunal characterization. *Ossa, International Journal of Skeletal Research* **3/4**:141-151.

1977b Characterization of faunal assemblages and the minimum number of individuals determined from paired elements: continuing problems in archaeology. *Journal of Archaeological Science* **4**:125-134.

1978 Faunal assemblages and the "wiegemethode" or weight method. *Journal of Field Archaeology* **5**:71-77.

Casteel, R. W., and D. K. Grayson
1977 Terminological problems in quantitative faunal analysis. *World Archaeology* **9**:235-242.

Chaplin, R. E.
1971 *The study of animal bones from archaeological sites.* New York: Seminar Press.

Clason, A. T., and W. Prummel
1977 Collecting, sieving and archaeozoological research. *Journal of Archaeological Science* **4**:171-175.

Coe, M.
1980 The role of modern ecological studies in the reconstruction of paleoenvironments in sub-Saharan Africa. In *Fossils in the making,* edited by A. K. Behrensmeyer and A. P. Hill. Chicago: University of Chicago Press. Pp. 55-67.

Coe, R. J., R. L. Downing, and B. S. McGinnes
1980 Sex and age bias in hunter-killed white-tailed deer. *Journal of Wildlife Management* **44**:245-249.

Collins, M. B.
1975 Sources of bias in processual data: an appraisal. In *Sampling in archaeology,* edited by J. W. Mueller. Tucson: University of Arizona Press. Pp. 26-32.

Cook, S.
1975 Subsistence ecology of Scovill. *American Antiquity* **40**:354-356.

Cox, C. B., and P. D. Moore
1980 *Biogeography: an ecological and evolutionary approach,* (third ed.). New York: Wiley.

Crabtree, D. M., C. D. Clausen, and A. A. Roth
1980 Consistency in growth line counts in bivalve specimens. *Palaeogeography, Palaeoclimatology, Palaeoecology* **29**:2323-2340.

Craw, R. C.
1979 Generalized tracks and dispersal in biogeography: a response to R. M. McDowall. *Systematic Zoology* **28**:99-107.

Custer, J. R.
1981 Comment on David Meltzer's "Paradigms and the nature of change in American archaeology." *American Antiquity* **46**:660-661.

Daly, P.
1969 Approaches to faunal analysis in archaeology. *American Antiquity* **34**:146-153.

Dart, R. A.
1957 The osteodontokeratic culture of *Australopithecus prometheus. Transvaal Museum Memoir No. 10.*

Dasmann, R. F.
1952   Methods for estimating deer populations from kill data. *California Fish and Game* **38**:225–234.
Daubenmire, R.
1968   *Plant communities: a textbook of plant synecology.* New York: Harper.
Delcourt, P. A., and H. R. Delcourt
1980   Pollen preservation and Quaternary environmental history in the southeastern United States. *Palynology* **4**:215–231.
Dennell, R. W.
1976   The economic importance of plant resources represented in archaeological sites. *Journal of Archaeological Science* **3**:229–247.
1979   Prehistoric diet and nutrition: some food for thought. *World Archaeology* **11**:121–135.
Dodson, P., and D. Wexlar
1979   Taphonomic investigations of owl pellets. *Paleobiology* **5**:275–284.
Ducos, P.
1978   "Domestication" defined and methodological approaches to its recognition in faunal assemblages. In Approaches to faunal analysis in the Middle East, edited by R. H. Meadow and M. A. Zeder, pp. 53–56. *Peabody Museum Bulletin* 2.
Duncan, O. D.
1966   Path analysis: sociological examples. *American Journal of Sociology* **72**:1–16.
Dunnell, R. C.
1980   Evolutionary theory and archaeology. *Advances in archaeological method and theory* (Vol. 3), edited by M. B. Schiffer. New York: Academic Press. Pp. 35–99.
Earle, T. K., and A. L. Christenson (editors)
1980   *Modeling change in prehistoric subsistence economies.* New York: Academic Press.
Efremov, J. A.
1940   Taphonomy: a new branch of paleontology. *Pan-American Geologist* **74**:81–93.
Elder, W. H.
1965   Primeval deer hunting pressures revealed by remains from American Indian middens. *Journal of Wildlife Management* **29**:366–370.
Emerson, T. E.
1978   A new method for calculating the live weight of the northern white-tailed deer from osteoarchaeological material. *Mid-Continental Journal of Archaeology* **3**:35–44.
1980   A stable white-tailed deer population model and its implications for interpreting prehistoric hunting patterns. *Mid-Continental Journal of Archaeology* **5**:117–132.
Emslie, S.
1978   Dog burials from Mancos Canyon, Colorado. *The Kiva* **43**:167–182.
Findley, J. S.
1964   Paleoecological reconstruction: vertebrate limitations. *Fort Burgwin Research Center Publication* **3**:23–25.
Flannery, K. V.
1967   The vertebrate fauna and hunting patterns. In *The prehistory of the Tehuacán Valley,* (Vol. 1) *Environment and subsistence,* edited by D. S. Byers. Austin: University of Texas Press. Pp. 132–177.
1968   Archaeological systems theory and early Mesoamerica. In *Anthropological archaeology in the Americas,* edited by B. Meggers, pp. 67–87. Anthropological Association of Washington, Washington, D.C.

1976 Empirical determinants of site catchment in Oaxaca and Tehuacán. In *The early mesoamerican village,* edited by K. V. Flannery. New York: Academic Press. Pp. 103–116.

Floyd, T. J., L. D. Mech, and P. A. Jordan
1978 Relating wolf scat content to prey consumed. *Journal of Wildlife Management* **42**:528–532.

Ford, R. I.
1979 Paleoethnobotany in American archaeology. In *Advances in archaeological method and theory* (Vol. 2), edited by M. B. Schiffer. New York: Academic Press. Pp. 285–336.

Freeman, L. G.
1973 The significance of mammalian faunas from paleolithic occupations in Cantabrian Spain. *American Antiquity* **38**:3–44.

Frison, G. C.
1974 *The Casper Site.* New York: Academic Press.
1978a Animal population studies and cultural inference. In Bison procurement and utilization: a symposium, edited by L. B. Davis and M. Wilson, pp. 44–52. *Plains Anthropologist Memoir* 14.
1978b *Prehistoric hunters of the high plains.* New York: Academic Press.

Gabel, C.
1967 *Analysis of prehistoric economic patterns.* New York: Holt.

Gamble, C.
1978 Optimising information from studies of faunal remains. In Sampling in contemporary British archaeology, edited by J. F. Cherry, C. Gamble, and S. Shennan, pp. 321–353. *British Archaeological Reports, British Series* 50.

Gauthreaux, S. A., Jr.
1980 The influences of long-term and short-term climatic changes on the dispersal and migration of organisms. In *Animal migration, orientation, and navigation,* edited by S. A. Gauthreaux, Jr. New York: Academic Press. Pp. 103–174.

Gifford, D. P.
1978 Ethnoarchaeological observations of natural processes affecting cultural materials. In *Explorations in ethnoarchaeology,* edited by R. A. Gould. Albuquerque: University of New Mexico Press. Pp. 77–101.
1980 Ethnoarchaeological contributions to the taphonomy of human sites. In *Fossils in the making,* edited by A. K. Behrensmeyer and A. P. Hill. Chicago: University of Chicago Press. Pp. 94–106.
1981 Taphonomy and paleoecology: a critical review of archaeology's sister disciplines. In *Advances in archaeological method and theory* (Vol. 4), edited by M. B. Schiffer. New York: Academic Press. Pp. 365–438.

Gilbert, A. S.
1979 Urban taphonomy of mammalian remains from the Bronze Age of Godin Tepe, western Iran. Ph.D. dissertation, Department of Anthropology Columbia University. University Microfilms, Ann Arbor.

Gilbert, B. M.
1973 *Mammalian osteo-archaeology: North America.* Missouri Archaeological Society, Columbia.

Gordon, J., and M. R. Carriker
1978 Growth lines in a bivalve mollusk: subdaily patterns and dissolution of the shell. *Science* **202**:519–521.

Gould, R. A.
1967 Notes on hunting, butchering, and sharing of game among the Ngatatjara and

their neighbors in the West Australian Desert. *Kroeber Anthropological Society Papers* **36**:41–66.

1980   *Living archaeology.* Cambridge: Cambridge University Press.

Grayson, D. K.

1973   On the methodology of faunal analysis. *American Antiquity* **39**:432–439.

1976a   The Nightfire Island avifauna and the altithermal. *Nevada Archaeological Survey Research Reports* **6**:74–102.

1976b   A note on the prehistoric avifauna of the lower Klamath Basin. *The Auk* **93**:830–833.

1977a   On the Holocene history of some northern Great Basin lagomorphs. *Journal of Mammalogy* **58**:507–513.

1977b   Paleoclimatic implications of the Dirty Shame Rockshelter mammalian fauna. *Tebiwa* 9.

1978a   Minimum numbers and sample size in vertebrate faunal analysis. *American Antiquity* **43**:53–65.

1978b   Reconstructing proximal communities: a discussion of Shotwell's method of paleoecological reconstruction. *Paleobiology* **4**:77–81.

1979a   Mount Mazama, climatic change, and Fort Rock Basin archaeofaunas. In *Volcanic activity and human ecology,* edited by P. D. Sheets and D. K. Grayson. New York: Academic Press. Pp. 427–457.

1979b   On the quantification of vertebrate archaeofaunas. In *Advances in archaeological method and theory* (Vol. 2), edited by M. B. Schiffer. New York: Academic Press. Pp. 199–237.

1980   Vicissitudes and overkill: the development of explanations of Pleistocene extinctions. In *Advances in archaeological method and theory* (Vol. 3), edited by M. B. Schiffer. New York: Academic Press. Pp. 357–403.

1981a   A mid-Holocene record for the Heather Vole, *Phenacomys* cf. *intermedius* in the central Great Basin and its biogeographic significance. *Journal of Mammalogy* **62**:115–121.

1981b   The effects of sample size on some derived measures in vertebrate faunal analysis. *Journal of Archaeological Science* **8**:77–88.

1981c   Towards a history of Great Basin mammals during the past 15,000 years. In Desert varnish: man and environment in the Great Basin, edited by D. M. Madsen and J. F. O'Connell. *Society for American Archaeology Papers* Vol. 2.

1981d   A critical view of the use of archaeological vertebrates in paleoenvironmental reconstruction. *Journal of Ethnobiology* **1**:28–38.

Guilday, J. E.

1970   Animal remains from archaeological excavations at Fort Ligioner. *Annals of the Carnegie Museum* **43**:177–186.

Guilday, J. E., H. W. Hamilton, E. Anderson, and P. W. Parmalee

1978   The Baker Bluff cave deposit, Tennessee, and the late Pleistocene faunal gradient. *Bulletin of the Carnegie Museum of Natural History* 11.

Guilday, J. E., P. W. Parmalee, and D. P. Tanner

1962   Aboriginal butchering techniques at the Eschelman Site (36LA12), Lancaster County, Pennsylvania. *Pennsylvania Archaeologist* **32**(2):59–83.

Gumerman, G. J., and D. A. Phillips, Jr.

1978   Archaeology beyond anthropology. *American Antiquity* **43**:184–191.

Gustafson, C. E.

1972   Faunal remains from the Marmes rockshelter and related archaeological sites in the Columbia Basin. Ph.D. dissertation, Department of Zoology, Washington State University, University Microfilms, Ann Arbor.

Guthrie, R. D.
1968   Paleoecology of the large mammal community in interior Alaska during the late
         Pleistocene. *American Midland Naturalist* **79**:346–363.
Hardesty, D. L.
1980   The use of general ecological principles in archaeology. In *Advances in archaeo-
         logical method and theory* (Vol. 3), edited by M. B. Schiffer. New York: Academic
         Press. Pp. 157–187.
Harris, A. H.
1963   Vertebrate remains and past environmental reconstruction in the Navajo Reser-
         voir district. *Museum of New Mexico Papers in Anthropology* 11.
1970   Past climate of the Navajo Reservoir district. *American Antiquity* **35**:374–377.
1977   Wisconsin age environments in the northern Chihuahuan Desert: evidence from
         the higher vertebrates. In Transactions of the symposium on biological resources
         of the Chihuahuan Desert region, United States and Mexico, edited by R. H.
         Wauer and D. H. Riskind, pp. 23–52. *U.S. Department of the Interior, National
         Park Service Transactions and Proceedings Series* No. 3.
Hastorf, C. A.
1980   Changing resource use in subsistence agricultural groups of the prehistoric Mim-
         bres River Valley, New Mexico. In *Modeling change in prehistoric subsistence
         economies,* edited by T. K. Earle and A. L. Christenson. New York: Academic
         Press. Pp. 49–120.
Haynes, G. S.
1980   Evidence of carnivore gnawing on Pleistocene and recent mammalian bones.
         Paleobiology **6**:341–351.
Heizer, R. F., and L. K. Napton
1969   Biological and cultural evidence from prehistoric human coprolites. *Science*
         165:563–568.
Hempel, C. G.
1966   *Philosophy of natural science.* Englewood Cliffs, New Jersey: Prentice-Hall.
Higgs, E. S., and C. Vita-Finzi
1972   Prehistoric economies: a territorial approach. In *Papers in economic prehistory,*
         edited by E. S. Higgs. Cambridge: Cambridge University Press. Pp. 27–36.
Hildebrand, M.
1974   *Analysis of vertebrate structure.* New York: Wiley.
Higham, C. F. W.
1968   Faunal sampling and economic prehistory. *Zeitschrift für Säugetierkunde*
         33:297–305.
Hill, A. P.
1978   Taphonomical background to fossil man—problems in palaeoecology. In
         Geological background to fossil man, edited by W. W. Bishop. Edinburgh: Scot-
         tish Academic Press. Pp. 87–101.
1979a   Disarticulation and scattering of mammal skeletons. *Paleobiology* **5**:261–274.
1979b   Butchery and natural disarticulation: an investigatory technique. *American An-
         tiquity* **44**:739–744.
1980   Early postmortem damage to the remains of some contemporary East African
         mammals. In *Fossils in the making,* edited by A. K. Behrensmeyer and A. P. Hill.
         Chicago: University of Chicago Press. Pp. 131–152.
Holbrook, S. J.
1975   Prehistoric paleoecology of northwestern New Mexico. Ph.D. dissertation,
         Department of Anthropology, University of California, Berkeley.

1977   Rodent faunal turnover and prehistoric community stability in Northwestern New Mexico. *The American Naturalist* **111**:1195–1208.

Holtzman, R. C.
    1979   Maximum likelihood estimation of fossil assemblage composition. *Paleobiology* **5**:77–89.

Hooykaas, R.
    1970   *Catastrophism in geology, its scientific character in relation to actualism and uniformitarianism.* Amsterdam: North Holland.

Hughes, W. W., and C. D. Clausen
    1980   Variability in the formation and detection of growth increments in bivalve shells. *Paleobiology* **6**:503–511.

Jochim, M. A.
    1979   Breaking down the system: recent ecological approaches in archaeology. In *Advances in archaeological method and theory* (Vol. 2), edited by M. B. Schiffer. New York: Academic Press. Pp. 77–117.

Jones, D. S.
    1980   Annual cycle of shell growth increment formation in two continental shell bivalves and its paleoecological significance. *Paleobiology* **6**:331–340.
    1981   Annual growth increments in shells of *Spisula solidissima* record marine temperature variability. *Science* **211**:165–167.

Kelker, G. H.
    1940   Estimating deer populations by a differential hunting loss in the sexes. *Utah Academy of Science, Arts and Letters, Proceedings* **17**:65–69.
    1943   Sex ratio equations and formulas for determining wildlife populations. *Utah Academy of Science, Arts and Letters, Proceedings* **20**:189–198.

King, F. B., and R. W. Graham
    1981   Effects of ecological and paleoecological patterns on subsistence and paleoenvironmental reconstructions. *American Antiquity* **46**:128–142.

Kirch, P. V.
    1980   The archaeological study of adaptation: theoretical and methodological issues. In *Advances in archaeological method and theory* (Vol. 3), edited by M. B. Schiffer. New York: Academic Press. Pp. 101–156.

Klein, R. G.
    1978   Stone Age predation on large African bovids. *Journal of Archaeological Science* **5**:195–217.
    1979   Paleoenvironmental and cultural implications of late Holocene archaeological faunas from the Orange Free State and north–central Cape Province, South Africa. *South African Archaeological Bulletin* **34**:34–49.
    1980a   Environmental and ecological implications of large mammals from upper Pleistocene and Holocene sites in southern Africa. *Annals of the South African Museum* **81**:223–283.
    1980b   The interpretation of mammalian faunas from Stone-Age archaeological sites, with special reference to sites in the southern Cape Province, South Africa. In *Fossils in the making,* edited by A. K. Behrensmeyer and A. P. Hill. Chicago: University of Chicago Press. Pp. 223–246.

Kleinbaum, D. G., and L. L. Kupper
    1978   *Applied regression analysis and other multivariable methods.* North Scituate: Duxbury Press.

Kranz, P. M.
 1974 The anastrophic burial of bivalves and its paleoecological significance. *Journal of Geology* **82**:237–265.
 1977 A model for estimating standing crop in ancient communities. *Paleobiology* **3**:415–422.
Lagenwalter II, P. E.
 1979 Prehistoric record of muskrat (*Ondatra zibethicus*) in the Mimbres River drainage, New Mexico. *Journal of Mammalogy* **60**:857–858.
Larson, P. A., Jr.
 1979 Archaeology and science: surviving the preparadigmatic crisis. *Current Anthropology* **20**:230–231.
Lasota-Moskalewska, A., and Z. Sulgostowska
 1977 The application of contingency table for comparison of archaeozoological materials. *OSSA* **3/4**:153–168.
Lawrence, D. R.
 1971 The nature and structure of paleoecology. *Journal of Paleontology* **45**:593–607.
Leach, E.
 1973 Concluding address. In *The explanation of culture change,* edited by C. Renfrew. London: Duckworth. Pp. 761–771.
Leechman, D.
 1951 Bone grease. *American Antiquity* **16**:355–356.
Lewontin, R. G.
 1978 Adaptation. *Scientific American* **239**(3):213–230.
Lowe, V. P. W.
 1980 Variation in digestion of prey by the tawny owl (*Strix aluco*). *Journal of Zoology, London* **192**:283–293.
Lyman, R. L.
 1976 A cultural analysis of faunal remains from the Alpowa locality. Unpublished M.A. thesis, Department of Anthropology, Washington State University, Pullman.
 1977 Prehistoric mammalian exploitation in the Lower Granite Reservoir Area, southeastern Washington. Paper presented at the Annual Meeting of the Pacific Northwest Bird and Mammal Society, Pullman.
 1978a Formation of the archaeofaunal record: a preliminary model. Paper presented at the 31st Annual Northwest Anthropological Conference, Pullman.
 1978b Prehistoric butchering techniques in the Lower Granite Reservoir, southeastern Washington. *Tebiwa* 13.
 1979a Archaeological faunal analysis: a bibliography. *Occasional Papers of the Idaho Museum of Natural History* 31.
 1979b Faunal analysis: an outline of method and theory with some suggestions. *Northwest Anthropological Research Notes* **13**:22–35.
 1979c Available meat from faunal remains: a consideration of techniques. *American Antiquity* **44**:536–546.
 1980a Bivalve molluscs in southern plateau prehistory: a discussion and description of three genera. *Northwest Science* **54**:121–136.
 1980b Inferences from bone distributions in prehistoric sites in the Lower Granite Reservoir Area, southeastern Washington. *Northwest Anthropological Research Notes* **14**:107–123.
 1980c Archaeofauna. In Prehistory and history of the Ojo Amarillo, edited by D. T. Kirkpatrick, pp. 1317–1388. *New Mexico State University Cultural Resources Management Division Report* No. 276.

1981   Archaeology, zoogeography, and paleoenvironments: theoretical implications and examples from the West. Paper presented at the 34th Annual Northwest Anthropological Conference, Portland.

Martin, P. S., and H. E. Wright, Jr.
1967   *Pleistocene extinctions: the search for a cause.* New Haven, Connecticut: Yale University Press.

Matthews, W. H., III
1962   *Fossils.* New York: Barnes and Noble.

May, R. M.
1980   Cree–Ojibwa hunting and the hare–lynx cycle. *Nature* 286:108–109.

Mayr, E.
1970   *Populations, species, and evolution.* Cambridge: Harvard University Press.

McDowall, R. M.
1978   Generalized tracks and dispersal in biogeography. *Systematic Zoology* 27:88–104.

McGuire, K. R.
1980   Cave sites, faunal analysis, and big-game hunters of the Great Basin: a caution. *Quaternary Research* 14:263–268.

Meadow, R. H.
1978   Effects of context on the interpretation of faunal remains: a case study. In Approaches to faunal analysis in the Middle East, edited by R. H. Meadow and M. A. Zeder, pp. 15–21. *Peabody Museum Bulletin* No. 2.

1981   Animal bones—problems for the archaeologist together with some solutions. *Paléorient* 6.

Medlock, R. C.
1975   Faunal analysis. In The Cache River archaeological project: an experiment in contract archaeology, edited by M. B. Schiffer and J. H. House, pp. 223–242. *Arkansas Archaeological Survey Research Series* No. 8.

1976   Determining the minimum number of individuals in archaeological faunal analysis. Unpublished M.A. thesis, Department of Anthropology, University of Arkansas, Fayetville.

Mellet, J. A.
1974   Scatological origin of microvertebrate fossil accumulations. *Science* 185:349–350.

Meltzer, D. J.
1979   Paradigms and the nature of change in American archaeology. *American Antiquity* 44:644–657.

1981   Paradigms lost—paradigms found? *American Antiquity* 46:662–665.

Miller, G. J.
1969   A study of cuts, grooves, and other marks on recent and fossil bones: 1. animal tooth marks. *Tebiwa* 12:20–26.

1975   A study of cuts, grooves, and other marks on recent and fossil bones: 2. weathering cracks, fractures, splinters, and other similar natural phenomena. In *Lithic technology: making and using stone tools,* edited by E. H. Swanson. Chicago: Aldine. Pp. 211–226.

Minnis, P. E.
1981   Seeds in archaeological sites: sources and some interpretive problems. *American Antiquity* 46:143–152.

Monks, G. G.
1981   Seasonality studies. *Advances in archaeological method and theory* (Vol. 4), edited by M. B. Schiffer. New York: Academic Press. Pp. 177–240.

Morlan, R. E.
1978   Early man in northern Yukon Territory: perspectives as of 1977. In *Early man in*

America from a circum-Pacific perspective, edited by A. L. Bryan, pp. 78–95. *Occasional Papers of the Department of Anthropology, University of Alberta,* No. 1.

1980   Taphonomy and archaeology in the upper Pleistocene of the northern Yukon Territory: a glimpse of the peopling of the New World. *National Museum of Man Mercury Series, Archaeological Survey of Canada* No. 94.

Mueller, J. W. (editor)
1975   *Sampling in archaeology.* Tucson: University of Arizona Press.

Munson, P. J., P. W. Parmalee, and R. A. Yarnell
1971   Subsistence ecology of Scovill, a Terminal Middle Woodland village. *American Antiquity* **36**:410–431.

Murie, O. J.
1957   *The elk of North America.* Harrisburg: Stackpole.

Myers, T. P., M. R. Voorhies, and R. G. Corner
1980   Spiral fractures and bone pseudotools at paleontological sites. *American Antiquity* **45**:483–490.

Nellis, C. H., S. P. Wetmore, and L. B. Keith
1978   Age-related characteristics of coyote canines. *Journal of Wildlife Management* **42**:680–683.

Noe-Nygaard, N.
1977   Butchering and marrow fracturing as a taphonomic factor in archaeological deposits. *Paleobiology* **3**:218–237.

Odum, E. P.
1971   *Fundamentals of ecology,* (third ed.). Philadelphia: Saunders.

Olsen, S. J.
1979   Archaeologically, what constitutes an early domestic animal? *Advances in archaeological method and theory* (Vol. 2), edited by M. B. Schiffer. New York: Academic Press. Pp. 175–197.

Olsen, S. L., and J. W. Olsen
1981   A comment on nomenclature in faunal studies. *American Antiquity* **46**:192–194.

Olson, E. C.
1980   Taphonomy: its history and role in community evolution. In *Fossils in the making,* edited by A. K. Behrensmeyer and A. P. Hill. Chicago: University of Chicago Press. Pp. 5–19.

Parmalee, P. W.
1979   Inferred Arikara subsistence patterns based on a selected faunal assemblage from the Mobridge Site, South Dakota. *The Kiva* **44**:191–218.

Parmalee, P. W., and W. E. Klippel
1974   Freshwater mussels as a prehistoric food resource. *American Antiquity* **39**:421–434.

Parmalee, P. W., A. A. Paloumpis, and N. Wilson
1972   Animals utilized by Woodland peoples occupying the Apple Creek Site, Illinois. *Reports of Investigations* 23. Illinois State Museum, Springfield.

Payne, S.
1972   Partial recovery and sample bias: the results of some sieving experiments. In *Papers in economic prehistory,* edited by E. S. Higgs. Cambridge: Cambridge University Press. Pp. 49–64.

1975   Partial recovery and sample bias. In *Archaeozoological studies,* edited by A. T. Clason. Amsterdam: North Holland. Pp. 7–17.

Perkins, D., Jr.
1973   A critique on the methods of quantifying faunal remains from archaeological

sites. In *Domestikationsforschung und Geschichte der Haustiere,* edited by J. Matolsci. Budapest: Akademiai Kiado. Pp. 367–369.

Perkins, D., Jr., and P. Daly
1968   A hunter's village in neolithic Turkey. *Scientific American* **219**:96–106.

Peterson, C. H.
1977   The paleoecological significance of undetected short-term temporal variability. *Journal of Paleontology* **51**:976–981.

Platnick, N. I., and G. Nelson
1978   A method of analysis for historical biogeography. *Systematic Zoology* **27**:1–16.

Poovaiah, B. P., L. K. Napton, and D. H. Calloway
1977   Inadequacy of coprolites and random fecal specimens as dietary indicators. *Contributions of the University of California Archaeological Research Facility* **35**:49–57.

Potts, R., and P. Shipman
1981   Cutmarks made by stone tools on bones from Olduvai Gorge, Tanzania. *Nature* **291**:577–580.

Pozorski, S. G.
1979   Prehistoric diet and subsistence of the Moche Valley, Peru. *World Archaeology* **11**:163–184.

Raup, D. M., and R. E. Crick
1979   Measurement of faunal similarity in paleontology. *Journal of Paleontology* **53**:1213–1227.

Read, C. E.
1971   Animal bones and human behavior: approaches to faunal analysis in archeology. Ph.D. dissertation, Department of Anthropology, University of California, Los Angeles. University Microfilms, Ann Arbor.

Reed, C. A.
1963   Osteo-archaeology. In *Science in archaeology,* edited by D. Brothwell and E. Higgs. London: Thames and Hudson. Pp. 204–216.

Redding, R. W.
1978   Rodents and the archaeological paleoenvironment: considerations, problems, and the future. In *Approaches to faunal analysis in the Middle East,* edited by R. H. Meadow and M. A. Zeder, pp. 63–68. *Peabody Museum Bulletin* 2.

Rice, L. A.
1980   Influences of irregular dental cementum layers on aging deer incisors. *Journal of Wildlife Management* **44**:266–268.

Roberts, J. D.
1978   Variation in coyote age determination from annuli in different teeth. *Journal of Wildlife Management* **42**:454–456.

Robison, N. D.
1978   Zooarchaeology: its history and development. *Tennessee Anthropological Association Miscellaneous Paper* **2**:1–22.

Roper, D. C.
1979   The method and theory of site catchment analysis: a review. *Advances in archaeological method and theory* (Vol. 2), edited by M. B. Schiffer. New York: Academic Press. Pp. 119–140.

Rossman, D. L.
1976   A site catchment analysis of San Lorenzo, Veracruz. In *The early mesoamerican village,* edited by K. V. Flannery. New York: Academic Press. Pp. 95–103.

Sadek-Kooros, H.
 1972 Primitive bone fracturing: a method of research. *American Antiquity* **37**:369–382.
 1975 Intentional fracturing of bone: description of criteria. In *Archaeozoological studies,* edited by A. T. Clason. Amsterdam: North Holland. Pp. 139–150.
Salmon, M. H.
 1976 "Deductive" versus "inductive" archaeology. *American Antiquity* **41**:376–381.
Salmon, W. C.
 1966 *The foundations of scientific inference.* Pittsburgh: University of Pittsburgh Press.
Schalk, R. F.
 1977 The structure of an anadromous fish resource. In *For theory building in archaeology,* edited by L. R. Binford. New York: Academic Press. Pp. 207–249.
Schiffer, M. B.
 1976 *Behavioral archaeology.* New York: Academic Press.
 1978a Taking the pulse of method and theory in American archaeology. *American Antiquity* **43**:153–158.
 1978b Preface. *Advances in archaeological method and theory* (Vol. 1), edited by M. B. Schiffer. New York: Academic Press. Pp. xiii–xv.
Schindel, D. E.
 1980 Microstratigraphic sampling and the limits of paleontologic resolution. *Paleobiology* **6**:408–426.
Schroedl, G. F.
 1973 The archaeological occurrence of bison in the southern plateau. *Reports of Investigations* No. 51. Laboratory of Anthropology, Washington State University, Pullman.
Scott, D. D.
 1977 Historic fact vs archaeological reality—a test in environmental reconstruction. Ph.D. dissertation, Department of Anthropology, University of Colorado. University Microfilms, Ann Arbor.
Selleck, D. M., and C. M. Hart
 1957 Calculating the percentage of kill from sex and age ratios. *California Fish and Game* **43**:309–316.
Shackleton, J. C., and T. H. van Andel
 1980 Prehistoric shell assemblages from Franchthi Cave and evolution of the adjacent coastal zone. *Nature* **288**:357–359.
Shawcross, W.
 1972 Energy and ecology: thermodynamic models in archaeology. In *Models in archaeology,* edited by D. L. Clarke. London: Methuen. Pp. 577–622.
Shipman, P. E.
 1979 What are all these bones doing here? *Harvard Magazine* **81**:42–46.
Shipman, P., and J. Phillips-Conroy
 1977 Hominid tool-making versus carnivore scavenging. *American Journal of Physical Anthropology* **46**:77–86.
Shotwell, J. A.
 1955 An approach to the paleoecology of mammals. *Ecology* **36**:327–337.
 1958 Inter-community relationships in Hemphillian (mid-Pliocene) mammals. *Ecology* **39**:271–282.
Simmons, A. H., and G. Ilany
 1977 What mean these bones? Behavioral implications of gazelles' remains from archaeological sites. *Paleorient* **3**:269–274.

Smith, B. D.

1974a Middle Mississippi exploitation of animal populations: a predictive model. *American Antiquity* **39**:274–291.

1974b Predator–prey relationships in the southeastern Ozarks—A.D. 1300. *Human Ecology* **2**:31–43.

1975a Middle Mississippi exploitation of animal populations. *University of Michigan, Museum of Anthropology Anthropological Papers* 57.

1975b Toward a more accurate estimation of meat yield of animal species at archaeological sites. In *Archaeozoological studies,* edited by A. T. Clason. Amsterdam: North Holland. Pp. 99–106.

1976 "Twitching": a minor ailment affecting human paleoecological research. In *Cultural change and continuity,* edited by C. E. Cleland. New York: Academic Press. Pp. 275–292.

1978 *Prehistoric patterns of human behavior: a case study in the Mississippi Valley.* New York: Academic Press.

1979 Measuring the selective utilization of animal species by prehistoric human populations. *American Antiquity* **44**:155–160.

1981 Wild animals: mammals. In Environment, Origins, and Population, *The Handbook of North American Indians* (Vol. 3), in press.

Speth, J. D., and D. D. Davis

1976 Seasonal variability in early hominid predation. *Science* **192**:441–445.

Spiess, A. E.

1979 *Reindeer and caribou hunters: an archaeological study.* New York: Academic Press.

Spinden, H.

1908 The Nez Percé Indians. *Memoirs of the American Anthropological Association* **2**:167–274.

Stein, W. T.

1963 Mammal remains from archaeological sites in the Point of Pines region, Arizona. *American Antiquity* **29**:213–220.

Stevens, S. S.

1946 On the theory of scales of measurement. *Science* **103**:677–680.

Steward, J. H., and F. M. Seltzer

1938 Function and configuration in archaeology. *American Antiquity* **4**:4–10.

Stewart, F. L., and P. W. Stahl

1977 Cautionary note on edible meat poundage figures. *American Antiquity* **42**:267–270.

Straus, L. G.

1977 Of deerslayers and mountain men: paleolithic faunal exploitation in Cantabrian Spain. In *For theory building in archaeology,* edited by L. R. Binford. New York: Academic Press. Pp. 41–76.

Strauss, L. G., G. A. Clark, J. Altuna, and J. A. Ortea

1980 Ice-age subsistence in northern Spain. *Scientific American* **242**(6):142–152.

Struever, S.

1968 Flotation techniques for the recovery of small scale archaeological remains. *American Antiquity* **33**:353–362.

Sullivan, A. P.

1978 Inference and evidence in archaeology: a discussion of the conceptual problems. In *Advances in archaeological method and theory* (Vol. 1), edited by M. B. Schiffer. New York: Academic Press. Pp. 183–222.

Tappen, N. C., and G. R. Peske
  1970   Weathering cracks and split-line patterns in archaeological bone. *American Antiquity* **35**:383–386.
Thomas, D. H.
  1969   Great Basin hunting patterns: a quantitative method for treating faunal remains. *American Antiquity* **34**:392–401.
  1971   On distinguishing natural from cultural bone in archaeological sites. *American Antiquity* **36**:366–371.
  1976   *Figuring anthropology*. New York: Holt.
Uerpmann, H. -P.
  1973   Animal bone finds and economic archaeology: a critical study of "osteo-archaeological" method. *World Archaeology* **4**:307–332.
Van Couvering, J. A. H.
  1980   Community evolution in East Africa during the late Cenozoic. In *Fossils in the making,* edited by A. K. Behrensmeyer and A. P. Hill. Chicago: University of Chicago Press. Pp. 272–298.
Vehik, S. C.
  1977   Bone fragments and bone grease manufacture: a review of their archaeological use and potential. *Plains Anthropologist* **22**:169–182.
Vita-Finzi, C., and E. S. Higgs
  1970   Prehistoric economy in the Mount Carmel area of Palestine: site catchment analysis. *Proceedings of the Prehistoric Society* **36**:1–37.
von den Driesch, A.
  1976   A guide to the measurement of animal bones from archaeological sites. *Peabody Museum Bulletin* 1.
Voorhies, M. R.
  1969   Taphonomy and population dynamics of an early Pliocene vertebrate fauna, Knox County, Nebraska. *University of Wyoming Contributions to Geology Special Paper* 1.
Vrba, E. S.
  1980   The significance of bovid remains as indicators of environment and predation patterns. In *Fossils in the making,* edited by A. K. Behrensmeyer and A. P. Hill. Chicago: University of Chicago Press. Pp. 247–271.
Walker, P. L.
  1978   Butchering and stone tool function. *American Antiquity* **43**:710–715.
Walker, P. L., and J. C. Long
  1977   An experimental study of the morphological characteristics of tool marks. *American Antiquity* **42**:605–616.
Watson, J. P. N.
  1972   Fragmentation analysis of animal bone samples from archaeological sites. *Archaeometry* **14**:221–227.
  1979   The estimation of the relative frequencies of mammalian species: Khirokitia 1972. *Journal of Archaeological Science* **6**:127–137.
Weaver, J. L., and S. W. Hoffman
  1979   Differential detectability of rodents in coyote scats. *Journal of Wildlife Management* **43**:783–786.
Western, D.
  1980   Linking the ecology of past and present mammal communities. In *Fossils in the making,* edited by A. K. Behrensmeyer and A. P. Hill. Chicago: University of Chicago Press. Pp. 41–54.

Wheat, J. B.
    1967   A paleo-Indian bison kill. *Scientific American* 216:44–52.
    1972   The Olsen–Chubbuck site: a paleo-Indian bison kill. *Society for American Archaeology Memoir* 26.

White, T. E.
    1953   A method for calculating the dietary percentage of various food animals utilized by aboriginal peoples. *American Antiquity* **18**:396–399.

Wilke, P. J., and H. J. Hall
    1975   *Analysis of ancient feces: a discussion and annotated bibliography.* Archaeological Research Facility, University of California, Berkeley.

Wilkinson, P. F.
    1976   "Random" hunting and the composition of faunal samples from archaeological excavations: a modern example from New Zealand. *Journal of Archaeological Science* 3:321–328.

Willer, D., and J. Willer
    1973   *Systematic empiricism: critique of a pseudoscience.* Englewood Cliffs, New Jersey: Prentice-Hall.

Wilson, M.
    1974   The Casper local fauna and its fossil bison. In *The Casper Site,* edited by G. C. Frison. New York: Academic Press. Pp. 125–171.

Wing, E. S., and A. B. Brown
    1979   *Paleonutrition: method and theory in prehistoric foodways.* New York: Academic Press.

Wolff, R. G.
    1973   Hydrodynamic sorting and ecology of a Pleistocene mammalian assemblage from California (USA). *Palaeogeography, Palaeoclimatology and Palaeoecology* 13:91–101.
    1975   Sampling and sample size in ecological analysis of fossil mammals. *Paleobiology* 1:195–204.

Yellen, J. E.
    1977   Cultural patterning in faunal remains: evidence from the Kung bushmen. In *Experimental archaeology,* edited by D. Ingersoll, J. E. Yellen, and W. Macdonald. New York: Columbia University Press. Pp. 271–331.

Yesner, D. R.
    1978   Animal bones and human behavior. *Reviews in Anthropology* 5:333–355.

Ziegler, A. C.
    1973   Inferences from prehistoric faunal remains. *Addision-Wesley Module in Anthropology No.* 43.

9

Nutritional Inference from Paleopathology

REBECCA HUSS–ASHMORE, ALAN H. GOODMAN,
and GEORGE J. ARMELAGOS

INTRODUCTION

Recent interest in paleonutrition has led to a proliferation of methods for the reconstruction of prehistoric diet. Although the technology of food procurement is a traditional archaeological concern, the role of food in changing human systems has only begun to be explored. Chief among the problems to be investigated is the nature and success of human adaptation. *Adaptation,* as defined here, is not simply the maintenance of homeostasis, but a dynamic interaction between human populations and the environment (including other human groups) (Thomas 1975). Because food procurement and consumption systems form a direct interface for humans with their habitat, these systems are critical components of the human adaptive complex. It is the purpose of this review to show how patterns of skeletal growth and pathology can be used to investigate changing patterns of human interaction with the nutritional environment.

Much of the effort in paleonutrition research has been directed toward the identification of dietary items. This has been approached through a variety of techniques for environmental reconstruction. Primary concerns have been the reconstruction of the resource spectrum that was available (Grayson 1974; La Marche 1974), and attempts to isolate the portion of that spectrum that was actually eaten (Kaplan and Maina 1977). Toward these ends, increasingly sophisticated refinements of floral, faunal, and fecal analysis have been

---

395

ADVANCES IN ARCHAEOLOGICAL METHOD AND THEORY, VOL. 5
Copyright © 1982 by Academic Press, Inc.
All rights of reproduction in any form reserved.
ISBN 0-12-003105-1

devised. Such research forms an essential basis for testing questions about ecological relationships. Unfortunately, most studies of dietary composition have remained descriptive documentation of the resources used. (For an interesting exception, see Kaplan 1973.) Processual questions, such as the role of nutritional status in subsistence change, have rarely been adequately addressed.

One recent approach to such questions has been the use of models from microeconomics and ecology to predict resource use and subsistence change. The simplest such models are essentially cost–benefit analyses for particular strategies of resource capture. This approach has been applied to the foraging behavior of hunter–gatherers (Winterhalder 1977) and to the adoption of agriculture (Cohen 1977a,b; Earle 1980). More sophisticated models of optimal foraging behavior have attempted to consider strategies for all essential resources simultaneously (Keene 1979, 1982; Reidhead 1980). Such models have the potential for expanding subsistence studies beyond mere description by predicting adaptive behavior for particular environments.

In general, these theoretical models are heuristic devices of greater or lesser realism, and are valuable for their ability to generate hypotheses about human–environment interaction. Their utility for solving specific problems is dependent on their testability. We would advocate the use of human skeletal populations as a source of data for testing dietary hypotheses. Although traditional archaeological methods have detailed with increasing accuracy the *nature* of human adaptations, the success of those adaptations can best be judged by their effect on the health and nutritional status of the population in question.

In light of its potential contribution, human skeletal material is an underutilized resource for studies of paleonutrition (Wing and Brown 1980). The history of skeletal studies, as well as the generalized nature of stress responses in bone is a major reason for this neglect. Although bone has traditionally been thought to reflect environmental conditions only tangentially, new approaches to skeletal biology provide the methods to overcome such drawbacks. Pathological conditions in prehistoric skeletons reflect disturbances of growth and repair in bone, and can therefore be used to infer the environmental stressors that caused them.

Stress is defined here as the physiological disruption of an organism resulting from environmental perturbation. The degree of physiological disruption is a function of both the severity of environmental stressors and the adequacy of host response. In keeping with our view that pathology and growth disruptions are "general" indicators of stress, a model developed by Goodman is utilized (Figure 9.1). Although stress cannot be directly observed in archaeological populations, the impact of that stress on the skeletal system can be determined. Past nutritional deficiencies may therefore be in-

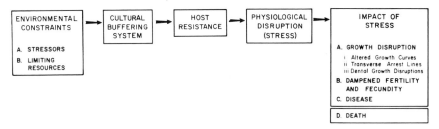

Figure 9.1. An ecological model of general stress. (From Armelagos *et al.* 1980.)

ferred from the pattern and severity of involvement within the skeleton and from the distribution of involvement within the population.

The realization that the skeletal pathologies of archaeological populations could aid in interpreting adaptation stimulated research in this area. Skeletal biologists have realized that patterns of growth and development, changes in morphology, and alterations in the morbidity–mortality profile of a group can be used to analyze its success in adjusting to its environment. Angel (1954), for example, used a number of features, such as stature and patterns of disease, to interpret the impact of changes in ecology on biological and cultural processes. These studies have given considerable time depth to our understanding of trends in human adaptation. Our purpose is to suggest methods for studying nutritional deficiencies in skeletal populations and to see how these techniques can advance our knowledge of nutritional factors in human adaptation. Our investigation of methods in paleonutritional research has two objectives: first, to help in delimiting the historical and geographical distribution of nutritional deficiencies in archaeological populations, and second, to understand the biocultural processes involved in the nutritional adaptation of prehistoric populations.

In the following sections, we briefly outline the processes of growth and repair in bone that are subject to environmental influence, and review the effects of nutrient deficiencies on those processes. We then examine how the results of nutrient deficiency, that is, pathologies and growth disturbances, can be used to identify malnutrition in archaeological populations. Individual stress markers are described and their utility is discussed.

GROWTH AND REMODELING IN NORMAL AND MALNOURISHED BONE

Normal Process

The traditional interest of paleopathology has been the recognition and diagnosis of disease from past human populations. Because bone is more frequently preserved than are other tissues, a wide range of skeletal pathologies have been catalogued. Meaningful interpretation of these phenomena and their use in cultural reconstruction depends on an understanding of the normal processes of skeletal growth and repair. Environmental factors may then be seen as influencing this process, either favorably, through diet, exercise, and the like, or unfavorably, through deficiency or other insults.

At the macroscopic level, the skeleton can be seen as an organ system in constant communication and cooperation with other systems. The primary functions of this system are support and locomotion, storage and regulation of minerals (and thus the ion concentration or acidity of body fluids), protection of the brain and spinal cord, and the production of red blood cells. This is a very diverse set of functions for a single system, and indicates the degree to which total body functioning is dependent on the maintenance of a functional skeletal system. The fact that other systems such as fat, muscle, and epithelium are affected relatively early in malnutrition, and that gross skeletal changes occur relatively late, indicates an adaptive response on the part of the organism. An organism that sacrificed its skeletal system to mild malnutrition would, at the very least, find itself hampered in its food quest.

At the histological level, McLean and Urist (1968:3) have defined bone as "a highly specialized form of connective tissue, composed of interconnected cells in an intercellular substance and forming the skeleton or framework of the bodies of most vertebrates." To this general definition, it should be added that bone functions as a support for other organs and shares with other connective tissue a matrix of collagen (i.e., protein fibers embedded in a ground substance high in mucopolysaccharides). The hardness of bone is attributable to crystalline salts, chiefly composed of calcium, phosphate, carbonate, and citrate, deposited within the organic matrix. Specialized cells mediate the deposition and withdrawal of this mineral component. The actions of these cells are essential to the growth, maintenance, and repair of bone, and give bone its dynamic quality as a living tissue.

Bone changes constantly throughout the life cycle and is most subject to environmental influence during periods of rapid development and growth. Insults during the embryonic period, when the first calcified tissues are formed, have the potential to radically alter the course of development. Insults during later fetal development are less severe, and the primary effect of undernutrition at this point appears to be retarded growth (Thomson and Hytten 1977).

Growth in the skeleton is primarily determined by the interaction of two processes—the laying down of bone by osteoblastic cells and the selective removal of bone by osteoclasts. The balance between these two processes determines the rate at which growth proceeds. Internal remodeling and repair of bone are likewise dependent on site-specific removal of bone and its replacement by new skeletal tissue. These elemental processes are altered by the lack (or occasionally the excess) of nutrients. For example, insufficient protein retards the formation of new bone matrix, whereas disturbances of calcium metabolism alter the mineralization of that matrix. Both may result in a relative deficiency of bone.

The dynamic interplay between osteoblastic and osteoclastic action continues throughout life and results in the configuration seen in the skeletons of archaeological populations. Interpretation of this record is complicated by the generalized character of bone response. Because bone responds to stress less dramatically than other systems, minor illness or mild nutritional deficiencies may be expected to have little lasting effect. Conversely, when gross deficiencies of bone are discovered, they may indicate a response to a stress so severe or so prolonged as to have exhausted the response potential of other systems.

Since the exact severity of environmental stressors is not always detectable, so also the nature of the disturbance may be difficult to elucidate. Many disturbances, by acting on the same process, may produce similar results, and the identification of a single causative agent may not be possible. This is particularly true in the case of nutritional deficiencies, in which the synergistic effect of multiple deficiencies, or of interaction with infectious disease, is frequently a complicating factor. It should become apparent from the following sections that the definitive diagnosis of a single dietary deficiency in a skeletal population is at best a hazardous undertaking.

Effects of Deficiency on Bone

Experimental studies of bone pathology in malnutrition have produced a voluminous literature, much of it inconclusive or contradictory. The ambiguous nature of the results in many of these studies reflects the difficulty of isolating specific effects for specific deficiencies. For example, stunting of growth and failure to gain weight are reported for most deficiency states. This may not mean, however, that the nutrient being investigated is solely responsible. Many animals subjected to nutritional imbalance are reluctant to eat, and thus suffer to an unknown degree from protein or energy deficit as well. A lack of protein can in turn materially affect the transport and utilization of vitamin A and calcium, further deranging the physiology of the organism. The level of a nutrient provided in the diet is thus not necessarily the same as the level physiologically available. Not surprisingly, single nutrient deficiencies are rarely encountered outside the laboratory setting.

Single deficiency diseases are also relatively rare in human populations. Some, such as scurvy among sailors, or rickets in northern industrial city dwellers, are directly traceable to specific environmental conditions. Beriberi, on the other hand, is primarily a technologically induced condition. Resulting from a lack of thiamine in polished-rice diets, it appears not to have been a problem before the introduction of highly efficient mechanized milling (McLaren 1976). Where rice is parboiled before milling, or fortified with vitamins, thiamine deficiency is once again a relatively rare disease. The distribution of pellagra is likewise limited. Occurring sporadically in the southern United States and southern Africa, it reached epidemic proportions in the early twentieth century (Goldberger *et al.* 1920; Roe 1973). Linked to a maize diet, it was shown to result from the abnormally low content in that grain of both available niacin and its amino acid precursor, tryptophan. Although outbreaks of pellagra ("disease of the mealies") continue to be reported in southern Africa; other populations for whom maize is a staple appear to have avoided the disease. Katz *et al.* (1974) have argued that the widespread New World practice of treating maize with lime (or other alkaline substances) enhances the nutritional quality of the grain. This is based on the work of Bressani *et al.* (1958), who found that heating and alkaline treatment significantly reduced the imbalance of amino acids in maize, making the limited tryptophan more effective. More recent experiments by Gontzea, *et al.* (1962) and Gontzea and Sutescu (1968) indicate that lime treatment increases the dystrophic effects of all-maize diets. These authors, along with Kaplan (1973), feel that prevention of pellagra and growth disorders requires the supplementation of maize with other sources of amino acids and B vitamins.

Even in clear-cut cases of deficiency disease, however, it is doubtful that only a single nutrient is lacking. An actual diet so restricted as to cause frank vitamin deficiency may be limited in protein, energy, or minerals as well. As in animal studies, the degree of interaction of multiple nutritional factors is difficult to assess.

Insofar as specific effects of nutrients can be identified in bone, they reflect the portions of the growth and repair process mediated by that element. Stewart (1975) has phrased this graphically, expanding on Mellanby's (1950) metaphor, which likened the skeleton to the walls of a citadel and osteoblasts to building operatives. Protein and energy, he notes,

> are essential for providing building materials and energy, and vitamin C ensures that the materials are used to provide a calcifiable matrix. Vitamin D controls calcification, insisting that all matrix deposited is mineralized even if older structures have to be destroyed to provide the inorganic salts. The continuing reshaping of bone necessary to ensure conformity with the final plan is directed by vitamin A, which exercises an overall control over the sites of activity of the osteoblasts and osteoclasts. Enzymes can be regarded as tools, and hormones as managers stimulating building, maintenance, and, where necessary, the destruction of the main structure (Stewart 1975:56).

It might be added here that enzymes and hormones, the so-called tools and managers, are themselves proteins, and are therefore influenced by dietary protein.

Protein-Energy Deficiencies

The effects of protein and energy deficits on the skeletal system appear to be broadly systemic and generalized. A condition of protein–energy malnutrition is therefore very difficult (perhaps impossible) to diagnose definitively, solely on the basis of skeletal pathology. Numerous experimental animal studies have shown the chief effect of underfeeding to be a slowing or even a cessation of growth. In the extended investigations conducted by McCance and his colleagues (Dickerson and McCance 1961; McCance 1960; McCance et al. 1962; McCance et al. 1961; Pratt and McCance 1958, 1960, 1964) on underfed piglets and cockerels, it was shown that the earlier the nutritional deficiency was introduced, the more severe and irreversible was the stunting.

If stress is not experienced until after weaning, normal growth can be induced by refeeding. However, rats underfed from birth remained stunted, even when later allowed unlimited access to food (McCance and Widdowson 1962). Examination of the bones of underfed animals showed several factors involved in growth failure. First, growth in length of long bones was greatly slowed. The cartilage growth plates at the ends of the long bones were unusually thin, and their cellular activity was disturbed. Remodeling activity increased in this area, with the amount of bone removed by osteoclasts exceeding the amount formed by osteoblasts. Growth in the width of long bones was likewise slowed, and the new bone formed was characterized by relatively thin protein fibers and small mineral crystals. In response to the generalized stress of dietary insufficiency, only a minimal amount of new bone was formed in order to maintain growth. At the same time, older bone was more rapidly removed, especially in the interior of the cortex of the long bones. This resulted in an increase in the diameter of the marrow cavity, and a concomitant thinning of the cortex (see Figure 9.2).

The dimensions and chemistry of the long bones in severe undernutrition have been well summarized by Dickerson and McCance (1961). Compared to well-fed age-mates, the humeri of piglets and the femora of cockerels were noticeably short and thin. The ratio of length to width, however, remained the same. The weight–length ratio of these bones was low in undernourished animals, reflecting the greatly reduced cortex. There was no evidence of a lack of calcium or phosphorus in the experimental animals; in fact the total amounts of mineral were similar to age-mate controls. The ratio of calcium to nitrogen was high in undernourished animals. Both of these findings reflect the lowered protein content of the bones, and therefore a *relative* hypercalcification of the cortex. Radiographically, this hypercalcification was seen as an increase in densely mineralized bands or "cement lines" surrounding resorption spaces, and as radiopaque transverse lines in the metaphyses, or growing ends, of the long bones. These hypermineralized bands were abnormal in that the matrix contained no collagen fibers.

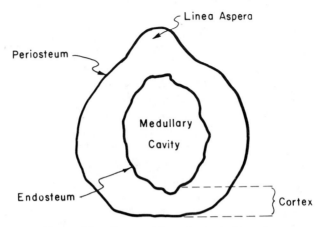

Figure 9.2.   Cross section of a typical long bone.

Although the long bones have been most intensively studied in undernutrition, they are not the only portion of the skeleton affected. Growth of the skull is retarded, and bones of the skull vault are thin (Garn *et al.* 1966). Growth of the mandible is relatively more retarded than that of the teeth, leading to crowding of teeth and impaction of unerupted teeth within the bone (McCance *et al.* 1961). It may be noted here that most abnormalities of bone structure and chemistry are eventually reversible if refeeding occurs during the growth period of the animal. Teeth, however, differ from bones in this regard; abnormalities of tooth structure resulting from undernutrition remain in spite of rehabilitation.

Many of the effects of underfeeding may be seen as not only a lack of energy, but also a physiological deficiency of protein. When the diet is restricted in calories, protein may be burned to provide necessary energy. Platt *et al.* (1961) have estimated that a 30–40% reduction in the amount of food consumed results in a 60% decrease in the protein value of the diet. Theoretically, therefore, even a high-protein diet could result in effective protein deficiency if fed in such small amounts that energy needs were not met.

When high-calorie, low-protein diets have been fed to laboratory animals, the resultant bone pathologies resemble those in simple undernutrition, but are generally more severe. Frandsen *et al.* (1954) showed that protein-deficient rats had severely retarded long-bone lengths, narrow epiphyseal growth plates, and fewer sites of actual bone formation. In rats fed a diet that was totally protein free, growth and ossification finally ceased, and the growth plate was sealed off with a thin layer of bone. The severity of these changes was undoubtedly influenced by the fact that these animals, although allowed unlimited amounts of protein-free food, refused to eat more than minimal amounts, and were therefore energy deficient as well. Pigs maintained on low-protein diets have shown skeletal changes similar to those in rats (Platt and Stewart 1962). Radiographically, the distal portion of the radius was rarified and contained numerous transverse "growth-arrest" lines. This osteoporotic appearance was considered to be a result of reduced matrix formation, and an imbalance in the activity of osteoblasts and osteoclasts. Skulls and vertebrae were also small and osteoporotic, with vertebral canals that were disproportionately large for their total cross sections. Protein-deficient dogs and monkeys showed similar changes (Jha *et al.* 1968).

Although rats on diets low in both protein and calcium lost mineral from their bones, simply supplementing the diet with calcium did not produce remineralization (El-Maraghi *et al.* 1965). However, the addition of protein to the diet resulted in significant increases in bone deposition, accompanied by greater osteoblastic and lesser osteoclastic action.

Taken together, these animal experiments indicate that bone changes in protein–energy deficiency are the result of decreased formation and increased destruction of bone matrix. The imbalance between the two processes can be viewed as part of the total adaptive response pattern of the body. In the face of protein and energy deficiencies, endogenous supplies can be liberated for use in maintaining growth and function. When deficiencies become severe or prolonged, even growth may be sacrificed. Thus the protein spared in nutrient-deficiency osteoporosis is theoretically made available for the maintenance of body systems, including bone.

Studies of living human populations show analogous skeletal changes in protein–energy malnutrition. Most notable of these are the reduction in stature and in total amount of bone. Children on diets low in energy, essential amino acids, or total protein, display disturbed growth patterns and a marked thinning of cortical bone (Garn 1966). In severe undernutrition, bone loss becomes systemic, involving skull, vertebrae, long bones of the limbs, and even the extremities. An increased number of Harris lines, or lines of growth arrest, are frequently seen. Poor mineralization is reflected in the large trabeculae and spongy appearance of the growing ends of bones. Ossification of secondary centers (epiphyses, wrist, ankle, etc.) appears to be delayed.

Garn *et al.* (1966) have suggested a development sequence for the skeletal changes in undernutrition. First, as energy intake decreases, growth requirements are increasingly ill met. Both longitudinal and transverse growth is slowed, whereas Harris lines become more frequent. Second, with continued caloric deficit, even the slowed rate of overall growth cannot be maintained. Although growth in length and width slowly continues, the amount of new bone added is insufficient, resulting in thinner bone cortices. Finally, as the child enters negative nitrogen balance and soft tissues become wasted, bone growth becomes even more economical. Not only is there a failure to add sufficient bone to maintain cortical volume, but existing bone may be "borrowed" to maintain growth and remodeling. The resulting volume of compact bone may be only half that expected for a given age.

Vitamin Deficiencies

Deficiencies of vitamins A, C, and D have been demonstrated to affect growth and development of bone. Probably the most visible and thoroughly studied of these for human populations has been vitamin D. In historic times at least, rickets has been one of the most important bone diseases of children in temperate climates. As early as 1660, rickets was attributed to damp climate and poor food (Stewart 1975). Although the curative effects of sunshine and cod-liver oil were known by the nineteenth century, the role of vitamin D was discovered only in the twentieth century through a series of laboratory experiments.

The clinical picture of vitamin D deficiency is well known. Viewed radiographically, the shafts of the long bones show a generalized rarefaction, with frequent deformities, such as bowing or twisting. Bones undergoing rapid growth are likely to be most severely affected. Trabecular patterns become blurred, and calcification at the growth plates becomes irregular. In addition to the deformities of the bone shaft, there are dramatic changes in the metaphyses. Remodeling of the funnel-shaped region of the metaphyses is disturbed, and a thick mass of uncalcified tissue develops. This overgrowth of matrix gives the ends of rachitic bones a swollen appearance, with a deeply cupped articular surface. As a result, rachitic subjects appear to have large knobby joints. Ribs are affected as well since long bones result in swelling at the costochondral junction. This "beading" of the ribs has been called the "rachitic rosary," and is a classic feature of the disease.

Vitamin D deficiency in adults results in osteomalacia, or softening of bone, with radiographic changes similar to those in rickets. In addition, adults may show symmetrical rarified transverse lines, or pseudofractures (Milkman 1930). If deficiency begins in adulthood, metaphyseal changes are not normally seen.

Histologically, both rickets and osteomalacia result from a failure of the osteoid matrix to calcify normally. Engfeldt and Hjertquist (1961) have reviewed the literature on the microscopic appearance of rachitic bone. The primary feature in both children and adults is the excess of uncalcified matrix. In children, islands of unremodeled cartilage may be seen in the bone trabeculae, surrounded by unmineralized osteoid. In adults, the Haversian system is poorly developed, with few osteons. Broad bands of subperiosteal osteoid remain uncalcified and unremodeled. The bowing deformities of rickets can be directly attributed to the effects of compression on this un-mineralized bone.

Bowing of long bones is also sometimes seen in vitamin C deficiency, or scurvy. Cortices of long bones become thin and radiolucent. In contrast to vitamin D deficiency, however, the osteoporosis of scurvy results from a reduced formation of calcifiable bone matrix. Fractures are common, due to the weakened cancellous bone in the metaphyseal area. Calcified spurs may be seen at the metaphyseal–diaphyseal junction, as remnants of old fracture callus. Subperiosteal hemorrhage is also a prominent feature of scurvy, and with periodic recurrence, may lead to a thickening of the bone shaft. Blood pooled beneath the periosteum may calcify during bouts of healing, eventually leading to a buildup of bone on the outer surface. This may occur on the superior surface of the orbits as well as in the long bones, resulting in a pitted appearance (Steinbock 1976).

Although significant bone changes are known to accompany experimental vitamin A deficiency, these probably have little relevance for human skeletal populations. Under normal conditions, humans store large amounts of vitamin A in the liver, and can synthesize it readily from dietary precursors. When severe deficiencies of vitamin A occur in modern populations, they appear to result from diets greatly restricted in variety as well as in amount. Symptoms in such populations primarily involve epithelial tissue, although neural changes have been suggested (Barnicot and Datta 1972; Rodahl 1966). The involvement of bone in human hypovitaminosis A remains speculative.

Bony changes demonstrated for rats (Wolbach 1947) and dogs (Mellanby 1938) are the result of disturbances in site and activity of osteoblasts and osteoclasts. In general, a deficiency of vitamin A promotes excessive osteoclastic activity on bone surfaces next to the marrow cavity, and excess osteoblastic activity on nonmarrow surfaces. This results in an enlargement of the marrow cavity and an increase in the total width of the bone; length of bones is not affected. Increases in diameter are most noticeable in the skull vault, mandible, long bones, and neural arches of the vertebrae.

Inorganic Nutrients

Calcium and phosphorus are undoubtedly the most important mineral elements for the growth and maintenance of the skeletal system. Bone serves as the primary mineral bank for the living organism, accumulating reserves during growth, and releasing them during periods of low intake or increased expenditure. The adult human skeleton may contain 1200 g or more of calcium and 500 g of phosphorus, as well as citrate, carbonate, sodium, magnesium, and traces of other elements (Stewart 1975). Deficiencies of these nutrients at the cellular level may be the result of impaired absorption or transport, as well as simple dietary insufficiency. Conversely, when intakes are low, transport may be enhanced such that serum calcium–phosphorus ratios are maintained (Winter *et al.* 1972). It should be emphasized that the ratios of available minerals are more important for skeletal maintenance than are absolute amounts.

Experimental feeding of diets low in calcium has generally been reported to produce osteoporosis, characterized by the development of normal bone in reduced amounts (Parsons and Hampton 1969). Growth may be slowed, and turnover rates increased. El-Maraghi *et al.* (1965) report increased osteoclasis, low ash values, and numerous intercortical resorption spaces for animals on low-calcium diets. Ratio of new bone to old bone also increased and was reflected in the decreased mineralization seen.

A variety of dietary and environmental conditions can interact with calcium intake to affect bone formation and mineralization. For example, protein–energy deficiency, vitamin D deficiency, and disuse can all exacerbate the effects of low calcium intake. Among the Eskimo, low levels of vitamin D and dietary calcium may interact to produce behavioral and skeletal changes. Compression fractures of the vertebrae are common in Eskimo populations, and age-related osteoporosis begins early in both sexes (Mazess and Mather 1974). It has been suggested that, in late winter, dwindling food supplies and lack of vitamin D may critically reduce available calcium, resulting in symptoms of arctic hysteria (Foulks 1973; Katz and Foulks 1969).

By contrast, high lactose diets have been shown to increase the efficiency of calcium utilization (Lengeman and Comar 1961), and an adequate supply of calcium reduces the amount of vitamin D necessary for bone mineralization. An ability to digest lactose would therefore appear advantageous in areas of low solar radiation, where vitamin D production may be limited. The use of fresh milk and a low incidence of lactose intolerance should therefore be theoretically advantageous for populations at high latitudes.

Calcium intake can also affect the utilization of phosphorus. Rickets has been induced experimentally in rats not only by deficiencies of vitamin D, but also by low phosphorus intakes, or by a calcium–phosphorus imbalance. The appearance of osteomalacia or rickets can be induced in rats by the addition of extra calcium to their diet (Stewart 1975). With a calcium–phosphorus ratio of 4, or 5:1, calcium combines with phosphorus to render it metabolically unavailable. The resulting bone is characterized by excessive osteoid formation, and poor mineralization.

Debate over the effect of dietary phytic acid on phosphorus utilization continues. The rachitogenic effect of many cereal-based diets has been noted, and attributed to high levels of phytate. Phytate is known to bind minerals, including phosphorus, and much of the phytate phosphorus ingested has been shown to be excreted intact (McCance and Widdowson 1935, 1942). This indicates that the full phosphorus content of the diet was not organically available. Cooking, however, can reduce the amount of phytate found in raw vegetable products, as does phytase, an enzyme occurring naturally in phytate-containing plants. The action of phytase is enhanced by acidity and heat (up to 70°C) (Gontzea and Sutescu 1968). Thus, prolonged yeast action and baking can reduce phytate content of whole wheat bread by 40%. Furthermore, there is evidence that humans can adapt to the ingestion of phytate and can release a significant portion of the bound dietary minerals. Because human digestive juices do not appear to contain phytase, it has been hypothesized that this is accomplished through the action of microorganisms in the intestine (Gontzea and Sutescu 1968).

Phytate has also been shown to lower the absorption of calcium, iron, zinc, and magnesium. This does not appear to adversely affect skeletal mineralization in individuals with access to a varied diet and sufficient vitamin D. However, in populations relying largely on unleavened whole-meal bread as a dietary staple, mineral deficiencies may occasionally become pronounced (Berlyne *et al.* 1973; Wills *et al.* 1972). In areas of the Middle East where abnormally high phytate diets have been combined with geophagy (ingestion of large amounts of clay), a distinctive syndrome of zinc-deficiency dwarfism has been reported (Halsted *et al.* 1972; Prasad *et al.* 1961; Ronaghy and Halsted 1975).

Manganese, copper, and iron have also been experimentally manipulated such that bone growth was disturbed. With the exception of iron (discussed in the following), it is doubtful that these experimental conditions are significant for human populations. Even marginal human diets generally contain enough of these elements to prevent frank deficiency.

NUTRITIONAL DEFICIENCIES IN ARCHAEOLOGICAL POPULATIONS

As can be seen from the previous section, the assessment of nutritional status is extremely complex and difficult, even for living populations. Although anthropometric measures have been useful for comparison of individuals and sample populations to growth standards, there are difficulties in assessing nutritional deficiency in these groups. Stature, for example, has been used as one indication of nutritional status. Other indexes that consider weight to height ratios have also been used. The anthropologist studying nutritional deficiencies in living populations has the advantage of examining soft tissues such as fat and muscle, which are more sensitive to nutritional changes. Even with the advantage of examining soft tissues, it is often difficult to select appropriate indicators of nutritional status, particularly when deficiencies are subclinical.

The skeletal biologist working with archaeological populations does not have the advantage of using most of the indicators available for living populations. There are, however, advantages to the use of archaeological skeletons in dietary reconstruction. Archaeological samples can provide large series of complete skeletons. Consequently, the physical anthropologist can examine the total skeleton to determine the effects of nutrition on the various bones of an individual. This will reflect the systemic effects of stress. In addition, skeletal biologists may have the total population at their disposal. One of the problems with much growth research, particularly in cases of malnutrition, is that most of the attention is focused on the survivors. Those who are most severely involved (i.e., those that die) are examined either superficially or not at all.

Specific Deficiencies Identified in Archaeological Samples

Steinbock (1976:322) reemphasizes the difficulty in ascertaining specific nutritional deficiencies from archaeological skeletal material. He states, "it should be emphasized that malnutrition is rarely selective for only one vital component. Malnutrition (including malabsorption and excessive loss of nutrients) is almost always multiple, resulting in deficiency of several or many nutrients to varying degrees." In addition, many of the nutritional deficiencies leave no skeletal changes. Beri-beri (thiamine deficiency), for example, is not detectable in bone, and humans with severe vitamin A depletion usually die of other causes before skeletal lesions become evident. Pellagra (niacin deficiency) is of considerable interest because it is found where maize is a staple crop. Despite the prevalence of maize horticulture in many areas of the New World, there is presently no evidence of skeletal involvement from pellagra. A variety of explanations can be advanced to account for this lack of evidence. Experimentally induced niacin deficiency in other animals has produced little information on the skeletal processes affected. Thus, effects may be so slight as to have escaped detection by normal analytic procedures.

Vitamin D and vitamin C deficiencies are also difficult to detect in archaeological bone. There is, however, some skeletal evidence from archaeological samples for vitamin D deficiency. Virchow (1872) argued that many features of the Neanderthal skull were due to deficiency of vitamin D, and Pruner-Bey (1868) ascribed lateral flattening of Cro-Magnon tibiae to the same cause. Wells (1975) notes that neither of these diagnoses could be sustained. Reports of vitamin D deficiency have been found in archaeological Danish populations (Furst 1920; Nielsen 1911). Møller-Christensen (1958) has a frequency of about 1% in a Danish monastery cemetery ($N = 800$) (Aebelholt) that was in use from 1250 to 1550 (Wells 1975:753). Gejvall (1960) found only one case in a sample of 364 individuals in the cemetery at Westerhus, Sweden. According to Wells, there is considerable controversy about the Precolumbian occurrence of vitamin D deficiency in the Americas. Although there are some reports from the earlier part of this century, there has been little evidence from more recent investigations in which the analysis is more systematic.

Wells believes that there is a positive correlation between rickets and urbanization in postmedieval, industrial Europe. In fact, historic sites in England show significant increases of the disease. Wells notes that almost a quarter of the 50 burials from Norwich show classic examples of rickets (1975:755), with individuals displaying severe bowing of the femora and tibiae.

There are similar problems with the analysis of scurvy (vitamin C deficiency) in prehistory. The most important diagnostic features are related to changes in soft tissue. Swollen, spongy, and infected gums and subcutaneous hemorrhages are some of the important diagnostic features of scurvy. Since these features are often difficult to diagnose in bone, obtaining archaeological evidence for this condition is likely to be problematic. Even with the problems of diagnosis, Møller-Christensen (1958) reports 78 cases of scurvy in 800 Aebelholt individuals, whereas Gejvall found only one case ($N = 364$) in the medieval Swedish cemetery at Westerhus (Gejvall 1960). Wells (1975:757) found about 7 cases (7%) in Anglo-Saxon burials from Anglia.

Steinbock (1976:254) is optimistic about the possibility of improving the diagnosis of scurvy in skeletal remains. The subperiosteal hemorrhages produced by the disease provide one of the most important diagnostic features. The ossification or calcification of these hematomas provides the archaeological evidence for vitamin C deficiency. Even when these subperiosteal hemorrhages are resorbed, the increased osteoclastic activity weakens the cancellous bone in the metaphyses. Steinbock reports that, on the basis of these diagnostic features, Saul (1972, 1973) found 27% of the 63 adult ancient Mayas to have ossified periosteal lesions, which he diagnosed as probable cases of scurvy. Saul speculates that this evidence of famine and disease may provide an explanation for the collapse of Maya civilization. More substantial evidence would be required, however, before such a conclusion concerning the Maya collapse would be warranted.

Although vitamin deficiencies have been reported from the archaeological record, the diagnostic problems of protein and energy malnutrition have been thought intractable. A typical comment is made by Wells: "No indubitable examples of kwashiorkor are known from ancient burial grounds and it is unlikely that any will be recognized unless some wholly unexpected method of identification can be devised" (1975:758). It is true that traditional methods have not proved successful in identifying protein–energy deficiency. However, the methodology that now offers promise in identifying protein–energy deficiency does not rely on new techniques, but on a systematic application of techniques that have been available for years.

The search for specific diagnostic skeletal markers of malnutrition has been unsuccessful since skeletal responses to nutritional stress are generalized and systemic. The systemic nature of these responses, however, can be used to interpret the nature of the stressors involved. Rather than searching for single diagnostic criteria, bone growth patterns, remodeling, infection, repair, and aging for an entire skeletal population can be examined. The occurrence of stress markers at different parts of the life cycle can also be examined and then compared to the mortality schedule of the group. Finally, information derived from direct examination of the skeletal remains can then be combined with environmental data to produce a more realistic picture of the nutritional status of the populations under study.

The following section outlines skeletal markers that have been used as indicators of nutritionally induced stress. Reconstruction of past dietary status requires the examination of many such markers for both subgroups at risk and the entire skeletal population.

Measures of Nutritional Stress in Bone

Long-bone Growth Curves

Although a variety of methods exist for determining nutritional status in children, the most widely used single measure is growth. Not only is growth sensitive to nutritional disturbance, but it is relatively easy to assess. Since growth in the skeletal system accounts for over 98% of an individual's total height, it is appropriate to view growth disturbances caused by malnutrition as disturbances of the skeletal system process. Growth in length of long bones reflects overall statural increase, and can therefore be used as a proxy measure.

Lengths of long bones have been plotted against age for a variety of modern and prehistoric populations. Comparison of the resulting curves (or formulas derived from them) can be used to indicate differences in timing or amount of growth of long bones in several modern populations, and Maresh (1955) has constructed growth curves from data on well-nourished American children. These form a standard against which growth in skeletal populations can be measured.

The construction of reliable growth curves from skeletal material requires the use of a large and well-preserved subadult population, and the use of dental age as an approximation of chronological age. Armelagos *et al.* (1972) have compiled such data for tibia, fibula, femur, radius, ulna, humerus, and clavicle from prehistoric Sudanese Nubia. Johnston (1962), Merchant and Ubelaker (1977), and Ubelaker (1978) have compiled growth curves from North American data. The growth curves for prehistoric populations may differ from the theoretical modern curves in two basic ways. First, the shape of the two curves may be similar, but the prehistoric population may display delayed growth (slower overall growth, later adolescent growth spurt, or later achievement of adult stature). Second, the shape of the curves may differ, indicating discrepancies in the growth *pattern*.

Delays in growth and maturation have been recognized in modern populations. Frisancho and Garn (1970) and Frisancho *et al.* (1970) believe that these delays are an adaptive response to chronic low nutrient availability. Thomas has shown that the delayed maturation evidenced in a highland Quechua population significantly reduces the population's energy (1973). Delayed growth, small adult size, and reduced sexual dimorphism all reduce nutrient requirements and may be a complex of adaptations to low nutrient availability (Thomas 1973).

Delayed growth curves have also been commonly observed in prehistoric populations. Using cross-sectional data from three prehistoric Sudanese Nubian populations, Armelagos *et al.* (1972) found a suggestion of retarded growth. Rapid increase in length occurred during the first two years, and again during the early teen years. Although it is difficult to isolate an adolescent growth spurt from cross-sectional data, these findings suggest that maximal growth may have been later than for modern populations. The finding that epiphyseal fusion is not complete in all individuals by the twenty-fifth year is further evidence of delayed maturation in this group.

Lallo (1973) presents a very similar growth pattern for the Dickson Mounds populations from the Illinois River Valley. The greatest postinfant increase in long-bone length occurs after the fifteenth year. Long-bones for individuals who died between the ages of 25 and 35 are significantly longer than those who died between the ages of 20 and 25. It therefore appears that growth often continued well into the third decade. Thus, the growth curves of preindustrial populations seem to differ from those of well-nourished modern populations in that there is a regular demonstration of delayed maturation in the former. These differences may be due at least in part to long-term mild or moderate undernutrition and may be seen as an "adaptive" response to low nutrient availability.

In contrast to growth delays, differences in the actual shape of growth curves between populations have received little attention. Where they are found, such differences probably reflect more severe and more acute disturbances. According to Tanner (1977), the theoretical pattern of growth derived from modern populations follows a smooth curve of the form

$$Y = a + b(x) + c \log(x)$$

When Bickerton (1979) plotted long-bone length against dental age for Dickson Mounds juveniles (0–7 years), all long bones showed a slight but perceptive slowing of growth around 2–5 years. When these data were fitted to a polynomial regression, it was found that the third-degree polynomial gave a significantly better fit than the second-degree polynomial (Goodman 1980). This indicates a fundamentally different growth pattern, accounted for by the early-childhood deceleration.

Observations of the Sudanese Nubian growth curves (Armelagos *et al.* 1972) and those from Indian Knoll, Kentucky (Johnston 1962, 1968) also reveal a similar slowing of growth around the ages of 2–6 years. Because weaning traditionally occurs at this age and is frequently accompanied by infection and refusal to eat, we hypothesize that this growth pattern reflects acute nutritional stress. Such stress should be most obvious in areas where suitable weaning foods are absent or low in protein.

A comparison with the growth curves for pre–nineteenth century Eskimo and Aleut bears out this contention (Y'Edynak 1976). These populations show no cessation of growth before the sixth year. Between 6 and 8 years, there is a marked growth retardation in females, which is later compensated by a preadolescent growth spurt of greater magnitude than that found in males. This pattern may reflect late weaning and a high-protein diet. It suggests, however, that females may have different patterns of activity or diet, particularly beyond 6 years of age.

Adult Stature

Despite the long tradition of anthropometry in physical anthropology, the relationship between adult stature and nutritional stress remains unclear. Small adult stature is frequently associated with chronic low nutrient availability, and it has been proposed that under such circumstances small body size may be an energy-efficient response (Thomas 1973). Determining the relationship between short-term nutrient stresses during the growth phase and later-attained adult stature is more problematic. Although growth is reduced when food intake is inadequate, refeeding has been shown to produce "catch-up growth" in both experimental animals and malnourished children (Himes 1978). This growth spurt can offset most, if not all, growth retardation resulting from short-term periods of undernutrition. Timing and degree of malnutrition are important; however, milder insults of short duration, or those occurring later in the growth period, are more adequately compensated by "catch-up growth."

Because there is such a strong genetic component to adult stature, researchers are understandably wary about attributing height differences between populations to environmental factors. One area in which comparison of mean height between skeletal populations has occurred is in the analysis of secular trends in height within countries and defined geographical regions (Acheson and Fowler 1964; Craig 1963). Reasons given for secular increases in adult stature include decreases in childhood–infancy disease, exogamy-produced hybrid vigor, less exposure to environmental stressors, and elimination of nutritional deficiencies (Dubos 1965:77–79). Of these factors, improvement in nutritional status is perhaps most frequently cited, and is generally thought to be the most important.

Differences in adult stature may be attributed to differential nutritionally induced stress only if reasonable control is given to genetic factors and other obvious environmental factors (high altitude, temperature, cultural factors, etc.). (See Haas and Harrison 1977 for a review of such factors.) This control is not often possible, but could be approached by the study of a single archaeological population that has undergone a change in subsistence patterns. Other confounding factors, such as loss of the most highly stressed subadults through mortality, and the variable effects of catch-up growth, make adult stature a relatively insensitive indicator of juvenile nutritionally induced stress. Adult stature, therefore, should be used with other indicators as a collaborative measure of stress.

Sexual Dimorphism and Other Measures of Adult Shape

Measures of adult shape, such as the degree of sexual dimorphism within a population, have similar problems as indicators of juvenile nutrient stress as do measures of adult stature. Shape measures may be largely genetic and are affected by a variety of environmental factors. However, Stini (1969, 1972, 1975) believes that certain shape differences between populations are at least partly the result of differences in nutrient availability. In attempting to document the effect of nutritional availability on sexual dimorphism, he has concluded that males are more adversely affected by undernutrition than females. This results from hormonal factors in females that help to maintain a more consistent growth pattern. It follows that in times of food scarcity, males will be smaller and dimorphism will decrease. For modern populations, at least, there appears to be strong association between nutrient availability and sexual dimorphism.

Lallo (1973) has tested this proposed relationship for the Dickson Mounds populations, from the Illinois River Valley. This population underwent a rapid change in diet. During a period of 400 years, they experienced a shift from hunting and gathering to a form of intensified agriculture. Using femoral and pelvic indicators of sexual dimorphism, Lallo was unable to show a significant difference in the degree of sexual dimorphism among the three Dickson skeletal populations. These results do not invalidate Stini's hypotheses. Rather, it may reflect difficulty in demonstrating changes in dimorphism in an archaeological population undergoing rapid changes in diet.

Other macroscopic measures of adult skeletal size and shape (humeral–femoral index, long-bone width–long-bone length, etc.) have similar limitations as diagnostic features. Greater control is needed to increase the validity of these measures; and even then, they are not likely to be the most sensitive indicators of nutritionally induced stress. They can, however, be employed in a multifactorial approach in which measures of greater and lesser sensitivity are combined to produce a pattern of skeletal involvement. Some of the more sensitive indicators of stress are discussed in the following sections.

Porotic Hyperostosis

Porotic hyperostosis, along with osteoporosis, is one of the best-studied stress markers available for studying archaeological populations. Although it is often difficult to uncover indisputable evidence of nutritional deficiency in skeletal material, recent evidence suggests that porotic hyperostosis may result from iron-deficiency anemia. In conditions of anemia, red cell production is increased, with a concomitant expansion of the marrow cavities of the thin bones of the skeleton. The skull in particular becomes thickened, as a result of significant expansion of the diploe. As the marrow spaces expand, the outer layer of bone becomes very thin, often exposing the trabecular bone of the diploe. The thickened bone and the porous, sievelike appearance are the most distinctive characteristics of the condition. The cranial bones most commonly involved are the superior portion of the orbits, the forehead portion of the frontal bone, and the parietal above the temporal line (Figure 9.3).

Moseley (1963) and Steinbock (1976:213–252) have discussed the problems of differential diagnosis in porotic hyperostosis. They note that most of the anemias show skeletal manifestations, but that the pattern and extent of involvement can usually distinguish between nutritional anemias and those caused by hereditary factors (Table 9.1). In general, the skeletal changes in nutritional anemias are less severe.

Earlier studies have emphasized hereditary anemias as the primary cause of porotic hyperostosis. Sickle-cell anemia or thalassemia has been the most frequent diagnosis of the condition. Eng (1958) was one of the first researchers to report that skeletal changes resembling hereditary anemias resulted from iron-deficiency anemia. Moseley (1965) further argued that the Precolumbian cases of porotic hyperostosis are the result of iron-deficiency anemia. In an important study of porotic hyperostosis, Hengen (1971) explained the

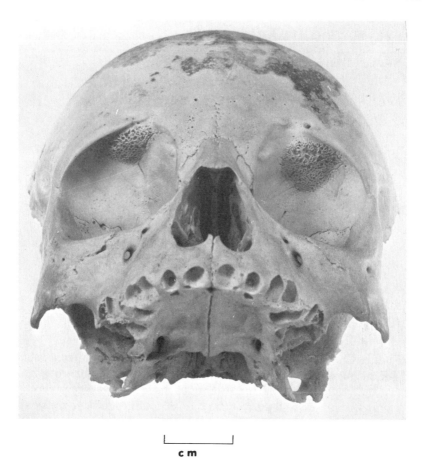

c m

Figure 9.3. Porotic hyperostosis (cribra orbitalia) of the orbital surface.

etiology of the condition in prehistoric populations, and isolated the various geographical and cultural factors associated with the condition. He argued that poor hygienic practices and parasitic involvement were responsible for iron-deficiency anemias, which resulted in porotic hyperostosis.

Another explanation advanced is that of Møller-Christensen (1953) who notes that in a group of 190 skulls from a leper cemetery at Naestved, Denmark, 45% of the adults and 83% of the children showed evidence of porotic hyperostosis of the orbits. Although Møller-Christensen argues that leprosy is the possible cause of the lesion, he does not specify how leprosy could have resulted in the lesion and does not attempt to link the infection with nutrition.

Although porotic hyperostosis is not by itself diagnostic of a specific anemia, it is a useful tool for investigating nutritional stress in an archaeologi-

TABLE 9.1

Partial List of Conditions That May Result in Porotic Hyprostosis of the Cranium[a]

Congenital hemolytic anemias
A. Thalassemias
1. Thalassemia major (Mediterranean disease, Cooley's anemia, erythroblastic anemia)
2. Thalassemia intermedia–severe heterozygous
3. Thalassemia minor–mild heterozygous
B. Sickle-cell disease
1. Sickle-cell anemia (Hemoglobin S-homozygous)
2. Hemoglobin C-homozygous
3. Hemoglobin E-homozygous
4. Hemoglobin S-C
5. Hemoglobin S-thalassemia
6. Other less common abnormal hemoglobins
C. Hereditary nonspherocytic hemolytic anemia
1. Glucose-6-phosphate dehydrogenase deficiency
2. Pyruvate kinase deficiency
3. Probably other deficiencies
D. Hereditary spherocytosis (spherocytic anemia, congenital hemolytic jaundice)
E. Hereditary elliptocytosis (rare)
Iron-deficiency anemia
Cyanotic congenital heart disease (rare)
Polycythemia vera in childhood (rare)

[a] From Mensforth *et al.* (1978). Adapted from Moseley (1965).

cal population. The use of such an indicator for nutritional inference should be undertaken within the context of an ecological analysis of a group's total adaptation. The distribution and severity of the lesion, the occurrence with respect to age and sex, and the reconstruction of the group's subsistence pattern should facilitate identification of nutritional anemias.

Using a paleoepidemiological approach, Carlson *et al.* (1974) undertook an analysis of porotic hyperostosis in a population from Sudanese Nubia. Carlson and his coworkers noted a high frequency of porotic hyperostosis (21%), which was restricted to the superior border of the orbit. The frequency among children aged 0–6 was 32%, significantly higher than in the population as a whole. The relatively mild involvement (affecting only the superior border of the orbits) and the age distribution argue against a serious hereditary anemia as the cause. The reliance on cereal grains such as millet and wheat, which are poor sources of iron, stress induced by weaning practices, and the probable high incidence of parasitic infection, suggest iron-deficiency anemia as the most likely cause of porotic hyperostosis in the Nubian case.

El-Najjar and coworkers (1976) reached similar conclusions in their analysis of porotic hyperostosis in prehistoric Native American groups of the Southwest. The reliance on maize (another cereal grain poor in iron) was believed to predispose these groups to nutritional anemias. Carlson *et al.* (1974) and El-Najjar *et al.* (1976) argue that iron-deficiency anemia results from a diet low in iron, foods that inhibit the bioavailability of iron, infectious conditions that reduce the absorption of iron, and weaning diarrhea. Thus, the interpretation of porotic hyperostosis requires an ecological perspective, both a reconstruction of the subsistence pattern of the archaeological population and a detailed paleoepidemiological analysis of the pathological conditions found.

Lallo *et al.* (1977) provided such an analysis for the Dickson Mounds population. The frequency of porotic hyperostosis increased as the subsistence pattern changed; as the population increased its reliance on agriculture, the frequency of porotic hyperostosis nearly quadrupled (from 13.6 to 51.5%, see Table 9.2). The increased reliance on maize may have increased the potential for iron-deficiency anemia. Maize is not only low in iron, but also contains phytates that can inhibit the absorption of iron. The major impact of the nutritional deficiency appears to have been on infants and children (Table 9.3). By using more refined age categories, Lallo and coworkers were able to determine the age of onset and the peak frequencies for nutritional anemias. Infants during their first year and children between the ages of 2 and 5 were shown to be at greatest risk. This is consistent with dietary patterns of modern populations, in which iron supplementation is recommended beyond the age of 6 months.

In addition, Lallo *et al.* were able to establish an association between the occurrence of porotic hyperostosis and infection. Infection was measured by the extent of periosteal reaction in the long bones. These researchers demonstrated that a synergistic relationship existed between porotic hyperostosis and periosteal reaction (Table 9.4). Individuals in this sample with both porotic hyperostosis and periosteal infection usually displayed a more severe manifestation of each condition. For example, if an individual displayed only porotic hyperostosis, it would likely be restricted to the orbit. However, if there was evidence of periosteal reaction, porotic hyperostosis was usually found to be more severe and more extensive (i.e., not restricted to the orbits, but involving the frontal and parietals as well). Similarly, in-

TABLE 9.2

Porotic Hyperostosis in the Dickson Mounds Population[a]

	N	Porotic hyperostosis	%
Late Woodland	44	6	13.6
Mississippian-acculturated			
Late Woodland	93	29	31.2
Middle Mississippian	101	52	51.5

[a] Modified from Lallo *et al.* (1977:476, Table 1).

TABLE 9.3

Age Specific Frequency of Porotic Hyperostosis for the Combined Samples from Dickson Mounds[a]

		Porotic hyperostosis	
Age	N	N	%
0–.9	79	16	20.3
1–1.9	45	13	28.9
2–4.9	43	20	46.5
5–9.9	45	28	62.2
10–14.9	26	10	38.5
Total	238	87	36.6

[a] Modified from Lallo *et al.* (1977:478, Table 2).

dividuals with porotic hyperostosis and evidence of reactive periosteal bone display a greater infectious involvement. The severity of the periosteal reaction was greater, and there were more bones showing evidence of infectious reaction (Figure 9.4). The mechanism of the synergistic reaction of nutrition and infection has been established in contemporary populations. Iron-deficiency anemia can inhibit the body's immunological ability to ward off infections. Conversely, infections can reduce the ability of the digestive system to absorb the nutrients necessary for survival.

Although the study by Lallo and his coworkers has clarified the relationship of porotic hyperostosis to both subsistence change and to infection, it has one major methodological drawback. This study did not distinguish between healed and nonhealed periosteal or porotic hyperostotic lesions. Analysis of healed and nonhealed lesions can provide the basis for evaluating the age of onset for nutritional anemias and for determining the impact on survival of those with the condition. For example, a finding in which 29% of second-year

TABLE 9.4

Frequency of Infectious Lesions (Periostitis and Osteomyelitis) and Porotic Hyperostosis[a]

Dickson population	N	Postcranial infectious lesions		Porotic hyperostosis		Porotic hyperostosis and infectious lesions	
		N	%	N	%	N	%
Late Woodland	44	9	20.5	6	13.6	3	6.5
Mississippian-acculturated Late Woodland	93	45	48.4	29	31.2	20	21.5
Middle Mississippian	101	74	73.3	52	51.5	41	40.6
Total	238	128	53.8	87	36.5	64	26.9

[a] Modified from Lallo *et al.* (1977:479).

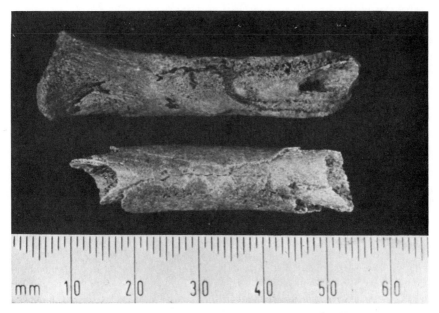

Figure 9.4.   Periosteal reaction involving the long-bone shaft.

mortalities showed porotic hyperostosis with evidence of healing would indicate that the condition occurred at an earlier age and the individuals sur-
vived the earlier episode of stress. We would assume that those who show no
indication of healing experienced a more recent episode of nutritional stress.

A more thorough analysis of porotic hyperostosis has been undertaken by
Mensforth *et al.* (1978), using more refined age categories and distinguishing
between remodeled and unremodeled lesions. Similar assessments were made
of the periosteal reaction in long bones. The analysis of porotic hyperostosis
and periosteal reactions in the same population provides the means for
establishing the relationship between anemia and infection with respect to age
of onset, duration, and decline of these conditions. The study was undertaken
on a Late Woodland ossuary sample from the Libben site (Ottawa County,
Ohio) composed of 1327 articulated skeletons, 452 of which were infants and
children.

The distribution of unremodeled porotic hyperostosis (Figure 9.5, Tables
9.5 and 9.6) indicates that the lesion does not occur before the age of 6 months
and occurs at a low frequency between the sixth and twelfth months. There is,
however, a dramatic rise in incidence between the first and third year, with a
frequency of about of 60%. From the third to the tenth year there is a leveling
off in frequency to about 20%. The highest frequency for periosteal reaction
occurs during the first year (Figure 9.6, Tables 9.7 and 9.8), in which half the

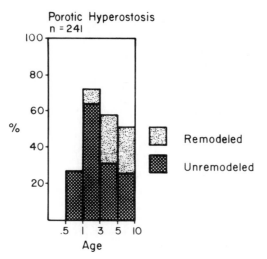

Figure 9.5. Age-specific frequency distribution of remodeled and unremodeled porotic hyperostosis among Libben infants and children (from Mensforth *et al.* 1978).

infants show evidence of infection. It should be noted that the first year is a period of high mortality for the Libben population. The rate of periosteal reaction decreases following the first year. Between the fifth and tenth year, the frequency of new cases of infection (as measured by unremodeled periosteal reaction) decreases to about 5%.

Age of onset, peak frequency, and age of decline are characteristics of porotic hyperostosis that are the result of nutritional anemias (Figure 9.7). Periosteal reaction begins earlier than hyperostosis and peaks between the ages of 6 months and 1 year. Porotic hyperostosis peaks around the third year.

The impact of the association of porotic hyperostosis and periosteal reaction can be demonstrated by examining the frequency and age distribution of

TABLE 9.5

The Frequency of Occurrence of Porotic Hyperostosis from Libben[a]

Age	N	Porotic hyperostosis			
		Present	%	Absent	%
0–6 mo	52	0	0.0	52	100.0
6–12 mo	38	10	26.3	28	73.7
1–3 yr	71	51	71.8	20	28.2
3–5 yr	26	15	57.7	11	42.3
5–10 yr	54	31	57.4	23	42.6
Total	241	107	44.4	134	55.6

[a] From Mensforth *et al.* (1978:29).

TABLE 9.6

The Frequency of Remodeled and Unremodeled Porotic Hyperostosis (Libben)[a]

Age	N	Remodeled		Unremodeled	
		N	%	N	%
1–3 yr	51	6	11.8	45	88.2
3–5 yr	15	7	46.7	8	51.1
5–10 yr	31	17	54.8	14	45.2
Total	97	30	30.9	67	69.1

[a] From Mensforth et al. (1978).

individuals with both conditions (Figure 9.8, Tables 9.9–9.11). A Yule's Q coefficient shows a strong positive association between both conditions in the 6–12 month and the 12–24 month period ($Q = +.63$; $x^2 = 7.79$, $p \leq .01$). After age two, there is no age-specific association. As Mensforth and his coworkers note, between the sixth and twelfth month, weanling diarrhea has been implicated as the leading cause of mortality in industrial and preindustrial societies (Gordon et al. 1963).

The Libben data indicate that the early onset of infections appears to be the factor that precipitates the nutritional deficiency in this population. The iron used by pathogens, the decrease in the ability of intestines to absorb iron during infection, and the increased need for iron during the intensive growth of

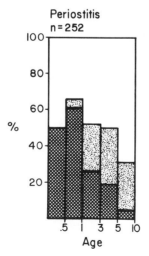

Figure 9.6. Age-specific frequency distribution of remodeled and unremodeled periosteal reactions (Libben). (From Mensforth et al. 1978:35.)

TABLE 9.7

The Frequency of Occurrence of Periosteal Reactions from Libben[a]

Age	N	Periosteal Reactions			
		Present	%	Absent	%
0–6 mo	52	26	50.0	26	50.0
6–12 mo	38	25	65.8	13	34.2
1–3 yr	67	35	52.2	32	47.8
3–5 yr	26	13	50.0	13	50.0
5–10 yr	69	21	30.4	48	69.6
Total	252	120	47.6	132	52.4

[a] From Mensforth et al. (1978:34).

the first 2 years of life are probably the most critical elements in the development of anemia in the Libben population.

The archaeological reconstruction of Libben suggests that diet is not the major factor in the etiology of porotic hyperostosis at this site. The available protein appears to have been adequate. The synergistic response of microbial infection, malabsorption due to weaning diarrhea, and nutrient depletion that occurs with rapid growth are the more likely causes of porotic hyperostosis in the Libben population.

In summary, we agree with Mensforth et al. (1978:47) in their conclusion that the partitioning of skeletal populations into broad age categories may obscure the pathophysiological factors contributing to porotic hyperostosis. Further, they convincingly argue that the physical qualities (remodeled and unremodeled) of porotic hyperostosis and periosteal reactions provide a method for estimating the impact of nutritional and infectious disease stressors on morbidity and mortality in prehistoric populations. Paleoepidemiological analysis of this sort, in conjunction with a thorough analysis of subsistence pattern, may provide a means for understanding the role of diet and disease in archaeological populations.

TABLE 9.8

The Frequency of Remodeled and Unremodeled Periosteal Reactions from Libben[a]

Age	N	Remodeled		Unremodeled	
		N	%	N	%
6–12 mo	25	2	8.0	23	92.0
1–3 yr	35	18	51.4	17	48.6
3–5 yr	13	8	61.5	5	38.5
5–10 yr	21	17	81.0	4	19.0
Total	94	45	47.9	49	52.1

[a] From Mensforth et al. (1978).

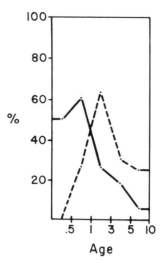

Figure 9.7. Age-specific frequency distribution of unremodeled porotic hyperostosis and periosteal reactions. Porotic hyperostosis, – – · – –; periostitis, — · —. (Libben) (From Mensforth *et al.* 1978:37.)

Osteoporosis as Dietary Indicator

Osteoporosis, defined as a decrease in bone mass, has been studied in contemporary (Garn 1970) and prehistoric populations (Armelagos *et al.* 1972; Carlson *et al.* 1976; Dewey *et al.* 1969; Ericksen 1976; Ortner 1975; Perzigian 1973). This wealth of research has demonstrated that bone loss is a normal

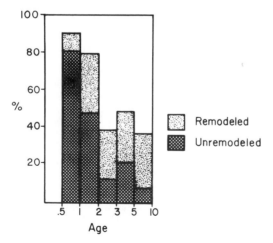

Figure 9.8. Age-specific frequency distribution of remodeled and unremodeled periosteal reactions, as they occur in individuals with porotic hyperostosis (Libben). (From Mensforth *et al.* 1978:40.)

TABLE 9.9

The Frequency of Occurrence of Individuals with Both Porotic Hyperostosis and Periosteal Reactions (Libben)[a]

Age	N	Porotic Hyperostosis and Periosteal Reactions			
		Present	%	Absent	%
0–6 mo	0	0	0.0	0	0.0
6–12 mo	10	9	90.0	1	10.0
1–2 yr	24	19	79.2	5	20.8
2–3 yr	27	10	37.0	17	63.0
3–5 yr	15	7	46.7	8	53.3
5–10 yr	31	11	35.5	20	64.5
Total	107	56	52.3	51	47.7

[a] From Mensforth et al. (1978).

feature of the aging process. In addition, however, there have been attempts to relate bone loss to differences in subsistence patterns. Perzigian (1973) specifically tested the hypothesis that change in diet may affect the rate at which osteoporosis develops. Although he found an increase in the size of medullary cavity (a common measure of osteoporosis) in agriculturalists as compared to hunter–gatherers, he did not believe this to be nutritionally related. Rather, he reasoned that agricultural populations have a more adequate nutritional intake, and, therefore, the increase in osteoporosis could not be explained on the basis of diet. Apparently, Perzigian accepted the assumption that agriculturalists are better fed. However, since there is historical and archaeological evidence that nutritional deficiencies increase in populations involved in intensive agriculture (Cook 1976; Cook and Buikstra 1979) this assumption may not be warranted.

Recently, Huss-Ashmore (1978) and Martin and Armelagos (1979) have in-

TABLE 9.10

The Frequency of Remodeled and Unremodeled Periosteal Reactions in Individuals with Porotic Hyperostosis (Libben)[a]

Age	N	Remodeled		Unremodeled	
		N	%	N	%
6–12 mo	9	1	11.1	8	88.9
1–2 yr	19	8	42.1	11	57.9
2–3 yr	10	7	70.0	3	30.0
3–5 yr	7	4	57.1	3	42.9
5–10 yr	11	9	81.8	2	18.2
Total	56	29	51.8	27	48.2

[a] From Mensforth et al. (1978).

TABLE 9.11

Values for the Association of Porotic Hyperostosis with Periosteal Reactions (Libben)[a]

Age	X^2	Yule's Q
6–12 mo	1.73	+.54
1–2 yr	6.62[b]	+.75
2–3 yr	.04	−.07
3–5 yr	.16	+.15
5–10 yr	1.64	+.36
6 mo–2 yr	7.79[b]	+.63
0 mo–10 yr	4.11[b]	+.29

[a] From Mensforth et al. (1978).
[b] Statistical Significance at 0.01.

vestigated the nutritional basis for premature osteoporosis in juveniles and young adults. Garn et al. (1966) have demonstrated that there is a reduction in compact bone thickness and bone mineral in modern children with protein–energy malnutrition. Measurement of radiographs of the second metacarpal showed a marked decrease in cortical thickness in undernourished children. Huss-Ashmore has suggested that the decrease in cortical bone noted in prehistoric Nubian juveniles may be evidence of protein–energy malnutrition in that group. Previous studies of long-bone growth in Nubian children (Armelagos et al. 1972; Mahler 1968) have showed some evidence of irregularities in growth at the earlier ages (1–5 years). However, the small sample sizes involved precluded a conclusive statement about the retardation of growth in this sample.

In an attempt to integrate bone growth with patterns of remodeling, Huss-Ashmore analyzed microradiographs of femoral cross section from 75 prehistoric Nubian juveniles, aged from birth to 14 years. She hypothesized that although the retardation of long-bone growth may indicate nutritional stress, decrease in cortical thickness may be a more powerful measure of dietary deficiencies. For the Nubian sample, long-bone growth (femoral length plotted against dental age) could be characterized by a generalized growth curve (Figure 9.9), with growth proceeding rapidly for the first 2 years, and slowing somewhat thereafter. The development of midshaft width (Figure 9.10) and a cross-sectional area (Figure 9.11) of the femur demonstrate a similar trend. Taken together, these figures suggest a relatively normal maintenance of growth in length and width of long bones. However, a comparison of cortical thickness with total midshaft diameter indicates some striking discrepancies (Figure 9.10). Cortical thickness not only fails to increase, but actually decreases after age 10. The impact of this aspect of growth failure may be seen by examining changes in percent cortical area, a more ac-

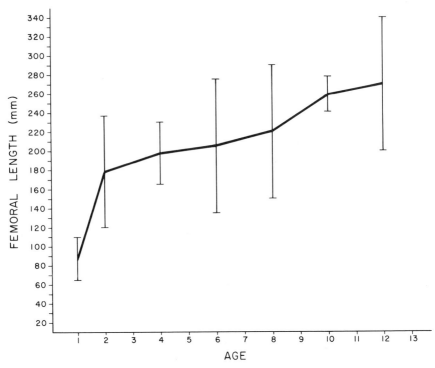

Figure 9.9. Growth in femoral length of Sudanese Nubian juveniles.

curate indicator of cortical bone development. Normally, the proportion of the bone cross section occupied by cortex increases until about age 30, and then declines slowly from then on (Garn 1970). The percent cortical area in the Nubian juveniles increases during the first 2 years of life and then declines sharply. Despite fluctuations, it is maintained at a relatively low level throughout childhood. A comparison with trends observed by Garn (1970) for a modern, well-nourished population is instructive (Figure 9.12). Garn's sample showed a steady increase in percent cortical area from birth. The analysis of the Nubian material suggests that long-bone growth in Nubians was maintained at the expense of growth in cortical thickness.

To examine the biological process involved, Huss-Ashmore extended her analysis beyond the macroscopic level. An analysis of microstructure was used to compare individuals near the mean for cortical area with those at least one standard deviation below the mean. The group below the mean showed marked differences at the endosteal portion of the cortex (Figure 9.13). The most salient feature of this area was the presence of large, active resorption spaces. Apposition of circumferential lamellar bone was maintained in most instances and was often the only cortical bone present. The ratio of formation

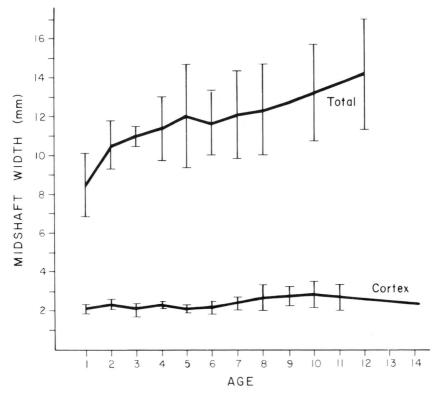

Figure 9.10. Growth in femoral midshaft width and cortical thickness of Sudanese Nubian juveniles.

to resorption spaces was determined in a small subsample of each group. For those near the mean, the amount of formation spaces exceeded resorption, whereas for those below the mean, resorption exceeded formation. This observation is consistent with Garn's (1966) study of bone loss in nutritionally related juvenile osteoporosis.

The occurrence of premature osteoporosis in young adults is difficult to interpret. The age at which bone loss begins is frequently obscured by the lack of sufficient adolescent skeletal material to establish a juvenile–adult continuum. However, despite small sample sizes and individual variability, histological analysis can reveal a pattern of growth and development that suggests an early onset of bone loss related to diet. Martin and Armelagos (1979) have argued that the evidence of premature osteoporosis in young adult females in an X-group sample (A.D. 350–550) from Sudanese Nubia may be a response to dietary deficiency. Microradiographs from 74 adult femora demonstrate significant gross and histological differences between males and

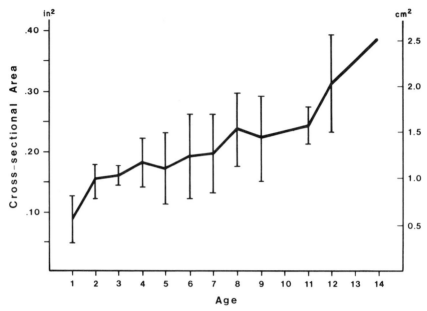

Figure 9.11.   Growth in the cross-sectional area of the femur of Sudanese Nubian juveniles.

females in osteoporotic bone loss (Figure 9.14). Quantification of the ratio between osteoblastic deposition and osteoclastic resorption provides a potential means for distinguishing normal from pathological development and for understanding the processes underlying macroscopic change.

Rates of remodeling can be calculated by quantifying the frequency of resorption spaces and forming osteons. Resorption spaces can be identified by rough, high-density edges with Howship's lacunae, whereas forming osteons are characterized by low density and relatively large Haversian canals (Figure 9.15).

The morphometric analysis of the 20–29-year-old Nubian females indicates an increase in resorption and a decrease in rate of mineralization. The decreased mineralization is reflected in the increased number of forming, low-density osteons (Figure 9.16).

Analysis of the rates of resorption and formation should differentiate changes in the endosteal region of the cortex. The ratio of periosteal formation to periosteal resorption is approximately 2:1. Although there are no significant differences in male and female resorption rates, females in the 20–29 age class show an increase in the number of forming osteons. The endosteal surface, however, shows the most interesting differences in rates of formation and resorption. The females in the 20–29 year age group display increased resorption, indicating extremely active remodeling (Figure 9.17).

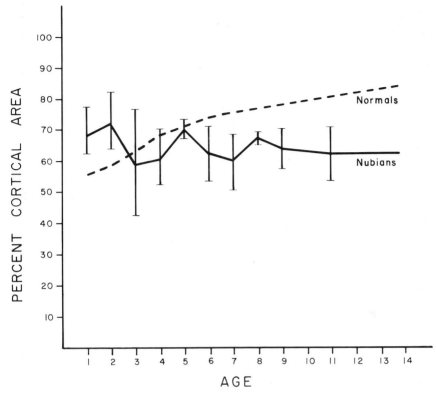

Figure 9.12.   Increase in percent cortical area of Sudanese Nubian juveniles as compared to the trend observed for modern American juveniles (Garn 1970).

The pattern of bone loss suggests that young adult females may be more stressed than males. That such stress occurs during the peak reproductive period suggests the possibility of nutritional involvement. Although bone is deposited during pregnancy, it is resorbed during prolonged lactation (Garn 1970). Females who are lactating can be deprived of 300 mg of calcium and 500–1000 kcal per day. Multiparous females are especially at risk, since their reserves of calcium and energy are likely to become depleted, with resultant bone loss. Premature osteoporosis in infants and children in this same population supports the contention that the demineralization of bone in young adult females is related to diet.

Although the results of these two studies are suggestive, their conclusions must be tested on other populations. Stout (1976) has estimated bone turnover rates for two Illinois Woodland populations undergoing dietary change. His results indicate an increase in bone turnover with the shift from hunting and gathering to maize horticulture. He has suggested that this physiological

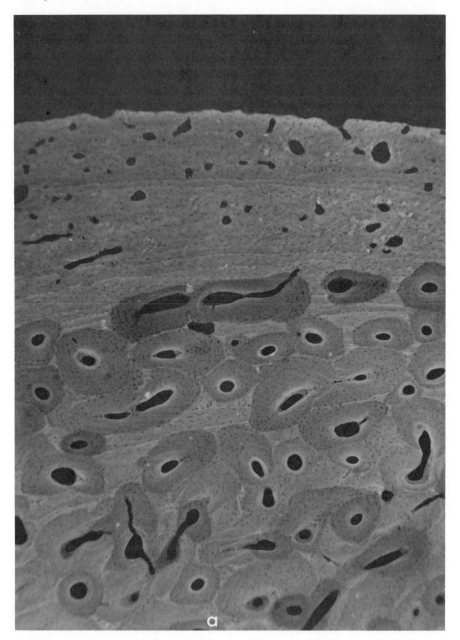

Figure 9.13.   Photomicroradiographs of femoral cross sections: (a) well-maintained cortex in a normal young individual, and (b) the cortex of an osteoporotic juvenile. Note the large resorption holes and deficient mineralization (dark areas) in the osteoporotic individual.

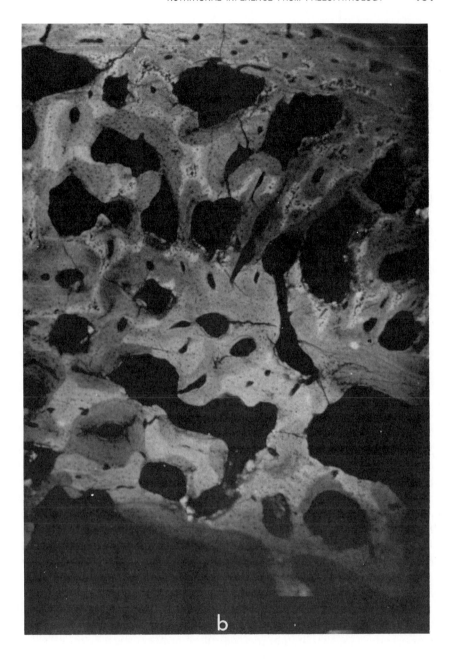

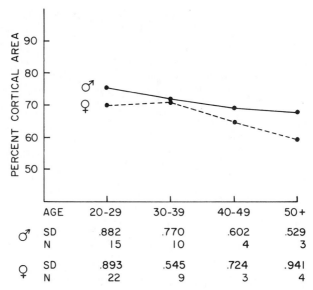

AGE	20-29	30-39	40-49	50+
♂ SD	.882	.770	.602	.529
N	15	10	4	3
♀ SD	.893	.545	.724	.941
N	22	9	3	4

Figure 9.14. Relationship between percentage of cortical area of bone and age in Nubian adults. (From Martin and Armelagos 1979:574.)

change is the result of secondary hyperparathyroidism, due to calcium deficiency with a high-maize diet. If applied to a series of archaeological populations, such morphometric analysis promises to be a useful tool in uncovering nutritional stress.

Osteophytosis

Osteophytosis, or the development of numerous exostoses, has been shown to result from the ingestion of particular dietary toxins (Stewart 1975). The most common of these are fluorine and the lathyrogens. Although moderate ingestion of fluorine has been credited with reducing osteoporosis, ingestion of large amounts (200–1000 ppm) can interfere with bone formation (Weatherell and Weidmann 1959). Osteoblastic activity is stimulated by high fluorine intake, with a consequent formation of excess osteoid and cartilage. Because fluorine interferes with calcium absorption, the osteoid formed may be poorly mineralized, and a condition of "pseudorickets" may occur. Serum calcium is maintained by resorption of bone from endosteal surfaces, with a consequent reduction in bone mass. Conversely, bone is laid down at points of muscle attachment. Such bone is rough and whitened, consisting of coarsely woven trabeculae that are not remodeled to normal cortical bone.

Lathyrogens, derivatives of a group of leguminous plants (*Lathyrus*), may also produce an overgrowth of bone at the points of muscle attachment. These exostoses are accompanied by pitting of the surface of the bone, produced by

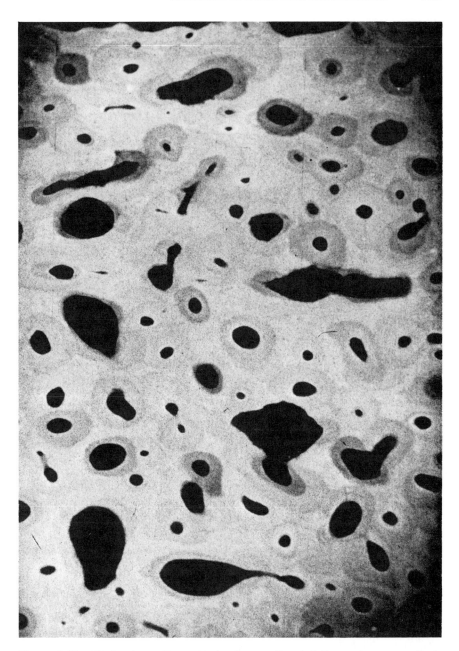

Figure 9.15. Photomicroradiograph of osteoporotic adult (femoral cross section) showing many resorption holes and forming osteons.

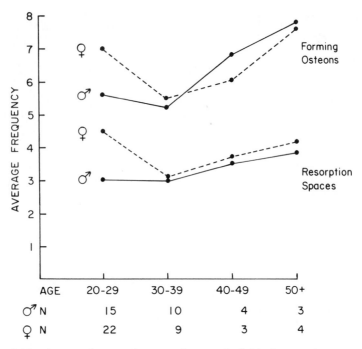

Figure 9.16. Average frequencies per microscopic field of resorption spaces and forming osteons for males and females from Sudanese Nubia (Martin and Armelagos 1979:574).

subperiosteal hemorrhages. It appears that the ingestion of a lathyrogen-rich diet interferes with collagen metabolism, and that such interference is more severe for young, growing animals than for adults (Geiger *et al.* 1933).

Two cautionary considerations should be introduced here. First, both fluoridosis and osteolathyrism are rare conditions in humans and unlikely to be prominent in skeletal populations. Second, other conditions, both hereditary and inflammatory, can produce an overgrowth of bone at the points of muscle attachment. A diagnosis of dietary osteophytosis should therefore be considered only when accompanied by overwhelming evidence from environmental sources.

Harris Lines

Although the existence of transverse lines in the growing ends of long bones has long been reported, their significance is still a subject of debate. These lines are commonly referred to as Harris lines, after one of the early researchers to extensively study their occurrence (Harris 1926, 1931, 1933) (Figure 9.18). The mechanisms of their formation are fairly well documented (Park 1964; Steinbock 1976), but their precise cause is still obscure. The interpreta-

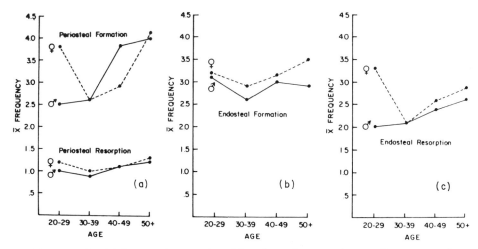

Figure 9.17. (a) Average frequencies of forming osteons and resorption spaces at the periosteum. Though periosteal resorption remains relatively constant, formation shows variability. (b) and (c) Average frequencies of forming osteons and resorption spaces at the endosteum. Endosteal formation shows slight variation. Endosteal resorption increases dramatically for Sudanese Nubian females aged 20–29 years. (From Martin and Armelagos 1979:575.)

tion of Harris lines in an archaeological population should therefore be approached with caution, and nutritional stress should be inferred only when there is supporting evidence from other skeletal indicators.

The controversy over Harris lines extends even to their nomenclature. Since Harris was neither the discoverer of the phenomenon nor the first to explore its cause, other researchers have objected to the use of his name (Garn *et al.* 1968) to describe the phenomenon. Other labels that are generally considered to be synonymous with Harris lines include "transverse trabeculae," "transverse lines," "radiopaque transverse lines," "bone scars," and "lines of arrested growth." Garn *et al.* (1968) are critical of these labels because the phenomena described are neither precisely due to arresting of growth, exclusively transverse, nor invariably linelike. Garn *et al.* prefer the use of the general label "lines and bands of increased density" (1968), a somewhat cumbersome phrase. We will continue here to use the term Harris lines, or simply lines, as a convenient short designation. However, the reader should be aware of the synonyms in other studies, and their explicit or implicit differences in meaning.

The most precise analysis of Harris lines is by densitometric analysis, involving the observation of adjacent longitudinal areas of bone for differences in density. However, Harris lines are more practically observable radiographically as lines or bands of increased radiopacity that can occur in all cartilaginous bone. In round bones (carpals, tarsals, etc.) these lines

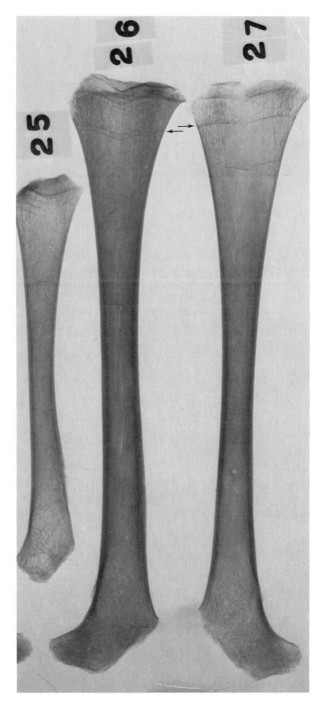

Figure 9.18. Harris lines in the distal femur of a Native American juvenile from the Pueblo period at Black Mesa. (Numbers are for identification.)

follow the topographic contours of the development of that bone. In long bones, the lines are transverse, or nearly so.

Few have studied the frequency distribution of these lines throughout the skeleton. Two researchers that have reported on such findings are in close agreement regarding the relative frequencies of Harris lines in different bones. According to Park, "arrest lines were most common at the anterior rib end, next at the upper and lower tibia ends with the lower end of the femur rating not far behind. The upper femur exhibited them less constantly. The lower radius followed next" (1964:830). Whereas Garn *et al.* find that "they are far more common in the distal part of the tibia than on any other bone or on any other part of the tibia. Next in order of frequency, they may appear on (1) the proximal tibia, (2) the distal femur, (3) the distal radius and (4) the metacarpals" (1968:61).

Thus, the precise relative frequencies of occurrence of Harris lines on different bones and bone ends need further refinement. It is generally agreed that Harris lines are most frequent in long bones and that the best bones to study are probably the tibia, femur, and radius. Because of the relatively high frequency of lines in these bones and their well-defined aging sequences, these bones are most frequently selected for examination of Harris lines.

Variation in lines is also evident, even within the same bone. Lines may be variable in thickness and in density. The relationship of line thickness and density and their cause is unclear. A tentative hypothesis is that thickness is a function of growth velocity and the length of the growth disruption. Density may be a function of the severity or the completeness of the growth disruption. However, the causes of line thickness and density have not yet been definitely investigated.

Lines are not always transverse and may be oblique (Garn *et al.* 1968). Often these lines do not transverse the bone in its entirety. The cause of oblique lines is not thought to differ from that of transverse lines. Their obliqueness is likely a function of the age dynamics of bone growth and remodeling (Garn *et al.* 1968).

Park (1964) and Garn *et al.* (1968) attribute Harris-line formation to episodes of growth disruption in which cartilage cell division slows or stops while mineralization is allowed to continue. The structure of the bones formed is abnormal, and may be resistant to osteoclastic removal. Therefore, when growth resumes, the long-bone cartilaginous plates move longitudinally, leaving rings of increased mineralization, density, and radiopacity behind. It should be added that these lines are not simply growth-arrest lines, but may more accurately be thought of as *recovery lines* (Park 1964).

The mechanisms of Harris-line formation in bone are similar to those of hypoplastic lines in dental enamel. Harris lines also seem to resemble enamel hypoplasias in that they are caused by a wide variety of environmental insults or stresses. Measles, scarlet fever, infantile paralysis, pneumonia, starvation, vitamin A, C, and D deficiencies, protein–energy malnutrition, kwashiorkor, and mechanical restriction have all been associated with the occurrence of Harris lines (see Park 1964 for a more extensive review).

Cartilagenous bone growth disruptions seem to be a "logical response" of the organism in the face of nutritional insufficiency and environmental insults of a less than chronic nature. Park states that "when nutritional disturbances in the young animal become so severe that nutrient material is inadequate to go around, in the economy of nature the bones are sacrificed. . . . In the crisis the bones simply cease to grown and, when the crisis is over, proceed to carry on again" (1964:815). Acheson suggests that "evidently the child in an adverse environment, instead of using his available amino acids for skeletal growth, is mobilizing them and redirecting them so that he can best deal with the stress to which he is adapting" (1960:87).

Two studies have attempted to associate the occurrence of Harris lines with that of enamel hypoplasias. The results of these two studies are contradictory. McHenry and Schulz (1976) did not find a significant association in a group of prehistoric Californians. Using a different statistical technique and a mixed archaeological population (North America), Clarke (1978) did find a significant positive association between Harris lines and hypoplasias. Further research on the relationship of Harris lines and hypoplasias must be undertaken to resolve this discrepancy.

As indicators of stress, hypoplasias and Harris lines have some important differences. First, Harris lines are generally more common and may be observed over a greater span of years (birth to 18) than hypoplasias (usually from birth to around 6 years). However, even controlling for this difference, McHenry and Schulz (1976) found Harris lines to be about 10 times as common. These results suggest that Harris lines are formed by insults that are not as severe or long lasting as those which cause enamel hypoplasias.

Second, bone is a more variable and viable substance in terms of growth and remodeling than enamel. The timing of enamel development is under stronger genetic control than that of bone (Garn *et al.* 1965), and the age of Harris-line occurrence must be estimated with less precision. Clarke (1978) presents a methodology for estimating within one year the time in life at which Harris lines develop (Table 9.12). His well-developed methodology is a conservative estimation of the precise timing of the occurrence of lines in an archaeological population.

Third, because of the remodeling process, many previously formed Harris lines are resorbed. Garn *et al.* (1968) have studied this problem extensively. Their major findings suggest that (*a*) the resorptive process has nearly equal effect on all portions of the bone, and (*b*) the thicker and denser lines will tend

TABLE 9.12

Chronology of Harris-Line Development[a]

	Female		Male	
Age	Percent per yr	Accumulated percent	Percent per yr	Accumulated percent
0	.193	.429	.178	.423
1	.125	.346	.119	.347
2	.087	.292	.074	.296
3	.066	.255	.059	.265
4	.057	.227	.050	.240
5	.052	.202	.044	.219
6	.049	.180	.052	.200
7	.052	.159	.042	.178
8	.054	.137	.045	.160
9	.057	.114	.059	.141
10	.047	.089	.045	.120
11	.043	.069	.040	.101
12	.033	.051	.037	.084
13	.027	.037	.052	.068
14	.019	.025	.034	.046
15	.014	.017	.037	.032
16	.025	.011	.038	.016

[a] Modified from S. Clarke (1978).

to persist longer. We would expect lines that are thicker and formed later to persist.

Anthropologists have attempted to associate Harris lines with (a) gender, (b) adult stature, (c) longevity, and (d) culture. The relationship between Harris lines and gender is not conclusive. McHenry (1968) and Nickens (1975) did not find significant differences in the frequency of Harris lines by gender for groups of prehistoric California and Mesa Verde Native Americans, respectively. Woodall (1968) (Casas Grandes population) reports that females had more lines than males. Wells finds fewer Harris lines in Anglo-Saxon males. He interprets this as a reflection of the protected position of males within Anglo-Saxon societies, affording them better care and nutrition (1961:528). However, Goodman and Clark (1981) found that males in their Dickson sample have more Harris lines than females. At present, it is not possible to specify the precise interaction of gender and cultural factors in the etiology of Harris lines.

The associations found between Harris lines and adult stature are also in-consistent. Blanco et al. (1974) found an inverse relationship between Harris lines and stature in Guatemalan children, and Perzigian (1977) implies that there is an inverse association between Harris lines and attained adult stature in the Indian Knoll populations. However, Goodman and Clark (1981) found that the taller adults (based on tibial length) in the Dickson population had a greater frequency of Harris lines than the shorter adults. This relationship is most pronounced for females.

Harris lines have been consistently associated with decreased longevity (McHenry 1968; Wells 1967), which is similar to the results of studies on dental hypoplasias. Those individuals that are better off nutritionally have a lesser frequency of Harris lines and a greater survival rate. Interpretation, however, is confounded by the resorptive process. Older individuals may show fewer lines simply because their lines have more often been resorbed.

The age at which Harris lines are formed is one of the aspects of this phenomenon most useful for interpretation. When Harris lines are graphed by their age of occurrence, interesting patterns are revealed. Wells (1967) finds a broad peak of increased Harris lines from approximately 2 to 7 years in his Anglo-Saxon population. Goodman and Clark (1981) found that the greatest frequency of Harris lines in the Dickson populations occurred around 2–3 years of age, with another period of increased frequency around age 13 (Figure 9.19). This earlier peak is very close to that found for enamel hypoplasias of the permanent dentition in this same population. It appears that the distribution of Harris lines provides additional evidence for stress

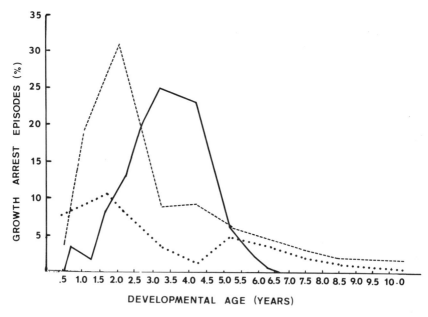

Figure 9.19.   Age-specific frequency of Harris lines (···· = distal and --- = proximal tibia) compared to enamel hypoplasias (—) at Dickson Mounds.

during weaning in this population. In summary, Harris lines should be considered an indicator of generalized stress during the growth stage. Many factors may produce stresses that are capable of causing Harris lines. Such stresses need not be particularly severe or prolonged. Thus nutrition, alone or in concert with other environmental disturbances, may be reflected in the formation of such lines.

Measures of Nutritional Stress in Teeth

The measurement and analysis of teeth have traditionally received a great deal of attention in studies of paleoanthropology. This disproportionate emphasis has resulted primarily from the fact that teeth are extraordinarily hard. They therefore remain for recovery and analysis when other tissues, including bone, are destroyed. The dental conditions most frequently studied for their relationship to diet are dental caries and dental attrition. Both conditions have been widely researched, and an extensive literature on each exists. Both conditions have been shown to relate to diet, but are not in themselves indicative of nutritional status. Caries, for example, is generally known to be positively correlated with dietary carbohydrate intake and dental attrition (Burns 1979; Leigh 1925; Turner 1979); but is negatively associated with malnutrition. The present discussion will emphasize those less well-known dental features that have empirically been shown to be systemically related to stress markers in bone: developmental enamel defects, asymmetrical dentition, and crowding and malocclusion of teeth.

Enamel Hypoplasia

Enamel hypoplasia is one of three developmental defects of the dentition that have been proposed as markers of nutritional stress in both modern and prehistoric populations. Along with enamel hypocalcification and defective dentin, enamel hypoplasia is a highly useful marker of physiological stress. Because enamel hypoplasia yields a well-preserved, relatively permanent record of growth disturbance, examination of them is a promising technique for dietary investigation. Enamel hypoplasia is usually defined as a deficiency in enamel thickness resulting from a cessation of ameloblast (enamel forming) activity (Figure 9.20) (Sarnat and Schour 1941). Other terms such as "congenital defects of the enamel" (Zsygmondy 1893), and "chronologic enamel aplasia" (Sarnat and Schour 1941) have been used in reference to the same phenomenon. Occasionally, the descriptive terms "ring" and "linear" are utilized, as in neonatal rings, tooth rings, and linear enamel hypoplasia. However, the term enamel hypoplasia is now widely recognized and will be used here as a generic name for disturbances in enamel development due to ameloblast activity.

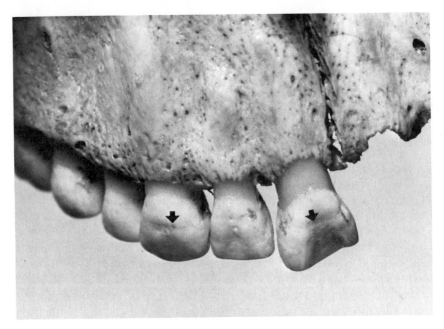

Figure 9.20. Enamel hypoplasia of the maxillary incisors and canine in a Native American individual from the Pueblo period at Black Mesa.

Enamel hypoplasias may be studied either by direct observation of the surface or by microscopic observation of enamel thin sections. Rose (1973) has presented a detailed account of the appearance, method of analysis, and utility of microscopic examination of enamel hypoplasias and other developmental defects. Microscopic examination is a sensitive indicator of stress, in that "pathological" phenomena that are not macroscopically evident can be examined and described. Macroscopic examination sacrifices some resolution for a savings in time, equipment, and the integrity of the tooth. The choice of which technique to use should be based on the relative importance of these factors for the specific project at hand (see Rose *et al.* 1978).

Enamel hypoplasia often occurs in concert with enamel hypocalcification, the other class of enamel developmental defects. Although these two developmental defects may be caused by similar environmental insults, they occur through different developmental mechanisms. Enamel is calcified in two stages. The first stage, matrix formation, accounts for approximately 30% of the calcified salts. Enamel hypoplasia is a result of a disturbance during matrix formation and is evidenced by the reduced thickness of the enamel. The second stage is maturation, during which enamel calcification is completed. If the enamel organ is disrupted during this stage, the resulting enamel will be of normal thickness but the calcified salt content will be reduced. This hypocalcification will be obvious by the opaque appearance of the enamel.

Although hypocalcification is easily discerned, it seems to be a less common phenomenon in the permanent dentition. It therefore requires a large population for meaningful analysis. Since hypocalcification is more frequently seen in the deciduous dentition, it is a useful indicator of prenatal stress. Cook and Buikstra (1979) have examined enamel hypoplasia, hypocalcification, and hypoplasia-related caries in the deciduous dentition of a Middle and Late Woodland skeletal series from Illinois. The high frequency of such defects was associated with skeletal evidence of anemia and infection, and high weaning-age mortality. This constellation of disturbances suggests the presence of nutritional deficiencies in Illinois Woodland populations.

Defects in dentin development are often similar in cause to enamel hypoplasia, and can be seen as an additional measure of general stress in the growing individual (Molnar and Ward 1975). Some of the dentin defects that have been identified are incremental lines of Von Ebner, contour lines of Owen, interglobular dentin, scattered cacospherite, or hypocalcified dentin. These can be studied in conjunction with defects of enamel to produce a more complete picture of stress.

Enamel hypoplasia may be the result of a wide variety of environmental stresses (Giro 1947; Kreshover 1960; Massler *et al.* 1941; Sarnat and Schour 1941; Schour and Massler 1945; Rose 1973; Vila 1949). Kreshover summarizes his review:

> ample clinical and experimental evidence exists to suggest that developmental tooth defects are generally non-specific in nature and can be related to a wide range of systemic disturbances, and any of which, depending upon their severity and the degree of tissue response, might result in defective enamel and dentin (1960:166).

In addition to their high validity as stress indicators, hypoplasias have other advantages. First, teeth are the most commonly found skeletal remains. Second, hypoplasias are unaffected by later life events and have a "memory" of earlier metabolic events; defects can also be related to future events such as morbidity. Third, the developmental timing of the defective enamel, and therefore of the stressful event, can be located, thus allowing for the formation of a chronological graph of the developmental timing of stressful events.

> The growing dental structure, particularly the enamel and dentin yield accurate, prompt and permanent records of both normal fluctuation and pathologic accentuations of mineral and general metabolism. Fortunately, these records are easily read by virtue of the orderly and rhythmic growth of these tissues in their daily, ringlike succession.
>
> In enamel hypoplasia the history of systemic disturbances is indelibly recorded by a cessation of ameloblast activity. A lack of enamel formation is noted in the particular portion of each tooth that is developing during the disease period (Sarnat and Schour 1941:1989).

Methods for the study of macroscopic enamel hypoplasia are poorly developed. The most promising are those in which chronology is explicitly considered. The time at which the hypoplasia developed is an important datum, and any method employed should take this into account. Otherwise, hypoplastic frequencies cannot be clearly related to frequencies of stressful events (Figure 9.21). Goodman *et al.* (1980) have explained at greater length why the chronological technique is vital, and have further described two chronological methods—the single tooth and the multiple-teeth.

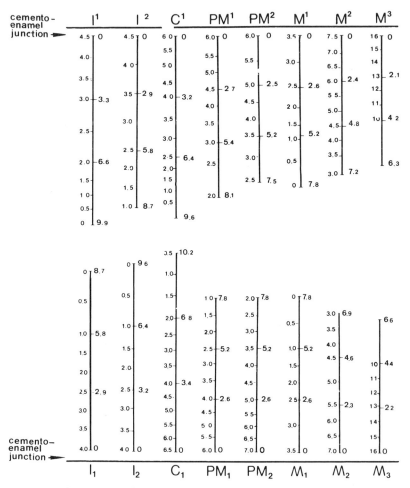

Figure 9.21.   Chronology of the development of macroscopic enamel hypoplasias. Numbers to the right are distances (in millimeters) from the cemento-enamel junction. Numbers to the left are corresponding ages at development. (From Goodman *et al.* 1980:520.)

The single-tooth technique utilizes only one tooth type for analysis. The tooth of choice is usually the mandibular canine (for examples, see Schulz and McHenry 1975). This tooth is selected because of its relatively long developmental time span and its relatively high sensitivity to environmental stress. Although this technique is very accurate and replicable, it cannot distinguish hypoplasias due either to nonsystemic environmental stress (e.g., those due to local trauma) or congenitally caused hypoplasias. Therefore, the technique loses some validity as a measure of general systemic stress.

The multiple-teeth technique examines all teeth present for the occurrence of hypoplasias. This technique offers a longer record of development, is able to distinguish nonsystemic defects and extends the sample size. However, these techniques are more complex, and may therefore lose replicability (Goodman et al. 1980; Swärdstedt 1966).

The overriding difficulty in this type of analysis is that it is not clearly known which teeth are most sensitive to environmental stress. Our data show that relative sensitivities change with developmental age. More precisely, for the Dickson populations the incisors, and specifically the central maxillary incisors, appear to be the teeth most likely to exhibit an enamel hypoplasia if the defect occurs before 3 years of age. If the hypoplasia occurs between 3 and 7 years of age, the canines are most likely to be affected. We have therefore suggested a "best teeth" technique, which combines the uses of canines and incisors. For the Dickson populations, 95% of the chronological growth disruptions are recorded in either the incisors or the canines. That is, the addition of premolars and molars adds only 5% more growth disruption episodes. It is therefore suggested that a multiple-teeth technique could be shortened to eliminate the postcanine teeth. We suggest the use of two of the canines and two of the incisors, with preference for the maxillary central incisors.

Although there have been few studies of the frequency and chronology of enamel hypoplasia in a population, a few types of inference are possible. These will be discussed with reference to (a) seasonality, (b) sex, (c) class, (d) culture, (e) longevity, and (f) age at hypoplasia formation.

Swärdstedt (1966) has devised a method of analyzing for seasonal occurrence of enamel hypoplasia by examining the chronological spacing of hypoplasias in individuals with greater than one occurrence of enamel hypoplasia. However, he did not find any support for a seasonal effect when his method was tested on an archaeological population from Westerhus (A.D. 1025–1375). Goodman et al. (1980) examined those individuals in the Dickson sample who had more than one hypoplasia. They found that the frequency of hypoplasias separated by a year was greater than that of hypoplasias separated by half a year (Table 9.13). They attribute these results to an annual cycle of stress.

Infante and Gillespie (1974) did not find a significant sex difference in frequencies of hypoplasias in a group of modern rural Guatemalan school

TABLE 9.13

Number of Cases in Which Two Hypoplasias are Separated by a Half Year and Number of Cases in Which Two Hypoplasias are Separated by a Year (Dickson Mounds)[a]

Population	0.5 Yr	1.0 Yr	Binomial 1-tailed probability[b]
Late Woodland	1	3	—
Mississippian-acculturated Late Woodland	5	12	.072
Middle Mississippian	10	14	.271
Total	16	29	.0336

[a] From Goodman et al. (1980:524).
[b] From Siegel (1956).

children. However, they cite unpublished data (Infante) on Apache children in which a greater prevalence of hypoplasias was found in males. Swärdstedt (1966) also found a significant increase in hypoplasias among the males of his Swedish medieval population. Goodman (1976), however, did not find a significant difference between sexes in his three prehistoric Illinois populations. Although sex differences in incidence of hypoplasia are variable, some of these results may reflect the fact that boys have lower nutritional reserves at birth, combined with a greater caloric need.

Two researchers have shown statistically significant class differences in the frequency of hypoplasias. Enwonwu (1973) found that the frequency of hypoplasias in contemporary Nigerian children of lower socioeconomic backgrounds was greater than that found in children from more affluent homes and villages. Swärdstedt found a significant difference among all three classes in his Swedish archaeological populations, with the lowest class having the lowest frequency of hypoplasias. Enwonwu points to nutritional differences in explaining the class differences that he found.

Swärdstedt studied four successive Swedish medieval "periods" extending from A.D. 1025 to 1375. He found a significant increase in the frequency of enamel hypoplasia over time. Goodman et al. (1980) also found an increase in the frequency of hypoplasias over time in their Dickson Mounds populations. This expected increase was explained by reference to the concurrent shift from a hunting–gathering economy (Late Woodland) to an economy based on maize horticulture (Middle Mississippian).

The relationship between early deprivation, stress, and developmental disruption, later morbidity, and mortality is poorly understood. Goodman and Armelagos (1982) and Swärdstedt (1966) have found that individuals with hypoplasias show a decrease in longevity. Although such results are intriguing, it is not known how universal this pattern is or why it occurs. It is possible that the same individuals in a population are constantly being exposed to stress, which results in hypoplasias during childhood and early mortality as adults. Alternatively, those individuals with hypoplasias may be "damaged" and therefore more susceptible to future stress.

As with Harris lines, the chronology of hypoplasia occurrence is a useful analytical procedure. Sarnat and Schour (1941:1992) have published a chronological graph for a group of Chicagoans that has come to be accepted as a modern standard. Their graph shows $\frac{2}{3}$ of all hypoplasias occurring before the first year, and that over 90% occur before the second year. This graph is assumed to reflect the pattern of stress and susceptibility in a modern population, and is the only such graph of which the authors are presently aware.

All three known graphs of enamel hypoplasias chronology in archaeological populations differ greatly from Sarnat and Schour's. Graphs for the Swedish medieval and prehistoric Illinois populations (Figure 9.22) show strong central tendencies around 2.5–3.0 years of age (Goodman and Armelagos, 1980; Swärdstedt 1966). A graph of incidence among prehistoric

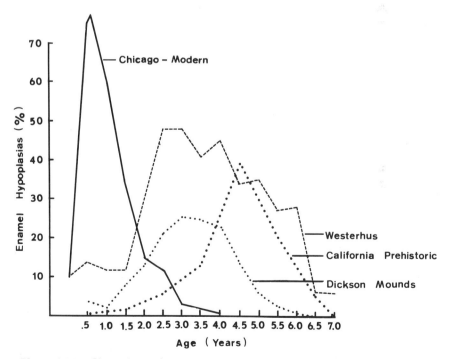

Figure 9.22. Chronology of enamel hypoplasias. (From Goodman and Armelagos 1980.)

Native Americans in California shows a central tendency around the fourth year (Schulz and McHenry 1975). All archaeological graphs follow a roughly normal, single-peaked distribution. We suggest that these delayed central tendencies in the archaeological samples are the result of increased infection and nutritional stress in the postweaning period.

Of the several developmental dental defects that may be related to general and nutritional stress, macroscopic enamel hypoplasia appears to be one of the more valid and reliable indicators. Graphs of the chronological age at occurrence of growth disruptions derived from macroscopic examination of enamel hypoplasias, can be used to isolate specific times of stress during the infant–childhood portion of the life cycle. It appears that examination of enamel hypoplasia will play a prominent role in the future analysis of the role of nutrition in population change.

Fluctuating Asymmetry

Asymmetry or lateral asymmetry refers to size and/or shape differences between sides in a bilateral organism. Fluctuating asymmetry or random asymmetry is simply asymmetry that does not favor either side, left or right. Although asymmetries may be studied for any bilateral structure, the dentition has been the most frequent choice for those interested in skeletal populations. Bailit *et al.* (1970) clearly present the methodology for studying fluctuating dental asymmetry. Siegel (1975) may be referred to for asymmetries of the appendicular skeleton. Jantz (1975), though concerned with dermatoglyphic asymmetries, provides a useful discussion of statistical procedure (see also Garn *et al.* 1979).

Mather (1953) and Van Valen (1962) were among the first to recognize that bilateral organisms might undergo selection to maintain and increase their bilateral symmetry. They and others have looked for both environmental and genetic variables that might increase or decrease the degree of asymmetry. DiBernardo and Bailit (1978) were unable to find intrapopulational differences in asymmetries that might relate to environmental stressors. Their study raises serious questions as to the critical period of environmental stress, prenatal or postnatal, and the type of stress that might cause asymmetries to increase. However, the view that environmental stressors are important factors in increasing fluctuating dental asymmetry has been given strong support by the study of Bailit *et al.* (1970). There is now a general consensus that fluctuating dental asymmetry will increase with increased stress. For example, Perzigian concludes, "it is suggested that fluctuating dental asymmetry represents a deflection of an organism off its genetically orchestrated course toward symmetry. The deflection results when nongenetic, environmental factors interfere with normal morphogenesis" (1977:87).

Fluctuating asymmetries have been studied in a variety of human populations. There is no consensus as to whether males or females show greater asymmetry. Niswander and Chung (1965) found that Japanese females were more dentally asymmetric than Japanese males. However, this result was not duplicated by DiBernardo (1973) for Japanese children, nor in any of Perzigian's samples (the Indian Knoll hunter–gatherers, the Campbell-Larson agriculturalists, and the Hamann-Todd population).

DiBernardo found an association between decreased socioeconomic status and increased asymmetry (1973). Suarez (1974) found greater asymmetry in a Neanderthal population than in a modern Ohio population. Doyle and Johnston (1977) showed that their Eskimo and Pueblo samples were also more asymmetric than Suarez's modern sample. Bailit *et al.* (1970) found asymmetry to be greatest among Tristanites, the Nasoi, the Kwaio, and residents of modern Boston, in that order. Perzigian (1977) found greater asymmetry in his Indian Knoll skeletal sample than in his Campbell-Larson or Hamann-Todd populations. He interprets these last results to mean that populations under greater environmental stress will demonstrate a greater level of asymmetry. Bailit *et al.* likewise state, ''asymmetry in the dentition is related to the general level of health and nutrition in each population'' (1970:636).

Malocclusion and Crowding of Teeth

Because dental development is less severely affected by environmental stresses than the bone in which it is located (Garn *et al.* 1965), the crowding of teeth may be an indicator of general and/or specific nutritional stress (Widdowson and McCance 1964). In a series of experiments on undernourished piglets, tooth development was shown to be only slightly retarded. However, the alveolar bone in which the teeth were located was noticeably stunted. This resulted in too little room for the developing teeth, with concomitant crowding and impaction of the molars (Trowell *et al.* 1954). We therefore suggest that the appearance of such a pattern in archaeological populations may indicate acute or severe nutritionally based stress.

Malocclusion has also been attributed to poor diet (Howe 1924), but much of the evidence for this has been taken from animal experiments. In malnourished children, the primary difference noted is a slightly subnormal angle of the maxillary incisors (Parker *et al.* 1952). Children with kwashiorkor show little evidence of undue malocclusion (Trowell *et al.* 1954).

Because there is a large genetic component to crowding and malocclusion, these measures should not be assumed to reflect nutritional status unless there is supporting evidence. To our knowledge, neither has been systematically employed in investigating archaeological populations. When used with other indicators of growth disruption, dental crowding and impaction could confirm a diagnosis of dietary involvement.

Bone Collagen Analysis as an Indicator of Nutritional Deficiencies

Preliminary work has suggested that the analysis of collagen recovered from the human skeletal system provides a method for assessing diet and dietary deficiencies. Collagen is a stable protein with a long half-life. Since collagen is synthesized in stages, its composition reflects diet during the various phases of individual development. It is possible to analyze collagen synthesized during the various development phases. This is accomplished by the serial extraction of collagen formed during various stages of the life cycle. For example, collagen synthesized just prior to death can be extracted from archaeological bone by dilute saline solution, whereas other substances can be used to extract collagen fractions developed earlier in life. The two types of collagen analysis that now show promise for dietary reconstruction are the analysis of trace elements and the examination of stable carbon isotopes.

Elemental Analysis

Chemical analysis of major, minor, and trace elements can provide an important technique for assessing paleonutrition. Elemental analysis has focused on those trace minerals that can play an important role in nutrition (Maugh 1973; Ulmer 1977). Studies of trace minerals have attempted to determine the impact of toxic levels or deficiency states. Gilbert (1977) and Wing and Brown (1980) have provided general discussions on the potential of trace-mineral analysis for paleonutrition. The incorporation of trace minerals into bones and teeth has been examined in a number of prehistoric populations (Boaz and Hampel 1978; Brown 1973, 1974; Gilbert 1975; Schoeniger 1979a, 1979b; Stedt 1979; Szpunar et al. 1978).

The analysis of trace elements related to diet is complicated by a number of factors. For example, there are often in vivo interactions between elements that can affect their distribution; post-mortem changes resulting from organic and inorganic exchanges will alter the concentration of trace elements (Hassan 1975; Hassan and Ortner 1977). The development of techniques to extract secondary carbonates should help to resolve these problems.

Although there have been a large number of elements tested, most studies have focused on variation in zinc, copper, manganese, magnesium, and strontium. These studies suggest that zinc and copper would increase in populations with a high dietary meat intake, whereas manganese, magnesium, and strontium would be higher in populations in which vegetables comprise a greater proportion of the diet.

Gilbert (1975) analyzed five trace minerals (zinc, copper, strontium, maganese, and magnesium) in 75 individuals from the Dickson Mound population in Illinois. This population was experiencing a rapid shift in subsistence from hunting–gathering (Late Woodland) to intensive maize agriculture (Middle Mississippian). Zinc concentrations did discriminate between the populations in the predicted fashion. Since zinc is related to protein consumption, the decrease in zinc levels would be expected in the maize-reliant Middle Mississippian population. Gilbert also found that zinc levels were related to the occurrence of pathology in some of the groups. For example, among the Late Woodland populations there was a negative correlation between zinc concentration and the occurrence of pathology. Bahou (1975) expanded on this aspect of the study and found relationships between trace elements and other pathologies.

The analysis of strontium has also been used to discriminate between meat and plant eaters. Although strontium and calcium react chemically in a similar fashion, most animals actively discriminate against strontium through renal excretion. Plants, however, accumulate strontium in their leaves and stems. Even though animals excrete strontium, the accumulation of strontium in bone may give clues to diet. Toots and Voorhies (1965) applied strontium analysis to discriminate herbivores and carnivores in paleontological samples. They found that herbivore skeletons had the highest concentration of strontium, whereas carnivores had the lowest concentration.

Brown (1973, 1974) has pioneered the use of strontium analysis as a dietary indicator. Using strontium–calcium ratios, she was able to assess the relative importance of meat and vegetables in the diet (herbivorous humans have a strontium–calcium ratio of 1:2000, whereas in carnivorous humans, the ratio is 1:4800). In addition she was able to assess differential access to meat by subgroups in the population. The impact of status differences on access to meat could thus be determined.

Schoeniger (1979a,b) used atomic-absorption spectrometry (AAS) and neutron-activation analysis to assess diet in prehistoric populations from Chalcatzingo, Mexico. Individuals with highest status had the lowest mean bone–strontium levels (more meat in the diet), whereas burials without grave goods had the highest mean bone–strontium levels.

The application of strontium analysis is not without its problems. Boaz and Hampel (1978) were not able to distinguish differences in strontium concentration in paleolithic samples that were heavily mineralized. However, Fuchs (1978) and Schoeniger (1978) suggest that there are methods for evaluating the impact of contamination. Fuchs (1978) argues that chemical separation can be used to distinguish, identify, and isolate fractions of bone mineral most representative of dietary strontium levels. Furthermore, by monitoring aluminum levels (aluminum is not incorporated into living bone, but *is* incorporated in interred bone), the presence of contamination can be determined (Szpunar *et al.* 1978).

Stedt (1979) used inductively coupled plasma–atomic emission spectrometry (ICP–AES) to analyze trace-element differences between Fremont ($N = 50$) and Anasasi ($N = 50$) skeletal samples, which she believed might result from differences in diet. Stedt measured 13 elements (sodium, potassium, lithium, phosphorus, calcium, manganese, barium, aluminum, iron, magnesium, copper, zinc, and lead) but found no conclusive evidence of trace-element differences that could be related to diet.

Stedt believes that factors affecting her results include the variability of trace elements in separate bones of the body (Gilbert 1975), variation in trace elements in different fractions of the same bone (Kuhn 1979), physiological state prior to death (Stedt 1979:89), and diagenic effects of soil and fossilization process. In addition, the use of samples from a large number of sites may have increased the variability found.

Although Gilbert (1977:94–96) has stated that AAS provided the best approach to trace-element analysis, recent advances in instrumentation of ICP–AES has altered this situation. The ICP–AES provides multielement channels (up to 40 elements), and greater precision, accuracy, and sensitivity. It thus has a greater potential than arc emission spectroscopy (AES), AAS, or neutron-activation analysis (see Fassel 1978).

The use of multielemental analysis would be difficult without methods for systematically analyzing the variation in concentration of various elements. Nonparametric recognition techniques have been developed, such as ARTHUR (see Harper *et al.* 1977), that can help to analyze such complex data. ARTHUR has the capacity to include other variables, such as pathology and archaeological information, that might be useful.

R. Barnes, in the Department of Chemistry at the University of Massachusetts, is presently using ICP–AES to test elemental variation in prehistoric Nubian bones. He will be collaborating with R. G. Brown to examine the concentration of 32 elements in the total bone sample, as well as the serial collagen fraction (dilute salt, guanidine hydrochloride, acetic acid, and gelatine fractions) extracted for stable-isotope analysis. This approach may help to clarify some of the confusion that centers around trace-element analysis and its use in reconstructing diets of prehistoric populations.

Stable Carbon Isotope Analysis

It is now possible to assess principal dietary components through the use of stable carbon isotopes. The ratio of the two stable carbon isotopes—^{12}C and ^{13}C—in animal tissue reflects the diet of the organism. Plant groups, because of differences in types of metabolism during photosynthesis, have different modal values for the ratio of stable carbon isotopes. (The following discussion is based on information supplied by Bumsted [1980] and personal communication.)

Nearly 99% of the earth's carbon is composed of the stable isotope ^{12}C whereas a little over 1% is composed of ^{13}C. The carbon content of a plant reflects the $\delta^{13}C$ value of its immediate carbon source, either atmospheric carbon dioxide or the aquatic bicarbonate or carbon dioxide pools. The $\delta^{13}C$ value is the ratio of ^{13}C to ^{12}C compared to a standard, and is always negative and expressed in thousandths (e.g., -38%) (see Lerman 1975 for a more detailed discussion). Carbon in plants is metabolized through three major pathways: C_3 (Calvin), C_4 (Hatch-Slack), and Crassulacean acid metabolism (CAM). During photosynthesis, plants will preferentially take up ^{12}C over ^{13}C. Although $\delta^{13}C$ values for plants may range from 0 to -38%, naturally occurring ratios are highly predictable, reflecting the metabolic pathway of the plant. C_4 (Hatch-Slack) plants take up more ^{13}C than do C_3 plants and will therefore have a higher (less negative) $^{13}C/^{12}C$ ratio. The modal value for C_4 plants is -12%, whereas for C_3 plants, the mode is -28%. CAM plants, with the ability to use both C_3 and C_4 pathways, are intermediate in value. Exact values depend on growth conditions.

The application of stable-carbon-isotope analysis to paleonutrition is based on controlled animal studies. This research has demonstrated that as carbon is passed along the food chain, the carbon composition of animals continues to reflect the relative isotopic composition of their diet (Bender *et al.,* 1981; DeNiro 1977; DeNiro and Epstein, 1978a,b).

The plants that comprise the diet of animals will have distinct ^{13}C values. Maize, a tropical New World cultigen, is a C_4 plant. On the other hand, the native flora of North American temperate environments is composed of primarily C_3 varieties. Therefore, a shift from indigenous gathered plants (C_3) to cultivated plants such as maize (C_4) will result in a shift in dietary isotopic values. Since $^{13}C/^{12}C$ ratios do not change after the death of an organism, archaeological remains can be used to assess diet. Food refuse, soil humus, or skeletal remains are potential sources of carbon for dietary reconstruction.

Interest in carbon isotopes has focused on their use in interpreting ^{14}C dates and in environmental reconstruction. Bender (1968) and Stuiver (1978) have used $\delta^{13}C$ analysis to correct radiocarbon dates. There have also been a number of attempts to apply stable isotope analysis to environmental reconstruction (DeNiro and Epstein 1978b; Lerman and Troughton 1975; Mazany 1978; Teeri and Stowe 1976; Tieszen *et al.* 1979).

There have been only nine stable carbon isotope studies published that are explicitly relevant to anthropology (Bender *et al.,* 1981; Brothwell and Burleigh 1977; Burleigh and Brothwell 1978; Craig and Craig 1972; DeNiro and Epstein 1978a; Herz and Wenner 1978; MacNeish 1978; van der Merwe and Vogel 1978; Vogel and van der Merwe 1977). Of these studies, six consider the problem of dietary reconstruction.*

Using a small sample of rib (seven individuals) from four sites in New York

---

*These six studies are Bender *et al.* (1981), Burleigh and Brothwell (1978), DeNiro and Epstein (1978a), MacNeish (1978), van der Merwe and Vogel (1978), Vogel and van der Merwe (1977).

state, Vogel and van der Merwe (1977) found a shift in the δ^{13}C values of hunting–gathering populations and horticulturalists. The average δ^{13}C value for hunter–gatherers was $-19.73^0/oo$, whereas the horticulturalists averaged $-14.43^0/oo$. Vogel and van der Merwe suggest that these stable isotope values indicate that maize comprised 40% of the diet of horticulturalists. Further, they argue that the shift to intensive cultivation occurred within 200 years of its introduction.

Van der Merwe and Vogel (1978) undertook a larger study (52 individuals) of 10 midwestern sites dated from 300 B.C. to A.D. 1300. Premaize sites gave average values of $-21.4 \pm .78^0/oo$, whereas maize-site samples averaged $-11.8 \pm 1.3^0/oo$. Females from these sites appeared to have less maize in their diet than males (64–75%). Further, Bender *et al.* (1981) have examined a sample of 46 individuals from archaic Hopewell, and Mississippian sites in the Midwest. Their study indicates that maize was of little importance in the Hopewell diet.

Carbon-isotope analysis of human skeletal material from the Viru Valley shows an increase in the use of maize in a diet that relied extensively on seafood (DeNiro and Epstein 1978a). Interestingly, the isotopic analysis of human remains reveals that maize was introduced at least 200 years before there is archaeological evidence for its use. Another Peruvian study has used the isotopic analysis of nonhuman remains to assess maize cultivation. From analysis of the hair of 10 Peruvian dogs, Burleigh and Brothwell (1978) were able to show that maize contributed 20–60% of the animals' diet.

MacNeish (1978) has used stable isotopes to reconstruct energy flows of prehistoric sites from the Tehuacán Valley of Mexico. The δ^{13}C values were used to determine the proportions of maize and animal protein in the diet of 75 individuals. This information, combined with archaeological reconstruction of diet, was used to estimate the production and use of energy.

These five studies indicate that stable-isotope analysis can be of use in reconstructing the diet of prehistoric populations. However, the actual determination of proportion of maize in diets is still controversial, and methods for this should be tested further. Although previous studies have dealt with the question of the importance of maize in the diet, there is a potential for using stable carbon isotopes to determine nutritional deficiencies in archaeological groups. For example, we may now be able to test the relationship of intensity of maize use to the increase in nutritional and infectious lesions in a skeletal population.

The effective use of stable carbon isotopes in paleonutritional research requires information on variation of δ^{13}C values within a population and the impact of variation on the health of individuals in the group. Preliminary studies by Vogel, van der Merwe, and their colleagues indicate that there are sex differences with respect to the use of maize. The effects of these dietary differences remain to be studied. Bumsted, Armelagos, and R. G. Brown (University of Massachusetts) are collaborating with Lerman (University of Arizona) on a stable-carbon isotope study of a large synchronic sample and a diachronic sample (from Sudanese Nubia), both of which exhibit excellent preservation of the biological remains (mummified skin, hair, etc.). These studies should provide information on the range of variation in these isotopes among individuals and between segments of the population (sex and age groups). The simultaneous analysis of stable carbon isotopes and specific nutritional diseases should clarify many questions about the effects on nutritional health of increased reliance on maize and other cereal grains.

Demographic Variables as Indicators of Nutritional Stress

Specific demographic variables, in conjunction with archaeological and skeletal indicators of nutritional stress, may be used to measure the impact of nutritional deficiencies on population. Nutrition has frequently been implicated in demographic change. However, without corroborative evidence from archaeology and skeletal biology, such change is difficult to interpret. Buikstra (1977) and Cook (1976) have provided a model for the analysis of demographic and dietary change. Their analysis considers multiple measures of stress in skeletal systems in conjunction with tightly controlled archaeological assessment of shifts in subsistence. In such controlled situations, it may be possible to measure the impact of nutritionally caused stress. If there is good archaeological and skeletal evidence of nutritional deficiency, the impact on mortality may be measured.

Mortality is a sensitive indicator of demographic change (Weiss 1973, 1975, 1976). Since the death of an individual is the ultimate example of maladaptation, it can be used to measure how well human groups adjust to their environment. The effect of mortality on the age structure of a population provides a key to understanding the impact of stress on that population.

The specific causes of death are extremely difficult to interpret in skeletal populations. In a few cases, severe trauma can be diagnosed as the cause of death. This information is not always necessary, however, since the pattern of mortality provides information for assessing various stressors. Although gross measures of mortality (i.e., percent of adults versus percent of children) have been used for demographic analysis, a more systematic analysis of mortality using life tables is desirable (Swedlund and Armelagos 1969, 1976; Weiss 1973). The life table is an effective method for assessing mortality differences between groups and changes within groups (Ascadi and Nemeskeri 1970; Moore *et al.* 1975; Palkovich 1978; Swedlund and Armelagos 1969; Weiss 1973). For example, increases in age-specific mortality can be a clue to the existence of a specific stressor. Cook (1976), using United Nations life tables for a prehistoric Illinois population, demonstrated that mortality data could be used to infer nutritional stress. Using Cook's method, Buikstra (1977) showed that mortality increased in the age groups predicted to be relatively more malnourished. Mortality in these age groups also increased with the intensification of agriculture from Middle to Late Woodland, and was associated with an increase in skeletal pathologies.

The relationship between pathology and mortality provides a potentially interesting vehicle for the study of nutritional stress. The physiological condition underlying pathology (even if it is not the immediate cause of death) can have an impact on mortality. In the Dickson Mounds population, Armelagos *et al.* (1980) and Bickerton (1979) have constructed life tables for the segments of the population aged 0–10 years, and computed life expectancies for the total sample, those with porotic hyperostosis, and those with periosteal involvement. Life expectancy data indicate that individuals with periosteal reactions experienced severe mortality. Individuals in whom periosteal reaction was present at birth could be expected to live 0.8 year. The sample with

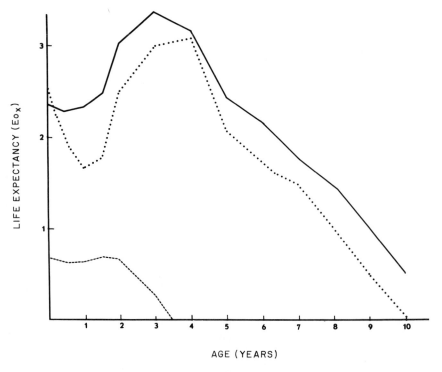

Figure 9.23. Life expectancy for the Dickson Mounds population for those dying within the first 10 years. Individuals with infection, - - -, or porotic hyperostosis, • • • •, showed reduced life expectancy as compared to the total population, —.

porotic hyperostosis also showed increased mortality when compared with the total sample. Between the ages of 6 months and 2.5 years, individuals with porotic hyperostosis had a life expectancy between 0.26 and 0.67 years less than those individuals without porotic hyperostosis (see Figure 9.23). After age 4, a difference in life expectancy is about 13 years.

In one of the most innovative analyses of the impact of underlying morbidity on mortality, Palkovich (1978, 1979) modified Preston's (1972, 1974, 1976) "dimensions of mortality" and applied it to an archaeological population. She found a significant association ($p < .02$) of pathology with mortality in several age classes. Porotic hyperostosis of the cranium and orbit, endocranial lesions, and general porosity were statistically related to increased death rates between the ages of 1 and 4.9 years, implying that poor nutrition is a predisposing factor for mortality in this group.

These few studies indicate the potential utility of demography for studying paleonutrition. The continued development of sophisticated demographic methods should provide more accurate measures of the effect of nutritional deficiency on the pattern of mortality. Imaginative use of these methods may then afford us insights into the evolutionary impact of malnutrition on human populations.

CONCLUSIONS

Our purpose in this chapter has been first, to outline the types of skeletal and population changes that accompany malnutrition, and second, to indicate pathologies and anomalies of skeletal growth that can be used to infer nutritional stress. A summary of these indicators is provided in Table 9.14. Obviously, not all stress markers are of equal utility, and we have attempted to point out limitations. The greatest drawback to the use of skeletal populations in nutritional studies is the generalized nature of their response to stressors. Growth is an excellent example of this. Severe deficiency of almost any nutrient will result in less than optimal growth. However, this same result can be produced by disease, malabsorption, altitude, genetic factors, or even social and physiological deprivation. Disturbances of growth are therefore measures of general stress, as are the results of growth—stature and sexual dimorphism. Used singly, such measures mean very little. Used together, they can indicate the presence of long-term mild or moderate stress. Growth curves and mortality schedules can additionally provide information on the timing and severity of stress.

Nutritional interpretation of skeletal pathologies depends on the use of more specific indicators. Harris lines, though sensitive measures of acute stress, need not be nutritionally caused. Enamel hypoplasias, porotic

TABLE 9.14

Summary of Skeletal Indicators of Nutritional Stress

Indicators	Parts of the population and skeleton required	Groups at risk	Severity and time of stress	General comments
Life tables and mortality schedule	Complete population or large representative sample—"agable" skeletons required	All	Chronic, severe	Best indicator of overall adaptation; may expect greatest nutritional involvement at times of greatest nutritional needs
Adult stature	Adult population, appendicular skeletons, especially lower extremities	Subadults	Summation of preadult factors	Short stature (small body size) may be a response to chronic undernutrition; must consider genetic and nonnutritional environmental factors.
Sexual dimorphism	Adult males and females; innominate used primarily, femur and other long bones secondarily	Subadults	Summation of preadult factors	Must consider genetic and nonnutritional environmental factors; sexual dimorphism decreases with increased nutritional stress.
Growth curves	Dental-aged subadults and subadult long bones	Subadults		
retardation			Chronic	May be adaptive in times of nutritional stress
shape differences			Chronic (1 year)	Can aid in estimation of time of greatest stress in an individual's life

458

Indicator	Skeletal location	Age/sex	Stress	Comments
Porotic hyperostosis	Cranium, particularly orbital regions	Both sexes 0.5–8 yr; females 20–30 yr	Acute to severe	Strong evidence for relationship to iron-deficiency anemia; potential synergist with infection; highest frequency before 5 yr
Osteoporosis	Femur and rib cross sections most commonly	Juveniles; Reproductive females; Senile	Acute to severe; Chronic to severe; Chronic	Evidence for increase in females at reproduction; may be related to calcium or protein-energy malnutrition
Osteophytosis	General skeleton, particularly joint regions and vertebrae	All or part	Chronic	May be specific to fluorine and lathyrogens
Harris lines	Adult or subadult radiographs of long bones (tibia, femur and others)	Subadults; adults	Acute stress; reoccurring stress	Experimental and naturalistic evidence for increase with decreased nutritional status; peak occurrence often near weaning
Enamel hypoplasia	Any teeth; permanent canines and incisors	0.5 in utero to 7 yr	Acute stress	Best indicator of seasonality; strong association with nutritional status and decreased longevity; peaks near weaning
Dental crowding	Maxilla and mandible with teeth in situ	Subadults	Chronic; severe	Must not be confused with genetic abnormality
Caries	Permanent or deciduous dentition, especially molars	All	Chronic; low	An indicator of a soft, refined carbohydrate diet; should be analyzed with consideration of missing teeth, attrition, and age

459

hyperostosis, and premature osteoporosis are probably the most valid indicators of nutritional involvement, but even they are not meaningful when used alone, or on single individuals.

Skeletal pathologies are most useful for archaeological reconstruction when a series of general and specific measures are analyzed for an entire skeletal population. In this way, both chronic and acute stress can be recognized, and the severity of each assessed. Meaningful statements about nutritional status depend on the demonstration of patterns of disturbance in the processes of bone growth and repair. They depend even more on the demonstration that such patterns are distributed differentially by age and sex within and between populations. We therefore advocate the simultaneous consideration of all measures available to produce a complete picture of populational stress response. Few such thorough studies have been undertaken to date, but the Libben site, analyzed by Mensforth *et al.* (1978) and others, may serve as an example of an integrated ecological and populational approach.

It should be noted that the most useful indicators of nutritional status are those applicable to the juvenile portion of a population. This reflects the fact that growing bone is most easily imprinted by nutritional disturbances, and that children are at greatest risk of malnutrition. The adult organism is buffered from mild malnutrition by its greater nutrient stores and more highly developed metabolic controls. When signs of nutritional involvement, such as premature osteoporosis, are seen in adults, they undoubtedly reflect severe conditions.

The future productivity of paleonutritional studies will require cooperation not only between anthropological subdisciplines, but between anthropology and a variety of other disciplines. Skeletal analysis, in particular, is increasingly oriented toward the techniques of chemistry and microbiology. Elemental analysis and the determination of $^{13}C/^{12}C$ ratios in bone, though only briefly reviewed here, are likely to be important in future studies. Such techniques are not in themselves radically new, but their application to archaeological material is an interesting and promising development.

It should be borne in mind, however, that the most sophisticated methodologies and the most precise techniques are only as good as the questions that are asked of them. The formulation of evolutionary questions is thus the first step to the productive study of paleoecological relationships. It is not enough simply to demonstrate change. Rather, it is in the causes and consequences of change that we are interested. Traditional methods of dietary reconstruction have documented change in diet. Skeletal studies have demonstrated change in patterns of human growth and pathology. It is now necessary to integrate these two aspects of our inquiry so that causal questions can be addressed.

The serious study of adaptation and dietary change will require information outside the traditional realms of archaeology and paleopathology. For example, we still do not know whether childhood malnutrition, or even life-long undernutrition, reduces biological fitness. This question is central to any discussion of nutritional adaptation and evolution and could be addressed in living populations. This is only one of the possible areas in which nutritionists and anthropologists could profitably cooperate, and students of paleonutrition should encourage such interaction.

The previous discussion has not attempted to cover all possible skeletal traits that have ever been assigned nutritional significance. Rather, we have outlined an approach to skeletal studies that may serve to integrate them into a larger bioarchaeological framework. By concentrating on the concepts of process and pattern, we have attempted to link environmental influences to markers in bone. Disturbances in process may thus be used to evaluate the success with which a population has adjusted to its nutritional environment.

ACKNOWLEDGMENTS

The analysis of the Nubian skeletal material was supported by grants GS7, GS286, and GS557 from the National Science Foundation. Subsequent analysis of histology of bone was supported by the National Institute of Health research grant NIH-1-R01-02771-01. The analysis of tetracycline was partially funded by the University of Massachusetts biomedical research and support grant RR07048. We also thank Debra L. Martin, John Curry, M. Pamela Bumsted, and Jeanette Goodman for their helpful comments on a draft of the manuscript.

REFERENCES

Acheson, R. M.
   1960   Effect of nutrition and disease on human growth. In *Human growth,* edited by J. M. Tanner. New York: Pergamon Press. Pp. 73-92.
Acheson, R. M., and G. B. Fowler
   1964   Sex, socio-economic status and secular increase in stature. *British Journal of Preventive Social Medicine* **18**:25-34.
Angel, J. L.
   1954   Human biology, health and history in Greece. *Yearbook of the American Philosophical Society,* pp. 168-172, 266-270.
Armelagos, G. J., J. H. Mielke, K. H. Owen, D. P. Van Gerven, J. R. Dewey, and P. E. Mahler
   1972   Bone growth and development in prehistoric populations from Sudanese Nubia. *Journal of Human Evolution* **1**:89-119.
Armelagos, G. J., A. Goodman, and S. Bickerton
   1980   Determining nutritional and infectious disease stress in prehistoric populations (Abstract). *American Journal of Physical Anthropology* **52**:201.
Ascadi, G. Y., and J. Nemeskeri
   1970   *History of human lifespan and mortality.* Budapest: Akademiai Kaido.
Bahou, W. F.
   1975   The relationships of particular trace elements to various bone pathologies in the Dickson Mounds skeletal population. Unpublished Senior Honors thesis, Department of Anthropology, University of Massachusetts, Amherst.

Bailit, H. L. P., P. L. Workman, J. K. Niswander, and C. J. MacClean
  1970 Dental asymmetry as an indicator of genetic and environmental stress in human populations. *Human Biology* **42**:626–638.

Barnicot, N. A., and S. P. Datta
  1972 Vitamin A and bone. In *The biochemistry and physiology of bone* (Vol. 2), edited by G. Bourne. New York: Academic Press. Pp. 197–229.

Bender, M.
  1968 Mass spectrometric studies of carbon 13 variations in corn and other grasses. *Radiocarbon* **10**:468–472.

Bender, M., D. Baerreis, and R. Steventon
  1981 Further light on carbon isotopes and Hopewell agriculture. *American Antiquity,* **46**:346–353.

Berlyne, G. M., J. Ben Ari, E. Nord, and R. Shainkin
  1973 Bedouin osteomalacia due to calcium deprivation caused by high phytic acid content of unleavened bread. *American Journal of Clinical Nutrition* **29**:910–911.

Bickerton, S.
  1979 Porotic hyperostosis in a prehistoric Amerindian population from Dickson Mound. Paper presented to the Northeastern Anthropological Association, Henniker, New Hampshire.

Blanco, R. A., R. M. Acheson, C. Canosa, and J. N. Salomon
  1974 Height, weight, and lines of arrested growth in young Guatemalan children. *American Journal of Physical Anthropology* **40**:39–48.

Boaz, N. T., and J. Hampel
  1978 Strontium content of fossil tooth enamel and diet in early hominids. *Journal of Paleontology* **52**:928–933.

Bressani, R., R. Paz y Paz, and N. S. Scrimshaw
  1958 Corn nutrient losses. Chemical changes in corn during preparation of tortillas. *Journal of Agriculture and Food Chemistry* **6**:770–773.

Brothwell, D., and R. Burleigh
  1977 On sinking Otavalo man. *Journal of Archaeological Science* **4**:291–294.

Brown, A. B.
  1973 Bone strontium as a dietary indicator in human skeletal populations. Unpublished Ph.D. dissertation, Department of Anthropology, University of Michigan, Ann Arbor.
  1974 Bone strontium as a dietary indicator in human skeletal populations. *Contributions to Geology* **13**:85–87.

Buikstra, J. E.
  1977 Biocultural dimensions of archeological study: a regional perspective. In *Biochemical adaptation in prehistoric America,* edited by R. L. Blakely. Athens, Georgia: University of Georgia Press. Pp. 67–84.

Bumsted, M. P.
  1980 The potential of stable carbon isotopes in bioarcheological anthropology. In *Biocultural adaptation—comprehensive approaches to skeletal analyses,* edited by D. L. Martin and M. P. Bumsted. Department of Anthropology Research Reports. University of Massachusetts, Amherst, in press.

Burleigh, R., and D. Brothwell
  1978 Studies on Amerindian dogs. I. Carbon isotopes in the diet of domestic dogs from early Peru and Ecuador. *Journal of Archeological Science* **5**:355–362.

Burns, P. E.
  1979 Log-linear analysis of dental caries occurrence in four skeletal series. *American Journal of Physical Anthropology* **51**:637–648.

Carlson, D. S., G. J. Armelagos, and D. P. Van Gerven
1974   Factors influencing the etiology of cribra orbitalia in prehistoric Nubia. *Journal of Human Evolution* **3**:405–410.
1976   Patterns of age-related cortical bone loss (osteoporosis) within the femoral diaphysis. *Human Biology* **48**:295–315.

Clarke, S. K.
1978   Markers of metabolic insult: the association of radiopaque transverse lines, enamel hypoplasias and enamel histopathologies in a prehistoric human skeletal sample. Unpublished Ph.D. dissertion, Department of Anthropology, University of Colorado, Boulder.

Cohen, M. N.
1977a   *The food crisis in prehistory: overpopulation and the origins of agriculture.* New Haven, Connecticut: Yale University Press.
1977b   Population pressure and the origins of agriculture: an archaeological example from Peru. In *Origins of agriculture,* edited by C. Reed. The Hague: Mouton Press. Pp. 135–177.

Cook, D. C.
1976   Pathologic stress and disease processes in Illinois woodland populations: An epidemiological approach. Unpublished Ph.D. dissertation, Department of Anthropology, University of Chicago, Chicago.

Cook, D. C., and J. E. Buikstra
1979   Health and differential survival in prehistoric populations: prenatal dental defects. *American Journal of Physical Anthropology* **51**:649–664.

Craig, H., and V. Craig
1972   Greek marbles: determination of provenance by isotopic analysis. *Science* **176**: 401–403.

Craig, J.
1963   The heights of Glasgow boys: secular and social influences. *Human Biology* **35**:524–539.

DeNiro, M. J.
1977   I. Carbon isotope distribution in food chains, II. Method of carbon isotope fractionation associated with lipid synthesis. Unpublished Ph.D. dissertation, Department of Anthropology, California Institute of Technology.

DeNiro, M. J., and S. Epstein
1978a   Dietary analysis from $^{13}C/^{12}C$ ratios of carbonate and collagen fractions of bone. *U.S. Geological Survey Open File Report* 78-701:90–91.
1978b   Influence of diet on the distribution of carbon isotopes in animals. *Geochimica et Cosmochemica Acta* **42**:495–506.

Dewey, J. R., G. J. Armelagos, and M. H. Bartley
1969   Femoral cortical involution in three archaeological populations. *Human Biology* **41**:13–28.

Di Bernardo, R.
1973   *Prenatal stress, developmental noise, and postnatal risk.* Unpublished Ph.D. dissertation, Department of Anthropology, City University of New York. University Microfilms, Ann Arbor.

Di Bernardo, R. and H. L. Bailit
1978   Stress and dental asymmetry in a population of Japanese children. *American Journal of Physical Anthropology* **48**:89–94.

Dickerson, J. W. T., and R. A. McCance
1961   Severe undernutrition in growing and adult animals: 8. The dimensions and chemistry of the long bones. *British Journal of Nutrition* **15**:567–576.

Doyle, W., and O. Johnston
1977 On the meaning of increased fluctuating dental asymmetry: A cross-populational study. *American Journal of Physical Anthropology* **46**:127–134.

Dubos, R.
1965 *Man Adapting.* New Haven, Connecticut: Yale University Press.

Earle, T.
1980 A model of subsistence change. In *Modeling change in prehistoric subsistence economies,* edited by T. K. Earle and A. L. Christensen. New York: Academic Press. Pp. 1–29.

El-Maraghi, N. R. A., B. S. Platt, and R. J. C. Stewart
1965 The effect of the interaction of dietary protein and calcium on the growth and maintenance of the bones of young adult and aged rats. *British Journal of Nutrition* **19**:491–509.

El-Najjar, M. Y., D. J. Ryan, C. G. Turner III, and B. Lozoff
1976 The etiology of porotic hyperostosis among the prehistoric Anasazi Indians of southwestern United States. *American Journal of Physical Anthropology* **44**:477–488.

Eng, L. L.
1958 Chronic iron deficiency anemia with long bone changes resembling Cooley's anemia. *Acta Haematologica* **19**:263–268.

Engfeldt, B., and S. O. Hjertquist
1961 Vitamin D deficiency and bone and tooth structure. *World Review of Nutrition and Dietetics* **2**:187–208.

Enwonwu, C. D.
1973 Influence of socio-economic conditions on dental development in Nigerian children. *Archives of Oral Biology* **18**:95–107.

Ericksen, M. R.
1976 Cortical bone loss with age in three native American populations. *American Journal of Physical Anthropology* **45**:443–452.

Fassel, V. A.
1978 Quantitative elemental analysis by plasma emission spectroscopy. *Science* **202**:183–191.

Foulks, E. F.
1973 The arctic hysterias of the North Alaskan Eskimo. *Anthropological Studies No. 10.* American Anthropological Association, Washington, D.C.

Frandsen, A. M., M. M. Nelson, E. Sulon, H. Becks, and H. M. Evans
1954 The effects of various levels of dietary protein on skeletal growth and enchondral ossification in young rats. *Anatomical Record* **119**:247–261.

Frisancho, A. R., and S. M. Garn
1970 Childhood retardation resulting in reduction of adult body size due to lesser adolescent skeletal delay. *American Journal of Physical Anthropology* **33**:325–336.

Frisancho, A. R., S. M. Garn, and W. Ascoli
1970 Population differences in skeletal maturation and its relationship to growth in body size (Abstract). *American Journal of Physical Anthropology* **33**:130.

Fuchs, A.
1978 Strontium/calcium ratios in bone: An assessment of their use in paleodietary research. *MASCA Journal,* pp. 10–11. University of Pennsylvania, Philadelphia.

Furst, C. M.
1920 *Närde de Döda Vittna.* Stockholm: Svenska Teknolog i Förlag.

Garn, S. M.
  1970   *The earlier gain and later loss of cortical bone in nutritional perspective.* Springfield: Charles C. Thomas.
Garn, S. M., P. E. Cole, and B. H. Smith
  1979   The effect of sample size on crown size asymmetry. *Journal of Dental Research* **58**:2012.
Garn, S. M., A. R. Lewis, and R. S. Kerewsky
  1965   Genetic, nutritional, and maturational correlates of dental development. *Journal of Dental Research* **44**:228–242.
Garn, S. M., C. G. Rohmann, and M. A. Guzman
  1966   Malnutrition and skeletal development in the preschool child. In *Preschool child malnutrition,* pp. 43–62. National Academy of Sciences, National Research Council, Washington, D.C.
Garn, S. M., F. N. Silverman, K. P. Hertzog, and C. G. Rohman
  1968   Lines and bands of increased density: their implication to growth and development. *Medical Radiography and Photography* **44**:58–89.
Geiger, B. J., H. Steenbock, and H. T. Parsons
  1933   Lathyrism in the rat. *Journal of Nutrition* **6**:427–442.
Gejvall, N. G.
  1960   *Westerhus.* Ohlssons, Lund.
Gilbert, R.
  1975   Trace element analyses of three skeletal Amerindian populations at Dickson Mounds. Unpublished Ph.D. dissertation, Department of Anthropology, University of Massachusetts, Amherst.
  1977   Applications of trace element research to problems in archaeology. In *Biocultural adaptation in prehistoric America,* edited by R. L. Blakely. Athens: University of Georgia Press. Pp. 85–100.
Giro, C. M.
  1947   Enamel hypoplasia in human teeth: an examination of its causes. *Journal of the American Dental Association* **34**:310–317.
Goldberger, J., G. A. Wheeler, and E. Sydenstricker
  1920   A study on the relation of diet to pellagra incidence in seven textile-mill communities of South Carolina in 1916. *Public Health Reports* **35**:648–713.
Gontzea, I., and P. Sutescu
  1968   *Natural antinutritive substances in foodstuffs and forages.* Basel: Karger.
Gontzea, I., P. Sutescu, V. Cosma, and D. Cocora
  1962   Cercetari asuptra posibilitatilor de contracarare a efectului distrofiant al prombului (Parts 1–3). *Igenia* **11**:281–302.
Goodman, A.
  1980   Polynomial regressions of dental age with long bone length for Dickson Mounds subadults. Unpublished ms., Department of Anthropology, University of Massachusetts, Amherst.
  1976   Enamel hypoplasia as an indicator of stress in three skeletal populations from Illinois (Abstract). *American Journal of Physical Anthropology* **44**:181.
Goodman, A., and G. J. Armelagos
  1980   The chronology of enamel hypoplastic growth disruptions in prehistoric, historic, and modern populations (Abstract). *American Journal of Physical Anthropology* **52**:232.
  1982   Childhood growth disruption and decreased adult longevity in a prehistoric Illinois population. Submitted to *Science.*

Goodman, A., G. J. Armelagos, and J. Rose
1980   Enamel hypoplasias as indicators of stress in three prehistoric populations from Illinois. *Human Biology,* **52**:515–528.

Goodman, A., and G. R. Clark
1981   Harris lines as indicators of stress in prehistoric Illinois populations. In *Biocultural adaptations comprehensive approaches to skeletal analysis.* Research Report No. 20, pp. 35–46. Department of Anthropology, University of Massachusetts, Amherst.

Gordon, J. D., I. D. Chitkara, and J. B. Wyon
1963   Weaning diarrhea. *American Journal of Medical Science* **245**:345–377.

Grayson, D. K.
1974   The Riverhaven #2 vertebrate fauna: comments on faunal analysis and on aspects of the subsistence potential of prehistoric New York. *Man in the Northeast* **8**:23–39.

Haas, J., and G. C. Harrison
1977   Nutritional anthropology and biological adaptation. *Annual Review of Anthropology* **6**:69–101. Annual Review, Palo Alto.

Halsted, J. A. *et al.*
1972   Zinc deficiency in man: the Shiraz experiments. *American Journal of Medicine* **53**:277.

Harper, A. M., D. L. Duewer, B. R. Kowalski, and J. Fasching
1977   ARTHUR and experimental data analysis: the heuristic use of a polyalgorithm. In *Chemometrics: theory and application,* edited by B. R. Kowalski. Washington, D.C.: American Chemical Society. Pp. 14–52.

Harris, H. A.
1926   The growth of the long bones in childhood, with special reference to certain boney striations of the metaphysis and to the role of the vitamins. *Archives of Internal Medicine* **38**:785–806.
1931   Lines of arrested growth in the long bones in childhood: correlation of histological and radiographic appearances in clinical and experimental conditions. *British Journal of Radiology* **4**:561–588, 622–640.
1933   *Bone growth in health and disease: the biological principles underlying the clinical, radiological and histological diagnosis of perversions of growth and disease in the skeleton.* London: Oxford University Press.

Hassan, A. A.
1975   Geochemical and mineralogical studies of bone material and their implications for radiocarbon dating. Unpublished Ph.D. dessertation, Department of Geology, Southern Methodist University.

Hassan, A. A., and D. Ortner
1977   Inclusions in bone material as a source of error in radiocarbon dating. *Archaeometry* **19**:131–135.

Hengen, O. P.
1971   Cribra orbitalia: Pathogenesis and probable etiology. *Homo* **22**:57–75.

Herz, N., and D. Wenner
1978   Assembly of Greek marble inscriptions by isotopic methods. *Science* **199**:1070–1072.

Howe, P. R.
1924   Some experimental effects of deficient diets on monkeys. *Journal of the American Dental Association* **11**:1161–1165.

Huss-Ashmore, R.
    1978   Nutritional determination in a Nubian skeletal population (Abstract). *American Journal of Physical Anthropology* **48**:407.
Infante, P., and G. M. Gillespie
    1974   Enamel hypoplasia in Apache Indian children. *Ecology of Food and Nutrition* **2**:155-156.
Jantz, R. L.
    1975   Population variation in asymmetry and diversity from finger to finger for digital ridge-counts. *American Journal of Physical Anthropology* **42**:215-224.
Jha, G. T., M. G. Deo, and V. Ramalingaswami
    1968   Bone growth and protein deficiency. *American Journal of Pathology* **53**:1111-1121.
Johnston, F. E.
    1962   Growth of the long bones of infants and young children at Indian Knoll. *American Journal of Physical Anthropology* **20**:249-254.
    1968   Growth of the skeleton in earlier peoples. In *The skeletal biology of earlier human populations,* edited by D. R. Brothwell. New York: Pergamon Press. Pp. 57-66.
Johnston, F. E., H. Wainer, D. Thissen, and R. B. MacVean
    1976   Hereditary and environmental determinants of growth in height in a longitudinal sample of children and youth of Guatemalan and European ancestry. *American Journal of Physical Anthropology* **44**:469-476.
Kaplan, L.
    1973   Ethnobotanical and nutritional factors in the domestication of American beans. In *Man and his foods,* edited by C. E. Smith, Jr., pp. 75-86. University: University of Alabama Press. Pp. 75-86.
Kaplan, L., and S. L. Maina
    1977   Archeological botany of the Apple Creek site, Illinois. *Journal of Seed Technology* **2**:40-53.
Katz, S., and E. Foulks
    1969   Mineral metabolism and behavior abnormalities of calcium homeostasis. *American Journal of Physical Anthropology* **32**:299-304.
Katz, S., M. L. Hediger, and L. S. Valleroy
    1974   The anthropological and nutritional significance of traditional maize processing techniques in the New World. *Science* **184**:765-773.
Keene, A.
    1979   Economic optimization models and the study of hunter–gatherer subsistence systems. In *Transformations: mathematical approaches to culture change,* edited by C. Renfrew and K. Cooke. New York: Academic Press. Pp. 369-404.
    1982   Optimal foraging in a non-marginal environment: A model of prehistoric subsistence strategies in Michigan. In *Hunter-gatherer foraging strategies: Ethnographic and archeological analyses,* edited by B. Winterhalder and A. Smith. Chicago: University of Chicago Press, in press.
Kreshover, S.
    1960   Metabolic disturbances in tooth formation. *Annals of the New York Academy of Sciences* **85**:161-167.
Kuhn, J. K.
    1979   Trace and minor elemental analyses of Sicilian skeletons by X-ray fluorescence. Paper presented to the American Association of Physical Anthropologists, San Francisco.

Lallo, J.
   1973   The skeletal biology of three prehistoric American Indian populations from Dickson Mound. Unpublished Ph.D. dissertation, Department of Anthropology, University of Massachusetts, Amherst.
Lallo, J., G. J. Armelagos, and R. P. Mensforth
   1977   The role of diet, disease, and physiology in the origin of porotic hyperostosis. *Human Biology* **49**:471–483.
La Marche, V. C., Jr.
   1974   Paleoclimatic inferences from long tree-ring records. *Science* **183**:1043–1048.
Leigh, R. W.
   1925   Dental pathology of Indian tribes of varied environmental and food conditions. *American Journal of Physical Anthropology* **8**:179–199.
Lengeman, F. W., and C. L. Comar
   1961   Distribution of absorbed strontium-85 and calcium-45 as influenced by lactose. *American Journal of Physiology* **200**:1051–1054.
Lerman, J. C.
   1975   How to interpret variations in the carbon isotope ratio of plants: biologic and environmental effects. In *Environmental and biological control of photosynthesis,* edited by R. Marcell. The Hague: W. Junk. Pp. 323–335.
Lerman, J. C., and J. H. Troughton
   1975   Carbon isotope discrimination by photosynthesis: implications for bio- and geosciences. In *Proceedings of the Second International Conference on Stable Isotopes,* edited by E. R. Klein and P. D. Klein, pp. 630–644. United States Energy Research Development Agency, Argonne, Illinois.
MacNeish, R.
   1978   Energy and culture in ancient Tehuacán. In manuscript.
Mahler, P. E.
   1968   *Growth of the Long Bones in a Prehistoric Population from Sudanese Nubia.* Unpublished M.A. thesis, Department of Anthropology, University of Utah.
Maresh, M. M.
   1955   Linear growth of long bones of extremities from infancy through adolescence. *American Journal of Diseases of Children* **89**:725–742.
Martin, D. L., and G. J. Armelagos
   1979   Morphometrics of compact bone: an example from Sudanese Nubia. *American Journal of Physical Anthropology* **51**:571–578.
Massler, M., I. Schour, and H. G. Poncher
   1941   Developmental pattern of the child as reflected in the calcification pattern of the teeth. *American Journal of Diseases of Children* **62**:33–67.
Mather, K.
   1953   Genetical control of stability in development. *Heredity* **7**:397–436.
Maugh, T.
   1973   Trace elements: a growing appreciation of their effects on man. *Science* **181**:253–254.
Mazany, T.
   1978   Isotope dendroclimatology: natural stable carbon isotope analysis of tree rings from an archeological site. Paper presented to the Fourth International Conference on Geochronology, Cosmochronology, and Isotope Geology, Snowmass-at-Aspen, Colorado.
Mazess, R., and W. E. Mather
   1974   Bone mineral content of northern Alaskan Eskimos. *American Journal of Clinical Nutrition* **7**:916–925.

McCance, R. A.
    1960   Severe undernutrition in growing and adult animals. 1. production and general effects. *British Journal of Nutrition* **14**:59–73.
McCance, R. A., J. W. T. Dickerson, G. Bell, and O. Dunbar
    1962   Severe undernutrition in growing and adult animals. 9. The effect of undernutrition and its relief on the mechanical properties of bone. *British Journal of Nutrition* **16**:1–12.
McCance, R. A., E. H. R. Ford, and W. A. B. Brown
    1961   Severe undernutrition in growing and adult animals. 7. Development of the skull, jaws and teeth in pigs. *British Journal of Nutrition* **15**:213–224.
McCance, R. A., and E. M. Widdowson
    1935   Phytin in human nutrition. *Biochemical Journal* **29**:2694–2699.
    1942   Mineral metabolism of healthy adults on white and brown bread dietaries. *Journal of Physiology* **101**:44–85.
    1962   Nutrition and growth. *Proceedings of the Royal Society of Britain* **156**:326–337.
McHenry, H.
    1968   Transverse lines in long bones in prehistoric California Indians. *American Journal of Physical Anthropology* **29**:1–17.
McHenry, H. M., and P. Schulz
    1976   The association between Harris lines and enamel hypoplasia in prehistoric California Indians. *American Journal of Physical Anthropology* **44**:507–512.
McLaren, D. S.
    1976   *Nutrition and its disorders* (second ed.). Edinburgh: Churchill Livingstone.
McLean, F. C., and M. R. Urist
    1968   *Bone. Fundamentals of the physiology of skeletal tissue.* Chicago: University of Chicago Press.
Mellanby, E.
    1938   The experimental production of deafness in young animals by diet. *Journal of Physiology* **94**:380–398.
    1950   *A Story of Nutritional Research.* Baltimore: Williams and Wilkins.
Mensforth, R. P., C. O. Lovejoy, J. W. Lallo, and G. J. Armelagos
    1978   The role of constitutional factors, diet, and infectious disease in the etiology of porotic hyperostosis and periosteal reactions in prehistoric infants and children. *Medical Anthropology* **2**:1–59.
Merchant, V. L., and D. H. Ubelaker
    1977   Skeletal growth of the protohistoric Arikara. *American Journal of Physical Anthropology* **46**:61–72.
Milkman, L. A.
    1930   Pseudofractures (hunger osteopathy, late rickets, osteomalacia). *American Journal of Roentgenology* **24**:29–37.
Møller-Christensen, V.
    1953   *Ten lepers from Naestved in Denmark.* Copenhagen: Danish Science Press.
    1958   *Bogen om Aebelholt Kloster.* Kobenhaven: Dansk Videnskabs Foring.
Molnar, S., and S. C. Ward
    1975   Mineral metabolism and microstructural defects in primate teeth. *American Journal of Physical Anthropology* **43**:3–17.
Moore, J., A. Swedlund, and G. J. Armelagos
    1975   The use of life tables in paleodemography. In Population studies in archeology and biological anthropology: A symposium, edited by A. Swedlund, pp. 57–70. *American Antiquity Memoir No. 30.*

Moseley, J. E.
  1963   *Bone changes in hematologic disorders.* New York: Grune and Stratton.
  1965   The paleopathologic riddle of symmetrical osteoporosis. *American Journal of Roentgenology* **95**:135–143.

Nickens, P.
  1975   Paleoepidemiology of Mesa Verde Anasazi population: lines of increased density. Unpublished ms., Department of Anthropology, University of Colorado, Boulder.

Nielsen, H. A.
  1911   Ydenligeve bidragtil stenalder folkets. *Anthropologi Aarb. Nord. Oldk. Hist.* (3rd Series) **1**:81–205.

Niswander, J. D., and C. S. Chung
  1965   The effects of inbreeding on tooth size in Japanese children. *American Journal of Human Genetics* **17**:390–398.

Ortner, D. J.
  1975   Aging effects on osteon remodeling. *Calcified Tissue Research* **18**:27–36.

Palkovich, A.
  1978   A model of the dimensions of mortality and its application to paleodemography. Unpublished Ph.D. dissertation, Department of Anthropology, Northwestern University.
  1979   Mortality patterns in paleodemography: exploring the cause structure of mortality. Paper presented to the American Anthropological Association, Cincinnati.

Park, E. A.
  1964   The imprinting of nutritional disturbances on the growing bone. *Pediatrics* **33** (supplement): 815–862.

Parker, G. S., S. Dreizen, and T. D. Spies
  1952   A cephalometric study of children presenting clinical signs of malnutrition. *Angle Orthodontics* **22**:125–136.

Parson, V., and C. Hampton
  1969   Phosphate deficiency and collagen metabolism. In *Nutritional aspects of the development of bone and connective tissue,* edited by J. C. Somogyi and E. Kodicek. Basel: Karger. Pp. 46–57.

Perzigian, A. J.
  1973   Osteoporotic bone loss in two prehistoric Indian populations. *American Journal of Physical Anthropology* **39**:87–96.
  1977   Fluctuating dental asymmetry: variation among skeletal populations. *American Journal of Physical Anthropology* **47**:81–88.

Platt, B. S., P. S. Miller, and P. R. Payne
  1961   Protein value of human foods. In *Recent advances in clinical nutrition,* edited by J. F. Brock. London: Churchill. Pp. 351–374.

Platt, B. S., and R. J. C. Stewart
  1962   Transverse trabeculae and osteoporosis in bones in experimental protein–calorie deficiency. *British Journal of Nutrition* **16**:483.

Prasad, A. S., J. A. Halsted, and M. Nadimi
  1961   Syndrome of iron-deficiency anemia, hepatosplenomegaly, hypogonadism, dwarfism and geophagia. *American Journal of Medicine* **31**:532.

Pratt, C. W. M., and R. A. McCance
  1958   Histological changes occurring in the long bones of chickens dwarfed by prolonged undernutrition. *Journal of Anatomy* **92**:655–658.
  1960   Severe undernutrition in growing and adult animals. 2. changes in the long bones

of growing cockerels held at fixed weights by undernutrition. *British Journal of Nutrition* **14**:75–84.

1964   Severe undernutrition in growing and adult animals. *British Journal of Nutrition* **18**:393–408.

Preston, S.

1972   Influence of cause of death structure on age-patterns of mortality. In *Population dynamics,* edited by T. N. E. Greville. New York: Academic Press.

1974   Demographic and social consequences of various causes of death in the United States. *Social Biology* **21**:144–162.

1976   *Mortality patterns in national populations.* New York: Academic Press.

Pruner-Bey, M.

1868   An account of the human bones found in the cave of Cro-Magnon in Dordogne: VII. In *Reliquiae acquitanicae, being contributions to the archaeology and paleontology of Perigord,* edited by E. Lartet and H. Cristy. Paris and Coaden: Bailliere.

Reidhead, V.

1980   The economics of subsistence change: a test of an optimization model. In *Modeling change in prehistoric economics,* edited by T. K. Earle and A. L. Christensen. New York: Academic Press. Pp. 141–186.

Rodahl, K.

1966   Bone development. In *Human development,* edited by F. Falkner. Philadelphia: Saunders. Pp. 503–509.

Roe, D.

1973   *A plague of corn: the social history of pellagra.* Ithaca: Cornell University Press.

Ronaghy, H. A., and J. A. Halsted

1975   Zinc deficiency occurring in females: report of two cases. *American Journal of Clinical Nutrition* **28**:831–836.

Rose, J. C.

1973   Analysis of dental micro-defects of prehistoric populations from Illinois. Unpublished Ph.D. dissertation, Department of Anthropology, University of Massachusetts, Amherst.

Rose, J. C., G. J. Armelagos, and J. Lallo

1978   Histological enamel indicator of childhood stress in prehistoric skeletal samples. *American Journal of Physical Anthropology* **49**:511–516.

Sarnat, B. G., and I. Schour

1941   Enamel hypoplasia (chronological enamel hypoplasia) in relation to systemic disease: a chronologic, morphologic, and etiologic classification. *Journal of the American Dental Association* **28**:1989–2000.

Saul, F.

1972   The human skeletal remains from Altar de Sacrificios. *Papers of the Peabody Museum of Archeology and Ethnology* No. 63. Harvard University, Cambridge.

1973   Disease in the Maya area: the Pre-Columbian evidence. In *The classic Maya collapse,* edited by T. P. Culbert. Albuquerque: University of New Mexico Press.

Schoeniger, M. J.

1978   Bone strontium and diet: methods and some possible sources of error. *American Journal of Physical Anthropology* **48**:435.

1979a   Dietary reconstruction at Chalcatzingo, a formative period site in Morelos, Mexico. *Museum of Anthropology, University of Michigan, Technological Reports* No. 9.

1979b   Diet and status at Chalcatzingo: some empirical and technical aspects of strontium analysis. *American Journal of Physical Anthropology* **51**:295–310.

Schour, I., and M. Massler
1945   The effects of dietary deficiencies upon the oral structures (Parts I–III). *Journal of the American Dental Association* **32**:714–727, 871–879, 1022–1030.

Schulz, P. D., and H. M. McHenry
1975   The distribution of enamel hypoplasia in prehistoric California Indians. *Journal of Dental Research* **54**:913–920.

Siegal, M. I.
1975   Stress and fluctuating limb asymmetry in various aspects of rodents. *Growth* **39**:363–369.

Stedt, P. G.
1979   Trace element analysis of two prehistoric populations: the Fremont and the Anasazi. Unpublished Ph.D. dissertation, Department of Anthropology, San Diego State University.

Steinbock, R. T.
1976   *Paleopathological diagnosis and interpretation: bone diseases in ancient human populations.* Springfield, Illinois: Charles C. Thomas.

Stewart, R. J. C.
1975   Bone pathology in experimental malnutrition. *World Review of Nutrition and Dietetics* **21**:1–74.

Stini, W. A.
1969   Nutritional stress and growth: sex differences in adaptive response. *American Journal of Physical Anthropology* **31**:417–426.
1972   Reduced sexual dimorphism in upper arm muscle circumference associated with protein-deficient diet in a South American population. *American Journal of Physical Anthropology* **36**:341–352.
1975   Adaptive strategies of populations under nutritional stress. In *Biosocial interactions in population adaptation,* edited by E. S. Watt, F. E. Johnston, and G. W. Lasker. The Hague: Mouton. Pp. 19–41.

Stout, S. D.
1976   Histomorphometric analysis of archeological bone. Unpublished Ph.D. dissertation, Department of Anthropology, Washington University, St. Louis.

Stuiver, M.
1978   Carbon-14 dating: a comparison of beta and ion counting. *Science* **202**:881–883.

Suarez, B. K.
1974   Neanderthal dental asymmetry as the probable mutation effect. *American Journal of Physical Anthropology* **41**:411–416.

Swärdstedt, T.
1966   *Odontological aspects of a medieval population in the province of Jämtland/Mid-Sweden.* Stockholm: Tiden-Barnangen Tryckerien.

Swedlund, A. C., and G. J. Armelagos
1969   Une recherche en paleo-demographie: la Nubie Soudanaise. *Annales-Economies-Societies-Civilizations* **6**:1287–1298.
1976   *Demographic anthropology.* Wm. C. Brown, Dubuque.

Szpunar, C., J. B. Lambert, and J. E. Buikstra
1978   Analysis of excavated bone by atomic absorption. *American Journal of Physical Anthropology* **48**:199–202.

Tanner, J. M.
1977   Human growth and constitution. In *Human biology,* edited by G. H. Harrison, *et al.,* (second ed.). New York: Oxford University Press. Pp. 301–385.

Teeri, J. A., and L. G. Stowe
    1976   Climatic patterns and the distribution of C_4 grasses in North America. *Oecologia* (Berl.) **23**:1–12.
Thomas, R. B.
    1973   Human adaptation to a high Andean energy flow system. *Occasional Papers in Anthropology* No. 6. Pennsylvania State University, University Park.
    1975   The ecology of work. In *Physiological anthropology,* edited by A. Damon. New York: Oxford University Press. Pp. 59–79.
Thomson, A. M., and F. E. Hytten
    1977   Physiological basis of nutritional needs during pregnancy and lactation. In *Nutritional impacts on women throughout life with emphasis on reproduction,* edited by K. S. Moghissi and T. N. Evans. Hagerstown, Maryland: Harper. Pp. 10–22.
Tieszen, L., D. Hein, S. Quortrup, J. Troughton, and S. Imbamba
    1979   Use of ^{13}C values to determine vegetation selectivity in East African herbivores. *Oecologia* **37**:351–359.
Toots, H., and M. R. Voorhies
    1965   Strontium in fossil bones and the reconstruction of food chains. *Science* **149**:854–855.
Trowell, H. C., J. N. P. Davies, and R. F. A. Dean
    1954   *Kwashiorkor.* London: Arnold.
Turner, Christy G.
    1979   Dental anthropological indications of agriculture among the Jomon people of central Japan. *American Journal of Physical Anthropology* **51**:619–636.
Ubelaker, D. H.
    1978   *Human skeletal remains: excavation, analysis and interpretation.* Chicago: Aldine.
Ulmer, D. D.
    1977   Trace elements. *New England Journal of Medicine* **297**:318–321.
Van der Merwe, N., and J. C. Vogel
    1978 ^{13}C content of human collagen as a measure of prehistoric diet in Woodland North America. *Nature* **276**:815–816.
Van Valen, L.
    1962   A study of fluctuating asymmetry. *Evolution* **16**:125–142.
Vila, F.
    1949   A review of the literature on enamel hypoplasia. *Journal of the Phillippine Dental Association* **2**(5):5–21.
Virchow, R.
    1872   Untersuchung des Neandertal schädels. *Zeitschrift für Ethnologie* **4**:157.
Vogel, J. C., and N. van der Merwe
    1977   Isotopic evidence for early maize cultivation in New York State. *American Antiquity* **42**:238–242.
Weatherell, J. A., and S. M. Weidmann
    1959   The skeletal changes of chronic experimental fluorosis. *Journal of Pathology and Bacteriology* **78**:243–255.
Weiss, K.
    1973   Demographic models for anthropology. *American Antiquity Memoir No. 27.*
    1975   Demographic disturbance and the use of life tables in anthropology. In Population studies in archeology and biological anthropology: a symposium, edited by A. Swedlund, pp. 46–56. *American Antiquity Memoir No. 30.*
    1976   Demographic theory and anthropological inference. *Annual Review of Anthropology* **5**:351–381.

Wells, C.
   1961   A new approach to ancient disease. *Discovery* **22**:526–531.
   1967   A new approach to paleopathology: Harris lines. In *Disease in antiquity,* edited by
           D. R. Brothwell and A. T. Sandison. Springfield, Illinois: Charles C. Thomas.
           Pp. 390–404.
   1975   Prehistoric and historic changes in nutritional diseases and associated conditions.
           Progress in Food and Nutritional Sciences **1**(2):729–779.
Widdowson, E. M. and R. A. McCance
   1964   Effects of nutrition and disease on growth. *British Dental Journal* **117**:326–330.
Wing, E. S., and A. B. Brown
   1980   *Paleonutrition. Method and theory in prehistoric foodways.* New York: Academic
           Press.
Winter, M., E. Morava, T. Horvath, G. Simon, and J. Sos
   1972   Some findings on the mechanism of adaptation of the intestine to calcium defi-
           ciency. *British Journal of Nutrition* **28**:10–111.
Winterhalder, B. P.
   1977   Foraging strategy adaptations of the boreal forest Cree: an evaluation of theory
           and models from evolutionary ecology. Unpublished Ph.D. dissertation, Depart-
           ment of Anthropology, Cornell University.
Wolbach, J. B.
   1947   Vitamin A deficiency and excess in relation to skeletal growth. *Journal of Bone
           and Joint Surgery* **29**:171.
Woodall, J.
   1968   Growth arrest lines in long bones of the Casas Grandes population. *Plains Anthro-
           pologist* **13**:152–160.
Y'Edynak, G.
   1976   Long bone growth in Western Eskimo and Aleut skeletons. *American Journal of
           Physical Anthropology* **45**:569–574.
Zsygmondy, O.
   1894   Beiträge zur Kenntnis der Entstehungsurache der hypoplastischen Emaildefecte.
           Transactions of the World's Columbian Dental Congress **1**:48–67.

Subject Index

Department of Interior, managing cultural resources and, 12–14
Development, of cultural resources management, 2–4

E

Erosion, impact on soils and sediments, 64–65

F

Faunal analysis, archaeological, 372
  purpose and goals, 373–374
  subsistence models, 374–376
Fire
  impact on archaeological sites, 62
  impact on soils and sediments, 68

H

Historic Preservation Act of 1966, 7–9
Historical archaeology
  archaeological science and, 164–168
  cognitive studies, 168–170
  development and emergence in America, 155–158
  historical supplementation, 158–160
  processual studies, 162–164
  reconstruction of past lifeways, 160–162

I

Impact(s)
  on archaeological sites, 55–56
    artifact movement, 56–59
    fire impacts, 62
    internal changes, 59–62
    summary, 62
  definition, 53–55
Impact studies, applications to archaeological research and resource management, 71–74
Internal changes, impact of, 59–62

L

Legal context, of cultural resources management, 4–7

M

Management of cultural resources
  Department of Agriculture, 14
  Department of Defense, 14–19
  Department of Energy, 14
  Department of Interior, 12–14
  research and, 19–20
    conserving cultural resources, 20–21
    management versus research, 21–22
    quality control, 26–27
    research designs, 22–25
    significance, 25–26

N

Native Americans, cultural resources management and, 33–35
Nutritional deficiencies
  in archaeological populations, 407–408
    bone collagen analysis as indicator, 450–455
    demographic variables as indicators, 455–457
    measures of nutritional stress in bone, 410–414
    measures of nutritional stress in teeth, 441–449
    osteoporosis as dietary indicator, 423–441
    porotic hyperostosis, 414–423
    specific deficiencies identified, 408–410

O

Osteoporosis, as dietary indicator, 423–441

P

Porotic hyperostosis, nutritional deficiency and, 414–423
Profession, of cultural resources management, 35–37

R

Research, management of cultural resources and, 19–20
  conserving cultural resources, 20–21
  management versus research, 21–22
  quality control, 26–27